IN THE SHADOW
OF THE PLANTATION

IN THE SHADOW
OF THE PLANTATION
Caribbean History and Legacy

IN HONOUR OF
PROFESSOR EMERITUS WOODVILLE K. MARSHALL

Alvin O. Thompson
Editor

Ian Randle Publishers
Kingston

In the Shadow of the Plantation
© The Department of History
The University of the West Indies
Cave Hill Campus
Barbados, West Indies

First published in Jamaica in 2002 by
Ian Randle Publishers
11 Cunningham Ave.,
Box 686, Kingston 6

ISBN - 976-637-082-6 paperback
ISBN - 976-637-098-2 hardback

A catalogue record of this book is available
from the National Library of Jamaica.

Cover design by Michael Brooks
Book design by Shelly-Gail Cooper

Set in StoneInformal 9pt
Printed and bound in the United States of America.

Contents

Section III: Forging a New Society

Section IV: Political and Socio-cultural Issues

Figures

Tables

Foreword

Caribbean History - A Work in Progress

My first reactions to the news conveyed by the editor of this book that the publication is in honour of Professor Woodville Marshall were that this statement by colleagues is most timely and appropriate, and secondly that the task in which he has been engaged throughout his career, and the task to which he is still committed is very much 'a work in progress'!

The project started in earnest when, in 1950, 'Miss Goveia began the preparation of a syllabus in Caribbean History for the final Examination' (Report of Department of History: 1950). The job of building capacity to research and teach Caribbean History got underway at Mona when the late Professor Elsa Goveia and her colleague, Professor Sir Roy Augier, felt that highest priority should be given to it.

Woodville Marshall had been one of the first students to be inspired by the sense of mission which characterised the writings and the teaching of Professor Goveia. His own career is in many ways a fitting tribute to the work of Goveia and her colleagues who worked hard to make Caribbean history the main business of the department. The latter also understood the need to establish a strategic alliance with schools across the region and to include West Indian history on the curriculum of every school.

Woodville graduated with First Class Honours in 1958. He was smitten by the Elsa Goveia bug and by then had developed a passion for the profession of historian. In a successful career that began with his return to the Caribbean and to the Mona Campus as lecturer in 1964, and continued after 1970 at Cave Hill, Professor Marshall has made a substantial contribution to the profession through his teaching, publications and leadership.

The list of authors and chapter headings in this book makes an important statement about the person in whose honour this publication is fittingly dedicated. The list of authors comprises former students and colleagues, all of whom have shared with Marshall the excitement of discovering something more about our historical experience, and sharing it with the public.

Several of us have benefited from Marshall's obsession with 'evidence'! No student or colleague is allowed to go unchallenged if the statement made is unsupported by the evidence. Equally, the analysis has to meet certain standards. Again, colleagues do not escape if they seem to be lacking in rigour when they develop an interpretation of the data. On such occasions, Woodville's intervention is introduced almost apologetically as he calls attention to 'a little point'. Invariably, the 'little point' torpedoes many an otherwise impressive argument and exposes the offending fallacy for what it is - flawed!

As teacher, historian and administrator, he has applied, with remarkable consistency, the principles which are the hall-mark of a good historian - commitment to truth, thoroughness of investigation, honesty in documenting research findings, clarity of thought and precision in communicating. For him, the historian has a great responsibility. He or she has a responsibility to give an accurate and intelligible account of the past. Wilful distortion of the story is forbidden.

I am delighted to have this opportunity to reflect and comment on the significance of the release of this publication in honour of Professor Emeritus Woodville Marshall. It is good to know that, having shed responsibilities for administration, he is concentrating on his research agenda. It is indeed a work in progress.

Sir Keith D. Hunte
Pro-Vice-Chancellor and Principal
University of the West Indies
Cave Hill Campus

Acknowledgments

The Department of History and Philosophy of the University of the West Indies, Cave Hill Campus, provided the main funds for this publication. However, the Campus Research Fund and the FAculty of Humanities and Education made significant contributions towards the publication, for which we are grateful. Thanks are also due to the Campus' Learning Resource Centre for placing the figures on disk, and to all those who assisted in any way in making this publication possible .

Abbreviations and Acronyms

ACH	Association of Caribbean Historians
Add. MS.	Additional Manuscript
BDA	Barbados Department of Archives
BMS	Baptist Missionary Society
BPL	Barbados Public Library
CID	Criminal Investigation Department, Trinidad and Tobago
Cmd.	Command
CMS	Church Missionary Society
CO	Colonial Office, Public Record Office, London
CS	Colonial Standard
CWM	Council for World Missions
DG	Daily Gleaner
DHA	Debates in the House of Assembly (Barbados)
DLC	Debates in the Legislative Council (Barbados)
EWC	Eric Williams Collection (UWI Library, St Augustine, Trinidad)
fol(s).	Folio(s)
E1/12	Anti-Slavery Papers, Rhodes House Library, Oxford
FP	Falmouth Post
GNA	Guyana National Archives
ILP	Independent Labour Party, Trinidad and Tobago
IRO	Island Record Office, Spanish Town, Jamaica
ISER	Institute of Social and Economic Research (UWI)
JAr	Jamaica Archives, Spanish Town, Jamaica
JA	Jamaica Advocate
JBMHS	Journal of the Barbados Museum and Historical Society
JDT	Jamaica Daily Telegraph
JP	Jamaica Post
JT	Jamaica Times
KCC	Kingston Cricket Club

LMS	London Missionary Society
LNES	Ladies Negro Education Society
MCA	Minutes of Legislative Council and Assembly (Barbados)
MCCBG	Minutes of the Combined Court of British Guiana
MCGB	Minutes of the Council of Government of Berbice
MCPBG	Minutes of the Court of Policy of British Guiana
MCPCJB	Minutes of the Court of Policy and Criminal Justice of Berbice
Mfm	Microfilm
MJ	Morning Journal
MMS	Methodist Missionary Society
MS(S)	Manuscript(s)
NAMDEVCO	National Agricultural Marketing Development Company (of Trinidad and Tobago)
NLJ	National Library of Jamaica
NWIG	Nieuwe West Indische Gids (New West Indian Guide)
PEG	Political Education Group, Trinidad and Tobago
PNM	Peoples National Movement, Trinidad and Tobago
PNP	Peoples National Party, Jamaica
PP	British Parliamentary Papers (House of Commons)
PRO	Public Record Office, London
RCI	Report of the Commission of Inquiry into the Condition of the Government Slaves in Berbice
SMS	Scottish Missionary Society
SPG	Society for the Propagation of the Gospel
St.	Sterling
STG	Stowe Collection, Grenville Papers (Huntington Library, San Marino, California)
T	Treasury documents, Public Record Office, London
TECA	Teachers' Economic and Cultural Association, Trinidad and Tobago
UNC	United National Congress, Trinidad and Tobago
UPM	United Peoples Movement, Trinidad and Tobago
UWI	University of the West Indies
WIRC	Report of the West India Royal Commission (1877-98)
WVS	Women's Voluntary Service for Civil Defence

Contributors

HILARY BECKLES is Pro-Vice-Chancellor of Undergraduate Studies at the University of the West Indies, Mona Campus, and Professor of History.

BRIDGET BRERETON is Deputy Principal of the University of the West Indies, St Augustine Campus, and Professor of History.

CARL CAMPBELL is Professor of History at the University of the West Indies, Mona Campus.

HENDERSON CARTER is a Part-time Lecturer in History at the University of the West Indies, Cave Hill Campus.

HEATHER CATEAU is a Lecturer in History at the University of the West Indies, St Augustine Campus.

AVISTON DOWNES is a Lecturer in History at the University of the West Indies, Cave Hill Campus.

JEROME HANDLER is a Senior Fellow at the Virginia Foundation for the Humanities, and Professor Emeritus of Anthropology and Black American Studies, Southern Illinois University, USA.

KUSHA HARAKSINGH is a Senior Lecturer in History at the University of the West Indies, St Augustine Campus.

B. W. HIGMAN is Professor of History at the Australian National University.

MICHELE JOHNSON is a Lecturer in History at the University of the West Indies, Mona Campus.

WINSTON MCGOWAN is Professor of History at the University of Guyana.

BRIAN MOORE is Professor of History at the University of the West Indies, Mona Campus.

RITA PEMBERTON is a Lecturer in History at the University of the West Indies, St Augustine Campus.

JAMES ROSE is Vice-Chancellor of the University of Guyana.

BRINSLEY SAMAROO is a Senior Lecturer in History at the University of the West Indies, St Augustine Campus.

VERENE SHEPHERD is Professor of History at The University of the West Indies, Mona Campus.

KELVIN SINGH is a Senior Lecturer in History at the University of the West Indies, St Augustine Campus.

ALVIN THOMPSON is Professor of History at the University of the West Indies, Cave Hill Campus.

NOEL TITUS is the Principal of Codrington College, Barbados.

KARL WATSON is a Senior Lecturer in History at the University of the West Indies, Cave Hill Campus.

PEDRO WELCH is Student Support Services Coordinator of Distance Education at the University of the West Indies, Cave Hill Campus, and a Part-time Lecturer in History.

SWITHIN WILMOT is a Senior Lecturer in History at the University of the West Indies, Mona Campus.

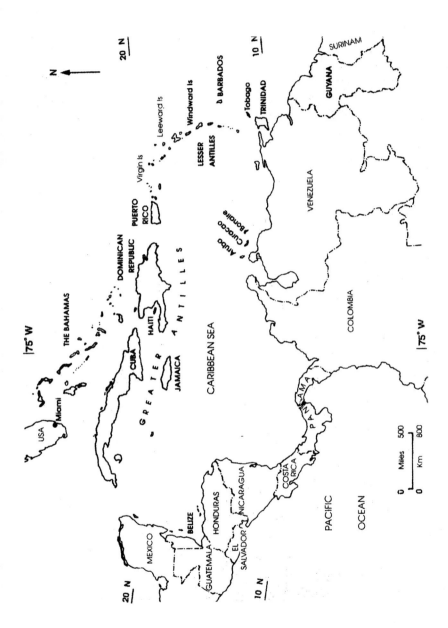

Introduction

Professor Woodville Marshall: A Short Biography

After more than 50 years of existence it is inevitable that the University of the West Indies (UWI) will bid farewell to more and more of its stalwarts: persons who joined the institution in the critical years of its early development, and who dedicated their entire working life to moulding, shaping and watching over its growth into the mature, world-class institution that it is today. In the process, their association with the university has assumed iconic dimensions and therefore it is virtually impossible to conceive of a UWI, or a Cave Hill, or a Mona, or a St Augustine, Campus without their presence.

On August 1, 2000 another such icon, Professor Woodville Marshall, took his formal leave, nudged into retirement by the calendar and the requirements of the university statutes. His has been an association that has spanned the gamut from student, to lecturer, to academic administrator, and finally to pro-vice-chancellor responsible for the university's outreach to the non-campus countries and for Distance Education.

Professor Marshall's relationship with the UWI began in 1954 when he left the sixth form at Harrison College in Barbados on a University College of the West Indies Open Scholarship and headed for Mona. He describes his student years there as exciting and intellectually stimulating, the pressure for intellectual vigour coming as much from the sharpness of his colleagues as from the demands of the teachers, 'We had excellent teachers like Elsa Goveia who had a way of making you feel that if you didn't do well you failed both her and yourself; and Roy Augier who introduced an element of rigour into writing and thinking which was important in my academic development.' But it was his classmates, 'people like the late Shirley Field-Ridley, Mavis Burke and P.J. Patterson who rubbed you intellectually,' he remarked.

After graduating with a First Class Honours degree, at the urging of Goveia and Augier, he decided against pursuing higher studies in economics, and began to contemplate an academic career as an historian. Awarded a university overseas scholarship, he enrolled at Cambridge in history in 1958. Five years later, after four years at Cambridge and a year in Nigeria teaching European history at the University of Ibadan, he landed a position in the History Department at Mona and finally returned there in 1964 to resume his love affair with Jamaica and the UWI as assistant lecturer in American history.

This was the early 1960s, in the wake of the break up of the short-lived West Indies Federation. It was a period of intense national consciousness in the Caribbean as the countries of the region began the march one by one into independence. And Mona was alive in every sense of the word. 'The History Department was a most exciting place. I had very good colleagues, most stimulating colleagues. Elsa [Goveia] and Roy [Augier] were still there, but there were a number of younger persons like Keith Laurence, David Buisseret, Kamau Brathwaite, and Walter Rodney who came when I was still there. It was a good group and there was a lot of scholarly activity going on.' Marshall became heavily involved in the community life of the campus.

With all the energy and daring enthusiasm of youth, Marshall launched himself into borderline political activity outside of the university as well. He was an active member of the Young Socialist League and the New World Group which were developing around that time. He was part of a team from the university which regularly participated in a news analysis and commentary programme on Jamaican radio produced by a Barbadian, J.C. Proute. Then came the Walter Rodney incident, which saw his colleague being banished from Jamaica in 1968 and suspicions raised about subversive activities by other non-Jamaican West Indian academics on campus, including Marshall. In the circumstances, he felt that he should return to Barbados.

When he finally arrived at Cave Hill Campus in 1970, Cave Hill, at seven years of age, was still a fledgling. The Mona he had left was a very active place 'in all sorts of ways.' The residential nature of Mona, where staff and many students lived on, or in very close proximity to, the campus, created a strong sense of community and a lot of social activity was therefore centred on the campus. It was also an intellectually strong community, thriving in terms of its own scholarship. 'I came out of a department where we had staff seminars, we were already doing some graduate training, people were showing each other their work, so that there was a sort of stimulus for individual scholarly activity.'

At Cave Hill, until that same year still a College of Arts and Sciences, he found a teaching institution in the early stages of development, and immediately recognised an opportunity and a responsibility to bring to the young campus some of what he had left at Mona. The timing was right because Cave Hill was in a growth phase, with additional staff and new disciplines or sub-disciplines being added, and other persons on staff who shared his keen interest in stimulating scholarly activity on the campus.

He found an early partner in another young Barbadian historian, Keith D.

Hunte (now Sir Keith, principal of Cave Hill Campus). Together they undertook a review and revision of the entire arts programme on the Campus, adding West Indian literature and West African history, among other subjects, to the offerings. Within a year, Marshall was appointed vice-dean of the Faculty (equivalent to the present-day dean) and soon after became head of the Division of General Studies. From this position of leadership, he was able to implement a number of important changes and initiatives, including staff/student seminars and graduate training. 'It was really a convergence of many things, including the presence of keen and willing colleagues, and I received a lot of support.'

He went on to play a major role in the development of the department and the faculty, serving in several administrative positions, including head of department, dean of the faculty, and university dean. When the Faculties of Arts and General Degree Studies were merged in 1972, he was a principal participant in the merger and became the first dean of the merged faculty. In 1977, he was elevated to the distinguished rank of professor.

In 1990, the university took a decision to strengthen the vice-chancellery through the establishment of a number of strategic support units. One of these was the Office of Academic Affairs, to provide policy support and advice to the vice-chancellor with respect to admissions, curricula, pedagogy, examinations and assessment, research, staff training and development, and links with other universities, among other areas. Professor Marshall was appointed pro-vice-chancellor in charge of this office and deputy principal of the Cave Hill Campus, the start of a move into full-time administration.

Under his watch the Office of Academic Affairs laid the groundwork for the introduction of student assessment of teaching; established mechanisms on each campus to support improvements in teaching skills; undertook preliminary work on the move towards the dual-mode approach to the delivery of the university's programmes; and advanced the establishment of linkages with several universities in North America and Europe. Another major achievement of his tenure as PVC Academic Affairs was the launching of the University Press.

Further adjustments to the university's management structure in response to the recommendations of the Chancellor's Commission on Governance saw the appointment of Professor Marshall to the post of pro-vice-chancellor responsible for the University's outreach programmes to the non-campus countries and for distance education in 1996. Under this umbrella he has held overall responsibility for the Tertiary Level Institutions Unit, the School of Continuing Studies and the Distance Education Centre. His tenure in this position witnessed the expansion of the University's distance education programme and the launching of the first full degree programmes by distance.

Professor Marshall helped to found the Association of Caribbean Historians and became its first president. He also played an important part in the development of the highly respected *Journal of Caribbean History* of which he was editor for nine years, from 1981 to 1990. 'Douglas Hall founded the journal and when he left in 1980/81 I took over as editor. We had a problem with the commercial publishers and I got the idea that the Departments of History could publish the journal. We started to publish it in 1981 and have been doing so successfully ever since.'

So from student, to teacher and researcher, to campus administrator, and finally university administrator, Professor Woodville Marshall has left his mark on nearly all major areas of the work of the university. It is with some excitement that he embraces the change which will allow him to return to the realm of the historian to complete some unfinished business.

The title and the essays

The title of this book, *In the Shadow of the Plantation: Caribbean History and Legacy*, has been chosen to emphasise both the historical and contemporary impact of the plantation on all aspects of Caribbean life. The plantation has dominated the landscape, economy, politics and culture of the islands and the northern mainland territories from almost the inception of staple cultivation on a large scale. For most academics, it was particularly the cultivation of the sugar cane as the major export crop from the mid-seventeenth century that gave a seemingly indelible character to the region as a plantation area,[1] some would say as a plantation writ large.

The impact of sugar culture on the region is often termed a revolution, and Barry Higman's essay details painstakingly how the concept of such a revolution evolved. He also notes that it is the only crop to which the term revolution has been attached. It is, of course, quite an irony, as Eric Williams observes, that 'an article like sugar, so sweet and necessary to human existence, should have occasioned such crimes and bloodshed!'[2] Maurice Lemoine, in his poignant documentation of the horrors experienced by migrant labourers on the sugar plantations in Cuba and the Dominican Republic in the post-war era, entitles his book *Bitter Sugar*.[3] Everywhere in the region sugar cultivation, especially on a plantation basis, has generated conflict, sometimes violently so. Such conflict is also part of the present-day scenario, whether on the plantations in the Dominican Republic or Guyana. It is witnessed every year, almost ritualistically within recent times, in Barbados in the struggle between trade union and management over wages during crop time, and also in the number of small disagreements leading to downing of tools and parking of tractors until a settlement has been reached. Sugar has therefore gained the reputation of a troublesome crop - for Akroyd a 'sweet malefactor;'[4] and for Nobel laureate, Vidiadhar Naipaul, 'a brutal plant,' 'an ugly crop 'with 'an ugly history.'[5]

A number of essays in this collection, especially the section entitled 'Production, Culture and Resistance in the Slavery Era,' detail the bitterness and brutality of the sugar revolution, in physical, emotional, psychological and other terms, and its exceptionally harsh impact on women and children. Verene Shepherd discusses the ubiquitous role of women in the struggle against slavery (and later other forms of oppression). Karl Watson looks at the way that lives were snuffed out frivolously, for such matters as stealing a bit of used clothing or a couple of chickens. But the essays also show that enslaved persons launched counter-revolutionary assaults on the slave systems, in a wide variety of ways, from the time of their enslavement in Africa, through the Middle Passage, and in the slave colonies. The high point of counter-revolution was reached in the successful revolt in St Domingue, modern Haiti, that not only overthrew the slave system but colonialism that spawned that system.

The impact of the plantation continued to be felt deeply and widely in the immediate post-emancipation period, for although emancipation theoretically gave 'freedom' to the former enslaved people, it did not in reality offer them scope to operate within a free society. They suffered from a battery of discriminatory laws, more subtle than under slavery but sometimes just as draconian. Impediments were placed in their way in respect of access to land, alternative forms of employment to the plantation system, migration to more attractive destinations, the right to combine in order to achieve wage increases, access to education, medical care, the franchise and representation in the colonial legislatures. They had to fight all the way to secure a niche as free persons for themselves and their children. They protested, demonstrated, withheld their labour, rioted and revolted in order to be heard - and they were heard, even though this was often not in the way that they intended. Their struggles are documented in this book in a number of excellent essays, under the theme 'Forging a New Society.'

The post-emancipation period saw the re-entry of contract labourers into a number of colonies in the region. These labourers came from Europe, Africa and Asia. The vast majority of them came from India, and helped to stabilise and expand the sugar economy, especially in Guyana, Trinidad and Suriname. The presence of the newcomers had a differential impact on Caribbean society and culture, but they eventually became part of the 'melting pot', symbolised so well by the hot temperatures for which the region is known. By the late nineteenth century, the struggle for rights was being engaged in on all fronts and by all oppressed groups, while the new generations of plantation owners sought to follow in the footsteps of their forbears by denying the people access to political and social rights, and the right to be recognised as citizens and not simply denizens of the Caribbean archipelago. This struggle is addressed in the section entitled 'Political and Socio-cultural issues.' The extreme vulnerability of the region's economy to external events as late as the Second World War is thrown into relief by Rita Pemberton's essay on the impact of that war on food supplies and marketing in Trinidad and Tobago. This study indicates clearly how the continued dominance of the plantation system placed that colony in a situation of food vulnerability, a situation under which the region as a whole still suffers, with some countries like Barbados and the Bahamas importing an estimated 80 per cent of the food that they consume.

The essays span the period from the sugar revolution to the post-war era. While most of them are time and country specific, they all have wider relevance, for by implication they speak to what was happening in the region as a whole. Thus, for instance, Jerome Handler's meticulously-crafted essay on the ways in which enslaved persons sought to achieve some small degree of space and autonomy through the individualisation of their homes and their garden plots, or Swithin Wilmot's essay on the struggle for political enfranchisement in Jamaica in the early post-emancipation period, can be translated *mutatis mutandi* to Trinidad, Barbados, Guyana, Antigua, or any of the former slave colonies. The same is true of Hilary Beckles' essay on Crop-Over and other festivals, of Aviston Downes' essay on the contestation of land space for recreational purposes in Barbados, or of James Rose's essay on the inequitable tax regime that bore hard on the working people in Guyana. In this sense, therefore, the essays reflect what was happening in the region as a whole. In identifying a few essays specifically in this introduction we are not suggesting that they are superior to the others; we have simply used them to illustrate the ways in which the collection as a whole has an underlying unity and a much wider appeal than the focus of each individual piece. We could just as easily use any of the other essays as examples.

The contributors to this collection have been academic historians for different periods of time; some have been in the profession for decades, while others have just entered the field. The choice of contributors has been, to some extent, deliberate, because this helps to reflect Professor Marshall's long tenure as an historian (still not completed), and the impact that his teaching and scholarship have had on both young and old scholars. Some of them have explicitly acknowledged their debt to him in their essays in this collection. Bridget Brereton's historiographical essay on his writings puts into sharp relief his contribution to historical studies on the Windward Islands and the peasantry. The guiding hand and mind of Marshall were experienced at undergraduate and/or graduate levels not only by Brereton herself, but by others such as Winston McGowan, Pedro Welch, Aviston Downes and myself. Many other colleagues have rubbed shoulders with him and been engaged in fraternal debates on historical issues. The list is long, but among these we should mention Keith Laurence, Keith Hunte, Roy Augier, Barry Higman, Hilary Beckles, Kamau

Brathwaite, and the late Walter Rodney, Elsa Goveia and Douglas Hall. His influence on the region's scholars, and especially those within the precincts of the University of the West Indies, has been deep. We are all grateful, and dedicate this work to him with joy and a feeling of having become better scholars by crossing historical paths with him.

Alvin O. Thompson
Department of History and Philosophy
University of the West Indies
Cave Hill Campus

March 2002

Notes

The first part of this introduction was adapted with the permission of the Office of Public Information, University of the West Indies, Cave Hill Campus, from an article entitled 'After Forty Years Professor Marshall is Packing His Bags,' in *Cave Hill News*, July 2000.

1. Lloyd Best, 'Outlines of a Model of Pure Plantation Economy', *Social and Economic Studies* 17.3 (1968): 283-326.
2. Eric Williams, *Capitalism and Slavery* (London: André Deutsch, 1944; 1964), 27.
3. Maurice Lemoine, *Bitter Sugar* (London: Zed Books, 1985).
4. W.R. Akroyd, *Sweet Malefactor: Sugar, Slavery and Human Society*, (London, Heinemann, 1967).
5. Vidiadhar Naipaul, *The Middle Passage: Impressions of Five Societies - British, French and Dutch in the West Indies and South America*, (London: André Deutsch, 1974), 62, 119.

Section I

Historiography

CHAPTER 1

Woodville Marshall and Caribbean History
Bridget Brereton

Introduction

Woodville K. Marshall was born in St Philip, Barbados, in 1935. Educated at Harrison College, the island's leading boys' secondary school, he went to the still very new University College of the West Indies (UCWI) at Mona, Jamaica, in 1954. Here he spent four years, being required to take the B.A. 'Intermediate' Year before embarking on the three-year honours degree in history, which he obtained in 1958. Armed with a first, he read for the PhD at Cambridge, which he was awarded in 1963 for a thesis on the Windward Islands in the decades after emancipation. After a year at the University of Ibadan, Marshall came back to UWI at Mona in 1964, lecturing in the Department of History there until 1970. In that year, he was 'repatriated' to Barbados, joining the Department of History at the Cave Hill Campus of UWI, where he became professor of history in 1977.

Marshall's formidable skills of persuasion, argumentation and administration marked him out as a leader early in his UWI career, and he served as campus or university faculty dean, or as head of department, for much of the 1970s and 1980s. In 1990 he became a full-time administrator when he was made pro-vice-chancellor, and Marshall continued to be a member of the University's senior management until his retirement in 2000. Unquestionably, his heavy involvement in academic administration negatively affected his scholarly productivity after his move to Cave Hill in 1970.

In assessing Marshall's contribution to Caribbean historiography, I have chosen to consider his writings under three categories: the history of the Windward Islands and Barbados between 1834 and 1865; the evolution of peasantries and villages in the British West Indies (especially Barbados) in the nineteenth and twentieth centuries; and the development of the historiography of the Anglophone Caribbean. Inevitably, there is a considerable overlap between my categories and a degree of arbitrariness in my assignment of individual pieces.[1]

The Windward Islands and Barbados

In 1963, Marshall completed his doctoral dissertation, 'The Social and Economic Development of the Windward Islands, 1838–1865.' The most important influence behind this thesis was that of Elsa V. Goveia, professor of West Indian history at Mona and Marshall's teacher and mentor; she suggested the topic, and 'effectively supervised the thesis' from 3,000 miles across the Atlantic, reading a draft and making extensive comments on it.[2] As its title suggests, the thesis is strongly oriented to social and economic history – again, Marshall tells us that it was Goveia who brought him to social history – but chapter seven includes considerable material on political and constitutional developments, and the 522-page dissertation provides a comprehensive analysis of the four islands' historical evolution in the post-emancipation period. Marshall explains in his preface that he excluded Barbados, even though it was linked administratively to the Windward group during his chosen period, because 'as before and since, its development has been altogether different from that of the other four islands.'[3] He did not, however, offer any explanation for not including Dominica, generally considered geographically part of the British Windwards; he simply stayed within the mid-nineteenth-century administrative grouping which linked Grenada, St Lucia, St Vincent and Tobago under a governor-in-chief based in Barbados, leaving Dominica in the Leewards group. Nor did he particularly attempt to compare the four islands' development or to establish the commonalities between them other than the administrative link. Writing over 30 years later, Marshall himself pointed to his failure (in the thesis and in subsequent articles or papers) 'to develop fully a base for treating the [Windward] islands as a homogenous whole.'[4]

No doubt Marshall's decision to research the four islands within the administrative group, excluding Dominica, was related to his heavy reliance on official sources for his thesis. This, of course, was not unusual in the British Caribbean historiography of the day; he was following the traditions and practices of the UWI Department of History which had initially trained him. Certainly, the great bulk of his material, as he points out, was derived from Colonial Office records and Parliamentary Papers. These rich sources were thoroughly exploited to produce a well-rounded, detailed analysis of his four islands' development in the decades after emancipation. Never published, the thesis represented a pioneering foray into the social and economic history of some of the 'smaller' islands of the British Caribbean, complementing the work of Douglas Hall, Sidney Mintz and Philip Curtin on Jamaica in the same period. It is still the major authority for Grenada, St Lucia, St Vincent and Tobago in the 1838–65 period; it has been mined by many, including, of course, the author himself.

Two important articles, both published in 1965 soon after Marshall's appointment to the Department of History at Mona, derived directly from the thesis.[5] The first was a general discussion of the social and economic development of the four Windward Islands, following the major themes in post-emancipation history which had been set out especially by Hall for Jamaica: land, labour, wages, tenancy, peasant development, popular unrest, and agrarian relations generally. In a way it provides a succinct summary of Marshall's doctoral thesis, giving readers (including students) relatively easy access to the major findings of that formidably long work (which was not, in the 1960s, available in the UWI libraries). The second article dealt with sharecropping (*metayage*) as a major adaptation to emancipation, especially in St Lucia and Tobago. This influential article, still the chief source on *metayage* in the period 1838–65, makes a significant contribution to the literature on post-emancipation agrarian relations in the Caribbean.

Most of Marshall's work, as he said in his 2000 Goveia lecture, has dealt with 'agricultural labourers, sharecroppers, peasants' and has had a social history orientation; his long 1971 article on the end of the apprenticeship in the Windwards and Barbados is a rare excursion into political history.[6] This excellent piece, subtitled 'an essay in colonial administration and politics,' considers the connections between events in Britain and reactions in the five islands and the effect of actions by the Colonial Office on the colonial legislatures, in the context of the hectic few months between January and July, 1838. Based on Barbadian newspapers and Assembly minutes as well as on the more familiar Colonial Office records, this is a thoroughly researched, closely written piece in which the careful analysis moves seamlessly between metropole and colony.

More generally representative of Marshall's work, however, is a group of five papers or articles on the Windward Islands which were all written between 1979 and 1989. His 1979 paper examined labour relations in the four Windward Islands in the first eight years after full freedom, in the context of the debate about the 'Labour Problem'.[7] Though this paper has not been published, it is a substantial piece of research which makes a significant contribution to that debate. Among other things, Marshall argued that labour relations during the apprenticeship were a crucial cause of the withdrawal from the estates after 1838, and he took this theme up in an article published in 1985.[8] Here he demonstrates that in the four Windward colonies, the planters' policies during the apprenticeship, and the apprentices' responses, were a key reason for labourers' actions after August 1, 1838. This article includes an interesting discussion on the phenomenon of apprentices' self-purchase in the months just before August 1, in opposition to well-meaning advice from magistrates and others; Marshall explains this as stemming from a search for status by the ex-slaves, as well as a profound mistrust of the white man's *bona fides*. A later article takes the analysis back into the period of slavery, examining the 'provision grounds complex' in the Windwards in the last 50 years of slavery.[9] Possibly Marshall's only publication dealing explicitly with the slavery period, it is less densely researched than the pieces on the more familiar post-emancipation decades, but it nevertheless brings together useful material and puts the analysis in the context of the literature on Caribbean internal marketing systems and slave subsistence patterns. He concludes that in the Windwards, as in Jamaica, the provision grounds and marketing allowed for the slaves' participation in independent economic activities and fostered attitudes and expectations which affected post-slavery labour relations. In this article, Marshall contributed to an important and lively debate in the literature on slavery, reinforcing the argument that enslaved persons shaped their lives and destinies.

The remaining two pieces in this series, though very different, both deal with specific islands. Marshall's article on the St Vincent labour protest of 1862 has become something of a classic piece, inspiring several other studies of post-emancipation unrest.[10] This is a model reconstruction of a popular protest, carefully examining its background, causes, course, motives and consequences. Despite the limitations of the sources, Marshall tries to enter the minds of his rioters, in the George Rudé or E.P. Thompson approach, and probe their consciousness and world-view. This article did not use the techniques or jargon of the 'new social history,' but it unquestionably made an important contribution to the literature on post-emancipation society and it did reflect the 'history from the bottom up' perspective. Marshall's article on the economic history of St Lucia in the nineteenth century is certainly a less significant piece[11] — it is the published version of a public lecture delivered in 1989—but it pulls together useful information on the St Lucian economy between the 1830s and the 1890s, information which (as Marshall observes) is very hard to find anywhere else.

Certainly the most important of all Marshall's publications on Windward Island and Barbadian history in the post-emancipation period, is his scholarly edition of the Colthurst Journal.[12] J.B. Colthurst served as a special magistrate in Barbados and St Vincent between July 1835 and September 1838, and wrote an extensive journal, during that time, which ended up in the Boston Public Library. Marshall's 40-page introduction provides a scholarly account of Colthurst's life, the work of the special magistrates, the state of Barbadian and St Vincent society in the 1830s, and the writing and subsequent fate of the journal itself. This is an excellent piece of archival research, and the text itself is enriched with many editorial notes. The publication of Colthurst's journal—a rich source which has been extensively used by historians—was a real service to Caribbean social history.[13]

Marshall has made a significant contribution to the historiography of the Windwards (excluding poor Dominica, of course) and Barbados in the nineteenth century.[14] It is a pity that the doctoral thesis remains unpublished, and he is perhaps correct in his auto-criticism that he has not clearly shown in what ways the Windwards may be seen as constituting a historical sub-region. A major work of synthesis on the Windwards (whether four or five) is still to come. Yet, taken together, his thesis, articles and papers, along with *Colthurst*, remain the single most important body of work on the Windward Islands between 1838 and 1865.[15]

Peasantries and villages

The evolution of peasantries and the development of independent village settlements after 1838 formed an important component in the studies on the Windwards and Barbados which I have just reviewed. But they also became the second major focus of Marshall's historical research, and he became an important contributor to the debate initiated by Sidney Mintz on the nature and significance of peasantries and villages in the post-emancipation Caribbean.

Marshall's 1968 article on peasant development after 1838, though a 'survey' rather than a piece of wholly original research, swiftly became a classic.[16] Marshall reviewed the relevant literature – not very extensive in the 1960s, but dominated by the classic 1936 pamphlet of Arthur Lewis and the later work by Mintz and Hall – and attempted a definition of a Caribbean peasant. He offered a survey of peasant development between the 1830s and the 1960s, proposing three stages – establishment (1838–1850/60), consolidation (1850/60–1900) and saturation (1900–1960) – and then considering the social role of the peasants and government policy towards them. Many of Marshall's UWI colleagues, condemned to read 30 years' worth of undergraduate essays trotting out the famous three stages whether relevant or not, have had reason to mutter darkly about this article; but it unquestionably came to dominate thinking and writing about peasantries in the Anglophone Caribbean after 1838. It was complemented by an article first published in 1972 which examined peasant development in more detail between 1838 and 1938.[17] Unlike the earlier article, this one looked at peasant organisations, and peasant protests of different types; Marshall concluded that direct action by Caribbean peasants was at least as important as government actions or official commissions in effecting change in their conditions.

Two briefer pieces continued Marshall's exploration of the peasantry. A 1970 paper discussed the relations between peasants and sugar plantations in the post-emancipation Caribbean.[18] Marshall concluded that, while antagonism between peasant and plantation was inherent in the historical realities, many (maybe most) West Indian peasants were closely involved in the sugar industry, as labourers, *metayers*, cane farmers, and producers of cheap, crude sugar for local consumers. Many peasants, he argued, wanted to continue to be involved in sugar, not only because they needed cash, but also because of status considerations. Marshall warned historians not to posit 'too extreme a discontinuity' in people's lives 'before and after' 1838. Some of these issues were taken up again in Marshall's brief commentary on a paper delivered by Mintz at a conference in Canada in 1979.[19] Marshall made the point that ex-slaves were not blindly reacting against the plantation nor indulging in an emotional, knee-jerk response to slavery when they faced the aftermath of 1838, and called for detailed research into their 'interests and expectations.' Anticipating his later piece 'We be wise to many more tings,' Marshall suggested that ex-slaves were interested in family organisation and reconstitution, wages no lower than during the apprenticeship, and continued access to their provision grounds. Probably, he wrote, they were more concerned with improving their standard of living than with seeking some abstractly defined 'independence.'

In the 1970s, Marshall became involved in a research project on village and peasant development in the nineteenth- and twentieth-century Caribbean, which he led. Three papers resulted from this project. The first, written in 1974, examined the evolution of the Barbadian peasantry, focusing on 1895–1920.[20] Though it was presented as preliminary research only, this paper was based on extensive primary sources held locally, including wills and deeds, Parish Rate Books, estate records and censuses, in addition to the more familiar Parliamentary Papers, Blue Books and commission reports and evidence. Detailed analysis was provided on the sub-division of plantations and subsequent sales of small plots to black Barbadians, especially after 1895 when this trend accelerated. More results of this research were presented in the form of a public lecture delivered in Barbados in 1987.[21] As with the earlier article, this piece analysed village development, both pre- and post-1838, but concentrated on the period after 1890. Marshall explained why the trend to sub-division and sale accelerated after 1890 and demonstrated how the process actually worked. He concluded by discussing the economic and social significance for Barbados of plantation sub-division and village formation. Among other things, he said, the villages were the cradles of the black middle class, the bases for political democratisation, and a major source of national identity. (Hence, he told his audience, Barbadians had no business to be changing historic village names like Sweet Bottom into Sweet Vale!)

While these two pieces dealt generally with Barbados, Marshall's 1977 paper on Rock Hall was a micro-study of a single village.[22] This outstanding paper, inexplicably never published, reconstructed the origin and early history of Rock Hall on the basis of newspapers, magistrates' reports, wills and deeds, slave registers, Assembly minutes, tax rolls, voter registers and oral sources. Marshall established that Rock Hall was the first 'free village' founded in Barbados and showed how these early post-1838 villages had considerable political potential which was exploited by some, notably Samuel J. Prescod. He succeeded, too, in making the early Rock Hall villagers as 'visible' as the sources permitted, in directing attention to the range of materials available for similar research, and in revealing the value of village studies to local and social history. Quite simply, this paper is a model of professional local history research.

Marshall's early articles on peasant development in the British Caribbean certainly helped to shape subsequent research and debate on the subject, and he contributed significantly to our understanding of the Barbadian case. His work here also linked him to the international scholarship on peasant studies worldwide, reflected in the re-publication of his 1972 article in a French-language volume on peasant movements (see note 17). Still, one feels a sense of disappointment that the 1970s research project on Caribbean peasantries did not yield a greater outcome. The Barbadian work, too, awaits a full-length monograph. Rock Hall gave us a glimpse of the potential here; though the 1977 paper remains unpublished, a video, 'Freedom Is,' was produced by the Barbados Government Information Service (1979), based on Marshall's research on the village.

The historiography of the British Caribbean

Following his teacher and mentor Elsa Goveia, Marshall has shown a consistent interest in historiography. An influential 1975 article reviewed historical writing on the British West Indies since ca. 1940.[23] Marshall examined the specialist literature falling into the genres of political/constitutional, economic and social history, and general works, including island histories, text books and so on. This was a very useful survey, sensible and workmanlike, with over 300 bibliographical references (no theses, but some unpublished papers, were included). He updated this survey in a brief 1989 paper,[24] which discussed how far the deficiencies he noted in 1975 had been remedied since, and proposed a research agenda for the historians.

In his two Elsa Goveia Memorial Lectures —at Mona in 1990 and at Cave Hill in 2000 —Marshall discussed the historiography of two of his major research themes: the 'labour problem' and village development.[25] In his self-deprecating style, Marshall told his Mona audience: 'Since in these matters [work on the labour problem] I might be considered more a historiographer than a historian, I am probably well placed to assess both the research output and the state of the debate.' He proceeded first to summarise the debate on the 'Labour Problem' since Hall's influential 1978 article,[26] giving a brief but trenchant overview and concluding that Hall's option for *push* over *pull* explanations had steadily gained ground as it acquired a firm empirical base. He then posited some crucial questions, which, he argued, needed to be addressed if the debate was to be advanced. Above all, he said, the debate needed more precision and rigour, more recognition of continuities before and after 1838, and many more micro studies (territories, districts, parishes, estates).

In his 'Outaugural Lecture' at Cave Hill (Marshall had already retired when he delivered it), he took up the historiography of the Caribbean village. After reviewing the 'state of play in historical studies of the village,'[27] he considered various definitions of the village used in the historical and anthropological literature and proposed his own. Marshall took his audience through a stimulating discussion of the main village types and sub-types, and then considered the place of the village in the historical literature. He concluded that the literature did not do justice to the village's importance to Caribbean history; neither anthropologists nor historians had followed Mintz's pioneering (1958) work on Jamaican free villages to any great extent (Barry Higman's *Montpelier* being a fine recent exception). There is, of course, an implied *mea culpa* here, especially when he says that, for village history to have really advanced, a senior scholar based at a university would have had to establish a research group and stimulate younger scholars to work on the topic.

Most of Marshall's research work was on the Windwards and Barbados, so it was not surprising to find him writing the chapter sections on the historiography of those islands for Volume VI of the UNESCO *General History of the Caribbean.*[28] He divided his piece on Barbados into four chronological periods during which historians and others wrote about the island's development: the golden age of the plantation, 1627–1740; the mature plantation, 1740–1838; disintegration and readjustment, 1838–1958; to nationhood and beyond, post-1958. In each period, Marshall carefully related the historical writers and their works to political, social, and economic developments, and the 'institutions' for the production and dissemination of knowledge about the past were also discussed. Between the academics and the 'public' historians organised in the Barbados Museum and Historical Society and the Barbados National Trust, he concluded, 'the foundations for all types of history-writing are now firmly laid in Barbados.' However, the situation was less satisfactory for the Windwards.[29] Very little appeared in Marshall's first two periods, which he characterised as insecure settlements to 1814 and these 'ruined islands' to 1958. His third period, 1958–98, saw a relative 'boom period' in historical writings on the Windwards, even if we exclude the over 400 titles on the Grenada Revolution. These aside, it turned out to be Dominica – on which Marshall has written little or nothing – which was best treated in the historical literature up to 1998. But significant gaps remained. Marshall concluded by noticing that the 'two Marshalls' (himself and Bernard) had attempted 'sub-regional history' but observed that their work consisted 'mainly of journal articles and book chapters and it [was] flawed by a failure . . . to develop fully a base for treating the islands as a homogenous whole' – another *mea culpa*, but this time explicit.

In an interesting article written for a *festschrifte* for Roy Augier, his long-time colleague, friend and sparring partner, Marshall took his historiographical interest closer to home: he surveyed the development of history teaching at the UWI.[30] This was not, he wrote, a memoir even though he was part of the developments from 1964; rather it was 'an attempt to reconstruct a story' using as sources UWI and University of London records, oral sources and personal letters. The essay was a piece of (recent) intellectual history, based on original research, authoritative because of his own involvement from 1964 (and as an undergraduate in the 1950s) but never slipping into celebration or reminiscence. It was a serious historiographical essay and an important contribution to UWI's self-documentation, which has become the major source for the role of UCWI/UWI in the professionalisation of West Indian history.[31]

Partly historiographical, but difficult to categorise in my tripartite schema, is Marshall's well-known essay on the ex-slaves' 'hopes and expectations' after 1838.[32] First delivered as a public lecture in 1988, and aimed at a general audience, it began with a critique of the historical literature: blacks' hopes and expectations did not 'figure prominently' in that literature, and even recent historians had generally failed to elucidate the *rational* hopes, fears and choices of the ex-slaves in the first generation of freedom. Marshall indicated the kinds of sources which might be used to reconstruct their 'hopes and expectations,' then discussed the 'range and nature' of these hopes on the basis of what they *did*, and (when this was recorded) what they *said*. He concluded—echoing his 1979 commentary on Mintz—that the ex-slaves wanted freedom of movement, family consolidation, 'just' wages, flexible labour arrangements and easy access to their grounds. It was the historian's business, Marshall exhorted, to retrieve the 'hopes and expectations' of the ex-slaves, to integrate 'all the elements of our past, particularly those that have been criminalized and submerged.'

This was a plea for history from the bottom up, and Marshall has been part of the historiographical trends towards 'subaltern studies,' research which focuses on the masses rather than the classes. Labourers, ex-slaves, sharecroppers and peasants have been his main subjects, as he said in 2000; social history has been his main *genre*. He has not been on the cutting edge of new techniques or unusual source materials, but he has written highly professional, analytical social (and economic, occasionally political) history and thoughtful historiographical surveys. It is true that we miss major works on the post-emancipation Windwards, on Barbadian villages, on British Caribbean peasantries. But, contrary to what he said in 1990, Marshall has been historian as much as historiographer; he has made a solid contribution to the literature on the themes and islands on which he has written. His scholarly output has not been large but it has always been of a high quality; I agree with Carl Campbell's view that he valued 'thoroughness over speed' in history writing.

Institution building

The skills of persuasion, mobilisation and administration which led to his second career as an academic manager at UWI also ensured that he would play a major role in building up the institutional infrastructure for historical work in the Caribbean. Here his contribution was significant.

The Association of Caribbean Historians (ACH) is largely his creation. The honour of first convening a meeting of historians from UWI and from the then Centre Universitaire des Antilles et Guyane belongs to Jacques Adelaide-Merlande. He organised a small meeting in Guadeloupe in 1969; Douglas Hall, head of the three-campus Department of History at UWI, sent Marshall, Neville Hall and Carl Campbell. (These three pioneers dined out for many years on stories of their hardships and adventures in 1969). Hall asked Marshall to organise a follow-up meeting in 1970, with Adelaide, in Barbados, and he was also co-organiser of the third conference in Guyana in 1971. From then on, conferences of Caribbean historians were held every year; and Marshall is, I believe, the only person to have attended every single one (1969–2002).[33]

Unlike Hall, who opposed institutionalising the conferences, Marshall saw the need to form a permanent body. He worked to this end in 1972–74, and was mainly responsible for writing the constitution of the ACH. It was formally launched in Puerto Rico in 1974, with Marshall being elected, predictably, the first president. He served as president (1974–77), and then was 're-cycled', first as vice- president (1990–92), then again as president (1992–94). Whether holding office or not, however, Marshall was – and is – a loyal and effective supporter of the ACH. While it has not achieved all its aims, it has unquestionably stimulated historical research and writing on the Caribbean, and forged strong and fruitful links among historians working in four different languages and based in many different countries.[34] Much of the credit goes to Marshall.

Marshall contributed to the survival and development of the *Journal of Caribbean History*, the only specialist English-language journal in its field. The organ of the UWI Departments of History, it was founded in 1970 with Douglas Hall as its first editor. Marshall took over in 1981 and was responsible for Volumes 18–23 (inclusive). Under his editorship the volumes were substantially enlarged and a regular book review section was begun. The *Journal* fulfilled its purposes and is still appearing, Volume 35 being the most recent at the time of writing. When discussions began about a UNESCO multi-volume *History of the Caribbean*, in 1981, Marshall was a leading actor, and in 1983 he was appointed a member of the drafting committee and its *Rapporteur*. He made an important contribution to the conceptualisation and planning of the six-volume *History*, though he had less to do with it once the volume editors began their work in earnest. He is, however, a contributor to Volume VI (1999) and is expected to write a chapter for Volume IV, still unpublished.[35]

These contributions to the institutional base for historical research and publication were complemented by Marshall's work 'behind the scenes' at UWI (and elsewhere) to mobilise resources for the Departments of History and for individual historians. He was a strong supporter of collaboration among the three History Departments after their formal (separate) establishment in 1972 and used his 'senior historian' status to make it a reality in the 1970s-80s. Always a force to be reckoned with in inter-departmental discussions, he helped to reshape the Caribbean history courses when UWI 'semesterised' itself. Though Marshall never formed a research 'school' around him, and in fact supervised very few successful graduate students, he did consistently use his eminence within the UWI system (as dean, head of department, deputy principal at Cave Hill, pro-vice-chancellor 1990-2000) to benefit the discipline, the historians, and their students.

Marshall has made, as I wrote earlier, a solid contribution to Caribbean historiography on his chosen themes, and has helped to build the infrastructure for teaching, researching and writing the region's history. But his publics await the major monographs and the works of synthesis which his many articles and papers seem to promise. There should be no idle retirement for this Barbadian and Caribbean scholar.

Notes

1. I am grateful to Carl Campbell, of the Mona Campus of UWI, for his helpful comments on a draft of this essay. I do not claim to have examined all of Marshall's publications, but I think I have reviewed all his major historical writings. A very recent paper appeared too late for inclusion in this essay: 'Henry James Ross of Grenada: A Pioneer of Tenant Farming Systems' (Paper presented at UWI School of Continuing Studies Conference on Grenada, Grenada, January 2002). It examines an 1842 pamphlet by Ross in which he advocates share-cropping, not wage labour, as the solution for the planters' post-emancipation difficulties.

2. See W.K. Marshall, ' "It is the Way We Live": the Village in Caribbean History' (Elsa Goveia Memorial Lecture, UWI, Cave Hill, Barbados, October 2000, unpublished typescript), 1-2. The official supervisors were first E.E. Rich, a specialist on Canadian economic history, and then Ronald Robinson of 'Robinson and Gallagher' fame. W.L. Burn was external examiner.

3. W.K. Marshall, 'The Social and Economic Development of The Windward Islands, 1838-65' (PhD thesis, Cambridge University, 1963), Preface.

4. W.K. Marshall, 'The Historiography of Barbados and the Windward Islands,' Parts A and B of Chapter 18, in *UNESCO General History of the Caribbean*, Vol VI, ed. B.W. Higman (London: UNESCO/Macmillan, 1999), 544–79. He coupled Bernard Marshall, author of a 1972 doctoral thesis on the Windwards between 1763 and 1823, in this criticism.

5. W.K. Marshall, 'Social and Economic Problems in the Windward Islands, 1838–65,' in *The Caribbean Transition*, ed. F. Andic and T. Matthews (Rio Piedras: University of Puerto Rico, 1965), 234–57, and 'Metayage in the Sugar Industry of the British West Indies, 1838–65,' *Jamaican Historical Review*, 5, (1965): 28–55.

6. W.K. Marshall, 'The Termination of the Apprenticeship in Barbados and the Windward Islands,' *Journal of Caribbean History*, 2, (1971): 1–45. This paper was first presented at the First Conference of the ACH, Guadeloupe, 1969.

7. W.K. Marshall, 'The Ex-slaves as Wage Labourers on the Sugar Estates in the British Windward Islands, 1838–46' (Paper presented at the Eleventh Conference of the ACH, Curaçao, 1979).

8. W.K. Marshall, 'Apprenticeship and Labour Relations in Four Windward Islands,' in *Abolition and its Aftermath*, ed. D. Richardson (London: Frank Cass, 1985), 203–24.

9. W.K. Marshall, 'Provision Ground and Plantation Labour in four Windward Islands: Competition for Resources During Slavery,' *Slavery and Abolition*, 12.1, (1991): 48–67. This was first presented at the Twentieth Conference of the ACH, St Thomas, 1988.

10. W.K. Marshall, ' "Vox Populi": The St Vincent Riots and Disturbances of 1862,' in *Trade, Government and Society in the Caribbean History 1700-1920*, ed. B.W. Higman, (Kingston: Heinemann, 1983), 85–115.

11. W.K. Marshall, 'St Lucia in the Economic History of the Windward Islands: The Nineteenth Century Experience,' *Caribbean Quarterly*, 35.3 (1989): 25–33.

12. W.K. Marshall, ed., *The Colthurst Journal* (Millwood, New York: KTO Press, 1977).

13. It was clearly a model for Roderick McDonald's introductory essay to his edition of John Anderson's journal. Anderson was also a special magistrate in St Vincent during the apprenticeship. See his *Between Slavery and Freedom* (Kingston: UWI Press, 2001).

14. For the sake of completeness, I note here two published lectures given in the mid-1980s on aspects of nineteenth-century Barbadian history: 'Amelioration and Emancipation (with special reference to Barbados)' in *Emancipation I*, ed. Alvin Thompson (Bridgetown: UWI, 1986), 72–87 and 'Nineteenth-Century Crises in the Barbadian Sugar Industry' in *Emancipation II*, ed. W.K. Marshall (Bridgetown: 1987), 85–101. Both are solid pieces, geared to general audiences as part of an

'outreach' series of public lectures.

15. Marshall noted in his 1989 lecture on St Lucia (note 11) that he was regarded as 'one of the few authorities on the economic history of St Lucia' on the basis of his PhD thesis written in the early 1960s.

16. W.K. Marshall, 'Notes on Peasant Development in the West Indies since 1838,' *Social and Economic Studies*, 17.3, (1968): 252-63.

17. W.K. Marshall 'Aspects of the Development of the Peasantry,' *Caribbean Quarterly*, 18.1 (1972): 30-46, 53-57; also published in *Les Mouvements paysans dans le monde contemporain* (Naples: 1976).

18. W.K. Marshall, 'The Peasantry and the Sugar Industry' (Paper presented at the Second Conference of the ACH, Barbados, 1970).

19. W.K. Marshall, 'Commentary I' on S. Mintz, 'Slavery and the Rise of Peasantries,' in *Historical Reflections/Réflexions Historiques* 6.1, ed. M. Craton (1979), 243-48.

20. W.K. Marshall et al., 'The Establishment of a Peasantry in Barbados, 1840-1920,' in *Social Groups and Institutions in the History of the Caribbean* (San Juan: ACH, 1975), 85-104. The paper was first presented at the Sixth Conference of the ACH, Puerto Rico, 1974.

21. W.K. Marshall, 'Villages and Plantation Sub-Division,' in *Emancipation III*, ed. W.K. Marshall (Bridgetown: UWI, 1988), 1-19. It was first delivered as a public lecture in 1987.

22. W.K. Marshall, 'Rock Hall, St Thomas: The Search for the First Free Village in Barbados' (Paper presented at the Ninth Conference of the ACH, Barbados, 1977).

23. W.K. Marshall, 'A Review of Historical Writing on the Commonwealth Caribbean since c. 1940,' *Social and Economic Studies*, 24.3,(1975): 271-307.

24. W.K. Marshall, 'Caribbean Historiography: Anglophone and British West Indian Scholarship in the last 20 years' (Paper presented at the Twenty-first Conference of the ACH, Guadeloupe, 1989).

25. W.K. Marshall, *The Post-Slavery Problem Revisited* (The 1991 Elsa Goveia Memorial Lecture, Kingston, Department of History, UWI, 1991); and see note 2.

26. D. Hall, 'The Flight from the Estates Reconsidered: The British West Indies, 1838-42,' *Journal of Caribbean History*, 10 & 11 (1978): 7-24.

27. He chose to cite only two of his own pieces, those cited here in notes 21 & 22.

28. See note 4.

29. Dominica was included in Marshall's coverage (as we saw, it was excluded from his Ph.D. research and from his subsequent publications on the Windward Islands). Works on Tobago were only considered if published before 1889 (subsequent studies were considered in the section on Trinidad and Tobago, by myself).

30. W.K. Marshall, 'History Teaching in The University of the West Indies' in *Before and After 1865,* eds. B. Moore and S. Wilmot (Kingston: Ian Randle Publishers, 1998), 49–76, 380–82.

31. It is interesting to compare Marshall's essay with the treatment of more or less the same subject in B.W. Higman's *Writing West Indian Histories* (London: Macmillan, 1999), chapters 4 and 5. Higman was a member of the Mona History Department 1969–94, and its most influential head after Douglas Hall.

32. W.K. Marshall, ' "We be wise to many more tings": Blacks' Hopes and Expectations of Emancipation,' in *The University of the West Indies' 40th Anniversary Lectures,* ed. F.R. Augier, (Mona: UWI, 1990), 31–46; republished in *Caribbean Freedom,* eds. H. McD. Beckles and V. Shepherd (Kingston: Ian Randle Publishers, 1993), pp. 12–20.

33. Fittingly, the person who has given the most papers at the Conferences is Adelaide-Merlande, according to Marshall.

34. Marshall presented seven papers to ACH conferences and chaired panels on innumerable occasions. He mobilised resources to keep the ACH operational and lobbied with UWI, UNESCO and other bodies for financial and other help.

35. This and the preceding two paragraphs are based on my own personal knowledge, though Marshall discusses the ACH, JCH and the UNESCO History briefly in 'History Teaching,' 68–76.

CHAPTER 2

'Petticoat Rebellion?': the Black Woman's Body and Voice in the Struggles for Freedom in Colonial Jamaica

Verene A. Shepherd

Introduction

On January 26, 1816, Matthew Gregory Lewis, proprietor of Cornwall Estate in western Jamaica, made the following entry in his Journal:

> Every morning my agent regales me with some fresh instance of insubordination. It seems this morning, the women, one and all, refused to carry away the trash, . . . and that without the slightest pretence: in consequence, the mill was obliged to be stopped; and when the driver on that station insisted on their doing their duty, a little fierce young devil, a Miss Whaunica, flew at his throat, and endeavoured to strangle him: the agent was obliged to be called in, and at length, this petticoat rebellion was subdued. . . .[1]

What the rather sexist Lewis referred to as 'petticoat rebellion,' arguably a metaphor for enslaved women's resistance, was not, of course, confined to Cornwall estate but was a standard feature of the slave system in colonial Jamaica, as indeed it was in the wider British-colonised Caribbean. Furthermore, even though the term 'petticoat rebellion' may have been used by early nineteenth-century planters as a way of peripheralising women's resistance, later developments proved how wrong they were to do so. Of course, that women played a fundamental role in the struggle for freedom and the eventual achievement of emancipation can no longer be in doubt, based on contemporary accounts of colonial Jamaica and the findings of modern researchers.

Bernard Senior, a British military officer active in the suppression of the 1831 Christmas Rebellion in Jamaica, in describing instances of malingering, insolence and the attempt to enforce moral economy on several plantations, admitted that 'women as well as men were alike defaulters.'[2] Several enslavers complained of intransigent females who thwarted the overseers and drivers in the field constantly, and of women who used a variety of strategies to subvert and destabilise the plantation system.

The majority of women may not have been in the vanguard of armed revolts, though they played other key roles; but their day-to-day strategies clearly bothered enslavers and their supporters and ultimately so undermined the efficiency of the plantation that they played an active role in the abolition of slavery, refuting the suggestion of harmless 'petticoat rebels.' In any event, as Hilary Beckles asks in *Centering Woman*, 'What is the political significance of an argument which says that physical combat in war should be privileged above broad-based ideological preparation?' Why should non-violent day-to-day strategies be marginalised and men's leadership of armed revolts be 'centred' as being more important?[3]

In addition to evidence of women's contribution to the freedom project in contemporary historical narratives, like those of Lewis and Senior, modern scholars like the pioneer feminist historian Lucille Mathurin Mair, along with Linnette Vassell and Beckles who have made women and gender analysis central to the historical discourse, have contributed much to our knowledge and understanding of women's participation in emancipation. These scholars have not only studied emancipation from that brutal slavery regime that for four centuries tyrannised millions of Africans and their descendants in the Americas, but also emancipation from systems of domination in the post-slavery and post-colonial periods.[4]

Despite continued cynicism in the academy about the legitimacy of gender-specific history, these radical scholars, attempting to compensate for past historiographical neglect, have emphasised that there was no homogeneous 'slave experience' and that analyses of the conditions of enslaved people, and indeed of the society influenced by the slave system, must take gender differentiation into consideration. As part of this project of differentiation, they have embarked on studies of the gender specificity of control and the struggles of the enslaved for freedom, showing that while the struggles of the slavery period were inherently collective, the gender relations of slavery determined actions in many ways. Their conclusion, then, is that the ideology of anti-slavery was not gender free, but implicated gender.

These scholars, among others, have shown conclusively that black women were to be found at various levels of the anti-slavery movement, formulating resistance strategies as non-violent protestors, Maroons, cultural leaders, and mothers. Such evidence now provides a counter-discourse to the racist and sexist assumptions of planters and other contemporary writers, some novelists, who represented enslaved women as being content with slavery and doing everything in their power to support white society.

For example, the enslaved women in the anonymously-written novel, *Marly, or a Planter's Life in Jamaica*, published in 1828, are made to voice support for the practice of white men taking black 'wives'.[5] Similarly, Catherine and Mary Ann, central female characters in Cyrus Francis Perkins' 1855 novel, *Busha's Mistress, or Catherine the Fugitive*, defend and support white men ('their bushas'), who abused them.[6] In 'Monk' Lewis' Journal, Mary Wiggins and the other enslaved people on Cornwall estate are made to seem grateful that they had a 'massa'; and it only took a threat that he was leaving for England '. . . never [to] return to Jamaica' to get the enslaved to beg him to stay. According to him, 'all hands were clasped and all voices were raised, imploring me not to leave them and assuring me that in future they would do their work quietly and willingly.'[7] A 'poor woman nearly 100 years old and stone blind' insisted on being taken to the Cornwall Great House so that she could 'touch massa [Lewis].' When she had done so, she is reported to have said: 'that was enough . . ., now me hab once kiss a massa's hand, me willing to die tomorrow, me no care.'[8] Cynric Williams' Diana, in his 1823 *Tour of the Island of Jamaica,* is content with her situation of enslavement though the central male figures, 'Sneezer' and 'Dollar', articulate clear anti-slavery opinions.[9]

Absent voices, ventriloquised voices

The fact that so-called 'petticoat rebels' constituted such a central feature of the Jamaican slave system should come as no surprise, given the central features of colonialism. Admittedly, there is limited access to the direct voices and written views of those who tried to liberate themselves. Instead, sources that ventriloquise their voices have to be tapped. The problems and pitfalls of ventriloquising the black experience and subjecting such experiences to a kind of disfiguring gaze are well known.[10] But finding enslaved women's written views is a very difficult task. Texts generated by enslaved peoples in the Caribbean do exist, forming an important part of the Caribbean literary tradition. However, unlike other Caribbean territories where letters written by enslaved women (like Dolly Newton and Jenny Lane,[11] and texts based on the narratives of enslaved people like Mary Prince,[12] Olaudah Equiano and Esteban Montejo) have come to light,[13] Jamaica has yet to discover comparable detailed letters and texts. Therefore, in order to access the voices of enslaved women in Jamaica, the historian is left with little choice other than to mine contemporary historical and literary texts, newspapers, reports of Commissions of Inquiry, records of trials of enslaved people, and court records generally. Skeptical as some scholars may be about their authenticity and the basis of their authority, these sources must be accepted as they allow historians to make some progress towards discovering how enslaved women participated in the project of emancipation.

These second-hand sources indicate first of all that slavery and colonialism provided enough justification for women's resistance. Caribbean history, like that of other former colonised spaces, has been characterised by imperial domination and systems of exploitation that have inevitably generated an opposing struggle for liberation. The emergence of Western Europe as the political centre of an Atlantic economy signalled the importance of imperial exploitation to its development. European colonial capitalism could see no way to ensure profitable economic activity other than with the mass deployment of servile labour. Beginning with Spain in the fifteenth century, six European nations proceeded to impose structural discontinuities upon indigenous Caribbean societies, to import and subjugate white servants from Europe after they had decimated the Taino and Kalinago peoples, and to kidnap, transport across the Atlantic and enslave millions of Africans. Among these African captives were Igbo, Akan, Ewe, Congo and other peoples from diverse regions of West Africa.[14] Quantitative studies reveal that during the period of the transatlantic trade in enslaved African captives to Jamaica, 1655 to 1807, the dominant sources of captives were (in order of numerical importance), The Bight of Biafra, the Gold Coast, West Central Africa, the Bight of Benin, Sierra Leone and Senegambia,[15] reinforcing recent views that the Igbo presence in Jamaica became stronger after the seventeenth century. Indeed, in the years 1792 to 1807, an estimated 49 per cent of enslaved Africans captured and shipped to Jamaica comprised ethnic groups from the Bight of Biafra, with West Central Africa (35 per cent) being the next significant.[16]

The majority of these enslaved Africans were male. Despite regional variations (with a significantly high proportion of women exported from the Bight of Biafra or present day south-east Nigeria), overall less than 40 per cent of enslaved African captives were female (compared to over 60 per cent in the trade to Muslim areas).[17] In the period 1658–1713, enslaved males made up 78.1 per cent of captives to Jamaica from Senegambia; 58 per cent from the Gold Coast; 61.7 per cent from the Bight of Benin; 51.2 per cent from the Bight of Biafra, and 60.9 per cent from West Central Africa.[18]

More cause for resistance: the abuse of women's bodies in the field

The abuse of women's bodies was a clear factor in their active participation in the emancipation project. While it is undeniable that both subaltern men and women suffered under the slavery system of domination, it is equally undeniable that women suffered ultra-exploitation. Their bodies became the site of power contestation, firstly as field labourers, and secondly, as a subsequent section will show, as domestics and concubines. Such abuse of women's bodies caused their resistance to take on unique, gender-specific forms, with the body being employed to full purpose. Despite the sexual disparity in the transatlantic trade in African captives, women outnumbered men in the field gangs that did the most arduous work. As in West Africa, production and productivity expansion eventually came to depend upon female labour. This was despite the fact that planters reportedly professed a preference for male captives, a factor that supposedly influenced the sexual composition of the trade in captives. Despite the reasons for the gender imbalance in the trade from Africa, in the Caribbean, men were valued for craftsmen skills or work in the semi-industrial processes of the sugar mill and were generally under-represented as field labourers.

Thus, while the majority of women worked in the fields, in the great houses as domestics, and nursed the sick in the hot houses, men had a wider range of tasks.[19] Women weeded, planted, harvested, worked in the sugar factories and generally contributed to the productive processes on sugar plantations. In addition to the physical demands on their bodies from field labour, any infraction of the slave codes or the law of the black slave-driver was followed by severe beatings and other forms of physical abuse of the enslaved female's body. The gender division of labour noticed on the large sugar plantations was replicated on non-sugar properties, for example, on coffee plantations and livestock farms (styled 'pens'). In 1784, 18 males compared to 40 females worked in the fields on Prospect Pen;[20] in 1822, 76 per cent of the women on St Jago and Paisley Pen were located in the field; and in 1802, 20 of the 55 men and teenaged boys worked in the fields on William Hewitt's coffee plantation in Clarendon compared to 39 of the women and teenaged girls.[21]

Sexploitation

The presence of more enslaved women than men in enslavers' (mostly white) households exposed women to mental, physical and sexual abuse. Therefore, in addition to the abuse of their bodies through the arduous physical field regime, women were open to sexual abuse – sexploitation – to a far greater degree than men. As Beckles has observed, 'Neither colonial statutes nor slave codes . . . invested slaves with any rights over their own bodies, but rather transferred and consolidated such rights within the legal person of the slaveowners.'[22] Male enslavers thus claimed violent access to enslaved women's bodies, and male and female enslavers to the sale of enslaved women's bodies for money upon the sex market. Not only did laws not allow the enslaved to refuse these sexual demands made by their enslavers, but they allowed for punishment of those who did not acquiesce.

Habitual rapists like Thomas Thistlewood, who owned and/or managed properties in western Jamaica, seemed to have believed that one advantage of coming to Jamaica was the chance of sexually exploiting many black and coloured women. Thistlewood kept detailed journals (over 10,000 folio pages) that reveal that while working for Mr Vassell on Vineyard Pen in Westmoreland and Mr Cope on Egypt plantation, he sexually abused practically every enslaved woman located on those properties: Betty, Chrissey, Hago, Juba, Marina, Phibbah and Sylvia. In his first year at Egypt Sugar Plantation, he raped 11 enslaved women on 53 occasions. At the end of 1753 he labelled Phibbah, the creole housekeeper at Egypt sugar plantation, as his 'wife' (but did not remain faithful to her). When he established his own property, Breadnut Island Pen, in 1768, he hired Phibbah from her owner as his concubine, taking her to his pen.

Thistlewood was not alone in his attitude towards, and treatment of, black women. In 1824, Robert Wedderburn, a freed man from Jamaica and son of a white Scottish planter, underscored the abuse of enslaved domestic women owned by his father, James Wedderburn, in the following way:

> My father's house was full of female slaves, all objects of his lust; amongst whom he Strutted like Solomon in his grand seraglio or like a bantam cock upon his own dunghill. . . . By him my mother [Rossanna] was made the object of his brutal lust. . . . My father ranged through the whole of his household for his own lewd purposes; for they being his personal property, cost nothing extra [for sexual favours]. . . .In short, among his own slaves my father was a perfect parish bull; and his pleasure was the greater, because he at the same time increased his profits [when enslaved women became pregnant].[23]

Examples abound of white men who sexually abused enslaved women or kept them as 'wives/mistresses': John Hartnole of Retrieve estate (who kept Coobah, Phibbah's daughter); William Crookshank of Egypt; John Filton, Thomas Fewkes, Mr Cope, Robert Gibbs, Christopher White, all of Egypt. These so-called 'sexual relationships' are also captured in novels like *Marly*, *Busha's Mistress* and *Harmony*, set during slavery in Jamaica. The author of *Marly*, while unwilling to take a 'slave wife,' describes the existence of the custom among other white men. Perkins links the enslaved women Catherine and Mary Ann with overseers Jackson and Waldy respectively, and Mary Gaunt writes of Hesba who had a son for Squire Thole of Harmony estate.

Robert Wedderburn also confirmed the practice of organised prostitution, noting that 'a planter letting out his prettiest female slaves for purposes of lust, is by no means uncommon.'[24] The commercialisation of enslaved women's sexuality as cash-receiving prostitutes was not unique to Jamaica as Beckles' analysis of the marketing of black women's sexuality in Barbados reveals.[25] Organised prostitution was particularly common in urban centres where the majority of black women were owned by female enslavers who profited from enslaved women's bodies as domestic labourers and prostitutes. The offspring of enslaved women prostitutes, usually sold, also brought in additional profits. Some gained freedom from such alliances, though such gratuitous manumission was never guaranteed.

While some women and/or their children were freed as a result of their sexual links with empowered white men, many others continued to exist within the context of unequal power relations. Cyrus Francis Perkins captured this historical reality in fictional form. Catherine, ostensibly the overseer Jackson's slave 'wife', knew that his frequent promises to free her were empty. Thus:

[I]t not today I hear the story talk of you buying me. S'pose you goin' buy me like Jack Mowatt buy Sally . . . buy him when him please an' sell him when he get tired of him. If you caan even buy me, you can buy de baby? If you get discharge 'spose I am to hand over to de nex Busha whether I like him or hate him. See Nancy Lewis, What she is come to.. a gal dat use to wear shoes and stocking when her fader was alive, an' could even read newspaper! I don't t'ink Nancy can all tell who is de fader of him two children. Tedder day me speak to him for him own good an' him say, "Pig ax him mumma wha' mek him mout' long so an' him mumma say "ta pickney tell yu mout long so to".[26]

The road to emancipation: the body in resistance

There is overwhelming evidence that enslaved women did not give their bodies for reproduction or productive labour willingly; neither did they accept passively the use of their bodies by white men. They used a variety of strategies to subvert the slavery system and liberate their bodies from brutal forms of enslavement and most of these are now common knowledge: malingering, lying, stealing, poisoning, self-purchase and running away. Marronage was a common form of removing the body from the site of oppression and the records are full of such examples. Nanny, of course, is now accepted as the quintessential rebel Maroon woman. But there were others. Abigail, Mary and Congo Sally would not be confined to his property despite Thistlewood's attempts and severe punishment. Sally, in particular, in whom Thistlewood had a sexual interest, ran away constantly, despite the difficulty presented by the post-1739 Maroon Treaty environment in western Jamaica.

As a result of the fact that their bodies were targeted in the enslavers' efforts to control them, enslaved women used their bodies, in addition to their voices and minds, in the emancipation project. They did so despite the physical consequences (some gender-specific), of such actions: floggings (such as those administered by Thomas Thistlewood to Mimba, Juba, Cynthia, Jenny and Deborah for theft of supplies on his pen); rape (as manifested in the actions of Thistlewood and James Wedderburn); hanging, transportation out of the island, imprisonment, branding with hot irons, gibbeting and dismemberment.

Women used body language to register their discontent with slavery. Cynric Williams, on his tour of Jamaica in 1823, tells us that among a party of enslaved people who were brought before the magistrate for misdemeanours was 'one damsel in particular who in her defence said she had been harshly used, on one occasion getting 230 lashings at one flogging.' As the magistrate doubted her story, 'the sable nymph without hesitation exposed her behind, whereupon there was no mark whatever; and it appearing that she had so done in derision and contempt, they ordered her a couple dozen.'[27] This use of the exposed 'behind' to express contempt for exploiters was not confined to Jamaican slave society, as Nemata Blyden has revealed in her analysis of Sierra Leone.[28]

The voice in resistance

Enslaved women raised their voices in liberation songs and used their voices to curse those who bought them at auctions or oppressed them generally. We learn from Mary Gaunt, author of the novel *Harmony*, that Maria, wrongfully enslaved and shipped to Jamaica and bought by a St Ann enslaver, resisted both the Middle Passage and her sale. Gaunt writes of the way in which Maria used tongue and body language to abuse her purchaser and his colleague and register her views about the injustice of her capture, shipment and auction. Speaking for her, Gaunt writes that Maria '. . . faced the two men [Thole and Ridley] and called them every vile name she could lay her tongue to; looked them up and down, noted their weak points [for example, baldness] and gave them the benefit of her observation aloud.'[29] Williams also reported that after being lashed by the driver, an unnamed black woman on an estate he visited, looked over her shoulder and said in a suppressed tone, but loud enough to be heard, 'Go to hell,' and walked off.[30]

Women petitioned attorneys to get unpopular or particularly harsh overseers dismissed and they also went on strike in order to force compliance with their wishes. Strikes were also resorted to when customary allowances, such as time to work provision grounds and to go to the markets, were reduced or withheld. The enslaved understood that negotiation for some measure of economic autonomy was not only a way of surviving enslavement, but also of asserting their power as workers on whom the productive activities of the sugar plantation and other properties depended. Thus the enslaved clearly practised forms of collective bargaining traditionally only associated with industrial wage workers.[31] Such activities were not confined to the large estates. Thomas Thistlewood, while on Vineyard Pen, seemed particularly disturbed about the extent to which the enslaved stole goods, at times as part of the activities of runaways, and described them as 'a nest of thieves and villains.'[32]

'Gynaecological resistance'?

After 1807, when the transatlantic trade in enslaved African captives was abolished, enslaved women's bodies became more crucial to the reproduction of the enslaved population and thus to the perpetuation of slavery. Armed with this knowledge, enslaved women sought to free their previously enchained wombs, refusing to bear children who would, themselves, be enslaved. Several enslavers attested to the use of abortive agents and the reluctance of enslaved women to bear children. Thistlewood recorded that enslaved females deliberately tried to abort their pregnancies by drinking various herbs. Mountain Lucy, for example, drank 'contrayerva' to abort her pregnancy.[33]

Matthew Gregory Lewis confirmed the trend of gynaecological resistance, commenting that 'I really believe that the negresses can produce children at pleasure; and where they are barren, it is just as hens will frequently not lay eggs on ship-board, because they do not like their situation.'[34] Domestic women also found various ways to harass and frustrate their female enslavers; and some women took the extreme action of dismemberment to remove the parts of the body necessary to give labour.

Bodies in motion: resisting sexual abuse

Women, whether kept by white men as mistresses or not, resisted sexual abuse, even though there were no laws to protect them from sexploitation. A close reading of Thistlewood's journals reveals that Phibbah was not easily seduced. Even though her 'relationship' with Thistlewood lasted for over three decades, she tried to maintain some autonomy over these years. Thistlewood's diaries contain evidence that Phibbah, even after becoming his 'wife', disregarded his overtures on occasions and withheld her affection periodically.

In *Busha's Mistress* (which is not as fictional as it might seem, as the author at one time may have worked on the estate on which the novel is set), Perkins tells us that Jackson, the overseer of Greenside estate in Trelawny, tried to punish Mary Ann because the latter refused his advances. Mary Ann complained that 'Busha persecute me all de time,' even putting her in the stocks, because she did not encourage him. Catherine upped and left Jackson, 'her' Busha, when she learnt of his interest in Mary Ann, making sure to check with the attorney that Jackson could not 'mek I lib wid him against me wishes.' Jackson's entreaties for her to return 'home' were met with a philosophical retort from Catherine:

> Home? Home! Has a slave any home? He is here today and there tomorrow.
> He is sen' to work any property Trustee please, an' praps seld if young Massa
> owe money. Look at me sister Sarah! Me eber see him since de day Marshall
> put handcuff on him an' drag him off de estate? An' didn't eberybody. Say
> Mr Hines was a rich man? De grave is de home for such as we.[35]

The author of *Marly* (who may have been a book-keeper on a Jamaican estate), tries to persuade his readers that there were women who encouraged their daughters to become white men's 'wives' because of perceived 'benefits'. Some of the women, he says, asked him constantly,'Why massa Marly not take him one wife like oder bukras? Dere is him little Daphne, would make him a good wife – dere is him young Diana – dere is him Venus – dere is him Mary Magdalene, and dere is him Phoebe.' But others refused white men's advances. Delia, of the fictional Water Melon Valley estate, refused overseer Adams' attempts to seduce her.[36]

The road to emancipation: armed revolt

Armed revolt was more infrequent than day-to-day strategies as a form of resistance, and when it occurred comparatively few of the enslaved participated in it. Still, despite the tendency to name armed rebellions according to their identifiable male leaders – Sam Sharpe Rebellion, Tacky's Rebellion, and so on – enslaved women, like rank-and-file enslaved men, played active, though apparently gender-specific, roles. Enslaved women in Jamaica were involved in the plots and violent rebellions of 1673, 1690, 1760 and 1824. In June 1824, at the height of the anti-slavery movement, the planters in the parish of Hanover reported that they had discovered a rebellious conspiracy of 'a very alarming nature' involving the enslaved on the sugar estates as well as on Argyle, Ramble, Burnt Ground, Silver Grove and Knockalva Pens. The plan had been for the enslaved to set fire to the properties in the parish and to kill any whites who attempted to put out the blaze. William Roach, an enslaved man on Argyle Pen, allegedly revealed the plot and prevented the revolt.[37]

In the 1831 'Christmas Rebellion', that has come to be intimately associated with Sam Sharpe, one of its outstanding leaders, women's roles have been recorded by contemporary observers. This rebellion erupted in St James. The main cause was enslaved people's belief that they were to be freed at Christmas, '. . . and that their freedom order had actually come out from England but was being withheld and that they only had to strike *en masse*, and they should gain their object.'[38] Enslaved men and women from pens and plantations in Trelawny and St James parish had apparently agreed that any attempt to force them back to work after the Christmas holidays was to be met by setting fire to the properties (though not their huts or provision grounds). After reports were heard that whites were attempting to break the strike on Salt Spring estate, John Dunbar, an enslaved man, set fire to the proprietor's house on Kensington. This triggered off, arguably, the most decisive rebellion on the road to emancipation in Jamaica and the British-colonised Caribbean.

Bernard Senior, who was a military officer in Jamaica when this crucial rebellion erupted, outlined three telling instances of female involvement in this armed struggle. First, at the height of the rebellion in western Jamaica, soldiers from the St Elizabeth and Westmoreland Regiments on the look-out for rebels, encountered an old, lame enslaved woman surrounded by numerous iron pots of provisions. Questioned about her activity, she claimed that she and other women were supposed to have been fixing breakfast for the rebels in a nearby camp. But on getting news that two regiments were close to the camp, the rebels fled, she knew not where. Because of her lame feet she could not descend the steep passes to escape, so she had made up her mind to stay put and deliver herself up to the 'bukras for pardon.'[39] The soldiers, however, became suspicious at the way in which, despite her alleged lameness, the old woman moved among the pots, stirring each in turn. It turned out that each pot of food was poisoned as a trap for the military, for it was hoped that they would be persuaded to consume it. Neither threats nor promises could induce the old woman to eat any of the food herself, reinforcing the soldiers' suspicions that the food indeed was poisoned.

Second, although a captain's detachment was posted in the vicinity of the provision grounds on Stracy Plantation, an enslaved woman named Susan, who wore an apron with the words 'My heart is fixed/I cannot change/I love my choice/ too well to range,' acted as a guide for a foraging party. Most of the party escaped with provisions, and only Susan and two enslaved men were caught.[40]

Third, a party of soldiers, tracking down rebels who had taken 15 white women captive, captured a young black woman who had abandoned her task of filling five gourds with water when she heard them approaching. According to Senior, the enslaved woman 'pleaded great penitence, acknowledging that she had long ago left her owner's service, without leave or cause, but (having been out so long) denied any knowledge of the insurrection.' She did admit that she had heard that as soon as Mr Burchell, the Baptist parson, returned from England, all the enslaved would be free. But she left the plantation because she thought there would be no harm in taking her freedom a little before the time appointed.[41] Asked why one person needed so much water, she said that she was living in the woods by herself and that day she was washing all her clothes and wished to carry plenty of water at once for the purpose. One of the soldiers decided that she was lying and commanded her to lead them to where the rebels were keeping the captives. She proceeded to do just that – or so the soldiers thought. She was in fact leading them away from the camp. But unfortunately for her, this was soon discovered, for one of the soldiers noticed that she carefully avoided every heavily travelled path, and invariably took those newly cut and little used. After going a 100 yards or so past a path with its entrance blocked with newly cut logwood branches (which the woman had passed without so much a glance), one of the soldiers insisted that he heard voices at a little distance in the wood.

According to Senior, 'she affirmed that it was quite impossible, as she knew every track in the neighbourhood, and the logwood had been cut by herself and placed there to prevent stray cattle from destroying her small provision ground, which they had latterly been in the habit of doing.'[42] The soldiers proceeded for a short distance further, but eventually became suspicious and decided to go back and explore the barricaded path they had passed. They also confronted the enslaved woman, accusing her of lying and held a gun to her head to force her to confess. She immediately fell on her knees, acknowledged that she belonged to a strong party of well-armed rebels and that what she had been doing was conducting them to the rebel retreat. She was confident that such a small group of white soldiers would have been easily killed by the slave rebels before they could retreat. At that precise moment of discovery, the soldiers were within a quarter mile of the rebels. She also admitted that the barricaded entrance led to where 15 white women were being held hostage.

What seems clear from these anecdotal accounts is that there was a gender division of roles during some armed revolts. While enslaved men led the armed, military assaults in 1831–32, women played non-military, supporting roles. Strategic manoeuvring was assigned to the women: supplying water, acting as guides to provision grounds; helping to guard captives, poisoning, and acting as look outs and even go-betweens in the final stage of the rebellion. It was Gardiner's wife, for example, who was sent to approach the British lieutenant to inform him that Gardiner wanted to give himself up, once he could negotiate terms for his life.[43] On livestock farms involved in the rebellion, women cooked food for the bands of rebels who stopped there for revictualling purposes. There was also a division of roles among the men. 'Daddy Ruler', Sam Sharpe, was clearly in overall charge, but, according to Senior, '. . . [Colonel] Gardiner took charge of all military movements; and being well acquainted with the characters of his juniors, knew well how to appropriate the squads.' Those in his 'squad' included 'Captain' Dove, M'Cail, M'Lenan, Trail, Largie, Haughton, Hurlock, Peterkin, Simpson, Bernard, and many other unsung, rank-and-file heroes.[44] Enslaved men and women thus worked together in this final rebellion before the passage of the Emancipation Act in 1833. By 1832, the writing was on the wall: if emancipation did not come from above, it would come from below, from the resistance activities of the subaltern.

The road to emancipation: not two types of labour at the same time!

In addition to contributing to emancipation through their activities of resistance, enslaved women contributed to freedom in two other ways. The abolition of the transatlantic trade in enslaved African captives in 1807 placed the British enslavers in a difficult position. They could not import fresh workers, though they could and did move around, internally, those that they possessed.[45] Their only hope was to get enslaved women to reproduce. We already know that some of the women did not agree to reproduce. But even assuming that the women would cooperate and have children, how could enslavers possibly deploy female labour in such a way as to encourage both reproduction and production? How could they ensure that women would perform both forms of 'labour' at the same time? This was a difficult position. Women were the backbone of the field activities, anti-slavery forces were clamouring for emancipation and the enslaved were fighting for freedom. One solution was to improve or ameliorate the conditions of women in the fertile age group. But this would mean scaling down the back-breaking gang labour performed by these women who also were in the most economically productive age group. In the end, it was clear that gender would affect emancipation, for labour and reproduction, though both needed at the same time, were clearly incompatible. To remove women from the fields would be to affect production severely; to keep them in the field for production, thus making reproduction difficult, would be to doom slavery anyway. Women's power to hasten emancipation was clear.

Gender in the British anti-slavery campaign: feminist sensitivity

As the anti-slavery movement gained momentum after 1807 and promoted its ideas by focusing on the exploitation of black women, the moral authority of enslavers came under intense scrutiny.[46] Among those who highlighted the condition of black women and agitated for their freedom were radical white women like Mary Wollstonecraft and Lucy Townsend. They expressed their concern for women and the family under slavery and opposed the ways in which slavery degraded women and prevented them from playing their proper role in life. They presented graphic evidence of the exploitation of women that served to align radical women in Britain with the emancipation cause and helped to step up the pressure for complete abolition.

Free at last?

Black men and women, then, played fundamental roles in their own liberation from slavery and enslaved black women presented slave society with a sustained feminist opposition. Despite the unquestionable importance of economic forces[47] and political reform, and despite the claims of humanitarian (e.g., church and missionary) activism as a factor in emancipation, it is now generally accepted by historians that sustained anti-slavery struggle on the ground, not the vigour of the British anti-slavery movement, sealed the issue of abolition. The enslaved gave the British government little choice but to respond with legislative emancipation in 1833.

The passage of the Emancipation Act in 1833 did not, however, end systems of domination. Consequently, women's activism in the cause of unambiguous freedom continued in the period 1834–38. Along with their male counterparts, they protested the introduction of the transition period of neo-slavery, euphemistically called the Apprenticeship System, scheduled to last until 1840 for praedial (field) workers and 1838 for non-praedials. Thomas Holt observed that the predominance of women among the leaders and activists during the apprenticeship years was especially ironic, given that the emancipation law was conceived and written in an unreflectively masculine gender.[48] Yet, since under slavery women comprised a disproportionate share of apprenticed field workers, it should come as no surprise that women offered the most militant resistance to the Apprenticeship System.[49] Many women refused to work in the non-compulsory hours allowed under the Apprenticeship System, even though wages were offered. Some sought to buy themselves out of the Apprenticeship System, while still others participated in violent and non-violent protests (such as strikes),[50] disrupted production as much as they could, brought numerous complaints to the stipendiary magistrates who were to act as mediators between former enslavers and apprentices, and used their bodies and voices to register discontent with plantation management. Holt reports that after some male apprentices on Belvedere estate were sentenced to prison and were being led away, a 70-year-old woman, 'with the most violent language and impassioned gestures,' called upon the other apprentices to prevent the police from taking her three children, who were among the prisoners, to the workhouse. Violence erupted as the workers tried to do just that.[51]

On the island's pens, a frequent complaint was that the apprentices were behaving in a disrespectful manner, especially to women employers, and were 'very much disposed to use unbecoming and saucy language to their masters and more especially to those among the small settlers.' [52] Eventually, the methods used to control women – the treadmills in the houses of correction – created such a furore that once again women's plight was placed at the centre of anti-slavery activism in England and added to the calls for the immediate end of Apprenticeship. 'Full Free' was finally conceded in 1838.

Women's activism in the post-slavery and post-colonial periods

The legislation that ended slavery in 1838 removed the legal authority that had enabled a small minority of whites to exercise virtually arbitrary power over the lives and activities of the large black majority. Interpretations of freed people's expectations of the new order by scholars like Woodville Marshall reveal that the emancipated hoped that the coming of freedom would provide the opportunity for them to take full control of their own lives and lay a completely new base for the society. They had hoped to realise the revolutionary potential of the legislation to abolish slavery by extending those social, cultural and economic values and institutions which they had cultivated zealously during slavery, particularly those relating to land acquisition and the re-interpretation of African/Christian cosmology.[53] In addition, black working- class women made it clear that they had no intention of conforming to the Victorian gender order and the gender systems of the new era that sought to confine women to the private sphere of uncompensated labour in the home.

Former enslavers and their imperial support groups had a different perception of post-slavery society and the free order. They had little interest in radically transforming Caribbean society. Thus the authoritarian society of slavery and oligarchic power continued into post-slavery society, diminishing the potential for radical transformation, especially in the realm of politics. Denied access to the rights of 'citizens' within the politics of freedom, and finding themselves still as labourers within the economics of emancipation, freed people inevitably found themselves in a 'border clash', a battle for terrain, with former enslavers. In this regard, the legacies of planter mentalities proved to be obstacles to Caribbean freedom and continue to do so. The revolutionary potential of land acquisition, for example, was too much for the power-holders to contemplate. While they were quite willing to encourage Indian indentured immigrants (initially imported to undermine the bargaining power of freed people), to settle by giving them land in lieu of repatriation (though we should be in no doubt about the conditions of such land for these exploited workers),[54] landholders tried to impede the development of the black peasantry. Redistribution of economic resources like land would threaten the social relations of production and the ideological arrangement of post-slavery society. Swithin Wilmot was thus forced to conclude that emancipation as a process, rather than as an event, remained 'in action' well into the mature years of the first generation of those born within it.[55] The class continuities of hegemony and subordination of the enslaved by the enslavers were reproduced in a new regime and were manifested in the class struggles on the sugar plantations and other properties. Freed men and women who had alternatives to plantation labour pursued these as much as possible.

The inequities of post-slavery Jamaican society ensured that the descendants of enslaved peoples would continue the struggle for complete emancipation, not just as an event, but as a condition of human progress. Protest action, the most notable being the 1865 Morant Bay Rebellion, was widespread in the post-1838 period and was attributable to the failure of post-slavery regimes to deliver on the promise of freedom by honouring freed people's claims to citizenship, civil rights and political enfranchisement. While the Morant Bay Rebellion has been associated with Paul Bogle and George William Gordon, women also played crucial roles, for example, organising many of Bogle's meetings. Wilmot tells us that Caroline Grant was referred to by a policeman at Morant Bay as 'a queen of the rebels.' Grant and Sarah Johnson ordered fleeing men to return to the scene of action. Elizabeth Taylor even beat Joseph Williams when he tried to run away.[56] Additionally, as Clinton Hutton tells us, women like Caroline Grant, Sarah Johnson and Ann Thompson raided police stations for guns and ammunition; and Elizabeth Taylor, mobilised support for the cause. It also seems that it was a woman who started the violence by throwing the first stone at the constable.[57]

Radical women joined their male colleagues in the decolonisation movement that intensified after 1865. For after the brutal suppression of the Morant Bay Rebellion, the state reacted by removing the elective principle in government and installing the Crown Colony system. The ruling elite believed that the potential for radical transformation would be considerably diminished once measures to curb the freedom of African-Caribbeans by retaining control of the government were effected. But, despite their optimism, protest action, far from decreasing, escalated after 1865. Indeed, the decolonisation movement intensified by the 1940s, fuelled by the radical ideology of Marcus Garvey, the great Pan-Africanist.

In one sense, Caribbean rebel women sacrificed their own feminist concerns initially in solidarity with their male counterparts during the height of the decolonisation movement. Despite the association of the Caribbean labour movement of the 1930s, the franchise movement of the 1940s and the independence struggles of the 1960s with men like Alexander Bustamante and Norman Manley, women were very much involved. Amy Jacques Garvey, Amy Bailey and Una Marson lobbied for universal adult suffrage. Catherine McKenzie, Amy Jacques Garvey, Eulalie Domingo, like Elma François and Audrey Jeffers in Trinidad and Tobago, lobbied for black self-determination, with François laying the foundations for three major trade unions. Gladys Longbridge (or Lady Bustamante, as she is called by most Jamaicans), Aggie Bernard, Edna Manley (like Mother Sellassie of St Kitts) – all supported protesters during the 1930s labour protests across the region, with Edna Manley joining Aggie Bernard and Adina Spencer to feed the rebels.

Women supported the movement for the legalisation of trade unions and rejoiced when that was achieved after the labour protests. They joined the unions as rank-and-file members and a few, like Edith Nelson and Gladys Longbridge, held important executive positions. Nearly all of the top leadership positions are, of course, still held by men. The introduction of (restricted) female suffrage in 1919 and universal adult suffrage in 1944 also represented a major victory for Jamaican women, the majority of whom had been denied the vote on the basis of gender before 1919. Of course, the lack of the franchise had not stopped black women from turning out at elections to support/lobby for male candidates and to try to influence the outcome of elections. Women of all classes and ethnicities exercised their franchise in the first elections held after universal adult suffrage was achieved. Women like Mary Morris Knibb, Iris Collins, Edith Dalton James, Rose Leon, and Rebecca (Rose) Williams also contested local and general elections before 1962, defying the political culture and gender conventions of the day.[58] When the British West Indies Federation collapsed in 1962 women were among those who lobbied for independence. The fact that some female politicians did not necessarily lobby for feminist issues should not detract from their pioneering roles.

The modern political order

Since the achievement of political independence in August 1962, Jamaican women have continued their political activism as voters, party workers and representatives in parliament, cabinet, senate and local government. Currently, as the majority of registered voters, they possess the potential to influence the outcome of elections; though as a minority in Parliament (nine out of 60 in the House of Representatives in 2001), their ability to influence legislation in favour of women may be limited. This under-representation of women in government is a global phenomenon. Statistics published in May 2001 reveal that in 178 countries surveyed, women form just 13.7 per cent of members of government in both upper and lower houses. That means that out of 40,819 members of parliament and senators, women members total 5,388. Predictably, their representation is just slightly higher in lower than in upper houses, 13.8 per cent and 13.1 per cent respectively. Among Caribbean states, Cuba leads the way, followed by Grenada, Dominica, Guyana, Suriname, the Dominican Republic, the Bahamas, Jamaica and St Kitts/Nevis (which tie at 46th on the world scale along with Israel and San Marino).[59]

Perhaps one of the biggest struggles for women in the post-colonial period was for the true emancipation of women from unequal power relations and gender discrimination at all levels of the society. All of the British-colonised Caribbean territories inherited a common legacy from the colonisers of a gender system that dichotomised public and private, work and family, and sought to confine women to the private sphere of uncompensated labour. Where women struggled against this Victorian gender order and entered the labour force, they were affected by the sex-typing of jobs and the paying of gender-discriminatory wages. The lack of formal education and skills training also handicapped women's economic and social advancement. These and other aspects of post-colonial Jamaican society that adversely affected women were targeted by individual women as well as women's organisations like the Women's Liberal Club, the Women's Social Service Club, and the Jamaica Federation of Women, though some of these were criticised for promoting the domestication of Jamaican black women. Before 1975 women's organisations were mainly concerned with social welfare issues. Women like Nellie Latrielle (of the Women's Social Service Club) and Amy Beckford Bailey were long among those contributing to social welfare issues.[60]

Since 1975, with the declaration of the Decade for Women, attention has been focused on the issue of equality. Thus many women and women's organisations have become involved in the International Women's Movement and have lobbied employers and governments for the establishment of women-oriented governmental machinery, the removal of gender-discriminatory practices and legislation; the introduction of gender-sensitive legislation such as maternity leave with pay; the increase of minimum wage for domestic workers, the majority of whom are female; and increased opportunities and resources to improve the conditions of women. Academic feminists like Lucille Mathurin Mair pioneered research on women's history, paving the way for the acceptance of gender analysis as a central tool of historical investigation at the tertiary level. The Women and Development Unit and (later) the Centre for Gender and Development Studies represent the initiative and energy of women who wish to ensure that a regional institution of the importance of the University of the West Indies should make a contribution to the promotion of women's development programmes. They aim also to provide research data that will help to promote awareness of women's condition.[61]

Conclusion

It should be clear from the foregoing analysis that Jamaicans can be justly proud of the role that women have played in the emancipation and larger liberation struggles of the colonial period that ended in independence in 1962, and in the struggle for rights and true citizenship in the post-colonial period. Yet, the need for women's activism is not over. Admittedly, post-modern society is one of individualism, but there is need – even a collective responsibility – for continued vigilance over aspects of the social infrastructure, political culture, justice system, crime-fighting strategies, tourist culture and economic climate that are unacceptable to civil society.

The descendants of enslaved people may now occupy the highest political offices in Caribbean societies, radically transformed by the slavery and post-slavery struggles for freedom and justice. However, the 'up from slavery' concept in public life is strong and indicates that there is a strong opinion that the process of emancipation to which women contributed so much is still incomplete.

Notes

1. Matthew Gregory ('Monk') Lewis, *Journal of a West Indian Proprietor Kept During A Residence in the Island of Jamaica* (1834; Oxford: Oxford University Press, 1999), 87.
2. Bernard Senior, *Jamaica As It Is, As It Was and As It May Be* (London: T. Hurst, 1835), 171.
3. Hilary McD. Beckles, *Centering Woman: Gender Discourses in Caribbean Slave Society* (Kingston: Ian Randle Publishers, 1999), 157.
4. See Lucille Mathurin Mair, 'An Historical Study of Women in Jamaica from 1655 to 1844' (PhD. thesis, UWI, Mona, 1974); Ibid., *The Rebel Woman in the British West Indies During Slavery* (Kingston: Institute of Jamaica Publications, 1975); Linnette Vassell, compiler, *Voices of Women in Jamaica, 1898-1939* (Kingston: Department of History, UWI, Mona,

1993); Beckles, *Centering Woman.*

5. Anon., *Marly, Or a Planters' Life in Jamaica* (Glasgow: Richard Griffin, 1828), 80, 133.

6. Jamaica Archives (JAr), Gifts and Deposits, L.G. Perkins, 4/26/6 and 4/26/7, Cyrus Francis Perkins, 'Busha's Mistress or Catherine the Fugitive: A Stirring Romance of the Days of Slavery in Jamaica' (1855). This novel was serialised in 20 installments in The Daily Telegraph and Jamaica Guardian in 1911. The novel is currently being edited and introduced for publication by Paul Lovejoy, Verene Shepherd and David Trotman.

7. Lewis, 88; Cynric Williams, *A Tour Through the Island of Jamaica* (London: Hunt & Clarke, 1823), 339.

8. Lewis, 212.

9. Williams, *A Tour.*

10. See Verene A. Shepherd, 'Locating Enslaved Women's Voices in the Colonial Caribbean: The Promises and Pitfalls of Ventriloquism' (Paper presented at the Workshop on Atlantic Crossings: Women's Voices, Women's Stories in the Caribbean and the Nigerian Hinterland, Dartmouth College, New Hampshire, 18 – 20 May, 2001).

11. H. McD. Beckles, *Natural Rebels: A Social History of Enslaved Black Women in Barbados* (New Jersey: Rutgers University Press, 1989).

12. For a discussion of this narrative, see Moira Ferguson, ed., *The History of Mary Prince: a West Indian slave related by herself* (1831; London: Pandora, 1987).

13. See excerpts from: Olaudah Equiano, 'The Life of Olaudah Equiano,' in *Caribbean Slavery in the Atlantic World,* ed., Verene A. Shepherd & Hilary McD. Beckles (Kingston & London: Ian Randle & James Currey, 2000), 822-28; Esteban Montejo, 'The Autobiography of a Runaway Slave,' in *Ibid.,* 829-42; Mary Prince, 'The History of Mary Prince: A West Indian Slave Related by Herself,' in *Ibid.,*843-58; Toussaint L'Overture, 'Speeches and Letters of Toussaint L'Overture,' in *Ibid.,* 858–67.

14. For a recent discussion of Igbo presence in the diaspora, see Douglas Chambers, 'Tracing Igbo into the Diaspora,' in *Identity in the Shadow of Slavery,* ed. Paul E. Lovejoy. (London & New York: Continuum, 2000), 55-71.

15. Philip D. Curtin, *The Atlantic Slave Trade: A Census* (Madison: University of Wisconsin Press, 1969), 144.

16. *Ibid.,* 160 and B.W. Higman, *Slave Population and Economy in Jamaica* (Cambridge: Cambridge University Press, 1976), 76.

17. David Eltis, *The Rise of African Slavery in the Americas* (Cambridge: Cambridge University Press, 2000), 85–113; Ibid., 'The Volume and Structure of the Slave Trade' (Paper presented at the Conference on

'Enslaving Connections,' York University, Toronto, October 2000).

18. Eltis, 251.

19. Barbara Bush, *Slave Women in Caribbean Society* (Kingston, Bloomington, Indianapolis & London: Heinemann, Indiana University Press & James Currey, 1990); Marrietta Morrissey, *Slave Women in the New World* (Lawrence: University Press of Kansas, 1989).

20. 4/b/4, Exeter University Library, Gale/Morant Papers.

21. See Verene A. Shepherd, ed./comp., *Women in Caribbean History* (Kingston: Ian Randle, 1999), 48-52; JAr, JB/1B/11/3/121, Inventory of William Hewitt, 1812, fols. 145-48.

22. Beckles, *Centering Woman,* 23.

23. Robert Wedderburn, *The Horrors of Slavery,* published as Ian McCalman, ed., *The Horrors of Slavery and Other Writings by Robert Wedderburn* (Kingston & Princeton: Ian Randle & Markus Wiener, 1991), 46–47.

24. *Ibid.,* 46.

25. Beckles, *Centering Woman,* 22–37.

26. Perkins, Chapter 2.

27. Williams, 339.

28. Conversation with Nemata Lyden, Dartmouth College, April 2001.

29. Mary Gaunt, *Harmony* (London: E. Benn Ltd., 1933), 19.

30. Williams, 13.

31. See Mary Turner, "Chattel Slaves into Wage Slaves: A Jamaican Case Study', in *From Chattel Slaves to Wage Slaves: The Dynamics of Labour Bargaining in the Americas,* ed., Mary Turner. (Kingston, London & Indianapolis: Ian Randle, James Currey & Indiana University Press, 1995), 33-47.

32. Lincolnshire Record Office, Thistlewood's Journal, Mon. 31/1, fol. 333.

33. Douglas Hall, *In Miserable Slavery: Thomas Thistlewood in Jamaica, 1750–1786* (London: Macmillan, 1989), 145.

34. Lewis, 41.

35. Perkins, Chapter 2

36. *Marly,* 133, 148.

37. See Verene A. Shepherd, 'Pens and Penkeepers in a Plantation Society' (Ph.D. thesis, University of Cambridge, 1988), 270; Ibid., 'Liberation Struggles on Livestock Farms in Jamaica,' in *Caribbean Slavery,* eds., Shepherd & Beckles, 896-904.

38. CO 137/181, Viscount Goderich to the Governors of the West India Colonies, 16 March 1832, enclosure.

39. Senior, 205-06.

40. *Ibid,* 212.

41. *Ibid.,* 215.

42. *Ibid.,* 216.

43. *Ibid.*, 255.

44. *Ibid.*, 264-65.

45. This is clear from the T71 Treasury Records (PRO, London), "Returns of the Registration of Slaves", 1817–1832.

46. See Clare Midgley, *Women Against Slavery; The British Campaigns, 1780-1870* (London: Routledge, 1992).

47. See the line taken by Eric Williams in *Capitalism and Slavery* (1944; Chapel Hill: University of North Carolina Press, 1994). For support for and opposition to Williams's view that economic forces ended slavery ultimately, see Section 17 of *Caribbean Slavery*, eds., Shepherd and Beckles.

48. See Thomas Holt, *The Problem of Freedom: Race, Labor, and Politics in Jamaica and Britain, 1832-1938* (Baltimore: The Johns Hopkins University Press, 1992), 64.

49. *Ibid.*; Swithin Wilmot, "Not Full Free": The Ex-Slaves and the Apprenticeship System in Jamaica, 1834-1838, *Jamaica Journal*, 17.3 (1984): 2–10.

50. CO 137/219, Smith to Glenelg, May 11, 1837, transmitting 'A Return of Complaints brought before the Special Magistrates.'

51. Holt, 62.

52. CO 137/210 (1), Sligo to Glenelg, April 2, 1836, enclosure from Stipendiary Magistrate Thompson.

53. See W.K. Marshall, 'We Be Wise To Many More Tings,' in *Caribbean Freedom*, eds., Beckles and Shepherd. (Kingston, London & Princeton: Ian Randle, James Currey & Markus Wiener,1993), 12–20.

54. For more on the conditions of indentured Indians, see Verene A. Shepherd, *Transients to Settlers: The Experience of Indians in Jamaica, 1845-1950* (Leeds & Warwick: Peepal Tree Press & The University of Warwick, 1994).

55. Swithin Wilmot, 'Emancipation in Action: Workers and Wage Conflict in Jamaica, 1838–1840,' in *Caribbean Freedom*, 48-54, eds., Beckles and Shepherd.

56. Swithin Wilmot, ' "Females of Abandoned Character?": Women and Protest in Jamaica, 1838–65', in *Engendering History: Caribbean Women in Historical Perspective,* Verene A. Shepherd, *et. al.*, eds., (Kingston, London & New York: Ian Randle, James Currey & St. Martin's, 1995), 291.

57. Clinton Hutton, '"Colour for Colour, Skin for Skin": The Ideological Foundations of Post-Slavery Society, 1838–1865,' (PhD. thesis, UWI, Mona, 1992); see also Ibid., 'The Defeat of the Morant Bay Rebellion,' *The Jamaican Historical Review*, XIX (1996): 30-38.

58. Shepherd, ed./comp., *Women in Caribbean History*; see also Linnette Vassell, 'Women of the Masses,' in *Engendering History*, 321, 322, 327,

Shepherd *et. al.*, eds.,

59. www.ipu.org/wnm-e/world.htm; http://www.ipu.org/wnm-e/classif.htm & http://hjem.get2net.dk/Womeningovernments/Jamaica.htm

60. See Vassell, *Voices of Women.*

61. Peggy Antrobus, 'New Institutions and Programmes for Caribbean Women,' in *Women of the Caribbean*, ed., Pat Ellis. (Kingston: Kingston Publishers, 1986), 131-34.

Figure 4:
The sugar cane in its four different stages

Old Plantation House at Drax Hall, St George Barbados

Figure 5:
An old plantation house at
Drax Hall, St George, Barbados

CHAPTER 3

The Making of the Sugar Revolution
B. W. Higman

A small number of key ideas dominate the conceptual field of Caribbean history. Of these few fundamental concepts, one of the most significant is the notion of a 'sugar revolution'. The colonial history of the Caribbean is commonly characterised by the intimate relationship of sugar (crop, commodity, symbol) and slavery (social relation, institution, mode of labour exploitation) and the defining moment of that relationship is located in the sugar revolution, beginning in Barbados in the middle of the seventeenth century. Although the sugar revolution is admitted to having its precursors, stretching back almost a thousand years and out of the Caribbean, and the Barbados revolution is in turn seen as providing a model for other places in the subsequent three centuries, these West Indian colonial events of the 1640s and 1650s, occurring in the midst of the 'English Revolution,' have come to occupy a foundational position in the historiography of the Americas and the larger history of the Atlantic World. It is the sugar revolution above all which has come to represent the vital watershed, starkly separating the history of the islands from that of the mainland, not merely in terms of agricultural economy, but in almost every area of life, from demography, to social structure, wealth, settlement patterns, culture and politics.

Modern historians generally have come to accept the sugar revolution as truly revolutionary, marking a genuine historical discontinuity. The sugar revolution is understood as a transition in which sugar monoculture swiftly replaced diversified agriculture, large-scale plantations replaced small farming, enslaved labourers replaced free workers, dense populations replaced dispersed settlement patterns, blacks came to outnumber whites, and the Atlantic economy was dramatically transformed. I have elsewhere offered a critical review of the historiography of the concept in the second half of the twentieth century.[1] In this essay, my objective is rather to trace the roots of the 'sugar revolution' as idea and term. Thus the aim is essentially historiographical, a search for origins. The project is worthwhile, I believe, because it may be argued that concepts only come to exist in their full form when expressed explicitly. Equally, it can be argued that the application of a label to a confusion of historical events serves to organise and naturalise, in this particular case to make the sugar revolution one of the class 'revolution,' an idea fundamental to much historical thought.

How did the sugar revolution come to occupy such a significant role in the historiography? It is a role for which sugar has no real rivals. Although tobacco, rice, cotton, coffee, and indigo transformed the colonial landscape – creating distinct cultures, mentalities, settlement patterns and specialised land use zones – historians have not given the names of these crops to revolutions or attributed to them the fundamentally transformative power associated with sugar.[2] Only sugar has been cast as the inevitable creator of systems of plantation slavery and large-scale slave societies. With other crops, the options were always greater and more real. Sugar stands alone as the truly revolutionary crop.

Who invented the sugar revolution concept, when and why? The historiographies of sugar, colonial America and the West Indies seem to hold no theories on the matter. Generally, foundational concepts often seem self-evident once stated and are quickly naturalised to their subjects, being used freely without reference to their origins. Citation-chains are difficult to establish or simply do not exist. Those who have employed the sugar revolution concept have consistently failed to identify their sources and, rather than choosing or simply forgetting to add a grateful footnote, seem genuinely not to know who the ancestors might be. This complicates the search for an ultimate creator but equally demonstrates the central importance of the idea and how naturally it has been assimilated.

Inventors

The sugar revolution, historians agree, occurred first in the English colony of Barbados ca.1645-60, in the French colony of Guadeloupe ca.1650-70, and then spread to other West Indian colonies. The concept of the sugar revolution emerged prototypically in the parallel colonial historiographies of the English and French from the seventeenth century to the early twentieth. It only emerged fully formed, however, after World War II, first in the literature of the French (initially as 'la révolution de la canne'), then in that of the English. Although the sugar cane was first introduced to the Caribbean by the Spanish, and cultivated and processed by them in Española and Jamaica in the early sixteenth century, these efforts produced no sugar revolution, and the Spanish only reluctantly adopted the concept into their historiography, drawing on the experience and literature of the English-speaking tradition.

The earliest identified use of 'la révolution de la canne' occurs in Gaston-Martin's general history of slavery in the French colonies, published in 1948. Gaston-Martin was professor of contemporary history at Bordeaux and his book appeared in a series 'Colonies et Empires'. He had previously published on other aspects of French colonial history, including the slave trade of Nantes.

Although Gaston-Martin paid great attention to traditional political narrative, the thematic structure of his history of slavery contributed to a search for organising concepts. The second chapter of the book began with sections on the chartered companies, Colbert, and the West India Company. These were followed by a section titled 'La révolution de la canne, la traite des noirs et la faillité des compagnies privatives.' In that section, Gaston-Martin outlined the introduction of sugar cane cultivation to the French West Indian colonies in 1640, sugar's displacement of tobacco as a medium of exchange, the profitability of the first plantations, and the search for a labour supply. According to Gaston-Martin, two factors determined the pattern of development: 'La canne à sucre demande une main-d'oeuvre nombreuse, en état de supporter toute la journée le soleil épuisant des regions équatoriales; et le produit brut n'est pas aisément transportable.' These essentially biological variables resulted in an intensive cultivation of sugar as a monoculture, the neglect of alternative crops, and an increasing dependence on enslaved African workers.[3] Having constructed this framework, Gaston-Martin directed his attention to a detailed account of the organisation of the slave trade to the end of the seventeenth century. He concluded that, in spite of a lack of initial capital, and vicissitudes of war and trade, 'la révolution de la canne a achevé à l'aube du XVIIIe siècle de transformer la vie des Iles et d'*imposer* l'esclavage comme seul mode rationnel d'exploitation de notre domaine "amériquain".'[4]

This was the only explicit reference Gaston-Martin made to 'la révolution de la canne' in his second chapter, but there is no doubt that he saw sugar's requirements as determinative and its consequences as revolutionary, even though the implications beyond slavery and the slave trade were not fully explored. He used the term just once more, in relation to the Code Noir, and then in italics and within inverted commas. This, perhaps, suggests that Gaston-Martin had found the term somewhere in the literature, but he provided no citations and his bibliographical note pointed only to general histories of French colonisation.[5] His narrative was completely French, making no reference to the parallel experience of the English West Indies.

In English, the earliest identified use of 'the sugar revolution' occurs in *A Short History of the West Indies*, a general text by John H. Parry and Philip M. Sherlock, published in 1956. Parry, an Englishman with a Cambridge doctorate, had wide-ranging interests in the history of oceanic empires, particularly Latin America. He was the first professor of history appointed to the University College of the West Indies, centred in Jamaica, and held that post from 1949 to 1956. Sherlock, a Jamaican, published on West Indian history and culture, and was director of Extra-Mural Studies and vice-principal of the University College. Parry and Sherlock titled their fifth chapter 'The Sugar Revolution,' giving it greater prominence and scope than had Gaston-Martin. In it they outlined the transformation of the English and French colonies beginning in the middle of the seventeenth century resulting from the shift to sugar. They traced the abandonment of tobacco, ginger and cotton, produced on small holdings by free and indentured white labourers, and the rapid establishment of sugar as a monocultural export crop commanding high prices in European markets. Experiments in sugar-making began in Barbados in 1642, backed by Dutch merchants, who supplied credit and technical knowledge derived from their experience in Brazil. By the end of the 1640s, sugar had a firm hold of Barbados, and spread quickly to St Christopher and Guadeloupe, to be followed soon after by Nevis, Martinique, Jamaica and St Domingue. After about 1650, sugar became 'the only product of importance.'[6]

The advantages of sugar as a colonial staple, argued Parry and Sherlock, were that it 'could be grown only in the tropics' (which is true of cane but not of the beet that later depressed the market), and 'could be grown by unskilled labour, for long periods on the same ground, without exhausting the soil.'[7] Like Gaston-Martin, they explained that the perishability of cane required its immediate processing, hence the need for the 'planter' to be manufacturer as well as grower, or at least to have access to a sugar factory. Sugar became 'a rich man's crop,' Parry and Sherlock argued:

> Considerable capital was needed to set up a factory; and a plantation, to run economically, had to be big enough to keep the factory supplied constantly with canes throughout the crop season. Once established, however, sugar plantations and factories soon became immensely profitable – far more so than, for instance, tobacco plantations.[8]

The outcome was that successful sugar planters bought out the failing tobacco growers. Barbados, formerly settled by small holders, 'became in a decade or so a land of relatively large estates' and by 1660 'almost the whole usable area of the island was cleared and in use.' The small holders were forced to emigrate. At the same time, the occupation of the land by large plantations meant that indentured labour could no longer be attracted by the promise of small holdings on the expiration of contracts. Attempts to fill the demand through persuasion and compulsion, including the transportation of Civil War prisoners, all failed to produce white labourers in the quantities required by the sugar planters. Their need for 'a large and well-disciplined labour force,' argued Parry and Sherlock, eventually led the English and French in the Caribbean to look to the slave trade from Africa. A demographic transformation followed. In 1645, Barbados had about 6,000 blacks and 40,000 whites; by 1685, 46,000 blacks and 20,000 whites. The whites of Barbados continued to dwindle, and other sugar colonies quickly came to show even greater concentrations of black slaves. By the early eighteenth century, whites had become 'a small garrison among the slaves' in the colonies of the English and French. From this unequal demographic and economic system flowed a hierarchical social structure rooted in colour, and systems of laws designed to keep the slaves in subjection. The sugar colonies became 'ideal' elements in mercantilist models of empire, and in the eighteenth century objects of European conflict.[9] It was with this theme that Parry and Sherlock closed their chapter on the sugar revolution.

Although the discussion of Parry and Sherlock was wide-ranging and touched on most of the features which were to occupy later studies, the term sugar revolution was used only once in the text of their chapter. This occurred in the section concerned with colonial politics: 'The sugar revolution did nothing to weaken the attachment of the British West Indians to the representative institutions and the legal guarantees of personal liberty which they had brought with them from England.'[10] Parry and Sherlock did however use the word 'revolution' and with more significance, saying that the establishment of the sugar monoculture was 'much more than the spread of a profitable crop and a new industry,' and constituted 'a revolution which changed the whole racial composition and social structure of the islands.'[11] Neither of these references has an economic focus, though pointing to the material foundation of the society. In their introduction to the *Short History*, Parry and Sherlock stated baldly that sugar 'entailed slavery,' and argued that the establishment of 'plantation slavery in the sixteenth and seventeenth centuries and its abolition in the nineteenth were social revolutions severe enough to alter the foundations of West Indian society and rob West Indian history of what little continuity it possessed.'[12] Thus, as with Gaston-Martin, their account of the sugar revolution was rooted in a crude version of crop determinism, allowing little space for other outcomes.

None of the items listed for the chapter on the sugar revolution in Parry and Sherlock's bibliography for the *Short History* yield the term.[13] In an earlier work, *Europe and a Wider World, 1415–1715* (1949), Parry had said only that the 'rapid development' of the sugar colonies had important 'consequences' for colonial policy, and that 'The considerable expenditure required for sugar production . . . dictated the division of the land into comparatively large plantations.'[14] In 1955, in a paper on the introduction of food crops to Jamaica, Parry had said sugar became 'the characteristic West Indian product,' that it was 'most economically grown on fairly large plantations, and its production demanded a large force of field labourers.'[15] Again there were no clear hints of the sugar revolution idea. The bibliography provided for chapter seven of the *Short History*, treating the slave trade, did however include Gaston-Martin's work of 1948,[16] and this perhaps provided the necessary inspiration.

Pioneers

The two contemporary accounts included in the bibliography of Parry and Sherlock's *Short History* – Richard Ligon's *True and Exact History of the Island of Barbados* (1657) and Père Jean Baptiste Du Tertre's *Histoire Générale des Antilles* (1667–71) – demonstrated an awareness of the momentous changes taking place in their time, but without calling them revolutionary. Ligon saw that the planting of sugar had 'grown to a high perfection' in the decade following his arrival in Barbados in 1647 and that sugar-making had become 'the soul of trade'. He observed the tendency to monoculture, saying that 'this commodity, sugar, hath gotten so much the start of all the rest of those, that were held the staple commodities of the iland, and so much over-top't them, as they are for the most part slighted and neglected.' Ligon also believed that 'when the small plantations in poor mens hands, of ten, twenty, or thirty acres, which are too small to lay to that work, be bought by great men, and put together, into plantations of five, six or seven hundred acres, that two thirds of the iland will be fit for plantations of sugar, which will make it one of the richest spots of earth under the sun.' These were essential elements of what Parry and Sherlock called the sugar revolution. On the other hand, although Ligon recognised that the 'Negroes' of Barbados were 'more than double the numbers of the Christians' he did not link the growth of the enslaved population to the spread of sugar.[17] Thus the social revolution was only partly represented in Ligon's account. Du Tertre had much more to say on the social and cultural life of enslaved people on the sugar plantations of Guadeloupe, Martinique and (French) St Christopher, following the introduction of sugar by the Dutch from Brazil, but was even further from a recognition of social or economic revolution.[18] Neither Gaston-Martin nor Parry and Sherlock made significant use of Du Tertre's four volumes, and it is Ligon who is most often seen as architect of the sugar revolution concept.

The bibliography of Parry and Sherlock's *Short History* included no works from the eighteenth and nineteenth centuries. By the middle of the eighteenth century, local historians were referring to the sugar-producing colonies as 'sugar islands', 'îles à sucre', indicating the dominance of the crop and the distinctive character of settlement flowing from its requirements, but the same was said of the 'tobacco colonies', for example.[19] The better known histories of the British and French West Indies produced in the eighteenth and nineteenth centuries did generally offer accounts of the impact and significance of sugar, and some introduced counterfactual arguments that laid the basis for later 'revolutionary' interpretations. Such counterfactuals often grew out of a questioning of sugar monoculture, the land monopoly of large plantations, and the racial balance of the population.[20]

Herman Merivale in his Oxford *Lectures on Colonization and Colonies* of 1839–41, emphasised the determining role of sugar in driving out small proprietors and creating ideal conditions for the large capitalist, part planter and part manufacturer. The result, said Merivale, was an 'unwholesome' or 'artificial' state of society, terminated inevitably 'either by rapid decline, or still more rapid revolution.'[21] Here Merivale was thinking of the revolution that ended the slave regime in St Domingue. It was a political rather than economic revolution. His interpretation was followed by Paul Leroy-Beaulieu, professor of political economy in the Collège de France, who argued in his general survey of European colonisation, first published in 1874, that the establishment of sugar cultivation in the English West Indies 'en changea complètement la physionomie et l'état social.' But Leroy-Beaulieu challenged Merivale's dating of the introduction of sugar to Barbados at 1670, correctly locating the origins of the sugar revolution in the 1640s.[22]

Merivale found it 'gratifying' to turn from the West Indies to North America whose colonial history was not cursed by the vicious institutions of sugar and the slave plantation. This was a comparison rooted in British imperial ideology, in which the ideal colony was one composed of Britons living lives similar to those of the motherland. Sugar made such an outcome seem impossible. Thus the English clergyman W. J. Gardner in his *History of Jamaica* published in 1873 argued that but for sugar the island could have developed much like New England. His counterfactual picture of Jamaica was dominated by 'English towns and villages, only changed so far as is requisite in semi-tropical climates, and of farms and gardens covering the country, occupied by men to whom occupation is a necessity, and who to their gorgeous island home would have brought those qualities which have placed Britain foremost among the nations of the earth.' Instead of this 'what might have been,' said Gardner, Jamaica became a place in which 'a few white settlers [were] surrounded by multitudes belonging to a different race and country.' The process which created this type of colony occurred in the last decades of the seventeenth century, 'colonists gave place to sugar planters, sugar planters required slaves, and gradually the island became a mighty aggregation of cane-fields, in which negroes toiled and white men were the taskmasters.'[23] Gardner saw climate as an insignificant variable; it was sugar that mattered in countering his alternate vision.

Charles Kingsley said much the same in 1882, arguing that the seventeenth-century decline in the white population of the West Indies was not so much to do with climate as caused by 'the introduction of sugar cultivation, at which the white man cannot work.' The extirpation of the white small holders, claimed Kingsley, 'helped to make inevitable the vicious system of large estates cultivated by slaves; a system which . . . brought its own Nemesis.'[24] Gardner agreed: 'An iniquitous system such as slavery could never be permanently prosperous.'[25] Here economic morality fought with biological determinism, the inevitability of the system of plantation slavery created by sugar containing the seeds of its own inevitable implosion.

An important contribution to the emerging historiography of the British West Indies was the appearance of *The Cavaliers and Roundheads of Barbados 1650–1652* by N. Darnell Davis in British Guiana in 1887. Born in Grenada, the son of a judge, Davis worked in the colonial service, but devoted much effort to transcribing material from West Indian and metropolitan archives. *Cavaliers and Roundheads* was intensely political, preserving a whiggish pride in the liberties of Englishmen and their right to colonial self-government. Davis dated the introduction of the sugar cane to Barbados at 1627, but believed that the sugar industry was 'thoroughly established' in 1645. The process of sugar-making was perfected only after planters visited Brazil, and the Barbadians were assisted by the Dutch in providing credit and slaves. Tobacco 'gradually gave place to sugar' and the colonies 'prospered mightily.'[26] But sugar, it was found, 'required many negroes and considerable quantities of land,' and once the industry was fully established, 'its effects upon the distribution of land became apparent.' The credit offered by the Dutch 'led some settlers into extravagance' and their properties 'fell into the hands of their more thrifty neighbours.' The displaced small holders migrated to other parts of the West Indies or North America. Thus, Davis successfully identified some of the major elements associated with what was to be called the sugar revolution, but maintained a moral attitude to the transformation and a preoccupation with its political consequences.[27]

Academic historians

The first academic historians of the West Indies generally gave greater weight to climate in the development of slave societies, but retained a transformative role for sugar. They also retained the political emphasis of their amateur precursors, and their imperial moral stance. Thus Charles P. Lucas, who divided his career between practical imperialism at the Colonial Office and scholarship at Balliol, argued in his *Historical Geography* of 1905 that tropical climates engendered monoculture and that the universal association of sugar and slavery created societies contrary to 'the true spirit and methods of colonization.'[28] Hugh E. Egerton, in *The Cambridge Modern History* of 1906, located the early history of Barbados in the context of Anglo-Dutch rivalry. The introduction of sugar about 1637, by a Dutchman, produced 'remarkable results' Barbados was 'seventeen times as rich as it was before the making of sugar,' said Egerton, but the population of fighting men was halved, and the island more difficult to defend.[29] Frank W. Pitman, the earliest significant United States academic historian of the British Caribbean and a student of Charles M. Andrews, contended in 1917 that sugar 'required a larger, more highly organized, and more continuous labour force than any other agricultural pursuit in the eighteenth century.' White labour seemed at first to be adequate and appropriate but quickly, said Pitman, the solution to 'the labor problem' was found in the slave trade. He traced the 'exclusion of small proprietors' into the eighteenth century, however, suggesting a process more gradual than revolutionary, particularly in the case of Jamaica where the expansion of sugar cultivation was 'an exceedingly slow process.'[30] In 1921, C.S.S. Higham, in his *The Development of the Leeward Islands under the Restoration*, similarly couched these developments in terms of a 'labour problem', resulting from the fact that 'sugar lent itself to the employment of large gangs of labourers on big plantations,' a demand increasingly filled by enslaved Africans rather than indentured whites, and followed by the amalgamation of holdings. By the eighteenth century, said Higham, the Leeward Islands were dominated by 'a system of large plantations, often owned by absentees, worked by vast gangs of slaves and supervised by a small number of whites.'[31] For these writers, sugar was determinative, but the process of transformation was portrayed as something less than revolutionary.

Clearer indications of an interpretation favourable to the notion of the transition to sugar as a fundamental discontinuity occurred in Vincent T. Harlow's *A History of Barbados 1625–1685*, published in 1926. Most of Harlow's book was concerned with political history, and sugar did not appear in its index, but a concluding chapter titled 'The Labour Problem' provided the beginnings of an economic history of the period. Following Ligon, Harlow observed that the years around 1650 witnessed the 'sudden expansion of a poverty-stricken island into one of the wealthiest English plantations in the New World, at a time when the Mother Country was in the throes of war.'[32] In introducing this transition in the course of his political narrative, Harlow was quick to locate it in the context of colonial idealism and moral economy, connecting his argument with that of Gardner and Lucas. Thus Harlow contended that 'this access of prosperity . . . eventually proved to be the main cause of the island's decline.' Before sugar, a large number of tenants worked small holdings growing a variety of 'small crops', forming a 'sturdy "yeoman" class, who swelled the ranks of the militia and were indeed the backbone of the colony.' Sugar changed this 'healthy condition of affairs' because, said Harlow, the crop 'requires large acres of land and a plentiful supply of cheap labour,' as well as 'the considerable initial expense of setting up a sugar factory.'[33] Harlow then argued that the establishment of large plantations and the amalgamation of small holdings depopulated Barbados, even though the black population increased massively, seeing the 'negro population' as 'a source of anxiety and weakness to every colony in which they were involved.' The emigration of white small holders 'reduced Barbados from the position of a populous, virile colony to that of a politically unimportant sugar plantation owned by absentee proprietors, and worked by negro slaves.' Thus, for Harlow, the transition which occurred in seventeenth-century Barbados was a 'two-fold process, whereby a sturdy English colony was converted into little more than one large sugar factory, owned by a few absentee proprietors and worked by a mass of alien labour.' This was 'the main feature of Barbadian history.'[34]

Importantly for the construction of this transition as revolution, Harlow located the vital events within the short period 1645–1665, two decades of fundamental change determined by sugar. His emphasis on sugar was at times tempered or even contradicted by a parallel argument that the transition from white to black labour in the West Indies was 'the triumph of geographical conditions,' in which the tropical climate made the white man 'an alien.' But

Harlow regarded climate as setting limits, rather than absolutely prohibiting alternative varieties of settlement, whereas sugar (always a tropical crop, always the product of large planters and slave labour) was determinative. A French reviewer of Harlow's *History of Barbados* in 1927, noting parallels between the experience of the French and British West Indies, observed the rapidity of change resulting from 'un véritable *boom* du sucre.'[35]

Maurice Satineau's *Histoire de la Guadeloupe sous l'ancien régime 1635–1789*, published in 1928, and cited by Parry and Sherlock but not by Gaston-Martin, offered something closer than Harlow to the concept of the sugar revolution. Satineau is the first writer identified to apply the word 'revolution' to the events. He divided the agricultural history of Guadeloupe into two periods. The first, 1642–64, was dominated by 'la petite propriété', and the second, 1665–1789, by 'la grande propriété charactérisé par la culture intensive de la canne à sucre et le développement de la traite des nègres.' These periods, said Satineau, 'correspondant à une révolution économique et sociale dont elle sera l'expression.'[36] In the first, agriculture was diverse, the most important crops cultivated being cassava, tobacco, indigo, ginger and sugar cane. Cotton and coffee came later. The second period, running to 'la Révolution', was marked by 'le régime de la grande propriété provoqué par une sorte de révolution produite dans l'industrie sucrière qui, elle-même, entraîna le développement de la culture intensive de la canne à sucre et de la traite des nègres.' However, Satineau followed by saying 'la transformation du régime économique de la Guadeloupe ne fut pas immédiate; elle est le résultat d'une lente évolution.'[37] In advancing this interpretation, Satineau cited Leroy-Beaulieu who had observed in 1874 that 'la culture de la canne changea toute l'économie de la société.' As in Barbados, sugar induced in Guadeloupe a rapid reduction in small agricultural holdings, growth of large plantations, absentee-proprietorship, monoculture, and slavery. Mercantilist policies underpinned the structure. For Satineau, sugar was certainly determinative: 'La culture de la canne qui, pour être productive, exige de vaste plantations, des travaux prolongés et rudes, la construction de sucreries, favorisa à la fois le développement de la propriété aristocratique et de la traite des noirs.' However, 'cette révolution économique' did not spread uniformly throughout Guadeloupe, in the way it did in Barbados, but dominated those areas favoured by large level plains, leaving the mountainous regions in the tenacious hold of small farmers and their crops.[38] The same was to be true of other West Indian colonies with varied terrain, such as St Domingue and Jamaica.

James A. Williamson, writing in the first volume of *The Cambridge History of the British Empire* published in 1929, and following Higham and Harlow, said simply that, 'Sugar rapidly transformed the social aspect first of Barbados then of the Leeward Islands.' This was the case because sugar production was 'best practised on large estates needing considerable capital for their equipment.' For Williamson, the transition occurred in Barbados between 1649 and 1660, but moved more slowly in the Leeward Islands.[39] His emphasis on the social aspect of the transformation was to prove significant. A French equivalent to *The Cambridge History of the British Empire* was published in the same year, the *Histoire des colonies françaises* edited by Gabriel Hanotaux and Alfred Martineau. The latter work was cited by Gaston-Martin and by Parry and Sherlock, all of whom ignored the British imperial opus,[40] but the *Histoire* offered only a political narrative for the Antilles in the seventeenth century, effectively ignoring the significance of sugar.

In 1930 Louis-Philippe May observed in his *Histoire économique de la Martinique 1635–1763* that 'une révolution s'opérait dans la culture' in the late seventeenth century which concentrated landownership in large plantations producing sugar.[41] Elsewhere in the same work May termed this transformation a 'révolution économique' but tempered his interpretation by saying that 'l'introduction de la canne transformait lentement toute cette économie.' Between the years 1660 and 1680, said May, the French colonists of Martinique became divided into two distinct and opposed classes, the rich sugar planters who engrossed the land of their neighbours and established expensive sugar factories, and the small holders who cultivated tobacco, cocoa and food crops in areas of the island unsuited to sugar. This 'transformation fondamentale' not only created antagonism within the colonising population, but also constructed a new settlement pattern dominated by the slave plantation, and affected trade, colonial markets, law, and government. For May, the outcome of this revolution was momentous: 'Le domaine sucrier était la cellule vivante du grand organisme nouveau: la société sucrière des îles.'[42] He gave Martinique and West Indian sugar large roles in Atlantic and French imperial history.

The British historians Harlow and Williamson edited a series of 'Pioneer Histories' published in the 1930s and designed to offer broad surveys of European expansion. The series included *The European Nations in the West Indies 1493–1688* (1933) by Arthur Percival Newton, Rhodes professor of imperial history in the University of London, who sought to cover the complete story, rather than simply the experience of the British. Newton had earlier written a study of Providence Island, which came to be seen as the site of a kind of rehearsal for the sugar revolution.[43] He saw the introduction of sugar and slavery to Barbados between about 1645 and 1650 resulting in 'an extraordinary and striking social change.' In place of 'a multitude of tiny holdings cultivated by small planters with but a few white labourers apiece,' said Newton, the large planters dominated the landscape and 'turned their indentured servants adrift, to replace them with wild, untamed negroes from the heart of darkest Africa.' The survivors became wealthy but the land 'passed into the hands of a comparatively small group of magnates and the small planting class of the earlier period was mostly dispossessed.' In the French islands, the 'change-over to sugar' was 'more gradual' and easier because the populations were smaller, but the process was essentially similar and determined by sugar.[44]

Although Harlow and Newton narrowed the period of the transition to sugar, at least for Barbados, and emphasised its dramatic character, neither of these writers associated the word 'revolution' with their interpretations. The first known writer in English to do so was C.M. MacInnes, reader in imperial history in the University of Bristol, in *An Introduction to the Economic History of the British Empire* (1935), seven years after Satineau. In a chapter titled 'Anglo-colonial trade before the Revolution' (meaning the American Revolution), MacInnes emphasised the significance of the West Indies and sugar in the triangular trade and the contribution made to British wealth in the eighteenth century. Before their concentration on sugar, the West Indies had produced a variety of crops on small holdings and the islands were seen as places 'in which Englishmen could work in the fields as they did at home.' This expectation was short-lived. According to MacInnes, 'It soon became clear that the course of West Indian economic development was to be of an entirely different character. In the middle of the seventeenth century an agrarian revolution took place in all the British West Indian settlements.'[45] The features of this 'agrarian revolution' were several. MacInnes emphasised the emigration of settlers and the shift to monoculture, but also pointed to the fundamental significance of West Indian demand in the African trade, including but not confined to the slave trade, and the role of the colonies generally in the 'great colonial trade' of the British. The unique feature of MacInnes's account was that his 'agrarian revolution' was allowed to extend beyond sugar and the West Indies. In a chapter on 'The African Trade' he argued that, as the seventeenth century advanced:

> It became clear that Englishmen were not by nature adapted to arduous and prolonged labour under a tropic sun. This fact, coupled with the growing recognition of the commercial value of tobacco and sugar, helped to bring about the agrarian revolution in the southern continental and West Indian colonies. Small holdings gave place to large plantations, and more and more there was a demand for abundance of cheap labour.[46]

Thus, although MacInnes was innovative in his identification of an 'agrarian revolution,' he did not consistently attribute it to sugar or confine it to the West Indies. In this his account is problematic, since his linking of tobacco and the plantations of the 'southern continental' colonies does not square with his reference to the 'tropic sun,' and his argument that an 'agrarian revolution' occurred uniformly throughout the British West Indian colonies in the middle of the seventeenth century is unsupported by the accounts of Harlow, Williamson or Higham. In any case, the 'agrarian revolution' formulation appears not to have survived in the literature. MacInnes was not cited by Parry and Sherlock or by Gaston-Martin.

Published the year after MacInnes's *Economic History*, the magisterial work of Charles M. Andrews, *The Colonial Period of American History*, was indeed cited by Parry and Sherlock, though not Gaston-Martin, but contributed little. Andrews included a chapter on 'Far Flung Barbados' in his second volume and argued strongly that 'the history of Barbados and the Leeward Islands is essential to any proper understanding of the constitutional and commercial development of the English colonies in America,' but his emphasis on the political was even greater than in the earlier work of Harlow. He did briefly notice events surrounding the introduction of sugar to Barbados and said that by 1660 it had become 'the staple of the colony.' He also noted the emigration of whites resulting from 'the gradual crowding out of small holders by the more wealthy planters and merchants,' particularly in St Christopher which became 'the land of large plantations' even more than Barbados and Antigua. As a consequence of this exodus, said Andrews, Barbados 'tended to become a single great sugar plantation controlled by the crown, owned by absentee planters, and worked by negro slaves.'[47] The importance of all this for Andrews lay in the alternative political histories suggested for the American colonies generally, not in the internal economic, social and demographic experience of the islands themselves. He was looking for the roots of a different revolution.[48]

An important French scholar of the early colonial history of the Antilles, Gabriel Debien, was mentioned by Gaston-Martin and cited by Parry and Sherlock for his *Les engagés pour les Antilles (1634–1715)*, first published in 1951. Building on the researches of Satineau, May and Banbuck, Debien traced 'une évolution' in the conditions under which the *engagés* worked that parallelled the economic development of the colonies. By the end of the seventeenth century, argued Debien, 'la grande culture de la canne à sucre' and the range of skilled and semi-skilled tasks associated with sugar manufacture, resulted in 'un nouveau cadre de travail, un élément de révolution sociale.' Debien did not term the larger shifts from indentured to slave labour and from diversified agriculture to sugar monoculture revolutionary, even if he saw the result in these terms, 'Un nouveau monde coloniale français était né.'[49] Earlier, in a review published in 1949, Debien had referred to developments in St Domingue as a 'pleine transformation économique et sociale [qui] se mettre largement à la culture de la canne et à la main-d'oeuvre noire.'[50]

Debien was, however, the essential empiricist, reluctant to impose overarching concepts on the chaos of the past. His English equivalent was Richard Pares and the two mutually admired one another's work. Like Debien, Pares accepted the determinative role of sugar yet never quite embraced the sugar revolution concept. Fernand Braudel praised the empirical contributions of Debien and, in 1948, referred to him as 'ami des *Annales*, disciple de Marc Bloch.'[51] In order to understand 'le problème du sucre,' however, Braudel believed a grander vision and a fuller comparative history were necessary, taking in the whole of the American tropics. Braudel attempted something like this in *La Méditerranée* (1949). In a now famous passage, arguing the importance of islands in the history of the Mediterranean and the Atlantic, Braudel took sugar as his example and traced the crop's dissemination from India to Egypt, Cyprus, Sicily, Madeira ('la première "île à sucre" de l'Atlantique'), the Azores, the Canaries, the Cape Verde islands, and thence to America. These islands were ravaged by sugar monoculture, their forests destroyed to make way for cane and to provide fuel. Madeira was a prime example of this transformation, said Braudel: 'Notez que cette révolution se fit uniquement dans l'intérèt d'une Europe insatiable et qu'il fallait approvisionner du précieux produit; et point pour le profit des insulaires eux-mêmes.'[52] Braudel attached this 'révolution' firmly to sugar, arguing that, wherever it went, the crop destroyed 'équilibres anciens' of demography, environment, resource use and labour.

Conceptual evolution

Although neither Debien nor Braudel embraced 'la révolution de la canne' of Gaston-Martin, they contributed significant elements to the development of the concept, particularly in Debien's emphasis on social revolution and Braudel's more comprehensive conception of the environmental impact of sugar. In these ways, they added to the notion of economic revolution first advanced by Satineau in 1928 and to MacInnes' idea of agrarian revolution. Further support for the determinative role of sugar came from the seminal work of the Trinidadian Eric Williams, who obtained his doctorate at Oxford in 1938. In *The Negro in the Caribbean*, published in 1942 when he was at Howard University in Washington, Williams said simply 'Sugar meant slavery.' In *Capitalism and Slavery* (1944) he contended that slavery 'had nothing to do with climate' (explicitly rejecting the interpretation of Harlow, who had supervised his D.Phil.) and, perhaps more important, advanced a broader crop-determinism in which cotton and tobacco were equal to sugar. Along the lines of the 'agrarian revolution' of MacInnes, Williams argued that cotton and tobacco were at the root of slavery on the mainland, sugar in the Caribbean, 'Sugar, tobacco, and cotton required the large plantation and hordes of cheap labour, and the small farm of the ex-indentured white servant could not possibly survive.' The poor whites of Barbados were forced to emigrate. Sounding more like Harlow, Williams said, 'King Sugar had begun his depredations, changing flourishing commonwealths of small farmers into vast sugar factories owned by a camarilla of absentee capitalist magnates and worked by a mass of alien proletarians.' Williams extended this 'British West Indian pattern' to the 'whole further history of the Caribbean.' It occurred first in the British and French islands, spreading later to the Spanish, but the outcome was repeated following the cycles of the plantation system.[53] Williams traced a similar pattern in the plantation economy of Virginia based on tobacco, but offered no account of cotton.

King Sugar provided a political metaphor for a crop determinism that paralleled the more refined historiographical idea of revolution. Modelled on the King Cotton of the South, what Debien in 1949 called 'le vieux culte du roi-sucre' seems to appear first in Caribbean historiography in the early twentieth century. Born in the Barbados of the English Civil War, the transformation wrought by sugar was to shift from a model based on monarchy to revolution, a revolution occupying a period almost exactly the same as the 'English Revolution' of 1642-60.[54] This shift marked the emergence of a more sophisticated historiography. But the sugar revolution was not democratic in its tendencies; rather, it installed autocracy, inequality and monopoly.

Other anthropomorphic models were available in the literature of the 1940s, most importantly in the lyrical *Contrapunteo Cubano del Tabaco y el Azúcar* (1940) of Fernando Ortiz, a work which greatly influenced Williams. Ortiz constructed an extended contrasting parallelism between 'Don Tabaco' and 'Doña Azúcar', which opposed the similarity described in *Capitalism and Slavery*. Thus Ortiz saw sugar as always preferring slave labour, tobacco free; sugar requiring vast plantations and factories, tobacco being produced on a garden scale with manufacture occurring separately in cities.[55] In this way, Ortiz gave sugar a much greater authority to transform society and economy, but his dramatic dialogue was relatively timeless and he offered neither a detailed description of the process nor a term with which to label it. His attempts to construct sugar as feudal and aristocratic, and tobacco and indigo as democratic, have been dismissed by many. Debien did so as early as 1949.[56]

In general, the sugar revolution concept was rarely applied to the Spanish Caribbean territories before the Cuban Revolution. When the essence of the concept was recognized it was generally derived from English-language literature and applied to the colonies of the English. Even the denomination 'sugar islands' (islas del azúcar) is seen as essentially English in origin.[57] Thus Ramiro Guerra y Sánchez introduced his influential history of Cuban agriculture, first published as newspaper articles in 1927, with quotations from Harlow's *History of Barbados* and an argument that sugar followed a 'set cycle' with identical consequences in every place it touched even if there were differences in chronology. The islands of the Caribbean constituted microcosms of this cyclical process, the 'sugar latifundium' repetitively substituting one population for another and crushing independent proprietors. Guerra's analysis of Barbados closely followed Harlow's, often word for word, but Guerra argued that 'the substitution of cheap slave labour for the small-scale landholder . . . was not the inevitable result of race or climate and beyond human control.' Rather, this substitution was a result of the capitalist sugar industry's 'search for unlimited profits.'[58] This was shown by the relatively slow and healthy development of Cuban agrarian society, said Guerra, 'proving that the wretched fate of the other islands was the result of human greed, and not of some inescapable geographical determinism.' Only in the late nineteenth century did the latifundium rise to destroy what had been nurtured for centuries in the process of developing a Cuban identity. The source of this destruction was industrial concentration derived from technological change and the penetration of United States capitalism. Guerra quoted Manuel Sanguily who in 1903 said the growth of these foreign influences constituted an 'authentic economic revolution' which would be followed by 'a social and political revolution.' Ultimately, said Guerra, Cuba would become merely 'a plantation colony . . . dependent for all its activity and life on the sugar industry, just as has occurred in the British West Indies;' the latifundium would create 'a society as simple as that of Barbados.'[59] Guerra believed he was living through this transformation, in the 1920s and 1930s, but described neither the Cuba of his own time nor the Barbados of the seventeenth century as experiencing a sugar revolution. His account was a polemic, a moral reading of this 'tragic drama' which played itself out time after time, predictable in its devastating consequences, yet inexorable and ineluctable.

In 1954 Mervyn Ratekin offered an account of the failed sugar industry of early Española, an interpretation that stressed the potential for transformation represented by sugar. For a brief moment, it seemed that the 'rich and populous villages' created by the *ingenios* might support a 'colonial nobility' or 'slave-owning aristocracy.' This outcome was prevented by the shift of Spanish interest to Mexico in the 1520s, but the tendency persisted in comparison to pastoral Cuba, showing, said Ratekin, 'the power of the sugar industry to create a peculiar social structure and to channel political power.'[60] The sugar revolution might have occurred there and then but did not.

Another notable absence occurs in Noel Deerr's *The History of Sugar* (1949–50), a work cited by Parry and Sherlock and which remains the most complete survey of its subject. Deerr, a sugar technologist, provided quite detailed accounts of the transformation of a series of Caribbean colonies consequent on the establishment of sugar, but he presented his material without much drama and imposed no explicit label or model. He did introduce an innovation by identifying 'a pre-sugar stage of development.' This pre-sugar period was dominated by smallholders, 'a condition which the advent of the cane altered, leading to the appearance of the capitalist planter.' Deerr also emphasised the similarity of experience of the English sugar colonies in the Caribbean, most differences being merely a matter of chronology, and extended this pattern to the French, the Dutch, and the Danish, whose experience was 'but a replica of that of the other northern European nations.'[61] Overall, Deerr's *History* was a compilation devoid of the passion of Ortiz, Williams and Satineau. It was a long way from offering a precursor of the sugar revolution concept, though important in giving sugar the beginnings of a commodity history.

The influential compilation of Sir Alan Burns, the *History of the British West Indies*, appeared in 1954, two years before it was listed in the *Short History* of

Parry and Sherlock. Born in St Kitts in 1871, Burns served as a colonial civil servant in Dominica, Nigeria, the Bahamas, and British Honduras, and had begun writing in Africa. In a section of his *History* titled 'King versus Parliament,' he described the establishment of sugar in Barbados at the beginning of the Civil War as 'a great development.' He then introduced the concept of revolution: 'The change over from the production of tobacco, indigo, cotton and other minor crops to the manufacture of sugar, besides bringing great wealth to Barbados, effected a social revolution in the island.' This 'social revolution' constituted the shift to large plantations at the expense of small holdings, the emigration of the former yeoman class and the consequent growth of a labour force of enslaved Africans. In his model, both crop and climatic determinism played a part, as in the earlier work of Harlow. Sugar cane, said Burns, 'is more conveniently grown on large estates and sugar can only be manufactured economically on a large scale,' and white men 'were unable to work under a tropical sun as hard and as quickly as the new crop demanded.'[62] In this way, he explicitly connected the idea of revolution with the determinative role of sugar, and emphasised the 'social' aspect of that revolution as Debien had done in 1951. The earlier 'agrarian revolution' of MacInnes and the 'révolution économique' of Satineau and May shared this social emphasis but without using the term in the same manner. The emphasis on 'social revolution' was maintained in Parry and Sherlock's *Short History* of 1956 and provided the core of their sugar revolution.

Why a 'revolution'?

Why did Gaston-Martin and Parry and Sherlock need the sugar revolution concept? What was lacking in the earlier formulations? There is no doubt that French social thought has been receptive to the notion of revolution in history, an attitude rooted in national political experience. After all, it was the French who first named the (British) 'révolution industrielle.'[63] Thus, it is not surprising that French historiography termed the West Indian transition to sugar a revolution more quickly than the British tradition, even when the transformation was recognised to occur first on British colonial soil. To this national receptiveness must be added the influence of the *Annales* school, particularly in the contributions of Debien and Braudel. The idea that a commodity, a crop, could cause and symbolise a social and economic revolution seemed natural in that tradition. It was a grand organising principle, an idea conceived in the historiography of the imperial metropolis, but emerging in the midst of decolonisation.

The English-language version of the sugar revolution, on the other hand, was more obviously colonial in its origin. Parry and Sherlock saw themselves writing a national history of the Caribbean, from a British colonial base, for an academic audience, and that they therefore needed to provide an appropriate conceptual framework. They sought to write a history in which the West Indies had a significant role in their own right, in which the controlling forces were not to be found in European imperial policy but in the internal experience of the region. The sugar revolution offered all of this. Although Parry and Sherlock explicitly argued that the sugar revolution interrupted the continuity of Caribbean history, the notion of discontinuity is much favoured by historians in the European and North American traditions. Indeed, revolutions and crises are the very stuff of the historiographies of those continents, and their historians regularly complain of plethora rather than dearth, arguing that each newly identified revolution devalues the currency. In the Caribbean, on the other hand, revolutions have been few and far between in the mainstream historiography. The Haitian and Cuban revolutions are the only two internal social and political revolutions generally admitted in the literature. Gaston-Martin and Parry and Sherlock wrote before the Cuban revolution occurred, and historians generally have been reluctant to admit the Haitian revolution.[64] Before 1960, the revolutions that mattered in Caribbean history were external, the capitalised American and French Revolutions. Thus Gaston-Martin and Parry and Sherlock were far from overloading Caribbean historiography with revolutions. Rather, in constructing the sugar revolution they provided a dynamic model around which the fabric of the region's history might be woven and given form to rival that of the imperial world.

The sugar revolution was a real innovation, not a mere mimicking of the imperial tradition. Its reference to a commodity, a crop, was original. The method of 'commodity history' was in its formative stages, the now classic work of Redcliffe N. Salaman, *The History and Social Influence of the Potato* of 1949, still seen as an eccentric contribution. In any case, although Salaman recognised the revolutionary impact of the potato and referred to a 'potato economy,' he did not construct a 'potato revolution.' The idea of commodity history became linked with staple theory in the 1950s, building as it did on the work of Harold A. Innis in *The Fur Trade in Canada* (1930) and *The Cod Fisheries* (1940). The Canadian link pointed to the West Indian relevance of the theory, for the French as well as the British, and its emphasis on the decisive role of the export commodity's production function suggested a variety of crop determinism. Equally important, staple theory and commodity history existed comfortably within the framework of a larger imperial history and pointed away from inward looking histories of particular colonies and communities. They fed into the notion of an Atlantic world, a world of economic growth and industrial revolution, the capital for which had been derived in large measure from sugar and slavery.[65] The combination of commodity history, imperial history, staple theory, and revolution brought together in the sugar revolution was truly unique. By giving the name of a commodity to a revolution, a number of features could be signalled together. The usual production function of sugar meant that the revolution was dual: it comprehended both an agricultural revolution and an industrial revolution. Yet it was also a social revolution, giving the idea added strength and an equality with the political revolutions of the modern era.

Diffusion

By 1974 K.G. Davies was able to claim that it was 'common to speak of the "sugar revolution" or "révolution de la canne" in the English and French colonies, denoting swift economic and social transformation.'[66] But Davies provided no examples of this supposed common usage and the works he cited do not easily yield up the terms.[67] Parry and Sherlock wrote no joint works after the *Short History* (Parry moving on to Nigeria in 1956), and their prolific individual publications seem not to make any further use of the sugar revolution term, though the concept survived. In 1966 Sherlock said that in Barbados a 'revolution' followed 'the change-over from tobacco planting to the double process of cultivating sugar-cane and the manufacture of sugar,' and in 1998, with Hazel Bennett, he said that in Jamaica after 1675 the 'changeover from smallholdings manned by white indentured servants and a relatively small number of African slaves to large estates manned by gangs of enslaved African labour was revolutionary.' But this was a return to earlier versions, looser than the sugar revolution.[68]

The first identified use of the sugar revolution term after the *Short History* occurred four years later in *The Making of the West Indies* (1960), a textbook directed at the new West Indian history syllabuses of the Oxford and Cambridge Examination Board and the Cambridge Syndicate. Like the *Short History*, the new text had multiple authors: F.R. Augier, S.C. Gordon, D.G. Hall and M. Reckord. Augier and Hall were West Indian men with British doctorates, while Gordon and Reckord were English women in the school system, all of them living in Jamaica through most of the 1950s, the last decade of the island's colonial history. As for Parry and Sherlock, Augier et al wrote with a consciousness that they were creating a West Indian history, a scholarly history written from a West Indian perspective, though they also recognised that their focus was more narrowly British than the pan-Caribbean work of Parry and Sherlock. The *Short History* was listed first among the texts cited in *The Making of the West Indies*, and was no doubt the source of the sugar revolution concept for the new work.[69]

The fifth chapter of *The Making of the West Indies* was titled 'Planters and Rulers' and its first section carried the subhead 'Sugar Revolution.' The first sentence announced, 'The change from tobacco to sugar planting was revolutionary.' Tobacco, said Augier *et al*, required intensive cultivation and careful attention to individual plants, could be produced on family small holdings and had minimal needs for capital equipment and buildings. Sugar was a gross crop, demanding immediate processing after harvest, 'an estate crop' in which 'production . . . for export demanded much land, much capital equipment and large gangs of skilled and unskilled labour.' Recognising variations in the pattern of transformation in the seventeenth-century English and French West Indies, the authors observed, 'A change of such magnitude could be neither immediate nor easy.' The emphasis was very much on the technological requirements of sugar, an advocacy of straightforward crop determinism, and only later did Augier *et al* introduce the shift from servants to slaves (seen as a rational economic choice) and the resultant creation of a 'slave society.' Thus the association of the sugar revolution with 'social revolution' was muted, as was the significance of monoculture, white emigration and the amalgamation of land holdings.[70] But Augier *et al* did set out clearly their grounds for believing the sugar revolution was truly revolutionary.

The first identified use of the sugar revolution term in French, after Gaston-Martin, occurred in 1961 in Guy Lasserre's doctoral dissertation on the geography of Guadeloupe for the University of Bordeaux. Interestingly, Lasserre referred to 'la révolution sucrière' rather than 'la révolution de la canne' of Gaston-Martin's formulation. In an extended treatment of the evolution of population, settlement and agricultural patterns, Lasserre twice referred to the shift from tobacco to sugar as 'la révolution agricole' and traced its profound consequences for the demographic history of Guadeloupe. He cited Gaston-Martin.[71] In discussing the development of land tenure, he described the crowding out of small holders lacking the capital needed to build their own mills: 'La révolution sucrière eut comme première conséquence l'absorption de nombreuses petites concessions primitives par les grandes habitations.'[72]

Apart from this use of the sugar revolution term for the changes of the seventeenth century, Lasserre also introduced the idea of 'la révolution industrielle' to refer to changes in mill technology and organisation that transformed the French West Indian sugar industry in the mid-nineteenth century. Indeed, he made more of this 'révolution industrielle' than of the earlier 'révolution sucrière' and divided it into two stages. This represents a further important contribution to the development of the sugar revolution concept. The first stage ('première forme de la révolution industrielle') was marked by the establishment of central mills, in the 1840s, without disrupting the pattern of plantation landholding. The second stage ('deuxième aspect de la révolution'), in the last quarter of the nineteenth century, was associated with economic crisis in the industry and had deeper consequences: 'la disparition des habitants sucriers et le règne de l'usine, appuyé sur un vaste domaine agricole.'[73] The formation of such 'latifundia' paralleled the impact of the seventeenth-century sugar revolution.

In 1966 the sugar revolution appeared in yet another general text, *Middle America*, by Robert C. West and John P. Augelli, American geographers. Citing

Parry and Sherlock's *Short History*, West and Augelli discussed the sugar revolution in some detail in a chapter titled 'Nature and Impact of the West Indian Colonial Plantation,' and their book is the first known to include 'sugar revolution' in its index. West and Augelli saw the colonial plantation as the principal instrument determining past and present 'patterns of land and people' in the English and French West Indies. They did not confine this influence to sugar, but it was sugar that 'caused a virtual revolution in the land-and-people complex of the Indies,' affecting land tenure, scale of production, demography, settlement patterns, capital and credit, and social relations. Barbados provided the model, variations elsewhere merely 'mirroring differences in the size of the territory, the date of the sugar revolution, the history of settlement prior to sugar, and other local conditions.' All of this followed closely the argument of Parry and Sherlock, but West and Augelli did introduce a new element (foreshadowed in Braudel), the impact of sugar on the environment and landscape. 'The very appearance of the land was altered,' they wrote, and 'as sugar planting expanded, the lowland forests were rapidly cut down and cane fields became the chief feature of the agricultural landscape.'[74]

The environmental interpretation of West and Augelli matched earlier remarks by David R. Harris, who in 1962 argued that the introduction of sugar to Antigua by 1650 'revolutionized the economy of the island and gave great impetus to the replacement of native vegetation by alien plants.' Forest clearance and an influx of alien plant species from Africa 'brought about the destruction or impoverishment of native vegetation over the whole island,' and had similar effects on the other Leeward colonies, even Barbuda and Anguilla which never supported large sugar plantations. David Watts, another geographer, reached similar conclusions in his 1966 study of the vegetation of Barbados, saying that the introduction of sugar 'caused a revolution in the island's agriculture' and that after 1665 'the Barbadian landscape was essentially open, dominated by large sugar estates set in a man-controlled environment.' The speed of the transformation from 'closed forest' in 1625 was very rapid, argued Watts, and the 'resultant open landscape was ripe for the introduction of alien species.'[75] Sugar cane covered about 80 per cent of the land of Barbados, so that 'alien' vegetation rivalled the demographic weight of 'alien' people consequent on the sugar revolution.

Another general text, D.A.G. Waddell's *The West Indies and the Guianas* (1967), used 'The Sugar Revolution' as a subheading. Waddell, who taught at the University College of the West Indies in Jamaica 1955–59, followed closely the arguments of Parry and Sherlock and of Augier *et al*, saying that the consequences of the shift from tobacco to sugar in Barbados in the 1640s 'were so rapid and far-reaching as to justify the use of the term "the sugar revolution" for the process.' Applying a simple technological determinism and emphasising the economic rationality of the shift, Waddell concluded that 'the coming of sugar transformed not only the economic basis of the non-Hispanic West Indian colonies, but their ethnic composition and their social system as well.'[76]

In 1968 Christian Schnakenbourg followed Lasserre in using the term 'révolution sucrière' in a paper on the origins of the sugar industry in Guadeloupe. Schnakenbourg identified two central 'conséquences humaines du développement de l'industrie sucrière.' First, the sugar planters emerged as 'une classe supérieure, une caste' around 1670 and within a decade they had effectively wiped out the small holders formerly producing tobacco and indigo. Second, between 1640 and 1670 'la 'révolution sucrière', et son corollaire, l'afflux massif d'esclaves' transformed the racial composition of Guadeloupe. Schnakenbourg observed, 'La même phénomène s'était produit à la Barbade quelques années plus tôt.' It is only in the demographic context that Schnakenbourg refers to the sugar revolution, and it was not until the eighteenth century, he argues, that Guadeloupe was covered by sugar cane, marking 'le triomphe du sucre-roi.'[77]

The sugar revolution spread even more slowly to the Hispanic Caribbean. In 1970 it was applied to Cuba by Franklin W. Knight.[78] He was probably the first to do so, and his roots were in the English-speaking Caribbean. Sidney W. Mintz's 1964 introduction to the English language edition of Guerra's work of 1927 talked of a 'technical revolution' ca.1880–1900 in Cuba, but not a sugar revolution. Much earlier, in 1953, Mintz had noted that Puerto Rico was 'technologically far behind' developments in the British West Indies in the later nineteenth century, where the sugar industry had been 'revolutionized . . . by the introduction of great, centralized grinding mills.' In 1956 Julian Steward, with Mintz and others, argued that in Puerto Rico the establishment of *centrales* in the 1870s had 'a revolutionary effect on the industry and on the way of life of the population,' particularly through the elimination of small-scale producers. Although Mintz did not apply the sugar revolution term to Cuba or Puerto Rico, and has remained reluctant to use it in other contexts, his work is suffused with the power of sugar. In 1964, he contended that the bimodal distribution of land in Cuba represented 'the difference between peasantry and proletariat . . . between highland and plain, between small and large, between other crops and sugar, and – some would argue – between white and black.' In this comprehensive ecological and social dichotomy, sugar was determinative: 'Sugar is a lowland crop, a plantation crop, a colonial crop.'[79]

The demographic consequences of the sugar revolution were further emphasised in Philip D. Curtin's *The Atlantic Slave Trade* of 1969. His index points to 'The Sugar Revolution' and his text identifies the coming of the northern Europeans, especially the Dutch, as the 'crucial event' in the slave trade of the seventeenth century: 'They brought the "sugar revolution" to the Caribbean and began the shift that was to make the West Indian islands the heart of the eighteenth-century South Atlantic System.' In the same year,

Richard B. Sheridan – colleague of Augelli at the University of Kansas, and doctoral student with Douglas Hall at the London School of Economics – published a paper on 'The Plantation Revolution and the Industrial Revolution, 1625–1775.' Apparently the first to use the term 'plantation revolution', Sheridan intended to encompass something closer to the 'agrarian revolution' of MacInnes, taking in a regional 'Plantation America' that spread beyond sugar to the 'slave triangle', Curtin's South Atlantic System and the larger Atlantic world as understood by Eric Williams.

Sheridan had mentioned 'the mid-seventeenth-century sugar revolution' in a paper published the year before, 1968, but in earlier writing in the 1960s had identified only 'the sugar boom of the 1640's and 1650's' and 'a remarkable transformation' that imposed sugar on Antigua in the first three quarters of the eighteenth century. His 'plantation revolution' of 1969 included tobacco, cocoa, coffee, indigo, cotton and sugar, all of which required the plantation – 'a factory in the field' – and 'combined and constant labour' that led to enslavement and hence 'large-scale units of production and control.' But Sheridan did not attach the label 'revolution' to any crop other than sugar, and it was Barbados that he chose to exemplify 'the prototype of a small tropical export economy,' in which 'the shift from small staples to a near-monoculture of sugar economy was a revolutionary phenomenon both in its external and internal features.' He twice referred to the 'sugar revolution' as something that spread from Barbados to other islands of the Caribbean and transformed the Atlantic islands as well. Sheridan concluded that, 'The plantation-based trading area, born in the crisis-ridden middle decades of the seventeenth century, thus became a remarkable engine of economic growth as it drew into its orbit the resources of four continents and scattered islands in the Atlantic basin.' In this larger scheme, the role of sugar was lessened and the crop's determinative power matched by others, but the sugar revolution provided the essential model that enabled Sheridan's plantation revolution to take its place alongside the price revolution and the industrial revolution.[80]

The first decades of scholarship following Gaston-Martin's, and Parry and Sherlock's, introduction of the sugar revolution to the terminology of colonial American historiography generated relatively few disciples. Only Augier *et al* (1960), Lasserre (1961), West and Augelli (1966), Waddell (1967), Schnakenbourg (1968), Curtin and Sheridan (1969), and Knight (1970), are known to have used the term, and none of these writers explicitly acknowledged Gaston-Martin or Parry and Sherlock or any other source. The concept must have seemed a natural development, springing easily from three centuries of narratives and twenty or more years of reference to the 'revolutionary' nature of the seventeenth-century shift to sugar. New elements were added to the concept, however, notably the environmental impact introduced by the geographers and the broader, Atlantic ramifications raised by Curtin and Sheridan which connected the sugar revolution with the theses of Williams and made it an 'engine of growth' leading to the industrial revolution. In these ways, the sugar revolution came to represent something much bigger and more important in the economic history of the western world, an event with implications stretching far beyond the internal histories of seemingly insignificant islands. It also helped to move the transformation wrought by sugar from its moral framework – in which yeoman and plantation, settler and slave, had been counterposed ideals – and to place it in the realm of pure economics.[81] These developments were to be given archival depth in complementary studies published by Carl and Roberta Bridenbaugh, Richard Dunn, and Richard Sheridan in the early 1970s, monographs in which sugar and slavery and the seventeenth-century sugar revolution were placed at the very core of West Indian social and economic history.[82] With these firm foundations, the sugar revolution came to earn a secure place in the historiography.

Notes

The author thanks Stanley Engerman, Howard Johnson, Franklin Knight and Barry Smith for comments on drafts of this paper, Gregory Bowen for research assistance, and Ira Berlin, Bridget Brereton, Michael Craton, Pieter Emmer, Richard Grove, Douglas Hall, Jerry Handler, Merle Higman, Ralph Shlomowitz and James Walvin for helpful suggestions.

1. B.W. Higman, 'The Sugar Revolution,' *Economic History Review*, 53, (2000): 213-36. For the broader historiographical context, see B.W. Higman, *Writing West Indian Histories* (London: Macmillan, 1999) and B.W. Higman, ed., *Methodology and Historiography of the Caribbean*, Volume VI of the *General History of the Caribbean* (London: Unesco Publishing/Macmillan Education, 1999).

2. There is a recent exception. Ira Berlin, in *Many Thousands Gone: The First Two Centuries of Slavery in North America* (Cambridge, Mass.: Belknap Press of Harvard University Press, 1998), 108-09, 142, 342-43, identifies tobacco, rice, and cotton revolutions, in the context of a series of 'plantation revolutions' that began with sugar. This new crop of revolutions remains to be tested, assimilated, rejected or ignored by the historiography. Cf. Ira Berlin and Philip D. Morgan, eds., *Cultivation and Culture: Labor and the Shaping of Slave Life in the Americas* (Charlottesville: University Press of Virginia, 1993), 4-5; Daniel C. Littlefield, *Rice and Slaves: Ethnicity and the Slave Trade in Colonial South Carolina* (Baton Rouge: Louisiana State University Press, 1981); T.H. Breen, *Tobacco Culture: The Mentality of the Great Tidewater Planters on the Eve of the Revolution* (Princeton: Princeton University Press, 1985), 21-23; Allan Kulikoff, *Tobacco and Slaves: The Development of Southern*

Cultures in the Chesapeake, 1680–1800 (Chapel Hill: University of North Carolina Press, 1986), 6, 37–38; Philip D. Morgan, *Slave Counterpoint: Black Culture in the Eighteenth-Century Chesapeake and Lowcountry* (Chapel Hill: University of North Carolina Press, 1998), 27–101.

3.   Gaston-Martin, *Histoire de l'esclavage dans les colonies françaises* (Paris: Presses Universitaires de France, 1948), 19.

4.   *Ibid.*, 23–24, emphasis in original.

5.   *Ibid.*, 32, 297.

6.   J.H. Parry and P.M. Sherlock, *A Short History of the West Indies* (London: Macmillan, 1956), 64–70.

7.   *Ibid.*, 63.

8.   *Ibid.*, 66–67.

9.   *Ibid.*, 66–80.

10.   *Ibid.*, 74.

11.   *Ibid.*, 66.

12.   *Ibid.*, vii.

13.   Arthur Percival Newton, *The European Nations in the West Indies 1493–1688* (London: Adam and Charles Black, 1933); J.B. Du Tertre, *Histoire générale des Antilles habitées par les Français* (Paris: Th. Jolly, 1654); Richard Ligon, *A True and Exact History of the Island of Barbados* (London: Humphrey Moseley, 1657); Stewart L. Mims, *Colbert's West India Policy* (New Haven: Yale University Press, 1912); Nellis M. Crouse, *The French Struggle for the West Indies 1665–1713* (New York: Columbia University Press, 1943); Eric Williams, *Capitalism and Slavery* (Chapel Hill: University of North Carolina Press, 1944); George Louis Beer, *The Old Colonial System 1660–1754* (New York: Macmillan, 1912); Melville J. Herskovits, *The Myth of the Negro Past* (New York: Harper and Row, 1941); C.A. Banbuck, *Histoire politique, économique et sociale de la Martinique sous l'Ancien Régime (1635—1789)* (Paris: Libraire des Sciences Politiques et Sociales, 1935); Maurice Satineau, *Histoire de la Guadeloupe sous l'Ancien Régime 1635–1789* (Paris: Payot, 1928); Agnes M. Whitson, *The Constitutional Development of Jamaica, 1660 to 1729* (Manchester: Manchester University Press, 1929); Lawrence A. Harper, *The English Navigation Laws: A Seventeenth-Century Experiment in Social Engineering* (New York: Columbia University Press, 1939). 'General works' listed by Parry and Sherlock, used for the whole volume, were W.L. Burn, *The British West Indies* (London: Hutchinson, 1951); Sir Alan Burns, *History of the British West Indies* (London: George Allen and Unwin, 1954); Gabriel Hanotaux and Alfred Martineau, eds., *Histoire des colonies françaises et de l'expansion de la France dans le monde*, *Vol.1*(Paris: Société de l'Histoire Nationale, 1929); Noel Deerr, *The History of Sugar* (London: Chapman and Hall, 1949–50); C.P. Lucas, *A Historical Geography of the British Colonies: Vol. 2, The West Indies* (Oxford:

Clarendon Press, 1905); José Antonio Saco, *Historia de la esclavitud de la raza africana en el Nuevo Mundo y en especial en los países Américo-Hispanos* (Havana: Cultural, 1938); A.W. Acworth, *Treasure in the Caribbean: A First Study of Georgian Buildings in the British West Indies* (London: Pleiades Books, 1949).

14. J.H. Parry, *Europe and a Wider World 1415–1715* (London: Hutchinson University Library, 1949), 114.

15. J.H. Parry, 'Plantation and Provision Ground: An Historical Sketch of the Introduction of Food Crops into Jamaica,' *Revista de Historia de Americas*, 39 (1955): 1–2.

16. Parry and Sherlock, 299.

17. Ligon, 46, 85–86.

18. Du Tertre, I, 436–39; II, 139–43, 487–534.

19. Edward Long, *The History of Jamaica* (London: T. Lowndes, 1774), I, 402; Bryan Edwards, *The History, Civil and Commercial, of the British Colonies in the West Indies* (London: J. Stockdale, 1819), I, xxxii; Hanotaux and Martineau, 448.

20. Long, I, 402–11; Herman Merivale, *Lectures on Colonization and Colonies* (London: Longmans, 1861), 79–82.

21. Merivale, 82, 93.

22. Paul Leroy-Beaulieu, *De la colonisation chez les peuples modernes* (Paris: Félix Alcan, 1908), I, 116 and n. 1; Merivale, 79.

23. W.J. Gardner, *A History of Jamaica* (London: E. Stock, 1873), 85.

24. Charles Kingsley, *At Last: A Christmas in the West Indies* (London: Macmillan, 1882), 384. Cf. W. Adolphe Roberts, *The Caribbean: The Story of Our Sea of Destiny* (New York: Bobbs-Merrill, 1940), 205–06; Frank Tannenbaum, *Slave and Citizen: The Negro in the Americas* (New York: Alfred Knopf, 1946), 40; Trevor Burnard, 'A Failed Settler Society: Marriage and Demographic Failure in Early Jamaica,' *Journal of Social History*, 28 (1994): 63–82.

25. Gardner, 319.

26. N. Darnell Davis, *The Cavaliers and Roundheads of Barbados 1650–1652, with Some Account of the Early History of Barbados* (Georgetown, British Guiana: The 'Argosy' Press, 1887), 70. See also Elsa V. Goveia, *A Study on the Historiography of the British West Indies to the End of the Nineteenth Century* (Mexico: Instituto Panamericano de Geografía e Historia, 1956), 163–64.

27. Davis, 80. Cf. the scattered treatment in Robert H. Schomburgk, *The History of Barbados* (London: Brown, Green and Longmans, 1847), 79–81, 141–45, 266–85.

28. Lucas, 61–70.

29. Hugh E. Egerton, 'The Transference of Colonial Power to the United Provinces and England,' in *The Cambridge Modern History, Vol. 4*, eds.

A.W. Ward, G.W. Prothero, and Stanley Leathes. (Cambridge: Cambridge University Press, 1906), 756.

30. Frank Wesley Pitman, *The Development of the British West Indies 1700–1763* (New Haven: Yale University Press, 1917), 61, 91, 108. Cf. Waldemar Westergaard, *The Danish West Indies under Company Rule (1671–1754)* (New York: Macmillan, 1917), 121-25, 216.

31. C.S.S. Higham, *The Development of the Leeward Islands under the Restoration, 1660–1688: A Study of the Foundations of the Old Colonial System* (Cambridge: Cambridge University Press, 1921), 143, 178-79.

32. Vincent T. Harlow, *A History of Barbados 1625–1685* (Oxford: Clarendon Press, 1926), 42.

33. *Ibid.*, 43.

34. *Ibid.*, 43–44, 153.

35. *Ibid.*, 292-93, 306-07, 310, 327-28; J. T[ramond], review of Harlow's *A History of Barbados 1625–1685*, in *Revue d'histoire des colonies*, 20 (1927): 622-23.

36. Satineau, 110, 112.

37. *Ibid.*, 112-13, 117; Leroy-Beaulieu, I, 164.

38. Satineau, 117-26.

39. James A. Williamson, 'The Beginnings of an Imperial Policy, 1649–1660,' in *The Cambridge History of the British Empire, Vol. 1: The Old Empire from the Beginnings to 1783*, eds., J. Holland Rose, A.P. Newton, and E.A. Benians. (Cambridge: Cambridge University Press, 1929), 210, 873. Cf. James A. Williamson, *The Caribbee Islands under the Proprietary Patents* (London: Oxford University Press, 1926), 154; Ibid., *Great Britain and the Empire: A Discursive History* (London: A. and C. Black, 1944), 33.

40. Gaston-Martin, 297; Parry and Sherlock, 303.

41. Louis-Philippe May, *Histoire économique de la Martinique (1635–1763)* (Paris: Marcel Riviere, 1930), 74.

42. *Ibid.*, 206-20, 268. Other historians of the French West Indies were less enthusiastic: Banbuck, 217-25; Crouse, 2; Mims, *Colbert's West India Policy*, 36, 45, 50, 282-83, 310.

43. Arthur Percival Newton, *The Colonising Activities of the English Puritans: The Last Phase of the Elizabethan Struggle with Spain* (New Haven: Yale University Press, 1914), 146-48. Cf. Karen Ordahl Kupperman, *Providence Island, 1630–1641: The Other Puritan Colony* (Cambridge: Cambridge University Press, 1993); Margaret Marion Spector, 'A.P. Newton,' in Herman Ausubel, J. Bartlet Brebner, and Erling M. Hunt, eds., *Some Modern Historians of Britain: Essays in Honor of R. L. Schuyler* (New York: The Dryden Press, 1951), 290-91.

44. Newton, *The European Nations in the West Indies*, 197-99, cf. xvii.

45. C.M. MacInnes, *An Introduction to the Economic History of the British*

Empire (London: Rivingtons, 1935), 70. The idea of 'agrarian revolution' may be traced to Arnold Toynbee, *Lectures on the Industrial Revolution in England* (London: Rivingtons, 1884), 27.

46. MacInnes, *Introduction*, 70–75, 78. See also C.M. MacInnes, *A Gateway of Empire* (Bristol: Arrowsmith, 1939), 176. Cf. Louis Bernard Schmidt, 'The Agricultural Revolution in the Prairies and the Great Plains of the United States,' *Agricultural History*, 4 (1934): 169–73.

47. Charles M. Andrews, *The Colonial Period of American History, Vol. 3: The Settlements* (New Haven: Yale University Press, 1936), 253, 260, 270–71.

48. Cf. Alfred D. Chandler who, in his first published paper, argued simply that the introduction of sugar 'completely transformed' the farm economy of Barbados, causing the emigration to South Carolina: 'The Expansion of Barbados,' *Journal of the Barbados Museum and Historical Society*, 13 (1946): 108–09.

49. G. Debien, 'La société coloniale aux XVIIe et XVIIIe siècles: Les engagés pour les Antilles (1634–1715)', *Revue d'histoire des colonies*, 38 (1951): 68, 257–61.

50. G. Debien, 'Les travaux d'histoire sur Saint-Domingue: Chronique bibliographique (1946–1950),' *Revue d'histoire des colonies*, 36 (1949): 303.

51. Richard Pares, *Merchants and Planters* (London: Economic History Society, 1960), 22–23, 58 n.16; G. Debien, 'Richard Pares,' *Revue d'histoire de colonies*, 45 (1958): 300–06; Fernand Braudel, 'Antilles et Amérique,' *Annales ESC*, 3 (1948): 537.

52. Fernand Braudel, *La Méditerranée et le monde méditerranéen à l'époque de Philippe II* (Paris: Librairie Armand Colin, 1949), 123.

53. Eric Williams, *The Negro in the Caribbean* (Washington: The Associates in Negro Folk Education, 1942), 12; Williams, *Capitalism and Slavery*, 23–26. Cf. Léon Vignols, 'Une question mal posée: Le travail manuel des blancs et des esclaves aux Antilles (XVIIe–XVIIIe siècles),' *Revue historique*, 175 (1935): 308–15; Edgar T. Thompson, 'The Climatic Theory of the Plantation,' *Agricultural History*, 15 (1941): 49–60; A.P. Thornton, 'The Organization of the Slave Trade in the English West Indies, 1660–1685,' *William and Mary Quarterly*, 12 (1955): 399–409.

54. Debien, 'Les travaux d'histoire sur Saint-Domingue,' 306; Westergaard, v; Geoffrey Parker, *The Military Revolution: Military Innovation and the Rise of the West* (Cambridge: Cambridge University Press, 1988), 146.

55. Fernando Ortiz, *Contrapunteo Cubano del Tabaco y el Azúcar* (Havana: J. Montero, 1940), published in English translation as *Cuban Counterpoint: Tobacco and Sugar* (New York: Vintage Books, 1947, 1970), 81; Williams, *Capitalism and Slavery*, 8, 21, 213–17. Cf. M. Delafosse,

'La Rochelle et les îles au XVIIe siècle,' *Revue d'histoire des colonies*, 36 (1949): 276.

56. Debien, 'Les travaux d'histoire sur Saint-Domingue,' 303–04. Cf. Pares, *Merchants and Planters*, 22–23.

57. Manuel Moreno Fraginals, *El ingenio: complejo económico social cubano del azúcar* (Havana: Editorial de Ciencias Sociales, 1978), I, 15.

58. Ramiro Guerra y Sánchez, *Sugar and Society in the Caribbean: An Economic History of Cuban Agriculture* (New Haven: Yale University Press, 1964), 1–5, 9–16.

59. *Ibid.*, 45, 73–75, 89, 96–97.

60. Mervyn Ratekin, 'The Early Sugar Industry in Española,' *Hispanic American Historical Review*, 34 (1954): 15–19.

61. Deerr, I, 160, 168, 213, 228, 244; Parry and Sherlock, 303.

62. Burns, *History of the British West Indies*, 232–33; Sir Alan Burns, *Colonial Civil Servant* (London: George Allen and Unwin, 1949).

63. D.C. Coleman, *Myth, History and the Industrial Revolution* (London: Hambledon Press, 1992), 3–4.

64. Gaston-Martin, 213, 219–20, writes only of 'la révolte des esclaves' and 'la révolte noir;' Parry and Sherlock, 164, 170, 176, 313, talk of a 'slave revolt' and 'Haitian revolt' in their text, though index 'slave revolution' and 'Revolution, Haitian.' Cf. Michel-Rolph Trouillot, *Silencing the Past: Power and the Production of History* (Boston: Beacon Press, 1995); Thomas O. Ott, *The Haitian Revolution, 1789–1804* (Knoxville: University of Tennessee Press, 1973); Carolyn E. Fick, *The Making of Haiti: The Saint Domingue Revolution from Below* (Knoxville: University of Tennessee Press, 1990).

65. Redcliffe N. Salaman, *The History and Social Influence of the Potato* (Cambridge: Cambridge University Press, 1949), 142, 220, 601; Harold A. Innis, *The Fur Trade in Canada: An Introduction to Canadian Economic History* (New Haven: Yale University Press, 1930); Ibid., *The Cod Fisheries: The History of an International Economy* (New Haven: Yale University Press, 1940); W.A. Mackintosh, 'Innis on Canadian Economic Development,' *Journal of Political Economy*, 61 (1953): 185–94; W.T. Easterbrook and Hugh G.J. Aitken, *Canadian Economic History* (Toronto: University of Toronto Press, 1956), 66; Douglass C. North, 'Location Theory and Regional Economic Growth,' *Journal of Political Economy*, 63 (1955): 243–58; Robert E. Baldwin, 'Patterns of Development in Newly Settled Regions,' *The Manchester School of Economic and Social Studies*, 24 (1956): 161–79; Melville H. Watkins, 'A Staple Theory of Economic Growth,' *Canadian Journal of Economics and Political Science*, 29 (1963): 141–58; Ralph Davis, 'English Foreign Trade, 1660–1700,' *Economic History Review*, 7 (1954): 162–63; Jacob M. Price, 'The Transatlantic Economy,' in Jack P. Greene and J. R.

Pole, eds., *Colonial British America: Essays in the New History of the Early Modern Era* (Baltimore: The Johns Hopkins University Press, 1984), 22-26; Williams, *Negro in the Caribbean*, 12-14; W. Arthur Lewis, 'Economic Development with Unlimited Supplies of Labour,' *The Manchester School of Economic and Social Studies*, 22 (1954): 173.

66. K.G. Davies, *The North Atlantic World in the Seventeenth Century* (Minneapolis: University of Minnesota Press, 1974), 180. Davis in *The Royal African Company* (London: Longman, 1957: 14), had stated simply that the introduction of sugar to Barbados set in train 'a dramatic transformation;' his 'Empire and Capital,' *Economic History Review*, 13 (1960): 105-10, discussing the work of Pares, similarly lacked the sugar revolution term.

67. Davies, *North Atlantic World*, 180-82. His citations included Harlow, *History of Barbados*; Richard Pares, *A West-India Fortune* (London: Longmans, 1950); Higham, *Development of the Leeward Islands*; May, *Histoire économique de la Martinique*; Deerr, *History of Sugar*; and Satineau, *Histoire de la Guadeloupe*. Davies' bibliography (pages 340-41) called Parry and Sherlock's *Short History* 'easily the best introduction to this region: it is one of the few books to treat the subject internationally.' Davies also (page 340) cited Gaston-Martin, *Histoire de l'esclavage*, for his chapter on the slave trade.

68. Philip Sherlock, *West Indies* (London: Thames and Hudson, 1966), 41; Philip Sherlock and Hazel Bennett, *The Story of the Jamaican People* (Kingston: Ian Randle Publishers, 1998), 89. Cf. J.H. Parry, *The Age of Reconnaissance* (London: Weidenfeld and Nicolson, 1963), 260-65; Ibid., *Trade and Dominion: The European Overseas Empires in the Eighteenth Century* (New York: Praeger Publishers, 1971), 40-50; Ibid., *The Spanish Seaborne Empire* (Harmondsworth: Penguin Books, 1973), 263; Philip Sherlock, *West Indian Nations: A New History* (Kingston: Jamaica Publishing House, 1973), 86-91.

69. F.R. Augier, S.C. Gordon, D.G. Hall, and M. Reckord, *The Making of the West Indies* (London: Longmans, Green, 1960), ix-x, 303. Cf. Howard Johnson, 'The "Jamaica 300" Celebrations of 1955: Commemoration in a Colonial Polity,' *Journal of Imperial and Commonwealth History*, 26 (1998): 120-37.

70. *Ibid.*, 43-46, 62.

71. Guy Lasserre, *La Guadeloupe: Étude géographique* (Bordeaux: Union Française D'Impression, 1961), I, 276 (and n.55), 290.

72. *Ibid.*, I, 343. Here Lasserre cited a 1916 thesis by P. Bernissant, 'Etude sur le régime agricole des Antilles françaises.'

73. Lasserre, I, 352, 356, 384, 388, 390-91, 401.

74. Robert C. West and John P. Augelli, *Middle America: Its Lands and Peoples* (Englewood Cliffs: Prentice-Hall Inc., 1966), 80-95. Cf. C.O. Sauer,

'The Agency of Man on the Earth', in William L. Thomas, Jr., ed., *Man's Role in Changing the Face of the Earth* (Chicago: University of Chicago Press, 1956), 63; David L. Niddrie, 'An Attempt at Planned Settlement in St. Kitts in the Early Eighteenth Century', *Caribbean Studies*, 5 (1966): 6.

75. David R. Harris, 'The Invasion of Oceanic Islands by Alien Plants: An Example from the Leeward Islands, West Indies,' *Institute of British Geographers, Transactions and Papers*, 31 (1962): 75-77; David Watts, *Man's Influence on the Vegetation of Barbados 1627 to 1800* (Hull: University of Hull Publications, Occasional Papers in Geography No. 4, 1966), 43-46, 62. Cf. J.H. Galloway, 'The Sugar Industry in Barbados during the Seventeenth Century,' *Journal of Tropical Geography*, 19 (1964): 35-41.

76. D.A.G. Waddell, *The West Indies and the Guianas* (Englewood Cliffs: Prentice-Hall Inc., 1967), 41-44, 137.

77. Christian Schnakenbourg, 'Note sur les origines de l'industrie sucrière en Guadeloupe au XVIIe siècle (1640-1670),' *Revue français d'histoire d'outre mer*, 55 (1968): 297-302, 311.

78. Franklin W. Knight, *Slave Society in Cuba during the Nineteenth Century* (Madison: University of Wisconsin Press, 1970), esp. chapter 2. Cf. David A. Lockmiller, 'Agriculture in Cuba during the Second United States Intervention, 1906-1909,' *Agricultural History*, 11 (1937): 185.

79. Sidney W. Mintz, 'The Culture History of a Puerto Rican Sugar Cane Plantation, 1876-1949,' *Hispanic American Historical Review*, 33 (1953): 228; 'Foreword,' in Guerra y Sánchez, *Sugar and Society in the Caribbean*, xxxix; Julian H. Steward, et al., *The People of Puerto Rico* (Urbana: University of Illinois Press, 1956), 54. The term 'sugar revolution' does not appear in Sidney W. Mintz, *Sweetness and Power: The Place of Sugar in Modern History* (New York: Viking, 1985).

80. Philip D. Curtin, *The Atlantic Slave Trade: A Census* (Madison: University of Wisconsin Press, 1969), 125-26; Richard B. Sheridan, 'Samuel Martin, Innovating Sugar Planter of Antigua, 1750-1776,' *Agricultural History*, 34 (1960): 127; Ibid., 'The Rise of a Colonial Gentry: A Case Study of Antigua, 1730-1775,' *Economic History Review*, 13 (1961): 43; Ibid., 'The Wealth of Jamaica in the Eighteenth Century,' *Economic History Review*, 18 (1965): 295; Ibid., 'The Wealth of Jamaica in the Eighteenth Century: A Rejoinder,' *Economic History Review*, 21 (1968): 61; Ibid., 'The Plantation Revolution and the Industrial Revolution,' *Caribbean Studies*, 9 (1969): 8, 11-12, 14, 18, 21, 23 (citing Watkins, 'Staple Theory'), 25. Cf. D.A. Farnie, 'The Commercial Empire of the Atlantic, 1607-1783,' *Economic History Review*, 15 (1962): 205-18; E.E. Rich, 'Colonial Settlement and Its Labour Problems,' in E.E. Rich and C.H. Wilson, eds., *The Cambridge Economic History of Europe, Vol. 4*

(Cambridge: Cambridge University Press, 1967), 340–44. For a discussion of the development of Sheridan's ideas, see Howard Johnson, 'Richard B. Sheridan: The Making of a Caribbean Economic Historian,' in Roderick A. McDonald, ed., *West Indies Accounts: Essays on the History of the British Caribbean and the Atlantic Economy in Honour of Richard Sheridan* (Kingston: The Press, UWI, 1996), 1–28.

81. Carville V. Earle, 'A Staple Interpretation of Slavery and Free Labor,' *Geographical Review*, 68 (1978): 65.

82. Carl Bridenbaugh and Roberta Bridenbaugh, *No Peace Beyond the Line: The English in the Caribbean, 1624-1690* (New York: Oxford University Press, 1972); Richard S. Dunn, *Sugar and Slaves: The Rise of the Planter Class in the English West Indies, 1624-1713* (Chapel Hill: University of North Carolina Press, 1972); Richard B. Sheridan, *Sugar and Slavery: An Economic History of the British West Indies, 1623-1775* (Bridgetown, Barbados: Caribbean Universities Press, 1974).

Section

II

Production, Culture and Resistance in the Slavery Era

Figure 6 : *Revolt on board a slave ship*

CHAPTER 4

The Origins of Slave Rebellions in the Middle Passage
Winston McGowan

Introduction

No subject in Caribbean history has attracted the attention of scholars and captivated the imagination of the public as much as slavery. In particular, the question of slave resistance, especially slave rebellions, has evoked considerable interest. Not only have slave revolts been the focus of many monographs, but also the leaders of several major uprisings have been exalted in modern times to the status of national heroes. Such status has been accorded to Kofi, Bussa and Sam Sharpe, the principal leader of the most formidable slave rebellion in the history of Guyana, Barbados and Jamaica respectively.

In striking contrast to the pronounced focus on slave uprisings on land in the Caribbean, very little attention has so far been devoted to rebellions on board ship before the captives reached the region, namely, on the coast of Africa before their departure and during the Atlantic crossing. Even authoritative studies of the Middle Passage,[1] one of the best-known aspects of the transatlantic slave trade, hardly address the question of rebellions on board the slave ships. Rather they focus on issues such as the number of slaves shipped, their ethnic and geographical origins, mortality from disease, ports in Africa and the Americas, the size, structure and ownership of the slave ships, shipping patterns, sea routes, sailing times, the experience of the slaves and the crew, and the various European national trades in slaves. This comparative neglect of rebellions on board the slave ships is particularly striking in view of the fact that such revolts were more frequent and more successful than slave uprisings on land in the Americas.

The greater frequency of maritime slave rebellions was due largely to two factors. Firstly, captives on board a slave ship did not have any other means of escaping alive from servitude than through a successful rebellion. It was not possible for them, unlike slaves on land in the Americas, to escape and remain alive by flight. The only place to flee at sea was overboard in what was in reality an act of suicide. Secondly, the higher incidence of slave revolts at sea was related to the fact that certain favourable circumstances gave them a greater chance of success than those staged on land in the Caribbean. Notable among the advantages which rebels at sea enjoyed were the ability to plan in secret below deck without detection, the smaller likelihood of betrayal by informers and the virtual inability of the captain and crew to summon the help of reinforcements to suppress the revolt.

Love of country

More revolts actually took place on board slave vessels on the coast of Africa before they sailed for the Americas than during the Atlantic crossing. This was because the slaves believed that they could more easily capture the ship, guide it to the shore and escape while it was on the coast than in the open sea. As John Atkins, a British slave trader, rightly observed, 'there has not been wanting Examples of rising and killing a Ship's Company, distant from Land, tho' not so often as on the Coast.'[2] His opinion was supported by Jacques Savary, an early authority on the French slave trade, who stated:

> It is necessary to observe that as soon as one has completed trading in slaves, and they have entered the vessel, one should set sail. The reason is that these slaves have such a great love for their country and despair seeing that they are leaving it forever, and that makes some die from much grief and I have heard it said to traders involved in this commerce in Blacks, that more die before their departure from the port than during the voyage . . . some throwing themselves into the sea . . . and when they lose sight of their country, they begin to be consoled, especially when they are entertained with the harmony of some instrument.[3]

At least one captain felt so relieved and secure when he left the African coast that he removed the handcuffs and leg shackles from his slaves, 'excepting a few offenders that were troublesome in the ship, and endeavouring to persuade the slaves to destroy the White Men.'[4]

The greater frequency of slave rebellions on vessels on the African coast has been confirmed by recent statistical analysis of the Rhode Island slave trade. Of the 17 slave revolts which took place on Rhode Island vessels between 1730 and 1807, eleven occurred on the West African coast, five during the Atlantic crossing and one in the Caribbean, while the location of the other rebellion is unknown.[5]

Second only to rebellions on the African coast were those within ten days' sail of that continent. One example of this occurred on board the *Clare Galley* in 1729. According to a contemporary report:

> The Clare Galley, Capt. Murrell, having compleated [sic] her Number of
> Negroes had taken her Departure from the Coast of Guinea for South Carolina;
> but was not yet 10 Leagues on her Way, before the Negroes rose and making
> themselves Masters of the Gunpowder and Firearms, the Captain and the
> Ship's crew took to their Long Boat, and got ashore near Cape Coast Castle.
> The Negroes ran the Ship on Shore within a few Leagues of the said Castle,
> and made their Escape.[6]

The view, however, which some slave traders and other individuals expressed that rebellions at sea by slaves only took place close to the African coast 'while they had a shore to fly to' was not true. Many revolts occurred several weeks after the slaver had left African waters. Nevertheless, it is clear that uprisings far in the ocean presented slaves with the difficult problem of directing the ship back to Africa with or without the assistance of the crew.

The possibility of the outbreak of slave rebellions made the Middle Passage a very dangerous undertaking, especially for the sponsors of the voyage and the officers and sailors in the slave ship. Slaves were the most dangerous cargo in the world. As Philip Drake, a notorious slave trader for 50 years, observed, 'Slavery is a dangerous business at sea as well as ashore.'[7] This risk was often emphasised in the instructions which sponsors of slaving voyages gave to the captains of the slave ships. For example, in 1759 the captain of a British slaver was told, 'We must recommend to you to have a constant watch on board your ship to prevent insurrection;' and a few years later an American captain was warned to be 'very careful in keeping a good look out and watchful of your Negroes to prevent Insurrection.'[8]

Security from slave insurrections and the health of the slave cargo were, in fact, usually the two paramount concerns expressed by owners of slave ships to their captains. Typical of such instructions were those given in 1755 to a Rhode Island captain who was told, 'Keep a watchful eye over 'em and give them no opportunity of making an insurrection, and let them have sufficiency of good diet, as you are sensible your voyage depends upon their health.'[9]

Slave insurrections were the main source of fear of the captains of slavers for they could endanger their own lives as well as those of the crew who could not be replaced at sea. Admittedly, in the Middle Passage they were normally responsible for only a small part of slave and crew deaths, which were due mainly to disease. Nevertheless, captains were much more fearful of the prospect of slave revolts than of disease. They were also conscious of the financial implications of rebellions. Uprisings increased the cost of slaving voyages before the vessel left Europe or North America for Africa by causing sponsors to take out insurance and to outfit it with a comparatively large crew as well as chains and shackles to control the slaves. They could result in the financial failure of the voyage if they caused the slaves to escape or many deaths among them or the loss of the ship. These consequences were noted by the English captain, William Snelgrave, who observed, 'I knew several voyages had proved unsuccessful by Mutinies; as they occasioned either the total loss of the Ship and the white Men's Lives; or at least by rendering it absolutely necessary to kill or wound a great number of slaves, in order to prevent a total Destruction.'[10]

Desire for freedom

The most fundamental cause of slave rebellions at sea was no doubt the natural desire of the slaves for freedom. This is easily understandable, especially as almost all the slaves had been born free, but had lost that cherished freedom because of the Atlantic slave traffic and wished to regain it. This desire was appreciated by some white participants in the slave trade. For example, a member of the crew of a Liverpool slaver described a rebellion which took place on it in 1749 as 'a design of recovering their natural right, Liberty.'[11] Similarly, Alexander Falconbridge, who served as a physician on slave ships in the 1780s, attributed the outbreak of slave revolts at sea to the fact that 'very few of the negroes can so far brook the loss of their liberty.'[12] He acknowledged that 'the unhappy Africans are not bereft of the finer feelings, but have a strong attachment to their native country, together with a just sense of the value of liberty.'[13]

The desire for freedom is said to have been particularly strong among the residents of the British colony of Sierra Leone which was established in 1788 as the much-vaunted 'Province of Freedom' where slavery and the slave trade were totally outlawed. Africans from Sierra Leone who were kidnapped and sold into the Atlantic slave traffic are known to have been prompted to rebel because of the supreme value which they attached to freedom. This was said to have been one of the main causes of a successful revolt late in 1824 or early in 1825 on board a French slaver, *Deux Soeurs*, shortly after the vessel left the Sherbro region.[14]

Desire to return home

In addition to their natural desire for freedom, the revolting slaves at sea, as Falconbridge observed, were influenced by their anger and grief over their removal from Africa. They were motivated by a strong desire to return to their beloved and sacred home, Africa, where their protective spirits and revered ancestors allegedly lived, and to rejoin their family, other relatives and friends. Their grief struck James Arnold, a physician on a British slaver, who reported that slave women on board often tearfully sang songs about 'their separation from their Friends and Country.'[15] It was also stressed by James Towne, an Englishman who had made two slaving voyages in the 1760s, during his appearance in 1791 before the House of Commons Committee which was investigating the slave trade. According to Towne, when he inquired from slaves why they had attempted revolts on his slaving vessel 'The reasons that were given me were, "What business had we to make Slaves of them, and carry them away from their own country? That they had wives and children, and wanted to be with them".'[16]

The desire to return home is said to have been a very strong incentive for rebellion by slaves who had come from the more accessible areas of West Africa. They felt that if they could gain control of the ship, they could direct it back to the African coast and be quickly reunited with their families. This pain of separation was believed by some slave traders to have endured with greater strength among male slaves than females, who in general were subjected to less inhumane treatment than the men during the Middle Passage.[17]

The willingness of slaves to revolt on the slave ships was also fuelled by the fact that many of them believed that if they died, especially during a rebellion, their spirits would return immediately to their beloved motherland, Africa. This was noted by John Atkins, an English surgeon who participated in several slaving voyages in the early eighteenth century. He observed:

> When we are slaved and out at sea, it is commonly imagined the Negroes' ignorance of Navigation will always be a safeguard; yet as many of them think themselves bought to eat, and more, that Death will send them into their own Country, there has not been wanting Examples of rising and Killing a Ship's Company distant from the land.[18]

Fear of white cannibalism

They were also prompted to revolt, as Atkins noted, by their fears that they were destined ultimately for an awful fate. They did not know that they were being taken to work on lands across the Atlantic. Rather, many of them believed that a horrible destiny awaited them across the ocean, such as being offered as human sacrifices to the gods of their captors, being murdered to provide blood to dye the red cloth bartered by European traders in West Africa, or, more commonly, to be killed and eaten by their captors or other white cannibals.[19] The prevalence of these erroneous beliefs was noted by Adam Starr, a sailor on a British slaver, while describing the frenzy among the slaves just before the vessel's departure from São Tomé for Jamaica in 1781. He observed that 'the blacks in their ignorance believe that the lands to which they are transported are filled with giant man-eating whites, and that they are carried across the sea to provide fodder for these monsters.'[20]

Starr's experience was confirmed 15 years later by another European, Mungo Park, the famous Scottish doctor and explorer who later became the first European to discover the source and direction of the Niger River. On his first expedition to Africa in 1796–97, Park recorded a conversation which he had with some slaves who were on their way from the interior to the coast to be sold to British traders at the Gambia River. According to him:

> They were all very inquisitive, but they viewed me at first with looks of horror and repeatedly asked if my countrymen were cannibals. They were very desirous to know what became of the slaves after they had crossed the salt water. I told them that they were employed in cultivating the land, but they would not believe me; and one of them, putting his hand upon the ground, said with great simplicity, 'Have you really got such ground as this to set your feet upon?' A deeply-rooted idea that the whites purchase Negroes for the purpose of devouring them or selling them to others, that they may be devoured hereafter naturally makes the slaves contemplate a journey towards the coast with great terror.[21]

This widespread belief that whites were cannibals is said to have been particularly strong among certain Africans, especially those resident in the interior and who had less contact with Europeans than the generally more informed inhabitants of the coast. Admittedly, however, many coastal residents, particularly those from Bonny and Calabar, two principal slave ports in modern Nigeria, also shared this view. For this reason some captains of slave ships kept the Bonny slaves 'under a stricter guard because they are more vicious and therefore more care is obliged to be taken against insurrections.'[22]

Thomas King, an Englishman who made nine slaving voyages from West Africa to the Caribbean between 1766 and 1780, told a Parliamentary investigating committee in 1789 that the fear of white cannibalism was one of the three principal causes of slave rebellions at sea. In his evidence he stated:

> There are other Nations again in Africa who have an idea that the White People purchase them with intent to take them to their own country, to kill and eat them. These Negroes are sometimes on board the ship a considerable time before they are perfectly reconciled.[23]

Many captives, however, never overcame this fear of white cannibalism. This was one of the principal causes of rebellions in the slave ships in the sight of land in the Caribbean and of the frenzy slaves demonstrated when whites in the Caribbean territories came on board to purchase them. This was emphasised by the French cleric, John Labat, who rightly asserted that 'it is principally at the sight of land, whether one is still on the coast of Guinea or in the sight of the Islands that revolts must be feared because the Negroes are possessed with the idea that they are being taken to the Islands only to eat them.'[24]

The reasons for the belief that whites were cannibals are not clear. At least four factors are believed to have contributed to its existence. Firstly, it was facilitated by the fact that some Africans were known or believed by others to be or to have been cannibals in the past. Secondly, the belief is said to have been spread through propaganda used by rival European traders in Africa. According to Labat:

> It is claimed that it is Europeans, jealous of our commerce, who have spread these false rumours, which it is very difficult to make the Blacks abandon. . . . Some enemies of the trade of our nation have spread among the Blacks that we are buying them only to eat them. . . . One has all the difficulties in the world to free those who go on board from this deception.[25]

Thirdly, the rumour that whites were cannibals was spread by African rulers and slaveholders, who used the threat of sale to alleged man-eating European slave traders as an effective means of controlling their subjects and slaves. According to Robert Norris, a captain and merchant who made five slaving voyages from the Gold Coast, 'the implied Crime of Witchcraft is still believed there, and is punished with Transportation . . . [that is], selling them to the White Traders, what is represented in this [Fante] Nation as the greatest Evil that can befal [sic] them, in order to deter them from Crimes.'[26]

The employment of a similar strategy by African slave masters to control their slaves was substantiated in the evidence given in 1789 to a British Parliamentary Committee on the Slave Trade by Poplett, an officer who served in the African corps in Senegal and the Gambia from 1779 to 1783. According to the Committee's report:

> Being asked whether the Slaves shew Reluctance or Pleasure at being purchased by the Europeans? Mr. Poplett replied, Great Reluctance; for the Masters or Priests hold out as a general Doctrine to their Slaves, that the Europeans will kill and eat them, if they behave so ill as they do to their respective Masters, by which Means the Slaves are kept in better Order, and in great Fear of being sold to the Europeans. This doctrine is generally believed in that Part of Africa, and has a very political Effect on the Minds of these People.[27]

Finally, the Africans' belief in white cannibalism and their misunderstanding of the purpose of the transatlantic slave trade were widespread because few slaves had returned to Africa from the Americas to inform their countrymen that they had been taken there to work. Francis Moore, the British agent at James Island in the Gambia River in the 1730s, correctly noted that the Fula of the inland state of Bondu 'generally imagined that all who were sold for slaves were generally either eaten or murdered since none ever returned.'[28]

In an attempt to dispel this false idea and to prevent rebellions on board, experienced slave captains went at length to try to explain to the slaves that they were being taken away from Africa to work and to give them other assurances.[29] According to Labat:

> It is necessary on these occasions to assure them that they are being taken to the Islands only to help us exploit the land; that they will be more happy there than in their own countries, that they will be taught to know the true God, and that being made Christians by Baptism, they will enjoy the same benefits as their masters.[30]

Often, however, these assurances were not believed by the slaves who, according to the English slaving captain, Thomas Phillips, had 'a more dreadful apprehension of Barbadoes than we can of hell.'[31] The result was rebellions, suicides and hunger strikes at sea. To overcome fears and prevent revolts and other forms of resistance, when ships reached the Caribbean, the captains eagerly welcomed African slaves on board so that they could calm the new arrivals by informing them that the true purpose of their enslavement was to work for the whites, not to end up in their stomachs. For many victims of the slave traffic, it was this encounter with fellow Africans which finally dispelled the myth of white cannibalism which terrified them during the Middle Passage and prompted serious resistance.

Poor conditions on board ship

Uprisings at sea were also a reaction to the terrible conditions to which the slaves were subjected during the Atlantic crossing – conditions to which male slaves are said to have had more difficulty adjusting than females. Prominent among these well-known conditions were overcrowding, close confinement, poor ventilation and sanitation, the loathsome stench of the ship, intense heat, hunger and famishing thirst, the changing weather, including storms, seasickness, the length of the voyage and exposure to disease and death. While these factors made the Middle Passage unbearable, for many slaves its most distressing feature was the ill treatment, including molestation of females, which they received from the crew.

Some experienced captains of slavers believed that maltreatment by the officers and crew was one of the principal causes of slave revolts at sea. For example, according to William Snelgrave, 'the Mutinies raised by them on board Ships, are generally occasioned by the ill Usage of the Sailors. . . . If a ship captain is well inclined, slaves are easily governed.'[32] This view was also shared by John Knox, who made eight or nine voyages to West Africa in the 1780s and was one of the few captains who did not place his slave cargo in irons during the Atlantic crossing. He stated, 'I depended on the good behaviour of myself and people towards them for the safety of my family and crew.'[33] Similarly, experienced French captains believed that one of the best means of forestalling slave rebellions was 'to treat them as humanely as possible.'[34] This view, of course, did not take sufficient cognisance of the other factors, such as the basic human desire for freedom and the desire to return to Africa, which helped to produce rebellions at sea.

The recognition of the inter-relationship between inconsiderate treatment and revolt made some ship owners emphasise this point in their instructions to the captains. For instance, in 1759 the captain of an English slaver was told by the owners:

> We must recommend to you to have constant watch on board your ship to prevent insurrection and that all your officers perform the several duties they have engaged in and that the negroes have their provisions regularly and be in no ways molested but treated with all the lenity that security will permit of.[35]

To forestall rebellions a few captains went as far as to promise the slaves justice if they reported maltreatment by the sailors. But even captains who believed that slave rebellions could be reduced significantly by considerate treatment admitted that certain slaves, especially Akans, could not be rendered docile by kindness, for they never became reconciled to their enslavement.[36]

The harrowing conditions of the Middle Passage, the pain of separation from country, relatives and friends, the natural desire for freedom, the shame and anger of enslavement and the fear of white cannibalism – all combined to produce in the slaves a psychological condition of deep despair which guaranteed rebellions at sea. This complex situation was described well by a sailor on a Liverpool slaver which experienced a slave rebellion on its way from the Guinea Coast to the Caribbean. He reported:

> They were shackled two and two together, pent up within the narrow confines of the main deck, with the complicated distress of sickness, chains and contempt; deprived of every fond and social tie and in a great measure reduced to a state of desperation. We had not been a fortnight at sea, before the fatal consequences of this despair appeared, they formed a design of recovering their natural right, Liberty, by raising and murdering every man on board.[37]

Opportunistic circumstances

Distressed slaves on the slave vessels were usually able to take advantage of at least one of four practical circumstances which often facilitated the staging of rebellions. These were: a safe environment for planning, the element of surprise, numerical advantage, and deficiencies in the ship's crew. On some occasions they also profited from the dominance of one ethnic group in the slave cargo and emergency situations which distracted the captain and crew.

Although some slave uprisings at sea seem to have been spontaneous, most of them appear to have been premeditated and often they were carefully planned. One difficulty which the slaves seem to have encountered in planning rebellions at sea was communication in the absence of a common language, except in the relatively rare case where all the slaves came from one linguistic zone. The communication problem, though overcome, must have been particularly challenging when the slave cargo, as frequently was the case, was obtained from numerous points along an extensive area of the West African coast. The slaves had the advantage of being able to plan rebellions in secret, often at night below deck, where they enjoyed the absence of white supervision. Betrayal by informers of plans to rebel was comparatively rare. This was partly because in the relatively short period on board the slave ship, there was usually not sufficient time for slaves to develop a special relationship with any member of the crew which would induce them to betray plans for rebellion to obtain a reward or for some other motive. As a result, few planned rebellions at sea were nipped in the bud.

Success in keeping plans for rebellion secret meant that in many rebellions at sea the slaves enjoyed the element of surprise which they sought to exploit. Typical of the reaction of the captain and crew to the initial outbreak of a slave uprising was that of Captain George Scott of the slaver, *Little George*, in 1730. He reported, 'On so sudden a surprize, we were at a loss what to do.'[38] Slaves often surrounded officers and sailors, surprised them with a sudden attack, overpowered and killed them, seizing their guns.[39]

The slaves often were emboldened to rebel, partly by awareness of their numerical dominance over officers and sailors. This consciousness, which helped to give the slaves courage and confidence, is said to have played an important role, especially in situations where the ship was undermanned or the crew was negligent. This factor featured prominently among the circumstances which gave rise to a rebellion on a French slaver, the *Augusta*, in 1827 when the slaves were instigated to revolt by one of their number who 'spoke to them about the small number of the whites and drew to their attention the constantly increasingly negligence of their guards.'[40] Slaves no doubt were aware that at sea the captain and crew were not in a position to secure reinforcements to suppress a rebellion, for it was very rare for slavers to encounter another vessel until they reached the Caribbean. This was in striking contrast to the situation on the coast of Africa where there were often other slaving vessels nearby whose help could be summoned to quell a slave revolt.

Many rebellions on board ships were prompted partly by obvious deficiencies exhibited by the crew, especially numerical weakness, imprudence, and sleepiness, which resulted in lax security that the slaves exploited. The paucity of sailors which some slavers experienced was due to deaths and sickness before the vessel left the coast of Africa, as well as during the Atlantic crossing. It was extremely difficult to secure replacements for such sailors in

West Africa, because of the small number of Europeans there, and impossible to do so at sea. Undermanned vessels often could not provide adequate supervision or observation of the slaves, with disastrous consequences, especially if the slave cargo was large.

Among the uprisings which witnesses attributed to slaves' exploitation of a favourable opportunity afforded by a depleted crew was one which occurred on board a London slaver, the *Don Carlos*, in January 1701, four days after it had left Cabinda, near the mouth of the Congo River, for Jamaica with 417 slaves. The vessel was severely undermanned as six sailors had died at Cabinda or at sea and several others and all the officers, namely, the captain, the supercargo and the first mate, were ill, 'the Air being very unwholesome.'[41] According to one source, 'this Condition of the Crew encouraged the Slaves on-board to revolt on the fifth day.'[42] A basically similar incident occurred on board another British slaver, the *Princess Caroline*, in August 1735. The vessel was at the time on its way from the Gambia River to Carolina with 116 slaves 'and but 13 Hands including Officers and Boys;' the captain, having died in the Gambia, had been replaced by the chief mate.[43]

Though slave vessels with a depleted or sick crew were prone to rebellion, many of them managed to effect the Atlantic crossing safely. Some captains used slaves on board to replace sick, disabled or dead sailors as well as to supplement a full crew in special circumstances, such as maritime emergencies occasioned by storms or attacks by privateers or pirates. The vast majority of vessels employing slaves in such a capacity during the Middle Passage experienced no mishap. On a few occasions, however, rebellions occurred as a result of this risky practice.[44] For instance, in 1752 a successful uprising took place on a British slaver, the *Marlborough*, three days after it left the coast of Africa when the captain brought 28 of the 400 slaves on board upon deck to help manage the ship. At the same time he sent several members of the crew below deck to perform duties. This proved to be an unwise move, for the slaves on deck seized some firearms and succeeded in taking possession of the ship.[45]

Thirteen years later, in 1765, an unsuccessful revolt occurred under similar circumstances on board a Rhode Island vessel. Its skipper, Captain Hopkins, is reported to have 'lost near or quite all his Men' on the West African coast, where 'a very great Mortality prevailed among the Shipping on the Coast,' causing him 'great Distress.'[46] According to Hopkins:

> soon after he left the Coast, the Number of his men being reduced by Sickness, he was obliged to permit some of the Slaves to come upon Deck to assist the People. These Slaves contrived to release the others, and the whole rose upon the People, and endeavoured to get Possession of the Vessel, but was happily prevented by the Captain and his Men, who killed, wounded, and forced overboard, Eighty of them, which obliged the Rest to submit.[47]

Experienced captains, conscious that sickness among sailors tended to encourage slaves to rebel, made the maintenance of good health among the crew a top priority, resorting even to inhumane action to achieve this important end. For example, when slaves contracted small pox, ophthalmia or some other communicable diseases, they often threw the victims overboard to prevent its spread not only to other slaves but particularly to the crew, so as to check the danger to the vessel's security. They resorted to such drastic action, especially if the slave cargo contained a sizable proportion of Africans from groups which had a reputation for valour and a tendency to revolt.[48]

Slave rebellions in the Middle Passage were also prompted and facilitated by indiscretions and negligence on the part of officers and sailors, who often failed to perform their duties efficiently. These weaknesses provided opportunities for resistance for which vigilant, alert slaves were watching and waiting, and were often quick to exploit. They were often disastrous for the sponsors of slaving voyages, especially if the ship was undermanned.

This imprudence was not limited to the decision by some captains to employ slaves as replacements for dead or sick sailors. Some captains also made the mistake of allowing the slaves to be without chains and shackles even when they were on deck, whereas the normal practice on slavers was to permit only women and children to be unfettered. This indiscretion was a major cause of a revolt in May 1750 on board the Bristol vessel, the *King David*. A newspaper reported that the slaves rebelled about 5.00 a.m., 'none of them being in Irons on board.'[49] Similar circumstances seem to have been partly responsible for a revolt in October 1765 in the Caribbean on the *Othello*, a Rhode Island brig, whose captain, Thomas Rogers, reported that it had occurred at a time when the slaves had been 'let out of their irons.'[50]

Another indiscretion which sometimes prompted rebellion was the practice of some captains of going among the slaves unarmed and without armed guards, especially at meal times. In 1722 it resulted in the death of Captain Messery, a newcomer manning a London slaver, who ignored the advice of William Snelgrave, an experienced captain.[51] Slaves, when afforded such an opportunity, sometimes attacked the captains, triggering off rebellions.

The most dangerous indiscretion that was committed by the officers and crew of slave ships was that of allowing the slaves to secure arms and other weapons which the slaves realised were indispensable for a successful rebellion. This was the case with the uprising which occurred on board the Bristol slaver, the *King David*, in which some slaves, out of irons, remarkably, were allowed to fraternise with the officers and crew and gained access to the ship's arms. According to an account of the revolt which was given by a member of the crew:

> the slaves on board the said ship rose about five o'Clock in the Morning, none of them being in irons. The Insurrection was contrived and begun by 15 that

had for a considerable Time been treated with the same Freedom as the white men; and a great many of the latter dying, encouraged them in the Design. As the chief of these Slaves spoke very good English, he often convers'd with the Captain in his Cabin, where all the Arms were loaded; and consulting with his Comrades, knowing the small Strength of the white Men, they at once flew into the Cabin, and secured the Arms in a few Minutes, killed the Captain and five of the people, thereby putting it out of the Power of the Remainder of the Ship's Crew to make any Resistance, so that they got down the Hold to save themselves.[52]

In some revolts the slaves managed to obtain weapons as a result of both the crew's imprudence and their own ingenuity. This occurred, for instance, in the case of the abortive rebellion in January 1701 on board the London vessel, the *Don Carlos*, four days after it left Cabinda for Jamaica. It was reported:

Most of them [the slaves] were yet above Deck, and many provided with Knives, which had been indiscreetly given them two or three Days before; the English not suspecting the least Attempt of that Nature. Others had Pieces of Iron, torn-off from the Fore-castle Door, as having premeditated the Revolt. They had also broken off the Shackles from several of their Companions' Feet, which served them as well as the Billets they had provided them with. In short, they had seized every Thing they could find , which was fit for their intended Enterprise. Thus armed, they fell in Crowds on the English on the Deck, and stabbed one of the stoutest of the Crew. They next assaulted the Boatswain.[53]

Slave rebellions at sea were also facilitated by the fact that the sailors, whose role was to serve as guards, often fell asleep. This was a common problem with seamen during the Middle Passage. The tiredness that led to sleep was a result of the physically demanding nature of their twin roles of sailors and security which often made their daily working hours very long. This was largely responsible for a successful revolt in June 1730 by the 96 slaves on board the *Little George*, a Rhode Island vessel, five days' sail from the Banana Islands, off the West African coast. About 4.30 a.m. a group of the slaves, who had managed to free themselves of their shackles and break through the bulkhead to the main deck, killed three dozing guards, threw them overboard, got rid of the other five crew members, took control of the ship and navigated it back to the Sierra Leone River.[54] The occurrence of sleeping guards also proved fatal to one Captain Holliday in another vessel two years before, in June 1728, when the slaves got loose and killed the whole crew with the exception of the cabin boy.[55]

The danger of sleeping guards was sometimes emphasised to captains of slave vessels in their instructions. For instance, the owner of a British slaver, while warning the captain of the dangers of the Middle Passage, told him, 'Let always a constant and careful watch be appointed . . . for the preservation of their own lives as well as yours . . . which per sleeping in their watches often proves fatal.'[56]

Slaves also profited occasionally from unforeseen propitious circumstances which distracted the crew from its crucial security functions. In 1571, for example, slaves revolted while their vessel was engaged with a privateer far out in the Atlantic, approaching the Caribbean. They succeeded in killing every member of the crew.[57] Similarly, in 1800 slaves on board a Rhode Island schooner on its way from the Guinea coast to Havana in Cuba revolted, exploiting the captain's efforts to escape from a pursuing British privateer. According to one report of the incident, 'On the passage, while the English brig privateer *Neptune*, Capt. Cockburn, was in chase of the *Flying-Fish*, all the slaves were let astern to trim the schooner, who embraced that opportunity to rise against the crew — a conflict ensued, in which Captain Packwood, his two mates, and two men, and ten slaves were killed.'[58] The slaves demonstrated masterly timing, commencing the revolt when the privateer drew alongside to claim the slaver as a prize.[59]

Some rebellions were facilitated by the presence on board of a preponderance of slaves from a particular group or area. This ethnic and linguistic homogeneity gave them not only ease of communication but also a feeling of solidarity which emboldened them. This was the case with a revolt in 1722 on board the *Ferrers-Galley*, a London vessel proceeding with 300 slaves purchased by Captain Messery from a group of prisoners taken by inhabitants of Setrue Kru in an attack on a neighbouring town in retaliation for economic grievances.[60] About 100 years later, in 1824 or 1825, similar circumstances are said to have been responsible for a successful rebellion on board a French vessel, the *Deux Soeurs*. According to a contemporary report, 'the catastrophe on board may be attributed to several of the slaves who had been employed as labourers and boatmen in this country [Sierra Leone] and who understand the English language.'[61]

Not surprisingly, experienced captains of slave ships warned newcomers to be extremely careful if they had on board many slaves from one group or area.[62] Sometimes, however, revolts staged by a numerically dominant group in a slave cargo failed because the other slaves refused to participate in the insurrection. This happened, for example, with a rebellion in January 1788 on board a Bordeaux slaver at sea between Mozambique and the Cape of Good Hope.[63] Understandably, in an attempt to prevent rebellions, some captains deliberately tried to secure a cargo comprising slaves from several groups or areas, with the hope that since they did not speak the same language, they would not be able to plan a rebellion.[64]

On several occasions expected slave rebellions never materialised because of inter-group friction and rivalry. This was the experience in 1819 of the French slaver, *Le Rodeur*, of Le Havre which sailed from Bonny with 160 slaves on its way to Guadeloupe. The slaves were presented with a favourable opportunity to revolt by an outbreak of ophthalmia which caused most of the crew as well as many slaves to become blind. However, 'the feared revolt did not occur, because the Negroes who had belonged to rival and hostile tribes, far from thinking to profit by their situation and number to assert their liberty, continued to indulge their mutual hatred, even in chains and were ready in their rage to tear each other in pieces.'[65]

The outbreak of slave revolts during the Middle Passage is also attributed partly to the influence of three special types or groups of slaves, namely, those who had enjoyed status in African societies, women and children, and individuals with great courage and determination. Slaves who before their enslavement had been chiefs, priests or distinguished warriors are known to have used their standing and reputation to instigate rebellions at sea. Thomas King, an experienced English captain, believed that there were three main causes of slave uprisings at sea, namely, the fear of white cannibalism, the desire of coastal Africans to be reunited with their relatives and friends, and the instigation of clerics. In 1789 he told a committee of the House of Commons that 'there are particular Nations which have religious Priests among them, that induce them to make those attempts [at rebellion] with the expectation that they should get the ship to some shore, where they would form a community of their own.'[66]

In 1827 a successful rebellion which was staged on a French slaver, the *Augusta*, was said to have been due to the instigation of Daouda, a famous warrior and slave trader, from Joal in the Senegambia. Daouda was kidnapped by a European slave trader whom he had supplied with slaves and sold into the Atlantic traffic. While on board, this proud man 'shut up with the other slaves, urged them day and night to make a serious effort to recover their liberty; he spoke to them about the small number of whites, and drew to their attention the ever increasing negligence of their guards.'[67] Eventually, the slaves rebelled, killed the entire crew and took possession of the ship.[68]

The organisation of many rebellions at sea was assisted by adult female slaves and sometimes children who, in most slave ships, were kept on deck, often without chains or shackles. Women, in particular, often made at least three important contributions to the staging of rebellions. Firstly, they supplied the men with valuable information about the strength, health or sleepiness of the crew. Secondly, they provided them with tools which the men used to free themselves from their shackles. Finally, they supplied the males with items which could be used as weapons. For example, the ability of the slaves in a French slaver in 1827 to remove their shackles is attributed to a small file given by a female slave on deck to her husband, the leader of the rebels. With this instrument the slaves slackened their shackles in such a way that the least effort would be sufficient to get rid of them when they went on deck. As a result, they succeeded in killing the entire crew and taking control of the vessel.[69]

The importance of the role of women and children in the outbreak of slave rebellions at sea was sometimes reflected in the warnings given to captains of slavers in their instructions. For example, in 1734 Samuel Waldo, the owner of the slaver, *Africa*, told his captain and crew to station many armed guards on board and 'not to put too much confidence in the Women and children lest they happen to be instrumental in your being surprised which may be fatal.'[70] However, in spite of the part played by women and children in some rebellions, the prevailing belief of slave traders continued to be that adequate security could be maintained during the Middle Passage without locking women and children in the hold of the ship.

Courage and determination

The outbreak of some rebellions is said to have been due to the great courage and resolution of slaves who were prepared to die rather than continue alive across the Atlantic. For example, an eye-witness account by a European of a revolt at sea in 1701 stated that 28 slaves were killed or 'leapt overboard, and drowned themselves in the ocean with resolution, showing no manner of concern for life.'[71]

This determination to resist servitude was also reflected in the behaviour of slaves who made repeated attempts to revolt during the Atlantic crossing. This was the case with a New London slaver in 1764. The slaves rebelled unsuccessfully in Senegal while the ship was weighing anchor to go to Gorée and again at sea on their way to the Caribbean. Furthermore, William Snelgrave, an English captain, gave an account of a voyage of the *Ferrers-Galley*, a London slaver, in which the slaves staged an unsuccessful rebellion ten days after it left the Guinea Coast for Jamaica. On their arrival in Jamaica they twice attempted to revolt before they were sold. Understandably, planters showed reluctance to purchase these rebellious captives, with the result that they had to be sold at lower prices than others.[72]

Such strong resolution was attributed by many slave traders, especially to a few groups, among whom were the Coramantines and Quaws. The Coramantines, as Akan-speaking Africans from the Gold Coast were often called, developed a fearsome reputation for staging rebellions at every phase of the slave traffic – on the African coast, during the Atlantic crossing and in the Americas. The Quaws, who were purchased by slavers at Bonny, had a similar reputation for determined resistance. According to the British captain, Hugh Crow of Liverpool:

> [The Quaws] were ever the foremost in any mischief or insurrections among the slaves, and from time to time many whites fell victims to their fury at Bonny. . . . The slave ships were always obliged to provide separate rooms for

these men between the decks and the captains were careful to have as few of them as possible amongst their cargoes.[73]

The principal objective of slaves in staging rebellions at sea was to secure control of the ship and navigate it to land, preferably in Africa. This was one reason why most slave revolts during the Middle Passage occurred relatively soon after the ship had left the African coast. If the uprising took place far out at sea, the slaves often decided to continue to sail rather than attempt to return to Africa. In that event they would seek to navigate the vessel to the nearest country in the Americas.[74]

Some slaves believed that they had the ability to navigate the ship back to Africa. Consequently, if their rebellion was successful, they killed all the officers and sailors or set them adrift and proceeded to make their way towards Africa. For example, in 1730 about 96 slaves on board the *Little George* slipped out of their chains and overpowered most of the crew, leaving the others who had taken refuge armed in a locked cabin, with the door guarded. They then concentrated on sailing back to Africa, accomplishing their goal in nine days.[75] Two years later, in 1732, slaves on board the *William* rebelled, killed the captain, set the crew adrift and returned to Africa.[76]

Sometimes, however, rebels encountered insuperable problems in their attempt to sail back to Africa on their own. For instance, on one occasion after a successful revolt on board a French slaver, many slaves lost their lives when they attempted to abandon the ship, which they were experiencing difficulties in managing, and take to the boat.[77]

More often than not, however, successful rebels preserved the life of at least one member of the crew on condition that he or they helped to steer the vessel to land. This was particularly the case if the rebellion took place far out at sea. On several occasions the decision to preserve these lives was made reluctantly or as an afterthought, modifying the original intention of the slaves. This was the case with the revolt on the *King David*, when slaves killed the captain and five members of the crew in the course of gaining control of the ship. They were about to throw the remainder of the crew overboard, but instead accepted the advice of some of their number to retain the chief mate to ensure that the ship was navigated properly.[78] Sometimes successful rebels preserved the lives of whites not only to steer the vessel, but also, if necessary, to use them as hostages in bargaining for their freedom when they reached land. As the English captain John Atkins remarked, 'some Negroes know well enough that the preserving one white man may answer their purpose in an exchange.'[79]

Careful planning

In planning rebellions slaves had a clear, well-conceived strategy which included several elements. They had to find an effective means of freeing themselves from the shackles which bound them to each other and hindered their freedom of movement. Furthermore, they needed to secure weapons. The achievement of these two critical initial goals without detection was often made easy because the slaves were below deck without white supervision. The experience of rebel slaves on a French slaver in November 1738 was typical of many others. During the night, unknown to the crew, they all managed to free themselves from their chains and shackles and to arm themselves with pieces of iron which they broke off without any noise.[80]

In short, before planned rebellions broke out, slaves usually tried to arm themselves with any item – wood, metal, knives, etc. – on which they could lay hold to serve as a weapon. Once the revolt had started, however, one of their chief aims was to gain possession of the ship's arms and ammunition, for that would determine the outcome of their battle with the ship's officers and crew.[81] The latter, on the other hand, realised that to prevent rebellions, it was crucial to prevent slaves from having access to anything which they would use as a weapon, especially the ship's arms. This was sometimes reflected in the captain's instructions. For example, as early as 1522 a Portuguese captain on a voyage to Benin was instructed thus, 'You must keep good guard and watch upon the arms that are in the ship, so that they do not come into the hands of the negroes, thus no mischief shall befall.'[82]

Apart from seeking to gain possession of the ship's arms and ammunition, the other frequent initial strategy of slaves during rebellions at sea was to kill the captain and the chief mate. The rebels no doubt recognised that the elimination of the ship's two principal officers would demoralise the crew and leave them deficient in leadership. In fact, on many occasions the initial act or sign of rebellion was an attempt by the slaves to seize and kill the captain. Typical of the commencement of slave rebellions was the following account of an uprising in October 1806 on a slaver a few days' sail from the Senegal River:

> Four or five days after the voyage commenced as the slaves were all together messing one day, the males and females apart, the males who were forward, one of them seized the master as he was pouring molasses into his food, some of the other males then rose, some of whom seized him.[83]

Slaves often consciously timed the outbreak of revolts to gain an advantage. Revolts usually took place at two times. Some of them occurred in the wee hours of the morning when the slaves assumed that the crew, with the possible exception of a few guards, was asleep and therefore incapable of making a prompt response. For example, the successful rebellion in June 1730 on board the *Little George*, a Rhode Island slaver, which profited from the fact that the three guards were asleep, began at 4.30 a.m.,[84] while the one about 20 years later on the *King David* of Bristol in May 1750 occurred 'about five o'Clock in the Morning.'[85] This tendency made slave-trading interests stress the need to be alert at night. According to Labat:

> To avoid them [rebellions] it is necessary to feed the slaves well and to treat them as humanely as possible, without however ceasing to be always on one's guard by day and night, especially at night, for it is normally this time that they take to revolt when they form the plan for it. [86]

Rebellions also often occurred when the slaves were allowed to come on deck for food, water, air or exercise, especially in situations where the crew was small, weakened by illness and death, negligent, and indifferent to the welfare of the slaves. This second occasion for rebellions highlighted the dilemma facing ships' captains who had to deal with the twin considerations of health and security which were not easily reconcilable. As William Littleton, an English captain, observed, 'it is a general rule to keep them on deck as much as we can consistent with prudence.'[87]

The danger faced when male slaves came on deck and the precautionary measures taken by experienced captains were emphasised by Captain Thomas Phillips in his account of the voyage which he made in 1693–94. According to him:

> They are fed twice a day, at 10 in the morning, and 4 in the evening, which is the time they are aptest to mutiny, being all upon the deck; therefore all that time, what of our men are not employ'd in distributing their victuals to them, and settling them, stand to their arms; and some with lighted matches at the great guns that yaun [sic] upon them, loaded with partridge, till they have done and gone down to their kennels between decks.[88]

Nevertheless, revolts occurred, as happened in May 1750 on board a Liverpool slaver, where 'the Slaves . . . being admitted to come upon Deck to air themselves, took an opportunity . . . and killed the Master and Mate of the ship, and threw fifteen of the Men overboard.'[89] Some rebellions took place at sea in close proximity to, and sometimes even in sight of, land in the Americas. As noted already, such revolts are believed to have been prompted largely by the deep fear engendered in the slaves by the apparent imminence of the awful fate awaiting them at the hands of white cannibals. These uprisings were problematic to the slaves in at least two ways. Firstly, in striking contrast to rebellions near the coast of Africa, the slaves did not know what precisely to expect in the unfamiliar Americas, if they decided to land the ship there, instead of attempting to sail back across the ocean to distant Africa. Secondly, even if their revolt was initially successful, there was no guarantee that they would ultimately gain their freedom, for the authorities there were likely to take action against them.

The problems which faced slaves who staged rebellions at sea in the Americas were illustrated in an uprising in 1750 on a Liverpool slaver near the French colony of Guadeloupe. The slaves rose, killed the captain and the first mate and threw 15 members of the crew overboard into a watery grave. They then sent the ship's boat and three or four of their number and two young sailors whose lives were spared 'to discover what land it was.'[90] However, before the boat arrived at its destination, news of the successful revolt reached Guadeloupe. In response, a commander of one of the island's districts 'immediately raised about 100 Men, and put them on board a sloop which went in pursuit of the Ship and in a few hours took her and carried her into Port Louis.'[91] Thus the slaves' freedom proved to be short-lived.

This was a likely outcome of slave rebellions in the waters of the Americas until the transatlantic slave trade was outlawed there in the nineteenth century by governments there and in Europe. It was this change of attitude and policy towards the slave traffic which made it possible for the slaves, who were involved in the famous rebellion in 1839 on board the Spanish schooner, *Amistad*, ultimately to gain their freedom when the vessel, unknown to the slaves, was deceitfully directed to the United States instead of Africa by the owner and a few members of the crew whose lives were spared for that purpose.[92]

Some reflections and comparisons

As long as the slave trade lasted, slave rebellions continued to occur during the Atlantic crossing. Successful revolts at sea depended on a combination of factors. Among them were imponderable ones such as the captives' implacable hatred of slavery, their courage, their disdain of death, and their solidarity which was often forged by common suffering. Also of crucial importance to the success of rebellions were circumstances of a more practical nature. These factors included good planning, the ability of the slaves to free themselves from their shackles, their acquisition of firearms and other weapons, the element of surprise which they enjoyed, their numerical superiority, the ship's inadequate security arrangements, the unpreparedness of the captain and crew, and their inability to summon reinforcements to their aid.

The sponsors of slaving voyages employed many expedients to prevent slave rebellions. They warned the ship's captain in his instructions about the possibility of revolts and provided chains, shackles and an unusually large crew to control the slaves. They also equipped the vessels with special armament, especially close-range weaponry, including the deadly swivel guns mounted on the railings at strategic locations about the main decks.

Similarly, the captains of the slave ships took measures to prevent slave uprisings. They did everything to ensure that the members of the crew remained healthy so that they could play their critical role in the system of security on board through vigilance, including the use of armed sailors as sentinels. They also tried to ensure the ethnic diversification of the slave cargo and to exploit these and other divisions among the slaves. Furthermore, they attempted to dispel the slaves' fear of the Atlantic crossing by informing them of the true purpose of their enslavement and used both propaganda and threats of severe punishment to dissuade slaves from rebellion. They also cleared the decks of anything which could be utilised by slaves as weapons and made special security arrangements for slaves suspected of planning rebellions, usually placing them under stricter guard. At the same time many captains tried to forestall revolts by treating the slaves as humanely as possible, given the need for security and within the severe limitations of the conditions normally found on slave ships.

Notwithstanding the wide range of mechanisms of slave control employed by the sponsors of slaving voyages and the captains of the ships, slave rebellions at sea continued, forcing sponsors to take out special shipping insurance to recover losses. The rebellions and other forms of resistance, such as suicide, demonstrated during the Middle Passage, were clear evidence that the captives resented their enslavement and yearned to be free. This resistance, which began in Africa and manifested itself during the Atlantic crossing, continued on the plantations and in the mines and cities of the Americas.

There are obvious similarities in the origins of the slave rebellions which occurred during the Middle Passage and those which took place on land in the Caribbean and other areas of the Americas. For example, the slave rebels at sea and on land both had the basic natural human desire for freedom and were angered by the terrible conditions of servitude to which they were subjected forcibly. Although there were some common elements, such as under-feeding and the sexual harassment of females, these conditions were not identical. Slaves at sea, for instance, knew nothing of the physical brutality and demanding labour from which many on land suffered, while the latter did not generally experience the chains and shackles, the close confinement, the poor sanitation, the insufficient ventilation, the frequent exposure to disease and other environmental hazards commonly faced by captives on board the slave ships. Furthermore, rebellions on land were not sparked off by the fear of white cannibalism. There were also differences in the objectives and organisation of slave revolts at sea and on land. The objectives of those on land, which sometimes were designed to achieve the improvement of slave conditions not liberty, were more diverse than maritime uprisings, which always had a single goal, namely, the capture of the ship and navigating it to land to gain freedom.

The planning and organisation of rebellions were more easily effected at sea, where they were done at night below deck, than on land where it was difficult for slaves to meet, especially in large numbers, without being detected and arousing suspicions. Nevertheless, it seems that there were more spontaneous slave uprisings at sea than on land. Furthermore, whereas the betrayal by slave informers of plans for rebellion was rare at sea, it was common on land, depriving rebels of the element of surprise and causing many revolts to be nipped in the bud. The element of surprise was, in fact, more critical to the outcome of rebellions at sea than on land, where the authorities and slaveholding interests were usually able to summon reinforcements to enable them to offset any reverses suffered at the beginning of the rebellion.

There were also differences in the attitude of these two groups of slaves to enslavement and resistance. Those on board the slave ships seemed less reconciled to servitude and more prepared to resist it than those on land. They were generally more vigilant, constantly watching for an opportunity to rebel. As John Newton, the English slave trader who later became a clergyman, noted:

> I was at first continually alarmed with their almost desperate attempts to make insurrections upon us . . . when most quiet they were always watching for opportunity. . . . One unguarded hour, or a minute, is sufficient to give the slaves the opportunity they are always waiting for.[93]

The slaves also believed that rebellions could be successful. On the other hand, slaves on land learnt by hearsay and personal experience that uprisings were very difficult to organise, were likely to fail and would result in severe punishment for the rebels. These considerations help to explain why there was a higher incidence of rebellions at sea and greater participation by slaves in them than on land. Admittedly, however, many slaving voyages were free from rebellions. Moreover, it was only a small proportion of the rebellions at sea that resulted in the slaves taking control of the ship. Ships' captains, however, always feared that this might happen. In short, while there were some similarities in the circumstances prompting and surrounding the outbreak of slave rebellions during the Middle Passage and on land in the Americas, the differences were more striking. Both types of rebellion, however, were ultimately expressions of the determination of the slaves to achieve freedom.

Notes

1. For example, Herbert Klein, *The Middle Passage: Comparative Studies in the Atlantic Slave Trade* (Princeton: Princeton University Press, 1978).
2. John Atkins, *A Voyage to Guinea, Brazil, & the West Indies in His Majesty's Ships, the Swallow and Weymouth* (London: C. Ward and R. Chandler, 1735), 175.
3. Jacques Savary, *Le Parfait Negociant ou Instruction Générale Pour Ce Qui Regarde le Commerce et L'Application des Ordinances* (Paris, 1679), Part II, 206–07.
4. Evidence of Mr James Fraser, January 29, 1790, in *Minutes of the Evidence*

Taken Before the Committee of the House of Commons, being a Select Committee, Appointed on the 26th day of January 1790 for the Purpose of Taking the Examination of such Witnesses as Shall be Produced on the Part of the Several Petitioners who have Petitioned the House of Commons Against the Abolition of the Slave Trade (London, 1790), Part I.

5. Jay Coughtry, *The Notorious Triangle: Rhode Island and the African Slave Trade 1700-1807* (Philadelphia: Temple University Press, 1981), 151.

6. *Boston, New England, The Weekly News-Letter,* September 18-25, 1729.

7. Cited in William Katz, *Breaking the Chains: Afro-American Slave Resistance* (New York: Macmillan, 1990), 12.

8. Cited in Charles MacInnes, *England and Slavery* (Bristol: J.W. Arrowsmith, 1934), 48-49; Newport Historical Society, Rhode Island, Peleg Clarke Letter Book, John Fletcher to Peleg Clarke, October 19, 1775.

9. William and Samuel Vernon to Caleb Godfrey, November 8, 1755, cited in Coughtry, 143.

10. William Snelgrave, *A New Account of Some Parts of Guinea and the Slave Trade* (London: James, John and Paul Knapton, 1734), 173.

11. Cited in Anthony Benezet, *Notes on the Slave Trade* (Philadelphia: Joseph Crukshank, 1781), 4.

12. Alexander Falconbridge, *An Account of the Slave Trade on the Coast of Africa* (London: J. Phillips, 1788), 30.

13. *Ibid.*

14. *PP,* 1826, XXIX, H. M.'s Commissioners at Sierra Leone to Canning, April 10, 1825.

15. *Report of the Lords of Trade of the Committee of Council Appointed for the Consideration of all Matters Relating to Trade and Foreign Plantations . . . Concerning the Present State of the Trade to Africa and Particularly the Trade in Slaves* (London, 1789).

16. Evidence of James Towne, February 8, 1791, in *Minutes of the Evidence Taken Before a Committee of the House of Commons Being a Select Committee, Appointed on the 23rd day of April 1790, to Take the Examination of the Several Witnesses Ordered by the House Respecting the African Slave Trade* (London, 1791).

17. *Report of the Lords of Trade* (1789).

18. Atkins, 175.

19. John Matthews, *A Voyage to the River Sierra Leone on the Coast of Africa* (London: Printed by B. White and Son, and J. Sewell 1788), 152; Philip Curtin, *Africa Remembered: Narratives by West Africans from the Era of the Slave Trade* (Madison: University of Wisconsin Press, 1967), 307-08; Winston. McGowan, 'African Resistance to the Atlantic Slave Trade in West Africa,' *Slavery and Abolition,* 11.1 (1990): 21-22.

20. 'Journal of Adam Starr, Seaman, 20th August to 6th September 1781,'

in Charlotte and Denis Plimmer, *The Damn'd Master* (London: New English Library, 1971), entry for August 21, 1781.

21. Mungo Park, *Travels in the Interior Districts of Africa, Performed Under the Direction and Patronage of the African Association in the Years 1795, 1796 and 1797* (London: Everyman's Library, 1969), 244-45.

22. Evidence of James Fraser, January 29, 1790, in *Minutes of Evidence* (1790).

23. Evidence of Thomas King, June 19, 1789, in *Abridgement of the Minutes of the Evidence, Taken Before a Committee of the House of Commons, Being a Committee of the Whole House, to Whom it was Referred to Consider of the Circumstances of the Slave Trade, Complained of in the Several Petitions Which were Presented to the House in the Last Session of Parliament, Relative to the State of the African Slave Trade* (1789; Chicago: Afro-Am Press, 1969).

24. Jean Labat, *Voyage du Chevalier des Marchais en Guinée, Iles Voisines, et a Cayenne; Fait en 1725, 1726 & 1727* (Paris: Guillaume Saugrain, 1730), II, 144-45.

25. *Ibid.* & Vol. III, 56.

26. *Report of the Lords of Trade* (1789), Part I, 13.

27. *Ibid.*, 26.

28. Francis Moore, *Travels into the Inland Parts of Africa* (London: Printed by E. Cave for the author, 1738), cited in Curtin, 57.

29. Snelgrave, 162-63.

30. Labat, II, 144-45.

31. 'Journal of Captain Phillips,' published in A. and I. Churchill, *Collection of Voyages and Travels* (3rd ed., London: Printed for Henry Lintot and John Osborn, 1744-46), VI, 235.

32. Snelgrave, 162-64.

33. Evidence of John Knox, June 9, 1789, in *Minutes of Evidence*, 1789.

34. Labat, II, 142.

35. Cited in MacInnes, 48-49.

36. Snelgrave, 168-72.

37. Benezet, 4.

38. *The Boston Weekly News-Letter*, April 29 – May 6, 1731.

39. Jehan Mousnier, ed., *Journal de la Traite des Noirs* (Paris: Éditions de Paris, 1957), 246-47.

40. *Ibid.*, 245.

41. Thomas Astley, *A New General Collection of Voyages and Travels* (London: Printed for T. Astley, 1745), III, 210.

42. *Ibid.*, 210-11.

43. *The Boston Weekly News-Letter*, November 22, 1735.

44. Coughtry, 159.

45. Derek Robinson, *A Shocking History of Bristol* (Bristol, 1973), 66.

46. *The Newport Mercury*, June 17, 1765.

47. *The Massachusetts Gazette*, November 28, 1765.

48. Isidor Paiewonsky, *Eyewitness Accounts of Slavery in the Danish West Indies also Graphic Tales of Other Slave Happenings on Ships and Plantations* (New York: Fordham University Press, 1989), 67, 69, 83.

49. *The Boston Weekly News-Letter*, September 6, 1750.

50. Cited in Coughtry, 156–57.

51. Snelgrave, 188–90.

52. *The Boston Weekly News–Letter*, September 6, 1750.

53. Astley, III, 210–11.

54. *The Boston Weekly News-Letter*, April 29 – May 6, 1731; Coughtry, 157.

55. Robinson, 66.

56. *Ibid.*

57. C. Munford, *The Black Ordeal of Slavery and Slave Trading in the French West Indies, 1625–1715* (Lewiston: The Edwin Mellin Press, 1991), II, 346.

58. *The Newport Mercury*, August 5, 1800; Coughtry, 158.

59. *Ibid.*

60. Snelgrave, 185–91.

61. *PP*, 1826, XXIX, H.M.'s Commissioners at Sierra Leone to Canning, April 10, 1825.

62. Snelgrave, 187–89.

63. Joseph Brugevin, 'Journal de Traite du Vaisseau la Licorne de Bordeaux,' in Patrick Villiers, *Traite des Noirs et Navires Négriers au XVIII Siècle* (Grenoble: Éditions des 4 Seigneurs, 1982), 152.

64. Anne Mountfield, *The Slave Trade* (London: Wayland Publishers, 1973), 29.

65. *Memoranda Respecting the French Slave Trade in 1820, Drawn up at the Close of that Year* (London: Ellerton and Henderson, 1820), 30.

66. Evidence of Thomas King, June 19, 1789, in *Minutes of the Evidence* (1789).

67. Mousnier, 243, 245.

68. *Ibid.*, 242–43.

69. *Ibid.*, 245–46.

70. Samuel Waldo to Samuel Rhodes, March 12, 1734, in Elizabeth Donnan, *Documents Illustrative of the Slave Trade to America* (Washington, D.C.: Carnegie Institute of Washington, 1930), III, 45.

71. Cited in Katz, 11.

72. Snelgrave, 189–91.

73. H. Crow, *Memoirs of the Late Capt. Crow of Liverpool* (London: Longman, Rees, Orme, Brown & Green, 1830), 200–01.

74. *The Boston Weekly News-Letter*, September 6, 1750.

75. Katz, 11–12.

76. *Ibid.*
77. Mousnier, 247–55.
78. Donnan, II, 486–87.
79. Atkins, 175.
80. 'Journal de bord de l'Africain, 1738–1740,' in *La Traite des noirs à Nantes du XVIIe au XIXe siècle* eds., X. Du Boisrouvray and M. Konrat, (Nantes: CRDT Nantes, 1981).
81. *Boston, New England, The Weekly News-Letter*, September 18–25 1729.
82. Cited in Alan Ryder, *Benin and the Europeans* (London: Longmans, 1969), 296–97.
83. Donnan, III, 400–01; Coughtry, 158.
84. *The Boston Weekly News-Letter*, April 29–May 6, 1731.
85. *Ibid.*, June 21, 1750.
86. Labat, II, 142.
87. Evidence of William Littleton, June 18, 1789, in *Minutes of Evidence* (1789).
88. "Journal of Captain Phillips."
89. *The Boston Weekly News-Letter*, June 21, 1750.
90. *Ibid.*
91. *Ibid.*
92. For a sample of the voluminous literature on the famous slave rebellion on board the *Amistad*, which became the subject of a trial before the United States Supreme Court, see John Barber, *A History of the Amistad Captives* (New York: Arno Press, 1969); Mary Cable, *Black Odyssey: The Case of the Slave Ship Amistad* (Baltimore: Penguin Books, 1977); Helen Kromer, *The Amistad Affair, 1839: The Slave Uprising Aboard the Spanish Schooner* (New York: Franklin Watts, 1973); Howard Jones, *Mutiny on the Amistad* (New York: Oxford University Press, 1987).
93. Bernard Martin and Mark Spurrell, eds., *The Journal of a Slave Trader 1750–54 with Newton's Thoughts upon the African Slave Trade* (London: Epworth Press, 1962), 80, 103–04.

CHAPTER

The New 'Negro' Business:
Hiring in the British West Indies 1750–1810
Heather Cateau

Introduction

Simon Taylor, one of the most prosperous and influential planters of the British West Indies, interestingly, seldom used the term slavery in his discussions about the economic system in which he operated. He used the expression the 'Negro Business' (see the Golden Grove Plantation Papers and Simon Taylor's Letter Books). He used the phrase to refer to all aspects of slavery, including the buying and selling of slaves. At no point did he define exactly what this 'Negro Business' involved. We know, however, that he was involved in not just the ownership of plantations but also the management of numerous estates, and several other concerns. All these business activities were connected in some way with the system of African enslavement. While studying the papers of the Jamaican plantation, Golden Grove, which Taylor managed, it became increasingly apparent to me that the 'Negro Business' to which he referred possessed another dimension which he also actively encouraged, and which was, in fact, a very important dimension — the hiring of slaves. If slavery was the 'Negro Business,' then hiring was certainly the new 'Negro Business' of the eighteenth century.

Traditionally, emphasis has been placed on purchasing practices as the means of maintaining and increasing the slave labour force. This discussion focuses on an additional method of labour acquisiton which was increasingly used by planters in the eighteenth century. It was referred to as 'hiring' or 'jobbing' — the terms were used interchangeably. Hiring consisted of using slaves who were not actually owned by the planter/employer to augment the labouring population at particular periods. Such labour was contracted from one of three sources: individuals, particularly the plantations' white tenants and employees who maintained labourers whom they hired out to the plantations; jobbing firms (i.e., establishments which owned gangs of slaves specifically for hiring); and estates/units with excess slaves. This last source was increasingly available in cases where a plantation was not doing well economically and could not maintain its labour force. In such cases hiring was a means of retaining ownership of one's slaves without selling them, maintaining one's slaves, and perhaps even making a profit from hiring them. In its most basic sense, hiring was a means of adding extra strength or skill to the labour force. This became extremely important in the light of increasing slave prices. In short, hiring allowed for a measure of flexibility in the management of the labour force. In all the British West Indian colonies examined to date, hiring was used to some extent. What varied was the extent of its use and the purposes for which it was employed.

By the middle of the eighteenth century, hiring of additional slaves, as opposed to purchasing them, had become an integral part of British West Indian plantation management, with far-reaching implications. Hiring and purchasing existed side-by-side; they were dependent on each other. However, although hiring was in many ways a natural part of the slave system (in fact, so natural that it has often been overlooked by historians), it was a qualitatively different mode of labour organisation. It involved two distinctively different forms: *self-hire* and *hiring-out*. While both can be described as hiring because they involved payment for labour, the forms were qualitatively different and affected quantitatively different numbers and categories of enslaved persons.

Self-Hire

Self-hire[1] involved slaves who, although owned by a particular individual, were allowed to hire out themselves. The slaves offered their services for rent to various persons, for which they were paid directly. In return for this 'privilege' the slaves paid a stipulated portion of their earnings to their owners. The slaves were free to use the rest of the money that they earned as they saw fit. Very often they also enjoyed much freedom of movement and exhibited greater degrees of independence than slaves attached to a particular plantation, household or other unit. In most instances they also provided for their own food, clothing and accommodation. Thus, these slaves functioned independently of the slave owner, often making contact merely to hand over the monthly or weekly payment.

This mode of hiring was more prevalent in the urban than the rural areas and became more widespread in the nineteenth century (after 1807). Howard Johnson points out that in the case of The Bahamas the system was widely used much earlier and was more firmly entrenched than elsewhere in the British West Indies.[2] Less frequent examples of the self-hire system can be found in the eighteenth century and in the rural economies in the rest of the British West Indies. Barry Higman suggests that self-hire was more an urban than a rural phenomenon, because the large plantations tended to be more self-contained and often did not possess the extra labourers who could be hired out under such a system.[3] He also suggests that the system was more prevalent in the urban areas because finding jobs for slaves in these areas would have been more time-consuming and cumbersome, particularly because of the nature of many of the occupations involved (e.g., when ships arrived porters would have had to be on the spot to get jobs). Further, slaves in the towns often did several jobs in one day.[4] These factors made policing the slave and collecting payments difficult and cumbersome. Self-hire, therefore, eased the administration of a system that might have been fraught with difficulties. Thus, the system benefited both owners and slaves. The owners received fixed sums on a regular basis without having to be concerned too much about other aspects of the slaves' lives, while the slaves were given the freedom to maximise any opportunities that came their way.

In both rural and urban areas, most of the slaves involved in self-hire were skilled persons. These included carpenters, masons, blacksmiths, joiners, coopers and sailors. In the towns, however, there were also many unskilled workers under self-hire, including porters, field labourers and petty retailers. In the case of women the self-hire system offered opportunities for prostitution. There were also limited opportunities in the domestic sphere, but because of their very nature these occupations tended to be more directly supervised.[5]

The benefits of self-hire can be exaggerated. It must be remembered that there were two primary charges on any money that the slaves made: payment to their owners and subsistence. Both Higman and Johnson suggest that many slaves had great difficulty in meeting the payments to their owners.[6] Some even resorted to theft in order to do so.[7] It was however a contract that most slaves were quite willing to make because of the increased freedom and independence which they gained. In the rural areas, particularly, slaves on self-hire were regarded as the most privileged of the plantation workers. In addition, through the system of self-hire some slaves were able to purchase their freedom.[8]

Most published works on the British West Indies have concentrated on this primarily urban system of hiring in the nineteenth century. According to Higman's statistics, the towns only had approximately ten per cent of the total slave population in the British Caribbean in 1807.[9] Thus, the majority of the enslaved population was concentrated in the rural areas. This essay will focus more extensively on hiring-out within the rural plantation system. This was, in fact, the prevalent system in the British West Indies for most of the slavery period. Hiring-out shaped the character of West Indian life in very significant ways. Yet much remains unknown about the system, and neither its importance nor its impact has been fully appreciated.

Hiring-out

Generally, there were three types of hiring-out contracts: by task, by the day, and for longer terms (often one month to a year). The owners of the slaves involved were usually paid for these services. In cases where slaves were hired out for extended periods payments were usually made by the 'head' or calculated at a percentage of the appraised value of the slaves. In most cases the lessees (i.e., the persons renting the slaves) were responsible for the maintenance and housing of the slaves. The owners of the slaves were sometimes responsible for supplying the required tools. There could be some variation in the details of the contract but all hired-out slaves were fed at the expense of the employer.

One can easily hypothesise that hiring-out of slaves was begun as an expedient by persons who owned more slaves than they could productively use on their own properties. However, it is more difficult to pinpoint the historical details regarding the origins of the system. Edward Long points to the end of the Seven Years' War (1756–1763) as a decisive period in the growth of the system, and accounts for the origins of the system in the following manner:

> I must not here omit taking some notice of an expedient espoused, with great alacrity, by several planters for supplying themselves with those recruits of labourers or slaves, which they were unable or unwilling to purchase at the advanced price and short credit at which they have been sold since the conclusion of the late war. . . . The planters who had been largely trusted during the war, and upon a long term credit, found the case suddenly altered, after peace had given a check to the career of our trade. The merchants called in their money, fewer Negroes were imported, and these were sold at higher prices, and much shorter credit; the planters, straining every nerve to pay off their old debts, were unable to contract new ones; the monied men therefore and others who had got good credit, first thought of making an advantage by the necessities of the planters. They bought up the major part of the Negroes, and leased them for a term of years, at the rate of from 8£ to 12£ per head, per annum, conditioned that all such as might happen to die, or be deficient, during the lease, should be paid for according to their original value at the time of delivery. By this contract the renter was able to make a most exorbitant interest on his money. . . .[10]

Long was clearly not referring to the hiring of a few slaves from a neighbouring plantation or even hiring slaves on a daily basis. He was clearly describing the evolution of the long-term labour contract. Hiring was evidently by this time more than an expedient; it was a new business venture.

Hiring was used in the British West Indies before 1763. However, Long may have been referring to an increase in the extent to which the system was used in general, as well as a specific aberration of the hiring mode. He was clearly referring to the hiring of a large number of slaves for an extended period of time. This was referred to as leasing and has been described above.

What is interesting, however, is the fact that the terms he outlined were precisely those used in hiring contracts of the later eighteenth century.

Hiring seems to have become more firmly entrenched and more pervasive in the British West Indies in the second half of the eighteenth century. The increase in its use may also be reflective of a qualitative change in the manner in which hiring was used on estates. There was probably increasing use of larger numbers of hired slaves for longer periods. This would support the impression gleaned from the documents that by the second half of the eighteenth century hiring had become a new business venture in the British West Indies. It, in fact, became an alternative means of making quick fortunes. Thus, while slaves were still involved and as such slavery remained the primary mode of production, elements of a 'proto-capitalist' mode of production were clearly visible.

Rates for hiring

There was much variation in the rates for hiring, according to the terms of the contract, that is, whether by task, by day, or on a long-term lease, and also according to the type of job which the labourer was hired to perform. A skilled slave, for example, would cost more than a field slave.[11] In some cases comparison is difficult because some tasks, such as holing, were paid for by the acre.[12] Rates also varied among the different islands and within particular islands.[13] Certain factors, for instance the availability of slaves for hiring in general or at particular times in the year (which was greatly affected by the increase in cocoa and coffee cultivation), also had the effect of increasing the price of hired labour over time.[14] However, on an average, it can be estimated that in the eighteenth century hired labour by the day in most colonies cost between one and three shillings local currency, and holing averaged about £6 per acre.[15]

Table 5.1 shows the average rates for hiring in several British West Indian islands. Of major interest is the wide variation in the rates from island to island. Rates were generally higher in Grenada, Dominica, Jamaica and St Vincent than in Antigua, Montserrat, St Kitts-Nevis, and Barbados. Indeed, hiring rates in the last island were the lowest, daily rates ranging from 10d. to 1s.1d., and payment by task or per acre from £3 to £3.10s. These rates were more than double in Grenada and Dominica where the average daily rate was 3s.; and task work or work paid for by the acre was between £8 and £9. These differences reflected the relative demand for hired labour in the colonies. They also indicate that the colonies in which hiring was most highly priced were the 'newer' or 'less developed' territories. Rates were lowest in the 'older' or longer established territories of the Leewards and Barbados. This supports the view that there was a greater demand for slaves in the more recently developed islands, leading to a greater reliance on hired labour in these colonies. These colonies were also the ones with more diversified economies, and thus there would have been a greater amount of cocoa and coffee production which, we shall see, competed with the sugar plantations for hired labour, driving the price up.

Table 5.1: Hiring rates collated for the British West Indies, 1750-1810[16]

Country	Daily rates	Yearly rates	Long-term rates (%)*	Task per acre
Grenada	3s.	£10–£15		£8–£9
Dominica	2s.–3s.	£12–£15	10-12	.£6.10s–£10
Jamaica	1s.10d.	£12–£15	8-10	£6–£7
St Vincent	3s.	£12–£16		£7
Antigua	1s.1d.	£10–£16		£6–£8
Montserrat	1s.6d.–2s.	n.a.	10-12	£5
St Kitts/Nevis	n.a.	£12–£14		£4.10s.
Barbados	10d.–1s.1d.	n.a		£3–£3.10s.

*Long-term rates are the percentage values paid per annum on the appraised value of the particular slaves.

Sources: Sheila Lambert, ed., *House of Commons Sessional Papers of the Eighteenth Century*, Vol. 69 (Delaware: Scholarly Resources Inc., 1975), pp. 210, 290, 322, 357, 368, 406-07, 427; see also William Dickson, *Mitigation of Slavery* (London: Longman, 1814), Part II, 262.

Advantages and disadvantages

Views on the advantages and disadvantages of hiring varied. The planters at different times made conflicting assessments, and often their espoused views were not reflected in their actions. The fact is that, in spite of inherent problems, hiring was of some utility to almost every West Indian plantation. Whenever money was short or expenses increased, the managers of estates tended to delay buying slaves. Instead, many of them increased their hiring of slaves, which enabled them to meet their immediate labour requirements. For example, the labour force owned by the Codrington plantations in Barbados between 1715 and 1731 in an average year numbered only 242, but hired labour made 'the Codrington labour force approximately equal in strength to that of an estate with 300 slaves.'[17] Plantation owners often instructed their attorneys in the West Indies not to expend money to purchase slaves, but to use hired labour instead to harvest the sugar crop.[18] Plantations therefore began to rely less on purchasing than they had previously.

Maintaining the enslaved labour force through purchasing was not as easy as it may have seemed. In difficult financial times many planters simply did not have the credit to make the necessary yearly additions. Moreover, a large number of newly imported slaves died during the seasoning period (some estimates state one in three), thus increasing the real cost of the surviving ones by as much as one-third. New slaves were also of more limited use than already seasoned ones who could be hired immediately. Further, without warning, an epidemic could deplete the labour force substantially. A brutal overseer or manager could also substantially reduce one's labour force in spite of one's best efforts. A gang of hired slaves would not be expected to have the high proportion of old, sick, maimed, intractable and infant slaves as would normally be found among the average plantation slave population. The planter was also freed from certain managerial concerns; for example, he did not have to pay taxes on hired hands.[19]

Various other scenarios, which were 'part and parcel' of plantation life, also encouraged hiring even further. Firstly, there were periods in the year, such as crop time, when hiring was most prevalent.[20] Many plantations required the extra labour to ensure that their crops were harvested within the necessary time period. Attorney James Craggs advised absentee planter Henry Goulburn that:

> [To] have . . . the advantage of that season, Negroes could be hired to assist in the taking off the crop if you did not wish to purchase so many, & I am of opinion that no hired labor is so well bestowed as to take off Canes when ripe that the crop may go early to market & the estates kept forward. . . .'[21]

As one may imagine, the situation (of hiring more labour) was further exacerbated on occasions when the crop proved to be an unexpectedly large one. In such cases the availability of workers became an issue because of the periodic increase in the demand.[22] When the price of sugar was high planters also tended to hire in an effort to ensure that they benefited from these fortuitous circumstances. It was with this mindset that Joseph Barham wrote to his attorneys Graham and Plummer:

> I quite agree however objectionable hired labour may be in general that under the present circumstances it will be advisable to avail ourselves of it as far as is proper as one would not be willing to let the crop down on acct of the high prices & yet on acct of the general uncertainty of prosperity one is not willing to lay out any sum in the purchase.'[23]

On other occasions managers found it necessary to use hired labour to expand production. One such instance occurred under the attorneyship of Racher Webb. In 1801, he wished to increase the fall acreage from 32 to 40 but noted that it could not be done 'without the assistance of hired labour.'[24]

Hiring was also resorted to as a means of acquiring the labour to do tasks which, although not directly related to the crop, were necessary for the long-term development of the plantation. Thus the permanent labour force of the plantations could be kept occupied in matters related to the harvest while hired labour performed other tasks. In 1797 hiring was the answer to one such problem on the Goulburn estate. James Craggs the attorney voiced the problem and the solution as follows:

> It is a thousand pittys some of our woodlands in a seasonable part of the Country could not be cleared & placed in Guinea Grass. It would be a vast saving to the property, the strength upon the estate is not equal to do it, but it might be done by hired labour & would cost about £12 per acre cleaning, planting and fencing. . . .'[25]

At times planters used hiring to ensure that they had the necessary requirement of skilled labour on estates. This dearth could not be filled simply by purchasing because such slaves had to be instructed over a period of time. Often, therefore, the only solution was to hire until one of the plantation slaves could be trained. Of course, this was not a short-term process and such slaves were more expensive to hire.[26] Hiring was also of great value in times of martial law when slaves were drawn from estates for defence purposes, or when mandatory labour from estates was required for public duties such as the building of roads and bridges. At these times the estates' labour force could be greatly weakened. At such periods plantation owners and managers were able to use hired slaves to ensure that productivity continued. Edward Long reported one such instance in 1779: 'When I was last at L. Valley the negroes & white people having been taken off during marshal law, had certainly put it back. I was therefore obliged to hire jobbers to assist the plantation Negroes in holing.'[27]

Particularly in the later eighteenth century, hired slaves were used as a means of preserving the permanent work force on plantations. Using this management technique, Joseph Barham wrote to his attorneys Wedderburn and Graham in 1796, 'I quite approve of your intention to have the mountain ground cleared by hired labour as it produces freshness among our own negroes for there is nothing which can tend to their health comfort & increase which I shall think ill bestowed & do now earnestly recommend you to adopt.'[28] Edward Long also shared this view. He intended 'giving some help in the holing by Job, [because] it will enable us to enlarge the plant, & save our Negroes some hard labour.'[29] Not surprisingly, therefore, in many cases hired gangs were employed to dig cane holes on the estates, one of the most strenuous and laborious tasks. Alexander Barclay claimed that holing, which was the hardest work on the estates, was often done by 'hired negroes.'[30] There are also many references in plantation documents to slaves being hired to hole ground.[31]

To complicate matters, slaves that were hired out to a plantation were often owned by attorneys, overseers, bookkeepers and even doctors, resident on the same plantation. Thus a planter who owned 350 slaves might hire 40 additional slaves from his attorney who lived on the same plantation and, in fact, kept the 40 slaves there.[32] It is clear, therefore, that in cases where the specific planter was absent, tricky situations often developed. There were numerous complaints that attorneys' slaves lived off the planters' estates free of charge, and that the attorneys overworked the planters' slaves while preserving their labour force in a far superior condition. In fact, such managers had a vested interest in ensuring that planters hired labourers, even if they did not actually need them. Attorneys often insisted that they had to hire to ensure that the plantation profited.

The problems inherent in such situations are clear. One may well ask, 'Why did planters allow such situations to develop?' To use hired labour was one thing, but to allow employees to own slaves, keep them on the plantations, and hire them to work on the same plantations was quite another thing. This meant that, as well as paying the attorney his salary, the planter paid him a charge for the hiring of his slaves. This sum was, in fact, often more than his regular salary. John Kelly was paid two sums of money on March 4, 1773. One was his salary as attorney on Golden Grove Plantation; the other was for his slaves, which he hired out to that plantation. The former was £300, the latter £566.[33] Clearly, for Kelly hiring was the more profitable occupation. Perhaps an even more important issue is whether the planter could trust such a person to manage his (i.e, the planter's) own labour force. It was, arguably, generally not in his interest to do so. This is reflected in Simon Taylor's complaint to absentee planter Chaloner Arcedeckne about the same attorney John Kelly:

> It would have been much for your Interest if Kelly had taken a little more Care of your Negroes by which means they would have lived, but then there would not have been any Jobbing for him, & that would not have been for his Interest, which has always been with him preferable to yours.[34]

There were also additional problems. A contemporary observer described the heavy dependence on hired labour as 'not always dependable in either attendance or performance.'[35] In situations where the hired slaves belonged to the manager or overseer, and often where there was little or no alternative to hired labour, he could hold the plantation owner at his mercy in cases of dispute, by threatening to withdraw his slaves. Such action could leave plantations without a source of hired labour when they needed it most, especially if there was no clear contract between the two parties.[36] This was also true in respect of task gangs not resident on the plantations.[37] Another major problem was the cost. Hiring was an expensive expedient. Large sums of money were expended yearly by plantations to support their hiring practices.

Some plantations expended between £500 and £1,500 per annum[38] on hired labour by the end of the eighteenth century. The figure increases in significance when we consider the fact that plantations were finding it increasingly difficult to balance their budgets during this period.

Problems of a different nature led to attempts to reduce hiring. Towards the end of the eighteenth century, particularly in Jamaica, there was an increase in cotton and coffee production.[39] This, in turn, led to a decrease in the availability and an increase in the price of hired labour, because many of the cotton and coffee plantations were owned by those who had previously let their slaves out for hire. Sometimes they themselves began using hired labourers. James Craggs summed up the situation in Jamaica to his employer when he explained that, 'the price of hired labour is now very high and greatly in demand from the great number of new coffee plantations now settling.'[40] Another attorney, Henry Plummer, voiced the same concern a year later.[41] Planters began to insist that 'the work of the Estate can be done without hired labour.'[42] Planters who adopted this view were influenced not only by the problems of availability and high prices which themselves were deterrents, but also by the impending abolition of the slave trade and the need to build up their own labour force.[43] Hiring, however, continued into the nineteenth century.[44]

Hiring, though extremely useful, could not replace purchasing in the slave plantation management schema. Once the permanent labour force had declined to a certain extent, it needed to be regenerated. It was a managerial error to ignore the importance of keeping up a supply of fresh labour inputs to counteract the decline of old ones. Many estates had actually become reliant on hiring to increase the labouring strength of their slave populations, which proved to be an extremely dangerous development. This was precisely the situation at Dunkenfield Hall Plantation, moving the owner to comment that:

> We have for a long time observed a vast expense the estate is put to for Job work, we suppose this is found necessary from the insufficiency of our own and to remedy this in part you have a full liberty to purchase 15 to 20 or 30 Negroes.[45]

Evidence suggests that the failure to maintain sufficient permanent hands in the working population was a constant failure in plantation management. One can cite the examples of the Codrington estates in Barbados, and Amity Hall and Dunkenfield Hall in Jamaica.[46] In all these cases hiring was used to fill the void when additional labourers were required. Clearly, hired slaves became almost as important to the plantation as slaves actually owned by the planter. However, hiring could be a destabilising factor.

Let us go back to the example of the Codrington estates. It is illustrative of a situation where the managers needed large additional numbers to achieve the complement required. Hiring slaves and purchasing creole slaves proved to be very expensive, and they often had no choice but to resort to newly imported Africans, in spite of the danger of heavy losses. A similar development was observed by Samson who described the situation at Amity Hall (Jamaica) in 1802 in the following manner:

> It is no doubt that Amity Hall Negroes from the Estate being for many years weak handled, and from having no supply of new Negroes as other Estates, they of course have been exposed to hard Labour which always will be against Negroe Females bringing an increase of Children than Estates in more easy circumstances, and naturally the aged will be kept longer at more laborious stations on the Estate from the want of young ones filling their places. By this means also a natural decrease will happen without the smallest instance of inhumanity.[47]

Samson went even further and suggested a solution: 'All these hardships on the slaves will be done away by the purchase of Negroes and when you see the Estate has been so very . . . short of what is necessary to cultivate it you will allow I have some difficulty to keep it up.'[48] Like Samson, the solution to many managers in distress was to purchase new African slaves, in spite of the high mortality risk.

In the eighteenth century, it was frequently noted that skilful management of the size of one's labour force included the timely purchase of small groups of slaves. The cheapest means to do this was through the purchase of new Africans. However, to reduce mortality these additions were to be made in small numbers. Good management, therefore, should have involved the timely injection of such slaves in order to ensure that the plantations never reached the stage of Amity Hall or the Codrington estates where immediate and often risky action was necessary. Edward Long stated that he thought that purchasing '6 good Negroes' every year would keep up his gangs; he added that he himself 'had lately purchased 3 young men & 3 young women, all prime people.'[49] For others who needed to augment their labour force, instead of simply maintaining it, he advised, '. . . 12 Negroes put on annually will raise the Gang very considerably.'[50] Bennett estimated that a similar number purchased per year would have solved Codrington's problems.[51] Hiring usually meant that these timely additions did not take place.

The planters were constantly in a balancing act. Once their labour force had declined to a certain degree, the problem was serious. Control of the numbers in one's slave population was essential to good management. Planters were committed to using whatever means they had at their disposal to procure the necessary number of energetic labourers to operate their estates at the optimal level. Therefore, according to their particular situation, they used a variety of techniques to do so. As noted above, many were forced to resort to hiring.[52] Plantations were placed in dangerous situations once the cost of hiring superseded that of annual purchases. Hiring could not be used as an alternative to purchasing. Such situations meant that they were expending large sums of money without increasing their capital investment[53] in an environment in which ownership of slaves was central to one's position/status. Further, though hiring produced additional workers, planters retained most of the responsibility for maintenance, in spite of the fact that they were *paying* for labour.

Some estates could support such policies, but managers who came to rely on hiring generally did not cater for contingencies, such as the sudden withdrawal of the hired labourers, or the sometimes highly inflated prices of hired labour.[54] However, many estates also benefited from the moderate use of hiring. It gave the owners/managers some flexibility in the management of their plantations. Even managers who mistrusted the system were forced in many cases to resort to its use.[55] Similarly, many who were committed to the upkeep of the plantation work force through purchasing saw some utility in hiring a certain proportion of the labourers required.[56]

The slaves

There are different viewpoints concerning the treatment meted out to hired and plantation-owned slaves. John Stewart agreed that the jobbers were usually employed in the hardest and most disagreeable work on the plantations.[57] Pares adds that hiring diminished the planters' sense of responsibility for the slaves' well-being.[58] However, the attorney at Dunkenfield Hall (the same John Kelly who had previously been at Golden Grove) expressed the view in 1809 that jobbers were in a better position than the slaves belonging to the estate because it was not customary for them to work at night and they regularly received their day to cultivate their provision grounds. On the other hand, plantation slaves did not get such time off. Thus, in contrast to the earlier sentiments, Kelly felt that hired slaves had comparatively light work to do all year round.[59] Somewhere in between the two extremes was Alexander Barclay who concluded that hired slaves were treated by the lessee precisely as his own because he had signed a covenant in which he agreed to pay for whatever reduction in the number and value of slaves occurred during the term of his contract.[60] Barclay may well have a valid point. In the final analysis, however, we can only judge by examples which have survived. No doubt much depended on the particular context as well as the qualities of both the owner of the hired slave (the lessor) and the owner of the plantation (the lessee). There are numerous examples where hired labour was clearly used for the most strenuous tasks on plantations. But, of course, no estate labour force was made up entirely of hired labourers. Thus, to some extent hired labourers must have been doing work in common with plantation slaves.

It is reasonable to assume that where the estate attorney owned the hired slaves they would usually safeguard their interest. However, the plantations provided a certain measure of conservation for their own slaves which hired labourers did not experience because of their very purpose. As noted already, hired slaves were usually hired with the intention of them performing the more strenuous or disagreeable tasks. Hired labourers were also less likely to benefit from ameliorative practices, particularly those implemented in the nineteenth century. One can therefore conclude that with the possible exception of cases in which an absentee-owned plantation was run by an attorney, who more or less operated as the owner and hired his slaves out to the same estate, the lot of the hired slave was more distasteful than that of the slave attached to a particular plantation.

Skilled slaves would have been an exception to the general rule. These slaves were often hired out as individuals under the system of self-hire and because of their value and talents were the beneficiaries of far more concessions than the hired-out field slaves. These slaves were also the most likely to receive a percentage of the earnings they were paid. These two forms of hiring existed side-by-side on West Indian plantations. The latter was a privilege accorded to a few trusted and skilled slaves. The former, however, was no more than a variation within the framework of plantation slavery, serving the interest of no one but the lessor and the lessee. The slaves in these instances were given no special consideration.

Owners of hired labour

Some plantation owners, usually smaller proprietors, used hiring as a means of gaining additional income. John Pinney of Nevis preferred to own plenty of tradesmen whom he hired out; many of them operated totally outside the plantation system.[61] Some owners specialised in hiring out slaves. As mentioned before, sometimes these establishments became so specialised that they were referred to as jobbing firms. As also stated previously, the slaves who were hired on a plantation were usually owned by resident managers, overseers, bookkeepers, or other white employees.[62] Many of the smaller white settlers also combined occupations such as managing/owning pens, carpentry, and masonry with jobbing. For example, in Jamaica, even after Thomas Thistlewood had accumulated enough money to purchase a pen, he continued to derive considerable income from hiring out his slaves.[63] There were even instances when individuals who owned too few slaves to hire out as a gang pooled their resources, rather like business partners, creating a gang of the size required.

In St James parish in Jamaica in 1744, 17 establishments focused solely on jobbing. On 24 settlements, jobbing was combined with other occupations, the most popular of which were pen-keepers, overseers, and tradesmen.[64] These firms which specialised in hiring out slaves could own as many as 500 of them.[65] Hiring was clearly a thriving business, which operated alongside and in fact depended on the plantation system. Young men who came to the West Indies to try and make their fortunes often began as apprentices on estates,[66] but many soon realised that the easiest way to accumulate property was to begin to purchase slaves to hire out. Having no plantations themselves, this was the ideal way to benefit financially from their newly acquired property in humans.[67]

The records of plantations also suggest that by the end of the eighteenth century, in some instances, money could be more easily made from hiring out slaves than from owning plantations. The relatively easy means of acquiring property in slaves, and in turn substantial yearly incomes, can be contrasted with the difficulty and risks involved in starting a plantation. Thus persons who came to the West Indies without much available money could begin almost immediately to make their 'fortune' through jobbing, although they could not realistically begin to think about owning a plantation.

Towards the last decades of the eighteenth century planters complained continuously about reduced profits. J. Chishlome reported that his Trouthall estate had not been able to earn him more than £700 in the last four years.[68] Several estates actually gave no returns and sunk further and further into debt.[69] In 1791 the accounts of Golden Grove Plantation reflected that the balance Chaloner Arcedeckne (the owner) owed was £800. In 1788 the debt had been as much as £2,983.15s.9d.[70] In contrast, plantation accounts suggest that white employees were able to make substantial profits in the second half of the eighteenth century, largely because they owned slaves whom they hired out to the plantations. In 1753 Grant Elcock, the attorney of the Codrington estates, earned approximately £469.10s. per annum from hiring out his slaves.[71] By the end of the eighteenth century it was possible to earn even larger amounts. Sums such as £600 and £700 do not seem to have been unusual for the more successful renters of labour.[72] In 1782 Simon Taylor, referring to John Kelly, noted that he had 'put between 6 and 7 hundred pounds into his pocket for every year of these ten years passed.'[73] It is reasonable to assume that tradesmen with gangs and jobbing firms received even larger returns.

Towards a theoretical framework

Any theoretical framework should take into consideration both modes of hiring: *self-hire* and *hiring-out*. In The Bahamas the system of self-hire was more prevalent than elsewhere in the British West Indies. Howard Johnson associates the rise and spread of the system there with the depreciating demand for labour because of the failure of the plantation system. Planters, therefore, could not keep their slaves fully occupied, and these became a financial burden. Johnson notes that maintenance costs came to exceed the income which the slaves generated.[74] The slave system was therefore in a state of transition and this was indicated by the entrenchment of the self-hire system.[75] To use Johnson's words, to survive, 'the slave owner commuted the labor service of his slave into cash payment.'[76]

Johnson's observations, based on the Bahamas, are of limited utility in explaining the growth of the self-hire system in the rest of the British West Indies in the nineteenth century. In most of these other areas the plantation system was still strongly entrenched. An examination of them shows that self-hire existed at the height of the profitability of the plantation system, albeit on a much smaller scale. The case of John Pinney clearly demonstrates this. Pinney was said to have a 'consciousness of possessing abundant labour,' which led him to have his own slaves trained 'not only for self sufficiency but also for the money to be made by hiring them out.'[77] It would seem, then, that the most important factor explaining the evolution of hiring, and more particularly self-hiring, was the availability of excess slaves whom the owners found it difficult to employ profitably, whether in a town or on the plantation. While the presence of such slaves is not necessarily indicative of a decaying plantation system, it can certainly be taken as a sign that the particular economic unit was not capable of making use of all its available workers. But we would also expect to see more cases of self-hire where the decay/decline in the plantation system is significant.

While noting the particular aberration of self-hire, as stated before, hiring-out was more prevalent in the British West Indies between 1750 and 1810. This was a period when the plantations experienced both profitability and indebtedness, but were still widely perceived as viable in most of the region. Hiring-out, therefore, can be associated not only with decline but also prosperity. In fact, hiring-out seems to have been very prevalent even in the heyday of the plantation slave system. We may need, however, to distinguish between the slave mode of production in particular and the plantation economy in general. Problems within the slave mode of production did not necessarily mean that the plantation system or the entire economy was in decay. There had to be a demand for workers in order for hiring-out to have become prevalent. The economies affected by such an operation reflect different stages of prosperity, decline and decay at different times, but in all cases the system of labour management was clearly deficient. It is therefore an important aspect of the transition from slave labour to free labour.

The process of hiring involved the injection of capitalist structures, language and, perhaps most importantly, new *thinking* into the slave mode of production. Initially, it was to increase the efficiency and ensure the survival of the slave system. However, it also highlighted the weaknesses in the system and showed that alternative labour systems might well be more profitable. Towards the end of the eighteenth century some planters clearly showed that if they could choose between ownership of slaves and renting (i.e., hiring), they would rent. Johnson notes that by 1784, when large-scale cotton production on slave plantations was introduced into The Bahamas, it created a huge demand for labour. He further points out that contemporary advertisements reflect that the investors in these plantations frequently preferred to hire gangs of slaves on a long-term basis than to purchase slaves.[78] Similarly, he notes that when production stagnated, creating once more an excess of slaves, slave owners sold their slaves, hired them out or allowed then to hire themselves out. Interestingly, he points out that the sale of the slaves was the least used of the three options because there was a better market for their labour power than their persons.[79]

Self-hire reflected a situation of too many slaves than could profitably be used by the owner, either because of economic failure, excessive maintenance costs or, in a few cases, a labour force that was larger than the immediate needs of the owner. Hiring-out reflected the need for more workers because of the failure to achieve natural increases, poor maintenance policies, a debilitating system, and the increasing price of slaves, especially after the end of the slave trade. Both modes, however, reflected the problems inherent in the slavery/plantation economic system and the advantages of aspects of the capitalist system where one pays for labour, does not maintain that labour, can dismiss workers deemed inefficient, and uses no more labour that one requires.

Conclusion

Hiring became an integral part of the slavery system in the British West Indies. Both forms of labour acquisition operated side-by-side and often in dependence on one another. Both were essential aspects of the late eighteenth-century business environment. Hiring was an easy way for jobbing firms to make quick money. It provided a means for those without the large outlay of cash needed to buy land, a large labour force, and other resources needed to start a plantation, to benefit financially from property in small numbers of slaves, which was more easily attainable. It attracted and maintained a wide catchment of white individuals in the West Indies who might otherwise have been discouraged by the lack of opportunities for making *easy money* and by the poor working conditions in the planting line. Hiring was more common among whites than the ownership of plantations, which was dominated by a smaller and wealthier class. Hiring spanned all class lines, and extended the ownership of slaves beyond the boundaries of the plantations and the planter class at a much faster rate than it might have been without this additional economic incentive.

Perhaps, however, the most important aspect of hiring was that it pointed the way to the future. It caused monetary values to be placed on labour and not just labourers. Thus it was no longer an issue of simply owning a slave who was worth a certain amount of pounds. The emphasis shifted from the value of the slave (the *persona*) to the value of the labour. Slaves who were hired also became aware of the monetary values placed on their labour for specific amounts of time and tasks. They also had the experience of short-term stints of residential labour, as opposed to long-term attachment to a particular unit. These were important lessons for the future and for the transition from the slavery mode to the free-labour mode. This training came not only from the urban setting where slaves operated almost as free persons of colour, but right from within the bowels of the plantation system, where it was very clear who was master and who was enslaved.

Notes

1. H. Johnson, 'A Slow and Extended Abolition,' in Mary Turner ed., *From Chattel Slaves to Wage Slaves* (London: James Currey Ltd., 1995), 172; see also B. Higman, *Slave Populations of the British Caribbean 1807–1834* (Baltimore: The Johns Hopkins University Press, 1984), 244.

2. H. Johnson, *The Bahamas in Slavery and Freedom* (Kingston: Ian Randle Publishers,1991), chap. 1.

3. Higman, *Slave Populations,* 245.

4. *Ibid.*

5. *Ibid.,* 232, 236–37; see also Johnson, *Slow Abolition,* 173–74.

6. Johnson, 'Slow Abolition,' 174–77; see also Higman, *Slave Populations,* 246.

7. Higman, *Slave Populations,* 245.

8. Richard Pares, *A West India Fortune* (London: Longmans, Green), 132.

9. Higman, *Slave Populations,* 226.

10. Edward Long, *The History of Jamaica* (1774; London: New ed, 1970), I, 399–400.

11. Harry Bennett, *Bondsmen and Bishops: Slavery and Apprenticeship on the Codrington Plantations of Barbados 1710–1835* (Los Angeles: University of California Press, 1958), 64.

12. *Ibid.*

13. *Ibid.*

14. CO 28/61, Answers to Queries, Barbados, 1788, fol.164; see also Goulburn MS. Ac 319/53, James Craggs to Madam (Mrs. Goulburn), 12 October 1798.

15. See Table 5.1.

16. Most figures were originally in local currency. The few that were not were converted using the exchange rate of: Barbados and Jamaica £1 St.=£1.4 local currency; other islands £1 St.=£2 local currency. Daily and task rates varied according to the circumstances and conditions in which the slave had to labour, as well as the type of job the person had to perform. When a range of prices was given the figures relevant

to field labour and holing were the ones recorded wherever possible; thus the figures do not apply to skilled labourers.

17. Bennett, 65.

18. Penhryn MS. 1261, Richard Pennant (Lord Penhryn) to Mr. Hering, April 28, 1781.

19. Bennett, 65–66.

20. Goulburn MS. Ac 319/51, James Craggs to Mrs. Goulburn, April 13, 1801.

21. Goulburn MS. Ac 319/53, James Craggs to Henry Goulburn, September 1, 1793.

22. Goulburn MS. Ac 319/51, James Craggs to Henry Goulburn, June 13, 1801; see also Bennett, 67.

23. Clarendon MS. Dep. C. 428, Joseph Foster Barham to Messrs Graham and Plummer, n.d. (but seems to be part of a letter dated July 7, 1798), fol.43.

24. Clarendon MS. Dep. C. 357, Racher Webb to Joseph Foster Barham, September 30, 1801, fol.3.

25. Goulburn MS. Ac 319/51, James Craggs to Henry Goulburn, June 5, 1797.

26. Pares, 129.

27. Add. MS. 12412, Edward Long to Mr. Wynter, November 20, 1799, in Long's notes on eighteenth-century Jamaica.

28. Clarendon MS. Dep C. 428, Joseph Barham to Gentlemen (Wedderburn and Graham), June 1, 1796, fol.36.

29. Add. MS. 12412, Edward Long to Mr. Wynter, May 13, 1780, in Long's notes on eighteenth-century Jamaica.

30. A. Barclay, A *Practical View of the Present State of Slavery in the West Indies* (London: Smith Elder, 1826), 319.

31. Add. MS. 12412, Edward Long to D.S. Mackenzie, July 26, 1778, in Long's notes on eighteenth-century Jamaica.

32. Bennett describes a similar situation on the Codrington estates in 1753 when an attorney, Grant Elcock, was hired. One of his major assets was 40 slaves whom he brought with him and hired out to the plantation (see Bennett, 68).

33. Vanneck-Arc/3A/1773/4, Simon Taylor to Chaloner Arcdeckne, March 19, 1773.

34. Vanneck-Arc/3A/1782/18, Simon Taylor to Chaloner Arcdeckne, May 8, 1782.

35. Goulburn MS. Ac 319/54, Thomas Samson to Mrs. Goulburn, August 7, 1802.

36. Ibid.

37. Add. MS. 12412, Edward Long to Mr. Wynter, April 21, 1778, in Long's notes on eighteenth-century Jamaica.

38. R55/7/125/1, John Tharp, 'Dr [sums paid] to Sundry for the following accounts paid since his departure from Jamaica to August 1, 1796.' The management at the Codrington estates came to depend on hiring to the extent that they neglected to implement a consistent stocking policy to augment their labour force. Instead, they relied on the stop-gap measure of hiring. By 1760 the estate was spending £1,200 every year on hiring. Further, by this time the permanent work force had been considerably reduced through deaths, low fertility rates, and the failure to purchase new slaves. It was only when they had arrived at this critical point that management returned to purchasing schemes (see Bennett, 180).
39. CO 28/61, Answers to Queries, Barbados, 1788, Question No. 10, fol.164; see also Goulburn MS. Ac 319/53, James Craggs to Madam (Mrs. Goulburn), October 12, 1798 and November 20, 1798.
40. Goulburn MS. Ac 319/53, James Craggs to Madam (Mrs. Goulburn), November 20, 1798.
41. Clarendon MS. Dep. C. 357, Henry Plummer to Joseph Foster Barham, February 1, 1799. fol.2.
42. Penhryn MS. 1349, Richard Pennant (Lord Penhryn) to Fraser (Fearon), October 30, 1804; see also Clarendon MS. Dep. C. 428, Joseph Foster Barham to Samuel Jefferies and William Rodgers, July 7, 1803, fol.78; Goulburn MS. Ac 319/51, Thomas Samson to Henry Goulburn, October 4, 1804.
43. In 1799, Henry Plummer advised Joseph Foster Barham to purchase 8 or 10 young 'Negroes' (Clarendon MS. Dep. C. 357, Henry Plummer to Joseph Foster Barham, June 10, 1799, fol.2; see also Goulburn MS. Ac 319/51, Thomas Samson to Mrs. Goulburn January 12, 1804).
44. Hiring-out of slaves actually continued right up to the end of slavery, in spite of efforts to curtail its use. The demand and the cost also continued to increase, particularly with the abolition of the slave trade.
45. Cooper Franks MS. Acc 775/945, Jacob Franks to George Scott, October 15, 1788.
46. Bennett, 63–74 (Codrington estates); Goulburn MS. Ac 319/51, Thomas Samson to Henry Goulburn, July 23, 1812 (Amity Hall); Cooper Franks MS. Acc 775/945, Letter to George Scott, October 15, 1788 (Dunkenfield Hall).
47. Goulburn MS. Ac 319/54, Thomas Samson to Mrs. Goulburn, August 7, 1802.
48. Ibid.
49. Add. MS. 12412, Edward Long to D.S. Mackenzie, July 26, 1778, in Long's notes on eighteenth-century Jamaica.
50. Ibid.
51. Bennett, 69.

52. *Ibid.*
53. Cooper Franks MS. Acc 775/945, Jacob Franks to George Scott, October 15, 1788.
54. Bennett, 68.
55. Example of Abel Alleyne, attorney at Codrington estates 1740–1746 (see *Ibid.*, 67); see also Clarendon MS. Dep. C. 428, Joseph Foster Barham to Messrs Wedderburn and Graham, September 18, 1789.
56. Example of John Smalridge, attorney at Codrington estates, 1718–1731 (see Bennett, 64–65).
57. J. Stewart, *A View of the Past and Present State of the Island of Jamaica* (London: Oliver and Boyd, Tweedale-House, 1823), 234.
58. Pares, 120.
59. Cooper Franks MS. Acc 775/928, John Kelly to Jacob Franks, October 28, 1809.
60. Barclay, 67.
61. Pares, 129.
62. Bennett,, 64.
63. Douglas Hall, *In Miserable Slavery. Thomas Thistlewood in Jamaica 1750-86*, (Kingston: Heinemann, 1982), 249.
64. Add. MS. 12435, A list of sugar estates and other properties in the parish of St James, September 1774, fol.3.
65. Vanneck-Arc/3A/1790/42, Arcdeckne MS.
66. Simon Taylor approved of a gift of slaves for one of the young white men he was training to hold a position of attorneyship, because he was of the opinion that they would be useful and profitable for him to hire them out (see Institute of Commonwealth Studies, Univ. of London, Simon Taylor to George Hill, May 6, 1800, Simon Taylor's Correspondence, Private Letter Book 1A: July 7, 1779–July 15, 1785). Thomas Thistlewood is an excellent example of a person who came out to the West Indies, established himself as an attorney, invested initial savings in slaves whom he hired out, and progressed to the point where he bought a piece of land, established a pen, and managed two complementary businesses — looking after the pen, and hiring out a jobbing gang (see Hall, xvi).
67. Dickson, 151.
68. Chishlome Papers, MS. 5476, J. Chishlome to William Henderson, March 7, 1810, fol.197; see also Penhryn MS. 1259, Richard Pennant to Mr. Hering, January 28, 1787.
69. Vanneck-Arc/3A/1782/28, Simon Taylor to Chaloner Arcdeckne, June 11, 1782; see also Long, I, 391.
70. Vanneck-Arc/3A/1788/12, Simon Taylor to Chaloner Arcdeckne, January 27, 1769.
71. Bennett, 68.

72. Chishlome Papers, MS. 5476, James Chishlome to William Anderson, January 30, 1802. fol.91; see also Tharp MS., William Hall to John Tharp, February 11, 1821.
73. Vanneck-Arc/3A/1782/18, Simon Taylor to Chaloner Arcdeckne, May 8, 1782.
74. Johnson, 'Slow Abolition,' 167-68.
75. *Ibid.*
76. *Ibid.*, 172
77. Pares, 125–26.
78. Johnson, *Bahamas in Slavery and Freedom*, 3.
79. Johnson, *Slow Abolition*, 171.

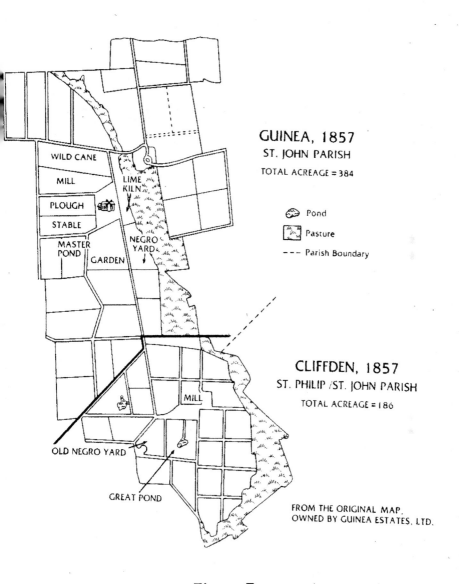

Figure 7:
Guinea and Cliffden (St. John), 1857, showing location of 'Negro yard' fields in relation to mill yard.

Figure 1: *Ashford plantation (St. John), Barbados, late 1830s, showing manor house, mill yard, windmill, pond and ex-slave/ apprentice houses in the centre, behind the pond.*
Figure 8: *Wattle-and Daub houses with thatched roofs*
Figure 9: *Stone house with thatched roof.*

CHAPTER

Plantation Slave Settlements in Barbados,
1650s to 1834[1]
Jerome S. Handler

Introduction

Professor Woodville Marshall has had a long-standing interest in the establishment of free villages in Barbados in post-emancipation times. In light of that interest, this paper describes the antecedents of many rural settlements in Barbados; it focuses on some of the major physical and demographic features of slave settlements, particularly on medium- and large-size plantations. Changes in some of these features are traced over the almost 200 years of plantation slavery on the island, and the possible influences of Africa or England on village layout and spatial arrangement of houses are considered. Some of the methodological and historical issues in establishing the number of plantation settlements during the slave period and of identifying the sites of former villages and plantation cemeteries in present-day Barbados are also explored. Finally, some of the sociological characteristics of the slave settlements as small communities are considered.

The slave settlement and plantation yard

In the late 1780s, Governor David Parry speculated that plantation slaves comprised about 88 per cent of the Barbadian slave population, assumed to be around 63,000 persons —although there were probably more. Barry Higman estimates that in 1834, when about 83,000 slaves were reported, aside from a relatively small percentage of town dwellers, 'no more than 78 per cent' lived on sugar plantations, while another 11 per cent lived on smaller farm units. There are no other overall estimates of the size of the Barbadian plantation slave population. Although the proportion who lived on plantations may have declined by emancipation, there is no doubt that at least from the 1650s to 1834, the majority of Barbadian slaves lived on plantations.[2]

Most slaves lived in plantation settlements that can be considered hamlets or small villages. Their work and leisure time, as well as their most important daily social interactions, were centred in these compact units. The settlements included the houses themselves, as well as the small plots of adjacent land (where subsistence and, occasionally, cash crops, small livestock and poultry were raised), and several other features not literally within the settlements, but geographically very close and socially and economically important: plantation fields where slaves were allocated small plots (in addition to or in lieu of house plots) for cultivating crops of their choice; water and wood supplies; and burial grounds. Toward the end of the eighteenth century, plantations built infirmaries or sick houses near the settlements and, occasionally closer to the emancipation period, chapels or schools.

The heart of the plantation and the focus of operations was the area known from an early period (until the present) as the plantation yard, mill yard or, simply and most frequently, the yard. Plantations of any consequence had in their yards at least one windmill, occasionally two or three, for grinding sugar cane. Situated close to the mill were other buildings essential to the processing and manufacture of sugar, molasses, and rum, e.g., the boiling house, curing house, and distillery, storerooms, workshops for tradesmen, stables, houses for white staff (if a larger plantation), and the owner's or manager's residence, variously called the mansion house, dwelling house, or simply the house (today called the great house). Very close and usually adjacent to the mill yard was the slave settlement itself.

The 'Negro yard:' name and location

From early in the slave period, the yard complex and its associated settlement appeared to European visitors, using the cultural models of their own geographical landscapes, as small villages or towns. 'Most of the plantations in the country,' wrote Antoine Biet, a French priest who resided in Barbados in 1654, 'are like as many villages whose size varies according to the number of slaves each plantation has.' In 1675, an English visitor described how 'every dwelling house, with the sugar work and other out housing, looks like a handsome town.' A few years earlier another English observer remarked how 'their buildings . . . at a small distance ordinarily present themselves like castles, and their houses built for making and preserving sugar and for other offices, with their Negro huts, show about 2 leagues at sea like so many small towns, each defended by its castle.'[3] Such reactions to the Barbadian countryside, regardless of the adjectives used to describe it, emphasise a settlement pattern that was at the core of the Barbadian landscape and social order: plantation yards and slave villages. Their essential physical features varied little from the last half of the seventeenth century to emancipation in 1834.

If the plantation yard and slave settlement together appeared to Europeans as villages or small towns, similar observations, stressing a more or less compact unit, were made when only the slave settlement was reported. For the Barbadian-born Anglican minister Henry Holder (a defender of the slave system), the slaves' 'small houses . . . are concentrated in little villages, inhabited solely by themselves.' Other writers also referred to the slave settlements as little villages, little towns, small towns, or the 'Negro town.' In fact, referring to the late 1600s or early 1700s, John Oldmixon, a British historian (who had never been to Barbados, but had gathered information from a variety of first-hand sources) wrote how 'every plantation look[s] like a little African city, and the planter's house like the sovereign's in the midst of it.' Dr William Douglass, who visited Barbados in 1717, observed that slaves 'live in contiguous huts like an African town.'[4]

Regardless of comparisons made with Africa, the slave houses were concentrated in a relatively small land area. By the late seventeenth century, and probably starting much earlier, this area was called the 'Negro yard'. This continued to be the most common designation, although occasionally terms such as 'Negro houses' or 'Negro land' were also used.[5] After emancipation, 'Negro yard' also referred to the villages of the ex-slaves before they were moved to newly established tenantries at the plantation peripheries.[6] When the houses of these new freemen or apprentices were placed elsewhere on plantation lands, their former village areas were usually converted to agricultural use. However, these new agricultural fields continued to be called 'Negro yard' or 'Negro yard field,' even though the areas no longer contained human settlements. In present-day Barbados, it is not unusual to find plantations with 'Negro yard fields.' Usually, these fields are employed agriculturally, but they are invariably situated close to the mill yard and mark the site of the former slave settlement.[7]

From early in Barbadian plantation history, slave settlements were placed very close to the plantation yard, and almost universally within ready sight of the mansion house itself. For example, in 1652, Heinrich von Uchteritz, a German indentured servant, observed that 'around the plantation yard stand the slaves' small houses.' In the 1780s, William Senhouse, the island's surveyor-general of customs and also the owner of Grove Plantation, noted how the 'ground immediately surrounding' the dwelling house was 'as usual in this island, appropriated for the use of the Negroes.' In early 1796, George Pinckard, a medical doctor with the British Army, also observed that slaves lived 'at a short distance' from the mansion house, a settlement pattern also reported in 1796 by Sampson Wood, the manager of Newton and Seawell plantations.[8]

The proximity of the slave settlement to the mansion house and plantation yard recorded in literary sources is also sometimes shown on plantation maps. Unlike Jamaica, where an abundance of plantation maps and plans exist, there are relatively few maps and plans of Barbadian sugar plantations dating from the slave or early post-emancipation period. Of those, only a handful actually show the slave/apprentice houses or identify the 'Negro yard,' and they invariably show the settlements adjacent to the yard or mansion house.[9] This settlement pattern is also indirectly corroborated by modern sugar plantation field names. From early in the island's history, plantations divided their acreage into fields of varying sizes and shapes, and assigned names to the fields. Field names, which could change over time, usually referred to former landholders or residents in the plantation vicinity, or agricultural, physical, and cultural features found on the plantation.[10]

It is often difficult to obtain literary or oral information on the history of specific fields, but many field names today seem to have existed for a very long time; sometimes these names, as with English field names, can be useful in reconstructing local history.[11] In Barbados, one such name is 'Negro yard' or 'Nigger yard' — the latter term being occasionally used today (although much more common 20 or more years ago) by elderly black and white Barbadians. Although the term 'Negro yard' once referred to the plantation area containing the slave village, many Barbadians are unaware of the origins of this field name.

Quite a few Barbadian plantations retain the field name 'Negro yard.' Even if a named 'Negro yard' no longer exists on a particular plantation, an elderly or retired manager or worker sometimes can remember which of the plantation's current fields was formerly called 'Negro yard.' Visual inspection of plantations with 'Negro yards' during my fieldwork in the 1970s, 1980s and 1990s, and examination of post-emancipation maps, almost invariably show the 'Negro yard' field located very close to, or adjoining, the mill yard — thus pointing to the area which had once contained the slave settlement (see, for example, figure 7). In general, then, all types of evidence converge to show unequivocally that the slave houses were situated very close to the mansion house and the mill yard (as seen in the cover illustration to this volume and Figure 1, showing Ashford Plantation, St John).[12] In Barbados, as throughout the West Indies, the areas for locating the 'Negro yards' were determined by the planters, not by the slaves; planters overwhelmingly chose these sites for reasons of their own personal comfort and security.

In many nucleated villages, typical of farming areas in England during post-medieval times, the houses of labourers and others who inhabited 'humble tenements' were generally close to the manor house. Although this settlement pattern began to change during the 1600s and especially the 1700s, it would not be surprising, albeit conjectural, if early English planters in Barbados transferred this general layout to the West Indies — as they attempted to do with other facets of life, including architecture.[13] In the West Indies, however, security issues relating to the slave population became an important factor — thus adding a New World variable to an Old World settlement pattern.

Inferential evidence for Barbados, and comparative evidence from elsewhere in the West Indies, strongly argue that security and surveillance were the major reasons why the slave settlement was located so close to the mansion house. For example, during the last half of the seventeenth century, several slave plots resulted in laws requiring regular searches of their slave houses for weapons, hidden fugitive or runaway slaves, or other signs of suspicious activity. It was also well known that slave plots could be hatched at dances, and these usually took place over the weekends in the 'Negro yards.' Although white fears of slave revolts had abated by the eighteenth century, plantation managements were still concerned about security issues ranging from the harbouring of runaways from other plantations to theft from plantation storehouses and workshops. The advantage of having the slave houses close at hand was sarcastically noted in 1796 by the manager of Newton and Seawell. In Barbados 'generally,' he wrote, 'the managers dwelling house is . . . situated where they enjoy the sight of all the doors of the [yard] buildings at one view; if nothing is wrong in the day time, all must be secure — they suppose — and from . . . their front door, they give their directions with a stentorial voice without the trouble of motion.'[14]

Was there any patterning to the direction in which the 'Negro yard' was situated with respect to the mill yard or mansion house? Ronald Hughes, a well-known Barbadian historian and authority on plantation history, has suggested to me that the slave village was located downwind, that is, to the leeward or west, of the mansion house so as to avoid the 'smoke and stench' from cooking fires. The same reason was also expressed by an anonymous late eighteenth-century author who was knowledgeable about the West Indies. Without mentioning a particular island, he observed that 'Negroes live in huts, on the western side of our dwelling houses . . . [so] that we may breathe the pure eastern air, without being offended with the least nauseous smell. Our kitchens and boiling houses are on the same side, and for the same reason.'[15]

My field observations on contemporary plantations and interviews with Barbadians who had personal knowledge of particular plantations, as well as an examination of plantation maps, yielded a group of 28 plantations which had identifiable 'Negro yard' fields or where the precise location of the former slave settlements could be established in relation to the mill yard or mansion house.[16] Of these 28 plantations, 19 (68 per cent) of the 'Negro yards'/ slave settlements were west of the mill yard/mansion house (11 were due west, while the remainder were either northwest or southwest); in three cases the 'Negro yard'—slave settlement was to the north; in four cases to the south or southeast; and in two cases to the east. These limited data support the view that slaves lived 'on the western side of our dwelling houses,' but they also suggest that this pattern was not universal in Barbados.

The 'Negro yard:' appearance and layout

By the time that the Barbadian plantation system was fully mature there were variations in the physical appearance of the slave settlements. Some, Pinckard reported, contained few trees or shade spots and were 'standing amidst the open fields, exposed to the full ardor of the sun;' others were 'shaded by the sea-grape,' or 'the broad and balmy leaf of the plantain,' or were 'protected by the umbrageous coco-nut.' In 1796, the Newton settlement contained 'a few shrubs' and 'no trees,' while at Codrington a few years later, 'the land all around the huts [was cultivated] with our luxuriant tropical vegetables;' trees were 'growing throughout the village.'[17]

Although visitors to Barbados had different reactions to the aesthetics of the slave village, some viewing it in pleasing terms, others much less so,[18] writers over a long period of time unanimously described the settlements as compact and congested. The individual, free-standing houses were clustered in close proximity, and to white observers they seemed to be arranged in an haphazard and disorderly fashion. Moreover, in their written comments — however brief and superficial — whites either imply or explicitly state that what they observed differed from European settlements of comparable scale. Father Antoine Biet noted that 'each household' had 'its own dwelling; they are all close to one another'; for William Douglass, over 60 years later, slaves lived 'in contiguous huts.' In the 1780s, Governor Parry compared the spacing of slave houses, which were 'so much nearer each other' with 'the lowest class of white inhabitants [who] live all separate from each other.' Pinckard contrasted one estate he visited with the more general pattern of slave settlement; the latter was a 'mean order, straggling . . . and bearing no kind of resemblance to the collective abode, constructed for the slaves of this estate.' During apprenticeship, Joseph Sturge and Thomas Harvey, British emancipationists viewed the 'huts' of plantation workers as 'crowded irregularly together,' while for J.A. Thome and J.H. Kimball, American emancipationists, houses were 'crowded thickly together.' The picture of a compact settlement is also conveyed by the few plantation maps that show slave houses, and other observers also stressed in one way or another that slave houses were 'concentrated in little villages' or 'crowded together on a small piece of ground.'[19]

The actual acreage of this 'small piece of ground' varied from plantation to plantation, but is actually known in only a few cases.[20] At Edgecombe in 1810 and 1812, the 'Negro yard' was reported as four acres and three acres, respectively,[21] while plantation maps indicate that the slave houses at Staple Grove in 1818 were on approximately five to five and a half acres, those at The Bay in 1822 on about two acres, and those at Sandy Lane in 1797 on about one acre. A 1719 map of Drax Hall shows the settlement divided into two portions of approximately eight acres each. Drax Hope, adjacent to Drax Hall, is also shown with an approximately three-acre village area. An 1845 map of Cottage Plantation (St George) shows the village on about five acres of land before it was removed. Despite the limited number of cases, these data suggest that the slave village area or 'Negro yard' averaged around five acres on medium to large plantations.

This five-acre figure is roughly supported by field data randomly collected on the acreage of 13 present-day 'Negro yard fields.' These fields ranged in size from about one and a half to 15 acres, but averaged around 6.25 (seven of the fields were between four and six and a half acres). If 6.25 acres is used as a rough average for present-day 'Negro yard' fields, it should be noted that this acreage does not significantly differ from the five-acre estimate derived from historical sources. However, although the locations of the fields called 'Negro yard' have not changed since emancipation, it is quite likely that their specific acreages (and shapes) shifted, and in most cases there is probably not a precise correspondence between the acreage of a present-day 'Negro yard' field and that of the village once located on it.

The congestion or crowding that Europeans observed was largely a function of the limited space that planters allotted for the 'Negro yards.' However, what Europeans considered a disorganised, even chaotic, layout of houses may have resulted from the inclinations of the slaves themselves and their cultural preferences in the use of space. Although planters determined the actual locale of the 'Negro yard,' the slaves generally chose their specific house sites within the yard. The Barbadian practice was probably very similar, if not identical, to that of Jamaica where, as Barry Higman has written, 'the masters simply set aside a tract of land for the village site and permitted the slaves to locate and construct houses as they wished.' In Barbados, as in other areas of the West Indies, it appears that 'most slave villages remained internally-ordered communities in which the planters rarely intervened.'[22] Although Barbadian planters, as those elsewhere, sometimes intervened in the internal arrangement of the settlements, this intrusion seems to have largely taken place during the later years of the slave period.

The evidence that Barbadian slaves followed their own inclinations in placing their houses and were, in effect, free to choose specific locations within the 'Negro yards,' is largely indirect and inferential.[23] For one, during most of the slave period, slaves were expected to build their own houses from locally-available materials on plantation woodlands, and there is no evidence that planters interfered with their choice of house sites. In addition, white observers, as noted above, describe or allude to a seemingly haphazard and non-geometrical arrangement of houses in the 'Negro yards.' Although post-medieval English settlements displayed considerable diversity, village plans fit into several major broad categories: one of these, 'the agglomerated village,' was composed of 'dwellings planted down almost haphazard, with no evident relationship to each other or to any visible nucleus.'[24] Seventeenth- and eighteenth-century English visitors to Barbados were familiar with such villages, but what they observed in plantation settlements clearly differed from the English 'haphazard' arrangement or irregular clustering of houses. It was not the irregularity of spatial relationships *per se*, but rather the configuration of this irregular and 'haphazard' arrangement (as well as, undoubtedly, the race of the slave inhabitants), that produced a settlement which struck English visitors. Their observations can be interpreted to suggest that slaves were not following European practices, but rather their own cultural notions of arranging space: these notions were probably shaped by African practices. The clustering of houses in relatively small spaces and in non-geometrical alignments would have conformed to common African spatial arrangements.

For most of the slave period, then, and provided plantation managements did not intervene, houses in Barbadian settlements were arranged, as in Jamaica, in 'irregular scattered layout rather than in geometric patterns.' Such a layout was more consistent with African village spatial arrangements than with European, particularly English, ones, even though African village configurations could also be, as Denyer has pointed out, 'quite formal or symmetrical.' The differences that white observers saw in slave settlements also attest their fundamentally African or African-like character. I am not suggesting that slave settlements exactly replicated African ones; rather that they were more African than European in their basic layouts. As in African communities, Barbadian slaves may have viewed their settlements 'as groups of people rather than as groups of buildings,' and in arranging their houses in the 'Negro yards' slaves placed emphasis on their social relationships.[25] In fact, writers such as Oldmixon and Douglass even explicitly likened the Barbadian slave settlements to African villages. The attorney for the Codrington plantations indirectly, albeit ethnocentrically, also made this point. Shortly after emancipation, he reported how the plantations' new settlements contrasted with the crowding of the old Negro villages; the latter, he believed, 'tend to keep up in the minds of the Negroes the idea of "savage life".'[26]

When planters directly intervened in the layout of the settlements and the placement of houses, they altered them to suit their notions of landscape order. As early as 1700, Father Jean Baptiste Labat, who visited Barbados for eight or nine days, reported that planters 'take care that their Negroes' huts are neatly aligned and uniform; this costs nothing and gives a good appearance.' However, this must have been exceptional since European-planned settlements tended to occur mostly toward the later years of the slave period. For example, in the 1780s, Philip Gibbes, a prominent planter, ordered that the 'houses be so situated as to preserve exactly the line upon which that row of houses is built,' and in 1787 William Senhouse ordered a new settlement at Grove Plantation in which the houses were 'disposed in regular streets, every house in the centre of a piece of ground 20 yards square.' Pinckard, in 1796, compared the more usual arrangement of the 'Negro yard' with an unusual one at a plantation he visited. He described it thus:

> A circular piece of ground had been appropriated as the Negro-yard, but instead of the slaves being left to construct their own habitations, sixteen very neat and uniform habitations have been erected . . . Placed in eight divisions they form a hollow octagon . . . The huts are neat, and the whole

premises wear an air of order, and of cleanliness, not common to the abode of slaves.[27]

Changes in England may have influenced some Barbadian planters in organising and planning their slave settlements. The creation and planning of English villages on lands held by institutional authorities and aristocrats have a long history, but during the seventeenth century and especially the eighteenth and continuing into the nineteenth, as Rowley has written, 'not a single settlement in the country remained untouched and many, perhaps the majority, were substantially altered.' Most planned villages simply replaced already existing ones, but many also involved 'completely fresh deliberate creations.' For example, in earlier periods the 'humble tenements' were generally close to the manor house, but now the landowner either rebuilt his own house on a new site or, 'more frequently,' removed 'all or part of the village' from near his dwelling to the outskirts of the estate, creating parks around the manor house. In addition, from around 1750 estate owners made greater attempts 'to landscape the new villages' and plan them according to formal aesthetic considerations.[28]

Some of the changes in England probably had some effect on planter intervention in the layout of slave settlements. However, this intervention seems to have primarily increased in Barbados, as Higman observed for Jamaica, because of general ameliorative trends in the West Indies and the increasing emphasis on slave health. Some Barbadian planters believed that slave health could be improved if housing was improved. Improvement in housing sometimes involved structuring the 'Negro yard' so that houses were less proximate and congested, or the entire settlement was removed to an area that planters considered healthier.[29]

Throughout the period of slavery, most Barbadian slaves were, as Pinckard noted, 'allowed to build themselves small huts to live in;' they constructed and repaired their own houses without planter intervention, and built their houses, as in Jamaica, 'according to their own fancy both in size and shape.'[30] The most common Barbadian dwelling, deeply influenced by West African architectural forms, was a small, low, rectangular wattle-and-daub structure with a packed earth/dirt floor and a pitched, thatched roof (see figure 8). There were many house types and architectural variations in West and West-Central Africa, but historical evidence from Barbados indicates that the wattle-and-daub house (also found in other areas of the Caribbean) was very similar to what Kwamina Dickson calls the 'Guinea forest house type, . . . rectangular, gable-roofed, and of wattle-and-daub,' that was widely distributed on the southern Gold Coast (modern Ghana), as well as in other tropical forest areas of West and West-Central Africa. This house was covered with oil-palm leaves. The wattle in the Barbadian slave house, as in others of this type, was formed by inserting (forked?) wooden posts or stakes into the ground to form a framework; this was then interlaced with twigs or slender tree branches. The wattle was plastered internally (and probably externally as well) with a mud or clay mortar. Roof thatching in Barbados was made from plantain leaves (especially in the seventeenth and early eighteenth centuries), palm leaves or branches and, what was the most common type, the leaves or trash of the sugar cane.[31]

Thatching on slave houses probably closely resembled, or was identical to, thatching on working-class rural Barbadian houses during the late nineteenth and early twentieth centuries (see figures 8 and 9). Some elderly Barbadians still remember the trash house, with its roof of thatched 'cane tops tied together.' During slavery, housing materials were largely obtained from plantation woodlands, and planters were sometimes advised to keep some of their land in 'wood for 'Negro houses;' occasionally plantations sold 'rafters and other sticks for building Negro-houses.'[32]

Wattle-and-daub was not only the earliest structural type; it remained the most typical slave house until emancipation. However, by the end of the eighteenth century and the beginning of the nineteenth, it co-existed with other house types as planters increasingly changed the structural materials and design of slave houses, and employed plantation carpenters and masons to construct them. The increased use of slave tradesmen to build slave houses often followed, as Higman has observed for the West Indies in general, 'standardized [architectural] plans chosen by the masters. This tendency toward master-controlled building often went together with the imposition of geometrical regularity on the settlement pattern.' Barbadian carpenters and masons constructed stone and wood plank (i.e., frame) houses, and these types increased in frequency. The latter was constructed of rough boards or planks (largely imported from abroad) nailed to wooden posts, the former from coral limestone, i.e., the stone-walled houses (see figure 9). Thatching continued as the major roofing material, although wooden shingles were also used occasionally. By 1850 in Barbados, as Thomas Cochrane observed, the 'small wooden [plank] houses resting on clumps of wood or blocks of stone' seem to have been very common among the working class, but stone houses also may have become more numerous. Both types, however, continued to be thatched, although occasionally they were shingled. In a sense, Barbadians today are correct when they refer to stone houses (the ruins of which are still found scattered about the island) as 'slave houses,' but it is erroneous to assume that such houses were typical slave dwellings. Stone houses were not numerically significant until the pre-emancipation decades of the nineteenth century, but were much fewer in number than wattle-and-daub ones.[33]

Houseplots and 'Negro grounds'

Barbadian slaves acquired most of their food through rations, usually distributed weekly, from plantation managements. Among the West Indian territories, Barbados fell somewhere between what the British emancipationist James Stephen called the home-fed and foreign-fed colonies, a distinction based on the degree of dependence on imported foods.[34] In Barbados, although foods were imported, considering the entirety of the slave period it appears that most food was locally produced and was cultivated on plantation fields called provision grounds. These grounds were collectively worked by slave gangs as part of their normal labour routines. In addition, many plantations gave adults or households[35] small plots of land on which they cultivated food crops (and later in the slave period cash crops as well) and raised small animals. These garden plots were usually worked on weekends or holidays, and their produce went directly to the producer. The produce was used to augment plantation food rations or exchanged in the island's markets for foods or material goods not provided by the plantation. Small garden plots were allowed slaves, starting around the mid-seventeenth century, but these plots were never codified in law; as Governor Parry reported in the late 1780s, they were given by 'long established custom.'[36]

There were two types of garden plots. One was a sub-division in a field that the plantation set aside specifically for slave use. This field was distinguished from other plantation fields upon which food crops were raised, i.e., the provision grounds, and was referred to as the 'Negro ground,' 'Negro land,' or 'Negro garden.' The 'Negro ground' was situated 'in the outskirts of the plantation' or adjacent to the village, but not literally within the "Negro yard'.'[37] The other type of garden, apparently meriting no special term, was adjacent to, or surrounding, individual houses within the 'Negro yard.' On these 'small patches of garden,' as Pinckard generalised in the 1796, 'it is common for the slaves to plant fruits and vegetables, and to raise stock. Some of them keep a pig, some a goat, some Guinea fowls, ducks, chickens, pigeons, or the like.'[38] The houseplots were small and hardly sufficient to raise much more than meagre supplements to plantation food rations; yet they were important features of the slaves' domestic economy.[39]

The distinction between the houseplot, on the one hand, and 'Negro ground,' on the other, is clearly expressed in a number of sources. For example, Governor Parry reported on the 'small portions of land annexed to each Negro house, but not assigned as part of their subsistence; and there is also in most plantations a field of land called the Negro ground, the profits of which are taken to the use of those who cultivate them, independently of the allowance they receive from their owners in common with other slaves.' Philip Gibbes also articulated the distinction: each house on his plantations had a small garden ground attached to it, and 'besides this spot of ground, a field is set apart in which each Negro is allowed to mark out his lot to any extent which he thinks he and his family are capable of cultivating.'[40]

The 'Negro garden' system is clearly illustrated in an 1835 map (the original survey dating to an earlier period) of Husbands (St Lucy). This map identifies two areas on the plantation as 'Negro gardens,' one of which is adjacent to the western portion of the mill yard, while the other is a few fields south of the mill yard and slave village. An 1825 map of Lowther also shows a seven-acre field named 'Negro garden;' after emancipation this field name was dropped and the field was sub-divided into two fields, each receiving a new name.[41]

The 'Negro garden' system was also evident at Ashford (St John) in 1809 when 6.5 acres were 'planted by the Negroes.' However, Ashford's records for the following year omit the separate acreage 'planted by the Negroes,' thereby suggesting that assignment of a field as a 'Negro ground' was not consistently followed from year to year. Yet, in 1812, there were nine acres at Ashford 'cultivated by the Negroes for their own use.' Also, a detailed account of land use on an unnamed plantation in 1822 shows that nine of the plantation's approximately 250 cultivated acres were designated 'Negro gardens.'[42]

Defenders of the slave system in Barbados usually emphasised that slaves were provided with gardens, but others questioned their universality. For example, Dr Caddell, a knowledgeable plantation medical doctor, reporting to a society of planters in 1812, observed that 'on many plantations the Negroes have no ground at all; on very few do they cultivate what they have; on none are they cultivated sufficiently to contribute materially to their comfort or support.' Also, an English emancipationist visiting Barbados in 1830, made a special effort to observe 'the small portions of ground allotted to them near their dwellings.' However, on visiting 'different estates' he found this 'only partially the case, many being certainly without this provision.'[43]

In summary, both types of slave gardens, the 'Negro grounds' and houseplots, date from at least the last half of the seventeenth century, and this dual system appears to have operated throughout the slave period. Both types could exist on the same plantation at the same time, but 'Negro grounds' may have been found mostly on the middle-sized to large plantations. Whatever the case, it is also clear that although houseplots were very common, they were not universal.

Water supplies

The earliest way that Barbadians ensured their water supplies was through the construction of ponds. 'This pond water, they use upon all occasions and to all purposes,' Richard Ligon wrote of the late 1640s, 'to boyle their meat, to make their drink, to wash their linnen.' Ponds were formed in natural depressions or were artificially constructed, usually taking advantage of an incline or slope in the terrain. In earlier periods, as Antoine Biet observed in

1654, 'great care' was taken 'to dig ponds in tree shaded spots so that they do not dry up too soon.' During slavery, as in post-emancipation times, plantations had both ponds and cisterns. Cisterns were constructed adjacent to the mansion house and collected the rain funnelled through roof gutters; however, except in emergencies, cistern water was largely for the plantations' white personnel. In early years, ponds seem to have been shared by blacks and whites alike, but as whites increasingly relied on cisterns, ponds continued to provide slaves (and, of course, the plantation cattle) with their main sources of water.[44]

Modern and early plantation maps, as well as my field observations, demonstrate that the major ponds were usually within or close to the mill yard, and not far from the 'Negro yard.' Pond depressions are common sights in the Barbadian countryside today, and even casual inspection of plantation yards and their immediate vicinities will often show these depressions, some of which still contain water; many of the empty depressions still have the capacity to be filled in the event they are needed.

Historical sources generally give the impression that, especially in the seventeenth and eighteenth centuries, slaves frequently shared their ponds with livestock, particularly during droughts, although this practice may have decreased by the later eighteenth century and pre-emancipation decades of the nineteenth.[45] Whether shared with cattle or not, the ponds could become seriously polluted by, for example, their use for bathing and their contamination with human waste, drowned small animals, and so forth. It is not surprising that slaves were especially vulnerable to parasitic worms and a variety of gastrointestinal disorders.[46]

Also, reliance on ponds could be precarious. Until well into the nineteenth century, rural Barbadians depended on ponds, and during a prolonged drought in 1870–72, 189 (74 per cent) of the 257 ponds in six parishes dried up. Conditions could not have been very different during slavery. Evaporation was a problem and when there was 'hardly sufficient [rain] to moisten the surface,' reported the visitor Arthur Anderson (director of the St Vincent Botanical Gardens) in 1783 or 1784, 'the lower class of inhabitants as well as the negroes are in great distress.'[47] Rain shortages or prolonged droughts were not infrequent in Barbados, and they sometimes caused serious alarm. In 1796, for example, the manager of Seawell (located in one of Barbados' lowest rainfall areas) reported that neither of the plantation's two ponds 'hold water through the year'; at the time, both were 'actually dry,' forcing him to 'drain every drop of water' from the plantation's well. In 1813, Robert Haynes, the plantation's attorney, complained that the drought was so bad that 'every drop of water . . . used by the Negroes and cattle at Newton and Seawell for many weeks has been drawn from the wells, not having any in the ponds;' 'the island is certainly in a most melancholy state,' he wrote eight years later, 'for the want both of rain and water in the ponds for our slaves and livestock.'[48]

In addition to cisterns and ponds, wells tapped underground streams formed by water percolating through the coral limestone. Wells may have been widespread on plantations by the late 1600s, and in the 1730s and 1740s, Griffith Hughes (the rector of St Lucy and a resident of Barbados for about 11 years during the period) wrote, there was 'not a parish . . . nor scarce a large estate' without a well, 'and a great many of these are very deep,' excavated to between 90 and 300 feet.[49] Slaves, of course, were compelled to dig these wells; yet, wells were not generally dug specifically for slave use, even though they occasionally had access to them.[50]

Wood supplies

Slaves preferred their meals cooked and warm (even though circumstances sometimes compelled them to eat their food cold), and fires also afforded some warmth during the chilly evenings of the winter months; in addition, as discussed earlier, most slave houses were constructed from locally obtained wood. With the expansion of sugar production and the plantation system, by the mid-1660s (perhaps even later in the seventeenth century), the indigenous forests of Barbados were virtually gone, and for the duration of the slave period the island's wood resources were limited. Barbados was unable to satisfy its timber needs in, for example, domestic and commercial building materials, windmill parts, barrels and other containers, carts, wagons, and so forth, and imported wood from other West Indian islands; increasingly wood came from North America and, later, from the Guianas.[51]

Although much forest land was removed, it bears stressing that plantations during the period of slavery had more of their acreage in food crops, pasturage, and woodlands than in post-emancipation and modern times.[52] The tropical climate and the island's soils permitted active tree and brush growth in fields and gullies. On most plantations, these wooded areas provided fuel for black and white Barbadians alike, as well as building materials for slave houses. In addition to woodlands, the widely-grown pigeon pea bush was used for fuel. However, by the late 1700s, and probably starting much earlier, firewood was in short supply, and slaves were commonly involved, observed a white Barbadian, 'in splitting up their bedding for firewood;' he urged the planting of more trees, and stressed how 'absolutely necessary' it was 'to forbid the cutting down and destroying of trees.' By apprenticeship, as a special magistrate reported in 1837, wood was a 'very scarce article here.'[53]

The charcoal or 'fuel wood' Barbadians used for cooking was imported or locally produced from trees or brushwood in the rural areas or plantations. Owners of plantations or small farms legally sold their own firewood in the towns, but some slaves (and poor whites) also illegally traded in charcoal or firewood they had stolen from plantation woodlands. Although wood and charcoal scarcities probably meant that slaves sometimes lacked cooking fuel or acquired it illegally, the wooded areas of many plantations were important sources of firewood and housing materials; although not literally in the 'Negro yard,' they definitely were features of the slave settlement.

Burial grounds

Apart from the houses, gardens, and water and wood sources, other features of the settlement complex were gravesites and cemeteries, and later in the slave period sick houses or plantation hospitals, as well as chapels and schools. Documentary evidence is very strong that the overwhelming majority of the several hundred thousand slaves who perished in Barbados from the seventeenth century to emancipation were buried on their plantations —either under houses within the slave villages or in separate cemeteries not far from the villages. In 1676, for example, Governor Jonathan Atkins wrote that slaves buried 'one another in the ground of the plantation where they die and not without ceremonies of their own.' Over a century later Governor Parry described, albeit in ethnocentric phrasing, how:

Negroes are superstitiously attached to the burial places of their ancestors and friends. These are generally as near as can be to the houses in which they live. It is frequent to inter a near relation under the bed-place on which they sleep, an unwholesome and dangerous practice which they would think it the utmost tyranny to alter . . . and to remove their habitations unto healthier spots, has been found, from that very attachment . . . a most dangerous experiment.[54]

Additional evidence for the interment of slaves in plantation cemeteries is to be found in replies to questions raised in 1828 by a London-based Anglican missionary society. The island's parochial rectors were asked, 'in what places are slaves usually interred?' Replies included, for example, the one from St Michael that 'slaves are always interred in places set apart for that purpose on each plantation;' in St Joseph, the 'slaves are usually interred in their burial-places on the estates;' and in St Lucy 'on the plantations to which they belong.' Even though Anglican influence far surpassed that of any other Christian denomination (e.g., Moravians and Methodists), its influence on slave burial practices was relatively small. For most of the slave period relatively few slaves, particularly plantation inhabitants, were baptised. Since baptism was a prerequisite to church burial, few slaves were buried in Anglican cemeteries. In brief, as Dr John Davy learned during his residence in Barbados in the late 1840s, the 'majority' of Barbadian slaves 'were not . . . interred in consecrated ground, but in some spot apart on the estate of the proprietor.'[55]

Archaeological research on Barbadian plantations during the early 1970s and in 1987 failed to provide evidence for under- or near-house burials, a practice of very clear African origin.[56] However, research at Newton discovered a slave cemetery close to the site of the former slave village. Importantly, the Newton cemetery is the only case that permits identifying the specific location of a slave cemetery on a particular plantation. I am unaware of any sources, such as maps or other documentary evidence, that show or describe the location of a cemetery on any specific plantation, although a few sources suggest an area in the general vicinity of the slave village or mill yard. Even the abundant documentation on Newton fails to mention the very cemetery whose existence was so clearly demonstrated by archaeological research.[57] Occasional oral information supplied by Barbadians also supports archaeological and historical data that plantation cemeteries once existed. Yet, such information is generally inconclusive with respect to the specific location of these cemeteries. Newton is the only case where oral evidence actually located a cemetery on a particular plantation. Field interviews as well as archaeological efforts in 1987 failed to locate another.

Historical sources provide no evidence that slave cemeteries were marked. Moreover, surface observations and field investigations on contemporary Barbadian plantations, as well as occasional oral evidence from plantation personnel, all suggest that slave graveyards lacked fences, gravestones or other readily observable features that identified them as burial grounds. The Newton experience indicates that earthen and stone mounds were occasionally constructed over grave sites, but the heavy grass cover on uncultivated fields in Barbados today makes it difficult to observe such mounds and be certain if they, indeed, contain burials or are not merely piles of rubble removed from a field.[58]

Planters determined the location of a cemetery area (as was the case when a 'Negro yard' was established), and then, as with house spots within the village, I assume slaves decided the specific grave sites within that area. These assumptions are based on, first, the fact that plantation managements dictated land use patterns, perhaps choosing as burial sites agriculturally marginal lands — as at Newton — and perhaps even taking into consideration the value that slaves attached to having their dead buried close to their villages. Secondly, it is important to stress that Barbadian slaves, as those elsewhere in the Americas, were relatively free to bury their dead according to their own customs and inclinations. Moreover, the likelihood that slaves decided specific burial sites within the cemetery area is also supported by the archaeological findings at Newton. Variation among the Newton burials and their scattering around the cemetery area (some were solitary field burials without mounds, others were interred in mounds) strongly suggest that the slaves themselves decided who would be buried where. How these specific decisions were made cannot be determined.[59]

In brief, although Newton remains the only slave cemetery yet discovered in Barbados (and to this day is still the earliest and largest undisturbed plantation cemetery reported in the Americas), documentary evidence clearly shows that Barbadian plantations contained separate areas for slave interments, and that most slaves (even some of the baptised minority) were buried in these cemeteries or within the village itself. Given the important role played by the dead or the ancestors, these burial sites were intrinsic and vital features of the village complex.[60]

Sick houses, chapels, and schools

Throughout the period of slavery, including the emancipation period, slaves largely attempted to care for their own medical needs. However, by the late eighteenth and early nineteenth centuries, with the impending, then actual, abolition of the slave trade, there was a growing planter interest in the natural increase of the slave population and its health and medical care. Barbadian slave laws did not provide for slave medical care (or for their housing or food); this was left to the inclinations of individual owners, and plantation medical expenditures were intimately linked to how planters defined their economic self-interests. Some expenditure went to hiring white medical practitioners; others to the purchase of medications or special foods; still others to the construction and maintenance of the so-called sick house or plantation hospital. As the term indicates, this was a small building in which ill slaves and lying-in women were confined. The sick house was administered on a daily basis by the sick nurse, usually one of the plantation's older, even elderly, female slaves (sometimes poor white women were hired instead). She was charged with cooking and otherwise caring for the hospitalised. The sick house was also visited by white medical practitioners when they made their regular plantation rounds, or when they were sent for on special occasions.[61]

There is little indication that sick houses existed in Barbados (or other areas of the West Indies) during the seventeenth century and for most of the eighteenth. However, by the late eighteenth century, and especially in the pre-emancipation decades of the nineteenth, sick houses were common on larger plantations, although they were probably lacking on many of the smaller ones.[62] The sick house was located in or near the plantation yard, within the general vicinity of the mansion house and not very far from the 'Negro yard.' Today in Barbados, there are still some plantations with a 'Hospital field;' this field is located near the plantation yard.[63]

Many sick houses were probably very dismal and similar to the one described in 1796 by Sampson Wood, Newton's manager, as 'a horrid unhealthy hole.' As elsewhere in the West Indies, they were generally poorly ventilated, hot, dirty, damp, and lacking rooms or compartments that separated people with contagious disease as well as by sex. Although sick houses improved somewhat during the few decades before emancipation, many left a great deal to be desired even by the standards of the period. The observations of J.B. Colthurst, a stipendiary magistrate, indicate what sick houses were like on many small plantations during apprenticeship; they also suggest what in earlier years must have been widespread on larger plantations as well. In his 1836 'observations upon the defective state of the hospital system, particularly upon small estates,' Colthurst reported:

> On the large ones, the hospitals are comfortable and airy buildings . . . but it is far otherwise on the small ones. They are wretched in the extreme . . . Indeed in many instances the sick apprentice, on going into the sick-house, becomes a close prisoner; the windows (if there happen to be any), closely shut, the door locked and the key taken away . . . This system is one of the remnants of slavery . . . It therefore sometimes happens that the apprentice, though ill, will continue to work, to the injury of his health, sooner than go into hospital. If he does go, he becomes a prisoner, and when the medical attendant says he is fit for labour he is compelled to resume it.[64]

Colthurst gives some insight into the negative reactions of slaves to these sick houses, and in the 1840s, Dr James Bovell also wrote how the plantation 'hospitals . . . were peremptorily abandoned by the newly emancipated, notwithstanding endeavors . . . made to induce the people to accept of medical aid and attendance free of expense to them.'[65] However comfortable whites might have viewed these structures, the evidence indicates that slaves felt otherwise and, as elsewhere in the West Indies, frequently resisted going to the hospitals, preferring to stay in their own houses when sick.

Plantation chapels and schools only began to appear in the last decade or so before emancipation; they were located near the mill yard. It is not known if special structures were erected for schools, but they were largely absent until the very late 1820s. They provided what planters considered appropriate Christian education, and sometimes reading instruction, primarily to slave children. By 1828, at least some plantations in all parishes (but a definite minority in each) afforded Christian instruction on a regular basis. In 1833, shortly before emancipation, approximately 50 plantations held daily schools, and many of the 50 included instruction in reading. Plantation chapels were rarer still. Aside from the one at Codrington, others were occasionally established very late in the slave period. For example, in returns by the parish rectors in 1830, most did not mention plantation chapels. However, in St James there was 'a small building on the estate of Sir Osborne Gibbes, where Divine Service is read every Sunday morning to the Negroes, by the overseer of the estate.' In Christ Church, there was 'one private chapel on the estate of Edward H. Senhouse, Esq. for the instruction of his slaves in religion,' and 'one Methodist chapel [for slaves] erected on the estate of William Reece.'[66]

Slave settlements: numbers and demographic features

This section addresses the possible number of plantation settlements in Barbados, the number of houses in each, and some of the basic demographic features of the settlements. There are no estimates of the number of such settlements at different periods of time, so the number must be estimated indirectly by ascertaining the number of plantations. The sources often identify many small land units in Barbados as plantations, but these units lacked sugar mills or 'sugar works,' and their owners milled their cane at neighbouring plantations. For purposes of this paper, land units with at least one sugar mill (some had two, a few had three) are considered medium and large plantations. Only a small set of figures give a direct idea of the number of such plantations at different periods: in 1683-84, there were 358; in 1717-21, 405; in 1771–73, about 400; and in 1822 and 1834, 302 and 399, respectively. Using these figures and estimates from narrative sources as well as maps, a simple method was devised for roughly estimating the number of medium and large plantations. On average, then, and despite fluctuations in ownership and acreage, I estimate that Barbados contained close to 400 medium and large plantations from around the late 1660s to 1834; by extension, there were probably a comparable number of slave settlements. However, many smaller plantation units had at least a few slave houses on them. If these smaller units were to be included in an estimate of plantation settlements, then obviously the number would be much greater than the 400 estimated for medium and large units.[67]

Statistics on the slave populations of individual plantations at various time periods yield some idea of settlement size. For the seventeenth century, a randomly collected sample of 20 plantations from 1650 to 1693 gave an average population of 64, ranging from seven to 150. Some 'Negro yards' were even larger: for example, Nicholas Abbey in 1686 had 157 slaves, and Antoine Biet claimed that some plantations in 1654 contained from 200 to 300.[68]

Another set of data, randomly collected on 177 plantations from 1727 to 1834, show that settlements averaged about 142 persons, ranging from 20 to 350; during the 1820s, another group of 20 plantations averaged 229 slaves per plantation. Four other plantations averaged close to 200 slaves during the approximately two decades preceding emancipation.[69] The size of slave settlements and their frequency distribution are also indicated by individual plantation statistics. For 197 plantations from 1650 to 1834, about one-third had 100 or fewer slaves, close to 50 per cent had from 101 to 200, and close to 16 per cent from 201 to 300; only 1.5 per cent had over 300 slaves.[70] In 1832–34, about 46 per cent of Barbadian slaves lived on holdings of 100 or fewer, 32 per cent from 101 to 200, 18 per cent from 201 to 300, and almost 4 per cent were on holdings that exceeded 300 persons.[71] Thus, from at least the 1700s to 1834, I estimate that most settlements on medium and large plantations probably held between 100 and 200 people, and a significant number had populations in the 200s; settlements exceeding 300 people were relatively rare.

How many houses were found in the settlements on medium and large plantations? Pinckard described one village with 'sixteen families,' and it can be assumed that each 'family' had its own house.[72] A 1719 map of Drax Hall and Drax Hope shows 27 or 28 houses and 6 houses respectively, but it is not known if the map-maker intended to depict the actual number of houses or merely to give a generalised idea of the village. The same problem exists with other plantation maps that detail the houses; on a sketch of Staple Grove in 1818, 12 houses are shown, while 18 houses are sketched for Cottage Plantation in 1845 (the latter, although post-emancipation, clearly shows the slave village before it was removed).

A more accurate idea of the number of houses in a settlement derives from data on a group of six plantations over the period 1796–1833. These are the only cases of which I am aware in which both the number of houses *as well as* the size of the slave population are specified for the same plantations. The number of houses ranged from 30 to nearly 80, averaging about 55. In addition, an 1838 inventory of the 203-acre Lightfoot Plantation (St John and St Philip) mentions 27 houses in the plantation's 'Negro village newly built;' although the inventory post-dates emancipation, the village was clearly constructed during slavery.[73]

Another idea of the number of houses in a settlement can be gained by applying estimates of household size. Following conventional social anthropological usage, by household I mean the residential unit, that is, the group of people who live together in the same house. Sometimes households contained members of the same family, sometimes not. In either case, data on household size are very limited. The six-plantation group mentioned above provides the best available data and yields an average of about 3.8 persons (range 2.9 to 5.6) per household (see note 73). This figure is independently supported by an estimate given in the 1820s by William Sharp, a prominent Barbadian planter; he reported 'an average number of about four persons inhabiting each house.'[74]

Assuming that slave households averaged about four persons, it can be roughly estimated that on many medium and large plantations there were fewer than 25 houses, and on a more consequential number of units, with populations from 100 to 200, the settlements contained from 25 to 50 houses. The significant number of settlements with populations numbering in the 200s contained up to around 75 houses. It is doubtful that many plantations exceeded 80 houses. In 1833, for example, Vaucluse was among Barbados' largest plantations, consisting of 'nearly 600 acres' and 'more than 300' slaves. At this time, less than 4 per cent of the island's slaves lived in population units of this size, and the Vaucluse settlement had 'nearly 80 houses.'[75] In any event, with so many plantations containing much more than just a handful of houses, it is not surprising that writers could refer to the settlements as 'little villages,' 'little towns,' 'small towns,' or the 'Negro town.'

Sex and age distribution

During the mid-1670s, the Barbadian slave population as a whole (including town dwellers) was about equally divided between males and females, with a slight preponderance of the latter. This island-wide demographic picture continued over the duration of the slave period and was reflected in the sexual composition of the average plantation settlement. As Governor Parry reported, 'most plantations' contained 'a greater number of females than males;' this estimate is generally supported by statistical data from individual plantations.[76]

There are no island-wide figures for the age structure of the slave population prior to 1817, but demographic data on individual plantations give an idea of the distribution of ages in the settlements. However, when the ages of slaves on individual plantations were recorded in earlier periods they were invariably given by the categories of men, women, boys, and girls. In a sample I collected at random on 43 plantations from 1781 to 1834, adults (presumably people 16 years or older) averaged about 59 per cent. In another study, Ronald Hughes presents data on 92 plantations from 1671 to 1816; adults averaged about 67 per cent on these plantations. And in the late 1780s, on a group of 22 plantations Barbadian authorities considered as representative, adults comprised about 61 per cent of the 3,116 slaves.[77]

Whatever the specific age structure on a given plantation at a particular period, the settlements contained several age groupings, including infants, small children, teenagers, young and mature adults, and the relatively elderly. Only the very first and very last of these categories were exempt from plantation labour, but all contributed, in one way or another, to the life of the community and the social roles within it.

The slave settlement as a small community

Reflecting a pattern found on sugar plantations throughout the Americas, the Barbadian slave settlement with its relatively small population, density, and the proximity of dwellings made for a compact social unit or community. Within this community it is unlikely that many activities went unnoticed, and there was great physical and, undoubtedly, psychological intimacy as well.

In 1796, George Pinckard provided a detailed, albeit romanticised and patronising, description of this community and its general ambiance. Observing that the crops slaves cultivated and the stock they raised in the settlements 'afford them occupation and amusement for their leisure moments,' he continues:

The negro-yard, viewed from a short distance, forms an object of highly interesting and picturesque scenery. It comprizes all the little huts, intermixed with, and more or less concealed by, the variety of shrubs and fruit trees ... ; likewise the many small patches of garden ground around them, and the different species of stock, some appearing in pens, some tied by the leg, or the neck, and some running at large. And if it be evening, you have also the crowd of negroes, male and female, as they chance to be seen, at rest, or moving in busy occupation, some passing from hut to hut, some dancing to their favorite music, some sitting at the door with the pipe in their mouths, and others smoking their loved sagar under the broad leaf of the plantain. The picture is also further enlivened by the groups of little black children; some running and skipping about, some seated, playing before the doors, in nature's ebon dress, and some, unable to walk, attempting little pedestrian excursions upon their hands and feet. Perhaps within so small a space, few scenes could offer so much to interest a contemplative mind; or to aid the pencil of a painter of the picturesque.[78]

Another idyllic and somewhat pastoral view of the slave village is illustrated in an early nineteenth-century engraving, although it shows details of slave housing and various activities.[79] Both Pinckard's description and the illustration mask a reality that was far less picturesque. They do not show the abject material conditions under which slaves carried out their daily lives, the dilapidation of their housing, their tattered and worn clothing, the hunger they often suffered, the blandness (and often inadequacy) of their food rations, the contaminated water they frequently drank. They also obscure the illness and infirmities that were widespread in the villages.

The village was central to the everyday life of plantation slaves and was a community in the sociological sense, viz. a 'distinct unit and of such a size that its inhabitants can all be personally acquainted.'[80] Small communities of this kind existed in all Caribbean sugar plantation areas, but in Barbados, with its many plantation and farm units, small land area, relatively easy topography and well-developed road network, the communities were not very far from one another and slaves from different plantations were in regular contact. Many leisure-time or recreational activities were not confined to the settlements, and despite laws designed to curtail their movements, slaves left their communities and attended markets in town or the countryside, weekend dances at neighbouring plantations, or visited kinsmen and friends elsewhere. Yet, on a day-to-day basis and outside of the plantation labour regimen during the work week, most of the activities in which slaves voluntarily engaged took place within their small communities.

Within these communities households were formed, crucial family connections could be established (though kinship or family ties often extended to other plantations or the towns), children were born and named, the dead were prepared for burial and interred, and various religious practices took place. Other leisure and domestic activities that occurred in the communities included food preparation and consumption, diagnosis and treatment of illness, nursing and care of small children, cultivation of garden plots, and making and repairing household utensils and furniture. Games and gambling, tobacco and alcohol consumption, musical activities, gossiping and visiting among kinsmen and friends also took place within the communities. The settlements were also places where revolts or other forms of resistance were plotted, runaway or fugitive kinsmen or friends from other plantations were hidden, and goods stolen from plantation storehouses or provision grounds were traded or consumed.

Although historical sources rarely provide explicit details on the internal organisation and life of the plantation community, they suggest an array of interpersonal conflicts that would be found in many small communities. Such conflicts could stem from, for example, sexual jealousies, disagreements over ownership of material goods, or the belief that food had been stolen from a garden plot. More generally, disagreements or conflicts within the communities could evolve into verbal arguments, physical assaults, or even murder. Indeed, interpersonal conflicts and community tensions were reflected in witchcraft or sorcery accusations, and the apparently frequent incidents of people believing themselves the victims of malevolent magical practices.[81]

However, cooperation between individuals or households was just as much a part of community life. For example, because of their high combustibility, houses were vulnerable to fire and, particularly when fanned by winds, fire could spread rapidly within the compact settlement. Cooperative endeavours were a community response to an ever-present threat of fire. Joseph Senhouse described how as soon as an accidental fire in a slave house was discovered, 'the bell was rung to alarm the neighborhood & the Negroes of the adjoining plantations as well as those of this estate (as is customary on such occasions) immediately repaired in crowds to the spot to give their assistance.'[82] Other cooperative labour forms may have extended to, for example, house construction, assistance in the care and nursing of infants and small children, and cultivation of the garden plots.

Within their communities, slaves had a variety of roles and specialties that were defined by their own cultural needs and were independent of the occupational roles that served plantation labour demands and interests. Such roles were associated with, for example, kinship, affinity, and friendship; music, crafts of one kind or another, haircutting, dentistry, storytelling, and midwifery. An important member of the community was the Obeah person or 'Negro doctor,' involved in the diagnosis and curing of illness; there were also people accused of practising evil magic. In the later years of the slave period, literate slaves taught others to read, and converts to Christianity proselytised among their peers. A Moravian missionary, for example, observed how one slave used his 'superior station' on the plantation to 'encourage the Negroes to come to church.'[83] Some people, through their personalities or special talents, were able to influence others in planning of revolts or other forms of resistance, and despite limited direct information, there were undoubtedly persons whose wisdom and advice were solicited on more mundane problems and in the adjudication of disputes with which plantation managements were not concerned.

Conclusion

Many features of the Barbadian plantation slave settlement were not unique to the island and were broadly shared by sugar plantations throughout the West Indies. In Barbados, as elsewhere, fundamental social and material patterns that emerged in plantation settlements during the era of slavery were to have considerable impact on post-emancipation rural life; major features of these settlements were to endure far into the post-emancipation period. The slave village, then, was a social unit of great significance to understanding the island's long history and particularly the impact of the slave era on rural life for many years after emancipation.

Notes

1. Ronald Hughes, Philip Morgan, and Fred Smith commented on earlier drafts of this paper, completed while I was a Senior Fellow at the Virginia Foundation for the Humanities, Charlottesville.

2. *PP*, XXVI (1789), Part 3, David Parry, Replies to Queries, in 'Report of the Lords of the Committee of Council . . . Concerning the Present State of the Trade to Africa . . .;' Barry W. Higman, *Slave Populations of the British Caribbean, 1807-1834* (Baltimore: The Johns Hopkins University Press, 1984), 50.

3. Jerome S. Handler, ed., 'Father Antoine Biet's Visit to Barbados in 1654,' *JBMHS*, 32 (1967): 55; Thomas Towns, 'An Extract of a Letter of Mr Lister Containing Some Observations made at the Barbadoes [March 26, 1675],' *Philosophical Transactions of the Royal Society of London*, X (1676): 400; CO 1/21, 'Some Observations on the Island Barbadoes,' 1667; see also, Jean Baptiste Labat, *Nouveau Voyage aux Isles de l'Amérique*, 6 Vols. (Paris: Theodore et Guillaume Cavelier, 1722), IV, 413.

4. Henry Holder, *A Short Essay on the Subject of Negro Slavery with a Particular Reference to the Island of Barbadoes.* (London: Couchman and Fry, for C. Dilly, 1788), 23; John Oldmixon, *The British Empire in America*, 2 Vols. (London, 1741), II, 131; William Douglass, *A Summary, Historical, and Political of the . . . British Settlements in North America*, 2 Vols. (Boston and London, 1755), I, 118; also, for example, George Pinckard, *Notes on the West Indies*, 3 Vols. (London: Longman, Hurst, Rees & Orme,

1806), I, 289; *PP*, XXVI (1789), David Parry, 'Extract of a Letter from Governor Parry to . . . Lord Sydney, August 18, 1788,' 17; Barbados Council, Replies to Queries, in 'Report of the Lords of the Committee of Council;' Estate Inventory of Robert Hooper, September 12, 1654, in 'Hooper of Barbados,' *JBMHS*, 7 (1940): 71.

5. E.g., Barbados Legislature, House of Assembly, *The Report from a Select Committee of the House of Assembly, Appointed to Inquire into the Origin, Causes and Progress of the Late Insurrection* (1817;London: T. Cadell and W. Davies, 1818), 32; *Barbados Mercury and Bridgetown Gazette*, June 11, 1805; BDA, R1/3a, b, Plan of a Section of Constant Plantation, St. George, 1739-1740 (see also, Deeds Record Book R1/90, fols. 128-29); J.W. Jordan, *An Account of the Management of Certain Estates in the Island of Barbados* (London, 1824), 4; University of London Library, Newton Estate Papers 523/129, 'Boiling House Account,' Newton Plantation, 1799; Ibid., 523/290, Wood, 'Report on the Buildings at Newton,' June 24, 1796; Pinckard, I, 287-88, 368-69; *Minutes of the Society for the Improvement of Plantership in the Island of Barbados, Instituted December 8th, 1804* (Liverpool: Printed by Thos. Kaye, 1811), passim; Raymond Richards Collection of Miscellaneous Historical Documents, University of Keele Library, Staffordshire, England, 'Minute Book of the Society for the Improvement of West India Plantership, 1811-1812 and of the Agricultural Society, 1812-1816' [June 1, 1811- April 6, 1816], passim.

6. E.g., Meliora, *Letters on the Labouring Population of Barbadoes* (London, 1858), passim.

7. Jerome Handler, *Searching for a Slave Cemetery in Barbados, West Indies: A Bioarchaeological and Ethnohistorical Investigation* (Research Paper No. 59. Carbondale: Center for Archaeological Investigations, Southern Illinois University, 1989), 17-19.

8. Alexander Gunkel and Jerome Handler, eds., 'A German Indentured Servant in Barbados in 1652: the Account of Heinrich von Uchteritz,' *JBMHS*, 33.3 (1970): 92; [William Senhouse], 'The Autobiographical Manuscript of William Senhouse,' [1787] *JBMHS*, 3 (1935-36): 14; Pinckard, I, 287; Newton Estate Papers 523/290, 'Buildings at Newton;' cf. Jerome S. Handler and Frederick W. Lange, *Plantation Slavery in Barbados: An Archaeological and Historical Investigation* (Cambridge: Harvard University Press, 1978), 60-61; Handler, *Searching for a Cemetery*, 17-18.

9. These maps include The Bay, Cottage, Dayrells, Drax Hall, Drax Hope, Lambert, Searles, Staple Grove, and Stepney (see note 16). Cf. B.W. Higman, *Jamaica Surveyed: Plantation Maps and Plans of the Eighteenth and Nineteenth Centuries* (Kingston: Institute of Jamaica Publications, 1988).

10. Handler and Lange, 43-45; see also Handler, *Searching for a Cemetery*, Figures 2-6.
11. See John Chandler, 'Plantation Field Names in Barbados,' *JBMHS*, 32 (1968): 133-43; J. Graham Cruickshank, 'Field Names in Barbados,' *JBMHS*, 2 (1935): 166; 'Old Plantation Customs,' *JBMHS*, 7 (1940): 109-15. The custom of naming fields, as well as the field system itself, undoubtedly derives from ancient English agricultural practices (see, for example, William Hoskins, *The Making of the English Landscape* (London: Hodder and Stoughton, 1988), 12, 22; Trevor Rowley, *Villages in the [English] Landscape* (London: Dent and Sons, 1978), 166; Christopher Taylor, *Fields in the English Landscape* (London: Dent and Sons, 1975), 78, passim.
12. The unique drawing of Ashford, captioned 'Ashford. The Estate of Henry Hart, Esq. Barbados' (see cover illustration and Figure 1 of this volume), was made by a teen-age girl between 1837 and 1845. However, the basic settlement pattern of the slave period is still quite evident. The drawing clearly shows the mansion house (still standing today, although modified over the years) and the yard, including the windmill, sugar buildings, pond, and, located between the mansion house and pond, the houses of some of the labourers or ex-slaves (I am grateful to Mrs Mildred Hart Higgins for permission to publish this drawing; for more details, see Handler and Lange, 297, note 3). For examples of plantation maps that show the location of the 'Negro yard,' see Handler and Lange, Figures 3 and 4; Handler, *Searching for a Cemetery*, Figures 2-7). In a well-known historical geography of the West Indies, David Watts errs when he writes that non-household slaves lived in houses 'placed at some distance away from the plantation house and mill complex' *The West Indies*, (Cambridge: Cambridge University Press, 1987) 193.
13. E.g., Rowley, 107; Richard S. Dunn, *Sugar and Slaves* (Chapel Hill: University of North Carolina Press, 1972), 262, 290-91.
14. Newton Estate Papers 523/288, Wood, 'Report on the Negroes [at Newton],' July 1796. As was reported in the eighteenth century for the West Indies in general, 'the habitations of the slaves, on every estate, are situated near the dwelling-house of the owner, or overseer; that they may be under more immediate inspection' (Robert Norris, *Memoirs of the Reign of Bossa Ahádee . . . and Short Account of the African Slave Trade*, 1789; London: Frank Cass, 1968, 176); also, for Jamaica, see Barry W. Higman, *Montpelier, Jamaica: A Plantation Community in Slavery and Freedom, 1739-1912* (Kingston, Jamaica: The Press, UWI, 1998), 100. Cf. Jerome S. Handler, 'Slave Revolts and Conspiracies in Seventeenth Century Barbados,' *NWIG*, 56 (1982): 5-43; Ibid., 'Escaping Slavery in a Caribbean Plantation Society: Marronage in

Barbados, 1650s-1830s,' *NWIG*, 71 (1997): 183-225.

15. Ronald Hughes, personal communication, March 1990; Native of the West Indies, *Poems on Subjects Arising in England, and the West Indies* (London, 1783), 11.

16. Modern plantation maps, copies of which were obtained from the plantations themselves, and/or interviews and field observations in the 1970s and 1980s provided information on Bissex (St Joseph), Burnt House (St Andrew), Claybury (St John), Four Hills (St Peter), Hanson (St George), Lancaster (St James), Malvern (St John), Morgan Lewis (St Andrew), Newton (Christ Church), Nicholas Abbey (St Peter), Parks (St Joseph), Todds (St John), Vaucluse (St Thomas), and Yorkshire (Christ Church). Plantation maps dating from the slave, apprenticeship, or post-emancipation periods (some depicting the slave houses themselves, rather than merely indicating the 'Negro yard' areas) and held by the BDA include Cottage (St George, 1845), Drax Hall and Drax Hope (St George, 1719), and Searles and Dayrells (Christ Church, 1815). Maps held by the Barbados Museum yielded data on The Bay (St Michael, 1822), Husbands (St Lucy, 1835), Sandy Lane (St James, 1797), Staple Grove (Christ Church, 1818), and Stepney (St George, 1794). Information also derived from post-emancipation nineteenth-century maps, usually based on earlier surveys, that are still privately held by the plantations themselves: Guinea (St John, 1857), Lamberts (St Peter/St Lucy, 1854), Lowthers (Christ Church, 1825), and Oughterson (St Philip, 1938).

17. Pinckard, I, 287; Newton Estate Papers 523/290, 'Buildings at Newton;' Society for the Propagation of the Gospel in Foreign Parts, *Annual Report* (London, 1836), 48.

18. E.g., Labat, 413; Pinckard, I, 368-69; Joseph Sturge and Thomas Harvey, *The West Indies in 1837* (London: Hamilton, Adams, 1838), 2, 62.

19. Handler, 'Biet', 289; Douglass, 118; Parry 'Extract of a Letter,' 17; Pinckard, I, 287; J.A. Thome and J. H. Kimball, *Emancipation in the West Indies* (New York: American Anti-Slavery Society, 1838), 56; Holder, 23; Society for the Propagation of the Gospel, *Annual Report*, 1836, 48; see also Barbados Council, Replies to Queries; James C. Brandow, ed., 'Diary of Joseph Senhouse' [1776-1778], *JBMHS*, 37 (1986): 403-04.

20. Historical data for individual plantations usually do not specify the 'Negro yard' acreage alone, but give a total for the mill yard and 'Negro yard' combined. This figure often includes roads and non-agricultural features. For example, none of Newton's records specifies the acreage of the slave village, but in 1796 the manager estimated that 'the Negro houses, buildings [of the yard], etc. stand on an area

of about twenty or twenty odd acres' (Newton Estate Papers 523/
290, 'Buildings at Newton'). A 1739-1740 plan (R1/3b) in the BDA
shows a portion of Constant (St George), and records as a little under
12 acres 'the land about ye sugar work, other buildings and the Negroe
houses.' For other typical examples, see *Minutes of Society for
Improvement of Plantership, 1804*, 85; Minute Book of Society for
Improvement of West India Plantership . . . 1811-16, 270, 290, 295.

21. *Minutes of Society for Improvement of Plantership, 1804*, 136; 'Minute
Book of Society for Improvement of West India Plantership . . ., 1811-
16,' 43.

22. Higman, *Slave Populations*, 219, 221.

23. The Barbadian situation does not seem very different from the one
described by Higman for a Jamaican sugar plantation: 'Whereas the
proprietors of Montpelier controlled the location of the villages and
held the ultimate authority to decide who should live within them,
they intervened much less in deciding how the houses should be laid
out and who should occupy each house. [But] they left no evidence of
explicit instructions on these questions' (*Montpelier*, 127).

24. Rowley, 33-36,110; Hoskins, 55. Cf. Brian K. Roberts, *Rural Settlement
in Britain* (Folkestone, Eng.: Dawson and Sons, 1977), passim.

25. Higman, *Jamaica Surveyed*, 244; Susan Denyer, *African Traditional
Architecture* (New York: Africana Publishing, 1978), 19, 20. Cf. Paul
Bohannan and Philip Curtin, *Africa and Africans* (Garden City, N.Y.:
Natural History Press, 1971), 120.

26. Oldmixon, II, 131; Douglass, 118; Society for the Propagation of the
Gospel , *Annual Report*, 1836, 48.

27. Labat, 413; Philip Gibbes, *Instructions for the Treatment of Negroes, etc.
etc. etc.* (London, 1786), 20; Senhouse, 'Autobiographical Manuscript,'
14; Pinckard, I, 289.

28. Rowley, 130-31, 133-35, 137. Cf. Hoskins, 17, 41-42.

29. Higman, *Jamaica Surveyed*, 244. Cf., for example, Society for the
Propagation of the Gospel, *Annual Report*, 1836, 48.

30. Pinckard, I, 287-88; Bryan Edwards, *The History, Civil and Commercial
of the British Colonies in the West Indies*, 4 Vols. (Philadelphia, 1810), II,
349. Cf. Edward Brathwaite, *The Development of Creole Society in Jamaica,
1770-1820* (Oxford: Clarendon, 1971), 234-35; Higman, *Montpelier*, 146
ff.

31. Information on Barbados house types is drawn from Jerome Handler,
'Housing, House Types, and Furnishings of Barbados Plantation Slaves'
(Unpublished Manuscript, 1997, BDA). See also Kwamina Dickson, *A
Historical Geography of Ghana* (London: Cambridge University Press,
1969), 51, 52, 61, 284, Figure 45. There are many more architectural
details available for Jamaican wattle-and-daub houses. For a discussion

of possible cultural influences on these houses (as well as other housing types), some of which is relevant to Barbados see Higman, *Montpelier*, 153-59, 182-90. Cf. Juanita Anderson, 'Houses of the Enslaved Africans in the Caribbean and Southern United States' (Unpublished Manuscript, Department of Anthropology, Southern Illinois University, Carbondale, 1978); Jay Edwards, 'The Evolution of Vernacular Architecture in the Western Caribbean,' in S.J.K. Wilkerson, ed., *Cultural Traditions and Caribbean Identity* (Gainesville: Center for Latin American Studies, University of Florida, 1980, Figure 4).

32. *Barbados Mercury*, March 4, 1788; William Belgrove, *A Treatise Upon Husbandry or Planting* (Boston, 1755), 31. Cf. Newton Estate Papers 523/290, 'Buildings at Newton;' 'Minute Book of Society for Improvement of West India Plantership . . ., 1811-16,' 111.

33. Handler, 'Housing;' Higman, *Slave Populations*, 220, 244; Thomas Cochrane, *Notes on the Minerology, Government and Condition of the British West India Islands* (London: Ridgway, 1851), 50. Cf. Ronald Hughes, 'Sweet Bottom, St. George, Barbados: An Early (1777) Non-White Freehold Village,' *JBMHS*, 36 [1981]: 270. For a similar progression of housing types in Jamaica, see Higman, *Montpelier*, 160-61.

34. James Stephen, *The Slavery of the British West India Colonies*, 2 Vols. (London, 1824-30), II, 261. At least by the nineteenth century, and probably for many years earlier, slave dependence on plantation rations was greater in Barbados than in the other West Indian territories (Higman, *Slave Populations*, 205, 210).

35. Some sources suggest that planters usually assigned plots to 'each adult Negro' or 'the grown people,' but the most common practice seems to have been allocating land to each household, regardless of household size (Joshua Steele, 'Queries from . . . Governor Parry, Answered by a Planter of 1068 Acres,' *PP*, XXVI (1789), 25; Beilby Porteus, *An Essay Towards a Plan for the more Effectual Civilization and Conversion of the Negroe Slaves, on the Trust Estate in Barbadoes* (London: Printed by T. Cadell and W. Davies, 1807) 195-96; Barbados Assembly, *Report of the Slave Trade*, 4; Barbados Council, *Report of Slaves*, 107, 113; Borome, ed., 'William Bell,' 34; Pinckard, I, 368-69; Report of Lords 1789, query 5; Society for the Propagation of the Gospel, *Annual Report* , 1827, 216-17; Alexander Gunkel and Jerome Handler, eds., 'A Swiss Medical Doctor's Description of Barbados in 1661: The Account of Felix Christian Spoeri,' *JBMHS*, 33.1 (1969): 17; 'Treatment of Slaves in Barbadoes,' 408.

36. Parry, 'Replies to Queries.' Aside from crops grown in their house or plantation gardens, slaves also raised small livestock and poultry, collected wild plants and land and marine animals, and acquired

food through trade in the markets and by theft; however, such activities played a minor role in their diets. Moreover, despite the occasional distribution of animal products, such as imported dried salt fish and meat, their fare was overwhelmingly vegetable. Food distributed by plantations was either imported or grown on the plantations themselves, but throughout the period of slavery the island depended less on imported food than on foods grown locally. Corn, primarily Guinea corn, was by far the most important food in the slave's diet (Indian corn, or maize, played a secondary role), although during the seventeenth century potatoes and plantains (the latter was particularly significant in the seventeenth and early eighteenth centuries) were also very important. The triad of potatoes, yams, and eddoes, collectively referred to as 'roots' or 'ground provisions,' also played an important role. The potato, in particular, was relied on as a back-up food when the corn crop failed or was insufficient. Plantations occasionally distributed other vegetables, but none played a significant dietary role, although some vegetables, particularly okra (a West African domesticate), may have been more widely consumed. Okra was probably one of the crops grown in the gardens (Jerome S. Handler, 'Food and Nutrition of Barbados Plantation Slaves,' Unpublished Manuscript, 1997, BDA; Ibid., 'The Domestic Economy of Barbados Plantation Slaves: Production and Distribution,' Unpublished Manuscript, 1997, BDA). Higman notes that among the West Indian territories, at least by the nineteenth century and probably for many years before, slave dependence on plantation food rations was the greatest in Barbados (Higman, *Slave Populations*, 205, 210).

37. E.g. Parry, 'Replies to Queries,' no. 10; George R. Porter, *The Nature and Properties of the Sugar Cane* (London: Smith, Elder, and Co., 1830), 326; Henry Drax, 'Instructions for the Management of Drax-Hall and the Irish-Hope Plantations' [written in the 1670s], in Belgrove, 56; 'Odd Pages from Old Barbados' [Letters between Seale Yearwood and A. Frere, March 1796 and 26 April, 1797], *JBMHS*, 16 (1949): 114-15.

38. Pinckard, I, 368. For similar comments, see, for example, Anon., *Authentic History of the English West Indies* (London, 1810), 41; Barbados Assembly, *Report of the Insurrection*, 42; Barbados Council, *A Report of a Committee of the Council of Barbadoes, Appointed to Inquire into the Actual Condition of the Slaves in this Island* (London: W. Sior, 1824), 107, 113; Borome, ed., 'William Bell,' *JBMHS*, 30 (1962): 34; F.W.N. Bayley, *Four Years Residence in the West Indies, During the Years 1826, 7, 8, and 9* (London: William Kidd, 1832), 92; John Brathwaite, Replies to Queries, 'Report of the Lords of the Committee of Council;' 'Treatment of Slaves in Barbadoes,' *The Christian Remembrancer*, 5 (1823): 408; Forster Clarke, 'Plan of Treatment of the Negroes on the

Estates in Barbados, 1823,' *JBMHS*, 2 (1934): 30; Henry Nelson
Coleridge, *Six Months in the West Indies in 1825* (London: John Murray,
1832), 125-26; Douglass, 118; Gunkel and Handler, eds., 'Swiss Medical
Doctor's Description . . .,' *JBMHS*, 33.1 (1969): 17; Holder, 21, 23;
Griffith Hughes, *The Natural History of Barbados in Ten Books* (London:
For the Author, 1750), 171; *PP*, 1790, XXX, Robert B. Nicholls, Testimony,
in 'Minutes of the Evidence Taken Before a Committee of the House of
Commons . . . for the Abolition of the Slave Trade,' 332; [William
Naish ?], 'Notes on Slavery, Made During a Recent Visit to Barbadoes,'
The Negro's Friend, No. 18 (London, 1830), 6; Oldmixon, I, 134; Porteus,
195-96; Thomas Rolph, *A Brief Account, Together with Observations made
During a Visit in the West Indies . . . in Parts of the Years 1832-3* (Dundas,
Upper Canada, 1836), 52; Senhouse, 'Autobiographical Manuscript,'
14; Society for the Propagation of the Gospel, *Annual Report*, 1836, 48.
39. Handler, 'Domestic Economy.' All sources emphasise the very small
size of house plots, but only a few from late in the slave period provide
actual dimensions. One source reports 'a square of 60 or 80 feet to
each house;' another notes that in a new village in 1787, each house
was 'in the centre of a piece of ground 20 yards square;' and in 1828,
a 'new' village at the Codrington plantations had '100 feet square to
each house.' These figures were offered as examples of liberal
management policies, but the extent to which they represent other
Barbadian plantations during the same time period is unknown (Philip
Gibbes, *Instructions for the Treatment of Negroes, etc. etc. etc.* (1786;
reprinted with additions. London: Printed for Shepperson and
Reynolds, 1797), 121-23; Society for the Propagation of the Gospel,
Annual Report, 1827, 216-17; Senhouse, 'Autobiographical Manuscript,'
14.
Although specifically referring to Antigua, Trelawney Wentworth
reported in the 1820s that house plots were 'rigidly define[d] by stones,
or trees, and shrubs,' and implied that his comments were also
applicable to Barbados, which he had also visited. In Jamaica, Higman
writes, slaves sometimes 'set out their houses in compounds or
'"yards,"' surrounded by fences' (Trelawney Wentworth, *The West India
Sketch Book*, 2 Vols., London, 1834, II, 218; Higman, *Slave Populations*,
219). There is no information if slave houses in Barbados were
surrounded by boundary markers; yet, the practice may have existed,
at least by the emancipation period. Demarcating house spots or yard
areas with brush, hedges or fences is characteristic of present-day
Barbados.
40. Parry, 'Replies to Queries,' No. 10; Gibbes, *Instructions* (1797), 121,
123. For similar comments, see Barbados Assembly, *Barbadoes: Report
of a Committee of the General Assembly upon the Several Heads of Enquiry*

&c. Relative to the Slave Trade (London, 1790), 4; Rolph, 53.

41. The Husbands map is in the Barbados Museum; for Lowthers, see Handler and Lange, 45.

42. *Minutes of Society for Improvement of Plantership 1804*, 85; 'Minute Book of Society for Improvement of West India Plantership . . ., 1811-16,' 38; Porter, 326-27.

43. Dr. Caddell, [Report on the Health of Barbados Slaves], Meeting of 14 November 1812, in 'Minute Book of Society for Improvement of West India Plantership . . ., 1811-16;' Naish, 6. Cf. Steele, 'Queries,' 25. During apprenticeship, plantations were no longer expected to distribute food to their ex-slaves, but the law required them to allow apprentices one-half acre for growing food. Because of this, some planters took away from their apprentices 'the small gardens around the huts' (*PP*, 1837, LIII (521-1), 'Papers . . . in Explanation of the Measures Adopted by Her Majesty's Government, for Giving Effect to the Act for the Abolition of Slavery throughout the British Colonies,' 393, 394, 398, 404).

44. Richard Ligon, *A True and Exact History of the Iland of Barbados* (London, 1657), 28-29; Handler, 'Biet,' 64; Hughes, *Natural History*, 44-45. Cf., for example, Towns, 'Extract of a Letter,' 229; Neville Connell, ed., 'Father Labat's Visit to Barbados in 1700,' *JBMHS*, 24 (1957): 171; Henry J. Cadbury, ed., 'An Account of Barbados 200 Years Ago' [by John Smith], *JBMHS*, 9 (1942): 83; Richard Gardiner, *An Account of the Expedition to the West Indies* (London: Printed by Z. Stuart, 1759), 38. In the 1790s, one of Newton's 13 fields was called the 'Negro pond field,' suggesting its function as a source of water for the slaves; it is likely that similar or identical field names existed on other plantations (Newton Estate Papers 523/129, 'Boiling House at Newton').

45. E.g., James Hendy, *A Treatise on the Glandular Disease of Barbados* (London: C. Drilly, 1784), 45; Robert Jackson, *A Sketch of the History and Cure of Febrile Diseases; more Particularly as they Appear in the West-Indies among the Soldiers of the British Army* (London: Baldwin, Craddock, and Joy, 1820), II, 252; Robert Poole, *The Beneficent Bee* (London: Printed by E. Duncomb, 1753), 229.

46. Early observers noted how slaves bathed or washed in the ponds after their labours (e.g., Ligon, 28; Hughes, *Natural History*, 227; Hendy, 32). For Father Labat, writing of his visit in 1700, pond pollution resulted from such conditions as 'crabs being drowned, by the beasts which water there, by the laundry done there and by the Negroes, who never miss going to bathe there as often as they can' (Connell, 'Father Labat's Visit,' 171). Cf. Jerome S. Handler, 'Health and Medicine Among Barbadian Slaves: Diseases and Disabilities' (Unpublished Manuscript, 1997, BDA).

47. Frank C. Ramsey, *Protein-Energy Malnutrition in Barbados* (New York: Josiah Macy Jr. Foundation, 1979), 12; Linnean Society of London, Burlington House, MS. 610, Arthur Anderson, 'Barbados' [ca. 1784-1785], 2.

48. Newton Estate Papers 523/291, Wood, 'Report on the Lands of Seawell,' July 16, 1796; Ibid., 523/ 694, Haynes to Lane, May 13, 1813; Ibid., 523/849, Haynes to Lane, May 7, 1821. See also, for example, Connell, 'Father Labat's Visit,'171; Huntington Library, STG, Box 25 (No. 26), Henry Grenville to George Grenville, February 20, 1751; Ligon, 28; Brandow, 'Senhouse,'403-04; Ibid., 'Senhouse Papers,'188-89.

49. Hughes, *Natural History*, 54; Ibid., 44-45; also Towns, 'Extract of a Letter,' 229; Henry Frere, *A Short History of Barbados* (London, 1768), 126.

50. E.g., Hendy, 45; Newton Estate Papers 523/291, 'Lands of Seawell;' Brandow, 'Senhouse' (1988),188-89; Towns, 'Extract of a Letter,' 400; Gibbes, *Instructions* (1786), 24-25; 'Minute Book of Society for Improvement of West India Plantership . . ., 1811-16,' 134. Cf. W.H. Garrod, 'Our Water Supply,' *JBMHS*, 19 (1952): 107-08.

51. E.g., David Watts, *Man's Influence on the Vegetation of Barbados 1627 to 1800* (Hull, Eng: University of Hull, Occasional Papers in Geography 4, 1966), 62; Council of Trade and Plantations to the Lords Justice, September 12, 1699, in *Calendar of State Papers-Colonial Series*, 1699 (London: Public Record Office), 435-36; Journal of Council of Trade and Plantations, November 16, 1699, in *Ibid.*, 527.

52. Plantation records do not separate woodland acreage from other non-agricultural acreage. Typical examples: in 1811, Lears had about 128 acres in 'wood, wasted lands, tenements, etc;' Joe's River included over 184 acres in 'wood, tenements, waste land, 'Negro yard,' water courses, etc;' and Colleton's had 179 acres in 'wood, waste, tenements, pasture, paths, etc.' ('Minute Book of Society for Improvement of West India Plantership . . . 1811-16,' 6, 18, 29).

53. J.W. Orderson, *Directions to Young Planters for their Care and Management of a Sugar Plantation in Barbadoes* (London: T. Bensley, 1800), 5, 22, 24; 'Papers . . . in Explanation of the Measures Adopted by Her Majesty's Government,' 412. Cf. CO 30/21, Act 497, 'An Act to Prevent the Cutting Down and Destroying of Trees for the Burning of Charcoal,' March 14, 1827.

54. CO 1/37, Atkins, 'Answers to the 32 Queries by the Lords of Trade and Plantations,' July 4, 1676; Parry, 'Extract of a Letter,' 17. The Barbados Council also commented on 'the injudicious situation of their houses, which it would be dangerous to alter, on account of their superstitious attachment to the burying places of their ancestors' ('Replies to Queries'). If such reports accurately reflect the intensity of

'attachment' to family grave sites, they raise the question of what might have happened in the immediate post-emancipation period when the 'Negro yards' began to be abandoned and plantation tenantries were established. Citing an 1838 letter from the Governor of Barbados, W. Emanuel Riviere writes that ex-slaves 'revered their burial grounds to the extent that a major ambition was to die on the estates where their relations had been interred, so that they too would be buried there' ('Labour Shortage in the British West Indies After Emancipation,' *The Journal of Caribbean History*, 4 (1972): 4). The movement to the tenantries, however, does not seem to have been marked by friction or a reluctance to abandon the 'Negro yards.' This, in turn, may suggest that house burials had significantly waned, if not disappeared, by the emancipation period.

55. Society for the Conversion and Religious Instruction and Education of the Negro Slaves in the British West India Islands, 'Returns to Questions Addressed to the Clergy of the Diocese of Barbados and the Leeward Islands, up to December 31, 1828: Island of Barbados,' *Report for the Year 1828* (London, 1829); John Davy, *The West Indies, Before and Since Slave Emancipation* (London: W. and F.G. Cash, 1854), 93-94.

A 'Graveyard' field is sometimes found on present-day plantations, but it is not a very common field name. However, the historical function of Graveyard field is ambiguous, despite its seemingly obvious association with burials; moreover, it is unknown if this field name existed during the slave period. Most Barbadians that I have queried specifically on this point were uncertain why Graveyard field was so named. Some informants speculated that Graveyard received its name because it had once contained a vault or tomb of a planter family. However, no historical, archaeological or physical evidence substantiates this reasoning, and in my experience a field with such a tomb would be called Vault field. Other informants suggested that 'old time people' had been buried in Graveyard fields, but they could not provide any evidence for their opinions. Perhaps some Graveyard fields were associated with the 1854 cholera epidemic, although the field name 'Cholera,' which is not uncommon in Barbados today, is a more explicit indicator of earlier function.

A few informants opined that Graveyard fields were thus named because in the 'old days' large animals were buried in them. Once again, these informants could not provide direct or hearsay evidence for the actual discovery of bones, or an oral tradition on the plantation. Others emphatically denied that plantation animals were buried in only one plantation locale; they maintained that animals were buried all over a plantation, wherever the soil was sufficiently deep to prevent carcasses from being easily exhumed by dogs. The historical function of Graveyard fields remains problematical. For a more detailed discussion of Graveyard fields, see Handler, *Searching for a Cemetery*, 18-19.

56. House burials clearly continued African practices. Although communal burial grounds belonging to particular family groups were common in Africa, interment in the compound of the deceased or under his house or room had a wide geographical range which included many cultural groups. Where house burial existed it was usually not the only type of grave site found in the society. Burials under the houses or in 'adjacent plots of ground' were also reported from elsewhere in the West Indies, and Douglas Armstrong has provided unique archaeological evidence for house burials in Jamaica (Wentworth, II, 219-20. Cf. Brathwaite, *Creole Society*, 216; Matthew Gregory Lewis, *Journal of a West India Proprietor*, London: John Murray, 1834, 97; Douglas Armstrong and Mark Fleischman, 'Analysis of Four House Area Burials from the African Jamaican Settlement of Seville,' *Syracuse University Archaeological Reports 6*, Syracuse: Department of Anthropology, Syracuse University, 1993).

57. Handler and Lange, *Plantation Slavery*, 58-60; Handler, *Searching for a Cemetery*. Documentation on Newton is described in Jerome S. Handler, *A Guide to Source Materials for the Study of Barbados History, 1627-1834* (Carbondale: Southern Illinois University Press, 1971), 158; Ibid., *Supplement to a Guide for the Study of Barbados History* (Providence, Rhode Island: The John Carter Brown Library and the Barbados Museum and Historical Society, 1991), 60; Ibid., 'Sources for the Study of Preemancipation Sugar Plantations in Barbados: Manuscripts Relating to Newton and Seawell Plantations,' *Caribbean Archives*, 5 (1976): 11-21.
In recent years, Lionel Ward, the principal owner of Newton, donated most of the cemetery area to the Barbados Museum. It is a grassland, not far from the yard, that is plainly visible against the surrounding cane fields. Merely looking at this field, however, would not suggest that it still contains many interments.

58. Handler and Lange, 104-17; Handler, *Searching for a Cemetery*, passim.

59. Handler and Lange, 104-32. Cf. Jerome S. Handler, 'An African-Type Healer/Diviner and His Grave Goods: A Burial from a Plantation Slave Cemetery in Barbados, West Indies,' *International Journal of Historical Archaeology*, 1 (1997): 91-130; Ibid., 'A Prone Burial from a Plantation Cemetery in Barbados, West Indies: Possible Evidence for an African-type Witch or Other Negatively Viewed Person,' *Historical Archaeology*, 30 (1996): 76-86.

60. For the role of the ancestors in slave life, see Handler and Lange,

passim.

61. Jerome Handler, 'Health and Medicine Among Barbadian Slaves: Medical Care and Treatment' (Unpublished Manuscript, 1997, deposited in BDA); Ibid., 'Slave Medicine and Obeah in Barbados, ca. 1650-1834,' *NWIG*, 74 (2000): 57-90. Even in the best of circumstances the medical care slaves (and whites) received from professional white medical practitioners, whether creole or foreign, was singularly deficient when judged by modern standards. Further, it is doubtful that the improvements in plantation health care during the early nineteenth century had a major impact on the health and longevity of the slave population (cf. Higman, *Slave Populations*, 260-61; Kenneth Kiple, *The Caribbean Slave: A Biological History*, Cambridge: Cambridge University Press, 1984, 154).

62. E.g., Barbados Assembly, *Report of the Slave Trade*, 5; Ibid., *Report of the Insurrection*, 46, 48, 51; Barbados Council, *Report of Slaves, 109*; Holder, 21; Parry, 'Replies to Queries.' Cf. Higman, *Slave Populations*, 267-68.

63. E.g., J. Harry Bennett, *Bondsmen and Bishops* (Berkeley and Los Angeles: University of California Press, 1958), 41; Newton Estate Papers 523/ 290, 'Buildings at Newton;' Ibid., 523/291, 'Lands of Seawell;' Handler and Lange, 48, 60-61; 'Old Plantation Customs.'

64. Newton Estate Papers 523/290, 'Buildings at Newton;' Higman, *Slave Populations*, 267; Richard B. Sheridan, *Doctors and Slaves* (Cambridge: Cambridge University Press, 1985), 268-91, *passim*; J.B. Colthurst, Monthly Reports for August and October 1836, in 'Papers . . . in Explanation of the Measures,' 387, 396.

65. James Bovell , 'Observations on the Climate of Barbadoes,' *The British American Journal of Medical and Physical Science*, 4 (1848): 170. Cf. Sheridan, *Doctors and Slaves*, 272, 285-86, 291.

66. Plantation schools, as well as others for slaves and free coloureds, are discussed in Jerome S. Handler, *The Unappropriated People: Freedmen in the Slave Society of Barbados* (Baltimore: The Johns Hopkins University Press, 1974), 172-89. For schools and chapels on the island around 1830, see the reports of parish rectors, in *PP*, 1831-32, XLVII (660).

67. For a description of my method for estimating the number of plantations, see Handler and Lange, 37-39, Table 4. As to smaller units, for example, a consequential number of the approximately 1,400 plantations reported in a 1712 census were, in fact, relatively small units, and Mayo's map, based on a survey between 1717 and 1721, identified 998 plantations, but only about 405 had sugar mills. In the 1770s and 1780s, William Dickson estimated that in addition to 'upwards of four hundred sugar plantations' there were 'a great number of places and other small possessions.' The farms of 'small free holders are called places,' he later wrote, 'to distinguish them

from the large sugar plantations;' 'places' had from 'one or two acres up to twenty or thirty,' and owners with 'eight or ten acres, or more, with slaves in proportion form a middle class between the sugar planters and poor whites.' Ronald Hughes calculates that in 1680 there were 259 plantations in Barbados of 100 acres or more, and notes that a comprehensive list of the island's sugar plantations and their acreages was not published until 1846 (CO 28/14, 'A List of the Inhabitants, Men, Women, and Children . . . Belonging to the Several Parishes of this Island,' August 16, 1712; William Mayo, *A New and Exact Map of the Island of Barbadoes in America*, London, 1722; William Dickson, *Letters on Slavery*, London, 1789, 8; Ibid., *Mitigation of Slavery*, London: Longman, 1814, 528; Ronald Hughes, 'Barbadian Sugar Plantations, 1640 to 1846,' Seminar Paper 1977-78, Department of History, UWI, Cave Hill).

68. Handler and Lange, 34-36; Handler, *Searching for a Cemetery*, 44; Ibid., 'Biet,' 65, 69. Ronald Hughes lists six plantations between 1671 and 1688. The average slave contingent was 81, with a range from 86 to 105 (Hughes, 'Sugar Plantations,' App. IX).

69. Sources for these various samples are given in Handler and Lange, 34; Handler, *Searching for a Cemetery*, 31, 35, 39, 44. Ronald Hughes independently gathered statistics from a variety of archival sources. For 88 plantations over the period 1715 to 1816, the average slave contingent numbered about 117, with a range from 35 to 281. Close to 70 per cent of the plantations averaged between 60 and 139 slaves (Hughes, 'Sugar Plantations,' App. IX).

70. Handler and Lange, 35, Table 3.

71. Calculated from Higman, *Slave Populations*, 439-41, Table S2.10.

72. Pinckard, I, 289.

73. The six plantations with the number of slaves and the number of houses are: Consett 1796 (169/30), Vaucluse 1833 (308/ 'nearly' 80), one unnamed plantation in 1816 (350/ 'upwards' of 70 houses), and three unnamed ones in 1824 (82/32; 118/41; 219/76). Sources: Consett (Bennett, *Bondsmen and Bishops*, 100-01); Vaucluse (Rolph, 53); unnamed, 1816 (Barbados Assembly, *Report of the Insurrection*, 41, 42); unnamed, 1824 (Jordan, *Management*). Lightfoot, BDA, RB 1, 295/287 (Ronald Hughes brought this inventory to my attention).

74. Barbados Council, *Report of Slaves*, 114. In the 1850s, a Barbadian planter described a 'Negro-yard' with 'some sixty-four huts or cottages,' containing a population of 'about three hundred,' yielding approximately 4.7 persons per household. Higman writes that 'generally' in the West Indies 'three to six slaves occupied each house,' but his data are not clear (Meliora, 29; Higman, *Slave Populations*, 222).

75. Rolph, 53.
76. For seventeenth-century statistics on males and females, see CO 1/ 36, Jonathan Atkins, 'An Account of His Majesty's Island of Barbadoes and the Government Thereof,' February 1676; Peter Colleton, Letter to Council of Trade and Plantations, May 28, 1673, in *Calendar of State Papers*, 1669-1674, 495. Cf. Ligon, 115; Parry, 'Extract of a Letter,' 18. On a randomly collected sample of 89 plantations from 1727 to 1834, females averaged close to 52 per cent. In slightly more than one-fourth of the sample males exceeded females, but the numerical differences between the two were very small (Handler and Lange, 36). Also, summarising data collected from archival sources on a group of 94 plantations from 1671 to 1816, Ronald Hughes concluded that up to 1780 this group was almost equally divided between plantations with more men than women and those with more women than men; however, from 1780 to 1830 'the number of women was significantly greater' (Hughes, 'Sugar Plantations,' 16).
   Although island-wide figures on sex are unavailable for the eighteenth century, during the decades preceding emancipation the entire slave population averaged 54 per cent females (Handler and Lange, 36; Handler, *Searching for a Cemetery*, 31, 35, 39, 44; Ibid., *Unappropriated People*, 24-25; Higman, *Slave Populations*, 413).
77. My sample was drawn from records in the BDA, Z9/11/5, Records of Drax Hall, 1803-04, and Estate Inventories, originals, 1780-1834. See also, Hughes, 'Sugar Plantations,' App. IX; *PP*, XXVI (1789), David Parry, 'An Account of 22 Plantations in Barbados, 1788 . . . Situated in Almost Every Different Part of the Island,' 39. For the age distribution of Barbadian slaves in 1817 and 1834, see Higman, *Slave Populations*, 462, 471, 477, Tables S4.1, S4.2, S4.3.
78. Pinckard, I, 368-69. For strikingly similar perspectives on Jamaican plantation villages, see sources quoted in Higman, *Montpelier*, 132.
79. This illustration (which space limitations prevent being shown here) appears in John A. Waller, *A Voyage in the West Indies* (London: Richard Phillips, 1820), facing page 20. A surgeon in the Royal Navy, Waller had been stationed in Barbados for about a year in 1807-08.
80. Royal Anthropological Institute of Great Britain and Ireland, *Notes and Queries on Anthropology* (6th ed. London: Routledge and Kegan Paul, 1954), 64. Cf. M.G. Smith, 'Community Organization in Rural Jamaica,' *Social and Economic Studies*, 5 (1956): 295.
81. Handler, 'Slave Medicine and Obeah.' Planters regularly complained about slave theft from plantation storehouses or fields, but there is little direct information on theft within the slave community itself.
82. Brandow, 'Senhouse,' (1986), 405. Cf. Parry, 'Extract of a Letter,' 15.
83. Handler, 'Slave Medicine and Obeah;' Ibid., 'African-Type Healer;'

Ibid., 'Prone Burial;' Jerome S. Handler and Kenneth Bilby, 'On the Early Use and Origin of the Term Obeah in Barbados and the Anglophone Caribbean,' *Slavery & Abolition*, 22 (2001): 87-100; Letter from J.G. Zippel, Mount Tabor, April 30, 1832, in *Periodical Accounts Relating to the Missions of the Church of the United Brethren* (London, 1832), XII, 223-24.

Figure 10: *A slave coffle comprisng adults and children*
&
Figure 11: *A slave driver about to inflict punishment*
on a slave woman holding her infant

CHAPTER 7

Enslaved Children in Berbice, with Special Reference to the Government Slaves, 1803–31[1]

Alvin O. Thompson

Introduction

In traditional African society children were regarded as the ones elected by their ancestors and the gods to carry on the heritage of the community. They were the embodiment of 'human wealth;'[2] the hope of better things. They were both the symbols and embodiment of new life out of the decaying bodies and minds of their elders, and were also the strength and vitality of the community. It is said that among the peoples of Central Africa there was often joy at the death of old people, with the following words being uttered, 'Now, a new child will be able to be born in our home!'[3] The deceased thus renewed human life in much the same way that seedlings renewed vegetation life. Both belonged to Mother Earth. Elaborate rites of passage marked the transition from birth to death, in a continuum that linked the living with the dead. According to Pierre Erny, the child was the principal reason for marriage in traditional African societies, and the image of the child was often 'full of sacred resonances.'[4]

In many African societies a grown-up female chronologically was believed to remain a girl until she had mothered one or more children. Erny writes, 'Only then was the stability of her union insured and only then did she receive the respect of others. . . . Love, consideration, prestige increase with their number.' The writer continues:

> Sterility, therefore, affects the woman in her greatest dignity. It almost always constitutes a case for divorce, regardless of the woman's qualities as a wife. The situation is dramatic and very often the unfortunate woman becomes a reject, despised in her own family and turned out by her husband's family.[5]

Maria Cutrufelli cites a popular Ghanaian song, attributed to barren women, that runs as follows:

> Ah, this womb of mine
> Is the cause of my fall

And brought dishonour to me
Yes, this womb of mine
Is the cause of my fall.[6]

Several African communities conducted elaborate fertility rituals to ensure the fecundity of the females, accompanied sometimes by prayers that the womb would be 'enlarged.' Among the Akan of Ghana one such prayer at the puberty rites was, 'May the elephant give you her womb, so that you may bear ten children.' Another prayer expressed at the time of the marriage ran, 'May all our Gods bless them and grant them good health and may the woman bear twelve children so that she may sleep in twelve beds.'[7]

Just as in the case of a woman, a man was not 'a real man' until he had fathered children. The Gagu of the Ivory Coast viewed a man without children as a person all alone.[8] Children were the ones mainly responsible for ensuring the appropriate funerary rites to the deceased so that they would not wander as restless spirits in the other world. In that world also their ancestral position depended heavily on descendants with whom they could communicate and exercise certain influences, and a family into which they could be reincarnated should they choose to do so. As Erny notes, 'The deceased one who does not have any children is "completely dead," his being disappears in nothingness.'[9] Cutrufelli informs us that among the Akan of Ghana a man dying without children was regarded as 'a taboo man.'[10] However, infertility was usually seen as entirely a female defect.

People alternately lived in the visible and invisible world. As hinted above, the birth of children was widely perceived as the reincarnation of ancestors, their return to the visible world, and children of dominant ancestors were often revered. The Senegalese poet Birago Diop writes:

Those who are dead have not gone forever
They are in the woman's womb
They are in the child who whimpers.[11]

While in a number of societies twins, albinos and other children not classified as 'normal' were put to death or left to die, in many more instances they were treated as special children, produced through involuntary coition of females with ancestral, water, forest and other spirits. These children were often treated with the greatest respect and sometimes feared for their 'supernatural' powers. Some of them were considered diviners, exorcists, etc.[12]

The concepts discussed above migrated with the Africans who came to the region as enslaved persons, though they became modified to fit the circumstances of slavery. In the Caribbean, as in Africa, children were the prized possessions of their mothers, and in many instances their fathers, who generally spared no effort to ensure that they were well looked after, within the resources (usually scanty in the case of slavery) of their parents. This is why it is difficult to accept without much more critical enquiry the widely asserted view that the practice of infanticide was prevalent among slave mothers.[13] This essay attempts to discuss aspects of the experience of children in Berbice. At the same time it calls into question the view that the birth and rearing of children were primary matters on the agendas of a significant number of slave owners in the period after the abolition of the slave trade, at least in the case of Berbice.

Berbice was a colony on the northern periphery of South America. It was a peripheral colony in the context of the slave societies of the New World. It hardly enters into the contemporary or present-day literature on discussions of slavery, and relatively few students of slavery are fully aware of its existence. Yet, in many respects it mirrored the slave societies elsewhere in the region. A small colony geographically and demographically, it was founded by the Dutch in 1627 and captured (not for the first time) by the British in 1803 during the Napoleonic Wars. At the Convention of August 1815 between Britain and the Netherlands, that followed the end of the war, the Dutch agreed to cede the colony to the British, along with Demerara its sister territory to the west. In 1831 these two colonies were united to form the colony known as British Guiana.

The slave population of Berbice remained small throughout the period of slavery. In 1796, when first captured by the British, it stood at 8,232. Under temporary British control its population increased to 17,885 by 1802 and climbed to at least 25,810 by 1806.[14] Cut off from further slave imports by the British slave trade abolition act of 1806 that officially prohibited slave imports into foreign colonies held by the British as a result of the war, its population declined gradually after that date. At emancipation in 1834 it stood at 19,359,[15] due to slave mortality and large numbers of planters transferring their slaves to the more dynamic settlement of Demerara.

Definition of the term 'children' in Berbice slave society

The definitive legal classification of the term 'children,' in respect to age, is the slave code of 1826 that defined them as persons under 16 years.[16] A law passed by the colonial legislature in 1810 concerning runaways imposed specific sanctions on persons 16 years and older, implying that adulthood started from that age. An official government document on the slave population in 1824 divided them into adults and persons under 14 years.[17] During the period of the slave trade persons above 15 years were regarded as adults, thus implying that younger persons were treated as children. In terms of the payment of the head tax in Berbice, persons under three years were exempted from payment, those between three and ten years were assessed at half of the sum paid for adults, and all others above that age were assessed as adults.[18] Other documents show that planters treated slaves between 12 and 15 years as children or adults depending on their physical size and strength. Maria III, Lucia III and Harriet I, for instance, were placed among the adults at age 13.[19] However, for purposes of discussion here we shall use the legal age (up to 15 years) set out in the slave code of 1826.

Population dynamics

Most of the hard data for the study of children in Berbice can be found in the documents assembled by a Commission of Inquiry appointed by the imperial government to look into the management of the *winkel* (literally 'shop') or artisan slaves belonging to the government and resident in the town of New Amsterdam in the mid-1820s. Among them are the 'Schedules of Examinations' that contain short portraits of the adults and older children, giving their ages, family connections, employment, etc., and briefer information on the very young ones. Still, the records on these enslaved persons are deficient in a number of ways.

For the colony generally, an even more serious lacuna exists in the data concerning the child population because of the haphazard way in which the records were kept. In 1817, following the promulgation of the slave registry bill, the Colonial Registry compiled the first, crude returns of the enslaved population. The Registry compiled a more comprehensive list in 1819, but it was still very defective. From then on, slave owners were required to make triennial returns. However, the copies of the registries deposited in the Public Record Office, London, list only the names of those who died or were born during the triennium, but do not give a detailed profile of the population. Apart from the triennial returns, the data compiled before 1824 were strictly for taxation purposes, in which slaves under three years were not listed, and those between three and ten years were listed as half an adult for such purposes.[20] From around 1825, government officials made some attempt to compile more accurate records of the total population based upon censuses taken by the militia officers and/or civil magistrates of the various districts. These records are also defective and, moreover, rarely provide a breakdown of the population according to age categories. When they do, some of the categories do not correspond to our working definition of a child. Bearing these limitations in mind, we have given some random samples of the child population as listed in the documents.

The population distribution of the four estates belonging to the Berbice Association in October 1803 (Dankbaarheid, Sandvoort, St Jan and Dageraad), at the time of the British government's takeover of them, shows that the child population constituted 17.9 per cent of the total population— 74 girls and 84 boys out of a total population of 881.[21] The returns for enslaved persons on estates in the entire colony in 1817 show that there were 2,698 girls, 2,636 boys, 6,752 women and 9,467 men, comprising a total population of 21,553.

The child population therefore constituted 24.75 per cent of the total plantation population.[22]

Table 7.1, that looks at the population trend of the *winkel* department between 1803 and 1825 indicates that, apart from the aberrant year 1803, the child population represented a fairly constant percentage of the total population. But the figures do not help us to determine the infant mortality rate over any period, a difficulty common in the records of all the slave colonies.

Table 7.1:
Children and adult winkel population for selected years, 1803–25

Year	Children	Adults	Total	% Children
1803	72	284	356	20.2
1812	104	251	355	29.3
1815	103	231	334	30.8
1819	91	228	319	28.5
1823	101	197	298	33.9
1825	85	212[a]	297	28.6

Sources: CO 111/73, 'List of buildings, crafts, materials and slaves of the shopkeepers department,' October 7, 1803; CO 111/79; 'Inventory of the Negroes and other slaves belonging to the Winkel Department,' August 7, 1812; *PP*, 1816, VIII (528): 36; T71/438; 'Return of slaves attached to the Winkel Department,' August 2, 1819, 723–32; T1/3481; Returns of Slaves belonging to the Crown, October 31, 1823, 816–19; T1/3483/1, Report of Commissioners of Inquiry (RCI), 1826, 12.

[a]Age not given but assigned by us to the adult category.

Of course, the main weakness in the data about the *winkel* people is that they were essentially an urban group of slaves, though they lived in a separate village on the outskirts of the capital. Researchers generally agree that urban slaves had greater opportunities than rural ones to order their own lives, and this was certainly true of the *winkel* people. Therefore, it is a moot point as to whether or not the demographic pattern of the *winkel* people reflected that in the colony at large where the vast majority of the population lived on plantations. In 1803, for instance, the *winkel* children constituted a higher percentage of their group than was the case with the children on the four estates of the Berbice Association (see above). As regards the child population of the colony as a whole, we do not have an exact tool with which to compare them with the *winkel* child population in any given year. The nearest comparisons are in respect of 1819 when the *winkel* child population under 14 years constituted 26.6 per cent of the total *winkel* population, and in 1825 when those under 16 years constituted 28.6 per cent. By comparison, the colony's population in 1824 under 14 years constituted 23.9 per cent of the total population.[23] The evidence presently available suggests that children consistently comprised between 24 per cent and 25 per cent of the enslaved population of the colony during the period under review (with some oscillation in numbers between males and females).[24] This suggests that the general average was somewhat below that of the *winkel* department.

Pro-natalist approaches

Up to the last decade of the eighteenth century, planters in Berbice and elsewhere generally found it more expedient to import fresh blacks than to rear them; it was cheaper 'to buy than to breed' was a popular adage in the slave colonies. It was largely the threat of the abolition of the slave trade, and its reality later on, that caused many slave owners to pay more attention to maintaining and increasing the numbers of their slaves by 'natural' factors, that is, excess of births over deaths. However, it was only in Barbados, within the slave plantation colonies of the Caribbean, that the slave population fully reproduced itself by natural births. Berbice experienced a brief period of slight excess of births over deaths between 1826 and 1828, and again in 1831.[25] It therefore remains a moot point as to the extent to which pro-natalist policies helped to increase the birth rate or reduce the infant mortality rate.

Any study of childbirth and child-rearing must begin with the parents themselves. One of the most significant features of the slave system that directly affected children was that their status followed that of their mothers exclusively. This was because throughout the slavery period the law regarded new-born children as the property of the persons that owned their mothers. Since it is commonly accepted that far more children were born to enslaved mothers in unions with free fathers than *vice versa*, in several instances it would have served better the interest of such children if they were allowed to take the status of their fathers. The official registration of births generally listed only the names of the mothers.[26] Thus, in this respect at least, matrilineage was reinforced at the expense of patrilineage, and it is generally far more difficult to trace the genealogy of slaves through the male than the female line.

For a long time scholars writing about the slave family accepted uncritically the view that children were generally neglected by their fathers who remained largely invisible and marginalised. However, several recent writers have noted that slave families, especially in the 'amelioration' period, were fairly stable, that there were co-residential and non-co-residential, nuclear and extended, units, and that children often had positive relations with their fathers.[27] Very little work has been done on the situation in Berbice, but the extant records of the Crown slaves there in the mid-1820s bear out this relationship of children with their fathers. Living mostly in the same suburban village, the enslaved people practised largely endogamy. However, there were important exceptions, where children were born through unions between *winkel* women and free black, and especially free coloured and white, men.[28] Twelve children were born from the union of the freeman (colour not stated) Tom Rose and the *winkel* woman Clarissa.[29]

The social system into which creole children were born and socialised was based upon convoluted notions of the value of epidermic distinctions. Thus light-skinned children stood a better chance of climbing the opportunity ladder than those of darker skin. George Pinckard, a surgeon just arrived in Berbice in the early nineteenth century, recorded a striking example of this ingrained tendency towards racism and rejection of the black skin and the individual in the castle of that skin. After playing with 'a fine black child, about a year old,' he tried to hand her to a young 'copper-skinned lady.' To his amazement, the latter absolutely refused to take the toddler. On enquiring the reason for this act of repulsion, the owner of the child responded, '*noire!*' Pinckard was astounded by three factors: first that the young lady was also an enslaved individual, second that the child was only a shade darker than herself, and third that the 'poor babe . . . all the time, looked up in her face, and solicited her attentions with a smile of heavenly innocence.' The owner told him that the young lady was a good nurse and loved children, provided they were at least as fair as she![30] Ultimately, it was not the young girl but the slave system that had created this social monstrosity. Such entrenched racism brings in its wake self-hatred, lack of self-confidence and social disarticulation, sometimes bordering on neurosis on the part of the victims.

Slave owners generally exempted 'coloured' children, like their parents, from field labour. Charles Kyte, a Berbice slave manager, testified that in his 20 years' residence in the colony he had never seen an enslaved coloured person put to such labour.[31] But coloured (and other) slave children benefited from the fact that they belonged to free fathers by being accorded greater material advantages, especially those resident in the urban communities. They were often provided with better clothing and (in rarer instances) a superior education to what was offered in the slave schools. Andries III, Edward, John Frederick, Richard I and Maria IV were children provided with superior clothing by their free fathers. The Commissioners of Inquiry in 1826 described Charles II, the mestee son of Juliana, as being 'very well dressed in clothes of a superior description given him by his father.' He also received instruction at a private school at his father's expense, and was thus able to read, say his prayers and recite the catechism well. Esdaile, son of Lucia II, was another lad sent to a private school by his father.[32]

Occasionally, children of enslaved fathers also enjoyed a higher level of material comfort than their fellow slaves, especially those artisans living in the urban communities. This was the case with the eight children of Louis, a boat-builder who was often on 'self-hire' (i.e., found his own employment for a fee). He is said to have made a good living. He himself testified that he had a comfortable house, and some money saved. Andrew McWatt, his manager, summed up his character thus: '. . . he is in every respect one of the best Negroes I ever knew, and his family are equally respectable.'[33]

Although children often enjoyed close relationships with their fathers, they were usually much closer to their mothers who were literally and figuratively at the centre of the reproductive system. While foetuses were sometimes deliberately aborted by pregnant women, a major reason was probably because, as the enslaved woman Ziemine alleged, the system of slavery was so draconian that they did not want to bring children into the world.[34] According to Hilliard d'Auberteuil, greedy masters did not wish to see their females pregnant, although children who survived to ten years would have earned their masters multiple times more than they would have lost financially through the pregnancy of the mother. If the females often aborted their foetuses it was because of the 'excessive tyranny' of their masters that caused them to 'smother their maternal feelings.'[35] African communities were known for the great emphasis they placed on children; the more children parents had the more blessed they were supposed to be by their ancestors and their gods. Children were also their security in old age, when their strength was gone and they became dependents for the second time.

Evidence from the *winkel* department in Berbice shows that some households had a large number of children, potentially or actually. For example, Suse had seven children, Susannah ten, Clarissa 12, and Maria I 13.[36] Several other mothers had four and more children. Even allowing for the deaths of several of these children, some households must have had a large complement of living ones. While these examples do not offer a definitive profile of the Berbice population as a whole, they reflect high levels of fertility, at least among some of the population, and also some retention of African traditions of having large families.

In African natalist philosophy, the child was a being that came into existence at conception ('hidden life'). Mothers were therefore expected to take great care to give the children in their womb the greatest opportunity of coming into the material world 'whole,' that is, without any visible physical or other defects. The birth of a child was usually the celebration of life and love by the parents, especially the first one, and more so if the child was a boy. Of course, in most African societies one had to wait for a short period of time after birth — in Ghana as in the Caribbean until nine days — to ensure that the child was not a 'ghost child' but would remain alive, before naming him/her and indulging in the usual festivities associated with such an occasion.[37] While abortion was well-known in traditional African societies, it tended to occur under special circumstances of stress or (belief in) impregnation by a malevolent spirit. Still, in these societies, and possibly also in the Caribbean, voluntary abortion was usually perceived as necrophilic, the very antithesis of life.

From the late eighteenth century slave managers began to latch onto the women's natural desire to bear children and to create the conditions for 'proper' slave births and the healthy rearing of children. These included the lying-in of pregnant mothers some weeks before delivery, the establishment of nurseries run by superannuated women, the granting of extra time during the day to lactating mothers to breast-feed their children, the assignment of special cooks to prepare meals for the children, and the granting of other indulgences. For every child that survived for a certain number of days, months or years as the case may be, slave owners now began to pay the mothers a small sum of money. They also began to exempt those with six or more living children from praedial or other heavy work, and sometimes from assigned work altogether.[38] The 1826 code made it compulsory for managers to give such rewards. It decreed that for every first child surviving for six weeks after birth to legally married or to reputed couples the owner must pay the mother 12 guilders (17s.2d.), and 15 guilders (£1.1s.5d.) for every other child. Every woman having six children under the circumstances mentioned above, the last of whom was seven years old, had to be exempted from field work and put only to light work. Managers were to be fined 300 guilders (£21.4s.3d) for every breach of these laws.[39] Already, before the promulgation of the code, slave mothers usually looked forward to and sometimes demanded these monetary and other rewards for child-bearing,[40] but it would be naive to suggest, as several writers do, that this was an incentive for them to bring children into the world or take greater care of them. The woman's natural instinct for her child's welfare usually ensured that this would be done, as we shall note more specifically later on.

In Berbice, as elsewhere, several slave managers pursued pro-natalist options. The Crown slaves and those of Wolfert Katz, the foremost planter in the colony, provide two notable examples. Between 1812 and 1816 the managers of the Crown slaves (a group of humanitarians in London, known as the Berbice Commissioners[41]), created new lying-in facilities on the estates and in the *winkel* department. They instructed their agents to assign the women only light work during their early pregnancy and, where necessary, to give them maternity leave in the last weeks of their pregnancy.[42] It took some years before their pro-natalist policy began to bear fruit, largely because De la Court, the first agent on the ground, paid little attention to the welfare of the enslaved people. However, with his dismissal and the arrival of James Walker as agent in February 1815 notable changes began to take place. Walker's pro-natalist measures are cited in the records as the chief reason for the elimination of stillbirths on the estates during the remainder of that year. Rev. John Wray, the London Missionary Society's (LMS) missionary, stated in April 1815 that on two of the estates, Dankbaarheid and Dageraad, the children were being well cared for and were receiving 'a large quantity of nutritious soup.'[43] In the following year he declared that the children on Sandvoort Estate 'that were almost sucked to death by chegoes & filth & the neglect of the Manager begin to be healthy.'[44]

Walker, as superintendent of the *winkel* department in the 1820s, placed a relative or close friend at the call of each mother in advanced pregnancy. He also gave a small sum of money to the women for each live birth. However, he did not always live up to the high expectations that the imperial government had of him. He refused to give any money to Matilda, with whom he had developed strained relations. He also kept Christina I, the mother of six children, forcibly in his domestic employment, although he alleged that she was not required to work in order to earn her keep.[45] He spoke often about building a separate nursery for the *winkels* but for years he made no efforts to do so, using instead one of the slave houses as a nursery. He also failed to assign adequate staff to the nursery for general nursing care. When the new nursery was completed in 1825 or 1826 he boasted that it was the envy of the colony.[46] In spite of his chequered administrative record, in the mid-1820s the children were almost completely free of permanent physical disabilities. In fact, only Hendrick (age 13), lame from birth, suffered any serious disability or physical defect — he was born crippled. The Commission of Inquiry noted that the children were healthy and 'remarkably fine.' It also declared that the young people as a whole were 'serviceable and well looking.'[47]

As regards Wolfert Katz, in 1826 his managers gave a most striking joint testimony of his pro-natalist policies. According to them, all pregnant women were removed from field work after about five months and put to light domestic tasks. About two weeks before the time of their delivery they were sent to the town of New Amsterdam and placed in the care of a qualified midwife who provided special lying-in facilities for them. During that time they were fed a variety of nutritious foods sent from the owner's estates, including rice, barley, plantains, sugar and pork, and also cordial, as the circumstances required. The managers also declared that several women took advantage of this situation, by claiming that they were in advanced pregnancy and were thus sometimes sent to town 10 or 13 weeks before the actual date of delivery. This entailed extra cost to their owner who normally paid the midwife 44 guilders (£3.2s.10d) for every birth.[48]

A fortnight or so after delivery they were returned to the estate where they and their infants were given the best of care. For the first month they were not given any work, but were allowed to attend their children. Then for the next three months, and sometimes as long as six months, they were put to light employment in the logies (sorting and/or curing houses) 'picking' cotton or coffee. Since they were allowed to keep their babies with them, they were able to feed them every hour. On sugar estates which offered little opportunity for working in logies, they were sent to the field after about three months. In such circumstances they were employed not far from the buildings and were allowed to begin their tasks one hour later and end them one hour earlier.

Meanwhile, the children were placed in nurseries or playgrounds under the care of specially assigned 'nurses.' 'Those nurses in the morning (when the Children are collected) wash them all, after that they are ranged before the Manager's door, to be examined if free from Chigoes & Ulcers; when a preparation of the Quassia Bitters is given them & they are sent off to the Nursery – the Nurses receiving at the same time a quantity of Plantains, Fish, Pork, Rice or Barley out of the Plantation Store . . . .' Mothers with daughters six to eight years old had the option of employing them as playmates and assistants to care for the new-born ones. Those without older children could select someone else to perform the same tasks. The most recent mothers became part of a 'Nursery establishment,' the main function of which was to breast-feed children whose mothers were absent at any given time or who had problems producing sufficient milk for their children.[49]

Katz appears to have been a shrewd businessman, both from the fact that he was the foremost planter in the colony, with seven estates, and he devoted much more time and money than the average planter to ensure that pregnant women gave birth to healthy children and were allowed the opportunity to give them quality care in their early months. The manager of Plantation Bohemia is said to have received 900 guilders (£64.5s.9d.) as bonus in 1822, while the manager of Plantation Vryheid received 800 guilders (£57.2s.10d.) between 1822 and 1824 'for every Increase of One to the Gang by the Birth of a Child.'[50] This statement is somewhat ambivalent: it might indicate either that there was a net increase of nine slaves (births over deaths) on Bohemia during 1822 or simply that nine children lived to the age of one year. Strangely, the fairly detailed deposition of the managers on the pro-natalist and other aspects of Katz's administrative policy did not indicate that any of the mothers received payment for bringing the children into the world or keeping them alive. This suggests that he considered the mothers mainly as 'breeding wenches' who were there to ensure the upkeep of the numbers of enslaved persons on his estates. For Katz, as for others, pro-natalism was shrewd business policy rather than philanthropy. The acid test of his pro-natalist policy would have been the increase in the number of his slaves through birth. However, this information is not currently available since he appears to have sold a couple of his estates. However, of the five estates for which full lists of the slaves are recorded for 1819 and 1831 —Overwinning, Vryheid, 's Gravenhage, Gebroeders and Cotton Tree — there was an overall decrease of 22 slaves (1,032 in 1819 as against 1,010 in 1831).[51] The verdict is therefore still undetermined on the success of his pro-natalist policy.

Table 7.2:
Number of births according to sex among the Berbice slave population, 1821 - 1828

Year	Males	Females	Total
1821	283	312	595
1822	266	230	496
1823	286	232	518
1824	272	246	518
1825	229	201	430
1826	213	201	414
1827	283	253	536
1828	254	205	459
Total	2086	1880	3966

Sources: CO 111/101, 'Statement of the Slave Population of the Colony Berbice with an account of Births and Deaths . . .,' January 1, 1821–January 1, 1825; CO 111/109, 'Return of the Population of the Colony of Berbice on September 15, 1829.'

No colony ever published a comprehensive body of laws relating to the general health of the slave population or any segment of it. Up to the end of slavery owners and managers still largely determined the health of their enslaved charges by the feeding, labour, punishment and other regimes that they put in place. These were reflected in the slow progression of the populations from disease-ridden to healthy bodies. They were also reflected in the mortality, and possibly in the fertility, rates of the enslaved populations.

Based strictly on the official government figures in Berbice, it appears that while there were fluctuations, as one would expect in any large population group, there was little or no improvement in the fertility rate of these people during the nineteenth century, until possibly the very last years of slavery. Between 1819 and 1822 inclusive the annual birth rate of the enslaved population was 20.7, while between 1825 and 1828 it was 21.3. These figures are lower than the birth rates in the last few years of the previous century. For instance, the rates were 22.6 in 1797, 21.6 in 1798, and 23.4 in 1799. However, in 1831 at 24.2 it was appreciably higher.[52]

We cannot accurately determine the frequency of children born to young mothers — children born to persons who were themselves legally defined as children — because the records are usually silent about children who were stillborn or who died shortly after they were born (and also about miscarriages). For instance, the *winkel* records for 1825 only mention the ages (and other details) of the five surviving children of the original 12 who were born to Clarissa (aged 52).[53] However, the figures available for the department suggest that childbirth hardly occurred before age 14. Of the 45 females who are listed with children in the 1825 census, three of them are listed as having their first child at 14 years, and two at 15 years. No actual childbirth is mentioned before these ages, though one miscarriage is listed at age 13. On the other hand, certain mothers are listed as having their first living child at 29 to 31 years (four mothers in all). A few mothers produced their last child at fairly advanced ages: Judith (41), Roosje (42), Rosalia (43).[54] The figures above suggest that either few children in the department were sexually active before they became adults officially, or that they took measures to prevent giving birth to children ('precocious motherhood') at an early age. We know that some of them were sexually active, as the cases of Julia, Catherine II, Matilda and Lucia III confirm.[55]

Higman states that there was significant under-registration of births in the slave colonies because slave owners did not generally include in the returns children who did not survive to one month and sometimes longer. Thus he suggests that, for instance, in Berbice between 1817 and 1821 perhaps only 67.9 per cent of the births were reported in the registration office in New Amsterdam. On that basis he calculates that slave births might really have been 35.4 (his 'direct estimate'), instead of the 24 indicated by the incomplete figures returned to the registry. According to his 'direct estimate,' the Berbice figures were higher than those of the sugar colonies of Jamaica (31.5 for 1817–20), St Vincent (31.5 for 1817–21), St Kitts (34.7 for 1817–21), Grenada (32.7 for 1817–20), Trinidad 27.8 (1816-19), Demerara-Essequibo (31.4 for 1820–22); and lower than those of Barbados (47.3 for 1817–20).[56] These figures only tell a small part of the story, for they need to be matched against child deaths. However, as noted in the previous paragraph, the under-registration of births and deaths makes these figures unavailable, so we cannot determine with any accuracy the quality of health care in the colonies in statistical terms. Nevertheless, during part of the period that the Berbice Commissioners ran the show (January 1812 to July 1816) the government slaves are said to have produced 107 children, 23 of whom died, giving a mortality rate of 21.5 per cent [57]

Demographers agree that there was a high infant mortality rate in all the sugar colonies, especially during the first year, with the possible exception of Barbados for most of this period. Scholars have advanced various explanations, human and natural, for this circumstance. They include parental and planter neglect, accidents, poor nutrition, managerial abuse and brutality, adverse disease environments, and imperfect understanding of the etiology of diseases.

Most of these factors are also used to explain the high incidence of mortality in the general population of enslaved persons.

The children's well being was also affected by the hard toil that many mothers had to undergo in the field. In several instances their workload was not reduced by virtue of the fact that they had nursing children. Susanna complained that she worked as hard as everyone else, although she had a sick child to tend.[58] The core of the problem was that mothers had restricted control over their children whom, in the words of Laura, they had brought 'with great pains in[to] life.'[59] The fact is that the children did not belong legally to their parents but to the slave owner. Fiscal Michael Bennett of Berbice wrote about 'two children belonging to Mr Elwes, the present proprietor' of the plantation Zelden Rust, not to their parents.[60] Thus it was the masters and their employees who made the most critical decisions concerning the children, who could brutalise them without the parents being able to do much about it, and who had the authority ultimately to dispose of them by sale or gift.[61] Therefore, when Zebith was sent several miles away from her young child who was not yet able to speak, as punishment for an alleged insolence on her part, she had no recourse to the law to right the wrong.[62]

A great deficiency in the plantation regime, even where pro-natalist policies were in place, was that it did not did not generally allow suckling children to receive regular breast-feeding from their mothers. The latter complained frequently about the lack of such provision and showed great anxiety over it. The list of such complaints is long but we shall cite only a few examples here. In 1819 Nettelje, Julia, Lea and Mietje of Plantation Gelderland, 'each with a little infant in arms,' complained that they were not allowed any time to suckle their babies. Just the day before manager Toel had caught Nettelje and Mietje suckling their infants, whom they had apparently carried into the field, and as a result he had flogged them, causing their clothes to become bloodstained. Julia, 'a young girl, with her first child,' was placed in the stocks for failure to complete her work.[63]

In the same year, Laura of Plantation no.6, Canje Creek, 'with a child at the breast,' expressed deep hurt at the refusal of her master to allow her to take her child into the field where she could breast-feed it more regularly. She complained that whenever the manager or overseer discovered that she had stolen away to feed her child he would flog her. She pleaded that since the child was 'of a weak constitution' it required regular maternal care.[64] In 1823 Catherine of Plantation Hampshire was traumatised by the fact that Cort, her master, did not show sufficient sensitivity to the fact that she had a sick child and needed to pay a lot of attention to it. She declared that 'he did not thank her for making children,' and that on two occasions when he found that she had stolen away from the field to feed her child placed in the nursery he had locked her up in the 'dark house.'[65]

The usual way of looking after infants whose mothers were in the fields was by placing them under the care of the elderly mothers, in association with a few young girls not yet ready to be put regularly into the fields or employed as domestics. Roxanna (77), for instance, was deemed to be well qualified to take care of the little ones; she had given birth to 13 children, and still performed multiple functions, including those of midwife and nurse to sick children.[66] Some managers and masters tried to effect a compromise between work and suckling by erecting special huts in the fields to allow the very young children to be fed by their mothers. Richard White, manager of Plantation Reliance, was one such person. However, the owners rejected the suggestion, opting to leave the children with the 'wet nurses' and giving the mothers an extra one and a half hours during the day to return to the nurseries and suckle their infants.[67] Joshua Steele, a plantation owner in Barbados in the late eighteenth century, stated that on his estates the 'sucking children' were 'attended in the field by two or three other older women as dry nurses; for I never allow the mothers to work with them at their backs, as they formerly used to do, when it was not uncommon, after a hot day, to bring the child home dead.'[68] There were clearly differences of opinion between managers and masters, and more especially between management and enslaved women, as to the best mode of providing for the nurturing of children during work hours.

Theoretically, feeding children away from the fields was a better solution, since it did not expose them to the elements of sun and rain, while it possibly offered them somewhat greater protection from diseases. However, the women were not satisfied with the care that the infants were likely to receive in the nurseries and so they preferred to take them into the fields with them, a practice brought over from Africa. The attitude of the majority of managers and masters towards the breast-feeding of infants indicates clearly that they still perceived the enslaved woman first and foremost as a labour hand and only secondarily as a mother. This viewpoint came out forcefully in the rejection of the manager of Plantation De Resolutie to the request of Ziemine and other women for more time to look after their children. He declared that he was not recruited to raise children; so he worked pregnant and lactating mothers as hard as everyone else.[69]

Failure to provide adequate time for infants to be breast-fed by their mothers, and the placing of their feeding in the hands of inexperienced nannies constitute a major health risk in any society and particularly in societies where there is a very adverse disease environment. T.P. Eddy's comment on Gambian children during the 1970s illustrates this point: 'The predominant form of illness in young children . . . is diarrhoea with marasmus . . . [T]his has been attributed to the deadly combination of a heavy load of infection with inadequate and early weaning caused by what is called "a shortfall of milk" in Gambian mothers, and the care of young weaning children by inexperienced child-minders whilst their mothers work in the rice-swamps.'[70]

He goes on to state that:

> Protein-energy malnutrition, or PEM as it is now known, has been called 'the
> most serious and widespread disorder known to medical and nutritional
> science.' . . . It is predominantly a disease of young children, because the
> younger the child the greater are its nutritional requirements, and as the
> child emerges from maternal protection it is increasingly exposed to
> environmental hazards for which it is still unprepared. Inadequate nutrition
> increases the vulnerability of the child and is recognized as a principal factor
> in high morbidity and mortality in childhood.[71]

It is now beyond doubt that poor nutrition had a lot to do with death and
disease in all Caribbean and American jurisdictions and all age categories
during (and after) the slavery era. Several excellent recent studies have been
done on this matter,[72] and so it is unnecessary in this short essay to revisit the
subject in any depth. Here we will focus largely on the quantities of food supplied
to children in Berbice and the complaints that enslaved persons made
concerning food, the second largest number of complaints after improper,
excessive and brutal punishments, as revealed in the reports of the Protectors
of Slaves.

The law specified that adults were to receive two 'good bunches' of
plantains, or as an alternative seven to nine pounds of rice, corn flour or
wheat flour weekly. Children were to receive half of these quantities. Not until
the last years of slavery did the law specify the amount of fish to be given, but
common practice was to give adults two pounds weekly and children half that
amount.[73] However, some managers breached the laws with impunity, not
bothering to give mothers a separate quantity of provisions for very small
children. They expected that if the children were under two years they would
be fed either in the nurseries or from their mothers' rations. For those above
that age half of the adult fare would theoretically be provided, but those
children elevated to the adult working category became eligible for adult
rations.[74]

A common complaint was that slave managers breached the law in regard
to both adults and children. The majority of the complaints of parents about
the shortage of food, while not mentioning children specifically, obviously also
included them, for any food shortage must have affected the family as a whole.
It appears that when food was in short supply, as happened periodically when
drought ensued or money ran short, the fare, especially of the children and
superannuated persons, would be cut back. There were several periods of heavy
rainfall and drought leading to critical food shortages or sometimes plantains
that were much smaller than usual. For a long time also the law failed to
specify the weight of a 'good bunch' of plantains, and this led to wide variations
in regard to the actual quantities given on various estates and at various times.

Some managers also deliberately gave their charges smaller allowances of plantains and fish, forcing them to go to the forest and rivers on weekends to supplement their rations.[75]

The enslaved persons belonging to the government not only complained about the general shortage of food but also that Walker gave the small children only half a bunch of plantains instead of a full one.[76] In 1811, manager John Trulock of Plantation Scotland frequently denied his charges the customary amount of food and clothing, and afforded them little time in which to prepare their meals. In 1819 Wilhelmina complained of shortage of rations, especially food and clothing, alleging that her master, Elwes of Plantation Zelden Rust, gave her children no allowances.[77] In the same year, several slaves of Mrs Ibon Sanders' woodcutting establishment in Upper Berbice complained of being given short supplies of food, clothing, etc. Lubin, William, Adam and Sam complained that the women and children did not receive any allowance and the people were punished if they complained about such practices. In response, Mrs Sanders claimed that 'food is dressed every day for the children,' and that the four field women of the establishment did not receive rations because they allowed the hogs to eat them.[78] Apart from shortages, there was little or no variation in the rations supplied by the managers. Thus enslaved persons were thrown back on their own resources, mainly through their small garden plots, to supplement their diets, especially in relation to protein.

Physical brutalities

There is no doubt that a lot of unrecorded misery visited all categories of enslaved people. However, charges of brutality to themselves and their children by mothers and expectant mothers were quite common. Up to 1811 the murder of an enslaved person was still not a capital offence. According to Lieutenant-Governor Gordon, Berbice was the only British-administered colony without such a law.[79] In spite of the fact that it became a capital offence shortly afterwards, managers still brutalised their charges to the point of death and in some instances actually killed them, knowing that they stood a good chance of escaping the noose because of a sympathetic justice system, especially in relation to capital offences.

Betsey of Plantation Berenstein complained to Manager Deussen in 1820 that she was unable to complete her work because she was pregnant. As a result Deussen continuously harassed her and once threatened to 'break her belly' with a *fufu* (corn meal or plantain) pounder. In his outraged contempt for what he viewed as her defiance, he overturned the pot in which she was cooking, while 'cursing and damming her' with his rasping tongue.[80] In 1823 Jacoba II, enslaved by the government, received 12 strokes when seven months pregnant which caused her to fear that she would miscarry.[81]

Confinement in the stocks was generally regarded as a more humane punishment for pregnant women, as De Quasy, manager of Plantation Reumzigt, smugly asserted, in what he obviously regarded as a humanitarian gesture (though he had no compunction about kicking women who were not pregnant in different parts of their body).[82] However, even strong men often bowed beneath the yoke of the stocks. They became weak, experienced cramps and suffered aching joints after confinement in such a way for some time.[83]

Several miscarriages actually occurred due to brutalities against pregnant women. In 1816, America of Plantation Sandvoort was brutally whipped at the command of Jacobus Overeem, her manager, and in his presence with 170 strokes for an alleged insult to his wife, resulting in a mangled body and a miscarriage.[84] Jenny complained in 1821 that when she was three months pregnant Betsey Atkinson, her mistress, accused her of trying to poison her, 'kicked her and trampled her on her belly,' placed her hands and feet in the stocks and 'licked [her] again on the back,' as a result of which she miscarried.[85]

C.J. Grade, manager of Plantation L'Espérance, surpassed Overeem and Atkinson in cruelty. What happened to Rosa (*alias* Roosje), an enslaved woman, was a particularly traumatic event. In 1819 she suffered a miscarriage after being beaten on the orders of her manager with *carracarras* ('tough' bush ropes) for failing to complete her field task on time. According to Zondag, the driver who administered the flogging, he advised the manager of the advanced state of the woman's pregnancy, but that individual responded, 'Give it to her till the blood flies out,' a testimony that corroborated that given earlier by the victim. As a result the foetus died in the mother's womb and the 'midwife had to force it' out. The ghastly remains showed extensive damage from the whipping, as several witnesses testified. '[O]ne eye was out, the arm broken, and a stripe visible over the head' was the way Rosa described her dead child. Marianna, the midwife, agreed: 'The child's arm was broken; one eye out, bruised and sunken in the head; it was a fine male child, quite formed; in every respect perfect.'[86] Even when children were not physically affected by such brutalities against their mothers, they must have suffered psychological damage.

Of course, the Berbice situation was only unique in the specific circumstances relating to such brutalities. Blake cites a case of a Jamaican slave mother's tragic loss:

> One infant fell to the ground dead as the mother gave birth on her fourth morning on the [tread]mill in St. Thomas-in-the-East. The overseer of the penal gang sent her to the hospital and she replied, 'Me cannot lef my dead pickanniny on the ground,' and she used a hoe to make a shallow grave for the child in the workhouse yard.[87]

The brutalities mentioned so far related to children within the womb and were directed specifically at the mothers. But a much larger number of incidents occurred in which brutalities and a wide range of other punishments were directed against children. In 1811 a case of cruelty came before the Court of Policy or colonial legislature (later called Council of Government) concerning manager John Trulock of Plantation Scotland, referred to above. He was in the habit of chastising all of his charges, adults and children alike, in the most cruel manner. Dr Lloyd, the military physician who examined the enslaved people there, testified that all those belonging to the plantation 'appeared to him to have been severely punished, particularly the woman Mary & two small Children, who were in a very deplorable state at the time he first saw them.' Mary testified that among the misdeeds of the manager was that she was a washerwoman and that he gave her no time off even on Sunday for herself or her child, 'that her child is not allowed to suck, as the Manager always orders her to work when she is giving her child the breast.' The minutes of the court indicated that the woman showed clear evidence of previous brutal flogging, and 'her child appears to be very much neglected and is extremely poor.'[88]

There were other live exhibits of Trulock's inhumanity. Betsey, described as 'a young girl,' told of a number of brutalities that he had meted out to her. She stated that the manager frequently punished her because of a key, for the loss of which she was not responsible, that he 'tied her up by the hands & flogged her & burns her feet & in various parts of the body.' The evidence before the court indicated that she had been severely flogged with a cart whip, but had now been healed. Two other children, Charles and Marcus, on the same occasion asserted that they had been denied their rations and had been severely flogged. The court noted that 'both of them appear to be very poorly.' The Commissaries of the Court were 'thoroughly convinced' of Trulock's cruelty, and 'more especially so of the Children,' and decided to refer the matter for criminal proceedings against him.[89]

In 1819, a number of persons including Wilhelmina and Avanturer (*alias* Quamina) complained to the Fiscal of several wrongs committed by Robert Elwes, the owner of Plantation Zelden Rust, and Fanny, his housekeeper/mistress, against them. According to the complainants, Fanny, an enslaved black woman, exercised considerable authority over the master's household. Wilhelmina stated that her four children — three girls, Anna, Betye and Philipintze (Phillipintje), and one son, Ordinance, all included in the household staff — were always treated badly by Fanny. Whenever they were ill and their mother brought them food Fanny would always throw it away. Both Fanny and the owner were in the habit of beating the children with *carracarras* or bush ropes. Fanny had recently flown into a rage because Betye was not cleaning the knives as quickly as she desired and had cut the child on her finger with one of them. On another occasion the owner had forced the same child to remove dung from near the bridge with her bare hands. He also worked them on Sundays, contrary to the law. Finally, she declared that her boy was somewhat retarded ('lingers very much') because of the ill-treatment meted out to him. The Fiscal noted that the three children who were present (Philipintze remained at home) were 'all naked, with the exception of a little piece of cloth for decency's sake,' and that they displayed marks consistent with whipping. Several other enslaved persons corroborated the complaints of Wilhelmina.

Avanturer, a boy eight to ten years old, complained that Fanny sent him very early every morning to milk the goats and that if she was dissatisfied with how speedily he performed this task she would whip him. Both she and his master often punished him by 'pulling him often in a cruel manner by the nose, and pinching his ears most inhumanly.' Also, he received no regular rations and had to survive as best he could. The Fiscal observed that 'the complainant proves by many old marks on his back and posteriors that his statement is not at all incorrect, and that he has often been severely dealt with.' In spite of this wealth of evidence, the Fiscal, himself a slave owner, viewed Elwes' actions as minor indiscretions. He simply warned him not to employ the people again on Sundays and prohibited the use of the whip in the presence of the gang.[90]

The punishment of females by whipping them on their naked bottoms was also one of the repugnant features of slavery visited on young girls. One case that came to the special attention of the imperial government was that concerning Carolina II, belonging to the Crown and 14 years at the time of the incident. This incident took place at the very time that the imperial government was seeking to get the colonial legislatures to abolish the practice of whipping females. In 1823, on the instruction of Walker, the superintendent, Carolina was punished on her bare buttocks, while she was menstruating, for refusing to go to work on the day following the Whitsuntide holidays. The punishment was administered by a teenage lad, in the presence of the superintendent. The Commissioners of Inquiry were persuaded that Walker himself had actually lifted up her clothes, as some of the witnesses testified. They viewed the event as being of a 'low and disgusting nature,' carried out in 'revolting circumstances of indelicacy.'[91] They referred the case to the imperial government that eventually dismissed Walker from office on this account.

The case of Matilda, also belonging to the Crown, calls for comment. Between 13 and 16 years at the time of the incident, she was one of those females who presented special management problems. But the manner in which Elizabeth Stanley, the schoolmistress, attempted to discipline her for poor work in the sewing room caused her to retaliate in kind. Stanley claimed that she slapped Matilda who 'returned me slap for slap, and tried to turn up my clothes to lick me.' Matilda's story was that the schoolmistress wanted her to kneel down and do a piece of work in the workroom but she was unable to do so because of a boil on her knee. As a result the schoolmistress beat her with a table foot and she returned the blow, for which action the superintendent punished her with a leather strap.[92] Even at this tender age Matilda attempted to assert her rights as a human being.

Female children should have been exempted from being whipped as a result of a circular letter from Earl Bathurst of June 12, 1823 to the governors of the West Indian colonies requiring them to publish a law to that effect. However, over a year later, Lieutenant-Governor Beard indicated to the Colonial Office that he had no hope that the legislature would consent to such a proposal. Therefore, while he instructed the Fiscal to cease whipping females as a form of judicial punishment, managers remained free to whip the females under their jurisdiction.[93] The slave code of 1826 finally outlawed such punishment for females, except for girls under 12 years who could be punished 'in such & the same manner for any fault or misconduct, by her committed in such & the same manner, and in such & the same extent, as any child of free condition may be and usually is punished and corrected in any school for the education of youth in this colony.'[94]

In 1810 a constable (*diender*) assaulted a lad named Mon Rose, as a result of which he suffered a broken thigh and other injuries.[95] In 1812 two young children came before the court in relation to a complaint that they had been brutalised by the owner or manager, Stewart. The court observed that one of them named Cotty 'had the appearance of having been punished with an extraordinary degree of severity' and further inquiry suggested that his brother had died from punishment. The court decided to investigate the latter complaint before taking any further action in respect of the two children. In 1821 Jenny's child Philip was so badly mauled by ill-treatment that, according to the Fiscal, he displayed 'marks of severe flogging over the whole body.'[96]

Whipping was not the only form of punishment meted out to enslaved children. Walker frequently used banishment to the distant plantation Berenstein, 20 miles upriver to punish both adults and children. Hendrick II, in his early teens and described as 'a decrepit Negro,' was sent there in July 1824 for six months, in the aftermath of a major dispute between his family and the superintendent. Maria III, only 11 years old, was probably also sent there because of an amorous connection. In the case of Maria, 13 to 14 years at the time, the superintendent explicitly stated that she was sent up for that reason ('a gross connection'). Clearly, banishment was not the solution to their problems, but rather counselling and maternal care. The decision was particularly insensitive because their banishment occurred during the period that William McConchie, a most immoral man, was manager of the estate. Matilda's banishment, along with her confrontation with the schoolmistress (mentioned earlier), punishment along with others for refusing to work on the day after Whitsuntide, and other events, left an indelibly negative impression on her mind, causing her to feel that the superintendent hated her.[97]

Sexual abuse of females by owners, managers and other persons having authority over them was one of the worst features of slavery. Females generally had no recourse to the law for redress of these (and most other) grievances, for they were regarded as the property of their owners, and (like other enslaved persons) without any legal personality unless they committed an offence. Female children were also commonly subjected to sexual abuse, though we cannot determine whether they were more liable to such abuse than adults. What we know is that many managers and owners paid little regard to age in their quest to satisfy their carnal appetites. Julia is a case in point.

About 15 years at the time and still classified in the records as a child, McConchie attempted to seduce her and when she rebuffed him he became very angry. His sexual passions ungratified, the same or the following day, a Sunday, which was a free day, Julia committed a minor breach of the slave laws by going to a neighbouring estate without a pass to obtain a 'hoe stick,' and this gave him the opportunity to release his pent-up feelings. He had her whipped on her naked buttocks 'until her bowels were affected' and she could not get up. The manner of the whipping needs comment. Called the Spanish whip, it entailed drawing up the knees while in a sitting position and placing the arms around them. The hands were tied and a stick was inserted between the arms and knees. Persons punished in this way were known to suffer death even from whippings with tamarind rods.[98] Julia, Betsey and others told the story of Manager McConchie frequently coercing the young women to bathe in the creek with, or in the presence of, the white youths from neighbouring plantations. McConchie once gave Sim, the brother of Julia, 50 lashes for objecting to the manager ordering her to go into the creek with these white lads.[99]

Robert M'Dermont, manager of Plantation Providence, was another abuser of children and females generally. On one occasion, in order to satisfy his carnal desires, he sent for one of the young daughters of Brutus. Let us listen to the complaint of Brutus to the Fiscal: 'The manager wants my daughter Peggy [aged 15]; I said no; he asked me three times; I said no; he kept the wife of Rule, and after having her a few nights, left her, therefore I refused.' Acquashiba (age unknown), one of the daughters of Brutus, told a more complete story of the manager's sexual proclivities:

> Peggy being sick, Acquasiba, her sister, attended; states, that manager sent aunt Grace to call Peggy, and to say if Peggy would not come, I must; we said, daddy said we must not, I was too young; Grace left us and went to daddy, shortly afterwards she returned, and tried to coax me to go, but I would not, as my daddy forbid it. Grace went and told the manager. The manager sent to call Fanny [aged 12]. Fanny went up and found him in his room, and all of us (the creoles) got orders to be watchmen at his door; I was watchman, Peggy, Fanny, and many more.[100]

The manager whipped Brutus the following day for his failure to comply with his orders, but under the pretext that the whipping had to do with neglect of work. The Fiscal believed that the manager had taken advantage of the young females, but simply admonished him to desist from such practices.[101] Doubtless, he continued to give orders to them 'to be watchmen at his door.' Many managers and owners considered having sexual relations with their female charges, consensual or otherwise, as a prerogative to be jealously guarded.

Education

Few masters paid attention to the education of their charges, and it was not before the second half of the eighteenth century, with the increasing humanitarian demand that education and Christian religious instruction be made accessible to the enslaved people, that the first consistent efforts were made in this direction. Within Berbice, again it was on the Crown properties that the first significant efforts occurred. In 1813 the imperial government, through the Berbice Commissioners, recruited Rev. John Wray to teach the enslaved persons on its estates and in the town of New Amsterdam. Most of the instruction was directed at the children, who were given special time off from their chores to attend classes. However, this instruction was carried out in the face of stiff opposition from both the managers on the neighbouring estates and the Crown ones, though in more subtle ways in the latter case. When, eventually, the imperial government agreed to return the estates to the Dutch proprietors, the educational work ceased within a short time. Wray alleged that the new (or renewed) management had turned the pulpit on Plantation Sandvoort into a cupboard and the chapel into the manager's house. Wray rued what had happened but could do nothing.[102]

Subsequently, he focused his attention on developing the town school, and this became by far the most solid effort at educational instruction in the colony up to the time of emancipation. While free coloured and free black children, and adult slaves formed part of the school population, his main focus was on the enslaved children. Other denominations such as the Anglicans, Lutherans and Reformed Church made hardly any effort to emulate the LMS work, and while Walker (after a breach with Wray) opened his own school, it was nothing in comparison with that of the missionary in terms of quality of instruction.[103] This is not to suggest that Wray's school offered a high-quality education; but it did offer the best quality of free education that was available at the time.

In January 1824 there were six private schools in the colony (excluding the *winkel* school) that catered to three slave boys, three slave girls, six free black boys, two free black girls, 38 free coloured boys, and 31 free coloured girls. Wray's public school — mentioned by Beard as disbanded — actually had only about a dozen children after the destruction of the LMS buildings, following an uprising in Demerara among the slaves belonging to that denomination in the previous month. Before that time he boasted a school with 62 children on the roll. It is interesting that no schools catering to whites are mentioned in the returns. The lieutenant-governor explained that white and 'respectable free coloured' children were usually sent abroad to receive their education.[104]

In March 1829 the first government free school was finally opened, after being mooted for several years and after suffering repeated delays because it depended to a large extent on contributions from the white population, most of whom were insouciant, and some of whom were antagonistic, to its presence. Officially, it catered to indigent free children of all 'races' from five to 11 years old. The school commenced with an enrolment of 16 boys and 20 girls. In 1831 it comprised 44 boys and 25 girls (total 69). In that year the LMS boasted an enrolment of 111 boys and 122 girls (total 233), but the vast majority of these were Sunday school children as the figures for 1830 indicate.[105]

The day schools catered largely to the free coloured, and to a lesser extent the free black, population, only three white and 88 enslaved children being listed among the population of these schools. Of the latter group, all but four of them belonged to the Lutheran estate, Augsburg, and the *winkel* department. Wray's day school's enrolment is the most surprising. It comprised only '3 or 4 slaves' out of 36 students 'fluctuating,' the remainder being classified as 'free,' but not indicating 'racial' groupings. Before the burning down of his chapel a significant number of enslaved children were on the roll. He was deeply depressed by the destruction of the chapel and intimidated by threats on his life. He begged the directors to reassign him to a non-slave colony.[106] When he finally came out of his trauma he must have decided that the day school would cater almost solely to free children, thus bending partially to the prejudice of the slave owners.

The pedagogy of the schools also demonstrated plantocratic fears about education becoming a revolutionary tool in the hands of enslaved and free black persons. The 1831 Blue Book summed it up as 'oral recital.'[107] It was much more loaded with religious texts and dogma than, for instance, one found in the curriculum of the early post-emancipation period when instructors were at greater liberty to teach other secular subjects. Take, for example, the curriculum of the two free schools in 1831: 'The 1st, 2d, 3d and 4th Parts Sunday School Union Spelling Books, the First Class Book, the Sunday School Reading Book, Crossman and Watts's Catechisms, the Testament and Bible and Prayer Book.' Instruction to the Lutheran enslaved children was even more concentrated on obedience to authority through religious dogma. It was described as 'catechetical tuition' and, in a slightly more elaborate description, 'Oral only. The nature of the instruction is inculcating to the children the Christian Religion and improving their morals.'[108]

The situation in 1830 was, if anything, worse than before 1823 when Wray and a few other teachers had been bold enough to teach a substantial number of them to read the Bible and other texts fluently. This was reflected in the 1826 report of the Commissioners of Inquiry concerning the government people. One of their prime examples was Louisa II (11 years): 'Reads in the testament very well – taught by Mr. Wray. Repeats the Lords prayer & Church Catechism very well – learned them at Mr Walkers – very perfect in her instruction.' They gave only a slightly less commendable citation of Christina II's (11) skills. A few enslaved children benefited from instruction under private tutors, usually paid for by their free fathers or, as in the case of Harriet (4¾), by some other benefactor. She attended a private school held by Mrs McIntosh, her godmother, and was showing good progress at the time of her examination by the Commissioners of Inquiry.[109]

In summary, on the whole the education offered to the small group of enslaved school children was at best only the first, timid steps in learning, while the vast majority of them remained completely illiterate.[110] Most of the school children were apparently taught to read haltingly, but a few of them were capable of reading well. The tragedy about all this is that the commissioners were firmly convinced that, while a few of the *winkel* children were dull, the vast majority were intelligent, and some even gifted.[111]

Conclusion

Child slavery in Berbice seems to have differed little, if at all, from adult slavery, in so far as it relates to the daily treatment of the enslaved people. While infants could not have been put to physical labour and therefore would not have suffered directly the trauma of the brutalities generally associated with that activity, they often suffered indirectly from as early as the womb through the brutalities meted out to their mothers. We have indicated that mothers were chastised, kicked and ill-treated in other ways, causing some of them to miscarry. Clearly, some of the children that were born under such circumstances must have suffered physical and mental impairment from the womb. Once out of the womb, their treatment was more direct. This is evident from the many complaints to the judicial authorities concerning ill-treatment to them by insouciant owners and managers, especially in relation to suckling infants. The incidents involving the children Peggy, Acquasiba, Anna, Betye and Avanturer also speak clearly to this point.

We have been unable to identify differences between managers and owners in their attitudes towards the children; so far our evidence suggests that the latter were as likely to mistreat children as the former. If we add to this picture the extreme brutalities managers and owners meted out to the rest of the enslaved population the picture becomes even starker. The genuinely sentient and caring managers and masters must have constituted a very small minority. Dyed-in-the-wool managers and owners found it very difficult to retreat from the use of the whip and other brutalities. Most of the amelioration that took place in the treatment of children and others was the result of pressure by the anti-slavery interests and the imperial government on the colonial authorities to bring to justice the perpetrators of brutalities against enslaved persons, though justice was often slow in coming and lenient in execution.

Government regulations seldom spoke directly to the situation regarding children, and so they rarely received specific legal protection in relation to a number of disabilities under which they lived. Arguably, it was easier for management to escape punishment for mistreatment of infants than adults, since those under three years did not appear on the official government records until 1819. In fact, until that time the entire enslaved population appeared simply as statistics in the crude censuses taken annually for taxation purposes. Evidence from Berbice and elsewhere also indicates that the births and deaths of infants up to a few months old were often not recorded in the triennial returns after 1819. Thus, some of the worst features of the slave system were revealed in the mistreatment of these very small ones who constituted the most vulnerable segment of the enslaved population. It was only with the inception of the apprenticeship system that those children under six years came in for special legislative protection. They were exempted from serving as apprentices, though mothers who felt incapable of maintaining them could apprentice them until they reached 21 years of age.[112]

Notes

1. Thanks are due to Professor Barry Higman of the Australian National University whose comments and suggestions helped me to improve this essay. Because of the constraints of space we have dealt with only a few aspects of the subject, omitting such issues as clothing, accommodation and manumission.
2. Pierre Erny, *Childhood and Cosmos. The Social Psychology of the Black African Child* (New York: Media Intellectics Corp., 1973), 103.
3. Cited in Erny, 110.
4. Erny, 102, 147.
5. Erny, 102–03.
6. Maria R. Cutrufelli, *Women of Africa. Roots of Oppression* (London: Zed Books, 1983), 133.
7. Cited in Cutrufelli, 134.
8. Erny, 103.
9. Erny, 103; see also Cutrufelli, 133.
10. Cutrufelli, 103.
11. Cited in Erny, 107.
12. Erny, 99–150; Cutrufelli, 134.
13. For a brief discussion of this subject see Barbara Bush, *Slave Women in Caribbean Society 1650–1838* (Bloomington: Indiana University Press,

1990), 146–48.

14. *Berbice Gazette*, September 30, 1815; CO 111/97, Beard to Bathurst, January 16, 1824. The figure for 1806 is taken from the taxation returns of 1815, but writers agree that the population did not increase after the abolition of the slave trade.

15. *PP*, 1806, XII (84), 'Order in Council Prohibiting the Importation of Slaves into America;' B.W. Higman, *Slave Populations of the British Caribbean, 1807–1834* (Baltimore: The Johns Hopkins University Press, 1984), 415.

16. CO 111/102, Slave Code of 1826, section 26, printed in *The Berbice (Royal) Gazette*, September 30, 1826. See also Henry Bolingbroke, *A Voyage to Demerary* (1807; Georgetown: Daily Chronicle Ltd., 1947), 48.

17. GNA, MCPCJB, April 2, 1810; CO 116/73, Blue Book for 1824.

18. *Berbice Gazette*, October 1, 1814.

19. CO 318/91, 'Schedules of Examinations,' 209, 212, 216. Beverley Blake indicates that Jamaican slaves were usually considered as adults between 14 and 15 years of age ('A History of Children in Nineteenth Century Jamaica,' M Phil. thesis, UWI, Mona, 1990), 5–9.

20. CO 111/94, 'Statement of the White, Free Coloured & Slave Population in the Colony Berbice (subject to the Capitation Tax) . . .,' 1812–1822.

21. CO 111/73, Inventories of former Berbice Association's estates, October 1803. The Berbice Association was the proprietor of the colony until 1795 when the Batavian Republic took over the colony. However, the estates remained (though disputably so) the property of the Association up to the time of the British takeover of the colony.

22. CO 111/88, Excerpt from MCPCJB, January 8, 1818.

23. T71/438, 'Return of slaves attached to the Winkel Department,' August 2, 1819, 723–32; T1/3483/1, RCI, 12; CO 116/73, Blue Book for 1824.

24. *Berbice Gazette*, April 12, 1820, 'An Abstract of the Slave Population of this Colony;' CO 116/173, Blue Book for 1824. The statistics used here are those reported by the Majors of the Militia Battalions to the Adjutant-General's office in December 1824. They differ by over a thousand from those compiled by the Receiver-General's office. The latter placed the total servile population at 20,734 (Ibid.). Beverley Blake states that in 1817 children comprised 29 per cent of the total Jamaican slave population ('History of Children,' 26).

25. See CO 111/109, Returns of births and deaths in Berbice, January 1, 1825–September 15, 1829 (two documents); CO 116/173-178, Blue Books, 1824-31; Higman, *Slave Populations*, 310.

26. However, in the case of the government slaves, in 1825 the Commissioners of Inquiry listed the names of all family members (see CO 318/91, 'Schedules of Examinations').

27. For more detailed studies on this topic see Bush, 84–93; Barry Higman, *Slave Populations*, 164–73; Ibid., 'The Slave Family and Household in the British West Indies, 1800–1834,' *Journal of Interdisciplinary History*, 6.2 (1975): 261–87; Michael Craton, 'Changing Patterns of Slave Families in the British West Indies,' *Journal of Interdisciplinary History*, 10 (1979): 1–35; Herbert G. Gutman, *The Black Family in Slavery and Freedom, 1750–1925* (New York: Pantheon Books, 1976).

28. See CO 318/91, 'Schedules of Examinations.'

29. Ibid., 196, 207.

30. George Pinckard, *Notes on the West Indies and the Coast of Guiana* (London: Longman, Hurst, Rees & Orme, 1806), III, 41–43.

31. T1/3483/1, RCI, 203, 206.

32. CO 318/91, 'Schedules of Examinations,' 196, 198, 207, 228–33.

33. Ibid., 181; T1/3483/1, RCI, 161.

34. *PP*, 1825, XXVI (476): 66.

35. Hilliard d'Auberteuil, *Considérations*, II, 64, 66, cited in William Dickson, *Mitigation of Slavery* (1814; Westport, Conn.: Negro Universities Press, 1970), 249. Wilma King makes basically the same point about the value to planters of children who lived to a certain age. She cites the following statement of Thomas Jefferson in 1819: 'I consider the labor of a breeding woman as no object, and that a child raised every 2 years is of more profit than the crop of the best laboring man' (Wilma King, ' "Suffer With Them Till Death." Slave Women and Their Children in Nineteenth-Century America,' in David Barry Gaspar & Darlene Clark Hine, eds., *More Than Chattel. Black Women and Slavery in the Americas* (Bloomington: Indiana University Press, 1996), 147.

36. T1/3481, Slaves belonging to the Crown in 1819, 1017; CO 318/91, 'Schedules of Examinations,' 196–99.

37. Erny, 120; Cutrufelli, 133.

38. William A. Green, *British Slave Emancipation. The Sugar Colonies and the Great Experiment 1830–1865* (Oxford: Clarendon Press, 1976), 132.

39. CO 111/102, Slave Code of 1826, section 21. The exchange rate during the period under review varied from 12 to 14.5 guilders to the £1 sterling.

40. CO 318/91, 'Schedules of Examinations,' 199, 211.

41. This group, selected by the Imperial Treasury to manage the properties from London, was headed by William Wilberforce and included James Stephen. They recruited Zachary Macaulay as their secretary/treasurer. They must be distinguished from the Commissioners of Inquiry who carried out a thorough investigation of the *winkel* department between 1825 and 1826.

42. *PP*, 1816, VIII (509), 'Copy of the Berbice Commissioners Instructions

to their Agent; dated the 27th August 1811,' 309; *PP*, 1816, VIII (528), 'Copy of the Report of the Commissioners Appointed for the Management of the Crown Estates in the Colony of Berbice . . .,' 31.

43. Thomas Rain, *The Life and Labours of John Wray, Pioneer Missionary in British Guiana, Compiled from his own Mss. and Diaries* (London: John Snow, 1892), 124.

44. *PP*, 1816, VIII (528): 20, 22; LMS. MSS, Box 1A, Wray to Burder, January 11, 1816; Rain, 116, 138–39; James Walker, *Letters on the West Indies* (London: Camberwell Press, 1818), 256.

45. CO 318/91, 'Schedules of Examinations,' 199, 211.

46. T1/3481, Walker to Harrison, November 10, 1820, 520; Ibid., Walker to Lushington, January 31, 1820, 148–49; Ibid., 'Return of slaves . . .,' October 31, 1823, 817; T1/3482, 'Observations by Walker . . .,' in Walker to Harrison, March 24, 1826, 189; T1/3483/1, RCI, 119, 177; CO 318/90, Day Books 2 & 3, July 31, 1822 & January 16, 1823, 326, 379.

47. T1/3483/1, RCI, 24.

48. CO 111/103, Katz's managers to Beard, February 14, 1826.

49. Ibid.

50. Ibid.

51. T71/438 and T71/444, Registration returns for 1819 and 1831 respectively.

52. CO 111/73, P. Eggers, Govt. Secretary, Total number of slaves in Berbice, December 1799; CO 111/97, 'Summary of the Slave Population of Berbice for 1822,' dated December 23, 1823; CO 111/101, 'Statement of the Slave Population of the Colony Berbice with an account of Births and Deaths . . .,' January 1, 1821–January 1, 1825; CO 111/109, 'Return of the Population of the Colony of Berbice on the 15th September 1829;' CO 116/178, Blue Book for 1831. For some years there are important discrepancies in the returns produced by the registry (see, for instance, CO 116/173–176, Blue Books, 1824–1828).

53. CO 318/91, 'Schedules of Examinations,' 12, 212, 217.

54. CO 318/91, 'Schedules of Examinations.'

55. CO 318/90, Day Books 1&2, October 29, 1821 & August 5, 1822, 222, 327; CO 318/91, 'Schedules of Examinations,' 204–05, 211, 212; T1/3481, 'Return of Slaves . . .,' October 31, 1823, 202; Ibid., Walker to Harrison, December 29, 1823, 196; T1/3482/2, 'Remarks on the evidence transmitted to Earl Bathurst . . .,' February 25, 1826, 222–23.

56. Higman, *Slave Populations,* 32. We have computed the 24 from the other data given by Higman. This figure is substantially higher than our calculation for 1819–22, using the returns in the Colonial Office records, rather than the slave registries that he used.

57. Walker, *Letters,* 253.

58. *PP*, 1825, XXVI (476): 36.
59. *Ibid.*, 24.
60. *PP*, 1826, XXVI (401): 13–14.
61. The slave code of 1826 prevented the separation of families (husband, wife and children under 16 years) in execution of debt, but did not prevent such separation by regular sale, bequest or otherwise (CO 111/102, slave code, section 26).
62. *PP*, 1825, XXVI (476): 63.
63. *Ibid.*, 13.
64. *Ibid.*, 24.
65. CO 111/104, Complaints made to Protector, July1 –September 1, 1827.
66. CO 318/91, 'Schedules of Examinations,' 240; see also CO 111/104, Complaints made to Protector, July 1– September 1, 1827.
67. *PP*, 1825, XXVI (476): 24. For a comparison with other Caribbean colonies see Higman, *Slave Populations,* 187.
68. Joshua Steele, 'Letters,' in Dickson, *Mitigation,* 14.
69. *PP*, 1825, XXVI (476): 66.
70. T.P. Eddy, 'Food Shortage as a Health Catastrophe,' in E.E. Sabben–Clarke, D.J. Bradley and K. Kirkwood, eds., *Health in Tropical Africa During the Colonial Period. Based on the Proceedings of a Symposium held at New College, Oxford 21-23 March 1977* (Oxford: Clarendon Press, 1980), 37–42.
71. Eddy, 37.
72. See, for instance, Higman, *Slave Populations,* 260–378; Kenneth Kiple, *The Caribbean Slave: A Biological History* (Cambridge: Cambridge University Press, 1984); Kenneth Kiple and Virginia Kiple, 'Deficiency Diseases in the Caribbean,' in *Caribbean Slavery in the Atlantic World, eds.,* Verene A. Shepherd and Hilary McD. Beckles. (Kingston: Ian Randle Publishers, 2000), 785–94; Richard Sheridan, *Doctors and Slaves. A Medical and Demographic History of Slavery in the British West Indies 1680-1834* (Cambridge: Cambridge University Press, 1985).
73. T1/3482/1, Bennett to Burdett & Kinchela, January 31, 1826, 107–08.
74. CO 111/110, Bird to Beard, September 1830, enclosure.
75. LMS. MSS, Box 1A, Wray to Directors, February 23, 1814; Ibid., Wray to Burder, October 25, 1817 & March 26, 1821; Alvin O. Thompson, 'The Crown Slaves of Berbice: A Study of Official Mismanagement 1803–1831' (PhD. thesis, University of the West Indies, Cave Hill Campus, 1998), 112–13, 301. For a more detailed discussion of this aspect, and of the protein and caloric values of the foods distributed to slaves in Berbice and Demerara, see Alvin O. Thompson, *Colonialism and Underdevelopment in Guyana 1580-1803* (Bridgetown: Carib Research and Publications, 1987), 119–23.
76. T1/3483/1, RCI, 18–23, 96–97, 303–04.

77. GNA, MCPCJB, May 6, 1811; *PP*, 1826, XXVI (401): 13–14.

78. *PP*, 1825, XXVI (476): 5–6.

79. GNA, MCPCJB, January 8, 1812.

80. *PP*, 1825, XXV (476): 36–37.

81. T1/3482/2, Burdett & Kinchela to Horton, August 13, 1825, 544–73.

82. *PP*, 1825, XXVI (476): 56. The sambo girl Betsey had an altercation with her mistress and so her master Obermuller flew into a rage and 'kicked her on her belly so that she could scarcely draw her breath' (*Ibid.*, 18).

83. *Ibid.*, 46–47.

84. *PP*, 1818, XVII (433), 'Further Papers Relating to the Treatment of Slaves in the Colonies,' 229–38. For a detailed study on this case see Alvin O. Thompson, 'The Chastisement of the Slave '"America,"' *Journal of Caribbean History*, 33.1 & 2 (1999): 146–61.

85. *PP*, 1825, XXVI (476): 45.

86. *Ibid.*, 26–27. For a more detailed account of this case see Mary Turner, 'The 11 O'clock Flog: Women, Work and Labour in the British Caribbean,' *Slavery and Abolition*, 20.1 (1999): 38–58. John Stedman mentioned a more brutal instance of the flogging of a pregnant mother in 1776 by an Italian named d'Onis, owner of plantation Hazard. He 'Ordered a Negro woman to be Flogg'd, Who was Advanc'd 8 Months in her Pregnancy till / it was said / her very intestines Appear'd through her Body And all this for having broke a Cristal Tumbler' (*Narrative of a Five Years Expedition Against the Revolted Negroes of Surinam*. Transcribed for the first time from the original 1790 manuscript. Eds. Richard and Sally Price, Baltimore: The Johns Hopkins University Press, 1988, 495).

87. Blake, 'History of Children,' 40–41.

88. GNA, MCPCJB, May 6, 1811.

89. Ibid. The minutes do not record the results of the criminal proceedings.

90. *PP*, 1825, XXVI (476): 16–18: *PP*, 1826, XXVI (401): 13–14.

91. T1/3482/1, Examination of Scott, March 30, 1826, in Kinchela to Horton, April 22, 1826, 376–79; T1/3483/1, Burdett & Kinchela to Bathurst, August 13, 1825, 536–41, 553, 562–68.

92. CO 318/91, 'Schedules of Examinations,' 211; T1/3482, 'Remarks on the evidence transmitted to Earl Bathurst . . .,' February 25, 1826, 222–23 .

93. CO 111/96, Beard to Bathurst, August 17& 25, 1823; CO 111/97, Extract from MCGB, January 10, 1824; Ibid., Beard to Bathurst, January 14 & September 16, 1824.

94. CO 111/102, Slave Code of 1826, section 14. In January 1834 only male and female children under 10 years could be flogged by their masters under the circumstances described in the 1826 code

(Ordinance establishing Inferior Courts of Criminal Justice in British Guiana, January 23, 1834, section 18, in *PP*, 1835, L (278–1), 'Papers Presented to Parliament by His Majesty's Command . . .,' 342–45).

95. GNA, MCPCJB, October 3, 1810.

96. Ibid., January 8, 1812; *PP*, 1825, XXVI (476): 46.

97. T1/3482/2, Walker, 'Remarks on the evidence transmitted to Earl Bathurst by the Commissioners of Inquiry ...,' February 25, 1826, 222; CO 318/90, Day Book 1, January 31, 1821, 179; CO 318/91, 'Schedules of Examinations," 209, 211; T1/3481, "Return of slaves ...,' October 31, 1823, 202.

98. CO 318/91, 'Schedules of Examinations,' 204–05. See R.A.J. Van Lier, *Frontier Society* (The Hague: Martinus Nijhoff, 1971), 130 for a description of this form of punishment.

99. CO 318/91, 'Schedules of Examinations,' 193, 204–05.

100. *PP*, 1826, XXV (401), 'Copies of the Record of the Proceedings of the Fiscals of Demerara and Berbice, in their Capacity of Guardians and Protectors of the Slaves ... from the 1st January 1814 ...,' 12–13. See T71/438, Slave Registrations, 1819: 329 for the ages of the children.

101. *PP*, 1826, XXV (401), 12–13.

102. CO 111/90, Wray to Goulburn (?), October 7 & November 26, 1817; Ibid., Extracts from Wray's journal, October 31 & November 3, 1817. For a fuller discussion of Wray's early educational efforts see Thompson, 'Crown Slaves,' 184–95.

103. CO 111/97, Wray to Beard, December 28, 1823; CO 111/97, Beard to Bathurst, January 10, 1824.

104. CO 111/97, Beard to Bathurst, January 10, 1824.

105. CO 111/107, Beard to Murray, July 8, 1829 & enclosure; CO 116/176 & 178, Blue Books for 1828 (sic.) and 1831. The Parliamentary Papers published by the imperial government on the educational establishments in the colony in 1830 listed two separate government free schools, one for boys and the other for girls (*PP*, 1831–32 (660), 'Return from all the Slave Colonies Belonging to the British Crown..,' 42–43).

106. LMS. MSS, Box 1B, Wray to Raynor, August 27, 1823; Ibid., Wray to Hankey, September 4, 1823 & February 6, 1826; Ibid., Wray to Directors of LMS, November 18, 1823; Ibid., Wray to Burder, May 29, 1824.

107. CO 116/178, Blue Book for 1831.

108. *Ibid.*

109. See, *for example*, CO 318/91, 'Schedules of Examinations,' 222, 224, 232.

110. CO 111/97, Beard to Bathurst, January 10, 1824.

111. CO 318/91, 'Schedules of Examinations,' 191–231.

112. Green, 134.

Figure 12:
Public Punishment of enslaved persons
&
Figure 13:
The execution of breaking on the rack

CHAPTER

Capital Sentences Against Slaves in Barbados in the Eighteenth Century: An Analysis
Karl Watson

Introduction

In his discussion of crime in eighteenth-century England, Douglas Hay in his preface makes the point that criminality, offences, offenders and myths are all central to unlocking the meanings of eighteenth-century social history. He states further that they are 'all centrally concerned with the law, both as ideology and as actuality and with that country's definition of crime.'[1] Similarly, John Styles, in a perceptive article in *History Today*, points out that quantitative analysis of crime enables the historian to identify changes over time in the level of prosecuted crime and prompts him to seek an explanation for those changes.[2] Laws, he argues, are a system of ideas which are influential in shaping people's understanding of the social order. He points out that belief in the rule of law was a striking feature of eighteenth-century England. Yet, these laws were invariably made by those in authority; in other words, the powerful, the propertied class, those who had substantial material goods to lose. Laws were punitive and constructed to protect property, in a century when the first tentative successes of the Industrial Revolution were creating significant property holdings for the upper and emerging middle classes. This view is supported by Sir Leon Radzinowicz who, in his examination of English criminal law, points out that the number of capital statutes grew from about 50 to over 200 between 1688 and 1820. Almost all of them concerned offences against property.[3]

In the West Indies, a special type of property had been created by the labour needs of tropical export agriculture. Sugarcane cultivation required large inputs of labour. When European indentureship failed, these labour needs were satisfied by massive imports of Africans, who were enslaved for life, as both the chattels and real estate of their owners. David Trotman, in looking at the case of nineteenth-century Trinidad, argues that plantation society generated its own particular rate and pattern of crime which reflected the nature of that society's polity and economy.[4] In her discussion of the West Indian slave laws, Elsa Goveia forcefully makes the point that slaves were only theoretically property. In reality, however, they were human beings with all the proclivities of humans, both good and bad. Therefore, a legal system had to be devised to police and control this special group in West Indian society. During the period of slavery, this legal system created a framework on which that society was constructed. Parameters were established in order that free and non-free persons could co-exist in a controlled and orderly fashion in an abnormal environment which ran counter to established human values. Of course, laws themselves are theoretical constructs, which establish guidelines for human relationships. They may or may not be obeyed. The phrasing of laws, their intent, the forces which led to their creation and the response of those at whom these laws are directed, all tell us a great deal about the dynamics of the society which framed them. All aspects of the workings of society are covered, moral, social, political, economic, etc. As intimated earlier, understanding a given legal system helps us to understand the power relationships within that system, and ultimately gives us a much better understanding of the society itself.

The raw data used in this paper were derived from a painstaking search of the minutes of the Council of Barbados for 1700 to 1800. From this material, it is proposed to do the following: quantify the executions at ten-year intervals and observe any fluctuations; establish a typology for capital crimes committed and see what specific patterns are revealed; examine the social status of the owners in order to see what correlations are present; determine, through inductive analysis, the possible world view of the slaves in respect of crime and punishment; see what linkages exist between this world view and the broader theoretical concept of slave resistance.

The compensation lists to Barbadian owners for the judicial execution of their slaves provide the main body of source materials for this paper. Petitions for compensation invariably included the name of the owner, the name of the slave executed and a brief description of the capital crime committed. Certain limitations should be noted at the outset. The following analysis concerns itself solely with capital offences. As stated clearly in Clause XII of the 1688 Act (see below), these included any offence which *'caused damages in excess of twelvepence'* (author's emphasis). The paper therefore does not consider all crime, since the evidence has not survived. Petty offences were invariably dealt with by plantation management or individual owners, and no systematic records of punishments were kept. Admittedly, this will introduce a degree of distortion in any conclusions drawn about the nature and frequency of crime in Barbados. However, the quantum set of 12 pence is so small that it serves to underscore the wide range of offences which were considered capital offences in the eighteenth century. Only very petty offences were excluded. Admittedly, these may have been very numerous. A glare, a raised voice, inappropriate body language, tardiness in carrying out an order could all have been interpreted as insolence. The documents frequently attest to a white aversion

197

to perceived insolence. In 1707, complaints were made to the governor and council about 'the daring insolence of the Negroes at this juncture.' Various individuals complained that:

> The Negroes were so impudent that they were afraid to go along the road for fear of being knockt down & robbed & that they were afraid to send their children to school & that Mr Glascock told him, he was pursued by several Negroes last Saturday night & was forced to run for his life & that daily complaints were made by ye poor inhabitants, that they went in danger of their lives.[5]

'Uppity' blacks with too much 'attitude' were not to be tolerated. Dr Robert Poole, who visited the island in 1748 and left a detailed journal of his experiences, provides us with the following eyewitness account of slave punishment for petty offences:

> As soon as it is determined to punish a Negro, one of these persons [a 'Jumper'] is sent for, and with a long, strong scourge, that leaves deep impressions at every stroke, they are scourged, having their thumbs or hands first tied together, and sometimes tied to an appointed place; and this scourging is so frequently used here, that hardly a day passes but the noise thereof is sounding in one's ears; and which to me, is indeed one of the most disagreeable things I have yet met with here.[6]

Judgement in slave trials

Laws designed to control aspects of slave behaviour had been sporadically enacted in Barbados from as early as 1643, but it was not until 45 years later, in 1688, that the House of Assembly drew up a fairly comprehensive code entitled 'An Act for the Governing of Negroes.'[7] Among its clauses, Nos. XII and XV are of specific interest to this paper. Clause XII states that, 'whereas many heinous and grievous crimes, as murder, burglaries, robbing in the highways, rapes, burning of houses or canes, stealing, wilfully killing or maiming of cattle (or any other form of livestock or poultry) are committed or attempted by slaves,' any criminal act which caused damages in excess of 12 pence would result in the arrest of the suspect and his arraignment before a justice of the peace, who was empowered to summon another justice of the peace and three freeholders in order to hold an enquiry and pass sentence. The slaves, according to the wording of the law, being 'brutish,' did not deserve 'for the baseness of their condition, to be tried by the legal trial of twelve men of their Peers or Neighbourhood.' After hearing and examining the evidence, if the suspect was proved guilty, the death sentence was to be pronounced and the execution was to be carried out immediately 'by some Negro to be pressed for that purpose, by any Constable.' Clause XV provided for damages and compensation to the interested parties after they presented a certificate to the council corroborating their claim for a sum 'which shall never exceed £25, to pay the damages to the party injured and the overplus if any to the owner, and if no person is injured, then the whole to the owner out of the Public-treasury.'

In 1692 the question of runaways, which had been omitted in the earlier Act, was addressed,[8] and an amendment was passed which stated that any slave who had lived on the island for over one year and had absented himself from his master's service for more than 30 days was to suffer the death penalty, compensation of £25 being paid to the owner.[9]

In 1739 a further amendment to the 1688 Act was passed, making provision for owners to appeal the mandatory death sentence for the offences specified in Clause XII, 'which in some instances hath been thought erroneous and many times by the malice or ill will of the Prosecutor.' In such instances, owners could file a Writ of Error before the Court of Errors, causing the execution to be stayed for ten days while the matter was being reconsidered.

The justices of the peace involved in slave trials were also instructed to try to bring about an agreement between the parties concerned, 'requisite and equitable, for saving the life of such slave or slaves,' provided, in their judgement, 'the matters charged are not of a heinous nature, nor the criminal or criminals to be an old offender or offenders and shall think him, her or them, an object deserving less severity.'[10] In the event that no agreement was reached, the justices of the peace would then submit the case to the governor and council who, after hearing the minutes of the trial, would either reverse or confirm the judgement.

A sampling of the executions recorded will show how lives were terminated for what today are considered very insignificant offences. In 1756, Mason was hanged for stealing 10s. In 1761, Wolley was executed for stealing 2s.6d. In 1737, George Dicke was executed for stealing a turkey cock valued at 3s.9d. In 1740, Bussoe and Bristol were convicted in separate cases of stealing 'wearing apparrell.' They paid with their lives for appropriating used clothing. Sometimes the offence was so minimal that even to the eighteenth-century mind the sentence must have seemed extreme. Thus, in 1742, John was convicted of stealing bread and other provisions worth £1.17s.6d. from John Little and sentenced to be hanged. Members of the Council of Barbados were dubious about the severity and fairness of the verdict. They set up an enquiry to determine whether 'the criminal was an old offender or not.' He was deemed a rogue and duly hanged, his hunger notwithstanding.[11]

On the other hand, some owners were able to obtain a reprieve for their condemned slaves by appealing the sentences under the provisions of the 1739 Amendment (mentioned above). The vast majority of these appeals were upheld. For example, in 1754, Dr William Cox filed a Writ of Error on behalf of his slave Cudjo who had been convicted and sentenced to death for stealing a cock and a hen from Joseph Thorne. The court, on the grounds that Cudjo was not an old offender and had returned the stolen poultry to Thorne, altered the sentence to 12 lashes with a cowskin (a plaited whip made of leather).[12] In 1748, William Thorne filed a claim on behalf of his infant relative, John Butcher, requesting the reversal of the death sentence which had been passed on the slave Macco. The sentence was reversed by a majority of four votes to three. However, Macco did not escape scot-free, but was sentenced to 39 lashes; 13 were given him in front of the custom house on July 7 and 13, in the market place on July 8, and the final 13 in front of Eldridge's tavern door on July 9. The minutes do not specify the nature of Macco's offence, but, since the plaintiff John Grant was awarded £4 damages, we can be fairly sure that Macco had been convicted of theft.[13]

In other instances, the sentence was simply reversed, as in the case of Thomas Newton vs Codrington Carrington, where the felony charge was dismissed and 'the Council ordered that the said Negro man Ben be discharged.'[14] Not all convicted individuals were as lucky, and this was especially true where a guilty verdict based on a murder charge had been given. In 1751, James Mahon filed a Writ of Error on behalf of his slave London, who had been found guilty of the murder of the slave Prince, the property of Dr James Sedgewick. After consideration, the verdict of guilty was reaffirmed and Prince was subsequently executed. In 1762, Nathaniel Haggatt appealed against the death sentence passed on his slave Dijon for the murder of Celia, the slave of one Elizabeth Bolton. Haggatt was supported in his appeal by Bolton who petitioned the governor directly, saying that she would prefer to see Dijon transported rather than executed. Both appeals were turned down and Dijon was executed. Governor Pinfold, in a testy comment on Elizabeth Bolton's appeal, observed, 'that the expectations of receiving a greater sum from the attorneys of Mr Haggatt's estates than what was allowed by law for an executed slave was the motive of her application to him.'[15]

The minutes recorded by the council are oftentimes terse in their commentary and do not always give us insights into the thinking of those passing judgement. However, a surviving proclamation issued by Governor William Spry in 1769 regarding the case of Pompey gives us considerable detail, and demonstrates that judgements were not arrived at capriciously, and could be overturned if a sound case was made for such a reversal.[16]

Pompey's owner, Henry Bishop, appealed directly to Spry for clemency for Pompey. In his consideration of the case, the governor contacted the body of freeholders and justices of the peace who had originally heard the case.[17] They explained to the governor that, having examined the evidence, they were agreed that Pompey was guilty of the murder of Will, a slave belonging to Issac Lavine, and so, according to the laws of Barbados, they had no alternative but to find him guilty and sentence him to death. However, they went on to advise Spry that:

Notwithstanding they thought the sd [sic] Negro Pompey guilty of the crime with which he stood charged before them, and therefore passed sentence of death upon him, yet, for as much as the sd Negro Pompey committed the sd act in a sudden transport and heat of passion, and was urged thereto, by some ill disposed person or persons then present, and the said Negro Pompey, being a youth but of about 17 years of age, and not an old offender, and before the commission of the act for which he lies under sentence of death, always bore a fair and honest character; they, the sd Justices and Freeholders therefore recommend him to me as a fit object of mercy.[18]

Acting on their recommendation, which was supported by a favourable report on the case from the attorney-general, and the formal agreement of the murdered slave's owner, Governor Spry issued a full pardon for Pompey.

Of some interest, because of its racial overtones, is the 1784 case of Padmore vs Columbus, in which an appeal had been entered on behalf of the slave Coley, convicted of the murder of James Columbus, a white man. Padmore had retained Gibbes Walker Jordan and John Beckles, two of the most eminent lawyers on the island, to argue his case and that of Coley. They had located a material witness, John Smith, who had not appeared at the previous trial. Against the objections of Matthew Coulthurst, Mrs Columbus' counsel, his evidence was considered.

Invariably, the murder or attempted murder of a white person by a black slave resulted in a conspicuous and horrific method of execution which, it was hoped, would serve as a deterrent. In 1763, Governor Pinfold made this abundantly clear when, at the end of the trial of the slave Joe for attempted murder, he ordered that 'the execution and destruction of the Barbarous Wretch may strike a dread and terror to the survivors that they may be deterr'd from perpetrating the like crime for the future.'[19] The security of the white population seemed to demand such an unequivocal deterrent. However, in the Columbus murder case, the powers that be determined that the homicide was a justifiable one. Despite the pleas of Sarah Columbus on behalf of her dead husband, the Council directed that Coley's sentence be altered to transportation. Two votes, those of Governor Ricketts and Mr Cumberbatch, were cast for full acquittal.[20]

How does one interpret these cases and dozens of similar ones? It appears that for a variety of reasons whites were prepared to risk the force of the law in order to protect blacks. In 1719, John Goodwin was charged with secreting the Negro slave Monsieur, for whom a warrant had been issued. He told Constable John Linscomb who was attempting to effect the arrest, 'you are a son of a Whore, Villain, Dog and Rascal, God Damn the Warrant and God Damn the Authority. God Damn you, you dog. There is the Negro, take him if you dare, if you do, I will shoot you through the head.' Such provocative language aroused the ire of the authorities, and Goodwin was found guilty and fined £10.[21] Years later, William Yard of Newton Plantation smuggled Billy Thomas, his favourite slave, off the island in order to prevent his execution.[22]

There seems to be a mixture of economics and eighteenth-century liberalism combined, which helps to explain shifting attitudes on the part of slave owners towards capital punishment. It is clear from the wording of the 1739 amendment, that the House of Assembly was concerned at the increased cost to the public treasury of compensation payments, and the bill was enacted at a time when executions were rising dramatically. However, there also seems to be genuine preoccupation at the callous waste of human life, and the case of Coley above clearly demonstrates that Barbadian whites from the mid-eighteenth century were prepared to accept provocation or justifiable homicide as a defence or mitigating circumstance, even when the murder crossed racial lines. This evidence of changing attitudes must be related to changing values in the broader Western world, as concepts embodied in the Enlightenment slowly spread.

On the other hand, it should be noted that blacks were also vulnerable to the whims, or drawn into the personal quarrels, of their masters. In 1721, for example, such an event followed an altercation between two white men, Richard Byrch and Cap. John Swan, over political differences. Byrch had drunk to the health of President Samuel Cox and his friends, 'whereupon the said Swan said to this deponent, God damn you, you son of a whore, you tell the President (the Honourable Samuel Cox meaning) he may kiss my arse like a son of a whore; for he And they (the said President's friends meaning) are a pack of dogs.' Swan then 'fell into a very great passion with this deponent.' He ordered his slave to 'mount his horse and draw his pistol and put himself upon a level with this Deponent, again calling this Deponent, "Son of a Whore" and threatened his said slave to shoot him, if he did not shoot this deponent.' This, of course, put the slave in a considerable dilemma. The choice was damming either way. Refuse and risk his master's ire at a point in time when tempers were flaring, or do as commanded and risk the wrath of the white community for wounding or killing a white man. The slave was saved by the intervention of others. Swan contented himself with striking Byrch and 'swore he would some other time kill this deponent.'[23]

Another example illustrating the extent to which slaves could be drawn into the personal affairs of whites occurred in 1761, when the owners of Lowlands Plantation were indicted for inciting slaves to take up arms against officers who had been instructed to levy on the plantation. The House of Assembly considered that their action had brought 'the very being no less than the well being of this community in danger.'[24] Again, in 1764, after Samuel Adams had been arrested for similar reasons, John Spencer, the marshal, reported to the governor that 'they were on the road met by Mr John Adams & his overseer Hutchinson who with several Negro slaves armed with drawn cutlasses & bludgeons did rescue and take away his prisoner Samuel Adams.'

Both Jonathan Blenman, the attorney-general, and J. Stone, the solicitor-general, were advised to 'consider the dangerous consequence of putting arms in the hands of Negroes in a country where the number of Blacks is so superior to the white inhabitants that our main security depends on the ignorance of their natural power and strength. If by the example of their owner they are thus taught to resist the arm of Justice, this community must sink.'[25]

Sometimes attempts were made by white offenders to implicate black slaves so as to mask their own involvement. The case of Peter Archer provides us with a good example of this. He was the guardian of Jonathan Franklin, a sensitive young man, who owned substantial real estate and slaves. The young man was forced by Archer to eat in the kitchen with the slaves and never at the family dining table. After abusing him physically and psychologically for some time, Archer determined to kill his ward and lay the blame on black slaves. He paid a man, John Warburton, to lie to the authorities, telling them that he had witnessed three slaves kill young Franklin. In reality, as the evidence later showed, Archer was the perpetrator. He had dragged the young man into a cornfield, cut his 'throat from Ear to Ear and so deep as to reach the Vertebrae of the Neck,' smashed in his head with a rock and thrown him into a marl hole, which he had then filled with rubbish in an effort to conceal the body. Charles, one of Franklin's slaves who was passing by, heard the cries of the young man as he was being killed and, on creeping closer, witnessed his final moments and Archer's disposal of the body. He went to the nearby house of a relative and reported what he had seen. The constabulary were alerted and Archer was taken into custody, still wearing his bloodied shirt. As the date of his trial approached, there was some nervousness on the part of the prosecutors, for slave evidence could not be used to convict a white man. Yet, as events unfolded, the guardians of the law were sensible and permitted a flexibility which, in a legal sense, was an anomaly since it did not create a precedent. Slave evidence in cases involving whites was not accepted in Barbadian courts until 1831. However, in this instance, Basil Thomas, the court prosecutor, included the eyewitness account of the slave Charles in his address to the jury, and used it in an exceptionally clever way, as the following section of his address demonstrates:

> For the reasons I have said, a slave cannot give Testimony, although he should see a Murder perpetrated — This is our Case, Gentlemen; and in such a Case not to allow of violent Presumption were doubly to take away the Law from the Friends of the Deceased; it would be a shuting [sic] of the Door against Justice and a Toleration for all Crimes whatever. Who then can be said to lie down with Safety on his Bed, or promise himself the Fruits of his Labor, if the Sword of Murder and the Hand of Rapine, can, under the Veil of Unbelief, and in the Breast of a Negro, at all Times remain concealed, and never come to light, because the positive Evidence is invalidated thro' any other means whatever ?[26]

In effect, Thomas' address to the jury, which included the detailed account of Charles, was tantamount to bringing him into the court. It pitted the evidence of a black slave against that of a white person. The crown's counsel asked the jury to disregard Warburton's evidence and give credence to that of Charles. Also, and quite deliberately, Thomas pointed out the anomalies of the legal system within the framework of slavery, which he highlighted with his remarks on the 'shuting of the Door against Justice and a Toleration for all Crimes whatever.' It was this eyewitness account, in addition to other supporting evidence, which assisted in Archer's conviction. He was taken to the usual place of execution, the Pierhead in St Michael, and 'hanged by the neck until dead.'[27]

Methods of executing the death penalty

Before examining the execution data in detail, it might be useful to look at the methods used to impose the death penalty as there was some variation relating to the nature of the crime committed, and the race and social status of the victim. The usual mode of execution was by hanging, not from a constructed stand, but from a nearby tree. This was publicly done and must have involved great trauma for those who witnessed it, especially friends and relatives of the executed individual. Nor did the psychological pain end there, for on most occasions the corpse was left to hang and rot in the wind and rain. Since there was no official hangman for slaves, the most convenient male slave was pressed into that deadly service, and so that individual must have felt a sense of complicity in his fellow slave's death. Notwithstanding the difference in eighteenth-century attitudes and the degree to which the average person was exposed to physical violence and trauma, there must have been some degree of mental scarring for these amateur and, almost certainly, unwilling hangmen.

If the crime being punished was premeditated murder, especially that of a white, then the guilty person would be suspended in a gibbet or iron cage in a highly visible location to starve to death slowly. Occasionally good fortune intervened, as in the case of Joe who had been convicted of attempting to poison Maynard Miller, a white man, and his family, and had been gibbeted in 'a convenient place least offensive to the neighbours.' Joe was pardoned because he implicated another slave named Consong. The latter, apparently an African-born slave, was judicially executed by gibbeting. He was used by the establishment to attack West African beliefs about the transmigration of the human body and soul, for as soon as he was dead Governor Pinfold ordered that 'his head be severed from his Body and put upon a poll in such a place... to convince the other Negroes of the absurdity and impossibility of his return to his own country after death.'[28] The slave Marcellus did not have Joe's good fortune. Having escaped from the gibbet in which he had been secured and suspended, he was recaptured and returned to the same gibbet which was reinforced this time. There he hung until he died.[29]

In more extreme cases involving prominent members of the white elite, or where the crime was considered particularly brutal, the individual was burnt alive. Governor Pinfold's directives in two cases illustrate this. Ann Odwin, a white infant, was taken from her home by her slave Cuffee on July 27, 1758. She was murdered by stabbing and the body hidden in some bushes. Cuffee was subsequently gibbetted and when dead was quartered, his limbs displayed and his trunk burnt at the site of the murder.[30] In the case of Miss Sarah Sutton, who was raped and murdered by the slave Sharper in early August 1764, Governor Pinfold ordered that he be:

> chained to a stake to be fixed for that purpose. That his privy members be then cut off and burned before his face and that afterwards he be burned alive . . . the whole carcase be reduced to ashes and those ashes dispersed in the air that no part of such a vilain may remain, and that the whole execution may be performed with such solemnity, that it may strike the spectators with the greatest awe and terror.[31]

Influences on crime

Table 8.1 shows clear fluctuations in the level of executions over time. One would expect crime figures to increase with the growth of the population, and this pattern occurs until 1779 when there is a dramatic decline in executions for the last two decades of the century.

Table 8.1: Slave executions in Barbados, 1700–99

Year	Male	Female	Total
1700-1709	51	6	57
1710-1719	38	1	39
1720-1729	31	0	31
1730-1739	55	1	56
1740-1749	94	1	95
1750-1759	87	7	94
1760-1769	62	3	65
1770-1779	82	4	86
1780-1789	2	2	4
1790-1799	13	0	13
Total	**515**	**25**	**540**

Source: BDA, Compiled from Minutes of the Council of Barbados.

Of 540 individuals executed between 1700 and 1799, 25 of them (4.63 per cent)were women and 515 (95.37 per cent) were men. Even though modern crime statistics indicate that the majority of crimes are committed by males, this statistic seems to be rather high, especially when one takes into account the fact that in Barbados, unlike elsewhere in the West Indies, the sex ratio among blacks was balanced from as early as 1680.[32]

The figures show that there was a tendency for executions to bunch in the period 1730–79 when 396 took place out of the total of 540. However, from 1780 to the end of the century there is a substantial decline in the numbers of slaves executed. For the last 20 years of the century, 17 executions are recorded. This was sufficiently noticeable for contemporary observers to comment on, as John Brathwaite did when giving evidence before the Board of Trade, when he intimated that this decrease was due to new sensitivities on the part of the planters.[33] Nathan Lucas, a Barbadian luminary who in the early nineteenth century made copies of the Council Minutes, was forced to comment in respect of the 1789 minutes, 'not one [order] for Negroes executed according to law and this source of expense seems to have dwindled to nothing for some time past;' and again in respect of the 1798 minutes, 'not one [order] for the execution of a slave — nor has there been one for some time, a proof certainly of improved manners. In former minutes they are very frequent.'[34]

Here we have two opinions put forward for the decline, 'greater humanity' on the part of the planters and 'improved manners' on the part of the slaves. Certainly, there is some degree of truth in both assertions. Let us now examine the variables which certainly did affect the propensity of people to prosecute and hence the rate of executions. In 1780, Barbados experienced what was from all accounts the worst hurricane in its history. Mortality was high, upwards of 4,000 slaves being killed.[35] This massive loss of life was extremely high in economic terms, and when combined with the market value of slaves meant that slave owners were increasingly reluctant to prosecute. The compensation rate of £25 set in 1688, when the price of a slave was much lower, could not match the £100 to £150 fetched by Barbadian-born slaves or the £50 paid for an African-born during the second half of the eighteenth century.[36] Moreover, it should be noted that by 1780 Barbados had a heavily creolised population and was no longer dependent on African imports. Therefore, given the fact that such a high percentage of the enslaved population was Barbadian-born and had a correspondingly high value, it is not surprising that slave owners were unwilling to risk execution and the corresponding loss of capital. Human life was no longer as cheap as it had once been.

Secondly, there is no doubt that Barbadian planters towards the end of the eighteenth century held a different view of crime and punishment than their predecessors. Whereas the seventeenth-century mentality allowed a man to be hanged for stealing a turkey, this was seen as too severe by the enlightened planter mind. Again, in this instance, West Indian planters, among them

Barbadians, have been victims of a widespread stereotype which portrayed them as complete ignoramuses who, if literate at all, hardly read. On the contrary, many planters were very well read, and the tenets of the Enlightenment with its emphasis on rational thinking contributed to their shifting world view.

There is a marked clustering of offences involving the theft of livestock in the first half of the eighteenth century, but these tend to be absent in the second half of the century. It is also significant that after 1756 there were no more executions for running away, despite the fact that runaways were constantly identified in newspaper advertisements during the latter half of the century. Moreover, the islands, and Barbados in particular, were becoming increasingly subject to criticism in Britain, as the humanitarians waged an increasingly effective public relations campaign directed at the slave owners. Many members of the resident Barbadian plantocracy were sensitive to this criticism and this is reflected in the marked decrease in executions.

Another factor to take into consideration, in addition to the slave owner's possible reluctance to prosecute in view of the changing international conditions, is that the decrease in executions might be a response to less criminal activity on the part of slaves. It can be argued that better treatment and diet in the last decade of the century, prompted in part by the activities of the humanitarians and the impending cessation of the slave trade, reduced the frequency of petty and praedial larceny, which had occurred so frequently in the first three-quarters of the century. Richard Sheridan supports this view, arguing that, 'beginning about 1760, certain Barbadian planters, motivated by economic self-interest, attempted to ameliorate the condition of their slaves in an effort to reduce mortality and encourage breeding. As part of this program, more land was planted in corn and ground provisions, and more attention given to raising poultry and pigs.'[37]

Violent crimes committed by slaves

There is a compelling and sometimes titillating aspect to crime. Violence repels yet at the same time draws us, as evidenced by the crowds which gather at accident scenes or to get a quick glimpse of a murdered individual. The Romans knew well the psychological importance of gladiatorial combats for their citizenry, and modern-day telecommunications thrive on this specialised voyeurism which has survived, undiminished, through the ages. Let us look at three accounts of criminal actions recorded in the past, one of robbery and two of murder.

Sometime between 8 and 9 o'clock on July 25, 1768, R. Manley was on his way to Bridgetown, when between the properties of Richard Salter and Neal's (the property of Jonathan Worrell) he was robbed by two cutlass-wielding men of his money, handkerchief and penknife. They also took his hat, which he requested them to return. They duly returned it, and he was then warned 'to go about his business and not to make any noise.' The alarm was raised by Manley on reaching town, and the council informed, whereupon, it offered a reward for anyone finding the 'perpetrators of this atrocious offence.'[38] The slave Sam Clift was arrested, tried and hanged in the following year for his role in the robbery.

In 1783, the murder of Dr John Horsham attracted great attention and was reported in great detail in the *Barbados Mercury* of Saturday, November 29. He was on his way to Tunkes Estate (now Waterford), when a shower of rain forced him to stop and shelter. Four men rushed at him. Nick, a slave from Tunkes, held his horse, while he was seized by Jeffrey and Prince of the Belle Plantation. Sambo, also from the Belle, then stabbed him in his neck and through his heart. His body was hidden in a cane ground, and Nick then took his horse to Anthony, the ranger at Tunkes, who handed it over to Francis Bayley, the manager. Horsham's family started to worry when he did not return home, and the following day, when his horse was sent to his house, they became frantic and raised an alarm. The next day 'vast numbers of people went in search of him.' His body was found, fully clothed, with his gold coins, jewellery and instruments intact. Robbery clearly, was not the motive. 'There are perhaps,' the editor of the *Mercury* wrote:

> few instances of barbarity and villainy to equal the murder of the late, unfortunate Dr Horsham: it does not appear that he gave any provocation to justify even an insult, his character and disposition are so well known as not to admit of the thought of his having, previous to the day of the assassination, given the murderers any ill usage, on the contrary, he is universally acknowledged to have gained the respect of both the white people and negroes wherever he practised. . . . [C]ruelty and the greatest wantonness . . . actuated the wretches to committ the horrid act! It is in fact, a matter of so extraordinary a nature, as in some degree to interest every inhabitant of this island, and in more particular manner at this time, when added to the personal insolence of the negroes which is every day experienced, we have such frequent and daring robberies committed, even in the metropolis.[39]

Sambo, Jeffrey, Prince and Nick were tried for murder. Nick and Sambo were sentenced to death by burning, while Prince and Jeffery were acquitted because the justices of the peace and freeholders considered that there was not enough evidence to convict them. This is interesting, given the notoriety of the case and the heightened feelings of the white community. One would have expected a kangaroo court, with verdicts of guilty being handed down to all those charged with the murder.

Also of interest is the subsequent comment of the editor of the *Mercury*, that circumstances of 'a dark and mysterious nature' surrounded the crime.

No full confession was ever obtained, despite a full day spent by the court in examining witnesses. The newspaper reported that three slaves were whipped for giving false evidence. Nick and Sambo were executed on Fontabelle Beach on Boxing Day.

From the journal of Amelia Culpeper *née* Gaskin (1820–92,) comes this fascinating account of the murder of M. Ogier, who in the 1780s kept a dancing academy in James Street, Bridgetown. This story was handed down through her family and recorded by her in later years. Ogier taught dance in Holetown and Speightstown once weekly. He would ride there, stopping at friends' houses both going and coming. He often stopped for breakfast at the house of Edmund Gaskin (the grandfather of Amelia Culpeper). Late one afternoon, Ogier rode up to Mr Gaskin's house, having previously dined at Gabriel Reeves, another friend, who was known more for the quantity of his liquid refreshment than the quality of his cuisine. Mr Gaskin refused to offer Ogier any more rum and sent him on his way to Bridgetown.

The road in those days hugged the coast. While riding through Batt's Rock, he was attacked by several men, who pulled him from his horse and robbed him. Subsequently, he was helped up from the ground, put on his horse, and told to go on his way. Unfortunately for Ogier, he recognised one of his attackers, Peter, a young slave of Mr Gaskin. The dialogue, as recorded by Amelia Culpeper, relying on her childhood memories, went as follows:

'Ah Peter,' Ogier said, 'I knew *you* would not hurt me!'

'Oh massa!' said Peter, 'you should never have known Peter!'

Then and there he was murdered and thrown over the rocks into the sea. When Peter went home, his father who was an old African, cried out, 'Boy, wah you bin doin'? I smell blood from you.'

What excuse Peter made I know not. On the discovery of the body which the waves had not washed away as the thieves had hoped, inquiry was made into the matter. Peter turned King's evidence, the rest were hanged. . . .

I have heard the name of the others, but I forget them now. When I was a child, the belief prevailed that at low tide the blood could be seen on the rocks. I have often had the spot pointed out to me where perished *le pauvre Mon. Ogier*.[40]

Crime levels compared in Barbados and St Ann, Jamaica

In the compensation lists of the total number of 484 crimes recorded for which 540 slaves were executed between 1700 and 1799, some 159 are listed simply 'no reason' or 'executed according to law,' while another 54 are simply described as 'felony.' Of the specific offences listed, theft accounted for 114; followed by murder at 109; attempted murder and assault, 25; arson, ten; running away, nine; and rape, four.[41] The figure for murder may be modified to read 130 cases, since there are 21 petitions recorded in which the plaintiff requested damages of £25 exactly, an indicator that the offence was murder, since the claims for other offences would show considerable variation in monetary value. In fact, of specific claims listed for felony, theft and assault during the entire hundred-year span, none ever amounted to £25.

Of the specified 109 murders committed during the century, 92 were perpetrated against blacks, and 17 against whites. Of the murders of blacks, there were 75 male slaves, ten female slaves, three not differentiated by sex, one described as an Indian boy slave, and three free black males. Of the whites murdered, 12 were males and five females. If one compares the ratio of murders of blacks to those of whites, it becomes apparent that whites are under-represented and blacks over-represented, given the average ratio throughout the century of three blacks to one white.

From these data, one may deduce that Barbadian slave society internalised its violence and directed it against fellow slaves. This finding agrees with recent North American studies of black communities which show a similar tendency for violence to be internalised rather than targeted against any other racial group, particularly one which could be identified as the oppressor. Also, there were fewer females murdered in both groups, ten (12.5 per cent) for the black group as opposed to five (30 per cent) for the white group. Therefore, although there was an excess of women over men in the general population for both racial groups, more men than women were murdered. It should be noted, however, that white women stood a greater chance than black women of being murdered.

The parish of St Ann's in the island of Jamaica provides us with comparative data for the period 1787 to 1814. These data are taken from the record book of the Slave Court of St Ann's. The parish is a large one, encompassing some 481 square miles, as compared to 166 square miles for Barbados. However, much of St Ann's is hilly or mountainous. Like Barbados, its economic livelihood depended on the production and export of sugar. The parish was dominated by large plantations which, according to Edward Long, numbered some 30, and were worked by a slave population which in 1789 totalled 4,908, although Higman notes that by 1800 the slave population of St Ann's had risen to 21,055. This contrasted markedly with Barbados which at the same time, had a slave population of 75,000 who worked 430 large plantations, plus other smaller holdings, which together amounted to some 976 holdings. (The best eighteenth-century map of Barbados, exceedingly useful for locating these holdings, is Mayo's 1722 map). There were also marked differences in the size of the white populations. St Ann's had an estimated white population of 1,600, as compared to over 18,000 for Barbados.[42]

During the period April 1787 to April 1814, some 277 cases were brought before the St Ann's court. When separated by type, they show the following pattern: aiding runaways (8), obeah (12), assault/threat (29), running away

(63), attempted murder (16), murder (17), theft of goods (60), theft of animals (63), unlawful possession of goods (3), arson (3), conspiracy to rebel (3).[43]

For the closest corresponding period for Barbados, that is, between 1772 and 1799, some 75 executions were recorded. There were 24 murders, three of the victims being whites. For St Ann's, Jamaica, 17 murder cases were brought to trial, one of which involved a white. For both areas, therefore, it is fair to conclude that blacks stood a greater chance of being murdered than whites. However, given the difference in population size, residents of St Ann's whether slave or free, stood a greater chance of being murdered. Some interesting differences manifest themselves. There was a far greater propensity for slaves to run away in St Ann's than in Barbados. Also, it should be noted that the incidence of theft in St Ann's was far greater than in Barbados. The fair question to ask is, what were the forces which prompted these differences?

Certainly the topography of the land in Jamaica must have been a factor. Also, one must take into account differing management practices and the arguably harsher treatment of slaves in Jamaica. Another factor which must have influenced running away was the high percentage of Africans in the Jamaican slave population (close to 40 per cent), as compared to the very low percentage in the Barbadian slave population (less than 10 per cent). Almost certainly related to this was the number of convictions in St Ann's for the practice of 'obeah.' No convictions were recorded for Barbados for the time period under consideration. Although Hall's *Laws* record an eighteenth-century act prohibiting the practice of obeah, it seems that the authorities in Barbados paid no attention to it. In an interesting questionnaire sent out by the British Board of Trade in 1788 to the Barbados Council regarding the conditions of slavery in Barbados, several questions relate to the practice of obeah in that island. In response to a query as to whether any laws existed for the suppression of obeah practices, the council replied disdainfully that 'they have been considered too despicable to come under the notice of any public law.'[44] However, in November 1806, the House of Assembly passed 'an Act for the punishment of such slaves as shall be found practising Obeah.' This was replaced in July 1818 by 'An Act for the Better Prevention of the Practice of Obeah.' Three convictions were subsequently recorded, two of the practitioners being transported off the island and the third executed.

To return to a consideration of the case of Barbados alone, it seems fair to conclude that the level of recorded capital crime for the slave population was very low, taking into account the size of the slave population which averaged some 60,000 (some 80,000 persons for the whole island when whites are included). Using the corrected figure of 130 murders committed by slaves during the period under review (see above) and adding to it the eight murders committed by whites against whites,[45] we arrive at a total of 138, which gives us a ratio of 1.38 murders a year or four homicides every three years.

Table 8.2:
Slave population on Barbados for selected years, 1712–73

Date	Population
1712	41,970
1747	66,670
1757	63,645
1773	68,548

Sources: Compiled from Richard Dunn, (1972), 87; BDA, Barbados Council Minutes, Vol.7, fol. 26; Karl Watson, The Civilised Land, Barbados (Bridgetown: 1979), 69.

The question of murders committed by whites against blacks must also be taken into account. This figure is much more difficult to ascertain. Does premeditated murder alone count, or is the slave owner who orders an extreme whipping from which the slave dies not also guilty of murder? The documents are quite silent on this issue. Since slaves, at least in legal terms, were property, masters were pretty much at liberty to treat them as they wished, even to the point of excessive ill-treatment which resulted in death. Undoubtedly, this did occur. In 1766, for example, Edward Murphy, overseer to Thomas English, complained to the Council that a slave by the name of Obrey, property of the said English, had been beaten to death by Benjamin Edwards of St Peter. Edwards was fined and bound over to keep the peace for two years.[46] This was clearly not an isolated incident. However, it is difficult to determine with what frequency such incidents took place. We know from contemporary accounts, especially those of travellers or of British officials stationed on the island, that there were sadistic masters or individuals who brutalised their slaves to the point of causing their death. Such actions would have been concealed as far as possible, and so not reflected in the official documents.

In 1802, Lord Seaforth, the newly appointed governor of Barbados, attempted to have the murder of a slave made a felony, but this recommendation was not put into effect by the House of Assembly. Seaforth attempted to protect the slaves by publicising examples of wanton murders, but white public opinion was very strong in its opposition to such efforts. Barbadian whites who supported such initiatives were viciously criticised. This is well illustrated in an earlier case of Joseph Denny, a free coloured man, who, in 1795, was found guilty of shooting John Stroud, a poor white. He was sentenced to hang, but was reprieved by the Crown on the recommendation of George Poyntz Ricketts, the Jamaican-born governor of Barbados.[47] Instead, Denny was sentenced to banishment. Philip Gibbes, the chief justice, observed at his trial that Denny's dark skin colour and the fact that he had killed a white man had 'raised a prejudice against him which was shown in too barefaced a manner not to be observed by every impartial person present at the trial.'[48] A white mob attempted to seize Denny, but ultimately acquiesced in the Crown's decision. Philip Gibbes, however, was made to pay dearly for his remarks. He was ostracised, forced to resign all his public appointments, and left the island for some time.

However, as we will argue below, the frequency of slave murders in Barbados was low. Contemporary opinion seems to support this assertion. Dickson, himself a supporter of abolition and hence no apologist for the planter lobby, claimed that despite overall bad treatment of slaves, 'their condition is less intolerable in Barbadoes, than in the other sugar colonies.' He went on to say that 'persons from the other islands sometimes ridicule the Slave discipline of Barbados on account of its lenity.'[49] Apart from considerations of respect for human life which, despite the stereotype of the callous and brutal slave master, were real considerations in the context of an admittedly brutal eighteenth century, the greatest restraining factor, we would again stress, was the cost of the slave. As previously demonstrated, their replacement costs, especially after 1750, were increasing considerably, and so one may conclude that economic factors probably more than any other variable acted as a deterrent to wanton murder.

If we take into consideration the premeditated murder of blacks, then the numbers are also very low. Although killing a slave was not declared a felony until 1805, the slave owner or interested parties could in the preceding years issue a formal complaint against the murderer, who would be forced to pay double the value of the slave in compensation to the owner, in addition to a fine of £25 to the Public Treasury, which was recorded. The guilty individual was also bonded with a sum of money as surety for good behaviour.

The following case illustrates this point. On August 21, 1761, Governor Pinfold laid before the Council a letter from Matthew Best and Joseph Leacock, both members of the Barbadian elite, giving an account of 'the cruel murder that Samuel Jordan of the parish of St. Peter had committed upon a Negro slave belonging to Ward Harris of the same parish.'[50] After investigation, Jordan was fined £25 and bound over in the sum of £1,000 for two years. Therefore, despite no punitive legal sanction, there was a strong economic disincentive for whites to kill wantonly in the eighteenth century: £185 paid up (£160 compensation, plus £25 fine) and £1,000 tied up in the legal system constituted a small fortune.

Perhaps more important was the impact of local white public opinion, particularly that of the elite. Jordan, himself a member of that class, had betrayed them by his behaviour and had to be subjected to sanctions. The strength of public opinion and the economic disincentive worked together to reduce the number of murders of slaves, and is reflected in the low number of less than 10 fines recorded in the Council Minutes for the premeditated murder of slaves.

If we look at the thefts, of the 114 listed, 45 (40 per cent) can be classified as praedial larceny, involving livestock or poultry, as illustrated by the following sample of executed persons:

1702, Toney for stealing swine from Issac Raggs.

1730, Mingo,for stealing a bull from Benjamin Elcock.

1739, Dick for stealing a sheep from William Gulstone.

1743, Furry for theft/butchering cow from John Wheeler.

1744, Norman for theft/butchering young bull from Edward Greaves.

1774, Tom Tom for theft of 11 turkeys from George Walker.[51]

One possible interpretation is that as many slave plantation diets were deficient in protein, slaves were forced to resort to stealing to supplement their diets. Contemporary accounts indicate that although slaves had access to fresh fish in season, particularly flying fish, there was a scarcity of red meat. Handler and Lange argue that the skeletal evidence from the slave burial ground excavated at Newton Plantation shows periods of malnutrition among the enslaved population.[52] This, however, may be too small a sample from which to make a generalisation applicable to the entire slave population.

Planter-slave relations

The slaves executed were owned by a total of 409 individuals. If we use two broad socioeconomic categories of elite and yeoman, then the lists show that 186 of these may be classified as elite and 223 as yeoman.[53] Criteria used to select elite individuals included family status and tradition (there is a wealth of information on the genealogies of elite, white Barbadian families),[54] land and slave holdings, and office holding (civil and military). By the turn of the eighteenth century Barbados had a well established elite, many of them fourth-generation and island-born. The formation of this class is ably discussed by Richard Dunn, who also points out that by 1680 there were approximately 2,996 slaveholders on Barbados, of whom 175 were large slaveholders (with 60+ slaves).[55] My projections for the eighteenth century show a core group of 175 individuals owning 100+ slaves, the difference between my calculations and Dunn's being accounted for by the growth of the slave population, changing management practices which increased labour inputs, and a decline among the whites in the last two decades of the seventeenth century.

To assess the total number of slaveholders is difficult, given the lack of adequate data, but if we use the 1680 figure as a base and subtract 20 per cent to compensate for that level of decline in the white population, we arrive at an estimated aggregate of 2,400 slaveholders throughout the century. That only 350[56] of these found it necessary to try and execute their slaves legally over a hundred-year span underscores the low level of criminality, and brings into focus other possibilities which are discussed elsewhere in this essay (free/non-free social relationships, control/policing, complicity, care and attention).

A survey of the elite surnames, moreover, shows that only a small percentage of the surnames of well-established planter families appear on the compensation lists. Yet, their origins in Barbados dated back to the early seventeenth century, they were continuously resident on the island throughout the eighteenth century and many of them owned more than 200 slaves. Were their management practices and relationships with their slaves, including better treatment, the factors that prevented their slaves from straying from the straight and narrow path? Certainly, many of them prided themselves on their paternal attitudes, thinking of their slaves as a sort of extended family with whom they had links over several generations. Did these dependent relationships inhibit legal action on the part of the masters? Did their paternalism allow them to develop a greater *laissez-faire* attitude?

An illustration of the type of protective relationship which existed between this class and their slaves may be seen from the following incident which took place on April 26, 1790. A slave of Sir Francis Ford, a powerful landowner, came to complain that a poor white named Allamby had beaten him. Sir Francis ordered one of his employees to investigate the matter, and if the circumstances warranted it to have Allamby prosecuted. As his diary entries show, Sir Francis followed up the matter, for on May 6 he recorded, 'rode to Town, Phillips had not arrested Allamby, promised to do so directly.'[57] The message being sent was loud and clear. Sir Francis Ford's 'people' were not fair game for any 'backra johnny' to brutalise.

What of the slaves themselves? Were they too honest, too contented, too complacent to 'tek from massa,' especially a 'massa' whose grandparents had known, played with and grown up with their grandparents? This sounds idyllic, utopian even, but cynicism over inter-racial relationships should not blind us to the fact that genuine friendships could and did exist within the limiting framework of the institution of slavery.

The sexual distribution of ownership shows that of the 409 listed owners, 340 were males and 69 were females, 14 of the latter being classified as widows. In terms of class, as noted previously, ownership was distributed as follows: elite, 186; yeomen, 223. If one looks specifically at the case of female ownership, 20 can be classified as elite owners and 49 as yeomen. It can thus be demonstrated statistically that even though elites owned most of the slaves, there was a greater propensity for yeoman-owned slaves to commit crimes. One possible explanation for this trend is that financially pressed yeomen may have found it difficult to maintain their slaves adequately, thus forcing them to rob in order to subsist. An argument along these lines was put forward in 1724 by a committee of the council, whose task was to submit amendments to the slave runaway act. The committee argued that on self-hire slaves, in particular, were put at risk because of unconscionable demands on them by their owners. Their recommendation was that 'there ought to be a clause inserted in it to hinder People from giving Negroes their own time for any money consideration which often puts the said Negroes under a necessity of committing great disorders to get it.'[58]

The vast majority of the slaves executed were from rural areas. Underscoring this is the fact that the Sephardic Jewish community, which was located in Bridgetown, accounts for only three executions for the entire period under analysis. Perhaps, one can argue that social control and monitoring of slaves were more effective in town, as the white population of Bridgetown was large, some 30 per cent of whites being concentrated there, and the slave population smaller, as households did not require the same ratio of labourers as did plantations.

Crime or resistance?

A broad question must be posed in respect of the slaves themselves. At what point does an act perceived as criminal by the whites become an act of sabotage and resistance by the enslaved black group? Does the syndrome of 'me no tief it, me tek it from massa' apply here? David Trotman, in his examination of crime in nineteenth-century Trinidad, makes the point that 'the tradition of appropriating the property of the upper classes [was] forged during slavery.'[59] The same holds true for Barbados in the eighteenth century, although, given the more complex nature of Barbadian society at this period, especially white society, limiting this generalisation to the upper classes only is not feasible.

In discussing slave resistance in eighteenth-century Barbados, Beckles and Watson have shown that one of the major factors controlling the level of slave resistance was the degree of compromise and restraint exhibited by blacks and whites.[60] It can be shown clearly that there were periods of relaxation on the part of the whites. In 1748, Governor Grenville found it necessary to issue a general proclamation to the public, which echoes those issued in 1692 and 1702, in which the justices of the peace and magistrates were excoriated for being lax in their duties and for not applying the slave laws strictly. The public was also blamed for their 'remisness and supiness' in reporting offences committed by slaves.

Grenville had earlier told the Council and Assembly that 'there was reason to apprehend the worst should the insolence of the Negroes be suffered to go unpunished.' He pointed out that despite the laws for 'keeping the Negroes in a due state of subjection . . . many insufferable disorders are still practised by them.' Moreover 'their daily insolence, their midnight Cabals and their frequent Robberies are now grown to such a height as to endanger the Peace of the Island and become a Reproach to the Government.'[61]

This ebb and flow of vigilance on the part of the whites was matched by an equal ebb and flow of pressure on the part of the blacks. Both sides were conscious of the stakes at play, both sides aware that the powder keg once lit meant destruction for all, hence the brinkmanship and jockeying for advantage. But as the details of the executions often show, individuals lost control and paid the penalty for isolated confrontation with the power structure.

What do we make of Daniel's gesture in 1732, when he burnt the canes of William Niblette and 'threatened to burn him also.' Arson, yes, but what of the circumstances which drove Daniel to act? Could it also be legitimate sabotage? What of Tom, who in 1740 attempted 'to kill T. Skeete, William Marshall and others' and died for it? What went through Jeffery's head in 1749 as he murdered Peirce Poor by throwing him down a well? This was a terrible act of vengeance and would certainly have been prompted by feelings of a profound nature. Their peers who stood on the sidelines and watched could only offer praise in death — itself a gesture of resistance against the system. The power structure knew and understood this and moved against it. Therefore, Governor Pinfold directed in 1763:

> That none of the family of the criminal be permitted on any Account or pretence whatsoever, to make or have any plays, Dancings, or Cabells or Riotting at any place whatsoever, in honor to or memory of the said criminal, and shou'd you at anytime hereafter hear of any such, that you cause the same to be supprest and the offender duly punished.[62]

However, just five years later, during the administration of Governor Spry, a proclamation issued in 1768 informed the public that Molly, executed for attempting to poison John Denny, 'had been attended to the grave with unusual Pomp by numbers of Negroes meeted together for that purpose.' This gathering constituted an 'open violation of the Laws, *a daring arraignment of the justice of the sentence by which she was executed* and a most outrageous insult to the person of a Public Magistrate and Member of the Legislature whose life had been endangered by the horrid attempts of this wretch.' Spry ordered that justices of the peace in future were to bury the bodies of those executed far out to sea, 'so that it may be impossible for the Negroes to take it up again.'[63]

In broad terms, then, one can generalise and say that many of the executions resulted not from criminal activity as we know it, but as specific acts of resistance. Within the construction of power relationships in the plantation system, even with the considerable imbalance which existed, which saw masters as the ruling class enjoying the benefits of power, slaves were able to provide challenges to the system. Paradoxically, they enjoyed the power of the majority. The laws designed to maintain social control over the slave population may be seen as manifestations of the masters' desire to rule with an iron fist. These laws were theoretical constructs, an ideal framework around which to construct the world of the slaveholders. Reality, however, dictated that some flexibility would occur, since the slaves also had a world of their own. Neither world existed as a discrete unit, but each impinged on, meshed with and affected the other. To deny, however, the existence of crime among slaves would be mistaken, but the task of distinguishing criminal from martyr among the 540 executed is an impossible one. We know only that both are there.

Notes

1. Douglas Hay *et al. Albion's Fatal Tree. Crime and Society in Eighteenth-Century England* (London: A. Lane, 1975), Preface.
2. John Styles, "Crime in 18th Century England," *History Today*, 38 (1989): 39.
3. Sir Leon Radzinowicz, *A History of English Criminal Law and Its Administration from 1750* (5 Vols., London: Stevens, 1948-68).
4. David Trotman, *Crime in Trinidad: Conflict and Control in a Plantation Society, 1838-1870* (Knoxville: University of Tennessee Press, 1986), 28.
5. BDA, Barbados Council Minutes, 21 November 1707, fols. 326-27.
6. R. Poole, *The Beneficent Bee or Traveller's Companion* (London, 1753; reprinted in *The Journal of the Barbados Museum and Historical Society*, xlvi (2000): 188-89.
7. Richard Hall, *Acts Passed in the Island of Barbados from 1643-1762, Inclusive* (London, 1764), 116-17.
8. An act governing runaways was first enacted in 1676, which stipulated the death penalty without any mention of compensation. However, it soon lapsed.
9. Hall, 130-31. Additional Act to an Act entitled 'An Act for the governing of Negroes.'
10. Ibid., 323-24. This alteration was largely due to the efforts of J. Dottin, a Barbadian, and the President of the Council.
11. The details of these trials and convictions are recorded in the Barbados Council Minutes. As noted, these minutes constitute the principal source for this essay.
12. BDA, Barbados Council Minutes, March 1754, Cox vs Thorne, Court of Error, Vol.24, fol. 195.
13. Ibid., June 1748, Butcher vs Grant, Court of Error, Vol.23, fol. 33.
14. Ibid., December 1747, Newton vs Carrington, Court of Error, Vol.22, fol. 402.
15. Ibid., July 1762, Vol.26.
16. G.H. Bancroft Collection, The Bancroft Library, University of California, Draft of the Governor's pardon for Mr. Bishop's 'Negro,' Pompey. Issued by Governor William Spry, Government House, 1769.

17. The jury was composed of the following individuals: William Worrell and Cumberbatch Sober (the two Justices of the Peace); Thomas Alleyne, Samuel Hinds and William Prescod (the three freeholders).
18. G.H. Bancroft Collection, The Bancroft Library, University of California, Draft of the Governor's pardon for Mr. Bishop's 'Negro,' Pompey. Issued by Governor William Spry, Government House, 1769.
19. Pinfold MSS, Library of Congress, Instructions of Governor Pinfold, March 10, 1763.
20. BDA, Barbados Council Minutes, July 1784, Padmore vs Columbus, Court of Error , Vol.30.
21. Ibid., February 17, 1719, fol. 224.
22. Karl Watson, *A Kind of Right to be Idle: Old Doll Matriarch of Newton Plantation. Rewriting History No.3* (Bridgetown: Department of History, UWI, and Barbados Museum, 2000), 21.
23. BDA, Barbados Council Minutes, September 6, 1721, Deposition of Richard Byrch, fol. 309.
24. Ibid., December 21, 1761.
25. Ibid., October 10, 1761.
26. *Barbados Mercury and Bridgetown Gazette*, December 26, 1772, 53–58. This publication gives a complete account of this trial.
27. *Barbados Mercury*, November 4, 1772.
28. Pinfold MSS, Library of Congress, Instructions of Governor Pinfold, March 10, 1763.
29. BDA, Barbados Council Minutes, December 10, 1743.
30. Pinfold MSS, Library of Congress, Letters written during Governor Pinfold's administration, August 5, 1758.
31. Ibid., August 10, 1764.
32. Watson, 69.
33. West Indies Collection, Main Library, UWI, Cave Hill, Barbados, Evidence of E. Brathwaite, in 'Papers on Trade and Treatment of Slaves,' Barbadoes, Part III A, No.2 , 1785.
34. BDA, Nathan Lucas, Marginal comments in copied Council Minutes, Vol.31, April 7, 1789, and Vol.32, October 16, 1798.
35. Robert H. Schomburgk, *The History of Barbados* (1847; London: Frank Cass, 1971), 47.
36. Watson, 74.
37. Richard B. Sheridan, 'The Crisis of Slave Subsistence in the B.W.I. during and after the American Revolution,' *William and Mary Quarterly*, XXXIII. 4 (1976): 635.
38. BDA, Barbados Council Minutes, July 27, 1768, fols. 131, 132.
39. *Barbados Mercury*, November 29, 1783.
40. Journal of Amelia Culpeper, *née* Gaskin (compiled between 1820 and 1892). This document is in the possession of Ms. Pat Layne, descendant

of the family, to whom I am indebted for drawing it to my attention and permitting me to quote from it.

41. BDA, Compiled from compensation lists, Barbados Council Minutes, 1700–1799.

42. Population data for Barbados are quite reliable. From as early as 1680, a thorough census was taken on the island. Counts continued through the eighteenth century and into the nineteenth century. The same cannot be said for Jamaica. The figure given for St. Ann's in this period is therefore an estimate. It was not until the 1844 census that a reliable figure of 1,186 whites was given (see B.W. Higman, ed., *The Jamaica Census of 1844 and 1861* [Mona, Kingston: Department of History, UWI, Social History Project, 1980]).

43. Janet A. Brown, 'Black Versus White: An Analysis of the Slave Court of St Ann, 1787–1814' (Caribbean Studies paper, History Department, UWI, Mona, 1989).

44. BDA, Barbados Council Minutes, October 21, 1788, fol. 76.

45. This figure may be underestimated, but not by much, as a careful search of the minutes and other sources, such as newspapers, does not reveal more cases.

46. Pinfold MSS, Library of Congress, Orders of Governor Pinfold, 1756–1767, Extracts of Barbados Council Minutes, January 21, 1766.

47. Ricketts, though a creole, did not seem to have the prejudices of most white Barbadians of the time. He shocked local white society by living with a coloured mistress at Government House.

48. Schomburgk, 354.

49. William Dickson, *Mitigation of Slavery* (London: 1814), 439.

50. BDA, Barbados Council Minutes, August 21, 1761, Vol.26.

51. BDA., Barbados Council Minutes, 1702–1744.

52. Jerome S. Handler and Frederick W. Lange, *Plantation Slavery in Barbados. An Archaeological and Historical Investigation* (Cambridge, Mass.: Harvard University Press, 1978).

53. Ideally, four categories should have been used: upper elite (100+ slaves), lower elite (30–99 slaves), yeoman (11–29 slaves), and freeman/poor white (1–10 slaves). This would have been quite feasible for the two elite groups, for whom there are adequate data. However, differentiation for the lower groups is more difficult. Hence, it was decided to reduce the classification to two groups.

54. See, for example, James C. Brandow comp., *Genealogies of Barbados Families* (Baltimore: Genealogical Publishing Co., Inc., 1983).

55. Dunn, 96.

56. This is an adjusted figure, moved upwards to compensate for the 63 cases where no owner is listed.

57. BDA, Copy of diary of Sir Francis Ford, entry for April 26, 1790.

58. BDA, Barbados Council Minutes, March 17, 1724, Vol.17, fol. 229.

59. Trotman, 155.

60. Hilary McD. Beckles and Karl Watson, 'Concessionary Politics: Slave Resistance in Eighteenth Century Barbados' (Department of History, UWI, Mona, 1984).

61. BDA, Barbados Council Minutes, Vol.22, fol. 94, Speech of H.E. Henry Grenville to Council and Assembly, November 16, 1748.

62. Pinfold MSS, Library of Congress, March 1, 1763.

63. BDA, Barbados Council Minutes, December 20, 1768.

Figure 14:
Parade of militia in Georgetown following the 1823 revolt.

CHAPTER 9

Reassessing John Smith's Influence on the Demerara Slave Revolt of 1823
Noel Titus

Introduction

The story of the trial and death of John Smith, a missionary of the London Missionary Society (LMS) to the British colony of Demerara, is well known in the history of the West Indies. It forms part of that saga of slavery and its abolition which has been told and retold from the 1820s until the present, with virtual unanimity about the injustice done to the non-conformist missionaries in the West Indies.[1] The story is set in one of those eras in Caribbean history which do not make pleasant reading, because of the cruelty and racism which they depict. But before going into any discussion on the place of Smith in the drama, it is necessary to review some of the literature on the subject. This literature might be divided into two segments: contemporary and modern.

The revolt attracted the hostility of the colonists who blamed it on the attempt of the British government to impose a new slavery policy on the colony. In a lengthy report of a meeting of that group which was carried by the *Guiana Chronicle*, they stated that the objectives of the revolt were 'the attainment, by force, of supposed privileges and immunities, but eventually the throwing off of all restraints of Law and Order.'[2] They criticised the interference of the missionaries, stating that the revolt had been 'accelerated by the pernicious pre-disposition occasioned by Missionary instruction and influence.' Even so, they highlighted the work of 'one individual' who, they alleged, had perverted portions of Scripture, and displayed a constant tendency towards opposition to the authorities, thus creating discontent among the slaves. To support their case, they argued that the trial did not reveal 'privation of comforts, excessive work, or ill treatment of any kind' that justified the revolt. The fact that the treatment of the slaves was not raised in the trial seemed not to matter to them.

The inhabitants professed themselves to be sympathetic to the religious instruction of the slaves, and referred to a petition which they had submitted to the government asking for parishes to be demarcated and ministers of the

Established Church to be appointed. In a striking display of apparent toleration, they resolved to ask for the licensing of ministers of the Dutch Reformed Church, the Established Church of England, the Presbyterians, and even the Roman Catholics. Their opposition to dissenting missionaries is evident from their resolution to request the Court of Policy to expel all current missionaries and prohibit the entry of all future ones. As a final nail in the coffin of the missionaries, they alleged that it was not religious instruction that drew the slaves to the missionaries, but the perception that the latter were working for their emancipation.

The LMS and several other contemporary religious bodies portrayed Smith as a martyr. The society itself, in its petition to the House of Commons, claimed that the uprising was unplanned and that the authorities in Demerara were using Smith as a scapegoat. Considering the 'evidence' against Smith as being trumped up, it called for an inquiry into the events.[3] The parliamentary debates of 1824 were used extensively, especially in the first biography by Wallbridge in 1848, to show that Smith was a martyr. His book contains the full text of Henry Brougham's opening speech on the issue — a panegyric of the LMS and John Smith. Brougham asserted that many persons were unwilling to address the issue, partly because of the remoteness of the events, and partly because of a lack of enthusiasm. His speech exposed several irregularities in the proceedings of the court, showing that the evidence against Smith had been fabricated. He concluded that Smith's warning had actually saved the whites.[4]

Subsequent writers have also portrayed Smith as one whom the slave system propelled to an early grave. F.J. Klingberg, for example, represented the planters as being alarmed by the general unrest among the slave population, and portrayed Smith as one who was destroyed by the vengeful spirit of the planters — a spirit that was not ultimately satisfied with the execution of large numbers of slaves. They could find Smith guilty of a capital offence yet could not execute him for lack of courage.[5] Klingberg's position has been replicated in the works of other scholars. W.L. Mathieson repeated the argument regarding planter concern about Smith's complicity in the uprising. He noted the findings of the court that the tendency, though not the intention, had been to foster discontent among the slaves.[6] Jakobsson surveyed the work of the LMS, assessing the relationship between the missionaries on the one hand, and officials and planters in Demerara on the other. He asserted that the missionaries were strictly observing their instructions and that, in so doing, they helped to preserve 'not only peace and order but also injustices and oppression in West Indian society.' He noted, however, that 'by raising up the new generation and giving them knowledge' they *indirectly* helped to bring about rebellion and revolution.[7] In examining Smith's case, he concentrated on the trial rather than on the teachings of the missionary. As a result, apart from Smith's opposition to slavery in his journal and letters, he did not demonstrate how the missionary helped to bring about the rebellion. C.A. Northcott only sketchily reviewed the work of the missionary, but raised a question about one aspect of his teaching, which he categorised as naïve. About this he wrote:

> He pursued his simple, unadorned approach to his ministry expounding the story of the Exodus and the entry into the promised land with an almost naïve boldness. Every negro slave and every plantation manager knew what the story meant for Demerara. But did Smith? Almost unconsciously he built up a catena of evidence that he was actively preaching freedom for slaves and putting ideas of insurrection into their heads.[8]

This conclusion about Smith's ingenuousness is correct, since none of the missionaries expected the slaves to draw any other conclusion than those which they themselves imparted in their teaching. But it does less than justice to the intelligence of the slaves.

Eric Williams cursorily reviewed the course of the rebellion, in which slaves demanded their immediate freedom. He agreed that the rebellion was so carefully and secretly planned that it took the planters unawares. However, while he spoke of the slaves' contribution to the ending of slavery, he did not attempt to look at the influence of the missionary on the slaves' actions.[9] Most recently, Emilia Viotti da Costa subjected the rebellion to its most detailed examination to date. Among points of interest that she noted were that: Wray and Smith had expected to meet ignorant 'babes' waiting to be saved; and that they found instead a people whose system of meanings they ignored and often took at face value.[10] In her view, the slaves had 'appropriated the missionaries' language and symbols, and turned their lessons of love and redemption into promises of freedom.'[11] The slaves were not just obedient servants of the missionaries, but retained their will to act in their own interests despite the efforts of the missionaries. They did not automatically trust the missionaries, but appealed to them since they had supported their cause.[12]

Da Costa's assessment has been taken a little further by Winston McGowan in a recent article. He attributed the rebellion to a number of causes, all of them deserving serious consideration. For him, the most basic cause was the 'natural human desire of the rebels for freedom,' sharpened by the severity of the system.[13] Secondly, he attributed the rebellion to overwork, which itself resulted from the switch to sugar from the formerly prevailing cotton culture. Because sugar cultivation was labour intensive, and the slave trade was abolished during the changeover, slave owners resorted to a variety of expedients in order to increase the workload of the slaves and maintain their profit levels.[14] Add to this the prevalence of absentee ownership, with the attendant abuses and physical brutalities, and the picture is one of stark cruelty and oppression. Thirdly, he considered the restriction of their attendance at Smith's chapel as one of the greatest stimulants to rebellion, and noted that Smith made this point in his correspondence with the LMS. Finally, he noted that some of the rebels drew a parallel between their own servile condition and 'several features of the history of the Jews as recorded in the Old Testament of the Bible,' particularly the deliverance of the Jews from slavery in Egypt.[15]

McGowan concluded, as most previous writers, that Smith did not incite the rebellion. Smith, he believed, might have been partly responsible for the revolt, but not in the way that the planters thought. While Smith detested slavery and might have encouraged the opposition of slaves to the system, he did not deliberately promote 'discontent and dissatisfaction in the minds of the slaves towards their masters, managers and overseers, as he was charged.' McGowan considered Smith's opposition to Sunday labour, his unwillingness to suspend weeknight services, and his irritation at having access to his slave congregation restricted as among the travails he endured. Planter association of missionaries with abolitionists added to their hostility towards Smith, and helps to explain their accusation against him. He did not incite the slaves to revolt, but rather tried to dissuade them from so doing. Nevertheless, McGowan thinks that Smith might have had knowledge or suspicion of the impending revolt shortly before it took place. He concluded that Smith's influence and role in the events were exaggerated.[16] Essentially, this is because McGowan has himself limited 'influence' to being directly responsible for putting the idea into the heads of the slaves, and there is no evidence of Smith doing this.

Only one of the portrayals attempted to look at Smith's influence on the action of the slaves, preferring instead to discuss the injustice of the colonial structures where he and other missionaries were concerned, and the guilt or innocence of this particular missionary. Not even the modern writers examine this aspect of the matter, except Da Costa, as indicated above. One is therefore left to conclude that sympathy for the missionary may have prevented them going all the way in their examination. We shall focus more attention on the influence of the missionary in due course, but it is necessary at present to remind ourselves of the charges against him. These were, first, that he deliberately incited revolt among the slaves by promoting discontent and dissatisfaction toward their masters, managers, and overseers. Second, that he conspired with Quamina, the leader, both before and during the rebellion. Third, that despite having prior knowledge of it, he failed to apprise the authorities of the slaves' intention to revolt. And finally, that he was associated with one whom he knew to be an insurgent, instead of 'securing or detaining' him as a prisoner or informing the proper authorities.[17]

The context of the revolt

The first task is to look at the context of the revolt, and at West Indian slave society in general. West Indian slave society was characterised by its arbitrariness. From the very beginning of the slave system, the African slave was regarded as a non-person. In the ships' manifests of the Spanish period, the slaves were often described as so many *piezas* or 'pieces' of 'negro.' In the British system which followed, the slaves were described as non-human merchandise comparable to sheep, cattle, horses and other similar merchandise in the ships' holds.[18] Slaves were therefore seen as the property of their owners, disposable chattels to be used, discarded, and replaced at will, with no consideration as to their humanity. This outlook had certain important implications for the general treatment of the slaves, as well as for their relations with clergy of the Church of England, as it was called then, and with the missionaries of the non-conformist churches.

In general, West Indian planters did not approve of the evangelisation of their slaves. They harboured concerns as to whether the baptism of their slaves implied to the latter that this made them free. These concerns had their roots in the view that one could not make a Christian a slave. But could one also make a slave a Christian?[19] The two ideas were not identical, but up to the early nineteenth century planters had taken comfort in the fact that the clergy of the Church of England and the Dutch Reformed Church had made very little effort to teach or baptise slaves. These clergymen were not models of energy in regard to either their regular parochial duties or their obligations towards the slaves in their parishes. They tended to conform to the wishes of those who, in many ways, controlled their lives by their control of the parochial purse strings. In addition, the parochial system encouraged in them a rather sedentary approach to ministry. In any case, the planters were not known to be patrons of the parish churches, even though the parish structure provided the basis for many of the civil functions which took place in the society.[20]

In common with other West Indian colonies, the plantation system in Demerara was a most repressive one. That repression may have been due partly to the relatively high incidence of absenteeism among owners of estates on the east coast where the rebellion originated.[21] This encouraged the kind of cruelty witnessed in several other Caribbean plantation colonies.

Only in the late eighteenth and early nineteenth centuries did Demerara become a player in West Indian sugar production.[22] Formerly a producer of cotton, the change to a new staple crop had certain implications for the slaves. In the first place, sugar-cane cultivation was considerably more labour intensive than cotton. This meant that those planters who made the change to sugar production needed to purchase more slaves than they would have required for cotton cultivation.[23] Especially during the crop season slaves were required to work longer hours since the grinding of the canes had to be continuous lest they became spoilt. Therefore, managers frequently overworked their slaves. Also, the development of the nascent sugar colony coincided with the period of intense debate about the abolition of the slave trade. When abolition became a reality it intensified the problem of slave maintenance to achieve an increase in the population by natural reproduction. A variety of circumstances affected the ability of the slave population to reproduce itself. There was gender imbalance, with males outnumbering females, and a consequential low birth rate. There were also 'high infant and adult mortality rates among slaves caused by the rigorous labour regime, inadequate diet, unhealthy working conditions in the fields and factories, and poor medical care.'[24] Planters therefore resorted to several expedients in order to ensure the same level of crop production as before, including requiring slaves to start work earlier in the day and to work harder. Planters often denied slaves Saturday afternoons off; the personal business of the latter had to be transacted on Sundays. Planters also paid less attention to the provision of grounds to grow food for their slaves whose nourishment became increasingly dependent on imports. The Dutch authorities had already enacted laws to deal with the problem, and these were re-enacted and amplified periodically by the British.[25]

It was into this human flotsam that the non-conformist missionaries sought to insinuate themselves. However, they had to navigate cautiously, for while imperial government policy favoured toleration in religious matters, it showed a distinct preference for the Established Church. A case in point was the memorandum of Lord Liverpool, secretary of state for the colonies, to the governor of Jamaica in 1810. The stated purpose of the memorandum was precautionary — to exclude from the exercise of ministerial functions 'all ignorant and ill designing persons who under the pretence of preaching the Gospel may disseminate principles inimical to the peace and good order of society.' To ensure that such breaches did not occur, it required that all preachers must be qualified and registered in the Supreme Court, that they should take the Oath of Allegiance and the Oath against Popery, and that meetings should be held only in places registered by the Supreme Court. Breaches of this order were punishable, as provided in the Act for the Suppression of Seditious Conventicles of 1682.[26] Three years later, another secretary of state, in his instructions to Sir Ralph Woodford of Trinidad, required that liberty of conscience and the free exercise of religion should be accorded to all, provided that they were peaceable and quiet and that they gave no offence or scandal to the government.[27] These instructions show that the British government associated non-conformity with sedition, and it is quite likely that the governors accepted and shared the same outlook.

In the eighteenth- and early nineteenth-century West Indies, governors were not merely representatives of the Crown of England; they functioned very nearly as though they were monarchs in their own right. In 1812 a Methodist missionary, arriving in Demerara and presenting himself and his credentials to Governor Bentinck, was precipitously returned to his ship.[28] Perhaps the most infamous of the governors in the 1820s was Sir Ralph Woodford of Trinidad. Any tolerance of which he might be accused was not applicable to his dealings with the missionaries. Among the qualities he found intolerable in them were: their assuming a right to function as ministers, developing too close associations with the slaves, permitting the slaves to preach, being irresponsible in baptising the children of slaves as though they were free, and having too short a residence in the colony, resulting in the removal of their records. The effect of the latter, according to him, was to prevent their being prosecuted for breaches of the local laws.[29]

Part of the problem likely to face the missionaries arose from the prejudices of the slave-owning class. This prejudice, that can be described as 'popular' prejudice, was often given statutory expression. The white inhabitants were opposed to the gathering together of any significant number of slaves, either because they believed them to be going somewhere other than the place they had indicated, or because they were convinced that any such gathering was for the purpose of plotting violence against their owners. The result was that laws were frequently passed prohibiting the practice of drumming and dancing, the most common activities associated with their assembling together. And when missionaries and other ministers became more energetic in their evangelisation efforts, not only did the slave-owning legislators pass laws to prohibit meetings between dusk and dawn, but the slave owners often refused to give their slaves the passes required by law in order to leave the estate.[30] This was the case, even though the planters themselves neither attended any place of worship nor gave their active support to the clergy of the established church.

In general, planters were not much inclined to encourage the evangelisation of their slaves. Hermanus Post, who initiated the practice on his estates, was in the minority, if not alone, in encouraging missions. The prejudice against the religious instruction of slaves, which was rife throughout the West Indies, facilitated the placing of obstacles in the way of persons who sought to perform such functions. While in Demerara non-conformist missionaries did not have the same problems with licences as in Jamaica,[31] the governors usually provided their own foil to the enthusiasm of the missionaries. Planters also viewed the missionaries with distrust, and increasingly so, as slave amelioration and the abolition of slavery grew closer to realisation.

Mindful of the hostility of West Indian societies generally towards missionaries, their parent societies provided them with detailed instructions as to how they were to conduct themselves in this sphere of work. These instructions were usually replete with caution, as the directors of missions sought to avoid conflict with those who held power in the slave colonies. The instructions given to Smith by the LMS warned him that his first duty was to preach to the slaves — the 'heathen' — as that was the first aim of the Society. They enjoined him to visit the slaves regularly in their huts, receive them in his home, converse with them, and teach them diligently. He was to ensure that he did nothing to endanger the public peace. His preaching was to render the slaves diligent and useful servants, thereby commending his ministry to the planters.[32] Some of these instructions were difficult for him to put into effect, for his ministry was encumbered by planter obstacles to religious instruction, excessive labour and harsh punishments, to name a few.

It was into this atmosphere that the imperial government's amelioration programme was introduced in 1823, following the passage of certain resolutions regarding slaves in the British Parliament. The amelioration programme was far-reaching, designed to ensure the humane treatment of the slaves, and to enable the latter to take a more active part in improving their condition and bringing cruel masters to justice. The despatches conveying these initiatives arrived in Demerara on July 7, 1823, and were therefore in the colony for several weeks before the local authorities took any action. In the meantime, the contents of the despatches had become known to the local slave owners and were being discussed by them in a stormy atmosphere. It is quite likely that the hostility of the slave owners exacerbated a growing desire for freedom on the part of the slaves. It is also possible that missionary inertia in confronting the slavery system encouraged in the slaves the belief that they must go it alone.

A number of incidents support this viewpoint. On June 15, 1823 a woman confided to Smith that she had been prevented from attending chapel for two years and had only recently been allowed to attend fortnightly by the manager. Smith advised her to be thankful for the liberty she currently enjoyed and to ask for permission to attend on sacrament days. One week later, Isaac of Triumph Plantation asked him whether the new law of the governor prevented slaves meeting on evenings to learn the Catechism. Smith replied in the negative, adding that the manager had no power to prevent them. He advised, however, that they should forego such assembly rather than offend and be punished. On July 25, the same year Quamina, a deacon in Smith's church on Plantation Le Resouvenir, inquired whether there was any truth in the rumour that the king had set the slaves free. Smith dismissed him with the observation that it was false. Quamina left unconvinced;[33] it appears that he was not alone in this. Leading slaves began to doubt Smith's sympathy with their cause. We do not know how far that doubt spread. What seems clear is that, at a certain point in the whole development, the missionaries were shut out of the confidence of the slaves concerned.

At this point I should like to depart from the well-trodden path of examining Smith's guilt or innocence with respect to inciting the insurrection, and attempt to examine his influence on the whole scheme of things. I believe that, in the anxiety to apportion blame for the uprising, the general influence of Smith has not been given sufficient consideration. That influence was positive in that it facilitated the conclusions which the slaves drew, even though Smith himself could not accurately be called the instigator. This approach imposes on the writer a degree of difficulty, exposing him/her to a charge of having accused Smith of incitement. But I am not doing that here. Smith did *not* deliberately incite the slaves to revolt, but his teachings might have provided a good foundation for doing so.

A major fallacy of Europeans, policy-makers as well as missionaries, was that the mind of the slave was a *tabula rasa* on which they were to inscribe the indelible truths of civilised society and religion. This approach carried with it unmistakable prejudice, suggesting that the slaves could not think for themselves. As indicated elsewhere with reference to the indigenous peoples of the Caribbean, it seems to have been the bane of their contact with people of foreign cultures.[34] An interesting variant of this theme was Gardner's explanation of the split in the Native Baptist movement in Jamaica. According to him, all the really good people went with the newly arrived English missionaries, while those of little account continued with their local leaders.[35] According to this view, therefore, good slaves were those who were ready for the inscription on their 'empty' minds of the teaching of the English clergy or missionaries, and would not revolt unless incited by missionaries and other 'evil' people to do so. The emphasis on incitement perpetuates the *tabula rasa* myth. Even Da Costa, who observes that Smith's teaching helped to reduce the level of violence (a defensive posture in favour of his innocence),[36] implies that the slaves were to some extent manipulated by the whites. The line of argument that I am pursuing challenges the fundamental error that the slaves were unable to arrive at any conclusions about the granting of amelioration or freedom by the imperial government, except through such a notion being instilled into their minds by the missionaries or other white persons. Rather, the evidence indicates that the slaves did exactly what they were *not* expected to do, given the precise instructions they received.

The missionary's teachings might, in fact, have directly or indirectly put ideas into the minds of the slaves and caused them to draw conclusions other than those of the teacher. To support my argument I will examine the subject and content of Smith's teaching, as reflected in the documents assembled at his trial and the letters that he dispatched to his superiors in London. These documents comprised entries from his journal, which consisted of references to passages which he employed in weekly Bible study, and texts forming the basis of sermons. Smith recorded most of these texts.

In carrying out this exercise, I had to contend with the fact that, while Smith indicated the text from which he preached or the passage forming the basis of his Bible study, he said nothing about what he had actually taught. One is therefore left to try and determine what message he might have intended to convey. Another impediment was the fact that several gaps occur in the records, sometimes at very critical points. For example, there is a gap between August 21, 1818, when the Bible study passage was Genesis 49:8–12, and December 6 of that year, when the text was Exodus 14:15. There are other gaps for most of the periods between March 12 and November 5, 1820, January 20 and August 5, 1822, and January 19 and May 23, 1823. Cumulatively, there is a loss of some 20 months when the missing information would have clarified a great deal. Therefore, the researcher cannot be sure whether Smith had dealt with certain topics in the intervals, repeating later what he had dealt with earlier. Yet, a cyclical pattern does appear in his teaching.

The contexts in which Smith taught the slaves varied with the activities that he scheduled for the congregation. He preached at the main morning and evening services on Sundays, as well as on Tuesdays and Fridays. However, prayer meetings — usually on Sunday mornings and other mornings during the week — offered the opportunity to teach from the Bible.[37] The attendance at these sessions was not as large as those for the main Sunday services. A contributory factor in all of this was the mental state of the missionary, although this issue has not been previously examined, except by Da Costa. What Smith taught might well have been affected by what he felt at particular times. It is significant that he suffered bouts of depression between October 1818 and January 1819, October and December 1819, in January 1821 and in August 1822.[38] Some of these times correspond with those when gaps appear in the records. This indicates that he was going through serious difficulties which might have required a change of scene. His problems might well have been brought on by physical difficulties such as the 'pulmonary inconvenience' of which he spoke in September 1822.[39] But his references to his state of mind seem to have made no impression on the directors of the society, for he received little or no response from them.

One cannot discuss the context of his teaching without reference to the prevailing plantation society in which he had to work. It was a society characterised by harsh treatment to those persons who provided the labour necessary for ensuring the sugar on which the prosperity of the planters depended. It was a society in which the slaves were regarded as the property of the slave owners, and in which the labour force was to all intents and purposes expendable. Put very mildly, the slaves in that society attended services or other religious activities under duress: threats from the masters and managers. Smith's journals abound with references to the slave owners' efforts, whether direct or otherwise, to prevent the slaves from attending the chapel. On several occasions he spoke of the slaves being forced to work on Sundays, or being severely punished if they refused to do so. The threat, if not the fact, of punishment was always pervasive. On occasion, the slaves were kept away from chapel because the owner was giving out rations on the Sunday, thus preventing their attendance at chapel.[40] It is not to be assumed, however, that the slaves themselves did not make the choice to stay away when they felt so inclined. Sometimes it was to go to the market,[41] when they needed to, or in one case to engage a fellow slave in helping him with a much needed task on his house.[42] The slaves sometimes took action on their own behalf, as, for example, when one or more of them stayed away from chapel as an act of protest against the missionary. The slave's position was represented thus, 'Massa, it come into my heart that you did not like me, because when I tell you we Manager lick me for not turning out so soon as the whip crack, you say, well, you ought to turn out quick.'[43]

The slave was making a decision about where the missionary's sympathies lay and acting on it. It was an ominous sign. Indeed, when they were expressly forbidden to attend the chapel in 1823, they disobeyed. It may have been an act of defiance or one of expectation, since the country was in some ferment because of instructions which had been received from London. They were not passively accepting their fate.

Smith was aware of the aversion of both the governor and the planters to the missionaries' teaching the slaves to read; yet he persisted in so doing, confiding to his diary his view that 'Whatever we do therefore must be by stealth.'[44] Such a comment would have been dangerous, if not conclusive of his guilt, had his letters been used in the trial. The plantocracy's attitude towards instruction in reading and missionary work in general was not satisfactory to Smith, who gave vent to his views, usually within the 'privacy' of his journal. The journal, however, was not altogether private, since such a document usually formed part of a missionary's report to his society, and often was exposed to public gaze when sections of it were published by the society as publicity regarding its activities.[45] When such materials reached the slave owners in the colonies the strain in relationships was further exacerbated to the discomfiture of the missionaries.

Smith's teachings frequently brought him into conflict with the planters, for instance, his denunciation of sexual liaisons between the latter and female members of the congregation.[46] The practice of marrying slaves was also not well received by slave owners, since it challenged the right of the owners to separate them.[47] Smith himself came into conflict with particular planters, such as a Mr Hamilton, whose behaviour in chapel and his sexual relations with one of Smith's converts led to the latter being dismissed from membership.[48] Later he would have difficulties with Captain McTurk, whose role in the events preceding the rebellion and subsequent to it would be detrimental to the missionary's cause.[49] Smith's position might therefore appear ambivalent owing, perhaps, to his desire to remain faithful to the terms of his instructions (see above). However, certain views emerge occasionally, and one is left to wonder whether Smith was completely successful in concealing his views from his slave audience. The following entries provide a very brief sample of his diurnal soliloquies:

September 3, 1817 — He expressed disgust at seeing slaves working in irons, one of them with a lacerated back. 'O Slavery! Thou offspring of the devil, when wilt thou cease to exist?' Then later in the same letter: 'I hail the day when slave masters shall be imbued with the feelings of men, & the slaves enjoy their birthright.'

July 12, 1818 — Commenting on the flogging of an old man, he was moved to speak thus of the injustice of the slave owners: 'The way here is frequently not to tell a negro of his error, but punish him first, & then tell him what to do.'

August 10, 1818 — He wrote of those who spent their time on Sundays with the bottle and the glass, cards and backgammon, who were haunted at night with hideous dreams and fearful forebodings, 'then rise to vent their arbitrary malice & authority – it may be upon the innocent.'

March 21, 1819 — 'I wish the negroes would say nothing to me concerning their treatment which arise from the severe usage of the managers, as it is not my business to interfere in such concerns, & only obliges me to treat such conduct with apparent indifference, & behave with coolness to those who relate it.' He ended with the remark that he had detected dissatisfaction among the slaves and would not be surprised if they revolted openly.

March 22, 1819 — He expressed concern about the cruel flogging of slaves, observing that they were likely to resent it, and concluded that he must speak to the rulers of the colony.

September 12, 1820 — He wanted to ask planters for land on which to build a chapel, but he was so badly treated by the first ones he approached that he determined to proceed with great caution thereafter.

Smith's assessment of the system of slavery, expressed as early as September 1817, was one which accorded with the sentiments of his evangelical colleagues in London. It was one which he had brought with him to his new ministry. As Da Costa observes, 'Before he arrived in Demerara, Smith was already prepared to see the planters as sinful, godless people, and the slaves as helpless and innocent victims of oppression.'[50] That outlook intensified during his stay in Demerara, so that by the fateful year 1823 he had already concluded that slavery could not be mitigated; it had to be abolished.

Analysis of the texts

As stated earlier, one cannot say anything concerning the content of Smith's teaching, except by way of inference from the subject matter of the texts listed. Smith's testimony at the trial suggests that he had made a conscientious effort to read through the Bible sequentially, with such exposition as he deemed necessary. He omitted passages that in his opinion might be considered open to misinterpretation by the slaves. For him, those passages, such as the patriarchal narratives of Genesis, were intended to highlight the goodness of God. His ultimate objective in utilising them was probably to bring the slaves to the point of conversion and commitment to God. If this were his aim, then the actions of the slaves were based on their own reinterpretation of his teachings, rather than on his incitement. In other words, he influenced them, but the course followed was of their own choosing.

Given what was said about Smith's approach, it should not be surprising to observe that his teachings were wide-ranging. For the most part, those focused on evangelical topics — the need to put behind one a life of dissipation and to choose a godly life;[51] to be truthful; to ensure that one did not 'grieve' the Holy Spirit;[52] to 'walk' in love, with such practical exhortations as avoiding drunkenness, paying attention to faithfulness in marriage, and avoiding insincerity.[53] Here and there one finds in the texts exhortations to the slaves to be obedient to their masters,[54] although this does not appear to have been a frequent topic of teaching or study. Firm action was taken against any slave who transgressed the moral teachings of the church, as when a slave woman agreed to become the mistress of her owner or manager. The slave was excommunicated, after efforts to deal with her circumstances had failed to dissuade her from her choice;[55] but there is no record of the missionary protesting to the manager against his immoral conduct.

A number of the texts used were susceptible to misinterpretation by anyone, and particularly by the slaves. In saying this, I am arguing that the slaves never seem to have regarded the passages as merely stories, but regularly applied them to their own circumstances. One can argue that Smith was aware and suspicious of the possibility of the slaves' application of these passages to themselves, hence his decision to exclude certain sections of Genesis from their instruction (see below).[56] Here are some of the passages that he actually used and that might have evoked special interest on the part of the slaves:

June 15, 1817 – Luke 12:32, 'Fear not, little flock; for it is your Father's good pleasure to give you the kingdom.'

June 22, 1817 – Galatians 6:7, 'Do not be deceived; God is not mocked; for whatsoever a man soweth, that shall he also reap.'

February 2, 1818 - Isaiah 60:22, 'The little one shall become a thousand, and a small one a strong nation: I the Lord will hasten it in his time.'

February 23, 1819 – 1 Peter 2:9-10, 'But ye are a chosen generation, a royal priesthood, an holy nation, a peculiar people; that ye should shew forth the praises of him who hath called you out of darkness into his marvellous light: Which in time past were not a people, but are now the people of God: which had not obtained mercy, but now have obtained mercy.'

December 31, 1819 – 1 Corinthians 7:29, 'But this I say, brethren, the time is short: it remaineth, that both they that have wives be as though they had none . . . .'

July 20, 1823 – Matthew 5:6, 'Blessed are they which do hunger and thirst after righteousness: for they shall be filled.'

August 17, 1823 – Luke 19:41-42, 'And when he was come near, he beheld the city, and wept over it, Saying, "If thou hadst known, even thou, at least in this thy day, the things which belong unto thy peace! but now they are hid from thine eyes."'

In referring to these in detail, it is not intended to suggest that Smith applied them specifically to the slaves' condition. Such application was probably always scrupulously avoided; but the passages were such that it would have been remarkable if the slaves had not extended their original meaning. A significant contribution to this discussion was made by Smith himself in his diary on September 10, 1822. In commenting on the flogging of certain slaves for attending chapel, he states, 'As Rogers complained of the insolence of some of the negroes in telling the late Manager of Clonbrook when he flogged them, that "he might kill the body but could not kill the soul," I questioned them as to the truth of it, & remarked that however true the doctrine was it did not become them to speak so to their Manager.' Smith was faced with a problem of the interpretation of a text which did not accord with his teaching about respect for those in authority. They had used the text with reference to themselves, a process which Smith reprobated at the trial; but Smith had not grasped that they were doing their own interpretation. It was an indication either that Smith was naïve or that he knew where his teaching was likely to lead. If the latter, he had played a dangerous game and lost.

The last group of texts to be examined consists of those which refer either directly or indirectly to the Exodus — the liberation of the Israelites from slavery in Egypt. Here one finds a remarkable circumstance. Smith seems to have given instructions on this topic on two separate occasions — from July to December 1818, and from October 1821 to January 1822. When one notes that there are several months for which there is no record of his teaching, it is quite possible that his teaching on this topic was more frequent than he acknowledged. Those slaves who testified that this was a frequent topic of instruction might well have been correct.

July to December 1818 seems to have been a period of extensive discussion on this aspect of Israel's history. Despite the gap in our records, it is feasible to suggest that teaching in sequence continued during the period. Two key passages emerged as sermon texts in July that year. They were:

July 19, 1818 – Exodus 3:7–8, 'And the Lord said, "I have surely seen the affliction of my people which are in Egypt, and have heard their cry by reason of their taskmasters; for I know their sorrows; And I am come down to deliver them out of the hand of the Egyptians, and to bring them up out of that land."'

July 26, 1818 – Hebrews 11:23–26, 'By faith Moses, when he was born, was hid for three months by his parents, because they saw he was a proper child; and they were not afraid of the king's commandment. By faith Moses, when he was come to years, refused to be called the son of Pharaoh's daughter; Choosing rather to suffer affliction with the people of God, than to enjoy the pleasures of sin for a season; Esteeming the reproach of Christ greater riches than the treasures of Egypt: for he had respect unto the recompense of the reward.'

The first text emphasises the fact that God viewed with displeasure the enslavement of his people and was prepared to act for their deliverance. The second emphasises the fact that Moses chose to be on the side of the oppressed, a text that the slaves might have viewed as a warning to those who collaborated with the oppressors. It is small wonder that some slaves testified that Smith had expressed his aversion to slavery. Yet it might not have been Smith himself but the texts; and the slaves conflated the texts and what seemed to them the views of the missionary. These texts provided fodder for fertile imaginations.

The circumstances surrounding the presence of the ancient Israelites in Egypt had been discussed frequently in Bible studies since June 1818. There was no specific reference to their escape from Egypt until December 6 of that year, when John Davies, Smith's colleague in Demerara, used as the text of his sermon Exodus 14:15, which reads, 'And the Lord said unto Moses, "Wherefore criest thou unto me? Speak unto the children of Israel, that they go forward."' It is a significant text, which could easily have been interpreted as an inspiration to the people to go forward with their plan rather than stand still in fear. Again, what matters is not what the preacher might have told his audience but the message which the text carried to his hearers. If the preacher had referred to the context of the passage — the historical circumstances in which Moses received his mandate — that would have carried enormous force. The remarkable identity of subject matter shows that Smith was not alone in addressing such themes, and such a circumstance might have encouraged the slaves even more.

Smith did not engage in further teaching on this subject until October 1821 to January 1822. The records show the following pattern of teaching:

October 1, 1821 – Exodus 4: Moses seeks assurance before approaching Israel, to tell them that God would deliver them from slavery in Egypt.

October 7, 1821 – Exodus 5: Moses and Aaron have their first encounter with Pharaoh, seeking deliverance for Israel. In retaliation, Pharaoh increases their work load.

October 21, 1821 – Exodus 7: The first of a number of plagues affect Egypt because of Pharaoh's failure to respond positively.

November 18, 1821 – Exodus 10 & 11: After a plague of locusts, Moses threatens the death of the first-born son of every Egyptian family.

December 16, 1821 – Exodus 14: The liberation of the Israelites begins. Pharaoh nevertheless pursues them, but the Egyptians are overwhelmed at the Red Sea.

December 31, 1821 – Exodus 16: The Israelites encounter harsh desert conditions and are shown how to gather food in the desert.

January 13, 1822 – Exodus 18: Moses finds it difficult to deal with the constant problems of the people and Jethro suggests a way to deal with them.

January 20, 1822 – Exodus 19: Israel arrives at Sinai, the end of the first stage in their journey of deliverance. Here they will receive the basis of the law – the *Decalogue*.

The recurrence of this theme suggests one of two conclusions: either Smith had suspended his teaching on the topic and was now continuing, or he was following a cycle. There were no entries in his journal for February to July 1822, but in August he spoke of being tired of repeating the same discourse. That circumstance, he said, had forced his discontinuance of the study.[57] The first suggests a strange lapse in the diligence which his journal would lead the reader to expect. The second points to an inclination to use colourful stories which he believed the slaves would understand more readily. It appears that he reverted to certain topics because the slaves showed enthusiasm for these narratives, reflecting their personal interests.

If, as the evidence suggests, the missionary favoured these patriarchal narratives and returned to them from time to time, it would explain why they became cemented in the minds of the slaves. With repetition came familiarity. But another explanation seems probable: the slaves had found that the stories spoke to their condition and gave them reason to hope and to plan their own deliverance. On that basis also it was easy for this event to become cemented in their minds. The event had its origins on the banks of the River Nile in Egypt, and Smith was teaching this story to slaves on the banks of the Demerara River in Guyana. He had no reason to expect the slaves to apply this story to their own circumstances, or to use it as a means of inspiration for their own liberation. He did not see a parallel in the circumstances of his audience — at least not to the extent that they should be considering an imminent liberation from their current state. He obviously did not see that only the names of the river and of the *dramatis personae* were different. His blinkered vision and his limited view of the capacity of the slaves meant that he could foresee no threat of rebellion on the basis of the 'simple' stories taught.

Smith's trial

It is now necessary to attempt a brief review of the evidence submitted at the trial of the missionary and, in so doing, to re-emphasise that the intention is not to determine Smith's guilt but his influence on the rebellion. One therefore need not go over the merits of the evidence since it is clear that Smith did not cause the slaves to rebel. The prosecutors relied heavily on the testimony of the slaves, creating the impression that Smith was, partially at least, convicted from his own mouth. One of the matters that needs to be addressed here is the roles assigned to slaves in the work of the mission. Slaves frequently held the offices of deacons and teachers, which ensured access to and influence over other slaves. It appears that deacons usually performed teaching duties in the chapel as teachers as well as their other leadership duties in sharing oversight over the congregation.

Teachers were located on a number of estates, and were either appointed by Smith or at the least approved by him.[58] The missionary took issue at the trial with the testimony of one slave who asserted that he appointed the teachers, asserting instead, 'The people themselves chose them, on their respective estates, without any interference from me.'[59] The testimony of the slave Bristol partially supports the missionary, in that the slave claimed to have appointed teachers with Smith giving approval to his choice.[60] Given the importance which the missionary attached to membership and leadership, to let the slaves choose their own teachers is surprising. It also suggests greater confidence in the slave leaders than one is led to expect, and the likelihood of slaves having a leadership all their own in contradistinction to the leadership of the missionary and those who were loyal to him. The teachers functioned on the estates, meeting the slaves, teaching them the catechism, and explaining to them the sermons of the missionaries, which they might not have understood. While one cannot prove that the teachers deliberately twisted the Scriptures to suit their own ends, one cannot overlook that possibility. This seems to have been the case with Quamina and Romeo, two leaders of Smith's congregation, who explained the missionary's sermons to their fellow-slaves.

Before dealing with the subject matter of Smith's teaching, we must note the pedagogical method which, by his own report, he used. His approach was to read through books of the Bible in sequence, and to give brief explanations of each passage which were 'of a moral and religious nature.' Even so, he occasionally omitted from his instruction such chapters of books as he thought susceptible to misinterpretation by the slaves. Thus he explained his omission of certain passages in Genesis 13 about promises to Abraham on the grounds that such promises might have been taken by slaves as applying to themselves. He did not omit that section of Scripture which related to the freeing of the Israelites from Egypt for a reason: 'the mercy, the power, and the providence of God, are signally displayed in that part of sacred history, and cannot fail to impress, with a sense of religious fear and trust, even the stupid mind of a Negro.'[61]

The evidence of a number of slaves was to the effect that Smith taught about Moses and the Exodus on several occasions. Some slaves such as Azor and Manuel barely remembered the outline of the Exodus story. In answer to a specific question, Azor was quite sure that Smith had not associated Egypt with Demerara. In answer to the question as to why God commanded Moses to take the Israelites out of Egypt, Manuel responded that 'God did not wish that they should be made slaves.' He also stated that Smith had made no application of the lesson to the experience of the slaves.[62] Bristol also testified to Smith's teaching on Moses, stating that such teaching took place up to three months before the revolt. He could remember what the missionary had said about Moses, but not what he had said about Joshua who immediately succeeded Moses.[63] These testimonies indicate a certain degree of selectivity on the part of the slaves regarding what they did or did not take to heart. What is interesting is that Bristol could not explain why the slaves spoke of no other part of the Bible except the Moses story, and why he appeared ignorant of the reason for their applying it to themselves. It may be that the answer was so obvious that Bristol felt no need to elaborate on it, or that he was astute enough not to mention it. This application of the text to themselves perplexed the court, and even Smith himself. Smith's explanation was ingenuous: 'If they themselves read the Bible and so apply it, the fault must be charged to their ignorance; and shows the necessity of their having more instruction.'[64] Smith had indicated early in his missionary career that he was not so imprudent as to teach the slaves to rebel.[65]

Another area of his teaching which the court noted was that concerning the observance of the Sabbath (Sunday). A number of slaves testified to his having impressed on them the need to keep it holy, though they differed in the details they sought to give. Smith had made it quite clear in his first address to the court that he was unalterably opposed to the non-observance of the Sabbath, except in extreme circumstances. His own view corresponded with the principle of the amelioration programme that slaves be employed on Sundays only for works of necessity, though he did not use the same terminology. As to whether they were under an obligation to carry out their owners' or overseers' instruction to work on Sundays, Smith's position was that it was the lesser of two evils to do as ordered. In an elaborate appeal to several scriptural texts, he illustrated that a missionary had no choice but to follow the precepts of Scripture, and the same was true for any Christian. Arguing against the 'violation of the Sabbath, by voluntary labour, which is not absolutely necessary,' Smith stated:

> In the face of so many precepts, could I tell the negroes there was no harm in working their ground, or in going to market on the Sabbath? was it for *me* to dispense with the commandments of God? surely not. Voluntary and unnecessary labour on the Sabbath I disallowed. I considered it a sin, and told them so; and if they are properly provided, by their owners, with the necessaries of life, as is asserted by all the planters, they can have absolutely no necessity for going to market on the Sabbath.[66]

Smith was forceful in his condemnation of the planters for their repeated unwillingness to facilitate their slaves' participation in worship; he was also strongly opposed to the slaves neglecting their sacred duty.

Several witnesses, including a free coloured slave owner, testified to Smith's use of Luke 19:41 as a text on the Sunday before the rebellion: 'And when he [Jesus] was come near, he beheld the city, and wept over it.' Again, the slave witnesses showed a vague recollection of what he said, except that Jerusalem was to be destroyed because the people did not believe in God.[67] The testimony of Romeo is interesting. According to him, Smith did not explain this sermon to his people. The reason he gave was curious as well as enlightening: the slaves were saying that Smith was making fools of them; he would not deny his own colour for black people.[68] Clearly, then, the confidence between missionary and slaves had declined considerably and the signs that they considered themselves to be on their own were ominous. Unfortunately, Smith's defence did not include a removal of the doubts which this text might have raised.

Conclusion

What conclusions can we draw from this brief examination of the events? The evidence of the slaves that Smith taught about the Exodus on more than one occasion was substantially established. The fact that the slaves could not remember precisely what he taught means that they paid less than due attention to what was actually being told them. It is quite likely that, where they were prepared to draw their own conclusions, the latter and his words were conflated to the extent that they were indistinguishable in their minds. The evidence says something of importance about their attitude to the missionary. When the crunch came, they were prepared to go their own way, rather than to confide in him or to accept his word. As a result, they did not accept his word that their 'free paper' had not arrived, and made their own plans to take freedom for themselves. In so doing, they were careful to conceal their plans from him, while having discussions with him on various matters. In other words, the slaves' relations with the missionary did not extend to their allowing him to determine their ultimate course of action. The bond between them was not as strong as missionaries generally projected, or as readers too easily assume.

Smith was denied the services of a lawyer and, not being one, was clearly out of his depth in such a situation. Even so, he expressed considerable doubt as to the probative value of the evidence presented. He spent some time demonstrating his conformity to the Instructions that he had received from his society, and to the fact that his teaching was 'calculated to instruct them in nothing but what was good, moral, and religious.' He therefore emphasised that neither he nor his teaching could have been the cause of the rebellion: 'I do as a minister of the gospel, in the presence of my God, most solemnly declare my innocence.' He defended the care that he used in ensuring that there was no perversion or misapplication of the Scriptures, so that if the slaves read the Bible and applied the Exodus story to themselves, 'the fault must be charged to their ignorance.' Before a court where slave-owning interests were not paramount, and where the officers were not determined to make an example of the missionary, an acquittal was the obvious verdict. But Smith was not before such a court. Yet what he demonstrated was not just his innocence, but his naïveté in thinking that the slaves could not draw conclusions other than those that he had sought to put into their heads.

On the face of it, the slaves were, and remained, independent of the teaching of the missionaries when it suited their purpose. It is clear that they listened and understood far more than their instructors gave them credit for, and that they effectively communicated their conclusions to their fellow sufferers. This was the danger in the use of the deacons. It is also evident that the slaves drew conclusions related to their own experience. No other conclusion seems possible when one considers the ease with which they remembered the story of Moses and the Israelites, yet their dim recollection of the other things he had taught them. It goes without saying that they kept their conclusions to themselves. Smith's testimony about the slaves' application of the lessons was, to say the least, condescending. In the long run, he seems to have had no higher opinion of them and their capacity than was common in his day.

Notes

1. See, for instance, Reginald Coupland, *The British Anti-Slavery Movement* (1933; London: Frank Cass & Co., 1964); Lowell J. Ragatz, *The Fall of the Planter Class in the British Caribbean, 1763-1833* (1928; New York: Octagon Press, 1971); F.J. Klingberg, *The Anti-Slavery Movement in England* (1926; Hamden, Conn: Archon Books, 1968).
2. What is stated in this and the following paragraphs derives from the resolutions passed at the meeting. The report is found in the *Guiana Chronicle*, February 27, 1824. See CWM Archives, fiche 792, Demerara, 1807-25.
3. CWM Archives, fiche 373, Petition of the LMS to the House of Commons. The petition is also printed in E.A. Wallbridge, *The Demerara Martyr* (1848; New York: Negro Universities Press, 1969), 159-65. It was presented to the House of Commons on April 13,1824.
4. There is a brief discussion by Wallbridge on the affair, eulogising those who spoke in favour of the resolution (*Ibid.*, 165-69, 215-72).
5. Klingberg, 218, 219.
6. W.L. Mathieson, *British Slavery and Its Abolition, 1823-1838* (1926; New York: Octagon Books, 1967), 143.
7. Stiv Jakobsson, *Am I not a Man and a Brother?* (Uppsala: Gleerup, 1972), 303. For his examination of the circumstances, see 293-369.
8. Cecil Northcott, *Slavery's Martyr* (London: Epworth Press, 1976), 52f.
9. Eric Williams, *Capitalism and Slavery* (1944; London: André Deutsch, 1967), 205.
10. Emilia Viotti da Costa, *Crowns of Glory, Tears of Blood* (New York: Oxford University Press, 1994), xvii.
11. *Ibid.*, xviif.
12. This point is made intermittently throughout the text. For the distrust of the missionary, see Da Costa, 114, 184, 212.

13. Winston F. McGowan, 'The Demerara Revolt, 1823,' in *Themes in African-Guyanese History* eds., Winston F. McGowan, James G. Rose, and David A. Granger (Georgetown: Free Press, 1998), 109, 110.

14. McGowan, 111, 112.

15. *Ibid.*, 114-17.

16. *Ibid.*, 124. McGowan examined the role of Smith in 120-24.

17. The charges are set out in *PP*, XXIII (158), Proceedings of a General Court Martial, 1824, reproduced in Irish University Papers, Slave Trade, Volume 66 (Shannon: Irish University Press, 1969), 53f. It is also printed in the LMS's *Report of the Proceedings against the late Rev. John Smith of Demerara* (1824; New York: Negro Universities Press, 1969), 2f.

18. Colin Palmer, *Human Cargoes* (Chicago: University of Illinois Press, 1981), 81f. Daniel P. Mannix, and Malcolm Cowley, *The Black Cargoes. A History of the Atlantic Slave Trade, 1518-1865* (London: Longmans, Green, 1962), 125-27 on the Zong case. The court ruled that slaves were more than merchandise.

19. For a reference to the issue in the West Indies, see Richard Ligon, *A True and Exact History of the Island of Barbadoes* (1657; London: Frank Cass, 1970), 50. For a broader discussion, see David Brion Davis, *The Problem of Slavery in Western Culture* (Harmondsworth: Penguin, 1970), Chapter 6.

20. Mary Turner, *Slaves and Missionaries, The Disintegration of Jamaican Slave Society 1787-1834* (Urbana: University of Illinois Press, 1982); William Dickson, *Letters on Slavery* (1789; Westport, Conn: Negro Universities Press, 1970), 58.

21. McGowan, 113.

22. The switch seems to have begun in the 1790s and was completed about 1815. See McGowan, 109; cf. Da Costa, 43.

23. Da Costa, 47, shows that up to 1813 the staple on the east coast was still cotton. See also *Ibid.*, 51.

24. See McGowan, 110; cf. Da Costa, 51.

25. Alvin O. Thompson, *Colonialism and Underdevelopment in Guyana, 1580-1803* (Bridgetown: Carib Research Publications, 1987), 120f. Elsewhere, Thompson devotes considerable space to discussing dietary provisions during the Dutch regime. He shows that under the Dutch things were not good (see 'Slave Society during the Dutch Regime,' in McGowan et al., *Themes*, 56-67). The problem, therefore, was not new.

26. 'Memorandum of Lord Bathurst on Religious Instruction for Negroes, March 1810,' in Eric Williams, *Documents on British West Indian History, 1807-1833* (Port of Spain: Trinidad Publishing, 1952), document 352.

27. Williams, *Documents*, document 345: 'Instructions to Governor Woodford,' n.d.

28. *Ibid.*, document 368: Governor Bentinck to Liverpool, January 6, 1812.
29. *Ibid.*, document 371: Woodford to Bathurst, August 4, 1816; document 376: Woodford to Bathurst, January 26, 1819.
30. For such laws, see Elsa V. Goveia, *The West Indian Slave Laws of the Eighteenth Century* (Bridgetown: Caribbean Universities Press, 1973).
31. Turner, 10-18, discusses attitudes in Jamaica towards missionaries and licensing.
32. The essence of the 'Instructions from the Directors of the Missionary Society to Mr. Smith, Missionary to Demerary' can be found in Da Costa, 131.
33. Smith's Journal, August 17, 1823; see also CWM Archives, fiche 787, August 20, 1823, Council for World Missions.
34. On this matter, see Noel Titus, *Conflicts and Contradictions* (London: Minerva Press, 1998), chapter V, and also Da Costa, 170.
35. W.J. Gardner, *A History of Jamaica* (1873; London: Frank Cass, 1971), 351, 357.
36. Da Costa, 198.
37. CWM Archives, fiche 364, Smith to Burder, May 7, 1817.
38. The reader is referred to Smith's journal entries for October 25 & November 20, 1818; January 21, October 3 & December 3, 1819.
39. According to Da Costa, 160, the LMS seldom responded to Smith.
40. CWM Archives, fiche 364: March 21, May 7 & October 14, 1817; fiche 365: March 18, 1818, January 20, March 2 & 19,1819, November 14, 1821.
41. Smith's Journal, November 28, 1821. Cf. Journal, August 9, 1822, where the missionary complains about Jack Ward, who frequently went to market, ignoring his warnings about the 'consequences of such wicked conduct.'
42. Ibid., December 3, 1820. Azor explained that his wife was near delivery and that he had no other help except on that day.
43. Ibid., January 8, 1821.
44. CWM Archives, fiche 372, Smith to Burder, February 28, 1823.
45. On one occasion, missionaries asked the LMS to temper its zeal in publishing extracts from their journals (See CWM Archives, fiche 365, Davies to the Directors, March 24, 1819; see also Ibid., fiche 366, Smith to the Directors, May 19, 1819).
46. Smith's Journal, March 5, 1820.
47. Ibid., July 19, 1818.
48. For references to difficulties with planters in the chapel, see Smith's Journal, November 16, 1817, February 26, March 15, July 23, November 24 & December 17, 1822. For the reprimand and later dismissal of Susanna, see April 15, May 13 & June 3, 1821. He had made an enemy of Hamilton in so doing.

49. See Smith's Journal, May 23, 25 & June 1 & 8, 1823.

50. Da Costa, 133.

51. Smith's Journal, April 3, 1818.

52. Ibid., October 28 & November 18, 1817.

53. Ibid., January 6 & 10, March 3, August 17, November 25, December 25 & 31, 1817, February 28, 1818 & September 21, 1819.

54. Ibid., March 24, 1818.

55. Ibid., April 15, May 13 & June 3, 1821.

56. Ibid., August 8, 1817. On November 8, 1818, Smith commented that some slaves had left the chapel during the sermon by his colleague Mercer, and that quite a large number were lying on the grass outside. This suggests some restiveness on their part.

57. Ibid., August 5, 1822.

58. LMS Report, 10, Azor's testimony.

59. Ibid., 64, Smith's first address to the Court.

60. Ibid., 22, Bristol's testimony.

61. Ibid., 67, Smith's first address.

62. Ibid., 11, Azor's testimony; 15, Manuel's testimony.

63. Ibid., 30.

64. Ibid., 68, Smith's first address.

65. Smith's Journal, February 17, 1818.

66. LMS Report, 16.

67. Ibid., Manuel's testimony; 12, Romeo's testimony.

68. Ibid., 12, Romeo's testimony.

CHAPTER 10

Crop Over Fetes and Festivals in Caribbean Slavery
Hilary McD. Beckles

Introduction

Enslaved Africans were concerned with much more than mere survival. They approached the experience of chattel bondage in the Caribbean and elsewhere with a determination to assert their humanity and cultural identities. They did this by redefining themselves, and refashioning the terms of social relations in creative ways that changed over time, and took a variety of forms in different societies. One result was that the African presence, despite its enchained circumstance, emerged as a vibrant and relevant cultural force. As enslaved people, then, Africans experienced neither cultural erasure nor absorption into the dominant ontological matrix of European enslavers.

From the outset, the dominant social and official postures of Europeans were determined by the need to promote cultural opposition to Africans as part of the strategy to establish and sustain the institution of chattel bondage. General cultural assimilation, then, was not the slave owners' intention. Had this been the case, it is unlikely that policy objectives would have been successful. Over time, when in some societies these postures softened, and slave owners sought to integrate Africans into European cultural institutions, such as missionary Christianity and monogamous family structures, they were soon to realise that projects of cultural assimilation would be the most difficult of all to accomplish.

For Africans, the enslavement of their labour and bodies was a process with discernible limits. It did not include their cosmological consciousness, from which site they imagined and identified themselves as intellectual and spiritually free social beings. Some traditional notions of cultural identity continued to inform their existential self and social living, and as a social reality functioned as a battleground of resistance and affirmation. It did so in much the same way that mountains and forests served to harbour maroon mentalities as invisible expressions of an unrelenting claim upon liberty.

The inner logic of cultural creativity in social life can be seen in the ways that the enslaved adopted and adapted the diverse heritages around them in order to strengthen this cultural assertiveness and sense of anterior freedom. In this way they developed attitudes and practices that drove the social dynamic and shaped the landscape and mindscape of Caribbean civilisation. What is now described, understood, and lived as the popular culture of the region, particularly the fetes and festivals of 'Crop Over,' is rooted in these persistent perspectives of enslaved ancestors. This is an important victory over the dehumanising intentions of chattel slavery, and speaks to the richness and creative flexibility of African culture.[1]

One way to examine the transatlantic slave trade is to consider it a mass transfer of traditional cultures from one continent to another, that is, as a forced migration of attitudes and values, art and science, as well as religion and technology. In this way it would be conceptually more coherent to begin an analysis of the diaspora experience from the perspective of Africans arriving with political, economic and social ideas that evolved. With this vision in place it would then be credible to begin by stating that the Caribbean experience posed a major challenge for the enslaved African to remain culturally relevant and dynamic. The celebration of survival and cultural emergence was an important part of the turbulent journey. The ritualisation of this triumph through the creative expressions of dance and song, using the formal format of seasonal festivals, was at the centre of much of what they did. For these reasons, and others, it has been said that Africans experienced a profound cultural remaking during this leg of their Caribbean journey. They met, for the most part and for the first time, large numbers of other Africans over a protracted period, from several different cultural and language groups. Of course, there was considerable movement of people throughout Africa. Long-distance trade and migration, as well as wars, displacement, and empire building, had seen to this. But in the Caribbean world, Africans from widely different backgrounds created households, kinship, and communities as the norm for the first time.

'Creolisation,' or the process of cultural adaptation, was as much an experience among Africans of different cultural groups as it was between Africans and Europeans. It was an encounter with Atlantic dimensions. It began on the African coast, as a social aspect of the transatlantic slave trade, continued in the Middle Passage, and flourished in Caribbean communities. As such, many of the enslaved who came to the Caribbean were 'creoles.' Some were persons already familiar with, and able to socially use, many aspects of European culture. These were equipped with a European language, and comfortable in the practice of European versions of Christianity.

Within this changing context African social cultures were challenged to remain relevant. The enslaved sought to create a community life of their own. They imagined a world that focused on issues beyond those of survival and invoked quests for cultural autonomy within social institutions built outside the reach and comprehension of the slave owners. Where they found it strategically necessary, they embraced and utilised both Amerindian and European cultural traits. This adaptation process worked in both directions. African cultural beliefs and practices crossed borders and facilitated the survival and development agendas of these ethnic groups. The enslaved demanded the right to free time, and to exercise autonomous control over its use. Inclement weather, Sundays, and Christian holidays were considered just reasons by slave owners to withdraw the enslaved from main-line production. Not all enslaved persons benefited on a regular basis from these concessions. Senior domestics, supervisors and artisans on the estates, as well as many enslaved urban workers, experienced a different rhythm in their labour-leisure cycle. Once the enslaved had achieved a customary right to leisure time, attention shifted to the more testing and vexing question of the manner in which it could be organised.[2]

Independent cultural living required that the enslaved would travel to other plantations or towns in order to participate in planned events and to sustain social relationships. This was done with and without the use of 'tickets' and 'passes' which were issued by persons with authority over them as proof of their legitimate travel beyond the confines of the property on which they were domiciled. Such travel documents were oftentimes forged, rendering this system inefficient and unreliable. Constables were empowered to stop black persons on the public roads and request that they produce travel documents. Failure to do so could lead to arrest and detention in facilities specially constructed for persons with no proof of legitimate travel.[3]

Evening dances became an important part of the popular culture of enslaved Africans in most colonies by the middle of the eighteenth century. William Dickson, reporting on the last quarter of the century, described the busy nature of highways in Barbados during the nights and early mornings as the enslaved sought to take full advantage of their leisure time. 'Their contubernal connections are unlimited as to numbers and local situations,' he stated. 'Both sexes are frequently travelling all night, going to or returning from a distant connection, in order, without sleep, to be in due time to go through a hard day's labour, after their nocturnal adventures.' Such pursuits, he tells us, included family gatherings, sexual relations, economic exchange, as well as the organisation and enjoyment of dances and festivals.[4]

Other Europeans wrote at length about the cultural expressions of the enslaved and the modalities they chose to be free in their social recreation. In 1790, G. Franklyn supported Dickson's observations concerning the movements of enslaved persons in pursuit of leisure. 'Nothing will,' he said, 'at any time, prevent them from pursuing their amours or their amusements.' Parties, he said, 'they are passionately fond of . . . [and] will travel several miles, after their daily labour is over, to a dance.' Finally, he said, 'after dancing the greatest part of the night, they will return to their owners plantations and be in the field at the usual hour of labour.'[5]

The conceptual tendency for Europeans to link the recreational and artistic culture of Africans to psychological escapism from the rigour and routine of hard labour, shapes and informs their literary narratives. This was so whether writers were travellers to the colonies or local chroniclers. Dr George Pinckard, who visited the islands on board a military vessel during 1795–96, wrote several accounts of Afro-Caribbean popular culture that were typical of the time. He too tells us that the Africans 'are passionately fond of dancing,' and that the 'Sabbath, offering them an interval from toil, is generally devoted to their favorite amusement.' He found it surprising, and irrational, that 'instead of remaining in tranquil rest, they undergo more fatigue, or at least more personal exertion, during their gala hours of Saturday night and Sunday, and during any four days of the week.'[6]

Their entertainment culture during the eighteenth century included the annual Crop Over festivals and weekend dances. Frederick Bayley, an Englishman who visited the islands for four years during the 1820s, tells us that whites who campaigned for the freedom of blacks, and who spoke of the 'groans of the negroes,' would not believe the spectacle of 'an assembly of these oppressed people on their grand day of jubilee,' which they called 'CROP OVER.'[7]

The Crop Over festival

According to Bayley, the Crop Over festival began on the 'day on which the last of the canes are cut on a sugar plantation,' during which 'flags are displayed in the field and all is merriment.' To initiate the ceremony, 'a quart of sugar and a quart of rum are allowed each negro on the occasion,' after which 'all authority, and all distinction of color ceases; black and white, overseer and bookkeeper mingle together in dance.' On the plantations, he added, 'it was common on occasions of this kind to see the different African tribes forming a distinct party, singing and dancing to the gumbay.'[8]

Crop Over was a West Indian festival. Mrs A.C. Carmichael, who witnessed the closing years of slavery in St Vincent and Trinidad, wrote in 1833 that Crop Over festivals were widespread. Robert Dirks notes, in addition, that the Jamaican Crop Over, rather than coming at the end of the harvest, was often put off until the conclusion of sugar-making, when the enslaved gangs assembled around the boiling house, dancing and roaring for joy. The overseer would distribute salt fish and rum, and the 'feast would be followed by a ball.'[9]

These planter-sponsored 'Harvest Home' celebrations afforded the enslaved opportunities to ritualise their relationships to the plantation world with song and dance. In Barbados, the Crop Over entertainment culture was well established by the early eighteenth century. One aspect of the festive proceedings was captured in satirical colonial literature, such as this verse from a 1754 poem by Nathaniel Weekes, a white creole Barbadian:

> There's not a slave,
>
> In spite of slavery, but is pleased and gay
>
> For this is their delightful, darling time![10]

Descriptions of Barbadian Crop Over celebrations, though few in number, are quite graphic. In 1798, Sampson Wood, manager of Newton Plantation in the Christ Church parish, reported that after the crop he would gather the enslaved and give them a 'dinner and a sober dance.' The reason he gave in justification of the financial expenditures was that it was 'a celebration of Harvest Home after the crop.' On the Codrington plantations, owned by the Church of England, the policy was adopted in 1819 to celebrate Crop Over with a holiday for enslaved persons.[11]

Generally, there were two types of Crop Over dances: those organised by, and held within, slave owners' households, and those convened by the enslaved —with or without their owners' permission. Pinckard offers limited comments on the second type. The enslaved, he stated, 'assembled in crowds upon the open green, or in any square or corner of the town, and forming a ring in the centre of the throng, dance to the sound of their beloved music.'[12] With respect to Jamaica, Trelawney Wentworth added more details:

> Music and dancing, the negroes love to their heart's core, although of late years, they have been taught by the missionaries to believe that they are inconsistent with morality. At this time, dancing was frequent in the negro houses in an evening, and once a week, a general assemblage took place under the auspices of one negro, who invited people from the neighbouring estates. On such occasions, it was customary to ask leave of their master to ensure a license for a greater duration of their obstreperous mirth, which, from the usual vicinity of his dwelling to the Negro-houses, he must necessarily hear.[13]

Wentworth also commented on the political and economic aspects of the enslaved persons' entertainment activities, and stressed that dances organised or engaged in by enslaved persons were not illegal when officially sanctioned by masters and mistresses. In most Caribbean colonies legal gatherings were permitted under the codes governing enslaved persons, and it was 'expedient,' Wentworth stated, for owners to 'admit them according to the character of the applicant.' Providing entertainment was also 'profitable to the negroes,' and slave owners tried to regulate activities so as to 'avoid monopoly by any one slave on the estates.' With respect to the financial arrangements, he stated:

> Each negro coming into the assembly paid half a bit, in order, partly, to meet the expense of a fiddler, who commonly charged as much as four and five

dollars; and who, if not to be found among themselves, was always to be engaged from among the slaves upon some other estate. If it happened, that the negro giving the entertainment has inferior accommodation, he would borrow a more eligible spot from another, the dancing taking place in the house, and in the adjoining plot of ground.[14]

Bayley's description of Crop Over fetes in Barbados, which he said were usually held in 'a negro hut,' speaks to the enslaved persons' commitment to an independent cultural order. According to him, 'tea and coffee are first handed round, after which the musicians, consisting of perhaps three fiddlers, a tambourine player, and a man who beats an instrument called a triangle, commence playing, and the dancing continues for a while in the most lively and spirited manner.' 'After the dancing,' he added, 'the group sits down to the supper table, the contents of which have all been stolen from the masters or mistresses.'[15]

At the end of the evening, Bayley continued, 'the parties separated and each returned home.' In general, he added, 'the masters know nothing of the matter. But if by chance any of them are charged the next day with having been on such an excursion, they do not hesitate in declaring that they never left the house.' Furthermore, he stated, the enslaved would 'assert, with the most impudent assurance, their total ignorance that such an occurrence was to take place.' These accounts offer insights into the social environment in which the enslaved carved out a celebratory and entertainment culture. They suggest the extensive nature of social and artistic expression, and indicate how the enslaved used cultural events and processes legitimately to display and promote an oppositional vanguard.[16] The musical expression of events often told of the ideological posture adopted by revellers. The legally outlawed drum was often invoked and legitimised within the context of cultural liberation. Sometimes whites sought to bring drummers to account before their magistrates. This was especially so during times of anxiety about the imminence of rebellion. They also discovered that it was sometimes wise not to interfere, and occasionally to participate.

The political role of slave dances

Enslaved persons never abandoned their hope for general emancipation. The 'dance parties' also provided opportunities for the enslaved to organise violent anti-slavery politics. In this regard, two types of gatherings are discernible — parties at which the enslaved ventilated social disaffection in a non-confrontational way, and those that constituted fora for the strategic negotiation and planning of anti-slavery revolution.

It may be said that these categories were political stages in anti-slavery designs rather than separate organisational types. But some dances were

251

organised specifically for the purpose of planning revolution and others were social gatherings innocent of revolutionary intentions. Official data on the 1816 Barbados anti-slavery rebellion and the 1824 Jamaica anti-slavery conspiracy illustrate the different natures and functions of dances, but locate the intentions of the enslaved in both situations within criminal law and the formal judicial system.

The Bussa rebellion in Barbados broke out on Easter Sunday, April 14, 1816, shortly after slave owners had taken the opportunity of the debate over William Wilberforce's Slave Registration Bill to reaffirm their unwavering pro-slavery stances. Over 10,000 enslaved persons took to arms in an act of revolutionary self-liberation. Slave owners claimed that they were shocked by the suddenness of the event, and that they had no signs to indicate that their human chattel possessed a mentality that could produce such a violent, bloody encounter. As a result, they looked within the nature of social relations of society in order to find an explanation. That the enslavement of over 80,000 people did not in itself constitute a viable explanation speaks more to the mentality of slave owners than any other factor. For over 100 years the island had not witnessed any large-scale, violent, anti-slavery rebellion coming from the black community. Slavery, they believed, could not be a compelling explanation in itself. Forces external to the society had to be in operation. The rebellion, therefore, could be seen as a social aberration, and the enslaved involved the victims of momentary delusion.

Having settled this matter through the identification of the metropolitan anti-slavery movement, particularly the campaign of Wilberforce, as the stimulus for rebellion, it was still necessary to identify the opportunities available to the enslaved to implement the politics of their delusion about freedom. How free were they to find the time and the space to engage in strategic discourse and planning? This was the question each slave-owner pondered. There were therefore detailed scrutiny and investigations of the daily lives of different categories of enslaved persons, as well as free blacks and free coloureds.

In any event, slave owners thought, the general circumstance of the life of the enslaved was shaped by anti-slavery tension and conflict. Not for a moment did they consider that the delusion was not with the enslaved but within themselves. They believed, and stated openly in their defence, that the extensive social and cultural liberties granted the enslaved ought to have protected them from such a violent onslaught. When the Investigative Commission reported on the causes of the revolt, the white community expected, therefore, that considerable attention would focus on the issue of blacks' cultural life and its socio-political implications.[17]

In this regard the report did not disappoint. It detailed the degree to which the enslaved population enjoyed extensive mobility throughout the colony, and explained this in terms of the willingness of 'slave owners' to allow them to develop cultural and kinship rights. It referred to the complex network of communications by the enslaved and the degree to which information passed between town and country, and through the estates that separated them.[18]

Several testimonies were received by the commissioners in which the view was expressed that the revolt was 'hatched' within the context of the cultural world of the enslaved that had gained a considerable degree of independence. The Crop Over festival was at the centre of this world, and by 1816 was a popular institution that shaped the social experiences of both whites and blacks. Fetes would begin long before the crop was over, and gained momentum during the harvest. Crop Over, then, was the culmination of a season of events. Between Crop Over seasons personal and family events, as well as Christian holidays, provided opportunities for fetes and ritual celebrations.

Edward Thomas, manager of Bayley Plantation, home of Bussa, the principal leader of the rebels, informed the commission that he had long provided many 'free' days for the enslaved to have 'dances' which, unfortunately, opened their appetite for greater rights.[19] Thomas Nurse, chief overseer at the River estate, argued that excessive social liberty and material comfort were the principal triggers of rebellion. It is a 'fact well known,' he informed the commission, that enslaved persons 'have had frequent dances and feasts, at which all were well (and some expensively) dressed.'[20]

Thomas Stoute, manager at Mapps estate, also explained the outbreak of violence in terms of the enslaved persons' extensive social activities. He told the commission, 'I conceive, as far as I am able to judge, that the Insurrection was produced by the negroes (in the first instance) abusing those indulgences which, for many years past, owners of slaves in this Island had been in the habit of granting them, such as having constant parties and dances on Saturday and Sunday evenings (at which they were most gaily attired).'[21]

James Maycock, physician in the parishes most physically affected by the revolt, stated that 'the frequency of dances, and other meetings of that kind, no doubt, enabled the disaffected to mislead their associates.' Lewis Young, doctor and estate owner, gave a similar account of the rebellion. He told the commissioners:

> As to the causes which produced the Insurrection, I am of the opinion that it was partly owing to the many indulgences– suffering them to keep cattle, and some own houses — to have large dwelling houses — great and frequent entertainments, with dancing, costly apparel, trinkets, etc. — had become more impatient of restraint. . . .[22]

Confessions taken from rebels before the courts martial, and from the depositions of enslaved witnesses, confirmed that revolutionary organisation was made possible on account of the frequent contact at parties, dances and other social gatherings.

Similar reactions were reported by Jamaican slave owners with respect to their enslaved workers' possession and use of 'free' time. On January 28, 1824, charges 'to enter into a rebellious conspiracy, for the purpose of obtaining, by force and violence, and by acts of resistance to the lawful authorities of [the] island, the freedom of themselves, and other such slaves' were heard in a Montego Bay, Jamaica, court-house.[23] The prisoners drew attention to three, and possibly more, dances and pre-Christmas parties they had attended for the 'dangerous purpose of exciting, encouraging, and maintaining each other, and other slaves in endeavouring by force, to obtain their freedom.' The prosecution spoke of the illegality of the dances within the contexts of their unauthorised and rebellious nature.

Parties and dances were given as the social events within which anti-slavery designs were organised. Reference was made specifically to two dances held at Mary-Ann's house and one at John Cunningham's in the pre-Christmas period, but general mention was made to gatherings, as early as August when it was common to celebrate the yam harvest. Mary-Ann's house was described as a regular dance venue with enslaved persons from distant estates attending to drink rum and dance into the early hours of the morning.

It was a trial in which Jamaican slave owners seized the opportunity to debate the extent to which enslaved persons had established a social life of their own. In court proceedings enslaved persons were described as having attained extensive social freedom. Images of enslaved persons freely holding nightly parties and interrupting their dancing to drink to 'Wilberforce 's health' were constructed for the jury by the prosecution. The defence sought to establish that parties were entirely permissible under the law, and that while there could have been some loose talk, typical of the season and oftentimes alcohol-inspired, there was no evidence of real conspiracy. The enslaved, in summary, were not rebels, but 'were merry-makers, mere dancers.'

The members of the jury were not convinced. They were instructed by Judge Vaughan that dances were permitted by the laws governing enslaved persons, and that free men of good character often attended such gatherings. The legal question before them, however, was whether these night dances were protective cover for the planning and encouragement of 'sedition, conspiracy or rebellion.'[24] Several witnesses, Judge Vaughan noted, provided evidence that enslaved persons did state at the dances in question that with respect to freedom they 'would fight for it,' and that 'they and the whites are now on a footing.' 'All these expressions,' he instructed the jury, 'must be termed criminal and rebellious,' but he implored them 'to consider that there was no overt act of rebellion proved; no proof of a sword being drawn, nor a threat against a white except by implication...In rebellion, you must have an overt act...' But in this case he concluded, 'there is only a disposition in the mind, a propensity of mind to crime.'[25] It took one hour of deliberations for the 12-man jury to reach its verdict after the three-day trial. Several of the enslaved were found guilty of 'attending meetings for the dangerous purpose of obtaining [their own] freedom, and the freedom of others by force.' Those found guilty of the most serious charges were executed; but many were whipped, imprisoned and deported as convicts from the island.

Some enslaved persons, then, were executed and others punished in several ways for using dances as venues for the planning and staging of anti-slavery activities. An enslaved person was not considered to be in a state of rebellion by virtue of harbouring recognisable anti-slavery thoughts, or even by the social articulation of such thoughts. Rebellion required actual physical action, as well as conscious organisation and planning. Their entertainment culture constituted a slice of everyday life over which the contest between hegemonic consensus and popular resistance played out. But dances were also attended by white persons, as well as free blacks and free coloureds whose pro-slavery agendas and ideologies were known to their enslaved hosts. Ideologically, then, the formal context of leisure organisation was complex with the free and the enslaved moving to the beat of different drums. In this sense, the dance party was in part an aspect of the pro-slavery apparatus that had to be internally subverted in order to serve anti-slavery purposes. For these reasons, the judge and jury at Montego Bay found it necessary to untangle the threads in order to separate the guilty from the innocent, the rebels from the revellers.[26]

Dances, therefore, were events designed for social amusement and recreation, as well as venues for political conscientisation and organisation. The notion of a social contract between slave owners and enslaved was ultimately a figment of some slave owners' imagination. Freedom in its fullest legal sense was never removed from the top of the enslaved workers' agenda. Slave owners' misrepresentation of the impact of paternalistic ideology was also in part the result of unfamiliarity with the nature and role of cultural action. While cultural activity among the enslaved took on an overt leisure-pleasure format, ultimately the process of celebration was about freedom from constraints, real or imagined.

Gombay and Junkanoo

The highlight of Crop Over and Christian holiday seasons was the colourful appearance and performance of the Gombay, a festive type of music and improvised dancing that had its roots in Africa. Blacks would paint their faces, decorate their heads with flowers and bright coloured ribbons, and go from house to house singing and dancing, and playing musical instruments. Sometimes they wore masks, and danced to the drumming of the 'Gombay'— a drum made with animal skin. The drummers were highly skilled, an art that was learnt, and was part of the African heritage of different ethnic groups.

Gombay was also the name given to a Caribbean festival that was seen yearly in many colonies, particularly Bermuda, the Bahamas, the Virgin Islands, Jamaica, Belize, and parts of the Leeward Islands. Most whites were hostile to

African festivals, and were particularly critical of the Gombay, but blacks refused to bow to their opinions of their culture. An editorial in the *Bermuda Royal Gazette* of December 26, 1837, for example, made the following hostile comment: 'the savage and non-sensical exhibition of the Gombay, practised here by the idle, should be done away with as a thing not suited to a civilised community, and highly dangerous to passengers on horses or in carriages.'

In the Virgin Islands, the government tried to control the Gombay festival, and in 1733 passed a law that all such 'fetes, balls, dances, and divertissments with negro instruments' should end at sundown or at 8.00 p.m. on moonlight nights. In St Thomas in the 1760s the governor extended the time limit to 10.00 p.m.; thereafter police permission was required, but in no circumstances was the use of 'Gombay drums permitted.' At all Crop Over and Christmas fetes the Gombay drum carried the beat.

These were events that allowed the enslaved persons to dress in fine clothes and fancy jewellery. In the Danish Virgin Islands, the government objected to enslaved persons dressing in silks and wearing gold. Only the white elites were expected to do so, and in 1780 a 'Sumptuary Law' was passed that prohibited enslaved persons from wearing 'gold, silver, and precious stones, silk, lace, and other expensive fabrics.' Enslaved persons caught wearing such items were arrested; the offending articles were deemed as stolen goods, and handed over to their owners.[27] Other colonies passed 'Sumptuary Laws' that prescribed the kind of clothing enslaved persons were to wear, and prohibited them from dressing in silks, lace, and fine cottons. Expensive jewellery was often confiscated by police and magistrates, but such action had little impact because of the determination of enslaved persons to dress elegantly on festive occasions.

Connected to the performance celebration of death, life and identity, were social expressions in dress, and the rituals of religious ceremony. During both the Christmas season and August Crop Over, Africans in Jamaica, Antigua and other places, performed the Joncanoe or John Canoe, a well-established cultural ritual. Using elaborate head dresses and masks, enslaved persons performed this ritual as part of their statement about the relationship between the spirit world and social living. It is said to have had its origins at Axim, a major slave trading port on the Gold Coast.

The Antigua 'Junkanoo' (Jonkonnu) was mostly a Christmas spectacle. In 1774, Janet Schaw described it as a rebellious affair that worried the whites: 'It is necessary, however, to keep a look out during this season of unbounded freedom; and every white man on the island is in arms and patrols go all round the different plantations as well as keep guard in the town.' In St Vincent, blacks also celebrated Crop Over and Christmas with the Junkanoo festivals. Mrs Carmichael described it during the early nineteenth century: 'They flour each other's black faces and curly hair, and call out, "look at he white face! and he white wig!" — with many other jokes of their own.' She also described an event on Christmas day: 'About eleven in the morning, a party of negroes from Paradise, the adjoining estate, came to wish us a good Christmas. They had two fiddlers, whose hats and fiddles were decorated with many-coloured ribbons.' Approvingly, she concluded, 'Negroes formerly used to be inclined, I was told, to rioting and fighting upon Christmas-day, but now they all go to church.'[28]

In the Bahamas Junkanoo had become established black arts and culture by the late eighteenth century and was associated with Christmas when 'negroes have been seen beating their tambourines and dancing the whole day.' A Mr Farquharson noted in 1832 that his enslaved workers 'go abroad to see some of their friends and some stay at home amusing themselves in their own way through the day, but all of them at home in the evening and had a grand dance and keep it up until near day light.'[29]

The Kumina dance, like Jonkonnu, was a core element of culture in Jamaica and other places with large Akan populations. It is a dance that allows the living to connect with spirit ancestors. Kumina emerged as a 'healer' dance, an invocation of the spirits which the rival doctors called forth with the help of gombay drumming. The Jamaican maroons integrated these rituals into their philosophy and science of life.

The Jonkonnu and other festivities in Jamaica's black community were related in origin to the seasonal Crop Over event. In a recent study of Afro-Caribbean cultural practices, Richard Burton argues that 'in many ways the annual Christmas extravaganza was an extension, elaboration, and intensification of the crop over celebration that, about August each year, marked the successful termination of the sugar harvest.'[30]

There are several descriptions of the Jamaica Crop Over festival. Most of these were written at the end of the slavery period by visitors to the island whose concern was to demonstrate that slavery was not as oppressive a reality as abolitionists suggested. The images of enslaved persons dancing, singing, and drinking rum in celebration of life, were meant to indicate that there was no serious anti-slavery sentiment within their ranks.

In 1826, Alexander Barclay noted that during the Jamaica Crop Over festival the enslaved persons on the plantation would gather in the evening 'in their master's or manager's house, and, as a matter of course, take possession of the largest room, bring with them a fiddle and a tambourine. Here all authority and all distinction of colour ceases, black and white, overseer and the book-keeper, mingle together in the dance.'[31]

In the anonymous novel, *Marly*, which was published in 1828 and depicts the closing years of the Jamaican slave system, the image of Crop Over presented is not one of paternal understanding and social consensus. While the interaction of slave owners and enslaved persons, blacks and whites, is set out as the formal arrangement, the subtext is one of cultural tension and subtle expressions of conflict. It is said, for example, that the enslaved do not arrive at the homes of white officials unless directly invited. Also, that they discern a fine distinction between an invitation and an instruction. In any case, it seemed, the enslaved knew that without them 'there could be no ball.'

Understanding that their presence was required at the Great House, the black belles, as the enslaved females are described in the novel, would arrive dressed 'in all the finery which they possessed.' In his narration of this text, Burton stated:

> White men dance with black women – there appear to be no white women on the estate — and then watch as 'sable fops' join 'black belles' to 'display their prowess in dancing.' When supper 'calls the Buckras from the ball,' the slaves dance by themselves until, supper over, the whites return and dancing continues until the early hours of the morning, whereupon 'all departed, if not happy, at least well pleased, and thus the black ball terminated' — in short, an enjoyable if less than ecstatic occasion during which, some minor infractions apart, the essential social and racial boundaries are observed by both sides.[32]

The practice of African religions at Crop Over

Throughout the region Africans practised, within the context of the Crop Over festivities, a range of religions that focused on the issues of everyday life. The belief in the power of mind over matter, and the use of spirit power to shape and determine destiny, resided at the core of religions such as myal, obeah, and voodoo. The intersection of art, science and religion within the entertainment process enhanced a political and social perspective among blacks that only ancestral spirits and gods, and not whites, should be feared. Whites who understood these thought processes lived in fear, as black spirit leaders expressed no awe for their political power.

Spirit-based religions integrated the black communities, and gave them philosophical identities as well as political leverage with respect to survival strategies. White governments outlawed these religions in all Caribbean societies and punished practitioners with death. But the criminalisation of black religion, in the form of anti-obeah and anti-myal laws, made little difference to belief systems within the black communities. Under the pretence of attending fetes and festivals, blacks visited their myal leaders, obeah and voodoo priests for cures for illnesses, the removal of curses and bad luck, blessings for children, insights into personal futures, and general counselling. They also visited myal leaders, seeking help in the settling of disputes and the administration of justice.

Moreover, operating within the entertaining contexts of festivals, spirit leaders were expected to foster the process of resistance to slavery by providing visionary leadership and a psychic advantage over the arms of white oppressors. In the case of Haiti, the role of voodoo in the revolution as a force in achieving solidarity, loyalty and extraordinary bravery in the face of death and destruction is well known. In Jamaica during the eighteenth century, myal was intertwined in festivals, fetes and maroon rebellions. Whites in the western areas, especially, were terrified of the influence of myal men who were called doctors. When they caught them they often condemned and brutally executed them.[33]

In Jamaica, myal doctors, who were shadowy figures within formal festive arrangements, incorporated some Christian beliefs and practices, as did voodoo leaders in Haiti. The force that led to the resurrection of the spirit was celebrated in dance and song during festivals. In more solemn circumstances, respect for this force was expressed in the practice of the Baptist faith, as voodoo found almost perfect synergy within Catholicism. In these ways Africans gave celebratory form to the philosophy that life, guided by the ancestral spirits — some good, some bad — was for the living. 'Living the life' was manifested in various festivals and carnivals that were social features of the plantation and urban worlds.

Some balls were formal events organised by the enslaved. They were called 'Dignity Balls' and were lavish affairs with an entry fee. Revellers could eat, drink and dance all night. Women were usually elegantly dressed in fine clothes and jewellery, and all kinds of alcoholic drinks were available. Whites would wonder from where these items came, and how enslaved women were able to obtain their flowing ball gowns. An officer in the British army described a 'Dignity Ball' in Bermuda in 1830 as follows:

> When dancing was over the company was ushered into the supper room, where a table was set out covered with a profusion of cakes, preserves, wines, etc; that the Black women appeared in full costume, lace, satin and flowers; and that, in short every thing was conducted with the same taste as in the higher circles of society. They had Spanish dances and quadrilles, country dancing not being considered genteel.[34]

The music was provided by black musicians who played violins, fiddles, flutes and drums.

James Stewart, writing in 1823, noted that in Jamaica some enslaved persons, particularly domestic ones, disassociated from African musical forms, and identified with those of the Europeans. He wrote:

> In a few years it is probable that the rude (African) music will be altogether exploded among the creole negroes, who show a decided preference for European music. Its instruments, its tunes, its dances, are now pretty generally adopted by the young creoles, who indeed sedulously copy their masters and mistresses in everything. A sort of subscription balls are set on foot, and parties of both sexes assemble and dance country dances to the music of a violin, tamborine, etc. . . .But this improvement of taste is confined to those who are, or have been, domestic about the houses of the Whites.[35]

Stewart's observations with respect to Jamaica speak to the Caribbean trend of adaptation within the logic of African cultural survival. With respect to Barbados, similar observations were made. Dr George Pinckard, writing in 1796, was clearly hostile to the African Crop Over culture as indicated in this statement:

> They assemble, in crowds, upon the open green, or in any square or corner of the town, and, forming a ring in the centre of the throng, dance to the sound of their favourite African yell. Both music and dance are of a savage nature, and their songs which are very simple, [are] harsh and wholly deficient in softness and melody . . . While one negro strikes the Banjar, another shakes the rattle with great force of arm, and a third sitting across the body of the drum, as it lies lengthwise upon the ground, beats and kicks the sheepskin at the end, in violent exertion with his hands and heels, and a fourth sitting upon the ground at the other end, behind the man upon the drum, beats upon the wooden sides of it with two sticks. Together with the man upon the noisy sounds, numbers of the party of both sexes bawl forth their dear delighting sound with all possible force of lungs, . . . a spectator would require only a slight aid from fancy to transport him to the savage wilds of Africa.[36]

Frederick Bayley, who visited Barbados during the 1820s, stated how the blacks, to the annoyance of whites, would 'sit' up during the greater part of the moonlight nights, chattering together, and telling 'nancy stories.' He added: 'A nancy story is nothing more or less than a tale of ghosts and goblins, which pass with the negroes by the appellation of Jumbees.' He then commented on the blacks' 'grand day of jubilee, which they call "crop over."' 'During the late eighteenth century,' he observed, 'it was common on "crop over" to see the different African tribes forming each a distinct party, singing and dancing to the gumbay, after the manner of their native Africa.' He added that the festival had now been made less African, with the fiddle and tambourine being used instead of drums, while 'black and white, overseer and book-keeper mingle together in dance.'[37]

There were other favourite pastimes among the enslaved. They enjoyed stick-fighting, particularly when contestants were competitive and prepared to dominate each other for a prize. Cock-fighting and card-gaming were also popular. Most societies passed laws prohibiting the enslaved from gambling with dice or cards, or betting on horses. Such laws had little effect in the face of determined communities. In effect, most things that enslaved did by way of organised leisure were criminalised by white legislators. Storytelling and the playing of 'warri' – an ancient African game — did not come under the legislators' wrath, largely because they were quiet, home-bound events.

Conclusion

Caribbean societies, then, were fashioned in important ways by the cultural expressions of enslaved Africans whose collective agenda was ontological freedom and ultimately legal emancipation. The arena of culture was the place where all blacks practised their freedom of mind and body as evidence of their refusal to accept slavery as an intellectual or spiritual experience. Crop Over festivals, and other related entertainment events, were symbols of resistance that stood in the way of the penetrative and corrosive power of chattel bondage. The persistence of these institutions of freedom indicates therefore that the existential reality of emancipation is still in the making, and that there remains a great deal about which to dance, sing and shout.

Notes

1. See Kamau Brathwaite, *The Folk Culture of the Slaves in Jamaica* (London: New Beacon Books, 1970); Robert Dirks, 'John Canoe: Ethnohistorical and Comparative Analysis of a Carib Dance,' *Actes du XLII Congrés International des Americanistes*, 6 (1979): 487 501; 'Slave Holiday,' *Natural History*, 84.10 (1975): 84–90; Jerome S. Handler and Robert Corruccine, 'Plantation Slave Life in Barbados,' *Journal of Interdisciplinary History*, 14.1 (1983): 65–90; Sidney W. Mintz, "The Plantation as a Socio–Cultural Type,' in *Plantation Systems of the New World* (Social Science Monograph, 7, Washington, D.C.: Pan American Union, 1959); Michael Craton, 'Decoding Pitchy Patchy: The Roots, Branches and Essence of Junkanoo' (Paper presented at the 26th Annual Conference of the Association of Caribbean Historians (ACH), Puerto Rico, 1994).

2. Robert Dirks, *The Black Saturnalia: Conflict and its Ritual Expression on British West Indian Slave Plantations* (Gainesville: University Presses of Florida, 1987), 145; Sylvia Wynter, 'Jonkonnu in Jamaica: Toward an Interpretation of Folk Dance as Cultural Process,' *Jamaica Journal*, 4.2 (1970): 34–38; Judith Bettelheim, 'Jamaica Jonkonu and Related Caribbean Festivals,' in Margaret Crahan and Franklin Knight, eds., *Africa in the Caribbean* (Baltimore: The Johns Hopkins University Press, 1979), 80–100; Richard Rath, 'African Music in Seventeenth Century Jamaica: Cultural Transit and Transmission,' *William and Mary Quarterly*, 3rd series, 50.4 (1993): 700–26; Sidney W. Mintz and Richard Price, *An Anthropological Approach to the Afro American Past: A Caribbean Perspective* (Philadelphia: ISHI., 1976).

3. See, for example, how Africans mobilised their economic culture: Hilary McD. Beckles, 'An Economic Life of Their own: Slaves as Commodity Producers and Distributors in Barbados,' in Ira Berlin and Philip D. Morgan, eds., *The Slaves' Economy: Independent Production by Slaves in the Americas* (London: Frank Cass, 1991), 31–48; Mary Turner, 'Slave Workers, Subsistence and Labour Bargaining: Amity Hall, Jamaica, 1805–32,' in *The Slaves' Economy* edited by Berlin and Morgan;

Sidney W. Mintz, 'Caribbean Market Places and Caribbean History,' *Nova Americana*, 1 (1980–81): 333–44; Hilary McD. Beckles and Karl Watson, 'Social Protest and Labour Bargaining: The Changing Nature of Slaves' Responses to Plantation Life in 18th Century Barbados,' *Slavery and Abolition*, 8 (1987): 272–93.

4. William Dickson, *Mitigation of Slavery* (London: Longman, 1814), 155–56.

5. G. Franklyn, *Observation occasioned by the attempts made in England to effect the abolition of the slave trade ... and also some particular remarks on a letter addressed to the treasurer of the society for effecting such abolition, from Rev Robert Boucher Nicholls* [Nickolls] (London: Logographic Press, 1789).

6. George Pinckard, *Notes on the West Indies*, 3 Vols. (London: Longman, Hurst, Rees & Orme, 1806), I, 263.

7. Frederick Bayley, *Four Years Residence in the West Indies* (London: William Kidd, 1832), 436.

8. *Ibid.*

9. A.C. Carmichael, *Domestic Manners and Social Conditions of the White, Coloured and Negro Population of the West Indies*, 2 Vols. (London: Whittaker, 1833), I, 175–76, Dirks, 146–47.

10. See Karl Watson, *The Civilised Island, Barbados; A Social history, 1750–1816* (Bridgetown: Caribbean Graphics, 1979), 84.

11. *Ibid.*

12. Pinckard, I, 263–64.

13. Trelawney Wentworth, *The West India Sketch Book* (London, Printed for Whittaker and Co., 1834), I, 65–67; see also 228–30; II, 240–42, 282.

14. *Ibid.*

15. Bayley, 69–71, 437–38.

16. *Ibid.*

17. Hilary McD. Beckles, 'Slave Drivers' War: The 1816 Barbados Slave Uprising,' *Boletín de Estudios Latinoamericanos y del Caribe*, 39 (1985): 85–111; Ibid., 'Emancipation by Law or War! Wilberforce and the 1816 Barbados Slave Rebellion,' in *Abolition and its Aftermath: The Historical Context, 1790-1916*, ed., David Richardson. (London: Frank Cass, 1985), 80–105; Michael Craton, 'Proto–Peasant Revolts? The Late Slave Rebellions in the British West Indies, 1816–1832,' *Past and Present*, 85 (1979): 99–125; Claude Levy, 'Slavery and the Emancipation Movement in Barbados, 1650–1833,' *Journal of Negro History*, 58 (1970): 1–12; Michael Craton, *Testing the Chains: Resistance to Slavery in the British West Indies* (Ithaca: Cornell University Press, 1982), 254–67.

18. Newton Estate Papers, 523/781, Senate House Library, London University, Robert Haynes to Thomas Lane, September 23, 1816; CO

28/85, Governor Leith to Lord Bathhurst, April 29, 1816, fol. 8; *The Report from a Select Committee of the House of Assembly, Appointed to Inquire into the Origin, Causes and Progress of the Late Insurrection* (1817; London: T. Cadell and W. Davies, 1818). For an independent report of the rebellion, see New York Public Library, MSS., Division A, Anon., 'An Account of the Late Negro Insurrection which took place in the island of Barbados on Easter Sunday, April 14, 1816.'

19. *Report from a Select Committee.*
20. *Ibid.*
21. *Ibid.*
22. *Ibid.*
23. *Report of the Trial of Fourteen Negroes at the Court-House, Montego Bay, Jan. 28, 1824* . . . *on a Charge of Rebellious Conspiracy* (Montego Bay, 1824), 4–5.
24. *Ibid.*, 43.
25. *Ibid.*, 49.
26. *Ibid.*, 31.
27. See Watson, *The Civilised Island*, 80–86; Orlando Patterson, *The Sociology of Slavery: An Analysis of the Origins, Development and Structure of Negro Slave Society in Jamaica* (London: MacGibbon and Kee, 1967), 230–59; see also Howard Johnson, 'Slave Life and Leisure in Nassau, Bahamas, 1783–1838' (Paper presented at the 26th Annual Conference of the ACH, Puerto Rico, 1994), 1, 9; Neville Hall, 'Slaves Use of their "Free" time in the Danish Virgin Islands in the Late Eighteenth and Early Nineteenth Century,' *Journal of Caribbean History*, 13 (1980): 22; Edward Brathwaite, *The Development of Creole Society in Jamaica, 1770–1820* (Oxford: Clarendon Press, 1971), 295–96.
28. Carmichael, II, 290–93.
29. Johnson, 'Slave life.'
30. Richard Burton, *Afro Creole: Power, Opposition and Play in the Caribbean* (London: Cornell University Press, 1997), 71–72.
31. Alexander Barclay, *A Practical View of the Present State of Slavery in the West Indies* (London: Smith Elder, 1826), 10.
32. Burton, *Afro-Creole.*
33. See Mervyn Alleyne, *Roots of Jamaican Culture* (London: Pluto Press, 1988), 76–106.
34. Cyril Packwood, *Chained to the Rock: Slavery in Bermuda* (New York: Eliseo Torres, 1975), 97.
35. James Stewart, *A View of the Past and Present State of the Island of Jamaica* (1823; New York: Negro Universities Press, 1969), 56.
36. Pinckard, I, 263–64.
37. Bayley, 84, 436.

Section III

Forging A New Society

CHAPTER 11

Post-Emancipation Adjustments in the Urban Context: Views from Bridgetown, Barbados
Pedro L.V. Welch

Introduction

*M*y main contention is that even after 150 years, the historical literature seems unclear about the nature and range of blacks' hopes and expectations of emancipation; therefore, we cannot fully understand how these expectations and the action they inspired affected the contours of post-slavery development. More important, this vagueness tends to obscure the extent to which frustration of expectations may have affected the consciousness and actions of blacks in decades after the ending of slavery, which is another way of saying that important features of our historical experience may not yet be fully in focus.[1]

The comments above of Professor Woodville Marshall, one of the most influential voices in the historiography of the post-emancipation Caribbean experience, offer a sharp reminder that we are not out of the woods yet in this area of historical discussion. Indeed, it may be argued that several aspects of the pre-emancipation reality which helped to shape the post-emancipation expectations of the formerly enslaved still remain obscured. Clearly, Caribbean historiography is hampered by the paucity of sources which give authentic voice to the ex-slaves. However, the way out of this morass might well lie in widening the search for that voice outside of traditional plantation sources. In that context, this essay focuses on the urban context of the ex-slaves' experience.

An examination of the historiography of the post-emancipation British Caribbean societies reveals a tendency to understate the place and function of the urban complex in the shaping of these societies.[2] This tendency is surprising, more so when it is noted that colonial towns in the Caribbean were home to a sizable ex-slave population. Indeed, on the eve of emancipation Bridgetown, the chief port and capital of Barbados, had a slave population of over 13,000 which represented the largest concentration of slaves in the island.

It is also important to note that throughout the Caribbean the urban environment represented a theatre in which specific kinds of challenge/ adjustments to the authority structure imposed by white slave owners might be identified.[3]

In this regard, Gary Puckrein, in observing the peculiarities of urban slave society in Bridgetown, has noted that 'urbanized blacks were exposed to all kinds of currents in the island's chief port of call.'[4] This contrasted sharply with the rural conditions in which slaves lived in 'comparative isolation.' Moreover, urban enslavers organised the labour of the enslaved in quite different ways from those typical of the rural plantation. They 'wanted slaves who could more or less work on their own.'[5] In fact, it may be observed that many urban slaves worked on self-assigned, own-account tasks, without any immediate supervision by whites.

Puckrein is not alone in recognising that urban slave society posed a dilemma to the maintenance of social distance between the enslavers and the enslaved. Barry Higman, Barry Gaspar, and Neville Hall have been foremost in identifying the urban complex as an important variable in understanding enslaver-enslaved interaction in the colonial Caribbean.[6] Gaspar has observed that urban environments provided a social mobility for the enslaved which was 'not ordinarily accessible to plantation slaves.' It was a mobility which offered the enslaved, particularly those who lived in the town, access to a wider world of values, ideas and experiences.[7] In Neville Hall's investigation of urban slavery in the Danish West Indies, he has observed that:

> The communal interaction of urban slave and freed men can be perceived not merely as pleasurable forms of inter-ethnic social commerce. In the important sense it existed also as a defence against the white's hold on hegemonic power; in another sense, as an offensive instrument aimed at containing that power's effectiveness or, under proper auspices, of defeating it.[8]

A useful contribution which may be considered here is that made by Roderick A. McDonald in his investigation of social adjustments in the Caribbean island of St Vincent during the Apprenticeship period. McDonald observes that the 'disparities between the urban and rural contexts reveal the priorities and values that guided the authorities' reconceptualisation of crime.' This observation takes note of the way that colonial elites interpreted the threat to social order posed by the peculiar conditions resident in the urban milieu. Indeed, McDonald comments further that 'the codification of laws experienced by agrarian apprentices, which were designed to control and extract work within the plantation gang system, reflected markedly different imperatives from those instituted to control town-based apprentices, whose patterns of residence and labour were so dissimilar to their rural counterparts.'[9] The

Bridgetown context will reveal similar considerations.

These brief comments point to the importance of urban research in mobilising a fuller comprehension of the expectations that ex-slaves and former owners held of the emancipation process. Indeed, it may be argued that to a large extent the controls which former enslavers put in place after emancipation were shaped by their pre-emancipation experiences with free coloureds, free blacks, and urban slaves operating in an urban environment which offered room-to-manoeuvre options not widely available in the rural milieu. It is within this context that we pay closer attention to the immediate pre-emancipation slave society in Bridgetown as an important antecedent to an examination of post-emancipation adjustments in this urban milieu.

Pre-emancipation antecedents of a post-emancipation dilemma

In considering the nature of pre-emancipation slave society in Bridgetown as an antecedent to post-emancipation adjustments, it is useful to focus attention on the practice of 'hiring out' slave labour. For many white and free coloured Bridgetown inhabitants (most of them female) who owned small units of slaves, hiring out the time and labour of the enslaved provided the sole source of income. Under the system, enslaver and enslaved often entered into an informal arrangement which permitted the latter relative freedom to seek his/her employer and to set the terms of negotiation for the purchase of labour. Under these arrangements, the enslaved often provided their own housing, food and clothing in return for a fixed remuneration to the owner. An interesting comment on the system of slave hiring in an urban slave community in North America suggests that it 'provided masters [and mistresses] with the profits of slave ownership without the accompanying managerial responsibilities.'[10] Whatever the advantage it brought the enslaver, the attraction it held for the enslaved was clear.

It is suggested that the enslaved actively sought these arrangements because of the following reasons. Firstly, blurred lines of authority could lead to a hirer being unsure of the extent of his/her disciplinary authority. The enslaved could exploit this to their advantage. Secondly, hirers might have little interest in the off-task activity of their charges, thus permitting a higher degree of autonomy than would have been possible under the owners' supervision. Thirdly, the flexibility created by the blurring of lines of authority may have forced owner and hirer to offer positive incentives to their social inferiors to ensure better compliance with their wishes.[11]

Quite apart from the hiring out of the enslaved, the port function of Bridgetown served to generate an occupational structure which differed markedly from that of the rural plantation. For example, there was a general absence of gang labour and a greater tendency towards individualised work.

Even where some elements of gang work may have existed as, for example, in the shipyard of John and Thomas Scott, where five ships' carpenters, seven caulkers, and six blacksmiths worked, the nature of supervision was still removed from the rural pattern.[12] It appears that the skills acquired by black craftsmen, who at times worked alongside white tradesmen, offered some autonomy in the work environment.

In short, the rhythm of urban occupational life was removed from the regimentation which was characteristic of the rural scene. From skilled slave to domestic and those involved in self-hire, marketing/selling, all found an ambience which offered room-to-manoeuvre options which impacted heavily on the nature of black-white interaction. Within the broad categories of urban occupations, slaves handled their owners' money and their own; they acquired skills which gave them some autonomy on the job; they were often in occupations which required unsupervised absences from the slave owners' residence. These were all factors in an evolving urban identity which had implications for the structure of discipline in the town. On the eve of emancipation, whites had no illusions as to the expectations of the enslaved. After all, there was enough evidence of those expectations in white creoles' interactions with those manumitted before 1834, operating as entrepreneurs (traders, tavern keepers, artisans etc.), and with the enslaved people operating in what was tantamount to a wage labour regime.

Even in the area of housing, the general image of town life is one in which the controls typical of rural society were loosened. In the case of the 'hired out' category of the enslaved, the practice was for owners or lessees to act as go-betweens in renting houses on their behalf. Some of the enslaved bought or constructed small huts on rented lands, in which case the name(s) of white patrons would appear in the St Michael (or Bridgetown) Rate Books, followed by the name of the actual renter(s). In other cases, the lessees or hirers would erect huts on lands owned by white, free coloured and free black town residents. Most of the districts where such housing was located were in the north-eastern quadrant of the town in such areas as Greenfields, Racoon Quarters, Upper Roebuck Street and Canary Street.[13] They were located out of the immediate vision of the slave owners. As Barry Higman states, 'even if the roof leaked more often and food was harder to come by, slaves on board wages were beyond earshot of their owners and able, to a relatively great degree, to set their own rules of behaviour.'[14]

Given the background presented, there is the clear suggestion that urban enslavers were faced with the need to develop disciplinary structures to cope with departures from the norms of plantation society. William Dickson refers to the 'Common whipper' or 'jumper.'[15] The absence of the driver or overseer so typical of the patriarchal authoritarian structure of the rural slave gang dictated the need for an alternative system. The jumper was a male hired by urban owners (the majority of whom were female) to carry out the punishments that some of them were incapable of administering themselves. This separation of physical discipline from the role of enslaver provides yet another feature of pre-emancipation urban society which had implications for the adjustments of the post-emancipation period.

There is some evidence that the employment of the jumper was inadequate in keeping order in the urban slave community. In 1814 and in the months immediately preceding emancipation, sub-committees of the vestry were selected to develop a 'town watch' to guard the town from the 'uncontrolled' and 'unruly' behaviour of free coloureds and slaves.[16] Even here, there was a tacit understanding that urban slaves had successfully challenged the disciplinary systems put in place by whites. In the 1814 report, the committee proposed that 'in case any watchman or watchmen be detected in taking a bribe or bribes from *any white or free-coloured person, or from any slave or slaves* . . . such watchman or watchmen on being convicted shall not only be dismissed from his situation but also forfeit the sum of £10.'[17] The fine and the dismissal of the watchman as proposed in the bylaws of the committee suggest that the authorities were faced with another problem. The monetarisation of services in the urban port economy and the widespread circulation of coinage among slave marketeers and hired-out slaves may have provided the financial resources to bribe a cash-strapped watchman. After all, the money itself was colour blind.

It seems clear, therefore, that on the eve of emancipation urban enslavers had had long tutelage in the likely response of their former charges to legal freedom. Bridgetown was the major locus of the free coloured and free black community. Also, the majority of the enslaved in the urban areas could not be classified as praedials and the prospect of an earlier emancipation than the field slaves meant that the earlier lessons learned from encounters with self-confident blacks would be widened. The lessons included the negotiations which skilled slaves had conducted on the level of wages to be paid for hired time. The control of the enslaved over the local provision market, based in the town, represented another area of insight into what issues might face a white establishment in the post-emancipation period. Given these realities, it is not surprising that some of the earliest responses to the dilemma of post-emancipation control came from the urban centre.[18]

As far as the enslaved were concerned, central to their expectations of freedom was economic and social autonomy. As Eric Foner has observed with respect to the experiences of freedmen in the post-bellum USA, 'the sole ambition of the freedman . . . [was] to control his own time and efforts without anything that [could] remind him of past sufferings in bondage.'[19] Given the experiences of the urban social context in the Caribbean, a similar philosophy was likely to sound a sour note to a white establishment intent on consigning the emancipated to a position as 'underclass.' The establishment of police forces in the towns of Barbados and the attempts by whites to limit the freedom of movement and employment choices of ex-slaves provide an arena in which tentative observations may be made of the way these realities were played out in the post-emancipation period.

Police control and black reactions in the urban context

The establishment of a police force in Bridgetown, Speightstown and Hole Town, as the first in a number of constabularies covering the island, represents an initial reaction of urban whites to the impending emancipation of the slaves. This reaction surfaced as early as December 30, 1833 when 79 of the leading merchants and other leading citizens of Bridgetown sent a memorial to Sir Lionel Smith, the governor.[20] In a lengthy preamble, they commended Smith for appointing a temporary constabulary 'for securing the peace of Bridgetown when by riot and insubordination, its tranquillity no less than its safety was reasonably to be apprehended from the same spirit of licentiousness which marked the holidays of 1832.'[21] The reference to insubordination expressed the concern of these persons for the maintenance of a social order built on notions of white racial superiority. The commendation was followed by a proposal for the establishment of a permanent, 'well regulated and effective police force.' Moreover, they were prepared 'to pay an additional sum to that already levied provided a satisfactory and well digested plan be adopted, which would secure to them the security of their property, the safety of the town, and the quiet of the country at large.'[22]

There is no specific reference to emancipation in the memorial. However, three months later the political representatives of this elite group in the vestry submitted a series of resolutions to the governor and assembly. They resolved to support a temporary police establishment in the town, 'anticipating with serious apprehension the great danger in which the town may be involved for want of a more efficient police to protect it through the eventful crisis following the 1st of August [Emancipation Day, 1834] next.'[23] The anxiety of the vestry in anticipating the legal dismantling of slavery is evident in the tone of the resolutions introduced by the vestrymen. They resolved that 'this vestry voluntarily and individually subscribe . . . a sum equal to what they are severally taxed for the support of the town watch.' In addition, they resolved that:

> The gentlemen of the island and proprietors generally be respectfully requested to act in concert with the aforegoing resolutions either by Parochial donations or individual subscription as an extended and well regulated Town Police must be important to the General interests of the Island by affording Protection to Produce and Plantation stores deposited in the Town and an effective means for the apprehension of absconding labourers and the recovery of their property. . . .[24]

The language of the extract was derived from the pre-emancipation experience. Bridgetown had been a mecca for runaway slaves who could merge with the free black population to escape capture. In addition, there had long been a charge that slaves, free coloureds and Jews in the urban environment had acted as conduits for stolen material from the plantations.[25]

Quite apart from the concern over the security of the town was the question of control of the emancipation process. An examination of the governor's response to the vestry's resolutions and to the memorial referred to earlier reveals that control over the establishment of the police force was a major plank in the effort of urban whites and their rural counterparts to derail the emancipation process. In a letter to the secretary of state for the colonies, Smith pointed out that he had raised the question of the town police with the Assembly. However, with respect to the appointment of magistrates to superintend the force he had 'no hope whatever that they will come into my suggestion of leaving the selection and appointment of magistrates to me.'[26] He was particularly surprised that the Assembly was unwilling to concede on this point, especially when he noted that the exports and imports of the town amounted to £1 million sterling, an indication, he felt, of the need to develop an effective security system.

In addition to the problems which the governor identified, he reported that he had received several complaints against the existing magistracy on the grounds of their inefficiency in controlling lawless mobs in town. The danger would be multiplied 'in proportion as general freedom may give numerical strength to the idle and dissolute resorting to the town.'[27] It seems, therefore, that the governor's perceptions of the security needs of the town were shaped by the perceived laxity of pre-emancipation discipline. More succinctly, however, his comments reveal a keen awareness of the intention of the urban slaveocracy to hijack the force to effect their own control. He summarised the philosophy which guided urban whites as, 'I have the right and power to punish my Nigger how I like . . . .'[28]

This was the reason why Smith appealed to the secretary of state to cancel Clause 32 of the Royal Instructions, which prevented him from appointing magistrates without the consent of the council. If armed with this empowerment, he would 'pledge . . . with the aid of the King's Magistrates [Stipendiaries] shortly expected from home, to form a more efficient police.'[29] At the core of Smith's argument was the need to appoint 'an independent magistracy; the existing magistracy being predominantly Members of Council or of the Assembly who [were] thus most useful in keeping up the frightful oligarchy which had so long governed this island by slavish systems.'

The governor's concerns were soon realised when the Assembly voted a Police Bill on July 29, 1834. The bill sought to give to the vestry the right to pass bye-laws governing the activities of the town police. In addition, it sought to limit jurisdiction over the police to a magistracy consisting of three persons 'not chosen by the crown.'[30] The Bill sought to permit vestrymen to hold the office of magistrate, a potential threat to the liberty of the ex-slave since the magistracy would have been drawn from those who had a vested interest in the continuing oppression of the freed population.

Smith's opposition to the Bill resulted in the alteration of the offending clause. The three magistrates were now to be appointed by the governor-in-council, with the power of dismissal resting in the governor's hands.[31] It was a hollow victory. When Smith selected magistrates 'uncontaminated by the abuses of slavery,' his nominations were overruled by the council which voted two men on whom they could rely for establishing a police force in 'the spirit of their . . . slave laws.'[32]

After considerable debate, marked by a voluminous correspondence between the governor and the secretary of state, the Bill received royal assent in December 1835. In its final form the Bill gave the Bridgetown Police Force, under the bye-laws of the vestry, control over the conduct of huckstering, peddling, portering, and the licences required for such activity. In addition, trafficking in the streets and 'unlawful assembly' in mobs were to occupy its attention. An examination of statistics in the Blue Books covering the period 1837-42 reveals that such issues constituted the majority of cases prosecuted before the police magistrates. For example, in 1841, under the heading 'felony,' 442 blacks and 11 whites were committed to trial, while under the heading 'misdemeanours' (which covered huckstering, etc.) 721 blacks and 51 whites were committed.[33]

The appointment of a police force in the towns was unlikely to terrorise a black population long schooled in pushing the boundaries of the urban disciplinary systems to the limit. There was a high rate of recidivism. In 1841, of those blacks committed for trial, a total of 119 had been imprisoned once before , 122 had been imprisoned twice before, and 77 had experienced three previous terms of imprisonment.[34] This represented some 30 per cent of the total brought to trial in that year. While the figures may represent police vigour in prosecuting cases, they also represent the disregard of the black working class for this new instrument of white control. One example of the willingness to confront police authority helps to illustrate the last point. It is drawn from an encounter in Speightstown.

On August 2, 1837, Police Superintendent Cummins reported to the council, through the magistrate of the town, that he had toured the streets to investigate the source of a 'great noise.'[35] The 'great noise turned out to be a pump dance' held by an ex-slave, Richard. Cummins reported that he had informed Richard that 'it was contrary to rule and regulation to hold a dance at so late an hour [7.30 p.m.].' Moreover, it appeared that there had been an earlier encounter between the two men as the council was informed that Cummins had reminded Richard on the previous Saturday that it was illegal to hold dances beyond 7 p.m.[36]

The legality of the dance was not the main reason for Cummins' report.

Following his advice to Richard, the dancers were addressed by Ben Greenidge, another ex-slave, who allegedly told them 'they would be dammed fools if they stopped dancing or went away, for no one could prevent them.' At this point the superintendent 'spoke to one of the music men and advised him to stop.' This action led to a physical assault on Cummins by 'one Edward Cozier' who 'chucked' him into the street. Cummins' request for assistance from Bowden Yearwood, a black Speightstown resident and owner of the land where the dance was held, was met with a refusal and a threat to 'blow his brains out,' followed by another push into the street.[37] The crisis was only averted by Cummins' departure. Later that night, Edward Cozier was arrested and held in the Speightstown jail. However, this action was to precipitate further confrontation. At about 9 a.m., the following morning, a mob of 200 persons attacked the jail with sticks and stones with the object of rescuing Cozier. The town police were hard-pressed to beat back the attack and were saved only because of the arrival of a detachment of 'rural police.'[38] The size of the attack and the willingness of those involved to take on the police establishment reflect the self-confidence of the urban freed persons in confronting what they perceived as an attack on their freedom.

Apart from direct confrontation of the law-and-order authorities, freed persons also resorted to other strategies to deal with unfair practices by post-slavery officialdom. In the areas of freedom of movement and choice of employment, the expectations of urban freed persons were clear. The controls, which the authorities attempted to place on emigration to other Caribbean territories, provide a backdrop to the next phase of this investigation.

Emigration control and black reaction

The strategies used by planters to restrict the freedom of movement of freed persons and to reduce wage levels in Barbados and the Windward Islands have been well documented in the historiography of post-slavery adjustments. The passage of legislation, like that of the Masters and Servants Act of 1840, was designed to tie freed persons to the former place of employment, but this appears to be more applicable to the rural than the urban context where the work experience was more individualised. However, despite some differences between the rural and urban conditions, the aim of the former owners was consistent — control of the working class by all means necessary. Attempts by freed persons to seek better working conditions elsewhere were bound to run into white opposition.

The 1841 edition of the *Blue Book for Barbados* gives wage levels as £1.13s.4d. per month for domestics (approximately 1s.4d. per day), 1s.3d. per day for praedials and 2s.6d. per day for tradesmen. These represented the higher levels of the wage scale, with the wages of most labourers falling somewhat below the 1s.3d. cited for praedials. In general, therefore, wages in the towns, where the occupational profile would have been heavily skewed towards the domestic and the skilled trades, were higher than those of the rural areas. When prices for basic commodities are factored into the discussion, the conditions facing the urban workers become clearer. Beef retailed at 1s. per pound, pork at 10d., mutton at 1s 3d., sugar at 3d., rice at 2d., and milk at 1s.8d. per gallon.[39] Given these facts, it is not surprising that the opportunity of migrating to higher wage environments would have been greeted favourably by urban freed persons. Indeed, Table 11.1 provides some general indication of the wage differentials which might have been factored into freed persons' reading of the opportunities elsewhere in the region. In particular, it is useful to note the lower end of the wage scales presented here.

Table 11.1:
Wages for field labour in the 1840s in selected territories

Territory	Wage Range
Trinidad	1s.4d. – 2s.1d.
British Guiana	1s.4½ d. – 2s.
Jamaica	9d. – 1s.9d.
Barbados	7d. – 1s.3d.
Antigua	6d. – 2s.1d.
St Kitts	6d. – 1s. 4d.
St Lucia	10d. – 1s.10d.

Source: Adapted from Walton Look Lai, *Indentured Labor, Caribbean Sugar*
(Baltimore: The Johns Hopkins University Press, 1993), 7.

On September 2, 1839, the Private Secretary to Governor MacGregor forwarded a circular to the respective police magistrates on the subject of emigration to British Guiana. The circular made reference to an advertisement appearing in *The Barbados Mercury* under the sponsorship of Thomas Day, agent for British Guiana interests. The advertisement was appended to an extract giving the governor's response to it and to the outcome of a meeting the governor had with Day. The following extracts provide useful insights into Governor MacGregor's approach to the emigration issue and also to the views of significant others among the ruling white elite:

Far from seeking to oppose the wishes of any of the Labouring Population really desirous of quitting this Colony, the Governor is anxious to leave them undisturbed in the free exercise of that discretion which they are unquestionably entitled to exert in selecting the scene of their future residence . . . but it is no less his Excellency's duty to protect this class of Her Majesty's subjects from becoming the victims of interested speculation and illusory statements.[40]

The apparent concern for the welfare of the masses displayed here is not consistent with other comments attributed to the governor in response to Day's advertisement:

His Excellency is therefore influenced by the tenor of Mr. Day's Advertisement to solicit your vigilant assistance in guarding [the freed persons] . . . against any imposition that may be attempted to be practised by this class of persons or by others acting under his direction. It is essential to mention for your further consideration that Mr Day verbally assured the Governor that he was actuated by a higher motive than the desire of procuring emigrants. His object being to raise the wages of labour in Barbados which he considered, himself, in condition to prove too low and that the governor observed in reply that this matter had better be left to find its own level . . . and [he] is consequently left to infer that Mr Day's ostensible mission may cover designs of which the authorities [in British Guiana] are unconscious.[41]

The governor's reaction to Day's proposal was clearly related to the issue of the wage levels raised by the latter. In a letter forwarded by Thomas Worsley, the assistant private secretary, on September 30, 1839, Day's commission as emigration agent was revoked. Nevertheless, this was not the end of Day's attempts to offer emigration to British Guiana as an alternative to freed persons. While it is unclear what personal interest Day held in the matter of working conditions in Barbados, it is clear that the bulk of his efforts centred on Bridgetown. It is also clear that he understood well the perceptions freed persons held of the post-emancipation environment. On February 7, 1840, he sponsored another advertisement which specified that in the event of conflict between migrants to British Guiana and employers there, the matter would be decided by 'magistrates sent from England and not by Police Magistrates who are themselves planters.'[42] It is not clear if this bait caught the attention of workers in Bridgetown. However, Bridgetown was the main theatre for emigration conflict.

Table 11.2:
Emigrants to British Guiana,
December 28,1839 to March 7,1840

Parish	Males	Females	Children	Total
St. Michael	78	16	9	103
St. Philip	35	10	10	55
Christ Church	23	-	-	23
St. Thomas	1	-	-	1
St. George	4	-	-	4
St. John	4	1	-	5
St. Andrew	2	-	-	2
St. Joseph	1	1	-	22
Total	**148**	**28**	**19**	**195**

Source: CO 28/118, Return of Church Wardens to Secretary of State, enclosure 8.

In commenting on the emigration issue, the secretary of state for the colonies recorded in a letter to the governor on October 24, 1839 that:

Your Excellency will observe that most of these Emigrants are . . . chiefly resident in Bridgetown and some of them have evidently been employed by Day as 'crimps.' In the exercise of their vocation however they have confined themselves, either from choice or necessity to the Town, which may account for the preponderance of this parish [St Michael, where Bridgetown is located] over the others.[43]

The observations of the secretary of state mirror closely those made earlier, on April 15, by Mr Jones, inspector of police, in a report to Governor MacGregor. In commenting on the nature of labour relations since the onset of full legal freedom on August 31, 1838, he recorded that:

I was in expectation that a considerable number [of the formerly enslaved] might have been induced to emigrate to the new colonies, but it has turned out otherwise; I believe more have gone from this parish [St Michael] than any other, but that few of them have been from the agricultural ranks, they being, for the most part, persons who could well be spared, many of them great vagabonds, whose absence I consider very beneficial to the community and are not likely to improve the morals any more than the agriculture of those places whither they have gone.[44]

Jones might have misread the factors underlying the demographics of the emigration movement. In the urban context, family ties were more fluid and the family structure was largely matrifocal. In that regard, men resident in the urban areas, who made up the largest cohort of the emigrants, might be less restrained in their *wanderlust*. In any case, his comments also reveal a perception of the threat which the urban non-praedials posed to the social order.

The governor's reaction to Day's statements on wage levels in Barbados was followed by a flurry of correspondence to the Colonial Office. Armed with correspondence from Governor MacGregor and other Caribbean officials, as well as the arguments of the Anti-Slavery Society which was concerned about the treatment of East Indian immigrants, Lord Glenelg, the secretary of state, issued an order barring would-be immigrants from entering into contracts in the host country. These contracts had to be concluded in the immigrants' country of origin.[45] This was used to subject would-be emigrants to a virtual inquisition before permission to emigrate was granted. The response of urban workers was to erect a wall of silence about the activities of agents such as Day and to involve family and friendship networks in a conspiracy to evade the questioners. The following encounters, extracted from the data, help to illustrate this response.

On October 25,1839, the secretary of state wrote to Governor MacGregor concerning Robert Clarke, a 'tradesman being desirous of emigrating to British Guiana.'[46] On April 28, Clarke had requested a certificate from the church warden of the vestry, clearing him for emigration. However, he had been refused because he had two children who, it was argued, would become charges of the state. If, the church warden stated, the mother of the two children would accept responsibility for their maintenance, the required clearance would be granted. Clarke lost no time in having a female make the required declaration. However, 14 days later 'another reputed wife . . . also with two children, understanding that their father was about to quit Barbados,' complained that their whole support would fall on her. By this time Clarke had left the island. The secretary of state was particularly concerned that intending emigrants 'who would be found principally among the able-bodied labourers would seize [the opportunity] with avidity, particularly such as may be circumstanced like Clarke.'[47]

The morality of Clarke's action is not at issue here. What emerges is a resourceful individual determined to escape the system which sought to 're-enslave' him. The secretary of state also noted that after the revocation of Day's commission, earlier emigrants who had been 'open and candid in their replies and grateful for the information they received [on conditions in the intended destination] . . . [now] equivocated and hesitated in the first and received the last with indifference.' Indeed 'one stated that he believed that the only reason for asking him questions was to keep him in Barbados.'[48] Conditions may have been difficult in British Guiana but that did not deter emigrants. As far as they were concerned, a fundamental tenet of freedom was the right 'to dance to a tune of their own making.' To give in to the controls imposed by whites was to deny the self-respect already earned though confrontations in the urban sector.

Thirty-five years later, the pattern of emigration from the island showed that the former enslaved urban people were exercising their options to vote with their feet by emigrating to other Caribbean jurisdictions. Like their rural counterparts, they had factored freedom of movement into their expectations of emancipation. In a situation of acute land shortage, where the plantations owned over 80 per cent of the arable land, and where land was at a premium in the urban areas, it was not surprising that one expectation of the process of adjustment consequent on the legal abolition of slavery, was the right to explore other options in the region.[49] After all, this was precisely what free coloured and free black kin had done in the pre-emancipation period.

Table 11.3: Emigration from Barbados, 1874–75

Parish	Males	Females	Total
St Andrew	23	10	33
Christ Church	88	38	126
St George	51	34	85
St James	27	3	30
St John	36	19	55
St Joseph	41	6	47
St Lucy	30	12	42
St Michael	350	152	502
St Peter	62	15	77
St Philip	40	4	44
ST Thomas	68	12	80
Strangers and 'Personators'	39	5	44
Total	**855**	**310**	**1,165**

Source: Report of the Superintendent of Emigration, 1874–75.

Conclusion

The interaction of slaves, freed persons, and whites in the urban complex in the pre-emancipation years and the creation of an urban typology of resistance represent the 'forgotten' dimension of Caribbean historiography. In our attempts to come to grips with the post-slavery experiences of the freed persons and their former owners an opportunity has been missed to engage the importance of this typology. In the towns of the Caribbean, more specifically in Bridgetown, the expectations which whites had of the emancipation process were shaped partly by a wide range of experiences with the enslaved persons who operated almost as wage labourers and marketeers, and interacted with freed persons. These experiences underlay the control strategies which the former slave owners thought necessary to put in place after emancipation. Two issues, namely, the establishment of police control and the control of emigration, have been identified in this essay as windows through which these dynamics may be viewed. Perhaps these represent the tip of the research iceberg but they identify freed persons also bringing to bear on the process of emancipation expectations and strategies born of a struggle to create room-to-manoeuvre options in the urban context.

It seems clear that freed persons read the options which were available in the post-emancipation period. These options included re-location to territories where the wage levels were significantly higher. In this regard, it may well be that the urban context, anchored as it was in sea port activities, provided the nexus for the transmission of information on wage levels elsewhere. Immigration agents from higher wage jurisdictions, like Thomas Day, might bring such information with them. However, it must be assumed that freed persons, particularly those resident in the urban maritime environments, had their own channels of information.

In addition to the emigration option, those freed persons who were forced by circumstances to remain in Barbados were not prepared to accept the new restrictions passively. Police forces might have been established in the rural and urban areas to suppress the freedom of movement and expression of the freed persons. However, the data relating to the charges levied on the labourers before the law courts show not only the extent of police success in prosecuting those arrested, but also the extent to which labourers were prepared to challenge the system which sought to suppress their freedom. In all of this, the urban context provides a useful arena within which to view more clearly the responses of freed persons to the conditions which followed full emancipation in 1838.

Notes

1. Woodville K. Marshall, ' "We be wise to many more tings": Blacks' Hopes and Expectations of Emancipation,' in *Caribbean Freedom,* eds., Hilary McD. Beckles and Verene Shepherd. (Kingston: Ian Randle Publishers , 1993), 12.

2. See, for example, the following articles in *Caribbean Freedom,* eds., Hilary McD. Beckles and Verene A. Shepherd, eds., *Caribbean Freedom* (1993): Marshall ' "We be wise to many more tings,"' 12-20; Rebecca

Scott, 'Former Slaves Responses to Emancipation in Cuba,' 21–27; Swithin Wilmot, 'Emancipation: Workers and Wage Conflict in Jamaica 1838–40,' 48–53; Rosamunde Renard, 'Labour Relations in Martinique and Guadeloupe 1848–70,' 80–91; O. Nigel Bolland, 'Systems of Domination After Slavery: The Control of Land and Labour in the British West Indies After 1838,' 107–23.

3. See Pedro L.V. Welch, 'The Urban Context of Slave Life: Views from Bridgetown, Barbados, in the Eighteenth and Nineteenth Centuries,' *Plantation Society in the Americas*, 5.2-3 (1998): 281–96.

4. Gary A. Puckrein, *Little England: Plantation Society and Anglo-American Politics 1627–1700* (New York: New York University Press, 1984), xiv.

5. Puckrein, xiv.

6. See Barry Higman, *Slave Populations of the British Caribbean* (Baltimore: The Johns Hopkins University Press, 1984); David B. Gaspar, *Bondmen and Rebels* (Baltimore: The Johns Hopkins University Press, 1985); Neville A.T. Hall, *Slave Society in the Danish West Indies* (Kingston: The Press, UWI, 1992).

7. Gaspar, 107, 230–34.

8. Hall, 87–109.

9. See Roderick A. McDonald, 'Urban Crime and Social Control in St. Vincent During the Apprenticeship,' in *West Indian Accounts,* ed., Roderick A. McDonald. (Kingston: The Press, UWI, 1996), 322.

10. Paul D. Lack, 'An Urban Slave Community: Little Rock, 1831–1862,' *Arkansas Historical Quarterly*, 41-3 (1982): 258-87.

11. *Ibid.*, 263–64.

12. BDA, Inventory of John and Thomas Scott, 1829.

13. Pedro L.V.Welch, 'The Urban Context of the Slave Plantation System' (Ph D. thesis, UWI, Cave Hill Campus, 1994), 339.

14. Higman, 257.

15. William Dickson, *Mitigation of Slavery* (1814; Westport, Connecticut: Negro Universities Press, 1970), 7.

16. BDA, Minutes of the St. Michael Vestry, July 12, 1814.

17. *Ibid.*

18. Mary Turner makes the important observation that the slaves' participation in the capitalist economy undermined the slave labour system. Moreover, their use of strike action and their 'tradition of bargaining for informal contract terms' formed part of a pattern of white-black interaction which impacts on the post-slavery adjustments (See Mary Turner, 'Chattel Slaves into Wage Slaves,' in *From Chattel Slaves to Wage Slaves* ed., Mary Turner (London: James Currey, 1995), 33–47.

19. Eric Foner, *Slavery and Freedom in Nineteenth Century America* (Oxford: Clarendon Press, 1994), 25.

20. CO 28/113, Memorial of Bridgetown Merchants to Governor Smith of Barbados, December 30, 1833.
21. Ibid.
22. Ibid.
23. BDA, Minutes of the St Michael Vestry, April 19, 1834.
24. Ibid.
25. Stephen Fortune, *Merchants and Jews* (Gainesville: University of Florida Press, 1984).
26. CO 28/113, Smith to the Secretary of State , February 10, 1834.
27. Ibid.
28. Ibid.
29. Ibid.
30. BDA, 'Public Acts in Force Passed by the Legislature of Barbados From the First of William IV.'
31. BDA, Amendment to the Police Act, in 'Public Acts in Force Passed by the Legislature of Barbados From the First of William IV.'
32. See CO 28/114, Smith to the Secretary of State; see also Alvin Carter, 'The Origins and Early Development of the Barbados Police Force 1835–45' (MA thesis, UWI, Cave Hill Campus, 1989), 34.
33. Barbados Blue Book, 1841.
34. Ibid.
35. BDA, Minutes of the Council, August 27, 1837.
36. Ibid.
37. Ibid.
38. Ibid.
39. Barbados Blue Book, 1841.
40. Mfm, 80B, BPL, Circular from Governor's Private Secretary to Police Magistrates in Barbados, September 2, 1839.
41. Ibid.
42. *Barbados Mercury*, February 7, 1840.
43. Mfm 80B, BPL, Secretary of State to Governor, October 25, 1839.
44. Mfm 80B, BPL, Report of Inspector Jones to Governor MacGregor, April 15, 1839.
45. Mfm 80B, BPL, Circular from Governor's Private Secretary to Police Magistrates in Barbados, September 28, 1839. Lord Glenelg's action is referred to as part of a series of general instructions concerning the activity of Thomas Day.
46. CO 28/118, Secretary of State to MacGregor, October 25, 1839.
47. Ibid.
48. Ibid.
49. See O. Nigel Bolland, *The Politics of Labour in the British Caribbean* (Kingston: Ian Randle Publishers, 2001), 54.

CHAPTER 12

British Aid and West Indian Education 1835–45
Carl Campbell

In the first decade after the abolition of slavery, primary education in the British West Indies received a tremendous impetus from the British government's decision to aid the development of education in all the islands and settlements to which the Abolition Act applied. This was a part of the emancipation settlement, and it was at the time of setting out its plan for the abolition of slavery that the government first pledged itself to this object.

In the House of Commons debate on May 14, 1833, Lord Stanley, secretary of state for the colonies, introduced five resolutions on the abolition of slavery, the fifth of which read:

> That His Majesty be enabled to defray any such expenses as he may incur in establishing an efficient stipendiary Magistracy in the colonies, and in aiding the Local Legislatures in providing for the religious and moral instruction of the negro population to be emancipated.[1]

This resolution was the origin of the Negro Education Grant which was voted annually by parliament from 1835 to 1845. Hereafter, in this study the grant will be referred to as the parliamentary grants, the name used in the West Indies.

The first grant was not made until 18 months after the beginning of the apprenticeship system. The delay may be explained by a number of factors. The staff of the Colonial Office was preoccupied with other aspects of emancipation, such as the recruitment of stipendiary magistrates and the colonial supplementary legislation necessary to implement the Abolition Act. Mr Stanley had drawn up the 'Heads of a Plan for promoting the Education of Youths in the B.W.I.,'[2] in late 1833, but, unlike other aspects of the change from slavery, education had no deadline to meet, and so was not pushed. Frequent changes at the Colonial Office also delayed the negotiations with the missionary societies. Within two years (May 1833–May 1835), three ministries fell, and the secretaryship of the colonies passed from Stanley to Spring Rice, to the Earl of Aberdeen, and finally to Lord Glenelg. It was Lord Glenelg who gave the final shape to the scheme of parliamentary aid, but not before the delays of the Colonial Office had disappointed and exasperated the missionaries. The secretary of the Wesleyan Methodist Society (WMS) wrote in April 1835:

> In answer to your inquiry respecting what government will do for the promotion of religious education among the negroes, I am unable to say anything satisfactory. We were in communication on the subject with the Colonial Secretary when the resignation of the Peel ministry took place. What will be done by the new Ministry, it is impossible to say. In the midst of the frequent changes in the Colonial Department, I am afraid not much attention is paid to such questions . . . . After negotiating with three Colonial Secretaries in succession on the subject, without any practical result, I begin to feel that 'hope deferred maketh the heart sick.'[3]

For 17 months after the parliamentary resolutions of May 14, 1833, the Colonial Office acted as if it had all the information about education in the West Indies from which to prepare a plan for the distribution of the parliamentary grants. Then just before leaving office, Spring Rice, on November 1, 1834, dispatched a circular to the West Indies asking for detailed returns of the church- and day-school facilities available. This procedure caused further delay because the Colonial Office awaited the returns from the islands before making a final plan. The returns began to arrive in early 1835, and were sent to the Rev. John Sterling, a well educated, freelance clergyman of the Church of England, whose leisure and practical knowledge of the slaves in the West Indies had recommended him to the Earl of Aberdeen as the person best qualified to analyse the voluminous returns and make recommendations to the British Government.[4]

In May 1835, Rev. Sterling produced a lengthy and valuable report, often quoted by scholars as a reservoir of upper-class English thinking about the education of black workers in the West Indies.[5] In July 1835, the Colonial Office asked the Treasury to place £25,000 on the estimates to aid 'negro education.' Parliament voted the money in August 1835, but four months of delay followed as the scheme had to be thoroughly explained to the missionary societies.

On September 10, 1835, Sir George Grey, under-secretary of state for the colonies, explained the essentials of the scheme to the secretaries of the missionary societies.[6] The sum of £20,000 was immediately available to help in building such new schoolhouses as the societies considered necessary. Before their applications could be considered, the societies not only had to provide the British government with information about the locality of the schoolhouse and the probable cost of its erection, but also had to undertake not to use the existence of the parliamentary grant as an excuse for withdrawing any part of the funds from their own resources which they had already committed to education. Each society had to underwrite a proportion of the cost of building each schoolhouse. Finally, all recipients of aid were expected to submit their schools to inspection by an officer appointed by the British government. The purpose of this, as Sir George Grey explained, was not to interfere with the religious instruction given in the schools, but only 'to ascertain that they really conduce to the moral and religious education and improvement of the negro population . . ..'[7]

There were certain points which some societies wanted the Colonial Office to clarify before they decided to participate in the scheme. Every society wished to retain full control of its schools and teachers in the West Indies, notwithstanding the acceptance of parliamentary aid. It was however the London Missionary Society (LMS) which specifically sought assurance from the Colonial Office that the inspectors would not be used to prevent the teaching of particular religious doctrines in the schools, and that schoolhouses built partly with the parliamentary grants would be the exclusive property of the society.[8] These were 'rights' which churches defended in the West Indies for the next 100 years. The Colonial Office willingly gave these assurances.

The missionary societies were most disquieted by the failure of the Colonial Office to state specifically in the letter of September 10, 1835 what proportion of the cost of each schoolhouse was to be borne by the societies. At that time the Colonial Office envisaged a situation in which the proportion to be borne by the British government would probably vary with the circumstance of each island.[9] At all events, the Colonial Office seemed to have been waiting for the societies themselves to give a lead by the nature of their request for aid. Obviously, the smaller the proportion to be borne by the British government, the more schoolhouses could be built with the £20,000. The object of the British government was to effect a speedy multiplication of the number of schoolhouses.

The Society for the Propagation of the Gospel (SPG) made the first proposal to the Colonial Office. In late November 1835, this society offered to pay half the cost of building the schoolhouses.[10] By virtue of its Special Fund for Chapel and Schools, the SPG was doubtless in a stronger financial position than any of the other societies. The Colonial Office readily agreed to this proportion, and the other societies were also asked to pay a half. The Church Missionary Society (CMS), the Moravian Missionary Society (MMS) and the LMS, however, objected to this proportion,[11] and not wishing to establish different proportions for different societies, the Colonial Office finally accepted the CMS proposal that the societies should pay one-third of the cost and the British government the remaining two-thirds.[12]

Having secured the cooperation of the missionary societies, the Colonial Office now had to decide how to allocate the grants. In the first three years what was foremost in the mind of Sir George Grey, who was responsible for making the allocations, was the need to distribute the funds fairly among the

West Indian islands. The scheme announced to the societies made no provision for the apportionment of any specific share to each colony. But, given the existing unequal distribution of missionaries and clergymen in the different islands, the consequence would have been to reinforce the disparities in educational facilities between the islands, by giving the largest sums to those islands which already had the largest number of missionaries.

Before any portion of the parliamentary grant was allocated, Sir George Grey had worked out two schedules[13] showing the sums which each West Indian island might fairly be given from the £20,000. The first schedule was calculated according to the number of stipendiary magistrates allocated to each colony. This allotment was originally based upon statistical returns of the size and population of the islands. As the total number of stipendiary magistrates was 154, Sir George Grey found that the grant of £20,000 would allow an allocation of £130 to each colony for every stipendiary magistrate employed. The basis of the second schedule was the number of enslaved persons recorded in the last registration. It gave a different result from the first schedule, and had the advantage of leaving £1,350 for the Cape of Good Hope and Mauritius. It was not the intention of the Colonial Office to be bound by either schedule. As Grey said, the schedules would 'only be a useful memorandum representing to the mind of the Distributors the interest and abstract claims of each particular island.'[14]

At best, then, the schedules were to be a guide. By the end of December 1835, and half-way through the allocation of the first parliamentary grant, the Colonial Office dropped the idea of using the schedule as a guide. In December 1835, the Colonial Office made some attempts to tell the earliest applicants what portions of their grants should be used in certain islands. The LMS was told to divide its £2,000 equally between Jamaica and Guyana,[15] while the CMS was advised to spend its £2,000 in the following manner: £1,334 for Jamaica, and £333 each for Trinidad and Guyana.[16] However, in early 1836 when the Colonial Office found it possible to give an additional £1,000 to the LMS and another £500 to the CMS,[17] it made no attempt to say where these sums were to be spent. Thereafter, the Colonial Office, in making allocations, usually disclaimed any desire to specify how much of the grant should be spent in each island, while reminding the recipients of the desirability of spreading the benefits of the grants as widely as possible.

In early 1836, the Colonial Office said this more pointedly than usual to the MMS. Sir George Grey, considering the proposal of the MMS, remarked, 'in the islands of St Kitts, Barbados and Tobago the building of schools is more urgently required than in Jamaica or Antigua, which latter islands are included in most of the applications which have been received from the co-operating Societies.'[18]

The MMS promised to comply as far as their longest established and extensive work in Jamaica and Antigua allowed them.[19] Since the MMS did not get enough money that year to build all the 21 schoolhouses it wanted to, its schedule had to be revised, and in revising it the remark of Sir George Grey apparently had some effect. Of the eight schools which the MMS now proposed for the West Indies, Jamaica was to have three rather than nine schools as in the first schedule. The earlier estimate had said that at least four were badly needed there. The first schedule also allotted Antigua four schoolhouses; the revised schedule gave it only one school.[20]

Generally speaking, however, the Colonial Office's policy of spreading the benefits of the grants was limited by the particular interest which most missionary societies had built up in certain islands to the exclusion, or at best marginal inclusion, of other islands. The missionary societies could not suddenly shift the whole balance of their operations to suit the Colonial Office. The cost would have been prohibitive; sentiment in some cases made it undesirable. It may be said that no missionary society, with the possible exception of the opening of the CMS Mission in Trinidad in the middle of 1836, went into an island not occupied by it before the period of emancipation because of the parliamentary grant for 'negro' education.

To spread the benefits of the parliamentary grants among the islands, the Colonial Office had to use other agents as well as the missionaries. One such was the governor of an island; another was the Mico Charity. Out of the first parliamentary grant, the Colonial Office by-passed the missionaries and gave £700 directly to the governor of the Bahamas, and £500 to Governor Hill of Trinidad.[21] These grants were used in aid of local resources, missionary or otherwise. St Vincent and Grenada were comparatively neglected by missionaries. Only the SPG had promised in 1836 to erect a schoolhouse in Grenada. No society included St Vincent in its application in 1836. The Colonial Office therefore gave £400 to Governor MacGregor to divide at his discretion between Grenada and St Vincent.[22]

The most successful method of spreading the benefits of the parliamentary grants was the use of the Mico Charity. For many years the bequest of Dame Jane Mico had been unused. In 1670 she had bequeathed £1,000 to redeem poor English slaves from the Barbary states.[23] The Court of Chancery declared in 1686 that the money should be invested and the profits used according to the intention of Lady Mico. A freehold wharf and premises were bought, but no general scheme of redeeming slaves was adopted. The matter was forgotten until the abolition of slavery in the British colonies. The Court of Chancery approved the scheme of using the Mico funds to educate the freed black persons in the colonies — a purpose, thought near enough to the intention of Lady Mico. A board of trustees was established and the Mico Charity came into being on July 19, 1835.[24]

The Mico Charity was just starting operations in Jamaica at the time of the distribution of the first parliamentary grant, and had not yet built up an interest in any one colony. Its mode of operating which was to rent rather than build schoolhouses, made it easier for the charity to work in several islands. The Colonial Office asked the Charity to establish schools in Trinidad, St Lucia, Dominica, Grenada, and St Vincent.[25] The Mico Charity's share of the parliamentary grant rose from £700 in 1835 for general purposes, to £4,000 in 1836, £14,000 in 1837 and finally to £17,000 per annum over the period 1838 to 1841. At this level the Mico Charity was getting more than half of the annual grant. Between 1838 and 1841 the Charity extended its activity successively from Jamaica (December 1835) to Barbados (1836), Bahamas (early 1837), Trinidad (April 1837), Antigua, Guyana, St Lucia, St Vincent, Tobago and Grenada (May 1838), and Dominica (April 1839).

It is not possible to say how much of the parliamentary grant reached the different islands through the Mico Charity or the agency of the missionary societies. What mattered to the Colonial Office was the spirit, not the letter, of the schedules. The policy of the Colonial Office was to spread the grants, and this was done by deducing from the annual amounts which the societies proposed to spend that some islands were comparatively destitute of schools. In this sense the allocations actually made may be said to have represented a rougher sense of justice to the islands than if they had been made in accordance with the schedules.

By 1838 the parliamentary grants had already become as widely distributed as they were ever to be. The benefits had reached all the British West Indian colonies[26] and Mauritius and the Cape. About this time there was a general change in the use which the missionary societies made of the grants. With the exception of the Mico Charity, all the societies had now stopped building schoolhouses with the aid of the parliamentary grants, and were consolidating their positions by using the grants to help in paying the salaries of teachers. These circumstances enabled the Colonial Office to change the basis for dividing the grants. What now became foremost in the mind of the staff of the Colonial Office was not the claims of the islands, but the claims of the societies *vis-à-vis* one another. So the Colonial Office did not direct the societies to use the grants for salaries in particular colonies.

Between 1838 and 1841 the total annual grant remained at £30,000, and all the societies except the Baptist Missionary Society (BMS) and the LMS remained in the scheme. The most unstable factor in the scheme was the fluctuation in the amounts which the societies requested each year. The Mico Charity distinguished itself by the manner in which its annual requests spiralled upwards from £20,000 in 1838, £21,045 in 1839, to £23,880 in 1840. Except for 1838 when it asked for £8,064, the SPG consistently requested £7,000 each year. The requests of the other societies are too varied to discern any clear patterns. Together the societies generally asked for more money than the Colonial Office was willing to give.

In 1838 the Colonial Office distributed a total sum of £29,500. Between 1838 and 1841 the societies annual grants were generally as follows: £17,000 for the Mico Charity; £7,000 for the SPG; £2,000 for the CMS; £1,000 each for the MMS and WMS; £800 for the SMS, and £700 for the Ladies Negro Education Society (LNES). The annual grants of the Mico Charity, SPG and LNES were held stable at £17,000, £7,000 and £700 respectively. Those of the CMS, WMS and MMS varied.

A number of considerations influenced the allocations made by the Colonial Office. As a rule the first aim of the Colonial Office was to give a society what it had received the previous year, provided the society itself did not ask for less. This meant that the allocations of 1838 served as guides to the approximate maximum sums which each society could get, consistent with the policy of leaving a small balance to meet emergencies. In cases where societies asked for considerable increases, the Colonial Office would not comply. Thus the Mico Charity, having received £17,000 in 1838 which was more than a half of the total annual grant, wanted £21,045 in 1839 and £23,880 in 1840. In 1841 Rev. Trew, secretary of the Mico Charity, simply asked for 'his share,' by which he meant £17,000.[27] The Mico Charity had now realised that the peak of its grants had been reached in 1838, and that thereafter the Colonial Office could not increase its share without cutting into that of some other society.

As far as can be gathered from the minutes of the staff of the Colonial Office, there was only one year in which the opinions about the value of the work of the societies influenced the allocations to a society. For three successive years the MMS received the laurels of praise. But in 1839 and 1840 admiration for their method of school management and their usefulness did not affect their allocation.[28] In 1841 when Rev. Latrobe applied for £600 for school expenses and also for an unspecified amount towards the liquidation of the Moravians' school debts,[29] George Hope, under-secretary of state for the colonies, tried to help them. In a minute to Lord Stanley he wrote:

> The Society which seem in the greatest actual difficulty is the Moravians, and looking to the opinion professed by Sir George Grey and Mr. Stephen, of the statements of their own application, it appears to be one of the most deserving and useful of all these Bodies. They ask for £460 less than they received last year (£600 instead of £1,000). The Scottish Churches ask for £200, and the Church Missionary Society for £250 more than they respectfully received last year, and I own I should be inclined to reduce those grants to what was given last year, and increase the Moravians to £1,000 . . . this distribution would still leave them with £60 less than they received last year, and allow a surplus on the whole of £774.15.11.[30]

Both Stanley and Hope had just come into office; but the former, unlike Hope, had not acquainted himself with the levels of allocations made in the past. Stanley therefore adopted the principle of giving each society what it specifically requested for that year. This was possible in 1841 when an unusual situation prevailed: the sums which the societies specifically requested were within the total at the disposal of the Colonial Office. Stanley was applying a general principle, not denying the merits of the MMS. Therefore, in October 1841 the MMS was given only £600. In the following month the case was reopened when Latrobe wrote two letters, one an official letter to Mr Hope, and the second (significantly) a private letter to James Stephen.[31] Latrobe appealed to Stephen as a friend to sponsor the Moravian application for additional aid. Stephen did not fail the Moravians. In a minute to Hope he praised the MMS as 'the very best Missionary Body the world has ever seen since the first Propagation of Christianity,'[32] and asked that an additional sum be given to it. Mr Hope was willing to do this; the matter was taken up with Stanley who eventually agreed that the MMS should be given £300 out of the balance of £724.15s.11d.

On other occasions the opinions of the staff of the Colonial Office about the work of the societies did not seem to have influenced the allocations. Mr Vernon Smith remarked in September 1840 that the Mico schools were 'very well managed, but I am not quite satisfied with their conduct towards the Roman Catholics.'[33] The Mico grant remained at £17,000. The Colonial Office was dissatisfied with the manner in which the LNES had presented its statement of expenditure in 1839, but this did not lead to any reduction in its share. In the same year the SPG was described by Sir George Grey as the society which extended on the largest scale and whose schools had been favourably reported on by Inspector Latrobe. This observation did not benefit the SPG. In April 1841 the Colonial Office announced that 'in the year 1842 and in each of the next succeeding four years the grants would be reduced by one-fifth of its present amount, after which it will entirely cease.'[34]

The Mico Charity immediately saw the need to effect a large-scale retrenchment of its operation in the West Indies. This could best be done if the trustees knew in advance what could be expected from the British government in the remaining years of the grants. The Mico Charity took it for granted that the amounts which would be allocated to societies in the years after 1841 would be reduced on the same principle as was to be applied to the total grant. On the basis of £17,000 in 1841 the charity expected £13,600 in 1842; and £10,200, £6,800 and £3,400 in 1843, 1844 and 1845 respectively. At the time of the announcement of the reductions, the Colonial Office was only thinking of reducing the total annual grant by £6,000 each year.

In 1842 Lord Stanley and Mr Higgins both thought of reducing the amounts to the societies in the same proportion as the total grant. This practice, however, was not adopted until 1843 when the societies were so informed. The principle was not applied in 1842 because the BMS made a request for a grant after staying out of the scheme for four years (1838–41); and also because some societies would have received more than they had requested. Lord Stanley saw no good reason to use the non-participation of the BMS for the previous four years as a ground for refusing a grant in 1842. But the only way to give the BMS a grant was not to apply the principle of reducing the allocations in 1841 by one-fifth, and to make arbitrary allocations to each society, in some cases of lesser amounts than had been requested. Table 12.1 shows the amounts given to the societies in 1841, the amounts requested in 1842, the amounts which each society — if allocated a fifth of the grants in 1841 — would have received, and what the societies actually received in 1842.

Table 12.1: British Government's education grants 1841–42 (£ sterling)

Societies	Amounts given in 1841	Amounts requested in 1842	Amounts on one-fifth ratio	Amounts received 1842
Mico	17,000	13,600	13,600	13,000
SMS	1,000	700	800	700
LNES	700	700	560	600
WMS	1,200	1,500	960	900
SPG	7,000	7,000	5,600	5,500
MMS	900	670	720	670
CMS	2,500	1,850	2,000	1,850
BMS	-	2,000	-	1,000

Source: CO 318/152, Correspondence on Negro Education Grants.

The allocations made in 1842 were successively reduced in 1843, 1844 and 1845, by a fourth, a third, and a half respectively. These were the proportions by which the total grant was reduced annually. It was not possible to adhere to the rule too strictly in 1844, when for the first time in the period 1842–45 there was no balance from the previous year. A distribution on the agreed principle would have called for £12,000 which was £110 more than the Colonial Office had at its disposal. The Colonial Office, in trying to distribute the 1844 grant as fairly as possible, clipped off on the average £13 from each society's grant. It was a simple matter in 1845 to halve each society's grant and terminate the parliamentary aid.

After 1842, the Colonial Office worked to a plan which obliged it to ignore completely the amounts requested by the societies. Because this plan was known to the societies, it also meant that the opinion of the staff of the Colonial Office about the relative value of the societies' educational work in the West Indies played no part in determining the allocations. In contrast to the earlier years, the allocations were now automatic. Indeed, it is difficult to explain why the Colonial Office, in its circular inviting the societies to participate in the grant of 1843, should have raised the hope that aid might be afforded that year to those societies whose West Indian schoolhouses had been destroyed or damaged in the earthquake of 1843.[35] No such aid was afforded. Another circular was sent two months later in which the Colonial Office hinted that there was no longer any need to request specific amounts of money.

All requests for special treatment in the period of reductions were dismissed. For example, in 1842 the LNES asked for a guarantee that its £700 per annum would be continued for the remaining years of the grants.[36] This was refused. The society hardest hit by the reductions was the Mico Charity. Emphasising that the Charity had expanded its operations in the West Indies at the invitation of the British government, Rev. Trew pleaded for a continuation of its grants of £17,000 per annum, or at least that the decision should be postponed if Lord John Russell was not able to approve it.[37] Again, in May 1843, the Mico Charity requested a special grant for a limited period for the exclusive purpose of maintaining teacher training schools.[38] This too was turned down. But the view that the Mico Charity, more than any other group, had a special claim to continued government support was evidently held in the Colonial Office. The Mico Charity was the only group which was faced with immediate abandonment of most of its schools as the only feasible alternative to government support. While unable to meet the Mico Charity's request from the finances of the British government, the Colonial Office, in its circular dispatch to West Indian governors informing them of the reductions and withdrawals of the parliamentary grants, specifically requested them to ask for financial support from the local legislatures for the Mico schools.[39]

In withdrawing the parliamentary grants the British government had not broken faith with the missionary societies. The circular of September 10, 1835 had not said how long the grants would last, and nothing was said subsequently to give the societies any grounds for believing that the scheme would be of longer duration. Indeed, the language of the annual circular inviting participation, as well as the annual character of the invitations, suggested that the scheme was susceptible to termination in any year. The decision of the Colonial Office to pay first a third and subsequently a half of teachers' salaries (whereas it had paid two-thirds of the cost of building schoolhouses) was based apparently on the uncertainty of the grants and the unwillingness of the Colonial Office to have the schools too heavily dependent upon the parliamentary grants for their maintenance. As usual, metropolitan money for capital expenditure was easier to obtain than for recurrent expenditure. Replying to Rev. Latrobe's expressions of surprise and disappointment at the proportion of teachers' salaries paid by the British government, Sir George Grey wrote that:

> His Lordship cannot however venture to predict for how long a period parliament may think fit to continue such annual grants; and it is chiefly in

reference to this consideration that it has been deemed proper to limit the proportion of the expense of the general maintenance of schools to be defrayed from the parliamentary grants to one-third.[40]

The official reason for withdrawing the grant was 'the improvement which has taken place in the condition of the Negroes since the date of their emancipation . . ..'[41] It seems certain, however, that the decision had more to do with the state of the public finances in England than with social improvements in the West Indies. Since 1839 the deficit in the public expenditure had been growing, and was expected to reach a new level of £2.4 million in 1842.[42] It was against the background of parliamentary requests for economy that the decision was taken to reduce and terminate the grants.

It is not clear whether the initiative to cut the grants came from the Treasury or the Colonial Office. It certainly did not come from any member of parliament; other items of colonial expenditure, but not the grants for education in the West Indies, were singled out for retrenchment by members. What is clear is that Lord John Russell, the secretary of state for the colonies, thought that the decision to cut the grants was proper. The ex-slaves, he thought, were in a better position to pay for the education of their children than the English labouring classes.[43] James Stephen agreed with the policy. His observation of the number of schools which the Baptist missionaries in Jamaica were able to support without the assistance of government led him to be hopeful for education after the discontinuance of the parliamentary grants.[44]

The practical question was not whether there had been social improvements in the conditions of the ex-slaves in the West Indies, but whether they were willing or able to make good the amounts which the British government had withdrawn; or whether the colonial legislatures would meet the deficit wholly or partly. Lord John Russell did not ask these specific questions until he had agreed with the decision to withdraw the grants. By the time the West Indian governors could reply to these questions Lord John Russell had demitted office, and the task of examining the replies fell to Mr Hope and Lord Stanley. The situation in Jamaica seemed the most hopeful. Governor Metcalfe wrote that 'the number of schools supported entirely by the contributions of the negro population will argue that the self-support of such institutions is not impossible, but . . . I do not expect that the decrease of funds in the National [Church of England] and Mico Schools will be remedied by negro contributions.'[45]

In the replies from the other colonies opinions differed, and sometimes the ex-slaves were declared capable of paying school fees, without anything being said of their willingness to do so. The general tenor of the replies from the local missionaries whom the governors had consulted was that the ex-slaves could not be depended upon to support the entire cost of the schools, while the governors generally said that there was not much hope of increased aid from the colonial legislatures.[46] Mr Hope optimistically saw 'nothing in these reports to show the gradual withdrawal of the grant to be improper, indeed the circumstances that in St Kitts and Tortola where little or no assistance has been given from the mother country, local funds have been provided, afford a strong argument in favour of the reductions.'[47] Lord Stanley himself wrote that his reading of the correspondence from Jamaica had left him with the impression that the policy of Lord John Russell should be allowed to stand.[48] The parliamentary grants were to end in 1845. Some 50 years were to elapse before the British government granted money again for education in the West Indies.[49]

Notes

1. *Parliamentary Debates* (House of Commons), 3rd series, XVII, Debate on May 14, 1833: 1230–31. This study is the only one which deals in a detailed manner with the division of the Negro Education Grants. Other studies have been written about the motives of the educators, the conduct of schools, and the response of parents and children to the new opportunities for schooling. See Shirley Gordon, *A Century of West Indian Education* (London: Longmans, Green, 1963); Shirley Gordon, *Reports and Repercussions in West Indian Education 1835-1933* (London: Ginn, 1968); Carl Campbell, 'Towards an Imperial Policy for the Education of Negroes in the West Indies after Emancipation,' *Jamaican Historical Review*, 7 (1967): 68–102; Carl Campbell, 'Social and Economic Obstacles to the Development of Popular Education in post-Emancipation Jamaica 1834-1865,' *Journal of Caribbean History*, 1 (1970): 57–88; M.K. Bacchus, "Education as a Social Control Mechanism,' *The Alberta Journal of Educational Research*, 25.3 (1979): 160–73; M.K. Bacchus, *Utilization, Misuse, and Development of Human Resources in the Early West Indian Colonies* (Ontario: Wilfrid Laurier University Press, 1990); Carl Campbell, *Colony and Nation. A Short History of Education in Trinidad and Tobago* (Kingston: Ian Randle Publishers, 1992).
2. CO 318/122, 'Heads of a Plan for Promoting the Education of the Youths in the B.W.I.,' 598.
3. Beecham to Chairman of Jamaica District, April 1, 1835, extract and Copies of Letters from the Wesleyan Missionary Committee to the Chairman of the Jamaica District (1834–65).
4. CO 318/122, George Grey to Secretary of the Treasury, July 21, 1835.
5. CO 318/122, Report of Rev. J. Sterling to the British Government, May 11, 1835. For studies on the Sterling Report see Campbell, 'Towards an Imperial Policy,' and Gordon, 'Reports and Repercussions,' 11–13, 46–48, 59–66; Bacchus, 240–41.
6. CO 318/122, George Grey to secretaries of missionary societies,

September 10, 1835. The circular was quoted subsequently by the Colonial Office and the missionary societies.

7. Ibid.

8. CO 318/122, Ellis to George Grey, November 24, 1835, LMS.

9. CO 318/122, George Grey to secretaries of missionary societies, September 10, 1835.

10. CO 318/122, Campbell to George Grey, November 23, 1835, SPG.

11. CO 318/122, Coates to George Grey, December 22, 1835, CMS; Ibid., Ellis to George Grey, December 15, 1835, LMS; CO 318/126 Latrobe to George Grey, January 7, 1836, MMS.

12. CO 318/122, George Grey to Campbell, December 31, 1835, SPG.

13. CO 318/122, George Grey to Glenelg, December 8, 1835 and December 11, 1835, 606.

14. CO 318/122, George Grey to Glenelg, December 8, 1835, 606. Gordon gives the impression that the grants were actually made according to the schedule based on the slaves, but this was not so (see Gordon, *A Century of Education*, 26).

15. CO 318/122, George Grey to Ellis, December 12, 1835. LMS.

16. CO 318/122, George Grey to Coates, December 30, 1835.

17. CO 318/126, George Grey to Ellis, January 20, 1836, LMS; Ibid., George Grey to Coates, January 9, 1836, CMS.

18. CO 318/126, George Grey to Latrobe, January 18, 1836, MMS.

19. CO 318/126, Latrobe to George Grey, January 23, 1836, MMS.

20. CO 318/126, Latrobe to George Grey, February 2, 1836, MMS.

21. CO 295/110, Hill to Glenelg, October 22,1836.

22. CO 101/81, George Grey to MacGregor, December 31, 1836.

23. Frank Klingberg, 'The Lady Mico Charity Schools in the British West Indies 1835-1842,' *Journal of Negro History*, 24 (1939): 295-97.

24. CO 318/138, Report of Trustees of Mico Charity, 1838. For studies on the Mico Charity see Carl Campbell, 'Denominationalism and the Mico Schools in Jamaica 1835-1842,' *Caribbean Studies*, 10.4 (1971):152-84.

25. E1/12, Anti-Slavery Papers, George Grey to Wainwright, August 26, 1836; CO 318/13, George Grey to Wainwright, July 11, 1837, Mico Charity.

26. But not the British Virgin Islands.

27. CO 318/152, Rev. Trew to James Stephen, September 8, 1841, Mico Charity.

28. CO 318/145, George Grey to Vernon Smith, October 9, 1839, 248; CO 318/152, Vernon Smith, September 25, 1840, 407.

29. CO 318/152, Latrobe to Vernon Smith, April 29, 1841, MMS.

30. CO 318/152, Hope to Lord Stanley, September 29, 1841, 428.

31. CO 318/152, Latrobe to James Stephen (private), November 9, 1841,

MMS.

32. CO 318/152, Stephen to Hope, November 11, 1841, 291.

33. CO 318/152, Vernon Smith to Lord John Russell, September 25, 1840, 407.

34. CO 318/152, Vernon Smith to secretaries of missionary societies, April 20, 1841.

35. CO 318/163, Hope to secretaries of societies, April 4, 1843, 275.

36. CO 318/156, Miss Smith to Lord Stanley, February 23, 1842, LNES.

37. CO 318/152, Rev. Trew to Vernon Smith, August 10, 1841, Mico Charity.

38. CO 318/163, Rev. Trew to Colonial Office, May 1843, Mico Charity.

39. CO 854/3, Lord John Russell to West Indies, April 25, 1841, 64.

40. CO 318/131, George Grey to Latrobe, August 21, 1837, MMS.

41. CO 318/152, Vernon Smith to secretaries of societies, March 18,1841, 420.

42. *Parliamentary Debates*, LVII, Speech of Robert Peel, April 30, 1841, 1328–36. For the condition of England, especially its turbulent politics and precarious finances in the 1830s, see Norman Gash, *Aristocracy and People. Britain 1815-1865* (London: Edward Arnold, 1976), chaps. 7-8.

43. CO 318/152, Lord John Russell to Vernon Smith, 420.

44. CO 318/152, Stephen to Stanley, September 24, 1841, 424.

45. CO 137/256, Metcalfe to Lord John Russell, September 20, 1841.

46. CO 71/98, Macphail to Stanley, October 25, 1841, enclosures; CO 7/68, Macphail to Stanley, September 18, 1841, enclosures; Ibid., Macphail to Stanley, November 13, 1841, enclosures; CO 7/69, Darling to Lord John Russell, August 19, 1841, enclosures.

47. CO 7/68, Hope to Stanley, November 5, 1841.

48. CO 7/68, Stanley to Hope, November 1841.

49. Carl Campbell, *The Young Colonials. A Social History of Education in Trinidad and Tobago 1834-1939* (Mona: The Press, UWI, 1996), 78-87.

CHAPTER 13

'Behold The Tax Man Cometh': Taxation as a Tool of Oppression in Early Post-Emancipation British Guiana, 1838–48

James L.G. Rose

Introduction

After 1807 the planter community became increasingly sensitive to the swing in popular opinion against slavery. Both the Registration Bill and the subsequent amelioration legislation telegraphed the turning of the tide in favour of the anti-slavery forces. The planters were convinced that the enslaved work force would not remain loyal to the plantation. They were therefore apprehensive of the survival of the cane-sugar industry and neither the 1833 Abolition Act nor the 1838 Emancipation Bill encouraged optimism. Panic responses, whether coercive or seductive, only aggravated the situation and, before long, nearly all the plantocracy accepted that, having lost control of the labour force, ruin appeared inevitable. In the ensuing struggle to regain control of the labour market, and to restore some measure of solvency to the plantation economy, the planters made extensive use of a fiscal policy aimed at curtailing the growing independence of the work force and inhibiting the labourers' development of a viable peasant economy.

During the early 1830s, the Colonial Office agonised over an emancipation formula which would free the enslaved African but would not, at the same time, destroy the plantation economy, the perceived mainstay of colonial civilisation in the Caribbean. Lord Howick, parliamentary under-secretary for the colonies, supported emancipation, but was not optimistic about the retention of the freed population as labourers on the plantations once slavery was abolished. He therefore suggested, in his 1832 proposals, that restraining measures be adopted, which would force the freed population to remain bound to the plantation.[1] His most potent means of immobilising the post-emancipation labour force was through the use of taxation. Howick's proposals were rejected, but some of his ideas persisted and influenced the policy of the planters in the years after 1838.

Taxation policy

The taxation policy began to take shape just about the time of emancipation. In June 1838 the half-yearly licence fee for hucksters was raised from 25 to 40 guilders.[2] Huckstering was a profitable activity in which the African had participated even before emancipation.[3] It was essentially a freed person's occupation, but these persons sometimes employed enslaved Africans to take their goods about the plantations.[4] In an effort to reduce the number of freed men who, because of their familiarity with this trade, might be enticed to take it up after emancipation, the half-yearly licence fee for huckstering was inflated by 60 per cent. The fee for a firearm licence was also increased in June,[5] and this was followed by increases in the licence fee for the use of boats, canoes, carts and mules.[6] A licence fee was also introduced for employment as a porter.[7]

In every case, the activity taxed offered an alternative to the plantation as a source of employment. They were all areas in which the labourer had functioned with a degree of success prior to emancipation. The indications were that, while revenue was an important motive, these increases and impositions were intended to inhibit the continued participation of the African labourer. The case of a charcoal manufacturer illustrates this contention. The individual had succeeded in establishing a prosperous trade when he was arrested for operating without a licence. He was jailed and the severity of the two-year sentence was intended to dissuade others from emulating his success.[8]

During slavery, the chief means of revenue accumulation was direct taxation. There was a poll tax on slaves, an income tax, a land and produce tax.[9] When slavery was abolished, the poll tax was scrapped and a new device for raising the necessary revenue became apparent. There was a concurrent need for an increase over the normal amount of revenue, because new establishments became necessary and new responsibilities had to be assumed in the wake of emancipation.

Prior to emancipation, public expenditure was restricted because the responsibility for the enslaved African rested almost solely with the master. Further, because the free coloured and manumitted black population was small and negligible, the state was not encouraged to provide even minimal social services for them.[10]

Table 13.1: Population of British Guiana, 1831

Town/County	Whites			Free Coloured & Black				Slaves			Colony
	M	F	Total	M	F	Total	Total Free	M	F	Total	Grand Total
Georgetown	962	658	1,620	1,625	2,743	4,368	5,988	3,209	3,407	6,616	12,604
Demerara (rural)	662	110	772	463	617	1,080	1,852	-	-	39,199	41,051
Essequibo	476	138	614	442	470	912	1,526	-	-	23,553	25,079
New Amsterdam	130	49	179	324	530	854	1,033	695	681	1,376	2,409
Berbice (rural)	289	55	344	130	177	307	651	10,220	8,501	18,724	19,375
Total	2,519	1,010	3,529	2,984	4,537	7,521	11,050			89,468	100,518

Source: Almanack and Local Guide of British Guiana Containing the Laws, Ordinances and Regulations of the Colony, the Civil and Military Lists with a List of Estates from Corentyne to Pomeroon Rivers (Demerary: The Royal Gazette Office, 1832), 479.

When the African was freed, the master was relieved of much of his pre-1838 responsibilities. These demands shifted to the colonial administration. Because the new services included the provision of hospitals and medical care, the administration of justice, jails, burial grounds, poor relief, education and religion, all institutions catering to the needs of civil society in which the African labourer enjoyed a numerical preponderance, a controversy arose as to who should shoulder the financial obligation of providing them. The Colonial Office proposed taxes on colonial produce to raise the required sum, but the planters protested.[11] They argued that if everyone benefited from a particular service then everyone should pay for it. On the other hand, when only a single class benefited, then that class should be obliged to pay.[12] In this way the planters intended to ensure that the unrepresented classes took on the expenses involved in the creation and extension of certain social services deemed necessary in post-emancipation society.

The anticipated increase in expenditure was great and continued to grow with each passing year. For example, the government spent about £812 on the police and the upkeep of the jail in 1833 and about £1,820 on health services in the same year. These sums had increased to £27,796 and £11,114 respectively by 1840. Total expenditure of £57,996 in 1833 grew to £125,209 in 1840.[13] In the place of the direct taxes proposed by the Colonial Office, the local assemblies, in which the planters enjoyed the preponderance, voted for indirect taxation and introduced higher import duties, a variety of high-cost licences and excise taxes to replace the outmoded poll tax.

From the very beginning, this strategy proved burdensome to the African labourer and in 1839 Governor Henry Light observed that the Combined Court had 'increased the duties . . . on objects of general consumption' by as much as 50 per cent in most cases, and by as much as 200 per cent in others. He pointed out that, according to his calculations, 'the labourers already contributed nearly three guilders or one Spanish dollar per annum by consumption per head of articles subject to an import duty.'[14] So effective was the conversion that a year after emancipation the import duty alone had just about equalled the head tax formerly paid by the planters for their slaves.[15] Just as significant was the fact that the planters had relieved themselves of paying taxes almost entirely. This was possible because indirect taxation was aimed at the African labourer who constituted nearly 90 per cent of the total population. The idea was that the items subject to the import duties should include the 'necessaries' of the African labourer's existence, whilst items peculiar to the planter class were often exempt from duties.[16] In 1833, direct taxes produced 76.5 per cent of the total revenue but by 1845 indirect taxes were producing 74.3 per cent of a greatly enlarged revenue. Direct taxes, on the other hand, had been reduced to an insignificant 4.5 per cent.[17]

Immigration

The withdrawal of the African labour force from the estates in 1838 by no means represented a mass exodus, but it was significant enough to force the planters to give serious consideration to a scheme of immigration. In an effort to attract public finance for this programme, the Court of Policy passed a Bill to raise the sum of £400,000 by issuing bonds in the name and on the security of the government and the Court of Policy.[18] In his objections to the measure, Sir Michael McTurk, a local planter, noted that the required amount could, and should, have been raised by normal taxation.[19] Governor Henry Light, on the other hand, took umbrage at the further burdening of the colony with a debt of such magnitude for the lengthy period of 40 years.[20] He was prepared to concede state assistance to a programme aimed at importing 2,000 agricultural labourers annually over a period of ten years.[21] This compromise proposal was rejected on the grounds that it did not adequately address the fears and needs of the planting community.[22]

It is perhaps true that the initial withdrawal of African labour — when females, children, the aged and the artisans ceased to perform on the estates and particularly in the field — was large enough to make Light's compromise proposal of 2,000 field labourers annually not much of a relief. Further, the curtailment of the working day by 1.5 hours reduced available labour hours and consequent productivity by one-sixth of its pre-1834 amount.[23] Finally, wages were increasing and the labourer now worked on the estates just long enough to satisfy his/her immediate needs for cash. Higher wages meant that the cost of labour was inflated even as the supply was contracting.

The planters were desperate and took their concerns to the Colonial Office, where they were again rejected.[24] The Colonial Office contended that it was unfair to use public revenue in support of a measure that was to the exclusive benefit of one section of the population. It was suggested that, since it was the planters who wanted an imported labour force, then it was for them to finance the scheme.[25] This was the same argument that the planters had employed against the Colonial Office's tax proposals for social services. When faced with the same argument, they petitioned the queen,[26] bringing forth Lord Russell's now famous reply: 'I am not prepared to encounter responsibility of a measure which may lead to a dreadful loss of life on the one hand or on the other, to a new system of slavery.'[27] Two years later, the Colonial Office reversed this position. According to Adamson, this was because of 'the growth of a conviction that the transition from slavery to freedom ought not to take place outside of the plantation context and that the personal dependence of slavery ought to be replaced by the economic dependence of the wage labour.'[28]

Henry Taylor, who was of the view that the freedmen were earning too much money and had too much spare time, both of which were misappropriated, supported the policy of the imposition of a heavy tax 'to relieve the hard pressed landed interest.'[29] It is important to note the insistence and determination of the planting interest to have the state involved financially in its attempt to secure an alternative labour force. This insistence derived from a conviction that the rehabilitation and perpetuation of the plantation system was essential to the survival of the colony. They argued that if the plantation went into bankruptcy, the planters would withdraw and civilisation would recede.[30] They also believed that all sectors benefited from the prosperity of sugar: the labourer who worked received an excessively high rate of wages; the commercial sector benefited from increased trade; and the immigrants were exposed to the civilising influences of the plantation, not to mention better working conditions than in their homelands.[31] There was an obtuse 'reasonableness' about this type of advocacy, but what it could not explain away was the fact that immigration aimed ultimately at replacing the African labourer on the plantation and immediately at reducing the wage rate. In spite of its oft-quoted benevolence, the Colonial Office seemed wedded to the idea of the advancement of one sector at the expense of the other.

There was still another aspect to this policy of indirect taxation. As the revenue increased, not only was the planters' share of it reduced, but every effort was made to get the state to subsidise the recapitalisation of the plantation economy from its surplus. The planters sought and obtained duty-free concessions for the mechanisation and modernisation process[32], scientific experimentation in the agricultural field processes,[33] in addition to the importation of an alternative supply of labour. The industry was passing through a series of crises and such assistance was perceived as crucial to its return to viability, competitiveness and survival. External capital assistance was inaccessible because of aggressive competition from more attractive forms of investment elsewhere, particularly in the expanding industries emerging in Britain, in international shipping, and in the booming railway industry.[34]

In 1840, a canal excavator capable of ditching all the trenches of an estate was put on show. It was estimated that it would save the planting interests up to 343,750 guilders annually, but it was priced at £74,000[35] and was consequently included in the annual estimates for 1841. This sum, coupled with £30,000 approved since 1839 as an annual subvention to immigration,[36] increased the local estimates by £104,000. The need to raise such a large sum entailed increased taxes for 1841. The planters increased the duty on plantains, flour, corn beef, pork, malt liquors and clothing, all necessaries of the African labouring class.[37] The planters did not increase duties on such items as ice, fresh fish, meat, fruit and vegetables, manures and machinery.[38]

Since there were few immigrants in the colony, and since these were bound by a contractual arrangement which guaranteed that their food be provided by the employer, it would seem reasonable to conclude that the African and the commercial sector were the ones expected to pay for the excavator and the immigration subsidy. But the commercial sector had a built-in relief valve since it was entitled to a mark-up on each item. By this expedient, it was able to pass on its share of the taxes to the labourer.[39] In the long run, therefore, the group that had the least to gain and the most to lose was made to pay the bulk of the increases.

When the £30,000 subvention for immigration was discussed, Mr Arrindell suggested that because it pertained to 'the planting or agricultural interests of the colony, as a matter of justice to the other interests . . . an impost on all exported produce'[40] should be levied to raise the required amount. The planters felt otherwise and adopted the alternative course of action. Ironically, not only did they reject Arrindell's suggestion, but in 1841 they increased the amount by 237 per cent for an object pertaining 'to the planting or agricultural interest of the Colony alone.'

In his opposition to the new taxes, Government Secretary Young accused the planters of an expensive bias when they decided to take the whole amount out of the pockets of the community instead of from the landed interests exclusively. He showed that the system of taxation was skewed to put the burden of running the country on the backs of the labouring classes. He noted that, when the total estimate of expenditure stood at £700,000, the produce and land tax stood at 2.5 per cent. With the proposed increase to £1,123,000 it stood at 3 per cent and not at 4 per cent where it should have been. Further, when £30,000 was the only allocation exclusive to the planting interest, the planters contributed 2.5 per cent by way of a land and produce tax. This sum was increased by £74,000 and the planters' contribution to the produce and land tax should have been 6 per cent, instead of the 3 per cent at which it was placed. There was a clear tendency for the planters' contribution to grow smaller as the total estimates grew larger.[41]

Production

In 1841, the land tax was manipulated to impede the acquisition of land by the labouring classes with agrarian aspirations. Between January 1840 and June 1841, 179 transports, valued under $1,000, were passed. Over the same period, 82 transports of a value exceeding $1,700 were also passed.[42] The Combined Court imposed a tax of from 4 per cent to 1 per cent *ad valorem* on all such transfers of ownership. What was significant, however, was the fact that the lower values of property received the higher taxes. When it is realised that such transfers were already affected by a 2 per cent fee at the Registrar's Office, the conclusion seems inescapable 'that the proposed tax has a strong tendency to obstruct the labourer in his attempt to attain to the station of a free-holder.'[43]

In 1841, 8,144 labourers were introduced into the colony.[44] A system of paying bounties for each immigrant had been introduced,[45] and a loan of £400,000 was made available to meet the cost of these bounties.[46] This increased the financial burdens of the planters and they, as always, were prepared to pass it on to the other sections of the community. The cost of essential goods went up again. George Ross was one of many who complained of the excessive taxes imposed by the Combined Court on articles of general consumption.[47] The *Royal Gazette* observed that the high cost of foodstuffs kept salaries of all officials and labourers very high. It noted that:

> This high price of food does not merely affect production by raising the wages of the labourers. Its effects are felt everywhere. It is the chief cause of the high cost of living in the Colony. It makes all salaries high, those of the public officers, of clerks, of attornies, of managers and overseers. It causes the wages of mechanics to be high, as well as the fees of lawyers and doctors, it produces a great necessity for profit in trade, in order to enable the trader to live. Its effects are felt in every direction from the amount of the Civil List which is so much complained of, down to the exorbitant prices of the Portuguese retail shops.[48]

In 1842, the planters attempted to reduce by 25 per cent the wage of the African labourer. But the labourers resisted this move, claiming that they could not exist on the reduced wage rate.[49] The point was that the planters, by attaching to the estimates at every turn expenses peculiar to the plantation, had created the high cost of living. The high cost of foodstuff acted as a disincentive to the production of sugar by the labouring class. The labourers, who had just become peasants or were in the process of becoming landowners, could have become cultivators of sugar or of ground provisions. They were, however, faced with the daunting prospect of cultivating a high-priced staple for a low-priced export market and of purchasing their own foodstuff at exceedingly high prices on the local market. Given the problems of sugar cane cultivation, the peasant quite reasonably chose to cultivate ground provisions which commanded a high price on the domestic market.[50] This choice provided a useful counter to the attempts of the planters 'to prevent the poorer classes from gaining a livelihood by any other form of labour than field work on the estates.'[51] When this counter was observed by Governor Barkley (as will be dealt with in greater detail later), he urged the planters to institute measures to disrupt it.

Governor Henry Light had other ideas. In a speech before the Court of Policy towards the end of 1842, he contended that 'the man who chooses to live the life of a savage and yet expect to have the protection afforded through the industry of others, should be made in some way to contribute his full portion to entitle him protection.'[52] This was a significant pronouncement. In the first place, the protection of which Light spoke was, by his own behaviour, rendered questionable. During the strike in the first months of that year, the labourers had sought that protection, but were denied it.[53] Light had promised them the questionable protection of the stipendiary magistrates,[54] but had proposed the use of his coercive forces against strikers.[55] He had even intended that the planters should eject striking workers from their premises on the estates, although he had earlier deemed such an intent on the part of the planters vicious and tending to produce unrest.[56] There was therefore no real protection for the labouring classes in post-emancipation society.

Further, as early as 1839, the planters had made it quite clear to Governor Light and to the Colonial Office that, if the social institutions peculiar to a civilised society and inclusive of the law enforcement agencies of a colonial government were to be established and maintained, the onus for so doing rested with the labouring classes.[57] Since then, the system of taxation had ensured that those social institutions, the society, and even the plantation system would become the charge of the labouring classes. Even Governor Light had protested the success of this strategy. His subsequent announcement would therefore seem to have come late but was interesting for what was to come later on.

In a speech in 1842, Light declared that if the African labourer 'should be forced to keep up roads in protection of his acreage and should be taxed according to his acres, he will then find his possessions not so desirable.'[58] Light knew that the planters had always objected to the maintenance of their allotted portion of roadway because of the recurring financial burden it imposed. For some time the planters had been trying to get the state to assume this responsibility. The point was that if the financial upkeep of the roads was a burden to the planters, it was going to be an even more severe stricture to the already over-taxed labourer.

Second, having restricted the alienation of crown lands by attaching a high price thereto,[59] Light was now introducing an aspect of Howick's 1832 emancipation proposal that land owned by the labourer be subjected to a special tax.[60] Local responsibility for the maintenance of roads, however objectionable, was not new but the context in which Light submitted the proposals suggested punitive intentions. Further, the idea of an acreage tax on small holdings was discriminatory since the planters had rejected such a proposal when it was put to them by the Colonial Office in 1838–39.[61]

Third (and this was crucial), Light's proposal aimed at inhibiting the further acquisition of land by the labouring class. It was Light who, in 1839, first spoke out against the burdensome and biased nature of the system of taxation.[62] That system had become even more particularistic and oppressive and had been the source of persistent protest. Yet it was Light who later proposed new and varied forms of discriminatory and punitive taxes. It was also significant that Light referred to the peasants as choosing to lead 'the life of a savage.' This allegation implied that they were not contributing their fair share to domestic development. He conveniently ignored the fact that, in Berbice alone, 1,223 families consisting of 4,646 persons had acquired 7,000 acres on which they had constructed 1,184 freehold cottages, all at a considerable cost.[63] Further, the glut on the ground provision market[64] was evidence of the industry and productivity of the peasant class.

Trading

The use of a licensing fee as a means of inhibiting the labourer's economic growth and independence of the plantation was significant, and is best seen in its application to the huckstering trade. The profitability of this trade was beyond doubt, as was the facility with which the African had always prosecuted it.[65] In 1838, the fee was raised from 25 to 40 guilders for a licence of six months' duration.[66] This was increased to 75 guilders in 1840, a further increase of 87.5 per cent on the 60 per cent increase of 1838.[67] In 1842, there were 1,179 licenced hucksters, the overwhelming majority of whom were Africans.[68] By 1852, the high cost of a licence was affecting the number of licence holders and most certainly the African's participation in the trade.[69] The number of licence holders declined, but the indications were that the number of evaders increased. What was significant was the growing prominence of the Portuguese in this trade. Of the 618 licences issued in 1852, 238 went to Portuguese.[70]

The significance of the upsurge of the Portuguese in this branch of trade was observed as early as 1843.[71] It was claimed that they were the recipients of credit on easy terms which made it possible for them to out-purchase and undersell the Africans.[72] Once they had moved the Africans out of the trade, they then proceeded to charge exorbitant prices for their goods.[73] This attack on the African was encouraged by the commercial community. Just as significant, however, was the assistance that the Portuguese received from the colonial administration that consistently manipulated the licencing fees, thereby undermining the extensive African participation in the trade. One of the consequences of this patronage was the development of acrimonious feelings between the Africans and the Portuguese. On a number of occasions, this antagonism exploded into disorderly and riotous behaviour.[74] The Africans perceived the Portuguese as their enemies,[75] but this was only partly true. The Portuguese, like the Africans, were trying to escape the plantation. The difference (and this became the advantage which went to the Portuguese) was that, because the planter preferred the African labour force to all others, he was prepared to undermine the Africans' effort in every other branch of economic activity leading to their independence from the plantation system. The Portuguese therefore became the beneficiaries of the planters' policy.[76]

It would seem, however, that because the Portuguese were physically and socially vulnerable, and because of their sharp business practices, the Africans chose to release their frustrations and anger on them, instead of the planting or principal commercial sector who sponsored the ascendancy of the Portuguese. The belief grew among a few Africans that, if the Portuguese were repatriated, the favour shown to them would be transferred to the Africans.[77] These few had failed to grasp the true dimensions of the plot aimed at recreating their former dependence on the plantation system.

In 1845, two ordinances on immigration signalled a further increase in the tax burden.[78] The 1841 bounty concessions necessitated a loan of $1,940,000, and of the 8,000 immigrants who came in that year alone, the government's share in the financial outlay was $213,317 or about $37 for each imported field labourer.[79] In 1843, Lord Stanley permitted a loan of £500,000, secured by colonial revenues, an added burden to the estimates.[80] Between 1841 and 1848, the public's contribution to immigration was in the order of £360,000, of which £232,000 was spent between 1846 and 1848 alone.[81] In the latter year the sum was £71,410, but it was reduced substantially in the next two years — to £3,829 in 1849 and £12,615 in 1850.[82] This subsidy was seen as 'a kind of reverse transfer payment' and 'an annual subvention to the planters' by the unrepresented classes.[83]

The anticipated tax increases were reflected in the 1846 Tax Ordinance and were the subject of a petition.[84] A committee was appointed to investigate the matter. The petition referred to 'the excessive duties on articles of food ..., the comparative inequality of the share of taxation to be borne by the separate classes and the injurious effects of both on the standard of living of the labouring population.'[85] It was significant that this petition was being presented by the commercial sector, which had always helped to oppress the labourer and had, by its indiscriminate mark-ups, contributed immensely to the high cost of foodstuffs. It seemed to have recognised the changing patterns of the labourer's consumption and was fearful for the future prosperity of the commercial sector, should the decline in labourer purchasing power continue.[86] The plantocracy saw the move by the commercial sector as an attempt to 'create discontent in the minds of the labouring population and to induce the ignorant and uneducated to believe that the Combined Court and the constituted authorities . . . combined for the purpose of oppressing them by levying on them excessive taxation.'[87]

Discontent

It was unnecessary for any one person, group or sector to create new areas of discontent in the ranks of the Africans. In 1842, John Scoble pointed out that the labourer knew that immigration was intended either 'to supersede their labour on the estates or to reduce the price of labour to so low a rate as to starve them.'[88] The planters had made it known that immigration, which was financed by public revenue to which the labourers were the chief contributors, aimed at undermining the Africans' monopoly of the labour market.[89] Light himself had noted that the labourers' awareness of this plan was one of the causes of the 1846 strike on the island of Leguan, on the Essequibo River.[90]

Similarly, it was unnecessary for the current dailies to cry out against the use of public revenue to provide an ice-house in Georgetown.[91] The labourers, no doubt, would have recognised this, and others like it, for what they really were: instances of unfair allocation of the public revenue.

The planters admitted to the 'soured' temper of the labouring classes[92] and Governor Light was forced to admit that this was true. He could not help but view it as the result of the excessive and unequal nature of the system of taxation to which he himself had drawn attention in 1839 and subsequently. In July 1848, he remarked that 'it has been the fashion to cry out against the burdens on the labourers, but if they choose to abstain from using imported produce no tax can reach them oppressively imposed by the Government....'[93]

It was significant that Light was not denying the oppressive nature of imposed taxation. Rather, he was suggesting a way of avoiding some of its worst effects. It is also noteworthy that when the labourers did, in fact, demonstrate a change in taste and habits induced by rising prices, they were ridiculed for retrogressing from civilisation.[94] The commercial sector had observed this trend towards reduced consumption, a factor which prompted them to suggest a reduction on the import duties. In 1842, when this fact and the possible consequences were first brought to the attention of Governor Light, he had expressed confidence that 'curtailment of some of its [the labourers] luxuries is hardly a reasonable incitement to violence; it is more probable that the labourer will be prompted to additional exertions by the diminution of his wages.'[95]

Essentially, however, Light was aware of the real purpose and consequences of the taxation policy. He recognised the discontent it generated and confessed that 'it was not at all uncommon for remarks, not of the civilest kind, being made by groups of the African labouring class on meeting carriages and horses of officials to the effect that they the people were taxed to pay such luxuries.'[96] This was an admission that discontent was seething and on occasion was openly voiced. Light could not have been happy about it.

Ignoring this fact, however, the Colonial Office proposed a punitive tax during the course of the 1848 sugar strike so as to fall principally upon that class of population whose 'unreasonable discontent'[97] created the need for the increased mobilisation of the police and raised the possibility of military intervention from the base in Barbados.[98] As a consequence of the recession in the sugar industry, aggravated by the 1846 Sugar Duties Act and the 1847 international financial slump, the planter body imposed a 25 per cent cut in colonial wages and salaries. The sugar workers rejected the imposition and adopted strike action. Unlike in 1842, however, when strike action had forced the planters to make speedy concessions, in 1848 the benefits of the immigration system had provided a sufficient body of immigrant labour to nullify the full effects of the strike action and after a few months the militant sugar workers capitulated.[99] What Grey suggested also embraced taxing the labourers to pay for the damages that were caused by the fires which occurred during the course of the 1848 protest.[100]

It was immaterial to Earl Grey, secretary of state for the Colonial and War Departments, that the origin of these acts of incendiarism had not been determined. He hoped that 'thus squeezed, they the African labourer, will betray their brothers in the struggle.'[101] This was yet another clear case of the oppressive application of taxation aimed at bringing the labourer to his knees. It failed in its particular purpose, but added to the overall system of oppression under which the labourer groaned. Grey's choice of the word 'squeezed' was an apt description of the purpose to which taxation had been put in British Guiana from 1838, and the success of the system encouraged both the prolonged and extensive nature of its application. In 1856, a head tax levied to reimburse the losses suffered by the Portuguese community after the communal violence of that year saw the impoverished working people vent their anger on the retiring governor, Wodehouse, in 1857. In 1864 the working people resisted the imposition of rates levied on their peasant acreage. Indeed, as late as 1926 the attempt to revamp the unequal system of taxation resulted in the criticism of the representative system of government and the eventual introduction of crown colony government in the colony in 1928.

Notes

1. Kenneth N. Bell and W.P. Morrell, *Selected Documents on British Colonial Policy* (Oxford: Clarendon Press, 1968), 383–89.
2. GNA, MCCBG, June 7, 1838.
3. *The Royal Gazette*, May 11, 1841. See also Henry Bolingbroke, *A Voyage to Demerara 1799-1806* (Georgetown: Daily Chronicle Ltd., 1947), 76.
4. Bolingbroke, 76.
5. GNA, MCPBG, Ordinance 19 (of 1838), June 28, 1838.
6. GNA, MCPBG, Ordinance 18, June 19, 1838.
7. GNA, MCPBG Ordinance 30, October 4, 1838.
8. GNA, *The Royal Gazette*, October 18, 1839.
9. Michael Moohr, 'The Economic Impact of Slave Emancipation in British Guiana 1832-1852,' *The Economic History Review*, XXV (1972): 592.
10. *Almanac and Local Guide of British Guiana* (Demerary: The Royal Gazette Office, 1832), 479.
11. GNA, Lord John Russell to Governor Henry Light, November 30, 1839.
12. GNA, MCPBG, February 16, 1836.
13. Moohr, 593.
14. GNA, Governor Henry Light to Marquess Normanby, May 2, 1839.
15. Ibid
16. Alan Herbert Adamson, 'The Reconstruction of Plantation Labor After Emancipation: the Case of British Guiana,' in *Race and Slavery in the*

    Western Hemisphere: Quantitative Studies, ed., S.L. Engerman and E. Genovese, (Princeton: Princeton University Press, 1975), 471.

17. Moohr, 605.
18. GNA, MCPBG, June 18, 1839.
19. Ibid.
20. GNA, Light to Normanby, June 26,1839.
21. Ibid.
22. Ibid.
23. A.R.F. Webber, *Centenary History and Handbook of British Guiana* (Georgetown: The Argosy Co. Ltd., 1931), l68.
24. GNA, Normanby to Light, August 15,1839.
25. Ibid.
26. GNA, MCCBG., December 21, 1839.
27. GNA, Lord John Russell to Light, February 15, 1840.
28. Adamson, 'Reconstruction . . .,' 459.
29. Henry Taylor, cited in *British Slave Emancipation: The Sugar Colonies and the Great Experiment 1830-1865,* ed., William A. Green. (Oxford: Clarendon Press, 1976), 187.
30. The Rose Report. See also GNA, Letter by Mr A.G. Fowler, *The Royal Gazette,* April 25, 1837.
31. This belief was bound up with the idea that the prosperity of sugar meant a prosperous colony.
32. Adamson, 'Reconstruction . . .,' 471. See also Adamson, *Sugar without Slaves: The Political Economy of British Guiana 1838-1904* (New Haven: Yale University Press, 1972), 79.
33. Henry Dalton, *The History of British Guiana* (London: Longman, 1855), I, 500-01.
34. Edgar J.E. Johnson and Herman E. Krooss, *The American Economy: Its Origins: Development and Transformation* (Englewood Cliffs, New Jersey: Prentice Hall, 1960), 166-69.
35. GNA, *The Royal Gazette,* May 2, 1840.
36. GNA, MCPBG, December 30, 1840, and *The Royal Gazette,* January 9, 1841.
37. Ordinance 11, Colonial Taxes, *The Royal Gazette,* June 22, 1841.
38. Adamson, 'The Reconstruction . . .,' 471.
39. GNA, *The Colonist,* May 13, 1853.
40. GNA, MCPBG, December 30, 1840, reported in *The Royal Gazette,* January 9, 1841.
41. GNA, MCPBG, June 7, 1841, reported in *The Royal Gazette,* June 8, 1841.
42. GNA, *The Royal Gazette,* June 12, 1841.
43. GNA, MCCBG., June 7, 1841, reported in *The Royal Gazette,* June 8, 1841.

44. Dwarka Nath, *A History of Indians in Guyana* (London: Nelsons, 1970), 219.

45. GNA, MCPBG, December 3, 1842. In the allocation of bounties for privately imported field labourers, $35 was offered for labourers from Sierra Leone, St Helena and Rio de Janiero; $30 for those from the United States; and $20 for those from the Spanish Main and Margarita.

46. GNA, MCPBG, Ordinance 7, May 18, 1843.

47. George Ross to John Scoble, 1842, *Papers of the British and Foreign Anti-Slavery and Aborigines Protection Society*, British Guiana, *Miscellaneous Papers*, Vol.1, 1812–49.

48. GNA, *The Royal Gazette*, September 22, 1842.

49. *PP*, 1842 (479): 656–57, Letter of labourers of Plantation Walton Hall to Stipendiary Magistrate.

50. GNA, *The Royal Gazette*, September 22, 1842.

51. Ross to Scoble, 1842, *Papers of the British and Foreign Anti-Slavery and Aborigines Protection Society*, British Guiana, *Miscellaneous Papers*, Vol.1, 1812–49.

52. GNA, MCPBG, December 12, 1842.

53. GNA, M.E.F.Young to George Bagot, January 5, 1842. See also Light to Lord Stanley, January 6, 1842.

54. GNA, Light to Stanley, January 6, 1842.

55. Ibid., January 26, 1842.

56. GNA, Governor's minute to Attorney-General H. Glouster and Solicitor-General W. Furlonge, January 2, in Light to Stanley, January 6, 1842.

57. GNA, MCPBG, February 16, 1836. See also Webber, 176.

58. GNA, MCPBG, December 12, 1842.

59. GNA, Light to Lord Glenelg, July 24, 1838 and September 1, 1838.

60. Bell and Morrell, 356–57.

61. GNA, Lord John Russell to Governor Henry Light, November 30, 1839; MCPBG, February 16, 1836.

62. GNA, Light to Normanby, May 2,1839.

63. GNA, *The Royal Gazette*, December 2, 1842.

64. George Ross to John Scoble, 1842, and John Dalgleish to Chamerovegen, November 23, 1854, *Papers of the British and Foreign Anti-Slavery and Aborigines Protection Society*, British Guiana, *Miscellaneous Papers*, Vol.1, 1812–49. See also GNA, *The Royal Gazette*, November 20, 1851.

65. GNA, *The Royal Gazette*, May 11, 1841.

66. GNA, MCCBG, June 7, 1838.

67. *Local Guide of British Guiana containing Historical Sketches, Statistical Tables and the entire Statute Laws of the Colony, in force, January 1, 1843* (Demerary: The Royal Gazette Office, 1843), cx.

68. GNA, Light to Stanley, April 7, 1845.

69. GNA, *The Royal Gazette*, August 15, 1842.
70. GNA, MCCBG, June 7, 1838.
71. GNA, *British Guiana Local Guide*, 1843.
72. GNA, Light to Stanley, April 7, 1845.
73. GNA, *The Official Gazette*, August 15, 1842.
74. *Ibid.*
75. GNA, *The Royal Gazette*, Tuesday, October 1843.
76. *Ibid.*, May 27, 1847.
77. GNA, Governor Wodehouse to Rt. Hon. Henry Labouchere, March 10, 1856.
78. GNA, MCCGB, Ordinance 2, January 13, 1845; *The Royal Gazette*, June 8, 1845.
79. Adamson, *Sugar Without Slaves*, 44
80. *Ibid.*, 45.
81. *Ibid.*
82. GNA, British Guiana Blue Books, 1848–50.
83. GNA, *The Royal Gazette*, March 2, 1845.
84. CO 111/234, Report of Committee Appointed to Investigate Petition — Tax Ordinance of 1846. This Report is stamped 'Received' at the Colonial Office on August 6, 1846.
85. Ibid.
86. CO 111/234, See Petition enclosed in Report on Taxation, 1846.
87. CO 111/234, Report on Taxation, 1846.
88. Scoble to Ross, 1842, *Papers of the British and Foreign Anti-Slavery and Aborigines Protection Society,* British Guiana, *Miscellaneous Papers*, Vol.1, 1812–49.
89. GNA, Light to Earl Grey, September 18, 1846.
90. In 1846 the field labourers on the island of Leguan on the Essequibo River took strike action (see CO 111/236, 'Report on Disturbances in Leguan, Essequibo 1846,' enclosed in Light to Grey, September 18,1846).
91. GNA, Editorial of *The Guiana Times*, October 18, 1847.
92. CO 111/249, Planters' memorandum, enclosed in Light to Grey, February 14, 1848.
93. GNA, State of the Colony 1838–48, in Light to Grey, July 1848.
94. CO 111/280, Miscellaneous Papers, Vol.2, 1850–53, 'The Report of the Commissioners appointed to enquire into and report upon the Condition and Prospects of the Colony of British Guiana, 1850.'
95. CO 111/237, Governor Light's comments on Ross' Outline.
96. CO 111/249, Light to Grey, February 14, 1848.
97. Ibid.
98. Ibid.
99. James G. Rose, 'The Strikes of 1842 and 1848,' in *Themes in African-*

Guyanese History, eds., Winston McGowan, James Rose and David Granger. (Georgetown: Free Press, 1998), 158–200.
100. Ibid
101. Ibid.

CHAPTER 14

'A Stake in the Soil': Land and Creole Politics in Free Jamaica – the 1849 Elections
Swithin Wilmot

Introduction

Significant changes in the distribution of landownership took place in Jamaica in the immediate post-slavery period when a new class of freed people established independent freeholds throughout the countryside. Between 1840 and 1845, the number of freeholds of fewer than 10 acres increased from 883 to 20,724 and several small freeholders acquired the £6 property franchise.[1] Contemporary historians have presented contrasting interpretations on the extent to which this new class of black and coloured small freeholders influenced the electoral process in post-slavery Jamaica. Mavis Campbell and William Green stress political apathy among the 'Negroes,' or the 'peasantry,' who withdrew because they either distrusted the white and coloured elites or their 'public awareness extended no farther than the local market.'[2] Conversely, Gad Heuman and Thomas Holt's more systematic accounts indicate that, although the male property franchise excluded the majority of the blacks and coloureds from the electoral process, small freeholders were still crucial to the outcome of the 1849 elections when black settlers supported 'Afro-Jamaican politicians' and white professionals, who comprised the Town Party which was led by free coloureds who supported the governor.[3] While Heuman and Holt's treatment better reflects the dynamics of the 1849 elections, neither writer details the process by which the new class of small freeholders ensured the success of coloured politicians in two sugar parishes, St Thomas-in-the-East and Westmoreland. Both authors also incorrectly assume that Charles Price, a black master carpenter, and Aaron Salome, a Jewish shopkeeper, both based in Kingston, successfully contested the elections as the Town Party's candidates in the rural parishes of St John and St Thomas- in- the-Vale, respectively. Also, the significance of the victory in St Dorothy of Moses Lyon, another Jewish retailer, over Peter Harrison, the coloured incumbent, passes unnoticed, perhaps because of incorrect assumptions about Harrison's racial status.[4] This essay explores the 1849 elections in the parishes mentioned above and underscores how class, colour and ethnic dynamics influenced creole politics in post-slavery Jamaica.

Representations by free coloureds

Once the free coloureds had attained full civil rights in 1830, they aggressively sought representation in the Jamaican Assembly that had been exclusively dominated by the white planter interests since its inception in the seventeenth century. The early free coloured politicians were mainly legal professionals, small merchants and newspaper editors whose political base was in the island's chief towns. Mainly government loyalists, the coloureds became a political force in the Assembly in the 1840s and were known by various labels as the King's House Men, the Coloured Party, the Liberals, the Town Party, and the Queens House Party. Their unifying theme was their creole identity that was built on their sense of being uniquely connected with Jamaica by their birth and that their future prospects were interwoven with the island's destiny. Few planters could stake such claims and the coloureds eagerly anticipated the time when the island's affairs would fall into their hands.[5] The financial and commercial crisis after the British government's adoption of free trade in 1846 provided the coloureds with an opportunity to demonstrate their *Amor patria*. Led by Edward Jordon, and supported by some white professionals in the Assembly, the coloureds stoutly resisted planters' reckless stratagems arbitrarily to cut public expenditure that undermined the integrity of the island's public offices, especially the judiciary. The coloureds' pro-government stances took on added significance after 1848 when absentee planters encouraged their contacts in Jamaica to orchestrate chaos in the island's finances so as to pressure the British government to abandon free trade.[6] The retrenchment battles culminated in June 1849 when the Legislative Council rejected revenue bills with appropriations that tied the hands of the government, and the planters in the Assembly resolved to abstain from 'further exercise of legislative functions' until the 'people' pronounced on their conduct, forcing the governor to call new elections.[7] The coloured candidates had mixed fortunes, as the planters pressed their campaign against the high salaries of public officials in the midst of a depressed economy and increasingly abandoned estates. Confronted by accusations that they were 'place hunters,' 'sycophantic timeservers' and 'the profligate opponents of the economy,' two coloured incumbents were defeated in the parishes of Metcalfe and St Dorothy, respectively, while in St Thomas-in-the-Vale, George William Gordon did not seek re-election. The coloureds made up for these losses by taking three seats from the planters, two in St Thomas-in-the-East and one in Westmoreland, where coloured professionals and shopkeepers, who articulated an aggressive creole nationalism that insisted on their entitlement to public office, defeated sugar planters whose supporters resorted to intimidation and racial abuse.[8]

Despite labour problems and the free trade crisis, the sugar estates held their own along the coastal alluvial plains and in the Plantain Garden River district in St Thomas-in-the-East. In 1852, 42 (i.e., 63 per cent) of sugar estates at emancipation were still in cultivation, and only the parishes of St James and Trelawny in the island's western sugar belt boasted more sugar estates. Accordingly, up to 1849, white planters monopolised the parish's magistracy and both Assembly seats, although coloureds had won a few seats on the vestry.[9] In the 1849 elections, the planters endorsed James Davidson and George Silvera, white and coloured Kingston merchants respectively, who had commercial links with estates in St Thomas-in-the-East. The former owned Stokes Hall and Hampton Court sugar properties in the Plantain Garden River district, and the latter had retail outlets at Bath and Morant Bay.[10] Determined to challenge the planter's political stronghold in St Thomas-in -the-East, the coloured political leadership brought forward John Samuel Brown, a merchant, and Henry Franklin, a solicitor, two coloured assemblymen who had difficult re-election campaigns in other parishes. By the time of the poll, the election took on added significance since Franklin had already lost his seat in Metcalfe to Dr Hinton Spalding, the leader of the Planter Party in the Assembly, and the planters in St James were confident of ousting Brown who had represented the parish in the Assembly since 1844. The coloureds canvassed aggressively and Franklin with 48 votes and Brown with 46 defeated Silvera and Davidson who received 36 and 28 votes respectively. For the first time since the free coloureds had won full civil rights in 1830 they had contested and captured the Assembly seats for St Thomas-in -the-East.[11]

Two considerations underscored this important victory. First, there was the political somersault of Alexander Barclay, the custos, who had represented the parish in the Assembly from 1830 until 1848 when financial difficulties forced his resignation. Subsequently, the governor appointed him to act as the island's receiver-general and, anxious to be confirmed, he canvassed support for Brown and Franklin and influenced other parish officials, including the Anglican rector and the clerk of the vestry, to support them. Not surprisingly, the planters accused Barclay of 'disgraceful treachery.'[12] More significantly, the coloureds in Morant Bay built a coalition with free blacks, free coloureds and freed men with small freeholds in rural districts, and their participation altered the parish's political landscape. Sixteen voters, including at least eight freed men, and who accounted for 39 per cent of the 41 freeholders who voted for Brown and Franklin, owned small freeholds in post-slavery settlements that emerged when parts of coffee, sugar and pen properties were subdivided. Eleven had their respective freeholds of under ten acres at Belle View, Dunrobin, Font Hill, Scotland, Spring Garden, Sunning Hill and York Land, areas to the north of Morant Bay from where men and women in 1865 were to assemble at Paul Bogle's chapel at Stony Gut and march to Morant Bay.[13]

Small freeholders from areas to the east of Morant Bay also participated in the election. Charles Stanford, whose two acres at Leith Hall formed part of the new village along the eastern road linking Morant Bay to the Port Morant and the Plantain Garden River districts, supported Brown and Franklin, as did James Lindsay and John Stevens, two freed men with small freeholds at Pleasant Hill which adjoined James Davidson's estate at Stokes Hall. Two other freed men, James Cameron from Port Morant, and J. William Francis, a former apprentice on Bowden, also voted for Brown and Franklin. At least 13 freed men participated in the election, and 12 supported the two coloureds from the Town Party, while Robert Miles, who had been enslaved on the Golden Valley estate, voted for Brown and George Silvera.[14] Joseph Sterling, a maroon from Hayfield, also endorsed Brown and Franklin, suggesting political links between that free black community and the 13 coloured artisans and shopkeepers in Morant Bay who supported the Town Party's candidates.[15] The electoral coalition between the townsmen and the small freeholders to the east and north of Morant Bay altered the social composition of voters in St Thomas-in-the-East. Indeed, the planters, previously unchallenged at Assembly elections, were jostled at the hustings by a crowd of men and women, mostly non-voters, who were also in Morant Bay to witness the historic victory of the coloureds over the planters.[16]

Two months later a by-election was held in St Thomas-in-the-East because John Samuel Brown, who also won his re-election battle against the planters in St James, opted to represent that parish in the Assembly. The coloureds were determined to consolidate their political gains and they brought forward Alexander Heslop, an Oxford-trained barrister and a prominent member of the coloured elite in the island, who had canvassed for a seat in Hanover in the general elections, but had withdrawn when planters' threats intimidated his supporters. Given this background, the coloured leadership was determined to put in Heslop for St Thomas-in-the-East, despite the governor's and the planters' search for a political accommodation because they were alarmed at the small freeholders' dramatic impact on the general election.[17] The planters again nominated James Davidson and on this occasion, given the governor's anxieties, Barclay, the Anglican rector, the clerk of the vestry and three others who had supported the coloureds two months earlier, abstained. Also, five black or coloured artisans or shopkeepers switched to Davidson after planters threatened to withhold patronage if they opposed their candidate again. However, a sufficient number of the coloureds in Morant Bay and the rural small freeholders stood firm and Heslop's 46 votes triumphed over Davidson's 35.[18]

The small freeholders' vote was again crucial to the outcome, since 15 men, who had not voted in the general election, endorsed Heslop in the by-election. Three were from the Blue Mountain Valley district, and two — Robert Ewing, a sawyer from Water Valley, and William Tailor, a carpenter from Font Hill — were freed men. Also among the new voters was John Davis, a black

Native Baptist minister in Kingston, who had a chapel at Morant Bay. His support for Heslop, as well as that of Andrew Duncan, one of the chapel's trustees who owned land at Stoney Gut and at Spring Garden, indicated that the Native Baptist network in the parish was already politically active before George William Gordon's campaigns in the 1860s.[19]

Heslop's victory underscored the strength of the coalition between the black small freeholders and the coloureds who prevailed in the face of planter intimidatory tactics. On election-day, Heslop's supporters waved placards proclaiming, 'Downfall of oppression, second defeat of Davidson,' and even the usually moderate coloured newspaper, the *Morning Journal*, praised the 'creoles' for their determined stance which had 'cleansed' St Thomas-in-the-East, 'a hitherto closed borough, that den of oppression, that hotbed of pseudo aristocratic insolence.'[20] George William Gordon's later political battles in the parish proved that this claim was premature, but the results of the 1849 elections demonstrate that Gordon inherited a political tradition whereby black and coloured small freeholders had twice combined to defeat the sugar planters in 1849.

1849 elections in Westmoreland

The election campaign in Westmoreland in 1849 was also acrimonious and it revived the recriminations of the 1830s when the coloureds in the parish's main port at Savanna-la-Mar championed abolition and protected the Baptists from the marauding Colonial Church Union.[21] The coloureds in Savanna-la-Mar first flexed their political muscles in 1835 when Aaron Deleon Snr., a coloured merchant, captured one of the two Assembly seats, and his two sons, also shopkeepers in that town, topped the poll in the election for the vestry, burying the white planters' political monopoly.[22] Illness shortened Aaron Deleon's political career and when John Samuel Brown and Charles Lake, two coloured merchants from Kingston, defeated two planters in the 1837 general election, the voting patterns reflected the class and colour cleavages in Westmoreland. Black and coloured artisans and retailers in Savanna-la-Mar, Jewish shopkeepers, as well as a white schoolmaster and a tailor, endorsed the two coloureds, while white planters, penkeepers, professionals and merchants in Savanna-la-Mar who were connected to the plantations, voted exclusively for the planter candidates.[23] This victory was short-lived as the 1838 Imperial Prisons Act, which transferred the administration of the island's prisons from local officials to the governor, split the coloureds in the Assembly. After heated debate, John Samuel Brown voted with the small minority to uphold the British Parliament's legislative authority over the Assembly's insistence on autonomy in matters involving local institutions.[24] When the Assembly refused to carry out its legislative duties until the Prisons Act was withdrawn, the governor, Sir Lionel Smith, dissolved the House and elections for a new Assembly were held in December 1838. The planters in Westmoreland capitalised on the coloureds' division and Hugh Whitelocke, who had been involved in sugar planting in that parish from 1821, ousted Brown from his seat. Since only 31 per cent of the coloured voters, including Aaron Deleon and his two sons, voted exclusively for the two coloured incumbents, and 43 per cent of the white electors voted for one of the coloured candidates, it is clear that the heated issue of the Assembly's legislative autonomy had bridged the class and race divisions that had given the coloureds both seats in 1837.[25]

Governor Metcalfe's conciliatory approach after 1839 settled the prisons issue, and the coloured political leadership adopted a more moderate attitude to the representation in the Assembly from the island's western sugar belt. By the early 1840s they were content to share the representation with the planting interest in St James and in Westmoreland, while in Hanover, Edward Jordon and Robert Osborn endorsed the candidacy of a white, creole planter over a coloured shopkeeper in 1841.[26] Also, the planters and the coloureds in the Assembly were either Anglican or Methodists and they were concerned by the growing threat to the Established Church from the Baptist-inspired Jamaica Anti-State-Church Convention. When Governor Elgin called a snap election in1844 to derail the Convention's voters' registration drive among the black peasantry, Charles Lake and Hugh Whitelocke, the coloured and planter incumbents in Westmoreland, faced the electorate as a team and the same 20 coloured or white voters returned them. Two years later, at the annual vestry election, whites, coloureds and Jews were re-elected without any contest or rancour, indicating that after the feuding and hostilities of the 1830s the whites and coloureds in Westmoreland had established a political *entente* by the mid-1840s.[27]

However, this accommodation camouflaged old prejudices and animosities resurfaced when the planters' and the coloureds' bitter differences over retrenchment set the tone for the general elections in Westmoreland in 1849. Hugh Whitelocke, pleading pressing property business, retired and warmly endorsed his close friend of 30 years, Benjamin Vickers, the proprietor of Belleisle, Fontabelle and Frome sugar estates on the Westmoreland Plains, and who was one of the island's most innovative planters.[28] The planters assumed that the coloureds would accept Vickers because he was willing to support the coloured incumbent, Charles Lake, despite his opposition to the planters' retrenchment proposals. However, Foster Davis, a young coloured solicitor in the adjoining parish of St Elizabeth where white planters and penkeepers monopolised the political posts, wanted an Assembly seat in Westmoreland, the parish of his birth.[29] Since he did not reside in the parish, Davis enlisted the assistance of John Deleon, one of the leaders of the 'radical' or 'democratic' party during the parish's turbulent politics in the 1830s. Together, they revived the nativist rhetoric of the coloureds' aggressive campaigns, insisting that they were the only true 'sons of Jamaica' and therefore entitled to a 'greater share in the administration of the affairs of their country.' If elected, Davis also unashamedly promised to 'elevate his coloured brethren' and 'to bring them forward in the Councils of the country whenever favorable opportunities occur.'[30] Davis' aggressive creole campaign incensed Whitelocke who exacerbated social tensions with 'indecorous remarks against the persons of colour' and others of the 'Whitelocke party' threatened coloureds that a vote against Vickers would jeopardise their children's career at the Mannings Free School in Savanna-la-Mar.[31] Stung by Whitelocke's prejudices and affronted by his supporters' vulgar threats, black and coloured voters lined up behind Lake and Davis who jointly polled 81 votes, defeating Vickers who received 59 votes. At least 58 blacks or coloureds voted and 85 per cent of them endorsed the two coloured candidates, while 88 per cent of the 40 whites so identified endorsed Vickers exclusively.[32]

Table 14.1:
Voters' location, Westmoreland, 1849

	Davis and Lake Voters		Vickers Voters	
District	Number	% of N[a]	Number	% of N[b]
Blufields	11	18.0	1	2.5
Darliston	8	13.1	5	12.5
Savanna-la-Mar	31	50.8	17	42.5
Westmoreland Plains	3	5.0	16	40.0
Whithorn	8	13.1	1	2.5
Not Known	17	-	19	-
Total	78	100.0	59	100.0

[a]Location known (N=61)   [b]Location known (N=40)

Sources: House of Assembly Poll Book, 1844–66; Jamaica Almanack, 1845; Land Deeds; Record of Voters, Westmoreland, 1849–66.

As in St Thomas-in-the-East, the voters' residential pattern in the 1849 election in Westmoreland reflected the growing political influence of the new class of black and coloured small freeholders who formed part of the parish's post-slavery social and economic landscape. Except for a white goldsmith, all Davis and Lake's 31 supporters in the port town of Savanna-la-Mar were black or coloured, and at least 14 were artisans and three were shopkeepers or liquor retailers.[33] In contrast, at least ten whites and three Jews in Savanna-la-Mar, merchants and wharfingers, who were associated with Westmoreland's planting interest, voted exclusively for Vickers.[34] Vickers' near monopoly of the votes from the Westmoreland Plains reflected the heavy concentration of some of the island's 'most flourishing' sugar properties in the areas along the lower basin and delta of the Cabaritta River. Hugh Whitelocke owned three estates in this area, Amity, Moreland and Blackness, and in 1845 he had also leased Paul Island, which bordered Vickers' estate at Belleisle. A baron of the 'sugar kingdom' on the Westmoreland Plains, Whitelocke ensured that his *protégé* triumphed handsomely there. Davis and Lake's three supporters from this area, two of whom, Williams Appleby and Robert James, were coloured artisans, owned small freeholds in post-slavery settlements at Blue Castle, Geneva and Meylersfield, respectively, which were encircled by sugar properties.[35] Clearly, the planters reigned on the Westmoreland Plains and Vickers' support there compensated for the coloureds' better showing in Savanna-la-Mar.

The coloureds' strong following in the mostly mountainous districts and uplands adjoining Bluefields, Darliston and Whithorn determined the outcome of the election. The post-slavery village at Whithorn was situated at the foot of the hill where the mountain road to Darliston intersected with the road between Savanna-la-Mar and Montego Bay. Whithorn bordered Deans Valley sugar estate which was abandoned after 1838. When its hillier sections that adjoined Caledonia estate and Mount Carmel Pen were subdivided in 1841, Robert Clarke, Robert Dixon and Alexander Lewis, all freed men, purchased four acres each which empowered them to vote for Davis and Lake in 1849. Two other freed men, Edward Campbell and Edward James, one black and the other coloured, both carpenters, had also voted for the two coloured candidates, having secured the franchise through the purchase of five acres that adjoined Caledonia and Cold Spring, which was also near to Whithorn. Three other coloureds from Whithorn, including Robert Jones, a liquor retailer in the village, also voted for Davis and Lake.[36] Dr John Tullis, a sugar planter, who had purchased parts of Caledonia estate after its previous owner had gone bankrupt, was the only resident from the Whithorn district who voted for Vickers. Thus, while the post-slavery village of Whithorn mushroomed on the decay of the adjacent declining sugar properties of Deans Valley and Caledonia, its residents and surrounding small freeholders made their presence felt in the new politics of Westmoreland.[37]

Davis' and Lake's 11 supporters from the Bluefields district were black or coloured artisans and small cultivators. Between 1838 and 1839, five of them, including at least two freed men, Nicholas Blake, a mason, and George Scott, purchased between six and ten acres each from Aaron Deleon Snr when he sold off sections of his Bluefields Mountain property on the steep interior road from Bluefields to Hopewell Pen. Three of the remaining six voters, Thomas Davis, Thomas Forbes and James McIntosh, a cooper, were freed men, and two others were free coloureds, one of whom, James Sloss, named his freehold

'Little Ease.' Since these voters resided in the area where peasants thrived on supplying provisions across Bluefields Bay for the Savanna-la-Mar market, it is possible that they had commercial linkages with the Deleon family and this translated into political support for the coloureds in1849. Significantly, Thomas Tate, the white penkeeper, who owned Shaftston, Bluefields, Mount Edgecombe and Auchindown Pens, was the sole supporter for Vickers from the Bluefields district. This speaks eloquently of the colour and class dimensions that determined voting patterns in the non-sugar areas of Westmoreland by 1849.[38] Similarly, Edward H. Clarke, William Harriet Cooke, and Rhodes Evans, three white penkeepers from the Darliston district in the uplands of the parish, who owned Enfield, Hermitage and Welchpool properties respectively, supported Vickers. His two remaining supporters (Table 14.1), James and Robert Riddock, were coloured penkeepers with smaller properties at Ramble and Sterling Castle.[39] In contrast, five of Davis and Lake's black or coloured supporters in the Darliston district were carpenters or sawyers, and one, who was a blacksmith and a liquor retailer, had married a freed woman.

Such overarching social linkages between free blacks and coloureds and freed people may well have provided a network of support for the coloured candidates since another voter in the Darliston district, William Cunningham, a coloured freedman, had been enslaved on Woodstock Pen when he married a free woman, and William Leslie, who named his 3.5 acres freehold, 'Content,' also voted for Davis and Lake. Moreover, John Laurie Pew, a coloured carpenter and schoolmaster, who was the clerk to St Johns Chapel at Darliston, may well have mobilised these small freeholders who journeyed up to about 18 miles to Savanna-la-Mar to record their votes against the planters and penkeepers.[40] Clearly, in the acrimonious contest between the coloureds and the planters in Westmoreland in 1849, the combined votes of free blacks, free coloureds, and freed men ensured an important victory for a coloured professional and a coloured shopkeeper over one of the island's premier sugar planters. With the small freeholders in the rural districts buttressing the coloureds' political base in Savanna-la-Mar, the planters from the 'sugar kingdom' on the Westmoreland Plains were sandwiched between the townsmen and the country voters in the upland and mountainous regions of the parish.

Charles Price and the elections in St John

Charles Price, a black builder and master carpenter in Kingston, also successfully contested a seat for the parish of St John in the1849 general elections. Price served his political apprenticeship in the Kingston Common Council, and along with Edward Vickars, who in 1847 became the first black member of the Assembly, strongly insisted on the blacks' entitlement to representation in Jamaica's public institutions.[41] St John was ideal for Price to fulfil his political ambitions. Before emancipation, large-scale coffee and sugar cultivation had declined in the steep, fertile and well-watered lands of the Juan de Bolas Mountains, and free black and free coloured small farmers, who combined a variety of crops such as coffee, pimento, provisions, fruit trees and hardwoods, had developed instead. This process accelerated after 1838 when freed people settled on abandoned coffee plantations and on the margins of pens, as well as along the old sugar road from Lluidas Vale to the shipping ports on the south coast, via the steep climb to Point Hill and down to Guanaboa Vale.[42] This altered pattern of land settlement found its political expression in the immediate post-slavery period and George Price, planter at Worthy Park and Custos of St John, noted that St. John's politics was dominated 'almost entirely [by] black men, mountain settlers.'[43]

In 1849, Charles Price jointly canvassed with Samuel Queensborough Bell, a coloured carpenter and a former bookkeeper, whose family roots were grounded among St John's settlers who had already elected him to the parish vestry. The settlers warmed to Bell and Price since they were members of the 'middle class' and were 'men from among themselves' who could be trusted 'to watch over and guard their interests.'[44] Their opponents were John Aris, a coloured sugar planter, who had represented the parish since 1841, and Francis Lynch, a white solicitor in Spanish Town, whose father-in-law, Dr William Turner, was the Custos of St Catherine and a member of the Legislative Council. Lynch, in particular, enjoyed the prestigious backing of the governor, Sir Charles Grey, who, with 'a select party of ardent adherents' to the Queens House Party, visited St John and canvassed support for him.[45] Indeed, Dr Charles Morales, the other incumbent, had been so impressed by the governor's entourage that he withdrew and accepted the invitation from the planters in Vere to represent them instead. However, Aris, who had also supported the planters in the Assembly, stood his ground. First, he was confident that his coloured status provided him with some modicum of political security, and second, he resided in Spanish Town and enjoyed cordial relations with some of Lynch's 'gentlemen' supporters there.[46] Since Bell, Lynch and Price opposed the planters' reckless retrenchment proposals, the coloured and white professionals from the Queens House Party in Spanish Town urged either Bell or Price to withdraw in favour of Lynch, whose pedigree as the 'son of a gentleman' differentiated him from the black and coloured master craftsmen. Both nurtured strong political ambitions and they refused, insisting that the majority of the 'blacks and browns' in St John preferred them. As the contest heated up, he and Lynch teamed up, despite their different positions on retrenchment, and St John's election became a mini-referendum on Bell and Price's suitability for public office over Aris and Lynch who boasted 'wealth' and 'social standing.'[47]

On election day, August 29, 1849, the four candidates and their supporters, accompanied by music bands, gathered at Point Hill for the poll, as did several 'visitors' from the five adjoining parishes who witnessed what proved to be a historic election. The two men who nominated the respective teams of candidates reinforced their different class origins. Adam Thoburn, a white doctor who trained at Edinburgh and who owned two properties, Lookout and Top Hill, that spanned the mountainous borders of Clarendon and St John, which together totalled 985 acres, nominated Aris, the coloured sugar planter, and Lynch, the white solicitor. In contrast, John Thomas Bell, a coloured artisan with 32 acres at Retirement in St John, and whose father had been manumitted as a child in 1790, nominated Bell, the coloured carpenter and former bookkeeper, and Price, the black master carpenter.[48] St John's black and coloured 'mountain settlers' handed victory to Price and Bell who received 51 votes and 50 votes respectively, while Aris with 43 votes and Lynch with 36 were defeated. It was an eloquent statement on how St John's political landscape had changed in the decade after emancipation that 40 (i.e., 85 per cent) of the 47 voters, whose racial identities have been identified, were either black or coloured, and two-thirds of them, including at least 11 freed men, voted for Bell and Price.[49] It is significant that 85 per cent of the 13 black or coloured men who voted for Aris and Lynch were either artisans or shopkeepers in Spanish Town or planters and penkeepers in St. John. The first group reflected the influence of the members of the Queens House Party in the island's capital, while the second group of Aris and Lynch's coloured supporters voted with seven white planters who also exclusively endorsed the two 'gentlemen' over the two craftsmen from the 'middle class.'[50] Since Bell, Lynch and Price shared similar views on retrenchment that differed from those of Aris, considerations of class and colour overlapped and the voters' respective holdings reinforced this.

Table 14.2: Voters' acreage in St John, 1849

Voter's Acreage	Bell and Price		Aris and Lynch	
	Number	% of N [a]	Number	% of N [b]
1 – 10	25	62.5	6	21.4
11 – 20	12	30.0	4	14.3
21 – 50	3	7.5	7	25.0
> 50	0	-	11	39.3
Not Known	7	-	4	-
Total	47	100.0	32	100.0

[a]Known (N=40) [b]Known (N=28)

Sources: House of Assembly Poll Book, 1844–66; *Land Deeds; Jamaica Almanack, 1840; Jamaica Almanack, 1845.*

Clearly, black and coloured small freeholders, several of whom were freed men who had established themselves after 1838, decided the election. For instance, nine voters for Bell and Price, including at least five freed men, purchased lots of up to six acres each after 1841, when James Williams, an absentee, sold off the upper regions of Watermount sugar estate, near to Point Hill. Also, between 1839 and 1842, 12 other supporters of Bell and Price with freeholds of up to 10 acres, purchased parts of ruinate coffee estates at Fellowship Hall, Hayle, Juan de Bolas and Lemon Ridge, as well as parts of Pratts Run, which incorporates the present-day Cudjoe Hill settlement. Two other black supporters for Bell and Price, Grant Bruce, a cooper, and Richard Wilson, whose freehold's locations have not been identified, also purchased their 2.5 and three acres respectively after 1838.

While the black mountain settlers ensured that Charles Price became the second black man to sit in the Assembly in Spanish Town, five whites and three coloureds were among Aris and Lynch's 11 supporters with holdings over 50 acres (table 14.2). Thomas Edbury and Stephen Hannaford, two of these whites who individually owned properties in St John that totalled over1,000 acres, personified the remnants of the planter class who were emphatically defeated by the mountain settlers in 1849, signalling an important shift in the political balance in the parish.[51] Accordingly, the planters were alarmed that a black 'uneducated Kingston operative tradesman' of 'slender means' had defeated two men of fine 'intellectual acquirements,' and echoing Henry Taylor's 1839 strategy for Crown Colony Government, some called for the abolition of the Assembly before 'every man of a white skin' was excluded.[52] Although the coloured leadership regretted Lynch's defeat, they embraced Bell and Price since they opposed the Planter Party's stance on retrenchment. Their success also compensated for the loss of two of the Town Party's coloured supporters, Peter Harrison, who had been defeated in St Dorothy, and George William Gordon, who did not seek re-election in St Thomas-in-the-Vale. They were replaced by Moses Lyon and Aaron Salome, two Jewish retailers, whose campaigns for lower taxation and 'rigid economy' in public expenditure, particularly on officials' salaries, elicited strong support from the small settlers in the respective parishes.[53]

Jewish representation

After 1838, while sugar and pen properties maintained their dominance in St Dorothy's lower regions, several freed people established themselves as small farmers in its mountainous areas. These 'mountain negroes' cultivated provisions — corn, yams, peas and plantains — which were sold by the 'cartload, hamper or head-load,' while others, utilising very rudimentary mills, manufactured sugar for local consumption and also grew coffee and pimento.[54] Their economic activity fuelled the market at Old Harbour Village which rapidly blossomed into an important interior trading centre by 1854 when at least eight Jews from Spanish Town, ten miles to the east, ran dry goods outlets or liquor shops there. Three of these retailers also set up branch stores at Bartons and Bellas Gate in the mountainous interior to the north of Old Harbour, thereby cementing the commercial ties between the Jews and the freed people with whom they traded dry goods for coffee and pimento.[55]

These business links had political implications, for the Jewish retailers, with the backing of black and coloured artisans and small farmers, replaced the planters and the penkeepers as the dominant political force on the local vestry in the 1850s. Moreover, between 1849 and 1865, six Jews from Kingston or Spanish Town, who had business and family ties with retailers in Old Harbour, represented St. Dorothy in the Assembly.[56] Moses Lyon, a tavernkeeper in Spanish Town, was the first to test his political fortunes in St Dorothy and since his candidacy in 1849 coincided with the retrenchment crisis, he endorsed the popular cry for public economy and lower taxation. He targeted Peter Harrison, a coloured shopkeeper at Old Harbour Bay, who had represented St Dorothy since 1844 and had supported the Town Party against the planters' retrenchment measures.[57] Stephen Hannaford, who owned estates and pens in St Dorothy, also coveted Harrison's seat, and the election became a three-way contest between a Jewish retailer, a sugar planter and a coloured shopkeeper, since the other incumbent, Francis McCook, a white sugar planter and a penkeeper, supported the Planter Party and was expected to be re-elected.[58] Lyon topped the poll with 35 votes, and McCook placed second with 31, while Harrison with 28 votes and Hannaford with 10 votes, were defeated. Moses Lyons' triumph was firmly grounded in the support of small freeholders, including at least eight freed men. The landholding for 25 of his supporters has been verified: 52 per cent owned less than four acres each, in the lower regions of the parish at Old Harbour Bay, or in the village by the Old Harbour Market, or in post-slavery settlements in the mountain districts, such as Bartons, Macca Tree, Orange Hall, Somerset and Stoney Hill.[59]

With the endorsement of the Jewish retailers and their clients among the peasantry in St Dorothy, Moses Lyon's defeat of the coloured incumbent and a white sugar planter marked a turning point in St Dorothy's representation in the Assembly. In the following year, when McCook died, David Brandon, a Kingston dry goods retailer, defeated Harrison and established the Jewish monopoly on St Dorothy's seats which survived the 1854 and 1860 elections, despite challenges from the planters in the parish. Clearly, in 1849 the Jewish retailers at Old Harbour Market and the 'mountain negroes' inaugurated a potent political coalition which terminated the coloureds' initial victory in 1844, and kept out the planters until the new franchise law undercut the influence of St Dorothy's small freeholders after 1860.[60]

Similarly, black and coloured freed men provided Aaron Salome, a Kingston Jewish retailer, with an impressive runaway victory in St Thomas-in-the-Vale in 1849. Salome, who had canvassed the voters in St Thomas-in-the-Vale for some time before the election, offered himself to the constituency as an 'unflinching advocate' of the reduction of the official salaries that were supported by 'oppressive taxation' on imported staples and on small settlers' animals. At the same time that he pledged 'more rigid economy in pubic affairs,' Salome demanded more support for education to benefit the 'poorer classes.'[61] With Salome successfully wooing several of the small freeholders, George William Gordon, the coloured incumbent, withdrew from the contest since the planters, who had assisted his election in 1844, abandoned him after he had voted with the Town Party on retrenchment, even though he had supported their immigration schemes.[62] The planters' also opposed Salome, insisting that the Jewish retailer from Kingston was 'a very unfit man to be a member for the parish' since he possessed no roots in the parish's 'aristocracy.' Accordingly, Dr Charles McDermott and Colin Chisholm, two planters, as well as James Dollar, a solicitor in Spanish Town, and William Lovesay, who may have been coloured and who echoed the Town Party's position on the 'vested rights' of officials' salaries, campaigned against Salome.[63]

Confronted by this political phalanx, Salome broadened his electoral base by forming a joint candidacy with Haim Barrow, a Jewish shopkeeper in Linstead, a thriving post-slavery market town in St Thomas-in- the-Vale which, by 1854, boasted 'a number of large well-furnished stores' that did a thriving dry goods business with the freed people who traded fruits, provisions and cash crops.[64] Salome topped the poll with 137 votes, which represented 76 per cent of those who participated. The landholdings of 85 of his supporters have been identified. Sixty-three owned freeholds of less than ten acres either in one of the mountainous districts around Above Rocks, Guys Hill, Redwood and Riversdale areas, or in one of the Baptist free villages at Hampshire, Jubilee Town, Sligoville and Victoria.[65] Clearly, Jewish dry goods and liquor retailers such as Lyon and Salome were central to the expanding commercial ethos of 'markets, traders and the rum shops' after 1838. Socially differentiated from wealthy Jewish merchants whose import-export business linked them to the plantations, or who were estate mortgagees or planters in their own right, the retailers were linked to strategic interior market towns such as Linstead and Old Harbour, and the freed men endorsed them whenever they championed their interests.[66]

Conclusion

In the 1849 elections, small freeholders, including freed men, had ensured that coloureds made significant inroads into traditional planter strongholds and a black master carpenter and two Jewish retailers triumphed in country seats. These shifts in the political landscape alarmed the governor and encouraged the planters to moderate their retrenchment strategies. Both were anxious 'to avoid the necessity of another general election' in which other 'representatives of the English and planting interest' would be successfully challenged by 'coloured or indigenous' candidates who enjoyed the support of the small freeholders.[67] Clearly, left to flourish, the black and coloured small free holders had the potential to alter profoundly the racial and ethnic composition of the Assembly. However, in 1858, the Planter Party, with the support of the governor and the increasingly conservative coloured elite, amended the electoral law. The new arrangements diminished the small freeholders' influence by imposing a registration tax on the franchise and also introduced a new voting qualification for salaried employees, thereby strengthening the planters and their merchant allies in subsequent elections. Still, the new class of black and coloured small freeholders maintained a keen interest in the island's political affairs and their political influence was finally checked when Crown Colony Government after 1866 slammed the door shut on the small freeholders' political participation.[68]

Notes

1. Douglas Hall, *Free Jamaica, 1838–1865: An Economic History* (London: Caribbean Universities Press, 1969), 2, 3, 160–62.
2. Mavis Campbell, *The Dynamics of Change in a Slave Society: A Sociopolitical History of the Free Coloreds of Jamaica, 1800–1865* (Rutherford, New Jersey: Associated Universities Press, 1976), 242; William Green, *British Slave Emancipation: The Sugar Colonies and the Great Experiment, 1830–1865* (Oxford: Clarendon Press, 1976), 321.
3. Gad Heuman, *Between Black and White: Race, Politics, and the Free Coloureds in Jamaica, 1792–1865* (Westport: Greenwood Press, 1981), 122–28; Thomas Holt, *The Problem of Freedom: Race, Labor, and Politics in Jamaica and Britain, 1832–1938* (Baltimore: The Johns Hopkins University Press, 1992), 216, 217, 229.
4. Heuman, 124; Holt, 229. Heuman claims that Peter Harrison was white, but marriage records confirm his coloured status (see Heuman, *Between Black and White*, 140, & JAr, 1B/11/8/3/35, Register of Marriages, St Dorothy 1826–43, fol. 3).
5. Heuman, *Between Black and White*, 56–60, 72; Holt, 219–22.
6. CO 137/301, Charles Grey to Earl Grey, February 19, 1849; *Morning Journal*, September 13, 1848.
7. CO 137/303, Charles Grey to Earl Grey, July 7, 1849; *Falmouth Post*, July 17, 1849.
8. *Falmouth Post*, July 17, 24 & 31, August 21, September 11, 1849, January 5, 1850.
9. CO 137/322, Barkly to Newcastle, May 26, 1854; B.W. Higman, *Slave Population and Economy in Jamaica, 1807–1834* (Cambridge: Cambridge

University Press, 1976), 18; Heuman, *Between Black and White*, 73, 100.

10. IRO, Spanish Town, *Land Deeds*, Liber 887, fol. 157, Liber 893, fol. 158; *Daily Advertiser*, January 4, 1854; *Morning Journal*, July 24, 1849.

11. JAr, 1B/11/23/19, House of Assembly Poll Book 1844–1865, fols. 53–55; *Falmouth Post*, July 24 & 31, 1849.

12. *Ibid*.; Glory Robertson (Comp.), *Members of the Assembly of Jamaica from the General Election of 1830 to the Final Session January 1866* (Kingston: Institute of Jamaica,1965), 34.

13. JAr, 1B/11/23/19, House of Assembly Poll Book 1844–1865, fols. 53–55; JAr, 1B/11/8/14/2 & 8, Register of Baptisms, St Thomas-in-the-East, 1817–25 & 1857–68; NLJ, Surveyors' Maps, St T. 519, St 531, St T. 538, St T. 1563; *Land Deeds*, Liber 853, fol. 189; Liber 913, fol. 226; Gad Heuman, *'The Killing Time' The Morant Bay Rebellion in Jamaica* (London: Macmillan, 1994), 3, 89.

14. JAr, 1B/11/23/19, House of Assembly Poll Book 1844–1865, fols. 53–55; 1844–1865; *Land Deeds*, Liber 844, fol. 113, Liber 849, fol. 120 and Liber 894, fol. 138; NLJ, Maps, St T. 1253; IRO, Dissenters Marriage Register; JAr, 1B/11/8/14/5, Register of Baptisms, St Thomas-in-the-East, 1833–1840.

15. JAr, 1B/11/23/19, House of Assembly Poll Book 1844–1865, fols. 53–55; JAr, 1B/11/8/14/5, Register of Baptisms, St Thomas-in-the-East, 1833–1840; *Land Deeds*, Liber 835, fols. 136; Liber 894, fol. 138; *Jamaica Gazette*, October 2, 1845, June 6 & September 3, 1846, June 28 & September 3, 1849, February 12, 1859.

16. *Falmouth Post*, July 24, 1849.

17. CO 137/303, Charles Grey to Earl Grey, October 8, 1849; CO 137/316, Charles Grey to Newcastle, April 9, 1853; *Falmouth Post*, July 24 & September 25, 1849.

18. JAr, 1B/11/23/19, House of Assembly Poll Book 1844–1865, fols. 98–100; *Morning Journal*, September 19, 1849.

19. JAr, 1B/11/23/19, House of Assembly Poll Book 1844–1865, fols. 98–100; JAr, 1B/11/8/14/5 Register of Baptisms, St Thomas-in-the-East, 1833–1840; *Land Deeds*, Liber 828, fols. 139, 231; Liber 901, fol. 136; NLJ, Maps, St T. 327, St T. 526, St T. 1531; Robert Stewart, *Religion and Society in Post-Emancipation Jamaica* (Knoxville: University of Tennessee Press, 1992), 161.

20. *Morning Journal*, September 19, 1849.

21. Mary Turner, *Slaves and Missionaries: The Disintegration of Jamaican Slave Society, 1787–1834* (Urbana: University of Illinois Press, 1982), 182–84.

22. Heuman, *Between Black and White*, 58; *Watchman*, January 17, 1835.

23. JAr, 1B/11/23/18, House of Assembly Poll Book 1804–43, fols. 176, 177; JAr, 2/7/1,Westmoreland's Militia List, 1828; JAr, 1B/11/8/16/3 & 4,

Registers of Baptisms and Marriages, Westmoreland, 1826–43 & 1844–54; *Jamaica Gazette*, June 22, July 13, August 24 & December 28, 1848.

24. Heuman, *Between Black and White*, 107–09.

25. JAr, 1B/11/23/18, House of Assembly Poll Book 1804–43, fols. 201–04; JAr, 2/7/1, Westmoreland's Militia List, 1828; JAr, 1B/11/8/16/3 & 4, Registers of Baptisms and Marriages, Westmoreland, 1826–43 & 1844–54; *Morning Journal*, December 1, 1838.

26. *Morning Journal*, September 10, 1841, January 1, 1842.

27. CO 137/280, Elgin to Stanley, September 7, 1844; JAr, 1B/11/23/19, House of Assembly Poll Book, 1844–65; *Jamaica Gazette*, January 22, 1846.

28. CO 137/322, Barkly to Newcastle, May 26, 1854; *Morning Journal*, August 2, 1849; *Land Deeds*, Liber 933, fols. 40, 41.

29. *Falmouth Post*, July 17, 1849.

30. *Jamaica Standard*, February 5, 1840; *Morning Journal*, August 2, 1849.

31. *Falmouth Post*, August 7, 1849; *Morning Journal*, August 7, 1849.

32. JAr, 1B/11/23/19, House of Assembly Poll Book 1844–66, fols. 61–63; JAr, 2/7/1, Westmoreland's Militia List, 1828; JAr, 1B/11/8/16/9, Register of Marriages, Westmoreland, 1826–37; IRO, Register of Baptisms and Marriages, Westmoreland, 1739–1825.

33. JAr, 2/7/1, Westmoreland's Militia List, 1828; *Jamaica Gazette*, November 12, 1846, September 29, & December 28, 1848, March 29, 1849, October 23, 1850, February 13, 1851.

34. JAr, 2/7/1, Westmoreland's Militia List, 1828; *Jamaica Gazette*, February 19, 1846, July 13, December 28, 1848, May 3, June 7, 1849, June 28, 1855.

35. CO 137/322, Barkly to Newcastle, May 26, 1854; JAr, 1B/11/23/19, House of Assembly Poll Book 1844–66, fols. 61–63; JAr, 2/7/1, Westmoreland's Militia List, 1828; *Land Deeds*, Liber 839, fol. 149; Liber 870, fol. 85; Liber 871, fol. 99; Liber 880, fol. 108; Liber 891, fol. 153; Hall, 14.

36. CO 137/322, Barkly to Newcastle, May 26,1854; JAr, 1B/11/8/16/2, Register of Slaves' Marriages, Westmoreland, 1827–34; JAr, 2/7/1, Westmoreland's Militia List, 1828; *Land Deeds*, Liber 830, fols. 135, 139; Liber 846, fol. 104; Liber 853, fols. 167, 170; IRO, Dissenters Marriages Register; *Jamaica Gazette*, April 13, 1854.

37. CO 137/322, Barkly to Newcastle, May 26, 1854; *Land Deeds*, Liber 835, fol. 115; Liber 906, fol. 101.

38. JAr, 1B/11/8/16/2, Register of Slaves' Marriages, Westmoreland, 1827–1834; *Land Deeds*, Liber 829, fols. 40, 41, 48; Liber 830, fols. 151, 155; Liber 852, fol. 210; Liber 882, fol. 202; Liber 895, fols. 56–58; Hall, 164.

39. JAr, 2/7/1, Westmoreland's Militia List, 1828; *Jamaica Gazette*, April

12,1849, *Jamaica Almanack 1845*, Returns of Proprietors, 80; *Land Deeds*, Liber 862, fol. 215; Liber 892, fol. 114; Liber 893, fol. 10; Liber 930, fol. 101.

40. JAr, 1B/11/8/16/2, Register of Slaves' Marriages, Westmoreland, 1827–34; JAr, 1B/11/8/16/4, Register of Baptism, Westmoreland 1844-54; *Land Deeds*, Liber 829, fol. 46; Liber 858, fol. 6; Liber 862, fol. 216; *Jamaica Gazette*, May 3, 1849.

41. Swithin Wilmot, 'The Growth of Black Political Activity in Post-Emancipation Jamaica,' in *Garvey: His Work and Impact*, eds., Rupert Lewis and Patrick Bryan. (Kingston: Institute of Social and Economic Research and Dept. of Extra-Mural Studies, 1988), 39-42; *Falmouth Post*, October 14, 1845.

42. Michael Craton and James Walvin, *A Jamaica Plantation: The History of Worthy Park, 1670-1970* (London: W.H. Allen, 1970), 3, 61, 208; Michael Craton, *Searching For The Invisible Man* (Cambridge, Mass.: Harvard University Press, 1978), 21-24, 48; Hall, 184; Higman, 34.

43. George Price, *Jamaica and the Colonial Office: Who Caused the Crisis?* (London: Sampson, Low, Son and Marston, 1866), 2, 3; Craton & Walvin, 227-30.

44. *Morning Journal*, January 13, September 3 & 6, 1849.

45. *Falmouth Post*, July 13 & August 24, 1849; *Morning Journal*, September 3, 1849.

46. JAr, 2/2/1, St Catherine's Tax Rolls,1846; *Falmouth Post*, August 24, 1849.

47. *Falmouth Post*, August 24, 1849.

48. JAr, 2/2/28, Register of Free Persons, St Catherine, 1789-1826; *Land Deeds*, Liber 804, fol. 205; *Jamaica Almanack 1840*, 199, 264; *Jamaica Almanack 1845*, Returns of Proprietors, 35; *Morning Journal*, August 30, 1849.

49. JAr, 1B/11/23/19, House of Assembly Poll Book 1844-66, fols. 92-94; JAr, 2/2/28, Register of Free Persons, St Catherine, 1789-1826; IRO, Register of Baptisms, St John, 1751-1825 & Register of Baptisms, St Catherine, 1764-1825.

50. Ibid., *Jamaica Gazette*, September 23, 1847, February 21 & September 22, 1848, December 12, 1850, May 27, 1852, February 10, 1853; *Jamaica Almanack 1845*, Returns of Proprietors, 31-35; *Falmouth Post*, August 28, 1849; *Morning Journal*, September 3, 1849.

51. IRO, Register of Baptisms, St John, 1751-1825; George Price, 2, 3; *Morning Journal*, September 3, 1849.

52. Holt, 109, 110; *Morning Journal*, September 3 & 13, 1849; *Falmouth Post*, September 14, 1849.

53. JAr, 1B/11/23/19, House of Assembly Poll Book 1844-1866, fols. 52, 53; *Morning Journal*, September 3 & 13, 1849; *Falmouth Post*, September

14, 1849.
54. CO 137/322, Barkly to Newcastle, May 26, 1854, report of S.M. Bell.
55. CO 137/284, Elgin to Stanley, September 2, 1845, report of S. M. Bell; *Land Deeds*, Liber 915, fol. 28; *Jamaica Gazette*, January 27,1848, December 22, 1853, January 26, 1854, April 5 & June 7, 1855, April 3, 1856, April 4, 1861; Hall, 25, 26.
56. CO 137/339, Darling to Lytton, October 25, 1858, report of S. M. Bell; CO 137/346, Darling to Newcastle, September 8, 1859, report of S.M. Bell; Robertson, 16, 17; *Jamaica Tribune*, July 7, 1860.
57. *Land Deeds*, Liber 840, fol. 78; Liber 916, fol. 211; *Jamaica Gazette*, June 28, 1849; *Falmouth Post*, July 24, 1849. Although Heuman claims that Peter Harrison was white, marriage records confirm his coloured status (see Heuman, *Between Black and White*, 140 & JAr, 1B/11/8/3/ 35, Register of Marriages, St Dorothy 1826-43, fol. 3).
58. *Falmouth Post*, July 18 & 24, 1849; *Jamaica Almanack 1845*, Returns of Proprietors, 4, 5, 18, 19.
59. JAr, 1B/11/23/19, House of Assembly Poll Book 1844-66, fols. 52, 53; JAr, 1B/11/8/3/22, 29 & 35, Register of Baptisms and Marriages, St Dorothy, 1826-35; *Land Deeds*, Liber 827, fol. 19; Liber 838, fol. 109; Liber 840, fols. 74, 75; Liber 844, fol. 165; Liber 854, fols. 47, 48, 113, 114, 115; Liber 856, fol. 213; Liber 888, fol. 211; Liber 907, fol. 9.
60. JAr, 1B/11/23/19, House of Assembly Poll Book 1844-66, fols. 11-13, 104-05, 120-21, 149-50; Robertson, 16, 17; Holt, 258.
61. *Morning Journal*, July 9 & 19, 1849. For incorrect suggestions that Salome ran on the Town Party ticket in 1849 see Heuman, *Between Black and White*, 124 & Holt, 229.
62. *Morning Journal*, July 9 & 19, 1849; Heuman, *Between Black and White*, 61. Edward Jordan later scolded Gordon for being a 'gallant coward' who had run 'away from his post in the hour of danger' in St Thomas-in-the-Vale in 1849 (see *Colonial Standard and Jamaica Despatch*, November 18, 1851).
63. *Morning Journal,* July 9, 19 & August 7, 1849. Lovesay voted for Edward Jordan in 1833 when he failed to win a seat in St Thomas-in-the-Vale. The coloured leadership in St Dorothy nominated Dollar for a seat in St Dorothy in 1854 (see JAr, 1B/11/23/19, House of Assembly Poll Book 1803-43, fols. 118, 119, and *Morning Journal*, September 25, 1854).
64. CO 137/323, Barkly to Newcastle, May 26, 1854; Thomas Harvey and William Brewin, *Jamaica in 1866* (London: A. W. Bennett, 1866), 8-9; Jacob Andrade, *A Record of the Jews in Jamaica form the English Conquest to the Present Time* (Kingston: The Jamaica Times Ltd., 1941), 30; *Daily Advertiser,* February 13, 1854.
65. JAr, 1B/11/23/19, House of Assembly Poll Book 1844-1866, fols. 72-74; NLJ, Map St T. 203, Plan of Palmetto Valley and Phillipsburgh, St

Thomas-in-the-Vale, 1842; *Land Deeds*, Liber 816, fol. 70; Liber 821, fols. 6, 9; Liber 823, fol. 204; Liber 824, fols. 34, 35; Liber 826, fols. 69, 142; Liber 828, fol. 195; Liber 829, fols. 123, 224; Liber 831, fols. 35, 179; Liber 834, fol. 98; Liber 835, fol. 48; Liber 836, fol. 177; Liber 837, fol. 239; Liber 839, fol. 114; Liber 840, fol. 24; Liber 842, fols. 130, 180; Liber 843, fols. 42, 196; Liber 847, fol. 109; Liber 848, fol. 40; Liber 850, fols. 3, 20; Liber 852, fol. 55; Liber 858, fols. 24, 25; Liber 864, fols. 54, 216; Liber 869, fol. 126; Liber 871, fol. 172; Liber 902, fol. 44; Liber 937, fol. 174, and Liber 940, fol. 2. The results of the poll were: Salome (137), Chisholm (78), Barrow (56), McDermott (33), Lovesay (32), and Dollar (3).

66. Glen Phillips, 'The Stirrings of the Mercantile Community in the British West Indies Immediately After Emancipation,' *Journal of Caribbean History*, 23.1 (1989): 75, 88; Hall, 23-26, 209-12, 234-35; Holt, 223.

67. CO 137/303, Charles Grey to Earl Grey, October 8, 1849.

68. Roy Augier, 'Before and After 1865,' *New World Quarterly*, 2.2 (1966): 21-40; Holt, 254-58.

CHAPTER

The Bridgetown Riot of 1872
Henderson Carter

Introduction

Barbadian historiography has benefited immensely from the incisive
scholarship of Professor W.K. Marshall in his pursuit to locate, identify
and explain the origins of the village movement in the nineteenth and
twentieth centuries. Recently, however, Marshall has urged young scholars to
conduct a systematic enquiry into the social dynamics of these village
communities in an effort to grasp the dominant ideas that permeated the
village, the nature of village life, and the factors which created cohesion,
solidarity and conflict within those communities. This essay seeks to address
some of these social dynamics, through the medium of a riot which occurred
in Bridgetown in 1872.

Historians have acknowledged the fact that the contribution of the 'crowd'
on the historical canvas to legislative and social reform has been largely muted
in the official records. The crowd never wrote, were hardly interviewed, their
views were hardly recorded by travel writers, and they never had the
opportunity to make speeches in a parliamentary setting. Through their actions,
however, it is reasonable to consider them as active participants on the socio-
political stage, and hence it is useful to use these episodes as barometers for
the creation of a better understanding of those who lived in urban villages in
Barbados in the nineteenth century.

This essay, therefore, has three main objectives: first, to describe a riot
which occurred in October 1872 in Bridgetown; second, to locate and discuss
the causes of the riot in the context of the poverty-stricken conditions which
existed and workers' views of moral economy; and third, to analyze the
significance of the riot in terms of the degree of threat that it posed to the
military authorities as well as its potential for the stimulation of socio-economic
changes. In so doing, the paper questions the validity of the nineteenth-century
Barbadian stereotypical image of docility and multi-racial harmony. At the
same time, it posits the view that rural dwellers developed notions of social

justice and were willing to launch a struggle in the pursuit of that goal.

In October 1872, the *Cuban*, a steamer belonging to the West Indies Steam Packet Company, on a journey from Liverpool to Colon, South America, arrived in Barbados in a stricken state. The steamer had broken a shaft about three miles off Barbados but the crew managed to bring it to the shallow waters of Nedham Point, where it sank with a cargo valued at £180,000.[1] The shaft was subsequently repaired, and the ship pumped out and taken to the usual anchorage on the wharf. The police created a guard post and the cargo, consisting mainly of textiles, was sold on the wharf site by the consignees, Messrs DaCosta & Co.

At about midday, October 28, 1872, an impatient and exasperated crowd which had assembled began their assault on the policeman on guard duty by throwing stones and broken bottles at him. By mid-afternoon John Clements, inspector-general of police, had requested 16 more men to be stationed on the wharf to maintain law and order, and by 5:00 p.m. the police had succeeded in clearing the wharf and blocking alleys leading to it. Feeling confident that the situation was under control, Clements returned home, only to receive the distressing news that a fresh and more vicious assault was being launched on his men. The Police Guard House was attacked, several windows were broken, and several police officers were injured.[2]

Police Magistrate Fleming noted that on hearing of a serious disturbance shortly after 7:00 p.m., he rode to the wharf in an attempt to clear the area. His buggy was pelted with two large stones, narrowly missing him and his son. According to Fleming, Officer Dean was struck by a 'large piece of brick, causing him to reel on his saddle and fall forward on his horse's neck, and that after being in the streets fully for over two hours, and being thoroughly worn out, I got out of the crowd, and went home.'[3] Not only did the crowd attack the civil law-enforcement authorities, but they also extended this assault to the properties of the mercantile establishment. The Ice House, the Colonnade, Sir John Arnott's store, Mr Drum's and Mr Girdwood's store were all broken, entered and looted, and street lamps on the wharf and Broad Street were also broken.[4]

After Clements realised that the police stationed on the wharf had been reduced to 17 and the city was in grave danger, he immediately rode to Government House, alerting Governor Rawson of the urgency of the situation. There he requested the use of the troops to restore law and order. Rawson did not hesitate, and immediately sent a letter to Colonel Chesney, the military commander, by Clements.[5]

At around 9.45 p.m., a detachment of 20 gunners of the Royal Artillery and two companies of the 29th Regiment were dispatched from the garrison at St Ann's and after encountering some stone throwing, succeeded in dispersing the crowd by the medium of a bayonet charge. By 1.40 a.m., Tuesday, October 29, the situation was brought under control and several arrests were made.

While the detachment of artillery returned to base, some 30 soldiers spent the night at Central Police Station, while the others remained at the scene of the riots until dawn, when they were marched back to the fort.[6]

The rioting, however, had only temporarily ceased. Later that day, the rioters renewed their efforts to pillage and destroy. A huge crowd, again assembled on the wharf, succeeded in pillaging goods and making threatening remarks to the merchants and their clerks, who had armed themselves the night before in an effort to contain the assault on business houses in the city. By 1.45 p.m. the plundering had ceased as the police and special constables stood guard. However, Governor Rawson took no chances, and requested the presence of the troops for the protection of the wharf and its immediate environs during the night.[7]

Socio-economic conditions contributing to the riots

The riot can be located within the depressed social and economic situation that characterised the Barbadian working people in the nineteenth century. Attempts by the planter-government to dominate and control the freedmen through political exclusion, vagrancy and contract legislation and anti-emigration regulations led to a negation of the freedom given in 1838. As a direct consequence of this, conditions for workers in terms of housing, health care, working conditions and education were far from satisfactory. While low sugar prices, drought and food shortage usually provided fertile conditions for unrest, these factors were definitely not present in 1872. Planters were once again receiving relatively good sugar prices and the absence of drought enabled both the planter and the small farmer to increase their production of provision crops.[8]

However, low wages, seasonal employment, unemployment and unequal distribution of wealth remained integral features of the socio-economic landscape for the working people. Conditions were more acute in the town. The steady trek of people from the rural areas in search of employment and better conditions created much overcrowding there. Many artisans and labourers roamed the streets looking for odd jobs, creating a huge class of urban folk existing in poverty-stricken conditions. Thus, in 1875, a Commission on Poor Relief noted that 'the gravitation of idlers to the city,' and scores of migrants who had left after 1863 returned home only to add pressure to the already volatile situation.[9] Even one Demerara newspaper, the *Creole*, drew reference to this poverty-stricken condition:

> News may reach us at any moment that quiet is restored and the whole affair will probably be put down to the accidental excitement produced by the wreck.... The present condition of the Barbados peasantry is, we learn on the best authority, truly deplorable. With little work on the estates provisions at

a ruinously high price, and the cost of living daily increasing, there are very many in that little Island, who fight a daily fight with starvation.[10]

Such a socio-economic predicament provided the general environment for the origin of upheavals in Barbados and the Caribbean. The evidence suggests, however, that poor conditions alone do not necessarily result in protest action and may exist for many years without concerted action. Political sociologists have argued that many revolts are triggered by certain events which may range from the arrest of a leader, police interference or perceived injustice, thereby placing the deplorable socio-economic conditions into a specific and reinforced context. In 1872, events associated with a wreck provided the triggering effect.

The argument emanating from the planter-merchant elite and the Barbadian middle class was that the excitement created by this sale triggered the upheaval which was carried out by the wayward and lawless elements in the city. According to the *Times*, the riot was 'caused by the light-fingered gentry, from whom the large packages and cases exposed on the coal wharf proved too strong a temptation.'[11] The *Globe* echoed the same sentiment pointing out:

> While the sale was going on, longing eyes and itching fingers were multiplying and ranging freely among the packages on the wharf. Thieving hands began to find occupation and it was soon manifest that darkness alone was wanted for the enactment of the bad old rule 'that they should take who have the power, and they should keep who can.'[12]

It is reasonable to suggest that some workers were eager to plunder some of the salvaged goods, but the evidence shows that it was not only this eagerness that triggered the upheaval. What precipitated the upheaval was the fact that the salvaged goods were sold to merchants and traders only. According to Governor Rawson, the police kept the mob out of the small yard in which the sales were held, thereby restricting the economic activity of workers, mainly women, who were eager to obtain good bargains.[13]

Such restrictions were further reinforced by workers' notion of moral economy. Workers had long held the view that wrecks were acts of God and that the goods salvaged from them could be plundered freely. In fact, for eighteenth-century England, E.P Thompson argues that workers did not necessarily respond when a bad harvest or a downturn in trade occurred. Rather, he suggests, they developed a notion of what was right or fair and the obligations of social groups within the context of the rural economy.[14] In 1863 those in Barbados exhibited this perception of moral economy and in 1872, according to Governor Rawson, they expressed the notion that 'Providence had sent them this windfall and that they ought not to be deprived of it by the Merchants and tradesmen purchasing the goods at high and speculative prices.'[15] Such an ideological position explains why some of the working people remained on the wharf the entire day (Monday, October 28) and walked away with some of the spoils in a nonchalant manner.

Challenge to law enforcement agencies

The treatment accorded by historian Claude Levy to this riot would tend to suggest that it was not a serious affair. We suggest, however, that in terms of the conflict with the authorities, the large number of participants and the amount of debate it generated, the riot must be taken as an important event which deserves special note within Barbadian historiography.[16] The evidence suggests that the riot manifested itself in a most brutal attack on the law-enforcement authorities. Thirteen police officers received serious injuries. Superintendent Sergeant DeRocha was knocked from his horse, sustaining injuries to the right arm, left shoulder and right side. Corporal Dash, of District A, received two severe wounds to the head and several blows about the body. Several days after the riot, Dash's condition was said to be 'poorly,' having received the most injuries. Eleven other officers were also admitted to hospital with injuries, mainly to the head, and several other men received minor injuries that did not immobilise them. In addition, five privates from the detachment of troops sent out from St Ann's fort sustained minor injuries.[17] Table 15.1 illustrates the nature of the attacks on the police.

Table 15.1:
Police officers injured during the 1872 riot

OFFICER	INJURIES
Sup. Sergeant Da Rocha	Knocked off horse, right arm injured, blow on left shoulder, right side injured
Corporal Dash	Two severe wounds on head, several blows about body
Corporal Corbin	Wound on forehead and other blows
Officer Goddard	Injury to head and body
Officer Bushel	Injury to face and body
Officer Goodridge	Injury to head and body
Officer Craigwell	Injury to hip
Officer Peirrepoint	Injury to body and knee
Officer Pollard	Wound on the face and ear
Officer Warner	Blow and bruised face
Officer Edghill	Injury to arm
Officer Johnson	Several blows and contusions about body
Officer Deane	Blows to the head and injury to stomach

Source: CO 28/217, Report of John Clements, Inspector General of Police, October 31, 1872.

There was also one civilian death. On the night of Monday, October 28, 1872, Isaac Barrow, a young man of 18 years, was shot in the chest in Trafalgar Square. Both the *Times* and the *Agricultural Reporter* pointed out that sounds of gunfire were heard along the wharf and Trafalgar Square on Monday, 28. The evidence suggests that when the rioting started, clerks from Girdwood and Company and Sir John Arnott's store armed themselves to stave off an assault on the warehouses.[18] It is not unlikely that Barrow, probably a rioter, was shot by one of these clerks. This shooting and the fact that no one was charged brought a stream of criticism from the *Times*. In condemning the action of the clerks, the paper stated:

> We find no word denouncing the illegal conduct of the person that deliberately discharged a pistol in the crowd on Monday night, mortally wounding a boy who has since died. Unless it be proved that the person, whose name has been freely banded about town acted purely in self defence, he is simply a volunteer in the eyes of the law.[19]

In addition to Barrow's death, Bayne, a clerk at DaCosta's, was shot in the back by another clerk, Mr Conch, while battling to protect the property of their employer. No charges were pressed by Bayne, but it is clear that the clerks were drawn into the struggle against the working people.[20]

The objectives of the rioters have always been a major theme of debate. The official view emanating from the governor was that no material hardship existed in the island to precipitate such pillage, and, more important, that there was an 'absence of combination' and 'a total absence of class feeling.' This was the normal position that governors in Barbados took. To have done otherwise would have been to admit that there was some degree of class conflict. Yet, the empirical data suggest that this was a conflict in which the workers were pitted against the ruling elite and their supporters in the quest for social justice.

It would seem, therefore, that the rioters aimed to obtain revenge on the police and the merchants for past and present wrongs done to them. The police, charged with the responsibility of securing the area where the sale was being made, were attacked. It was the first time since emancipation that the police were subjected to such a serious assault. On the other hand, the mercantile body, who most probably suggested that the working people be excluded from the sale, and who were the principal beneficiaries of the bargains, also came under attack. Their stores were looted and the clerks who tried to defend the property were attacked. Thus, the breaking of street lamps and the smashing of show windows and doors along Broad Street were not merely diversionary tactics designed to lure the police away from the wharf, but punitive measures aimed at exacting revenge for perceived injustices. It is certainly reasonable to infer that the pattern of the riot is indicative of some degree of class conflict.

We have so far examined the actions and motives of the rioters, but it is necessary at this juncture to analyse what George Rude calls the 'faces in the crowd' in order to understand the composition of the crowd. First, the crowd was estimated by the inspector-general of police and several newspapers at about 2,000.[21] This large number, drawn mainly from the ranks of the working people, comprised labourers, artisans, hucksters, the unemployed and children. While this was essentially an urban riot, with the urban folk comprising the majority of the rioters, there is some evidence to suggest that the rural folk from St Philip and Christ Church spearheaded the attack on the police and business houses. According to the *Times*, 'Towards the afternoon a great crowd mustered and showed signs of disorder, and about 7 o'clock in the evening large numbers of "roughs" assembled on the spot, in the vicinity of the goods, evidently bent on mischief.'[22]

Governor Rawson, in a despatch to the secretary of state, pointed out that the merchants in the city had great apprehension. As Rawson explained, 'When after dark the roughs who have come in from St Philip and Christ Church, where they have been accustomed to pillage wrecked vessels, find that there is none of the cargo exposed and open to their attacks, [they] may attempt to force those warehouses in which the goods already landed and sold are stored.'[23]

The *Globe* declared with considerable conviction that 'amphibious people' from St Philip and Christ Church formed the spearhead of the assault and reported that 'we have authority for stating that some of the champion appropriators from St Philip found their way to Bridgetown on Monday and communicated the element of dogged daring to the new and erring spirit of plunder.'[24] Although the rural folk might have given impetus to the attack on the authorities, the newspaper article does imply that the urban folk were incapable of carrying out such an assault by themselves. However, the evidence suggests that the urban folk had begun to plunder the goods from the wharf even before the 'roughs' arrived and that they returned the following morning to resume their assault.

Women, who had been active participants in slave revolts and protest movements after slavery, played a significant role. They assembled in large numbers and participated in the stone throwing and plundering. Many of them might have been attracted to the wharf site by the many broken packages of muslin dresses, shirts and handkerchiefs, and would have been obviously disappointed at being prohibited from participating in the sale.

In the House of Assembly, Mr Greaves, while speaking on the Police Bill, charged that the wharf women were the first to initiate the riot and called for the prohibition of the loitering of women on the wharf. According to the *Agricultural Reporter*, 'By 1 p.m. upwards of a thousand women were assembled and these began to be very noisy and riotous, shouting and singing, half-stripping themselves and snatching articles from broken packages.'[25] The

Agricultural Reporter, probably influenced by sexist bias, went on to describe the participation of the women on October 29:

> It is marvelous to witness the courage and pertinacity with which dainty ladies, who ordinarily [would] be shocked by the rude contact of the common herd, will elbow their way through odoriferous crowds, or their dexterity in crossing such an abyss as the stanchion over the molasses cistern of a sugar store, or to see their activity as displayed in ascending the step-ladder of some lift converted for the entry into a salesroom.[26]

Children, too, between the ages of nine and 13 years, played an active role in the riots, assisting in the transportation of the plundered articles. Indeed, the police reports reveal that over 40 per cent of the rioters arrested and charged were women and children, showing the extent of their participation in the struggle.[27]

The intervention and continued presence of the military effected a rather swift suppression of the riot and probably prevented the extension of the upheaval to the country districts. It is noteworthy that this event occurred only six years after the Colonial Office had pressured the local legislatures into developing their own para-military units for internal defence, as Britain considered the withdrawal of its standing army from the region.[28]

Yet, the use of the volunteers in the suppression of the riot was fraught with many difficulties. After the first day of rioting Governor Rawson requested that the volunteers assist the police in maintaining law and order. Over 300 merchants and clerks offered themselves for duty as special constables, but when Rawson announced that they would be prohibited from carrying firearms, many declined to be enlisted, reducing the number to about 90.[29] With lack of full support from the merchants and clerks, Rawson was constrained to place the 29th Regiment at the Central Police Station, where they could be quickly deployed to suppress any disturbance in the city during the night.[30]

It is clear that mercantile establishments were bent on swift and telling justice and declined to offer full protection unless fully armed. Governor Rawson was no doubt cognisant of the 'gun-play,' which resulted in the shooting of one man and was determined not to allow the situation to escalate into a 'blood-letting' scenario. He had the full support of the attorney-general and the commander of the troops, Colonel Chesney, who insisted that his men would not be used as sentries, merely protecting private property.[31] Thus, the evidence suggests that the major problem in the suppression exercise was the attitude of the mercantile body. The police and the military acted with great restraint, although they came under a serious attack from the rioters.

Governor Rawson decided to meet with the merchants on Tuesday, October 29, and urged them to remove all the goods from the wharf and not to land any more broken packages. This was, as he put it, 'to remove the temptation to plunder and pillage.'[32] On November 1 he informed the Assembly of the seriousness of the riot that had now all but subsided and renewed his call for an increase in the size of the police force to prevent similar disturbances in future. Lord Kimberly, secretary of state for the colonies, approved of Rawson's measures to maintain law and order and expressed great satisfaction with the conduct of the police.[33]

When order was restored, over 100 persons had been arrested. Forty-one were convicted, reprimanded and discharged, five were placed on a six-month bond to keep the peace, one man was fined 15 shillings for discharging a pistol, 10 boys were flogged and discharged, and 52 were remanded for trial.[34] At the court hearings held in December 1872 several men were sentenced to imprisonment. For instance, Samuel Sandiford, Charles Walcott, James Williams, William Jordan, John Gaskin, Alexander Holder and Henry Boyce were convicted for their participation in the riot and each received a 12-month prison sentence with hard labour.[35]

While the upheaval was a two-day affair and was suppressed by the prompt intervention of the military, it was dismissed by some as frivolous, merely the work of the idle and reckless. Yet, the empirical data suggest that this particular upheaval constituted a serious breakdown of law and order in the island's main port town. While the ruling elite had always endeavoured to trivialise such workers' actions, they were nevertheless compelled to admit that the 1872 upheaval was indeed serious. Police magistrate, C.W. Fleming, in his report to Governor Rawson, observed that 'a serious disturbance between the people and the officers had taken place.'[36]

The *Agricultural Reporter*, the conservative mouth piece of the planter-elite, also recognised the seriousness of the event when it stated that 'it has become our painful duty to record that which can only be regarded as a public disaster of the gravest character.'[37] More important, for the first time in the post-slavery era the police force had been stretched to the limit, their guard-post wrecked, several officers seriously injured, and Bridgetown for a brief period left without an effective civil law enforcement agency. This situation, in itself, confirms the seriousness of the upheaval, as riots, when unchecked, had often spread far beyond the area of formation, evolving into large-scale movements. The stark poverty and deprivation in the country would have provided fertile conditions for the seed of unrest to germinate and flourish.

The 1872 riot, unlike other upheavals in the post-slavery epoch, not only necessitated the urgent request for the military's presence but also the active involvement of a strong military unit. That the imperial troops had to be used in active combat and patrol points vividly to an upheaval of serious proportions.

The reaction of the middle class and the ruling elite reveals their perception of the riot as well as procedures to deal with future upheavals. The *Times* and the *Globe* echoed middle class sentiments on the futility of the riot, condemning the action of the rioters. The *Times*, in particular, lashed out at the working people who 'were not satisfied to obtain articles of merely nominal prices, but rendered the Wharf and Broad Street the scene of most disgraceful riots and disturbances.'[38]

The *Globe* also pursued the punitive trajectory, declaring, 'We have no sympathy with thieves, we hold the circumstances to be a serious aggravation and intensifying of the guilt.'[39] The *Agricultural Reporter*, deeming the upheaval 'a public disaster of the gravest character,' denounced the workers for resorting to violence and lawlessness without any grievances and merely for the sake of plunder.[40] It is noteworthy that because of the somewhat less conservative ideological position of the middle class, it could not sanction the use of violence to achieve change. The ruling elite, however, from its conservative position not only deplored the use of violence, but went a step further to underscore the absence of workers' grievances.

Much of the coverage given by the media to the riot dealt with aspects of its suppression, which included the conduct of the volunteers, the performance of the police and the punitive measures taken by the ruling elite. The *Times*, especially, was extremely critical of the 'leniency' shown towards the rioters by the law enforcement agencies. The paper pointed to the 'impunity with which the rioters were permitted to beat and stone the police which simply encouraged them to recommence their work of rapine with redoubled energy and increased audacity.'[41] In addition, it charged that fines ranging from one cent to 10 shillings were imposed, instead of two months' hard labour. As a deterrent, the paper called for 'a scratch from the cat, or a lengthened term of imprisonment with hard labour.'[42]

But perhaps the harshest press criticism of the police came from an editorial in the *Agricultural Reporter*, which spoke of the 'utter incompetency of the police force, which had completely broken down and proved itself untrustworthy in any emergency.' Thus, the editorial concluded that '[in] the prolonged struggle for mastery between mob and police, the mob won.'[43] However, it is possible that what seemed like ineptitude could have been deliberate class solidarity by black police officers, a feature which was certainly evident during the 1876 rebellion.

The *Globe* also criticised the performance of the police during the riot, but directed much of its remarks towards the conduct of the merchants and their clerks. Several long editorials and letters denounced 'the parading of firearms,' pointing to the potential dangers of such activity as well as its illegality.[44] The *Globe* was supported by the *Times* which argued that the troops themselves did not have the authority to fire upon the crowd, and charged that unauthorised and irresponsible individuals must not be permitted to perambulate the streets and discharge firearms with impunity.[45] As one would have expected, the *Agricultural Reporter* took an entirely different stance and lauded the clerks at the Broad Street stores for protecting the properties. The paper spoke of 'the credible conduct of the Broad Street clerks who turned out in force, ably assisting the police, and defending the property of their employers.'[46]

The ruling elite held fast to its conservative ideological position on what should be done to deal with riots. Since this position emanated from the view that the violence was without justification and motivated by greed and excitement, efforts to improve policing and punitive measures were naturally devised. The first measure was the re-introduction of the Flogging Bill of 1863. The 1872 Bill was an identical piece of legislation, specifying incarceration and a flogging for males. This time, however, the Bill was to be a permanent feature on the statute books. The auditor-general, while speaking on the Bill, admitted to the severity of the punishment (39 lashes for males with no less that three months' hard labour), but pointed to the desirability of such a law to curtail riotous conduct.[47]

The measure found some support in the *Times* editorial of November 15, 1872 which stated, 'These reckless spirits don't care a rush for the gaol. Many of them are quite familiar with its precincts. But they wince at the idea of the cat and stand in great dread of that animal as a rat does.'[48] On the other hand, the *Globe* asserted that the Bill was an unnecessary piece of legislation, which would only endanger the reputation of the colony. Thus, one *Globe* editorial stated, 'In the name of the character of the country — where life always has been secure and property sacred, we protest against panic legislation being resorted to, giving strangers an idea that something hideous has occurred, calculated to endanger our peace, threatening the security of property, and jeopardising the credit of the colony.'[49]

While the 'Flogging Bill' passed the legislature with great ease, another, the Police Bill, requesting an addition of 50 men to the force, was debated with much acrimony in the Assembly. Mr Spencer, who brought the Bill to the floor of the House, argued that the force was woefully inadequate and that on the night of Monday, October 28, 'only six men were left in the Barracks.'[50] He castigated the planters for withdrawing their support because they had very little at stake in the town. On the other hand, the planters in the Assembly deplored the move to augment the police force. One of them, Mr Gill, charged that the problem with the force was not inadequate manpower, but that the policemen were not 'disciplined enough and efficient.'[51] Gill added that some of the officers performing postal duties could be brought back into active service. H. Pilgrim also echoed Gill's sentiments, stating that 'the inefficiency of the force was in large measure due to the laxity of discipline.'[52]

Concessions

The riot forced the ruling elite, for the second time in nine years, to re-examine the efficiency of the island's law enforcement agency with a view to upgrading the capability of that agency to respond to crisis situations in an efficient and effective manner. Such is indicative of workers' actions which created sizeable cracks and crevasses in the oppressive sociopolitical control apparatus devised by the ruling elite in the 1830s. More important, what the workers saw as ineffectiveness of the police in Bridgetown generated a feeling of supreme confidence among them and a perception that in an organised assault launched against the ruling elite they could, by sheer numbers, seriously challenge the civil law enforcement authority. Four years later this confidence was transformed into action and the police force was again found wanting.

As a statement of protest against injustice, the riot kept alive the issue of poverty and social injustice on the political agenda in Barbados, stimulating considerable debate in and out of parliament on the plight of the worker and what might be done to remedy such a condition. After denouncing the working people for their misconduct, the *Globe* gave expression to workers' grievances when an editorial observed, '. . . we should fail in our duty to the state and to ourselves as a member of the fourth estate of the realm, if we did not speak with equal plainness of wrong, culminating in crime, on the other side. Thousands of the lower orders are known to be in a state of pinching distress....'[53]

Thus, while the ruling elite sought to strengthen their control mechanisms, it also recognised that some concession had to be offered in order to achieve a measure of social stability. This concession was related to the migration of workers from the colony. As early as November 15, 1872, Governor Rawson urged the Assembly to revive or re-enact the 1864 emigration law, which had become inoperative in 1867. As Rawson explained, 'the circumstances of the present time resemble in some respects those which led to its enactment,' alluding to the 1863 riots and the resultant 1864 Emigration Act.[54] Rawson realised his wish on December 3, 1872, when another Emigration Act was passed by the Assembly. The law focused primarily on regulating emigration from the island in an attempt to deal with some abuses that were detected. The governor was given the power to appoint emigration agents and a superintendent of emigration, thereby pre-empting the possibility of 'fraudulent agents' luring labourers away from the island.[55] This concession allowed hundreds of workers to leave the island, finding employment in St Croix, Antigua, Trinidad and Guyana. The governor saw it as being politically and economically prudent to allow several hundreds to leave the island rather than to risk mass rebellion.

Conclusion

The 1872 Bridgetown riot must be seen, then, as a significant episode in the history of the island. It was a clear statement of protest, which brought workers' conditions to the fore. It placed enormous pressure on the socio-political system, threatening its stability and forcing the ruling elite to make a concession with respect to emigration. This protest clearly refutes and exposes the notion that nineteenth-century Barbadians were docile and acquiescent, and chose to accommodate rather than resist. It tells us as well that the village community, whether urban or rural, exhibited signs of harmony, cohesion and solidarity in order to mobilise for, and implement, such devastating action. Furthermore, the 1872 struggle was not a detached or isolated episode, but rather a link to similar struggles in 1863 and 1876, representing the continuation and intensification of the struggle for justice and socio-economic betterment for the workers.

Notes

1. CO 28/217, Rawson to Kimberley, October 29, 1872.
2. CO 28/217, Police Magistrate Fleming to Rawson, November 4, 1872.
3. Ibid.
4. Editorial of *Times*, October 30, 1872.
5. CO 28/217, Rawson to Kimberley, October 29, 1872.
6. CO 28/217, Report of Inspector Clements, in Rawson to Kimberley, October 29, 1872.
7. CO 28/217, Rawson to Kimberley, October 29, 1872.
8. Henderson Carter, 'Resistance and Protest in Barbados, 1838–1904' (Ph D. thesis, UWI, Cave Hill Campus, 2000), 24–90.
9. Report of Commission on Poor Relief, 1875–1877 (Bridgetown, 1878) 10–27.
10. *Creole*, October 30, 1872, reprinted in *Globe*, November 11, 1872.
11. *Times*, October 30, 1872.
12. Editorial of *Globe*, October 31, 1872.
13. CO 28/217, Rawson to Kimberley, November 7, 1872.
14. E. P. Thompson, 'The Moral Economy of the English Crowd in the Eighteenth Century,' *Past and Present*, 50 (1971): 71–76.
15. CO 28/217, Rawson to Kimberley, October 30, 1872. The 1863 (June) riots started in St Philip after the police had tried to prevent the looting of the *Confederate* schooner. Rioting quickly spread to the parishes of Christ Church, St George and St Thomas, where potato fields were raided. By early September, the police had brought the spate of rioting under control.
16. Claude Levy, *Emancipation, Sugar and Federalism: Barbados and the West Indies, 1838- 1876* (Gainesville: Florida University Press, 1980), 134.
17. CO 28/217, Report of John Clements, in Rawson to Kimberley, October 24, 1872.
18. Editorial of *Times*, October 30, 1872.
19. *Ibid.*
20. CO 28/217, Clements to Rawson, enclosed in Rawson to Kimberley, November 7, 1872.

21. CO 28/217, Clements to Rawson, enclosed in Rawson to Kimberley, October 29, 1872.
22. Editorial of *Times*, October 30, 1872.
23. CO 28/217, Rawson to Kimberley, October 29, 1872.
24. *Globe*, October 30, 1872; CO 28/217, Report of Inspector Clements, in Rawson to Kimberley, October 29, 1872.
25. *Agricultural Reporter*, October 29, 1872; CO 28/217, Rawson to Kimberley, October 29, 1872.
26. *Agricultural Reporter*, October 29, 1872; Report of Commission on Poor Relief, 1875, 10–27.
27. CO 28/217, Report of John Clements to Governor, enclosed in Kimberley to Rawson, November 7, 1872.
28. BDA, Carnavon to Walker, August 4, 1866, in Minutes of the Barbadian Assembly, 1866.
29. CO 28/217, Rawson to Kimberley, November 7, 1872.
30. CO 28/217, Rawson to Kimberley, October 29, 1872.
31. CO 28/217, Col. Chesney to Rawson, enclosed in Rawson to Kimberley, November 7, 1872.
32. CO 28/217, Rawson to Kimberley, November 7, 1872.
33. CO 28/217, Kimberley to Rawson, December 2, 1872.
34. *Agricultural Reporter*, November 1, 1872.
35. *Agricultural Reporter*, December 20, 1872.
36. CO 28/217, Fleming to Rawson, November 4, 1872.
37. *Agricultural Reporter*, October 29, 1872.
38. Editorial of *Times*, October 30, 1872.
39. *Globe*, October 31,1872.
40. *Agricultural Reporter*, October 29, 1872.
41. Editorial of *Times*, November 2, 1872.
42. *Ibid*.
43. *Agricultural Reporter*, November 1, 1872. In the 1876 Confederation rebellion, a struggle launched by the workers in support of Governor Hennessy's confederation proposals, police officers from Districts 'A' and 'F' stations defected from the force and rallied to the assistance of the workers. The rebellion was suppressed by the imperial troops after nine days of fighting. For a discussion of this rebellion see Levy, 148–55; Hilary McD. Beckles, *A History of Barbados. From Amerindian Settlement to Nation-State* (Cambridge: Cambridge University Press, 1990), 120–26.
44. *Globe*, October 31, 1872.
45. *Times*, October 30, 1872.
46. *Agricultural Reporter*, October 29, 1872.
47. Assembly's Report, *Times*, November 9, 1872.
48. Editorial of *Times*, November 15, 1872. The Bill was passed at the sitting

of the Assembly on Tuesday, November 5, several days after the riot had been put down. The editorial's statement that the Bill led to the quelling of the riots seems to suggest that there was some degree of pillage even after October 30.

49. *Globe*, November 11, 1872.

50. Assembly's Report, *Times*, November 2, 1872.

51. Assembly's Report, *Times*, November 9, 1872.

52. Assembly's Report, *Times*, November 9, 1872. In this period, policemen were required to perform post office and other duties not related to law enforcement.

53. Editorial of *Globe*, October 31, 1872.

54. BDA, Rawson's address to the Assembly, in Minutes of the Barbadian Assembly, November 15, 1872. The 1863 legislation made provision for labourers to emigrate as a means of relieving the excess population in the island. Over 1,000 labourers took the opportunity and left for St Vincent and Antigua.

55. An Act to Amend the Laws Relating to Emigration from this Island, December 3, 1872, in C.V. Archer and W.K. Furgusson, *Laws of Barbados, Vol. 1, 1667-1895* (Bridgetown: Barbados Advocate,1994), 128.

Section IV

Political And
Socio-cultural Issues

Figure 15:
Caricature of the Amateur Cricketer
&
Figure 16:
The West Indies Cricket Team that toured England in 1906

CHAPTER 16

Challenging the 'Civilising Mission': Cricket as a Field of Socio-cultural Contestation in Jamaica 1865–1920

Brian L. Moore and Michele A. Johnson

Introduction

The period of Jamaican history between 1865 and 1920 is, peculiarly, one of the most understudied in Caribbean historiography. Most historians have focused on the immediate post-emancipation period (up to 1865), the lure of which is the fact that it marked perhaps the greatest transition in Jamaican society before the cataclysmic events of 1938. But significant developments occurred between 1865 and 1920 which helped to shape Jamaican society in a very dramatic manner. Four 'popular' disturbances reminded the colonial authorities that they presided over a potential powder keg: Morant Bay in 1865, Montego Bay in 1902, Kingston in 1912, and anti-Chinese riots in 1918. Consequent on the Morant Bay disturbances, the political face of Jamaica was fundamentally changed with the imposition of Crown rule. The plantation economy, in decline even before emancipation, was almost rendered a death blow by the most prolonged depression that faced British Caribbean sugar from the 1880s to beyond the turn of the twentieth century. Poverty and squalor, both in town and country, were getting worse; and these were aided and abetted by widespread alleged ignorance based on the fact that formal education was still not reaching the majority of the population.[1]

Jamaican society was further 'troubled' by a seemingly rising tide of 'indiscipline and immorality.' Coarse and uncouth behaviour in public spaces appeared to be the norm; people of all classes were generally 'loud and lewd,' some gathering at street corners abusing 'decent, innocent passers-by,' using indecent language, fighting, showing scant regard for, or courtesy to, fellow users of the public thoroughfares,[2] keeping noisy nightly dance parties and balls, wakes, and 'revival' meetings without consideration for their neighbours.[3] Marriage was declining, illegitimacy and prostitution were on the increase; so too were drinking and gambling;[4] while the belief in and practice of obeah remained widespread despite draconian laws sanctioning heavy fines, imprisonment and flogging.[5] The Jamaican people in some respects seemed ungovernable.

But there were some 'positive' signs. The people had taken to Christianity and demonstrated, on occasion, an abundance of piety, charity and goodwill, and there was the hope (though not the promise) that their daily lives would one day attain the exalted standards of Christian Victorian morality. To achieve this, however, it was believed that even more effort by way of religious proselytisation was required, reinforced by a more universalistic system of education that would reach all parts of the island, and an injection of a goodly dose of pure Victorian culture and moral values. As 'good imitators,' the people were expected to learn by example and copy from their 'social betters.' Great importance was thus placed on importing British Christian culture into the island, lock, stock and barrel, with a view to 'civilising' the Jamaican people.

British culture was also alluring to the elite classes who increasingly regarded it as a critical indicator of good social breeding. Furthermore, it fostered a growing cultural affinity with the motherland which was considered highly desirable in the heyday of British imperialism, and was psychologically reassuring in underscoring their belief that they were islands of civilisation in a sea of abominable superstition and immorality. It reinforced their sense of Britishness (they felt as British as their cousins at home), and distinguished them from, and elevated them above, the rest of society. British culture was uplifting, and it also bolstered their innate sense of social superiority.

The post-emancipation nineteenth century, thus, witnessed the wholesale importation of cultural items and symbols from Victorian Britain into colonial Jamaica. This ranged from Christianity and celebration of the monarchy, ideas and values, customs and behaviour, books, magazines and newspapers, dress and furnishings, food items, music and dance, to entertainment and sport. Altogether, this constituted a cultural invasion of unprecedented proportions aimed at reinforcing 'the Britishness of Jamaica,' and anglicising and civilising its people. The message was conveyed by every possible medium, most particularly from the pulpit, in the classroom, and through the press. A broad-ranged campaign was conducted, designed to indoctrinate the working people into believing that British culture was superior and should be embraced with a view to making them better persons and earning them a measure of social respectability.

But this was an uphill task, rendered more arduous by the difficult topography of the island, a grossly inadequate education system, and the poverty and squalor in which many Jamaicans lived. A generation of preaching, cajoling, castigating, and in some instances even coercing the people to conform, had not yielded much by way of 'progress.' Social engineering of this magnitude required the *voluntary* participation of the people. This could best be achieved by means of providing rational and civilising activities that offered some degree of pleasure and enjoyment which the people would willingly adopt and pursue, even in the most remote districts.

This requirement coincided with a sporting revolution among the Victorians in Britain as working people there enjoyed more spare time. Under middle class leadership and guidance, 'rational recreation' was deemed necessary to ensure that 'the lower orders' adopted socially approved leisure activities. In this context, organised sports and other forms of entertainment attained premium importance. Games were standardised by 'social' rules and regulations stipulating not only how they were to be played, but the conduct and dress of the players; and governing bodies were set up under middle class leadership to oversee each sport. Special attention, however, was paid to team sports which emphasised the value of team work and the importance of subordinating individual ambitions for the good of the whole unit. But of all the newly organised sports, the Victorians glorified cricket because they believed that it instilled such ennobling social attributes as discipline, self-sacrifice, fair play and honesty, gentlemanly behaviour and decorum, mental and physical toughness, courage in the face of adversity, respect for oneself, one's team mates and even for one's opponents, and obedience to the authority figure (the umpire). These were considered tremendously important social values of benefit to the local community and wider society at large. Cricket was a civilising and socially refining agent that would train young boys and men to be future leaders and empire-builders, and it was consequently enthusiastically adopted by the leading public schools, elite universities, the churches, and the imperial armed forces. It was the products of these institutions who were mainly responsible for exporting cricket to the British colonies.[6]

Cricket was introduced, adopted and popularised in Jamaica with those very same characteristics. As in England, this 'manly' sport was swathed in many positive qualities purportedly of benefit to young men and to society at large. It not only provided entertainment in an island where that was very limited, but it also encouraged healthy athleticism in the youth. According to the *Falmouth Post*:

> Cricket . . . is a sport which is mostly prized by those who are accustomed to confined and sedentary occupations, — and it is clear that where healthy bodily relaxation is required there is nothing to equal it. Not only does it afford exercise, to hands and legs, but it offers an agreeable mental stimulus in the emulation and competition which are engendered between the rival clubs. . . . There are few prettier sights to be seen at the present time than a well contested game at Cricket in which youth and manhood contend for an honorable mastery under circumstances which promote good fellowship and mental exhilaration, and which neither financially nor morally, leave any bad results behind, however the game may eventuate. Whatever side wins, it wins by virtue of some quality inherent in the players, and this quality whatever it may be is sure to be afterwards imitated and turned to good account by the losing side.[7]

As in Britain, Jamaican cricket was reputed to instil other useful character-uplifting values as well:

> It prevents any addiction to intoxication, because those who wish to excel, must to a certain extent, if not entirely, eschew excess. Its characteristics, too, [are] in the cultivation of a fine healthy and athletic exercise in the open air; a mingling . . . of all grades, the one with the other, combined also with the knowledge that if a man desires to stand well either as an operator in the game or with his superiors, his habits must be regular and steady, and his conduct and demeanour respectful and proper. There is nothing so good as to let a man discover, by mixing with his betters in the common pastimes of his country, with those to whom he ought to look up, that course of conduct which it is best for him to pursue.[8]

In making the presentation of the Senior Cup in 1916, Brigadier-General Leonard Blackden, commanding officer of the imperial troops, praised the game for developing teamwork, and:

> . . . for making the player think of playing for his side rather than for himself. Cricket, in a word, played in the right spirit, is a practical simulator of unselfishness. This community want[s] nothing more than it does men who will think more of their side, or rather of the community, than of their own gain or fame, and if Cricket add[s] to that element it does well by the community. It can, however, only do so if it is played in the right spirit.[9]

No greater testimony of the game's virtues in promoting courage in the face of adversity could be proffered than by an anonymous enthusiast who, despite having his thumb broken by the ball and suffering other injuries, asserted that there was 'no better game to improve a man's physical condition: it strengthens one's sinews too.' Cricket, for him, was a healthy amusement and he gloried in it.[10]

Elite cricket

Although an early form of cricket had been played in the island since the days of slavery,[11] it was not until the 1860s, in the wake of its organisation in England, that it really began to take off in a significant way. The military, who were largely responsible for transmitting the sport in the first place, continued to play a major role in its promotion throughout the nineteenth century. The garrison at Up Park Camp in Kingston was a major centre of sports, especially cricket, and visiting warships also provided sporting teams which played against both the garrison and local clubs. Cricket was, in fact, one of the major sporting events during the annual visits, in February–March, of the British North

American and West Indian Squadron — 'the Fleet.' It was teams of military and naval officers, therefore, which formed the main opponents of the local clubs when they were first formed.[12]

From the 1860s elite 'gentlemen' in various parts of the island began to form cricket clubs. The Kingston Cricket Club was established in 1863,[13] and this was followed by similar elite clubs including Falmouth (1868);[14] St Ann,[15] St James, and Hanover Western Interior Club[16] (ca. 1869); Lucea[17] and Plantain Garden River Club of St Thomas (ca. 1872);[18] Vere and Clarendon, Manchester[19] and Phoenix of Trelawny[20] (ca. 1873); Spanish Town[21] and Westmoreland[22] (ca. 1875); St Elizabeth[23] and Paradise of Westmoreland[24] (ca. 1876); Santa Cruz[25] (ca. 1877); Vere (1878);[26] Kensington,[27] Jamaica Cricket Club[28] and St Andrew[29] (ca. 1879); Old Harbour (ca. 1880);[30] Portland, Linstead, and St Thomas ye Vale (ca. 1880-81);[31] Manchester Union (ca. 1885);[32] Norman of Kingston[33] (ca. 1888) [named after Governor Henry Norman]; Blake of Montego Bay[34] (ca. 1891) [named after Governor Henry Blake]; Port Antonio,[35] Asylum of Kingston,[36] and (in Port Royal) the Victoria[37] and United Service[38] clubs (ca. 1892).

Some elite clubs, however, especially in the rural areas, had difficulty sustaining themselves and were short-lived. This was largely due to their small and exclusive memberships which could not finance and upkeep the expensive facilities and paraphernalia required for cricket — club house, grounds and equipment. Membership fees were high, largely with a view to keeping out 'social undesirables.' Less than five years after its foundation, the Falmouth Cricket Club had become dormant;[39] and while a new club was formed at Port Maria in 1880, it was feared that, like its predecessor, it would not last very much longer than it would take the half dozen members to 'wear out the ball and their patience too. . . .'[40] Cricket also languished in Portland until the 1890s for the same reasons.[41]

But the Kingston Cricket Club (KCC) was to prove enduring, largely because of the staunch support it received from the *crème de la crème* of the island's wealthy elites. Much of the success of cricket in Jamaica was, in fact, attributed by these elites to the KCC which assumed the mantle of the sport's leadership in the colony. This gave its members a decided advantage over the other clubs because visiting military, naval, and international teams automatically played against the KCC; and it also attracted to its membership young cricketers from British public schools and universities.[42] But even this club suffered periods of waning interest, most notably in 1890 when its energetic captain, Lawrence R. Fyfe, left the island for Grenada; and such was its influence on the domestic scene that whither Kingston, so went the entire island.[43] But the club and Jamaican cricket in general survived this decline. Its membership fluctuated, but stood at 222 in 1919, despite the high subscription fees of £2 8s. per annum.[44]

By the late nineteenth century, the KCC was big enough to possess at least three teams which visited different parishes to play against local clubs and promote the sport. The colours of the club were sky blue and white, and the cricket dress was flannel trousers or knickers, shirts and straw hats with turbans of the club's colours. The first practice ground was at McIntyre's Pen, later called Winchester Park. After the sale of that site, the club used the Race Course until 1877, then moved to Paradise Pen, before renting Sabina Park in 1879. In 1894 a new two-storied pavilion was erected at Sabina at a cost of £280.[45]

Although by the early 1890s cricket was regarded by many as 'the national game' of Jamaica, its dominance was never taken for granted. There were periods when interest in it seemed to wane, and other sports/activities, especially football (soccer), athletics, bicycling, yachting and 'volunteering' (military service), drew away its devotees. But the elite press were united in their support of this 'good old English game' that was considered 'one of the branches of genuine sport which are so essential to the physical development of the rising generation.'[46] The *Colonial Standard* argued that there was room enough for the pursuit of all sports in Jamaica without affecting cricket: 'A good Cricketer will, as a rule, prove a good Yachtsman, and a good Volunteer.'[47]

Cricket not only had the unwavering endorsement of the elite newspapers. It was fully supported by 'the wealth, intelligence and respectability' of the island — the colonial establishment, both civil and military (see above), the merchant and planter class, the legal and medical professions, and the churches.[48] The leading members of the elite clubs came almost exclusively from those socio-occupational groups, and some were products of the English public schools where cricket was almost a religion.[49]

Because of its ascribed social significance, cricket in Jamaica received official endorsement. Some elite clubs enjoyed the patronage of the governors and custodes. The KCC, for instance, routinely had the governor as its patron,[50] while Kensington enjoyed the patronage of the commanding officer of the imperial forces in the island.[51] In the rural parishes, Robert Nunes, the custos of Trelawny, and Judge Davidson were founding members of the Falmouth Club in 1868, which also benefited from a large donation by Major-General O'Connor, acting governor, towards its startup funds.[52] Likewise, Custos Gibb was a founding member of the Vere Club in 1878.[53] William Kerr, the custos of St James, donated cricket equipment to the Phoenix Club in Trelawny in 1873, while Colonel Sir Henry E.F. Johnstone, a former commander of the imperial forces, shipped a marquee from England to that club.[54] In 1890, Colonel Ward, the custos of Kingston, donated a handsome cup to the newly formed Norman Club.[55] The fact, too, that at least three cricket clubs during this period were named after governors is testimony to their influence on the sport locally, as well as a yearning on the part of the local elites to identify with symbols of British imperial authority.[56]

The governors further supported the game by attending cricket matches.[57] Governor Sydney Olivier, at the golden jubilee dinner of the KCC in January 1913, stated that although he had not personally taken an active part in local cricket, his interest in the game had never flagged because he realised that there was no more splendid or manly sport than cricket 'for young men and young middle aged men.' He had played the game at school and college, and he thought that he owed his current position as governor to the administrative training he had acquired as captain of his school's second XI, particularly the independence and despotism that it afforded him.[58]

Governor Augustus Hemming, however, went further than most by actually playing the game while in office — much to the annoyance of the 'radical' black newspaper, the *Jamaica Advocate*.[59] So involved was he in promoting the game that he publicly censured Rudyard Kipling, the famous English poet, for referring to cricketers as 'flannelled fools at the wicket':

> We know that the greatness of our Empire, and the success which has attended the Anglo-Saxon race wherever it has spread, are largely due to the manner in which it has always known how to combine a love of sport with the sterner business of life. I say that the words that I have quoted are an insult not only to the sportsmen of Great Britain, but to all our colonies also. Who have been more ready to come forward to offer their hard work and their lives in the service of their country than the cricketers of Great Britain, of Australia, of Canada and of South Africa[?] . . . I do say that the sports and games of Great Britain have, far from doing harm, largely contributed to make our race what it is.[60]

So much a part of the local cricket fraternity was Governor Hemming that he was invited to chair the local committee to select three Jamaican players for consideration for the first West Indies tour of England in 1900.[61] That a British governor should play any role in the selection of a West Indian team did not strike the Jamaican elites as odd. As far as they were concerned, there was, in fact, no distinction between being British and Jamaican/West Indian; and the cricket tour of the 'homeland' would serve to certify their credentials as good loyal British subjects.

As in Britain, cricket in Jamaica was also endorsed by some clergymen who were themselves practitioners of this 'manly' exercise.[62] The English clergy, from among whom many of the influential local priests were recruited, were convinced that 'a vast moral good is to be achieved by a general introduction of the game amongst all classes;'[63] and in Jamaica, clergymen were encouraged to do likewise because cricket seemed capable of promoting godliness along with healthiness — what was referred to in Britain as 'muscular Christianity':

> [There are] many instances where the dissolute have, by being allowed to meet their pastor and the gentlemen of their neighbourhood at Cricket, become excellent members of society. . . . those who instead of attending to religious worship, [and] have on the contrary, spent most, if not the whole, of a Sunday

in a public house, [subsequently] turn from their ways and become regular recipients of religious instruction by a constant occupation of a seat in the Parish Church. . . . men whose dispositions have from untoward circumstances been of a wavering character as between honesty and dishonesty, by being permitted to mingle with those above them in point of wealth and station [have] become fixed in the former. Surely, then, the Clergyman who adopts such a course as shall lead to the accomplishment of these objects does no more than perform one portion of the duty of his sacred calling.[64]

Cricket clubs were thus formed in association with some local churches which organised matches, not only as good character building, community-oriented activities, but as fund-raising entertainments too.[65] And clergymen took the game into the schools for which they were responsible. Thus, as in England and elsewhere in the British Caribbean,[66] cricket became part of the staple educational diet in elite schools such as the Collegiate, the Church of England, and Wolmer's High Schools, St George's College, and Jamaica High School (later Jamaica College) in Kingston; Potsdam in St Elizabeth; York Castle and Walton in St Ann; and Titchfield in Portland. Indeed, it was the old boys of the Collegiate School who established the KCC in 1863, and that school's cricket club was fully integrated into the KCC in 1868, thus serving as a nursery of good young players for the senior club.[67]

As many of the masters in these elite schools were drawn from the ranks of the English public schools and elite universities, they were imbued with the same philosophy towards games as their peers back home. As the *Colonial Standard* put it, 'the education of the body is, in some respects, as necessary as that of the mind, and the trite Latin quotation "*mens sana in corpore sano*" has been appropriately styled "the golden rule of education."'[68] The colonial elites evinced the same desire to have their sons active on the playing fields as if they were attending English public schools; and the playing of cricket, in particular, was fostered by the elite clubs (especially the KCC) which fielded second- and third-elevens to play against the schools.[69]

The early cricket matches in Jamaica, however, were little more than social gatherings which brought together the elites from nearby districts for a day's entertainment and socialisation where they could reaffirm their Britishness. Such entertainment took second place to their economic well being, and so the staging of matches, especially in the rural areas, depended on the state of the sugar crop. In February 1870, for instance, a match planned between the St James and Falmouth clubs was fixed for Monday, the 28th, because it was impossible for the planter community to travel on any other day during crop time. Although that posed problems for their merchant friends who stood to lose business, the latter eventually agreed to close their establishments on that day in order that the match could be played.[70]

Certainly up to the end of the nineteenth century, in the absence of other forms of entertainment, the day fixed for a cricket match, especially in the rural areas, was a red-letter day both for the elites and the masses. The venue would be thronged with people of all classes — 'ladies' splendidly bedecked arriving in carriages, 'gentlemen' on horseback, and the plebeians on foot. Special attention was paid to the accommodation of the ladies to make their attendance pleasant and comfortable. Marquees were erected to provide them with shade from the broiling sun, and their presence was evidently greatly appreciated by the men, not least of all by those who were on the field. These events were usually accompanied by bands of music which played during the breaks. An ample luncheon was generally provided, and some ladies helped to serve refreshments to the players. At the close of play, the teams paid their respects to the ladies who would commend the players for the amusement staged. Then they would leave the gentlemen to partake in a sumptuous dinner, complete with choice viands, wines, brandy and champagnes. These gala dinners were concluded with 'the usual loyal and patriotic toasts,'[71] which further served to reinforce their sense of being British.

The emphasis of these affairs was on sociability and lavish hospitality. It did not matter if a team won or lost; in fact, up to the 1890s it was rare for entire teams to amass more than 100 runs in an innings. Far greater emphasis was placed on playing the game for its own sake, and on the accompanying fun and feasting. What mattered most was the spirit in which they played the game. Cricket was an amateur sport, designed to promote camaraderie and *esprit de corps* among rivals, not competition. Reporting on a match in St Thomas in September 1872, the *Morning Journal* commented:

> The sociability, order, and happiness of every one were characteristic of the good feeling that existed; and there can be no doubt that the Saint Thomas men did everything that was in their power to make their guests happy and comfortable. . . . These gatherings tend to bring out the bright side of human nature; and, perhaps, none so much as Cricket, where all the energies of mind and body are called into play in friendly rivalry.[72]

Middle class Victorian manners and etiquette, however, were not easily inculcated by the Jamaican elites, even though they avidly sought to align themselves culturally more closely to their British 'cousins.' As integral constituents of and nurtured in a creole/plantation social environment characterised by aggression, raucous and coarse behaviour, the elites did not always live up to the demands of their newly adopted ethical code. It is not surprising, therefore, that occasionally disputes arose over cricket. Perhaps the most notable was the occasion of a match between Falmouth and St James in June 1870 over the dismissal of a batsman off an alleged no-ball. It was claimed that the umpire was influenced by a bet he had placed on the game. Out went the noble ideal of unquestioningly obeying the umpire's decision, and a fracas ensued between the two teams involving their supporters in which 'fists were freely made use of in the presence of a large number of Ladies.' It took a platoon of police armed with rifles and fixed bayonets to quell the white mob.[73]

Owing to the generally sunny weather in Jamaica, cricket was played all year round, but more matches were played on holidays, particularly Easter, the queen's birthday, Whitmonday and during the Christmas season. Until virtually the dawn of the twentieth century, there were no formally organised competitions among the clubs, so most matches were informal affairs, so-called 'scratch matches.' This accounts for the unevenness of participation in the sport and the generally poor level of performances until the end of the century. However, once cup competition was started, those matches were scheduled from February to October each year.

Regional and international competition

Jamaica, being so far away from the other British Caribbean colonies, did not play against any of them until 1891 when a Barbadian military team visited the island. In 1896 Jamaica sent a team to Guyana and Barbados but lost all three matches. It was not until 1905 that Jamaica next played against any of its sister West Indian colonies, but again fared badly against Trinidad and Barbados.[74]

Before 1920, therefore, the main exposure Jamaican players had to high-level competitive cricket was through the visits of American and English teams. In 1888 an American team toured the island and played against the Kingston, St Elizabeth and Garrison clubs.[75] In March 1895 an English team led by R. Slade Lucas played in Kingston, Montego Bay and St Ann's Bay. Although the visitors won all their matches, elite Jamaica seemed more bedazzled by their presence than the bad results, and the Legislative Council adjourned for a week 'in order that the members might have an opportunity of witnessing what one hon[ourable] gentleman termed "an event in our lives."'[76] This was regarded as a learning experience from the English masters for which Jamaicans should feel privileged: 'Let the local cricketers go with the idea of copying the best methods, of following the examples of the best men in the visiting team,' pronounced the *Gleaner*.[77]

Jamaica's catastrophic losses in Guyana and Barbados in 1896, however, served as a wake-up call. The *Gleaner* observed that usually the best trained men won at cricket:

> The men who have developed those intellectual and physical qualities, and have those frequent opportunities that lead to a thorough mastery of the principles of the game and their practical application. Our cricketers as a rule, do not take the trouble to train themselves properly. . . . This course

involves a certain amount of self-denial and perseverance but the cricketer who wishes to excel must face the sacrifice or have his efficiency impaired.[78]

Yet, when in 1897 Lord Hawke's English team won all its matches in Jamaica (although they had lost several in the other Caribbean colonies), there was no outcry. Instead, the *Jamaica Post* was content to say that there was no reason for falling into despair: 'On the contrary, every lover of the great English game in this colony owes a debt of gratitude to Mr Priestley [the visiting captain] for having given our players an object lesson in the art of cricket as it ought to be played.'[79] This was colonial sycophancy at its highest; and to compound the grovelling, John S. Brown published a poem/song entitled 'Toast to the English Cricketers' in the *Gleaner* extolling their greatness.[80]

For the elites, their cultural and kinship ties with the mother country were valued much higher than beating their English 'cousins' at cricket; and there was no greater expression of ecstasy than when Lord Hawke proposed that a West Indian team should tour England in 1900. The *Jamaica Daily Telegraph* saw this as a golden opportunity to draw the West Indian colonies and the mother country more closely together: 'This island is a loyal British colony: and we hope it will always remain a loyal British colony. And what we hope for Jamaica, we hope for the rest of the British West Indies.'[81] Moreover, as Aviston Downes has put it, 'The presence of a West Indian team at "home" in England was to be the ultimate symbolic test of the state of West Indian civilisation. What better symbol could one project of social stability and the "natural order of things" in the region than a mixed West Indies team dutifully led by a white captain?'[82]

Elite Jamaican cricket was also characterised by intense insularity. Despite Jamaica's consistently poor record of performance against all regional and international competitors, Jamaicans were aghast that only one Jamaican, M.M. Kerr, was originally selected to tour England with the West Indian team in 1900. The island's cricketing authorities threatened to withdraw if the colony was not accorded more than one representative on the touring team.[83] 'Interested' argued that to accept only one team member was an insult to Jamaica, and would be a humiliating admission of its inferiority to Demerara, Barbados and Trinidad which the island could not concede.[84] The storm only blew over when a Barbadian, H.G.B. Austin, withdrew from the team to go to South Africa, and Jamaica was offered his place.[85]

The fortunes of elitist Jamaican cricket, however, did not change. R.A. Bennett's English team won all its matches in February 1902.[86] This prompted the *Jamaica Times* to observe that 'We faithfully maintained our reputation for losing matches to our English visitors to the very last. . . .'[87] The island fared slightly better in 1905 against Lord Brackley's XI, losing one match rather badly but drawing two;[88] and against a visiting American team from Philadelphia in 1909, Jamaica finally shared honours, winning one match, losing one and drawing the third.[89] This encouraging trend was maintained against a Marylebone Cricket Club team in 1911 when Jamaica tied one match and drew the other two.[90]

The black and coloured challenge

The principal problem with organised cricket in Jamaica before the First World War was that it was *exclusive of* the black masses and *exclusive to* the elites, white and coloured. That base was too small to sustain top-quality performances at the highest level. The Jamaica Cricket Committee needed to expand its range of selection to include the mass of the population, but this was especially difficult in a society riddled with colour and class prejudices. The Jamaican elites were so self-absorbed in their own narrow class-based sporting entertainments that they had failed to notice the emergence of talented black and coloured cricketers even without formal training, proper facilities and equipment. Although quick to criticise other West Indian whites for refusing to play against blacks,[91] they were themselves guilty of at least ignoring the latter.

Black and coloured Jamaicans had long shown an interest in cricket, and were always among the spectators at elite matches. As Moore has observed, 'The Creoles, cognizant of the importance attributed to the sport by the leaders of society, voluntarily sought inclusive participation; for they thought it would confer social respectability on them, if not ultimately social equality.'[92] Black cricket, however, was confined to rough patches of pasture or to the lanes and streets with make-shift equipment because, as Downes has noted for Barbados, notwithstanding elite adherence to the view that the spread of cricket could be beneficial to society at large, they made very little effort to provide recreational spaces for the working classes.[93] When the latter resorted to playing in the streets, this aroused elite hostility. For instance, in 1892 the *Colonial Standard* complained about young 'idlers,' aged between 13 and 16, who were playing 'bat and ball' in Duke Street, and urged the police to stop the practice.[94] As late as November 1910, five lads were arrested in Port Royal for playing cricket in the street.[95]

Once cricket became popular among black Jamaicans, they began to play from childhood. Howard Pyle in 1890 observed black boys playing cricket on the green near the Mandeville parish church and 'for a moment it seemed all like a piece of old-time English life,' except for their black faces in the burning afternoon sun.[96] The Quakers noticed that the boys at Amity Hall always played cricket for their recreation;[97] and Bessie Pullen-Burry too commented that 'swings and cricket seemed most popular amongst the small blacks. . . .'[98]

By the late nineteenth century, virtually every district in the island had its local cricket club, and on Saturdays and public holidays teams could be seen going in different directions, sometimes walking as many as 12–14 miles to play a match. They were accompanied by bands of musicians playing drums, tambourines and fifes made of bamboo. Women fetched beverages and food: water, lemonade, rice and peas, yams, breadfruit, fish, roasted pork, etc. Throughout the game, there was music and dancing, and after play ended, there was feasting and singing. The shaking of hands brought the day to a pleasant end. As a rule, the playing equipment was rudimentary — there were rarely gloves and pads for the batsmen and wicket-keepers.[99] This may have tempted a few to steal equipment in order to play.[100] Those elites who bothered to watch blacks playing cricket, however, recognised their raw talent. S.C. Spencer Smith, for instance, observed that in a match between Fonthill and Hodges estates in 1899, 'The negroes catch and field very well: & bowl well: but it is . . . always a *shy* & a terrific pace.'[101]

Some became so addicted to the game that the black newspaper, the *Jamaica Advocate,* warned that it might induce more harm than good:

> When it is so followed as to become the daily pursuit of scores of our young men we become apprehensive that it is giving rise to habits of idleness, which will, in time, become fixed, and thus produce a type of character which will add very little to our future development, even if it does not become a stumbling-block in the way of our future program [sic].[102]

The need to make organised cricket in Jamaica more inclusive was clearly expressed by M.M. Kerr on his return from the tour of England in 1900. He observed that the two best West Indian players were both black, Charles Augustus Ollivierre of St Vincent and Learie Constantine (Snr) of Trinidad: 'I need hardly say that the blacks were the favourite[s] of the British public.' He added, 'We ought to search for new talent in Jamaica as vigorously as they do in the other colonies, and we ought to encourage black players as they do.... There are, I believe, plenty of black cricketers in Jamaica who would do credit to the Island if they were only given a decent chance.'[103]

That chance would not be forthcoming so long as blacks and coloureds were excluded from the leading cricket clubs such as Kingston. Denied equal opportunity, they were obliged to form their own clubs if they hoped to play the game at a high level. Thus in 1892, well-to-do coloureds established the Melbourne Cricket Club, but they in turn employed the same methods of relatively high membership fees and screening of applicants to deny those who were less well-off and of darker hue from joining. Not to be denied, some black artisans in Kingston decided to form a club of their own, and Lucas Cricket Club (named interestingly enough after R. Slade Lucas, the English cricketer) was born.[104]

At the turn of the century, therefore, just when the elites had taken steps to organise local cricket around the Senior and Junior Cups competitions, the coloureds and blacks were about to enter the fray and test their skills and wills against their 'betters.' Lucas' dominance in the first two decades of the century astounded the elites and shattered the racial myth of black inferiority/white superiority upon which Jamaican society had been premised since the days of slavery. They proved that if literally given a level playing field, they could be better at the imperial game than those who had brought it, and they introduced a new aggressive attitude and determination to win that had been theretofore absent.[105] There could be no pretence at forging camaraderie with the elites because the latter refused to socialise off the field with members of the Lucas team. Clear evidence of this was to be found in the fact that Lucas was the only major sports club not represented at the golden jubilee dinner of the KCC in 1913.[106] Even the Melbourne coloureds were guilty of this kind of social snobbery towards the Lucas players. So there was only one thing left for Lucas — to win.

So successful were they that the elites began to complain about their aggressive attitude and that of their supporters. In 1908 Frank Cundall opined that 'there is perhaps a tendency to placing the winning of a match above the playing the game.'[107] No longer were cricket matches involving Lucas and other working-class teams the quiet and decorous affairs of old. Their matches were marked by raucous barracking and shouting, while drinking and gambling became even more prevalent than before.[108] Violations of the cricket code were frequently manifested in disputes, rows, abusive language, intimidation and fights.[109]

In 1905, the *Gleaner* reported that the captain of Lucas was himself under official investigation for misbehaviour. There were also complaints about a gang of Lucas supporters who:

> attend all the cup matches in which their favourites appear. At times, the conduct of these men is simply disgraceful. Every means short of actual assault or interference is used to intimidate and fluster players on an opposing side: yelling, waving of hats and all kinds of pantomime gestures are indulged in when a catch is about to be made with the hope of distracting the player's attention and frequently the language used is of such a character that were the 'barracker' heard in the public thoroughfare, he would be arrested, taken before a Justice of the Peace and fined.[110]

Nor did the Lucas players adhere steadfastly and unquestioningly to the imported Victorian code of ethics. The umpire might be the supreme authority in the game, but his decisions, if perceived to be wrong, were likely to be vociferously challenged, and he was likely to be subjected to abuse and harassment.[111] For instance, in 1905 a young Lucas cricketer reportedly made use of very 'unbecoming language to one of the umpires;'[112] and in 1914, J. Nelson Barclay, an umpire, complained about the abuse often heaped on his kind by people as a result of their having lost bets on matches.[113] This sort of (mis-)conduct prompted the *Jamaica Times* to plead that:

> It is essential in sport that when the game goes against us we take it like men, and that the person and decision of the umpire be regarded there with the respect and obedience given in other departments to the rulings of a judge. Unless that wholesome view is resolutely upheld sport will surely become a rottenness and abomination.[114]

Occasionally disagreements on the field of play had to be resolved in the courts of law. The elites lamented these developments. The *Gleaner* opined that if trivial disputes on the cricket field were dragged into the law courts, it would not be good for cricket in Jamaica: 'Now, this sort of thing is not cricket. It is not playing the game fairly. . . . Let us have the great national game played fairly and squarely or not at all. We cannot afford to have it thus brought into disrepute.'[115]

If elite players had, as we have seen, occasionally broken the game's code of conduct, this was more the norm with the members of Lucas and other lower-class clubs who constantly felt obliged, given their accustomed underprivileged position in society, to challenge the stifling dominant ethos and to fight for what they felt was justly theirs. The 'gentleman's' world of cricket was being turned on its head. It was being proletarianised *and* further creolised and, not surprisingly, the officers of His Majesty's forces withdrew from Senior Cup Competition in 1909; while Melbourne, their duskier companions at arms, ever so sensitive of their undesired social proximity to their Lucas 'cousins,' threatened to follow suit. The reasons proffered were the fiercely competitive manner in which cup cricket was being played and the unacceptable behaviour of supporters.[116] A deeper reason might have been that the representatives of colonial authority and elitism could not allow the 'benighted' people over whom they ruled to beat them at the quintessentially imperial sport. It also points to what Downes regards as an underlying ambivalence of the ruling classes[117] who, while recognising the social benefits that could accrue from the inclusion of the lower classes in cricket, were at the same time unwilling to socialise with, and certainly to be defeated by, them.

The rise of Lucas was symbolic of a process of democratisation which constituted a challenge to the existing social order of black inferiority/white superiority that was reinforced by the 'civilising mission.' This challenge was just beginning in Jamaican cricket. Blacks no longer acquiesced in their relegation to the sidelines, or behind fences; they were at centre stage and their supporters made quite sure that everyone knew that. However, that they chose the imperial game *par excellence* to mount their challenge to the *status quo* was itself laden with inherent contradiction. For while *demanding* recognition and respectability within the colonial order, they were required to adopt some of its cultural forms, symbols and values. Moreover, as Moore has noted, 'When the Creoles embraced cricket . . . they were consciously or unconsciously adopting its ideology' of the superiority of things white and British.[118]

In this sense, their challenge to the 'civilising mission' was ambivalent. On one hand, they had to adhere to the laws and rules of the sport and its underlying system of values. But, at the same time, they brought to it the values and behaviour of the streets and yards of the towns and rural villages where they lived and were nurtured, which threatened to subvert the Victorian code of ethics in which cricket had been enveloped. This opposition of value systems rendered Jamaican cricket a major field of socio-cultural contestation in the years before and after the First World War.

By 1920, however, organised cricket was no longer a white preserve. Both coloureds and blacks had forced their way into the sport at the competitive level, and had proved themselves to be masters of this quintessentially British art form. By then cricket was arguably the national sport of Jamaica, played by elite and poor, in town and country. The process of popularisation of cricket was accompanied by that of creolisation. While cricket sought to instil the Victorian code of ethics in its practitioners, that code was not wholly inculcated, especially by working class players and spectators who, instead, introduced many of their own creole values into the sport. Cricket, like so many other aspects of life and culture in Jamaica, reflected two different systems of ethics — one modelled on an imported Victorian culture, the other based on an indigenous Jamaican cultural fabric. But while providing a field of contestation between the two, cricket also facilitated their commingling which gradually obfuscated the boundaries that differentiated them.

Conclusion

Cricket, as a prominent item of the imported Victorian culture of the nineteenth century, provides an important window through which to view the attempts at the 'civilising mission.' As bearers of the 'high culture' which British culture constituted, the Jamaican and expatriate elite strove to impart the ideals of 'gentlemanly' behaviour that cricket was supposed to teach, develop and stimulate. Through the clubs, churches and schools, the cultural elite sought to demonstrate their superiority by excluding 'unworthies' from their clubs, and from their social space. At the same time, however, they sought to 'elevate' the masses by teaching them the fundamentals of a game which would inculcate discipline, team-work and an absolute respect for authority — characteristics which they agreed the Jamaican people sadly lacked. Not only were sports, and cricket in particular, expected to help to civilise the children of the ex-slaves, but there was every belief that an abiding sense of 'Britishness,' and a prevailing respect for the empire would be natural outgrowths of the process.

What the cultural elite had not counted on, however, was that the Jamaican people would adopt their game, but not the entire cultural package that accompanied it. They had not anticipated that they would, in time, be challenged and even lose within the parameters of a sport in which they had vested so much social and cultural significance. They watched, in abhorrence, as one of the mighty symbols of the 'superior' British culture was turned on its head, as blacks in white flannels played aggressively, played to win, questioned and sometimes defied authority, and arrived with their 'exuberance' intact into the hallowed spaces where whites had once ruled unchallenged. Faced with such insurgency from those they sought to civilise, some of the elite decided to withdraw from playing with or against blacks on the grounds that the latter were bringing the game into disrepute. The reality, though, was that the blacks were playing a 'creole cricket' that was not at all what their 'civilisers' had had in mind and, even worse, they were beating them at their own game. The 'civilising mission' was indeed under siege.

Notes

1. Brian L. Moore and Michele A. Johnson, eds., *The Land We Live In: Jamaica in 1890* (Kingston: Social History Project, UWI, 2000); also Brian L. Moore and Michele A. Johnson, eds., *'Squalid Kingston,' 1890–1920: How the Poor Lived, Moved and had their Being* (Kingston: Social History Project, UWI, 2000).
2. See, for instance, *DG*, July 29, 1875, January 23, 1885, April 10, 1885, September 4, 1885, January 21, 1886, May 18, 1894; *CS*, October 16, 1885, November 26, 1890.
3. See, for instance, *DG*, November 6 & 8, 1884, July 29, 1887.
4. Brian L. Moore and Michele A. Johnson, 'Conflicting Moralities: Sex and Illegitimacy in Jamaica at the turn of the twentieth century' (Paper presented at the Workshop on 'Control and Resistance in the Post-emancipation Caribbean,' University of Warwick, Coventry, UK, July 2000); Ibid.,' "Fallen Sisters": Attitudes to Female Prostitution in Jamaica at the turn of the Twentieth Century,' *Journal of Caribbean History*, 34.1 & 2 (2000): 46–70.
5. See, in particular, the obeah laws, numbers 5 of 1898, 23 of 1899 and 8 of 1903.
6. See Richard Holt, *Sport and the British: A Modern History* (Oxford: Oxford University Press, 1989); J.A. Mangan, ed., *The Games Ethic and Imperialism* (London: Viking, 1986); Ibid., *Pleasure, Profit and Proselytism: British Culture and Sport at Home and Abroad 1700–1914* (London: Frank Cass, 1987); Keith A.P. Sandiford, 'The Victorians at Play: Problems in Historiographical Methodology,' *Journal of Social History*, 15 (1981): 271–88; Ibid., 'Cricket and the Victorian Society,' *Journal of Social History*, 17 (1983): 303–17; Benny Green, *A History of*

Cricket (London: Barrie and Jenkins, 1988).

7. *FP,* August 27, 1869. This paper regarded cricket as a manly sport which should be encouraged (*FP,* October 3, 1873) because it would lead to the social, moral and intellectual improvement of the Jamaican people (*FP,* October 5, 1869).

8. Article in 'Denison's Cricketing Companion,' quoted in *FP,* October 5, 1869.

9. *JT,* October 28, 1916.

10. *FP,* August 27, 1869.

11. Douglas Hall, *In Miserable Slavery: Thomas Thistlewood in Jamaica 1750–86* (1982; Kingston: University of the West Indies Press, 1999), 256.

12. See, for instance, *FP,* July 11, 1862, March 13, 1868, July 27 & August 6, 1869, February 21, 1873; *DG,* October 28, 1879, August 31, 1880, March 15, 1888, January 18, 1896, & January 13, 1897; *CS,* January 6, February 27, March 12, & August 26, 1880, February 22 & December 28, 1881, February 28, March 23 & June 14, 1882, July 20, 1883, June 30, 1884, May 8, 1886, July 9, August 23, November 19, & December 29, 1887, March 7 & 20, May 18, September 5, 1888, February 19, May 15, November 8 & 19, 1889, September 30, 1890, February 2, 1891 & February 23, 1892.

13. The founding members of the KCC were Caleb Hall, James Allwood, R.S. Haughton, George Pearce (Postmaster for Jamaica), W.A. Payne, Lawrence R. Fyffe, E. Sanguinetti, Thomas Harty, A.H. Jones, S.R. Whitehorn, R. Livingstone, F.L. Harris, J.B. Jones, & W. Smith (See John Coleman Beecher, *Jamaica Cricket 1863–1926*, (Kingston: Gleaner, 1926), 10.

14. *FP,* August 25, 1868.

15. *FP,* August 27, 1869; *MJ,* September 3, 1869.

16. *FP,* June 8, 1869.

17. *FP,* November 29,1872.

18. *MJ,* September 26, 1872.

19. *MJ,* November 21, 1873.

20. *FP,* November 11, 1873.

21. *DG,* March 10, 1875.

22. *MJ,* November 5, 1875.

23. *DG,* July 6, 1876.

24. *DG,* October 20, 1876.

25. *DG,* August 7, 1877.

26. *DG,* May 29, 1878.

27. Beecher, 18–24.

28. *DG,* January 15, 1880.

29. *CS,* January 27, 1880.

30. *CS,* February 10, 1880.

31. *DG*, May 24 and 30, 1881.
32. *DG*, April 2, 1885.
33. *DG*, August 3, 1888.
34. *CS*, April 20, 1891.
35. *DG*, August 3, 1892.
36. *CS*, February 16, 1892.
37. *CS*, December 5, 1892.
38. *CS*, April 21, 1892.
39. *FP,* October 3, 1873.
40. *CS*, March 6, 1880.
41. *DG*, August 3, 1892.
42. *CS*, September 23, 1887.
43. *JP,* September 13, 1890.
44. See *DG*, December 19, 1919 and *Handbook of Jamaica for 1921* (Kingston: Government Printing Office, 1921), 549. The subscription fee had, of course, risen over the years. In 1886, for instance, it was £1. 1s. for honorary members and £1. 16s. per annum for playing members. At that time the membership was 191 (See *Handbook of Jamaica for 1886-87*, Kingston: Government Printing Establishment, 1886), 482. Membership rose to as high as 275 in 1894 (*DG*, January 25, 1894).
45. *DG*, June 12, 1894. The ground floor of the new pavilion was 35 feet by 17 feet and contained an entrance hall, lavatory, dressing room, store room and locker, and bar. The floor was of cement and from the entrance hall were doors leading to all the other rooms and to the back. In front was an open verandah of cement running along the entire width of the building. The upper storey was the same size and contained a general meeting room and a verandah. The exterior was painted and above the first floor verandah was the shield in the club's colours bearing the letters KCC. There was also a flagstaff with the club's flag.
46. See, for instance, *DG*, July 11, 1881 & October 5, 1893; *FP,* October 5, 1869; *CS*, March 1, 1882; JP, November 19, 1894.
47. *CS*, September 23, 1887.
48. *FP,* October 5, 1869.
49. Public school graduates were so very prominent among the professional, intellectual and administrative classes that during the 1880s and 1890s an annual match was played between the Kingston Club and the 'Public Schools.' A fairly wide range of such schools were represented in the colony, e.g., Cheltenham, Glenalmond, Harrow, Malvern, Marlborough, Rugby, Sherbourne, Uppingham, Westminister, and Winchester (See *DG*, March 5, 1889 & August 26, 1892).

50. 'Jubilee Dinner of Kingston Cricket Club at Myrtle Bank Hotel,' *DG*, January 8, 1913.
51. *CS*, November 30, 1883.
52. *FP*, August 25, 1868 & October 5, 1869.
53. *DG*, May 29, 1878.
54. *FP*, November 11, 1873.
55. *JP*, October 25, 1890.
56. Two, Norman and Blake, have been cited in the text above. The third was Musgrave of Ipswich (ca. 1902), named after Sir Anthony Musgrave, governor, 1877-83 (See *JT*, March 22, 1902 & June 6, 1903).
57. See, for instance, *CS*, September 10, 1889.
58. 'Jubilee Dinner,' *DG*, January 8, 1913.
59. *JA*, October 5, 1901. It is ironic that this newspaper, under the editorship of Robert Love, the black 'radical,' should have upbraided the governor for playing cricket on the grounds that by doing so with 'inferior officers of the service and others who are not his equals,' he was lowering his prestige in the eyes of everyone. As governor he had no equals, and as such 'It is not dignified to see a Governor bowling for Peter Jones, the bar-keeper, or stripped to the shirt and shouting huzzahs for the batting of Thomas Claxton, the book-keeper. Still less comfortable is it to see the Governor laughed at like an ordinary clown for his awkwardness, or scorned, like a dolt for his ignorance. And nothing would surpass the disgrace of seeing a Governor slip and sprawl on the ground, as the result of an unsuccessful attempt at agility.'
60. *DG*, February 10, 1902. The occasion was a luncheon in honour of a visiting English cricket team to the island.
61. *DG*, January 17, 1900.
62. Among the clergymen who played cricket in Jamaica were Thomas Harty (later Canon) – one of the founding members of Kingston Club, C.T. Husband for Vere (*DG*, January 7, 1880), Hogan and MacCormick for Stoneyhurst and Beaumont College (*CS*, November 21, 1891). In 1880, one E. Nuttall played for Rugby against St. Andrew's (*CS*, April 2, 1880). It is probable that this might have been Enos Nuttall who in the same year was elected Anglican bishop of Jamaica and later Archbishop of the West Indies. If so, this is clear testimony to the linkage between cricket and the church. However, Downes has found that in Barbados at the same time there was resistance to promoting cricket by the clergy of the Anglican Church, notwithstanding encouragement from the bishop (See Aviston D. Downes, ' "Flannelled Fools"? Cricket and the Political Economy of the British West Indies c.1895-1906,' *The International Journal of the History of Sport*, 17.4 (2000): 59-80.

63. *FP,* October 5, 1869.

64. Ibid.

65. See, for instance, NLJ.MS 2089, Minutes of St Paul's Presbyterian Church, July 6, 1909; JA 5/5 (Periodicals), Report and Statistics of the Moravian Church in Jamaica – for Salem, 1912. The rules of one church-linked club, the Nazareth (Moravian), specifically forbade indecent language, foul expressions and unnecessary shouting on the grounds on pain of instant dismissal; and members were required to abide by the laws of the Marylebone Cricket Club (imperial cricket's governing body). The entrance fee was four shillings, and the monthly subscription was six pence (JA 5/5/S/6, Moravian Church Records: Rules of the Nazareth Cricket Club ca. 1923).

66. See Keith A.P. Sandiford, *Cricket Nurseries of Colonial Barbados: The Elite Schools 1865-1966* (Kingston: The Press, UWI, 1998); Brian L. Moore, *Cultural Power, Resistance and Pluralism: Colonial Guyana 1838-1900* (Kingston: The Press, UWI, 1995), 78; C.L.R. James, *Beyond a Boundary* (1963; London: Stanley Paul, 1980).

67. *DG,* June 12, 1894.

68. *CS,* March 1, 1882; see also *MJ,* August 20, 1872.

69. See *CS,* March 1, 1882, December 3, 1880, March 5, 1881, March 7, April 5, November 7 & December 7, 1882, April 23, June 13 & 17, 1883, June 29, 1886, June 27, 1888, November 27, 1889, November 21, 1891, May 5, July 6, 1892, December 5, 1893, January 15, 1895; *DG,* June 23, 1875, October 7, 1876, November 20, 1879, February 18, March 4 & 5, 1881, September 24, 1889; *JT,* June 12, 1909.

70. *FP,* February 22 & 25, 1870.

71. See, for instance, *FP,* July 11, 1862, March 13, 1868, July 27 & August 6, 1869, March 4 & April 22, 1870, September 25, 1874; *MJ,* November 21, 1873; *CS,* February 27 & September 13, 1880, March 31, 1881, April 22, 1882, August 6, 1887, February 16, 1892.

72. *MJ,* September 26, 1872.

73. In this instance, a batsman was adjudged 'out' off an alleged no-ball, but the umpire called 'no-ball' after the stump had been dislodged. One of the St James' players 'made use of very insulting language respecting the Captain of the Falmouth Club,' who attacked the offender and provoked the general disturbance (See *FP,* June 17, 1870).

74. See Jimmy Richards and Mervyn Wong, *Statistics of West Indies Cricket 1865-1989* (Kingston: Heinemann Caribbean, 1990).

75. *CS,* 11, January 20-23 & February 2, 1888; *DG,* January 14 & 18, 1888.

76. *DG,* February 15, April 1-4 & 16, 1895.

77. *DG,* March 30, 1895.

78. *DG,* September 24, 1896. Jamaica lost the first match by an innings

and 45 runs, and the second by one wicket.

79. *JP,* March 30,1897.

80. *DG,* March 30, 1897. The poem read as follows:

<u>1</u>

Charge your glasses ye sons of Jamaica and drink,
To the sons of old England we are bound by the link,
Of common affection for Country and Throne,
Their Island is ours and ours their own.
We are sons of that banner which sports in the breeze,
The ruler of wintry and tropical seas
Our Kingdom is one on which sun never sets,
Its sovereign one, whom no Briton forgets.
Chorus: Then stand up! Stand up, and pledge it,
Stand up with a hip, hip, hip, hurrah!
To the toast of the night, our glasses we'll drain,
We'll fill them and drink it again and again.

<u>2</u>

A welcome as warm as the tropical sun,
Has been theirs since the day our acquaintance begun;
We've pledged them the hand, we've pledged them the heart,
'Tis joy to have met, 'twill be sorrow to part;
Though as foemen in battle we've fought on the field,
Our friendship as kinsmen, for ever is sealed;
For every man 'Jack' is a Son of a gun,
A Briton, a Sportsman and second to none.
Chorus:

<u>3</u>

To battle they've been with the willow in hand,
Breaking duck's eggs, on West Indian land;
Catching mosquitoes, grasshoppers and gnats,
Not above catching West Indian Bats;
Game in the morning, and game all the day,
Game, but now crowing, though game in the play;
Wickedly toasting the Indian host
At cricket, by having him neatly on toast.
Chorus:

<u>4</u>

'On Stanley on'! Is their motto they say,
Their fight in the leeside in Priestley array;
With willow in hand and in Cricketing hoods,
They drive all our balls straight to Bush or to Woods;
With Stout Heart they play, every man on the tour,
Is equally good; not a 'Pal-a-rite' lower;
When Williams and Elliot, have 'Balled 'em' at play,
All meet at the 'Bar-at' the end of the day.
Chorus:

<u>5</u>

Then here's to the Captain and here's to his men.
We Indians hope that we'll meet them again,
And when next they play a West Indian Match,
May they raise a farm-yard with the ducks that they hatch,
Jamaica will furnish the land for the farm,
To raise their young ducklings and keep them from harm;
In comfort and safety, in features they'll walk,
For the Isle of Jamaica will harbour no 'Hawke.'
Chorus:

<u>6</u>

Then fill your glasses and give them one cheer,
Though the joy of the toast may be marred by a tear;
Life's a strange combination of joy and of pain,
We meet and we part and meet not again.
Though often in Cricket they have shouted 'good bye,'
With a laugh, when they know they were wiping their eye.
We are perfectly sure when we bid them adieu,
They'll be wiping the eye with a sentiment true.
Chorus.

81. *JDT*, July 10, 1899.
82. Downes, 73.
83. *DG*, February 26, 1900. A minor crisis was created by Jamaica's threat to withdraw from the tour.
84. Letter by 'Interested,' *DG*, January 22, 1900.
85. *DG*, March 12 & April 9, 1900. The second Jamaican on this tour was G.V. Livingstone.
86. See *DG*, February 8, 10, 13, 14, 17 & 24 , 1902; *JT*, February 8, 1902.
87. *JT*, March 1, 1902.
88. *DG*, January 13–14, 16 17 & 20–22 , 1905.

89. *DG,* February 13, 16–20 & 22, 1909; *JG,* February 11, 1909.

90. *DG,* March 25, 27–30, April 4 & 6, 1911.

91. In 1880 the *Gleaner* chided the Trinidadians for refusing to play against a team from St Vincent because some of the players were coloured/black. Said the newspaper: 'We had no idea that complexional prejudices ran so high in Trinidad or that one class of Creoles could not compete in friendly rivalry with another at a game of cricket without loss of dignity. Such conduct inevitably stamps the objectors as *parvenus.* The same may be said of other Colonies in the West Indies' (*DG,* December 9, 1880).

92. Brian L. Moore, 'Colonialism, Cricket Culture, and Afro-Creole Identity in the Caribbean after Emancipation: The Case of Guyana,' *Journal of Caribbean History,* 33.1 & 2 (1999): 54–73.

93. Downes, 77.

94. *CS,* February 29, 1892.

95. *DG,* November 4, 1910. In this instance, the five were acquitted when it became apparent that the arresting constable had lied.

96. Howard Pyle, 'Jamaica, Old and New,' *Harper's New Monthly Magazine,* LXXX (January–February 1890): 391.

97. JA 5/8/78/5949, *Friends Jamaica Mission,* VI.1 (1898).

98. Bessie Pullen-Burry, *Jamaica as it is, 1903* (London: T. Fisher Unwin, 1903), 119.

99. JA 7/12/160, Jamaica Memories of C.G Bailey, November 18, 1959; JA 7/12/181, Jean Calvin, n.d.; JA 7/12/288, L.U. Williams, n.d.

100. In one instance, the thief, David Brown, was apprehended and taken to court for stealing a cricket bat worth ten shillings. He was sentenced to three months' hard labour (*DG,* March 8, 1889).

101. JA 4/9 #9.1, Rough diary of S.C. Spencer Smith, March 1899. A 'shy' is when the ball is thrown with a bent elbow as opposed to when it is bowled with the elbow straight.

102. *JA,* October 8, 1898.

103. *DG,* September 8, 1900.

104. Beecher, 27, 38. Slade Lucas had brought the first English team to Jamaica in 1895. The founding members of Melbourne were G.C., G.M. & L.H. Gunter, R.H. Fletcher, J.S. Campbell, M. Dunn, *et al.* David Ellington was the principal person behind the establishment of Lucas.

105. Lucas won the Senior Cup cricket competition in successive years from 1904 to 1906, in 1911, and again successively from 1913 to 1915. Since no competition cricket was played in 1907 (the year of the catastrophic earthquake), this means that Lucas won 7 times in 11 years. This outstanding record brought immense pride to working class black Jamaicans in town and country who regarded the Lucas players as heroes. According to Beecher, 'The name Lucas became a household

word in every part of the Country. All who were wise welcomed them and befriended them because they had furnished for the game its latest and most important advance. Every man spoke of them, many dreamed of them, everyone felt the effect of the new injection of iron into our cricket life, and every eleven feared them. They strode along victoriously' (Beecher, 38).

106. See 'Jubilee Dinner,' *DG*, January 5, 1913. All the leading cricket clubs were invited to this event, except Lucas.

107. NLJ.MS 934, Frank Cundall, 'The West Indies Today' (MS 1908), 206.

108. See *JT*, February 12, 1910; letter by J. Nelson Barclay in *DG*, October 3, 1914. Drinking and gambling, as we have seen, had always been a feature of cricket in Jamaica, but it seemed to attract more negative attention when indulged in by the black working classes.

109. See *JT*, February 28, 1903; *DG*, October 21, 1904. This type of behaviour was not confined to Kingston. In 1903, for instance, a free fight broke out between two teams from Collington and Crook River which ended in the court room (See *JT*, 2 February 1903).

110. *DG*, April 28, 1905.

111. See, for instance, *JT*, August 22, 1908. In a match between Melbourne and Lucas, a decision that the crowd disputed led them to abuse the umpire with such terms as thief, robber, cheat, etc.

112. *DG*, April 28, 1905.

113. *DG*, October 3, 1914.

114. *JT*, August 22, 1908.

115. *DG*, June 6, 1907.

116. *DG*, May 4 & 6, 1909. In his letter to the Jamaica Cricket Challenge Cup Committee, Lieut. T.B. Nicholson, captain of the Garrison Club, claimed that since the introduction of cup competition cricket had become very competitive and was no longer being played for the sake of the game. Besides, 'Cup competition also seem to affect a portion of the crowd of spectators whose actions are at times not entirely impartial. It is a game which can, and should be played without bias, and the too keen feeling which on occasions almost amounts to unfriendliness should be absent.'

117. Downes, 77.

118. Moore, 'Colonialism, Cricket Culture,' 63.

CHAPTER 17

The Contestation for Recreational Space in Barbados, 1880–1910
Aviston Downes

The plantation sector and the problem of access to land

The issue of access to land has been a dominant theme in the exploration of capital-labour relations in the historiography of the Caribbean. This essay will, however, complement this economic focus with an examination of the recreational use of land in the Barbadian context. Social class was defined not only in terms of control over the economic factors of production, but also access to disposable time and recreational space. In other words, the dominant land-owning agro-commercial bourgeoisie also constituted the 'leisure class.' Not surprisingly, then, bourgeoisie-proletarian contention in colonial Barbados also revolved around the issue of access to recreational time and space.

But the nature of the social relationship between the white, rural-based planter class and the black agro-proletariat was not the sole determinant. Indeed, the quest for recreational space originated in the urban context. That quest was motivated initially by a concern for the labour conditions of white-collar employees in commercial establishments in Bridgetown, most of whom were whites. However, this concern soon extended to include all those outside the traditional white elite 'leisure classes,' especially those residing in urban and peri-urban areas. Expatriate educators, clergymen and colonial officials combined with local liberals to spearhead the campaign for popular public leisure spaces. These campaigners were influenced by trends in Victorian England where recreational reformism was being promoted among workers. These social reformers believed that officially approved working class leisure pursuits could serve to arrest potential proletarian protest. The Barbadian social elite was not convinced and often refused to provide publicly financed popular leisure spaces. Even when such spaces did emerge, the white elite ensured that 'aesthetic distance' and social differentiation would be upheld.

The report of the 1897 West India Royal Commission described the situation in Barbados as 'markedly different from that of any other colony of the West Indies . . . very thickly populated . . . no crown lands, no forest, no uncultivated areas.'[1] In this tiny island of 166 square miles, with one of the highest population densities in the British Empire, the local plantocracy was vigilant in its control over land as a critical mechanism to exploit the majority black working class. This was particularly effective in Barbados, where, as Marshall, *et al.* have clearly demonstrated, the emergence of an independent black peasantry was severely retarded up to the early twentieth century.[2]

In 1897, one estate owner boasted that planters in Barbados were more successful than their counterparts elsewhere in exercising control over black labourers. He observed:

> The Barbadian negroes are most civil as a rule, especially in daylight in Barbados, to us and to the managers, but you will see the same nigger goes down in a fortnight afterwards to Demerara — he will stand and look at the manager and whistle in his face, and 'cheek' him in any kind of way. It is that in Barbados we have such an ample command of the labourer, there is such a lot of them that they must work and must behave themselves, and it is their home-place; that is why we get hold of them, and they know they may lose the ground.[3]

The majority of the Barbadian working class were not freeholders but lived as 'located labourers' on plantation tenantries, working under exploitative conditions. A mass exodus from plantation tenantries was hardly practicable. Moreover, since property ownership was an integral qualification for a limited franchise, this ensured that members of the majority working class were rendered politically powerless through the formal political structures.

Planters and officials conspired to convince the Royal Commissioners in 1897 that there was not an extensive land hunger among would-be peasants. Representatives for the working class, however, observed that 'there has always been a disposition on the part of agricultural labourers to acquire land but hitherto, the difficulty for him was to find parties willing to sell the acre, more or less, which he may desire to acquire.'[4] As Mr Alleyne informed the commissioners: 'It is the ambition of every Barbadian to own a piece of land' but they were being denied such an opportunity.[5] In 1854, Britain had passed an Encumbered Estates Act to facilitate the transfer of heavily indebted estates to new ownership, but Barbadian planters established their own Chancery Court in an attempt to keep the ownership of estates from passing to British-based corporations. Although a mortgagee could take possession of an estate and receive the rents and profits, there could be no immediate sale of an indebted estate outside the Court of Chancery. The court appointed a receiver and, after one year, seven appraisers — 'agriculturalists of repute'— were appointed to assess the value of the land, buildings, implements and the cultivated crop.[6] These 'agriculturalists of repute' protected their vested interest as a class and ensured that land prices remained artificially high in spite of the depressed state of the economy. The appraisal system was therefore a farce. In his report of 1897, the colonial secretary observed, 'I do not think it will be controverted that the appraisement (whether it represents the true value of the land, as is often argued, or not) is generally much in excess of any sum likely to be paid for it.' The effect of the system was that:

> It has so far resulted in keeping fitful life in the bankrupt estate, in keeping the owner still owner in name and in holding out a will-o'-the wisp fantasy to owners and mortgagees that some day things will be better . . . The manifest objection to the system is that it puts obstacles in the way of new ownership, and of possibly fresh capital.[7]

Spokesmen for the working class accused Mr Chandler, master-in-chancery, of 'having decidedly set his face in opposition to any partition sale,' that is, selling plantations in lots.[8] An irate Mr Walter Marston argued that the Chancery system was 'rotten to the core. The appraisement should be swept away and estates sold at the hammer.'[9]

But even when land was sold grudgingly, its price bore no resemblance to the real market value which was about £20 an acre in 1897. Land *en bloc* was sold by planters to fellow white land speculators who resold lots at 50 per cent to 200 per cent above the purchase price.[10] Mr Dowridge recalled that his father paid $400 (£104) per acre to one of these speculators, just to secure a house spot. His father-in-law in St Thomas paid $800 (£208) per acre for agricultural land. It was clear to Mr Daniel, as to others, that 'The "fancy prices" paid for land in this country has been brought about in order to prevent a peasant proprietary body from rising in our midst.'[11] It was therefore not surprising that there were only 8,500 freeholders possessing five acres or less in 1897.[12] The West India Royal Commission recommended that British West Indian governments should facilitate the expansion of peasant proprietorships but the response of the Barbados government was terse: 'The question of a peasant proprietorship need not trouble us in Barbados.'[13]

The generally onerous conditions in the planter-controlled rural areas catalysed the rural-to-urban migration in the 1880s and 1890s as persons sought alternative employment in Bridgetown or opportunities to emigrate. This urban drift was facilitated by the subdivision of unprofitable estates into villages or urban tenantries in the parish of St Michael. The peri-urban areas of this parish, outside the statutory limits of Bridgetown, witnessed the greatest population growth. The population of St Michael increased from 17.2 per cent of the entire population in 1881 to 19.3 per cent in 1891, and 23.7 per cent by 1911.[14]

In the wake of this urban drift, many merchants who had previously resided on the same premises as their establishments, retreated, along with other members of the white middle class, to the arboreal suburbs of Belleville and Strathclyde. The population of Bridgetown proper declined by 20.7 per cent between 1891 and 1911, while the parish of St Michael increased in population by 15.8 per cent in the same period.[15] One visitor observed that St Michael was 'a place of striking contrasts, a region of surprises.'[16] There were uninterrupted rows of 'dingy-looking cottages' on both sides of the road for hundreds of yards, contrasted with the 'pretty villas' along 'several long avenues shaded by rows of palms.'[17] The contrast also extended to the social provision for leisure, an activity which itself became a definer of social status.

The struggle for recreational space

The campaign to secure public recreational space had emerged by the 1880s and was first articulated in the urban context. It was driven not only by a sense of urban congestion but also by a challenge to the notion that 'leisure-class' status was the sole domain of wealthy property-owning whites. It was perhaps more than coincidental that the debate emerged at a time when Belleville, and later Strathclyde were developing as model 'modern' middle class suburban residential districts with their provision of leisure facilities. Both of these districts hosted tennis clubs and Belleville was the initial home of Spartan — the cricket club of upper middle class coloureds. These were, however, virtually 'gated communities' which jealously guarded their exclusivity well into the twentieth century. Belleville residents, for instance, set up a committee to consider employing a watchman, 'with a good fat stick,' to ward off 'hooligans' attracted by the sports in the district.[18]

Commercial workers in Bridgetown, therefore, agitated for their own leisure time and space. A letter reaching the *Barbados Herald* in August 1880 railed against the absence of recreation for the clerks and shop assistants in Bridgetown:

> The employers do not know, or knowing, do not seem to mind, that 'All work and no play makes John a dull boy.' It would, I believe, be difficult to name a place where so little attention is paid to diversion and recreation for the above class of employees as in this island. It is one monotonous tune. Work! work! all through the year.[19]

For six days a week between 7.00 a.m. and 5.00 p.m., and in some cases from as early as 6.00 a.m. to as late as 6.00 p.m., city workers toiled as long as the agro-proletariat in the country. For some clerks and shop attendants early Sunday morning was neither theirs nor the Lord's; from 6.00 a.m. until 9.00 a.m., drug stores and outlets selling ice, fresh fish, and meat opened to serve the public.[20]

In November 1880, 600 commercial workers petitioned the merchants of the Commercial Committee and Mr Inniss, a representative for the constituency of Bridgetown, to support the extension of the Bank Holiday Act to commercial workers. Barbados' Bank Holiday Act of 1873 made the first day of January, Easter Monday, and the day after Christmas, inviolable holidays for bank employees and public servants.[21] The only days to which other workers had some statutory right were the holy-days of Good Friday and Christmas. The draft bill introduced by Inniss was rejected in the Legislative Council on technical grounds,[22] but in 1884, a similar petition was reintroduced by Grannum, senior representative for the city, and supported by 44 merchants.[23] That bill was passed in the House of Assembly,[24] and the Legislative Council added the first Monday in August (already in the English Act)[25] to the statutory holidays.

By the 1870s the game of cricket had emerged as a very popular activity. Wanderers Cricket Club was the first Barbadian club to secure a cricket ground; it established itself at the Bay Estate, St Michael in 1877. This club catered to the local white elite planters, merchants and professionals. It was Wanderers' elitism which forced the white merchant and civil servant clerks of obviously lower social rank to resort to the Royal Artillery grounds for lunch-time tournaments in late 1882. Following a number of meetings by them at the public library, the Pickwick Cricket Club was born with about 30 members.[26] By 1882, then, social struggle for leisure time and space, informed by both colour and class considerations, had emerged.

By 1884, the Bridgetown commercial clerks had won their statutory right to bank holidays, but there was no indication that the planter-merchant oligarchy had any interest in promoting government-funded recreational spaces. This omission in public policy was underscored by the *Herald* newspaper in 1883. It contended, 'In all civilized communities some such resort is to be found, provided at the public expense. Barbados is singularly devoid of any such; nor does there appear to be any effort made towards doing any such thing.'[27] There was the Fountain Gardens, a few square yards of Trafalgar Square, where a fountain had been erected in 1865, four years after piped water reached Bridgetown.[28] However, it was not until 1882 that some semblance of a garden was laid out, but its recreational use was negligible. Bridgetown still needed 'a place of resort easy of access and affording a means of retreat for a few hours from the confinement and dust of the City.'[29]

In 1887, a committee petitioned the House of Assembly to consider laying out part of the land at Government House, the residence of the governor, as a public garden to commemorate Queen Victoria's Golden Jubilee.[30] There was, however, a cynical suggestion that such a suburban facility would exclude the black working classes. 'The Upper-ten have their own gardens,' the *Bee* newspaper noted: let the People have theirs and not a mock combination for the benefit of the few to the detriment of the majority.'[31]

The editor of the *Barbados Herald* reiterated, 'With a teeming population overflowing her boundaries, she [Bridgetown] has no public parks or gardens to which either the adult or youthful population may go to snatch an hour's enjoyment in the open air.'³² As a result of the campaign, a portion of land opposite the St Mary's Anglican Church was acquired as a garden to honour Queen Victoria's Golden Jubilee. While this facility did not answer the need for sport, it became a centre by July 1892 for Police Band Concerts on Friday evenings. In reference to this facility, the *Times*, newspaper of the coloured middle class, warned that no 'vexatious regulations' should be implemented to exclude the masses from a 'public place.'³³ The concern of the *Times* was not misplaced because in nineteenth-century Barbados white colonial officialdom represented public spaces, and especially urban streets, as 'dangerous' places, potential political sites for mass mobilisation and rebellious actions. Such fears can clearly be discerned from the various Vagrancy Acts and the urban regulatory legislation of 1891.³⁴ Even the Salvation Army ran afoul of the law in June 1898 for attracting crowds to an open-air meeting in Beckwith Square, Lower Bridgetown.³⁵ It was the latent fear of the gathered masses by the ruling class which partly served to constrain the provision of public recreational space.

Social exclusion characterised the recreational facilities controlled by the elite. For instance, a committee consisting of the white elite secured exclusive supervision over Hastings Rocks on the south coast of the island. That group erected fences and gates which the *Wesleyan Watchman* asked to be speedily dismantled.³⁶ A schedule of admission fees was implemented at the Rocks, justified on the claim that a caretaker and the transportation of the military band had to be paid.³⁷ Such justifications did not alter the perceptions by the working class that this was an attempt to exclude all but 'a favoured few.'³⁸ As a correspondent to the *Taxpayer* observed, it was an attempt 'to debar the hardworking people who form the bulk of the population from enjoying this delightful and refreshing spot by putting up posts and gates, and barbed wire fence, and thus reserving the use of this place for a few idle, highly paid, pampered 'I am better than thou' Pharisees? — too often whited sepulchres.'³⁹ Harry Franck observed as late as the 1920s:

> Thus in negro-teeming Barbados there is scarcely a suggestion of African parentage to be seen at this stately entertainment on Hastings Rocks. It is partly the sixpence admission that keeps the negroes outside, but not entirely.... The English sense of dignified orderliness and the negro's natural gaiety, his tendency to 'giggle' at inopportune moments, do not mix well, and the Hasting Rocks concert is one of those places where African hilarity must be ruthlessly suppressed.⁴⁰

The aesthetic distance between Hastings Rocks and the Jubilee Gardens was emphasised by the employment of the white British regimental band at the former, and the relegation of the multiracial, ill-equipped and maligned Police Band to the latter. It was only when the removal of the British Regiment from Barbados became imminent that the local Police Band got their opportunity to play at the hallowed Hastings Rocks in March 1902.[41] Originally relegated to playing to children and nurses at the Jubilee Gardens, the Police Band was belatedly offered a chance for 'improvement' by playing to an 'intelligent and critical audience.'[42] Its instruments which had long been in use were expeditiously replaced when a vote of £130 was passed by the House of Assembly in 1904 for that purpose.[43]

Unlike a number of other Caribbean colonies, the Barbadian government controlled very little land. As table 17.1 clearly indicates, the planter class owned at least 85 per cent of the country's land space, with the government, church and freeholders jostling for the remaining 15 per cent. The last vestiges of original forest, as well as other geographical and geological sites which often attracted leisurely interest, were mainly privately owned.[44] Government could find a mere two sites from which to offer the Barbados Theatre Company Limited a home in 1894.[45] The government's limitation in providing recreational spaces was again evident during the debate considering the site for an extended Free Library.[46]

Table 17.1: Land use in Barbados, 1896–97

Owner	Acreage	% Total Land Space
Plantations (440)	90,890	85.37
Imperial War Dept	238	0.22
Anglican Church (Glebe)	221	0.21
Govt. & non-plantation freeholds	15,121	14.20
Total	106,470	100.00

Sources: Calculated from memoranda and evidence given before the WIRC, 1897, 157; memos, 213, 214; Barbados Blue Books, 1896–97; MCA, 1904–05, doc.188, War Department Lands, etc.

The Norham Devise

The planter class had so great a control over land resources that the provision of parks and playing fields would almost necessitate the benevolent paternalism of that class. But even when such benevolence was extended, there were other hurdles to surmount. This point is well illustrated by the refusal of the majority of the members of the House of Assembly to honour the will of George William Carrington in 1896. Carrington's will provided that five years after his death, his 'Norham House' and three lots of almost eight acres of land were to be bequeathed to government 'to be used and kept forever as open spaces and recreation grounds for the special benefit and use of the classes of persons in the Island now comprising the tenants of the said Welches Estate namely persons of the labouring and domestic servant classes.'[47] The Welches estate (now Carrington Village) had been subdivided into a tenantry in the 1880s and, in the wake of increased rural-to-urban migration, swelled into one of the largest working class peri-urban tenantries. At least one correspondent hailed Mr Carrington as a landlord attuned to the social needs of his tenants who had installed roads, erected toilets and a market square, and had plans for a school and church.[48] The upper working and middle classes who were lobbying for government-sponsored urban renewal, including recreational spaces, had envisaged that the Norham bequest could possibly become a centre for sport and a reading and lecture room for the improvement of the working people.

This was not to be realised because the bill was rejected in the House of Assembly on the premise that the bequest was aimed to benefit a specified class in one parish.[49] While the conservative *Agricultural Reporter* supported the argument upon which the House of Assembly voted against accepting the bequest,[50] Dr T. Law Gaskin pointed out that such an argument was not raised when the legislature approved a large sum of money to secure property for Harrison College.[51] Founded as the Harrison Free School in Bridgetown in 1733 as a 'Public and Free School for the poor and indigent boys of the Parish,' it was reorganised in 1870 as a 'good grammar school' for the education of 'the better classes.'[52] It was relocated from the heart of the city, a year later, in order to have access to a playing field. Members of the House of Assembly argued then that 'such an adjunct [playing field] is considered in the mother country to be absolutely necessary to the success of a good school.'[53] Obviously, as Gaskin pointed, such notions did not extend to the working class whose communities and schools remained bereft of playing fields. Dr Gaskin and about 3,400 persons petitioned the House of Assembly to reconsider their total rejection of the Norham bequest.[54] C.P. Clarke subsequently attempted to have the House rules suspended to enable the previously defeated motion to be discussed and voted upon again but his effort failed.[55]

This was not, however, the end of the matter as pressure continued upon the Barbados legislature by a cross section of community interests, including local working class leaders, English expatriates and local middle class reformists. In fact, about 110 petitioners, including the head teachers of Harrison College, Lodge, and Queen's College, the bishop of Barbados, and several merchants and doctors, expressed their willingness to make an annual subscription to assist the government in maintaining the Norham property.[56] The executive referred the matter to the Vestry of St Michael to ascertain whether it would be willing to raise £100 annually to support the project. Following a heated debate which went until near midnight on Wednesday, March 5, 1896, the rate payers of St Michael voted 50 to 22 in favour of accepting the Norham bequest.[57] C.P. Clarke once again tried to revive the issue in the House of

Assembly but he failed to secure an endorsement of an address to the governor-in-council to postpone any final decision on the matter.[58]

There was obviously no clear government policy on what role public recreation could play in the inculcation of dominant ideologies and promoting social order amongst the working class. *The Barbados Globe* expressed the opinion that members of the legislature seemed more willing to support coercive mechanisms such as prisons and policemen than to spend money in maintaining non-coercive measures, as had been envisaged under the Norham project.[59]

With the rejection of the Norham bequest by the legislature, Dr Gaskin spearheaded the formation, in April 1896, of an association 'to promote the establishment of play grounds and other means of pure and wholesome recreation for the people.'[60] The association included T. Roberts of the Reform Club; Rev. Clark Holman of the Church of England; Walter Marston, indefatigable agitator for working class interests; F.N.A. Clairmonte, a coloured master tailor; J. Bovell, superintendent of the Botanical Station; Horace Deighton, headmaster and a pioneer of muscular Christianity at Harrison College; and C.L. Elder, a clerk in the colonial secretary's office.[61] The association secured the permission of the government to utilise the estimated nine-acre Reef Ground in lower Bridgetown[62] to develop it into a public recreation space. This former dump was progressively transformed into a playing area for working class sports and also a fair ground for itinerant circuses and amusement shows. By September 1901, $1,000 had been raised and spent on this facility over a five-year period from $1 subscriptions and grazing fees.[63]

Up to the early 1900s, government had refused to invest in public recreational space, especially for the masses. This was in spite of the fact that there was an explosion of organised working class sporting activity —especially in cricket — from the late 1890s. For instance, in October 1899, the recently developed Reef Grounds was the venue for a cricket match between printers and tailors and on St Stephen's pasture there was an encounter between the teams of Sealy and Downes.[64] One newspaper report around Christmas 1904 observed, 'There was much cricket among the peasantry, some pastures having several teams batting at the same time.'[65]

In early 1903, Frederick Martinez, a merchant of Jewish ancestry, established the Frame Food Competition for working class cricket clubs and donated a 25 -guinea challenge cup.[66] Among the teams which participated in the first year were Fenwicks, Hyde Park, Quakers, Volunteers, Sportsman's, Glenville, St Martins, Police, Railway, W. I. Regiment, Wranglers, and Hunters. The majority of these black working class teams were from around the urban areas but attracted large crowds, even though forced to play on inadequate rab land.[67]

The withdrawal of the British military base from Barbados in 1906 made a number of War Office properties available to government. The estimated

238 acres offered some hope for recreational allocation for the public. Hastings Rocks and the Garrison area had already become the focus of recreation for the local elite. Queen's House, the former official residence of the commander of the British troops, along with its outbuildings and land, as well as the Retreat quarters and ground, together consisted of about 19½ acres in easy reach of the urban population. The advocates for working class recreational spaces seized the opportunity to urge the St Michael's Vestry to lease Queen's House and its grounds from the government. At a public meeting held at Carnegie Hall, Rev. Sealy of the African Methodist Episcopalian Church moved a resolution, seconded by Washington Harper, the shipwright, that the property be acquired by the St Michael Vestry for the purpose of a park, especially for the poorer classes who, unlike Strathclyde and Belleville residents, were short of recreational facilities. The resolution was passed, aided by the usual agitation of Washington Harper and Walter Marston — both accused of using 'threatening language.'[68] A Board of Parks Commissioners was appointed and with the keen involvement of Lady Carter, the wife of Governor Gilbert Carter, Queen's Park was designed and laid out. In June 1909, Lady Gilbert formally opened the gates of the park which became the venue for the annual exhibition, Police Band Concerts, the Christmas promenade and a host of public activities.[69]

While working class leaders had assisted in securing Barbados' first substantial public park, C.P. Clarke, representative for St Peter, and Walter Reece, the coloured representative for St Lucy, fought the permanent occupation of the Garrison Savannah by local white elite clubs. In January 1907, a bill was introduced to the House of Assembly to empower the governor-in-council to concede exclusive control over the former parade ground at the Garrison Savannah to one private club.[70] It was bad enough that the Turf Club, Polo Club, Football Club and other white elite clubs were already exercising *de facto* control of the Savannah, which the government was paying the British War Office £150 out of the public purse to lease. As Reece pointed out, 'I happen to know that even now, when the Savannah is under the control of the Executive Committee, a certain club called the Polo Club arrogates to itself certain rights and privileges with respect to a certain part of the Savannah.'[71] In theory the idea of having one amalgamated club that would regulate the use of the Savannah seemed rational enough, but again Reece was extremely doubtful: 'I know this country sufficiently well to know that it will simply mean this: that particular club will have the entire use of the piece of land and only those persons whom they favour will have any use of it.'[72]

This perception of favouritism towards the white elite was not misplaced. Indeed, within months, Reece was arguing against the adherence to the1897 Vagrancy Act to the gambling which took place on the Savannah on race days.[73] Reece's argument prevailed in the House of Assembly (Lower House), but the Legislative Council (Upper House) upheld the invidious original draft, absolving only the Pari Mutuel of the Barbados Turf Club from the sanction of the proposed Vagrancy (Amendment) Act of 1907.[74] The various games of chance operated by the working classes received no legislative protection, and were left to the merciful discretion of the police.

The Church and leisure spaces

In England the church played an important role in the promotion of 'wholesome recreation.' In Barbados, the Moravians and Wesleyan Methodists were in the forefront in organising tea meetings, concerts, excursions and other forms of 'rational recreation' especially directed at the working class. By the 1890s the Salvation Army and the Christian Mission churches added to those efforts. However, owing to their limited land ownership, these denominations were restricted in their ability to provide public playing spaces. The Church of England, however, was a significant landowner with an estimated 221 acres across the island. In St George, alone, that church possessed 50 acres of Glebe land and in St Philip, 45 acres. Moreover, Anglican parish priests were *ex-officio* members of the vestries which were charged with the upkeep of public parochial facilities such as schools. In these roles, Anglican ministers had greater potential influence over the big landowners in the parishes. Yet, the Anglican clergy failed to use their political power and influence to secure concessions of elementary school playing fields from planters.

Instead, the local Anglican Church served as another instrument of advancing and protecting the white minority planter interest. Not surprisingly, the attitude of many clerics was similar to the agro-commercial bourgeoisie. There were, of course, notable exceptions. For instance, Bishop Swaby and Rev. Clark Holman were committed campaigners for public grounds and threw their energies behind the work of the Reef Grounds Association. Bishop Swaby in his address to Synod in 1901 observed that, 'little beyond direct church work is done,' and the statistical report showed that a mere nine churches sponsored outdoor activity, two of which sponsored a cricket club.[75] The governor also found this situation unacceptable.[76] Local clergy were incensed at what seemed to be charges of indolence levelled against them and given tacit support by their own head, the bishop. The response given to Canon Watson's speech at a special meeting of the Anglican clergy summed up their general mood and attitude:

> I was not ordained to organise Cricket Clubs, (Cheers) in order to hold the young, nor Men and Women's Institutes and Church Lad's Brigades (Applause.) That is not my work . . . We would, as it were, be neglecting the word of God to serve tables (Cheers) . . . I do not think we ought to be ashamed because we have not got Cricket Clubs. (Cheers). I do not object to them. They are very useful and helpful, and I should be well pleased if there were ladies and gentlemen in my parish to take them in hand. I would give them all

encouragement, but they demand means and men and personal instrumentality which are available in England, but which are not to be had here. Cricket Clubs, Institutes, Lads Brigades and Guilds, all imply money.[77]

Canon Watson's position was an untenable excuse disguised as a reasonable explanation. Clearly, these clergymen shared the same prejudices and predilections of the social elite who still harboured doubts that any good could result from the mass *participation* of working class blacks in organised leisure activities. Recreation was still perceived as a means of building character in the children of the upper sections of society and preparing them for exercising leadership and authority. Any activity aimed at promoting the gathering of blacks in non-work situations continued to be viewed with suspicion.

Conclusion

The eventual securing of public recreational spaces such as the Reef Grounds, Queen's Park and the Garrison Savannah represented a hard-fought victory by an alliance of the working and some sections of the middle classes. This essay also clearly demonstrates that the ruling class and their functionaries were often divided on the social significance of leisure. In other words, leisure was an ideologically contested cultural terrain. This fact, in essence, means that leisure could not be simply mobilised as a mechanism of social control, as is suggested by some historians. Referring specifically to the game of cricket, Cashman has cautioned that one should take cognisance of divisions among the elite which often blunt any hegemonic agenda.[78] While reformists often argued that approved working class leisure activities could serve as diversions from potential labour unrest, the agro-commercial bourgeoisie in Barbados remained unconvinced. The control of land and the use of coercive measures had been so long entrenched that it was difficult to embrace a new *modus operandi*. It was not until the post-1937 period that the provision of community playing fields became entrenched in government social policy.

Notes

1. *PP*, 1898 (c.8657), L, *Report of the West India Royal Commission* (hereafter, WIRC), 29.
2. Woodville Marshall, Trevor Marshall and Bentley Gibbs, 'The Establishment of a Peasantry in Barbados, 1840-1920,' in *Social Groups and Institutions in the History of the Caribbean* (Proceedings of the Sixth Conference of the Association of Caribbean Historians (ACH), Puerto Rico, April 4-9, 1974. San Juan: ACH, 1975), 85–104.
3. *PP*, 1898 (c.8656), L, WIRC, app. C, pt. 1, para. 2103.
4. *PP*, 1898 (c.8657), L, WIRC, app. C pt. 3, Memorandum of J. Henri

Field (237), 217.

5. *PP*, 1898 (c.8657), L, WIRC, app. C pt. 3, para. 933.
6. *Ibid.*, paras. 444, 450.
7. *PP*, 1898 (c.8650–29), LIX, Barbados Blue Book for 1897, 19.
8. *PP*, 1898 (c.8657), L, WIRC, app. C pt. 3, Memorandum of J. Henri Field (237), 218.
9. *Ibid.*, para. 943.
10. *Ibid.*, para. 875.
11. *Ibid.*, para. 913 and Memorandum of George Gay Daniel (239) B.
12. *Ibid.*, para. 212.
13. *PP*, 1899 (c.9046–30) LXI, Barbados Blue Book for 1898, 27.
14. MCA, 1911–12, doc. 162, Census of Barbados (1891–1911), 6.
15. Ibid., Table 1.
16. George H.H. McLellan, *Some Phases of Barbados Life: Tropical Scenes and Studies* (Georgetown: Argosy, 1909), 75.
17. Charles Augustus Stoddard, *Cruising Among the Caribbees: Summer Days in Winter Months* (New York: Charles Scribner's Sons, 1895), 172.
18. *Standard*, September 16, 1911.
19. Letter to the editor from 'One of Them,' entitled 'Clerks and Shop Assistants' Holidays,' *Herald*, August 30, 1880.
20. Letter to the editor from 'A Humble Layman,' entitled 'A Plea for the Sabbath,' *Herald*, March 9, 1893. The legal provision for the sale of these 'essential' items on early Sunday morning was enshrined in an Act of 1827.
21. 1873–1874, Cap. XII, Bank Holidays Act, secs., I, V and Schedule.
22. 'Summary for the Mail,' *Herald*, November 8, 1880; Letter to the editor from 'An Old Clerk,' entitled 'Mr. Inniss' Bank Holiday Bill 1880,' *Times*, March 30, 1892.
23. 'Legislative Summary, Bank Holidays Act Extension Bill,' *Herald*, March 9, 1885.
24. 'House of Assembly,' *Herald*, March 12, 1885.
25. 1884–1885, Cap. XV, 'The Bank Holidays Act, 1873, Extension Act, 1885.'
26. J.M. Woodroofe, 'A Brief History of the Pickwick C. C.,' *Barbados Cricketers Annual*, 1907–1908.
27. 'Echoes of the Week,' *Herald*, December 17, 1883.
28. Warren Alleyne, *Historic Bridgetown* (Bridgetown: Barbados National Trust, 1978), 93–94.
29. *Herald*, January 14, 1886.
30. 'The proposed Public Garden,' *Herald*, October 27, 1887.
31. *Bee*, August 19, 1887.
32. *Herald*, November 14, 1887.
33. *Times*, July 6, 1892.

34. Vagrancy Acts: 1840, Cap. I; 1897, C.14; Bridgetown, Speightstown, and Hole Town Act, 1891, C.41, and Police Act, 1890, C.19.
35. See, for example, the arrest of Captain Widgery, *Weekly Recorder,* June 11, 1898.
36. *Bee,* June 13, 1887.
37. See letter to the Editor from 'Another Subscriber,' *Herald,* September 8, 1892.
38. See letter to the editor from 'Truth,' responding to such a charge from an editorial in the *Wesleyan Watchman,* in *Herald,* January 16, 1888.
39. Letter from 'New York,' *Taxpayer,* October 28, 1892.
40. Harry A. Franck, *Roaming through the West Indies* (London: T. Fisher Unwin, 1921), 366–67.
41. 'Hastings Rocks Committee,' *Globe,* March 12, 1902.
42. *Globe,* March 14, 1902.
43. 'House of Assembly, Tuesday Feb. 16, 1904,' *Agricultural Reporter,* February 20, 1904; MCA, 1904–1905, doc 156, A.B.R. Kaye, 'Report of the Police Force for 1904.'
44. For a description of many of these sites, see J.H. Sutton Moxly, *A West Indian Sanatorium and a Guide to Barbados* (London: Sampson Low, Marston, Searle, & Rivington, 1886), 58–122.
45. Theatre Act, 1894, C.4, preamble.
46. DHA, *Official Gazette,* 34.25 (March 17, 1904): 247–51; *Official Gazette,* 39.29 (March 31, 1904): 267–69.
47. BDA, RB4/88, Will of George William Carrington, February 20, 1891; DHA, 'The Carrington Bequest Bill,' Speech of Hon. W.H. Greaves, January 14, 1896.
48. Letter to the editor from 'Observer,' entitled 'A Philanthropic Gentleman,' *Taxpayer,* May 29, 1886.
49. DHA, January 14, 1896.
50. *Agricultural Reporter,* January 21,1896.
51. T. Law Gaskin, 'The Norham Bequest,' *Agricultural Reporter,* January 21, 1896. See also *Agricultural Reporter,* January 28, 1896 for his riposte to that newspaper's support for the decision of the legislature.
52. Ralph A. Jemmott, 'A Brief History of Harrison College, 1733–1983,' in *Harrisonian: 250th Anniversary Commemorative Issue* (Bridgetown: Harrison College, 1983),12. See also, 'Education Committee's Scheme for Restoring Harrison's School,' July 16, 1869, reproduced in Shirley Gordon, *A Century of West Indian Education* (London: Longmans, 1963), 96–97.
53. Preamble to Act of 1870 to reestablish the School, quoted in Ralph A. Jemmott, 'A Brief History of Harrison College,' 12.
54. MCA, 1895 1896, doc. 60, 'The Norham Devise.'

55. DHA, February 4, 1896.
56. See *Agricultural Reporter*, February 21 & 25, 1896.
57. 'The Norham Bequest,' *Herald*, March 5, 1896.
58. DHA, March 10, 1896.
59. *Globe*, January 27, 1896.
60. 'Recreational Grounds,' *Herald*, April 18, 1896.
61. Ibid.
62. The Constitution Swamp and the Reef (Vesting) Act, 1894, C.4.
63. 'An Appeal on Behalf of the Recreational Grounds,' *Agricultural Reporter*, September 14, 1901.
64. 'Bank Holiday Cricket,' *Bulletin,* October 11, 1899.
65. *Agricultural Reporter*, January 2, 1904.
66. *Weekly Recorder,* May 30, 1903, 6.
67. See *Barbados Cricketers Annual*, 1904–1905: 157–58.
68. *Weekly Recorder,* May 18, 1906.
69. See Henry Fraser, *et al. A–Z of Barbadian Heritage* (Kingston: Heinemann, 1990), 143; John Gilmore, *Queen's Park: A Brief History and Guide* (Bridgetown: National Cultural Foundation, [1990]).
70. See DHA, 'Savannah Regulation Bill,' January 29, 1907.
71. DHA, January 29, 1907
72. Ibid.
73. DHA, May 21, 1907.
74. DLC, June 4, 1907.
75. Bishop Court Papers, November 14, 1901.
76. See correspondence between Governor Hodgson and Bishop Swaby, laid before the House of Assembly, in MCA 1902–1903, doc. 213.
77. *Supplement to the Agricultural Reporter*, March 28, 1903.
78. Richard Cashman, 'Cricket and Colonialism: Colonial Hegemony and Indigenous Subversion?' in *Pleasure, Profit, Proselytism: British Culture and Sport at Home and Abroad 1700–1914,* ed., J.A. Mangan. (London: Frank Cass, 1987), 258–72.

CHAPTER 18

Another Grounding: Peasants and Citizenship in Trinidad and Guyana

Kusha Haraksingh

Introduction

The aim of this paper is to explore some aspects of the environment in which, and the mechanisms whereby, early cane and rice growers in Trinidad and Guyana sought to assert a sense of citizenship in the last decades of the nineteenth and the early years of the twentieth centuries. For present purposes this is conceived of as an approach to their general situation which demonstrates a notion of belonging to the local polity and which served as a platform on which claims could be grounded and particular demands made. In this sense, this idea has as its points of departure the powerful observation made by Woodville Marshall, in his seminal *Notes on Peasant Development in the West Indies Since 1838*, that 'peasant development was emancipation in action.' Since most, but not all, of the growers with whom we are concerned were originally indentured immigrants from India, we can rephrase Marshall's image to make it more inclusive by referring to 'freedom in action.' The search for a grounding in a new land on the part of Indian growers was informed by ideas with which they were familiar and by behaviour to which they were accustomed. In particular, it would appear that they had their own ideas of the purposes of the state and of the obligations both of the citizen and of those who held the reins of power. However, in the established story it is really only when this search assumed conventional forms linked to the development of political associations and organisations and to participation in formal politics that it begins to be recognised.

Thus there is something of a gap in the historiography between two successive pictures: that of Indians on the one hand as plantation workers where labour disputes and contractual rights and expectations define the ambit of their demands, and that of them on the other hand as participants in formal politics where they are neatly packaged into 'conservatives' (those supposedly concerned only with sectional interests) and 'radicals' (those who are considered prepared to deal with issues affecting the so-called larger society).

This compartmentalising, apparently on the basis of different attitudes towards culture, religion and the dictates of westernisation, would, with an air of seeming inevitability, stimulate scholarly condemnation for the first group and some praise for the second one. However, the limitations of this analysis were often cruelly exposed as one year's radical turned out to be a subsequent year's conservative. By itself, this ought to indicate that such a way of framing the analysis is to ignore some streams of 'indigenising' which this paper seeks to discuss. We will focus on those Indians in transition who were no longer full-time plantation workers but who still sought a living off the land, and who had not yet begun to speak in the ordinary terms of an emergent literate grouping.

Historians of this particular experience have to wrestle with the tools of their trade in a more self-conscious fashion than if they are concerned with either the earlier 'plantation worker' or the later 'emergent middle class' picture. This is especially the case if they wish to advance the proposition that this community of cane and rice growers were not only the 'done to' but also the 'doers,' that they were not only 'acted upon' but were also the 'actors,' and that they had a significant role to play in establishing the parameters of their own destiny. This is because when Indians completed their indentureship and, still more, when they ceased to reside on the sugar estates officialdom lost some, though not all, interest in them, and until Western education had made a sufficient impact they themselves hardly spoke in accents recognisable by the wider society. There are few petitions or letters to the editor which one can safely assume to be representative. Thus, one has to discover their voice in unorthodox ways, itself an emancipation of the history. This relates to the entire stretch of their history in the Caribbean but arguably is a task more pressing when one is dealing with the transition period with which we are here concerned.

Their personal tale is often obscured by some of the concepts embedded in the accepted story, and the first task is therefore to reassess certain notions. One has to reconsider especially the classification of host and immigrant, the former usually a code word for African and the latter for Indian and both clearly inapplicable in the Trinidad and Guyana context where the truly indigenous population was small or marginalised. These designations inexorably permit the formulation of the idea of 'contribution to the society' which, although it is hardly seen to be doing so, really puts the contributors on the one side and the society on the other. In this light matters internal to the contributors are not seen as matters affecting the society but as purely sectional issues. This emerges most clearly in discussions of the social ordering of society where the general conclusion is that Indians were relegated to the bottom of the heap. That was not their own ranking, but the ranking of others. To rely on that, then, as a statement of social hierarchy, is obviously to ignore the views of a significant group in the population and seemingly to fail to acknowledge that the Indians were themselves members of the society. One consequence of this approach is an emphasis on the formation of stereotypes, itself an important area, but often expressed in such a way as to carry the flavour of an 'exogenous' history, that is to say, of making what others thought of the Indians pass as the history of the group. One has, in addition, to reconsider the categories of economic and political activity, particularly when it is clear that the cane and rice growers did not themselves think of their world in that dichotomous light. From this perspective, to argue that rice growers in Guyana, for example, did not at first participate in politics because they were busily earning a living,[1] is perhaps to force on to the growers a concept of politics which they had not yet assimilated. True, in Guyana there were formidable ecological problems which could be tackled only by costly and complex drainage and irrigation schemes,[2] but it is precisely here that the growers would confront the meaning of status, authority and the proper role of government. Indeed, with a cultural baggage fashioned in rural India, it would be surprising if these were not the things that sprang to mind as they sought to wrest a livelihood from coastal swamp and upland creek. As a consequence, it is still more dangerous to suppose that lack of competence in English, admittedly the local language of public discussion, deterred Indians from participation in politics. Language problems might complicate the task of qualifying for the franchise or might, as in the case of the secret ballot introduced in Guyana in 1898, render it impossible for some to make a selection of a particular candidate,[3] but there was nothing in the life experience of Indians to cause them to suppose that was the centre of politics.

In a word, then, one has to discover the struggle for citizenship in the arena where the growers themselves located it and not where the analyst, from a vision external to the growers, might suppose that it resided. This becomes clearer if we look at the usual approach in the literature to formal organisations. The magic of form — constitution, chairman, delegates — often accords a spurious weight to political activity, and in a turn of the card its absence ordinarily serves to indicate a lack of activity. Not surprisingly, then, so much attention is directed at the debates of associations, the minutes of their meetings and the resolutions which are passed: sometimes, the attention conveys an approach so close and exact as would startle even the most ardent deconstructionist. But modern political activity in small countries should lead us to be cautious. It is not unusual for party groups to exist simply on paper for conventions and conferences, or for resolutions to be devised on the day for the day, often as a matter of form. What passes as substance is often show. The preoccupation with formal political activity, as indeed with formal trade union activity, when it makes its appearance, to elucidate the struggles of working peoples, is thus potentially misleading on at least two grounds: it tips the scale towards the magic of form more heavily than is warranted, and it downplays informal activity in favour of constitutionality more substantially than is justified.

In the case of early cane and rice growers, then, the task is the problematic one of assessing informal activity. The stray petition, or violent episode, or even spontaneous strike would leave a more or less definite trail. Even if the trail were exclusively official there would be enough to read against the grain to ground a reconstruction which permits the participants to tell at least part of the story.[4] But peasant history proceeds not from one great turning point to another and thus due attention must be given to the minutiae of peasant life.[5] Since the daily grind consumed the bulk of their exertions, it is pointless to look for a struggle for citizenship elsewhere. It is the daily grind itself that tells the story.

Cane farming in Trinidad

The stranglehold which sugar planters in Trinidad were able to establish and maintain over both their indentured and ex-indentured workers permitted them generally to dictate the pace and range of cultivation operations on their own fields. Their dominance over free labour, in particular, was achieved partly by manipulating earnings and this naturally stimulated a search by the workers for a sideline activity to supplement the income which they received from estate employment. The planters were able to guide that search through the control which they enjoyed, by ownership and by influence in the legislature, over the release of estate and Crown land. By helping to select which areas to make available the planters determined where the labourers would live, and by attaching conditions to the rental of estate land they determined what use would be made of it. The planters aimed at ensuring, firstly, that the sideline activity of the workers was attractive enough to keep a sufficient pool of labour in the vicinity of the estates but not so profitable as to detract from estate employment, and, secondly, that it helped to reduce the cost of sugar production. Both of these aims were realised under the system of cane farming.

The initial experiments with cane farming — whereby on lands made available by the estates individual growers cultivated and reaped canes which they then sold to the mills — were prompted by falling sugar prices in the early 1880s. The idea quickly took root, and in the later 1880s and the1890s, increasing numbers of planters turned over their idle land for their workers to engage in cane farming as a part-time activity. Also, some ex-indentured workers who commuted their return passages to India for land in the country established themselves as cane farmers on their own plots. The country's expanding rail system which continued to link new areas more closely to the central factories added a further stimulus to the spread of cane farming. By 1898 cane farmers, some of whom were ex-indentured workers, were supplying 20 per cent of all the canes crushed at the mills. The share of the crop which they provided continued to grow in the early twentieth century, and by 1914 it amounted to 33.5 per cent of the canes processed at the factories.

The major advantage of cane farming to the planters was that it allowed them to feed their mills more cheaply than if they had cultivated the canes on their own estates. This was secured through the pricing system. The returns which the grower obtained for his produce could vary, depending on several factors, for example, whether the canes were grown on his land or on plots rented from the estate; or whether he or the estate cut and delivered the canes to the mills or to outside purchasing stations. Not infrequently, the condition of the canes was also called into account; stale or over-ripened canes or canes heavily laced with trash were assessed at lower rates. Many farmers were convinced that the final determination was arbitrary and some complained that the decisive factor was merely the whim of the millers.[6] These misgivings led to the introduction in 1895 of a sliding scale for determining the price of farmers' canes: under this mechanism a relationship was supposed to exist between the returns to the growers and the London price for muscovado sugar. The scale, however, showed more of a tendency to slide downwards rather than upwards from the stated minimum price. The growers continued to express their displeasure with this arrangement and in 1916 the government established a Sugar Prices Committee to review the pricing system. None of the subsequent arrangements was totally satisfactory to the growers who more than once would turn to the courts in their attempt to obtain a better deal. In 1922 the growers would take a test case all the way to the Privy Council in England to challenge the pricing policy.

The ability of the planters to dictate the price paid to the farmer sprang directly from conditions within the sugar industry. The millers actively minimised the competition among themselves for farmers' canes. The crop obtained on lands rented from an estate was tied by the condition of the lease to the estate factory. Those growers who had borrowed money from estates to meet the expenses associated with cane cultivation were similarly circumscribed. In theory the farmer who possessed his own land or who rented from persons not connected with the sugar estates could sell his canes where he pleased, but in practice his freedom was limited by transportation costs and other logistical considerations, such as what was referred to as his ' "donkey distance" from the nearest factory or tramway siding.'[7]

Even in the face of this unequal relationship, the number of cane farmers and the acreage which they cultivated continued to increase. There were many reasons for this situation. Though never satisfied over the price fetched by their canes, the farmers were clearly attracted by the possibilities of obtaining ready cash which was useful in discharging debts which they had incurred during the growing season, and which represented more than the pure monetary value of returns from sales. In estimating the profitability of cane farming they did not count the cost of their own and their family's labour and so were led into believing that this enterprise was more remunerative than it really was. Further, the ability of the lands to sustain ratoons for long periods eased the burden on the cane farmers. In addition, they knew that once they had land at their disposal — never mind the implied or explicit terms of lease — they could exploit it to the fullest. In time they devised an efficient system of inter-cropping which allowed them to sow and reap food crops while the canes were in the early stages of growth. Finally, notions of status were involved; in the countryside the cane farmer enjoyed a higher social standing than the pure estate worker.

In these circumstances, it was the planters themselves who limited the expansion of cane farming. Obviously, it did not make sense to encourage it beyond the point where farmers' and estate canes combined exceeded the processing capacity of the factories or where the farmers began to compete with the estates for hired field labour. And though farmers' canes could be bought at a price lower than the cost of cultivation on the estates, the planters up to 1917 had a pool of unfree labour which was better employed growing estate canes than not at all. Most importantly, however, the planters felt that they needed to guard against giving the growers the advantage in determining cane prices; thus, they were not inclined to allow their mills to become too dependent on farmers' canes. These considerations were weighed against the substantial saving to the estates represented by farmers' canes in terms of cost of cultivation and also in terms of maximising operating time at the factories. In arriving at the right balance, the planters always seemed to have the upper hand.

Rice growing in Guyana

Some of the same trends observable in the previous section can be discerned in the case of rice growing in Guyana. There also the planters attempted to control the pace and extent of activity, and to ensure that the cultivation of rice proceeded in a manner that was complementary to the interests of the sugar estates.[8] Before the 1880s, Indians resident on the sugar plantations were generally not permitted to grow rice on estate land. Where it was allowed, careful steps were taken to limit the amount of land per head or per family unit so that the estate labour supply was not adversely affected. Following the depression of the mid-1880s, however, the planters began to see the financial sense of allowing their labour force to produce some of their own food supply. At the same time changes in cane husbandry, especially the gradual elimination of the Bourbon variety, rendered it feasible for cultivation to be pushed further back from the estate front lands which thus became available for rice growing.

The abandonment of sugar cultivation on some estates made more land available, as did the opening up of riverain Crown lands in 1898 on what for some were manageable terms of purchase. By 1900 government interest was being channelled through the Board of Agriculture which conducted experiments in different rice varieties and supplied seed to the growers. A major objective was to develop a uniform grain size to reduce wastage in the milling process and by 1908 this had been substantially achieved. All of this stimulated further expansion so that, whereas in 1891 the land under rice amounted to only 4,000 acres, there was a ten-fold increase in the following two decades, and by 1917 for every ten acres planted in sugar in Guyana, eight acres were planted in rice.[9]

Expanding rice acreage was accompanied by the mushrooming of small mills. In 1914 there were 86 of them in existence. They were hardly elaborate structures but they were linked to the large mercantile firms in the capital and they controlled growers in the villages through a system of advances. Many of the millers, like many large rice growers, were Indians who employed Indian labour, and the evidence suggests that ethnicity hardly guaranteed favourable treatment.[10] This was why, often in Guyana's rice villages, the first skirmish in any struggle for citizenship had to be waged in one's own backyard.

The search for citizenship

From the foregoing it is clear that in terms of the struggle for citizenship on the part of Indian cane and rice growers, the first decisive move was the decision to forego the return passage to India guaranteed under indenture contracts and to remain in Trinidad and Guyana. This was tantamount to letting down one's bucket, or even voting with one's feet. The planters' attitude towards the return passage is well documented. They seemed at least irritated that they had to make a choice between the productive work of Indians as labourers and the harmful moral effects which their presence had on the larger Christian society. But since considerations of profit were paramount, it is not surprising that, as a leading spokesman of the plantocracy in Trinidad put it, the provision of a return passage to India was an arrangement much to be regretted and an 'evil to which we must subsist.'[11] Little wonder, then, that sustained attempts were made to escape the obligation and to undermine the spirit of the provision, including schemes to make returnees pay for their children and successful efforts to make them contribute towards the cost. The planter stratagems have been so well illuminated that one can sometimes be forgiven for thinking that the planters effected the choice. But considerable numbers of Indians, in both Trinidad and Guyana, elected to return to India, so it would be inappropriate to see the planters as themselves determining events.

It is difficult from written sources to identify reasons for staying. Two arguments predominate in the literature, one relating to economic prospects and the other to social difficulties. It is often claimed that Indians must have concluded that a better life was possible in the New World, but that view cannot be disassociated from planter anxiety to prove that the regimen of work on their estates was not harsh and that a spirit of contentment prevailed. Additionally, some play is made of problems relating to regaining caste membership on return to India but this seems doubtful as an influential factor. The process of re-incorporation has been misunderstood and has been made to appear more complex and expensive than was actually the case. It was really more a matter of removing ritual pollution which could be accumulated even without leaving India. More importantly, caste inhibitions are not uniform across the spectrum;[12] if, therefore, concerns about caste validity were paramount one would expect some skewing in the profile of the returnees, but they are drawn randomly from across the range. Perhaps, then, accounts of social resentment and antipathy suffered by returnees were simply an indication of the imperfect understanding of the caste system current in the nineteenth century and attributable to an emphasis on prescriptive texts and not on actual practice, or perhaps the accounts were designed or at least exaggerated with the aim of persuading Indians to stay.

If the recollections of surviving Indian immigrants can shed any light on decision-making, it would appear that their concept of a space in which they had come to feel grounded and which they recognised as 'home' was decisive. Typically, they offer the explanation that they had no one in India, and that their family was located in Trinidad or Guyana.[13] This is really a reference to immediate family, both natural and ascriptive, and reveals a definition of homeland as the space where one's family resided. This particular concept was accorded little credence by the planters who continued to see Indians on the whole as transients. In retrospect, this was probably a reflection of the planters' own lack of commitment to any definite space, a legacy of generations of absenteeism, education in metropolitan centres, money in external banks, and familial, social and commercial contacts that rendered territorial boundaries meaningless. The planters set the tone and their views on this matter were absorbed uncritically by press and literate opinion in the colonies, so that an important aspect of the struggle for citizenship was the need for Indians to establish, over and over again, that their commitment to their new space was genuine. What made it harder was that Indians were so easily doubted. The stereotypical view that they lied on oath without compunction was freely translated to support the belief that they lied freely anyway. Even those who underwent religious conversion, in what sometimes must have been agonising moments of personal crisis, were widely suspected of insincerity.[14]

The belief that free Indians, even those working on their own cane or rice plots, were not subjects on a par with others, helps to explain official insistence that they should remain under the wardship of the immigration department. This was not as beneficial as it might appear: it precluded them from receiving assistance which was generally provided, so that for example in Guyana, they had on occasions to spend their own money poldering their lands while non-

Indians were able to benefit from the common budget.[15] The high watermark of this bifurcated approach was the proposal contained in the Trinidad Immigration Ordinance of 1897 to style all Indians, even those who had for long resided in the colony, as immigrants, and to authorise their arrest if found outside the estates without a certificate of exemption from labour. Under this provision Indian cane growers who wished to employ other Indians, perhaps at planting or harvest time, could not do so without ensuring that they had seen the required pass. The Ordinance of 1897 stimulated an intense agitation and considering that violence was seen in some quarters as a real possibility it is clear that the Indian peasantry was bristling.[16]

By the 1890s they were bristling too under the appellation 'coolie'; self-definition was obviously an exercise which they had carried out and were now demanding that fellow subjects adjust their sights accordingly. The cane or rice grower, especially if by his moderate personal standards a success, was not only claiming status in a social or economic sense but was also, in denying a designation appropriate to bonded labour, asserting his readiness to claim political rights. But unfortunately for him, by choosing to stay in the colony he provided the authorities with grounds for concluding that he was contented, which in turn reinforced officialdom's predisposition to ignore his claims.

Almost as big a step as electing to stay in the colony was the decision to move off the estates. Several factors were usually taken into account, including the quality of the estate management, the availability of opportunities for extra earnings, health and housing conditions. In Guyana, in particular, the health factor seemed to count for a great deal, with the drier estates retaining their resident labour force for longer periods than those where the rainfall was heavier. Of course, individual characteristics such as age and enterprise also played a part. The move off the estates was usually coupled with the acquisition of property, either through the commutation of return passages or the purchase of Crown land. At times the rate of land acquisition seemed to generate misgivings. Complaints that Indians have an earth hunger were not uncommon, and in Trinidad in 1906 people were actively debating whether the sale of Crown land should be discontinued.[17]

For Indian cane and rice growers, title to property provided a platform to make demands on the government. This has to be understood in the context of the traditional Indian view that the State had an obligation to protect the rights of people on the land, and to champion the interests of the cultivators. In rural India it was in the sphere of property relations that the government's presence was most immediately felt in land assessment, settling rates of taxation, deciding on competing rights, providing in return for a share of the crop, adequate water management, and maintaining access roads and traces.[18] These were precisely the areas which the new titleholders in Trinidad and Guyana began to address. For them this was the essence of the relationship between citizen and government, and this was why in meeting places, which included the village rum shop, these were the issues which were the focus of comment and discussion.[19]

The acquisition of private property naturally foreshadowed efforts to redesign the landscape. Rice growers who had acquired lands on abandoned sugar estates had more of a physical restructuring to accomplish than cane farmers, for the ecological requirements of both crops differed, but both sets of growers altered the environment in similar ways. The trees which they chose to plant around their homesteads, including religious vegetation,[20] constituted a statement about belonging; so too were the temples and mosques constructed in emergent villages and the sanctifying of selected places as sacred sites.[21] Many cane and rice growers raised domestic cattle. Some of them, as those in the Mahaica and Mahaicony creeks in Guyana, managed to accumulate herds of 90 to 100 heads. These animals, in Indian terms, could hardly be abandoned easily, or even sold; they represented therefore some form of commitment to the locality on the part of their owners. The growers dug ponds and constructed tanks, diverted watercourses and cleared land, and named or renamed various places. When all of this is put together it is hard to resist the conclusion that Indian cane and rice growers had begun to think of Trinidad and Guyana as their homeland long before general opinion in the colonies had awakened to that as a possibility.

One group that was obviously not too anxious to extend the idea of citizenship to the cane and rice growers, more than was strictly necessary, was the millers. Partly for this reason, the relationship between the growers and the millers was marked by conflict and tension. Common areas of dispute included methods of weighing and measurement, and of computing transport costs and the ultimate price for the crop, as well as delays in payment. In the case of rice growers, exorbitant rates of interest on advances provided by millers, who also operated as moneylenders, furnished grounds for strife. In the rice villages, rival millers stimulated village factionalism and the politicisation of the rice growers.[22]

While some rice growers could aspire to set up their own mill, as a group of them in a village in the Mahaica-Abary coast were able to do,[23] it was hardly likely that cane growers could amass the money necessary to acquire a sugar factory. A large cane-growing family in Trinidad did eventually acquire a small mill, interestingly enough called Hindustan, in the south of the island, but that was exceptional. The sugar factories remained in mercantile hands, and the unavoidable conflict between grower and miller represented a clash in which the realities of status and power were often nakedly displayed. This was nowhere clearer than in a remarkable piece of litigation which reached the Privy Council on appeal from Trinidad in 1922 but which revealed conditions which had been in existence for some time.[24]

The facts of the case were as follows: in January 1919, the Ste Madeleine Sugar Company Limited circulated a notice offering to buy canes from growers on their list of suppliers at a certain price per ton; in December 1921, two weeks before the start of the harvest season, the company issued a new notice offering a lower price; the growers proceeded to supply the company with canes and claimed the original price but the company insisted on paying the reduced rate. The growers thereupon took a test case to court to claim the difference. On the face of it this was a case about the validity of a contract and the Privy Council applied the usual analysis of dissecting the facts into the constituents of offer, acceptance, revocation of the offer and consideration. They held that an offer could be withdrawn at any moment before it was accepted, that no contract had come into existence until the canes were actually delivered to the company's mills, and that the 1919 offer, therefore, had been validly withdrawn. They found no merit in the growers' contention that the company's offer had been accepted when cultivation commenced, and that as a result it could only be varied by mutual consent or reasonable notice.

In strict law, of course, the Privy Council was right but that was cold comfort to a grower induced to cultivate his plots by the 1919 notice. He might not have understood the mysteries of part-performance and the equitable doctrine of estoppel had not yet emerged, but he knew that he had relied on the company's word. Like many appellate cases, this one turned partly on use of English — the literal meaning of 'cane' and 'canes,' of 'supply' and 'grow,' matters which undoubtedly would have appeared excessively arcane, especially to those whose first tongue was not English. Contract cases have a way of being dissolved into a simple maxim: keep your promise; and many of the growers must have felt therefore that the company was being allowed, with impunity, to renege on its obligations. The judgment turned a blind eye to the realities of cane growing with its long rationing periods and its in-built lack of manoeuvrability, factors which ensured that reasoning drawn from cases involving ordinary commercial contracts was bound to favour the millers. The court found that until the delivery of the canes no contract was concluded and justified this by pointing out that the growers were not themselves bound to sell their cane to the company; this was strictly true but it ignored the monopoly conditions imposed by arrangement between the various sugar millers which presented the grower with no real alternatives except, as the lawyer for the plaintiffs argued, to grind the canes 'with his own molars.' There is little doubt that the Privy Council's decision would have confirmed the growers' belief that some people could get away with anything, that wealth, privilege and connections in England (for the Privy Council had reversed the local Court of Appeal) obscured justice and fair play, and that the whole commercial and legal establishment was out to rob them of their just desserts. This was politics with a vengeance.

Conclusion

In this paper we have examined cane and rice growers in Trinidad and Guyana in the context of their decision to remain in the colonies, to move off the estates and to acquire property, to refashion the landscape according to their own demands, and to order their relationship with middlemen and millers. The period occupied by these developments was a time of transition and it was in these activities that the search for a grounding and the struggle for citizenship resided. The lines seemed remarkably similar, even though ethnographic evidence generally prepares us for sharp differences between cane and rice cultivators.[25] It may be that in this period these differences were subsumed under a common understanding held by Indian cane and rice growers of the role of government and the obligations of subjects. This might help to explain why the cherished goal in both rice and sugar villages was to ride the line of progress from landless labour to tenant to proprietor. The magic of property was the badge of belonging and the key to raising claims.[26]

In this period of transition, however, it was a set piece of planter wisdom that only those with a substantial stake in the colonies could be allowed any participation in political decision making. Indian cane and rice growers were not yet judged to have acquired a stake, let alone a substantial one. The most successful among them, as in the case of millers in Guyana or certain large cane farmers in Trinidad, had all too easily adopted the extractive inclinations of the plantocracy. This allowed them to begin by 1900 tentatively to put forward assessments of the Indian contribution to the local economy as a framework for supporting demands in recognisable political battles: franchise, representation, and so on. The tabulation stressed that Indians had rescued the economy, that they were licence—and rate-payers, proprietors and depositors with money in the bank. Ostensibly these points were made on behalf of all Indians, but in reality the spokesmen were usually speaking for themselves. Thus, new political alignments were already becoming noticeable.

Notes

1. T. Ramnarine, 'The Issue of East Indian Political Representation in British Guiana During the Latter Part of Indenture, 1890-1917' (Paper presented at Eleventh Conference of the Association of Caribbean Historians [ACH], Curaçao, 1979), 5.

2. C.Y. Thomas, *Plantations, Peasants and State: A Study of the Mode of Sugar Production in Guyana* (Los Angeles: Center for Afro-American Studies, University of California, 1984), 5.

3. Ramnarine, 1979.

4. A.C. Milner, 'Colonial Records History: British Malaya,' *Modern Asian*

Studies, 21.4 (1987): 773–92.

5. W. Rodney, *A History of the Guyanese Working People, 1881–1903* (Baltimore: The Johns Hopkins University Press, 1981), 75.

6. H. Warner, Paper on 'Cane Farming,' in *Proceedings of the Agricultural Society of Trinidad and Tobago*, Vol. I (Port-of-Spain, 1894).

7. *Council Paper No.13 of 1906: Report of the Labour Committee, Legislative Council of Trinidad and Tobago* (Port-of-Spain, 1906), 71.

8. L.M. Potter, 'The Paddy Proletariat and the Dependent Peasantry: East Indian Rice Growers in British Guiana, 1895–1920' (Ninth Conference of the Association of Caribbean Historians, Barbados, 1977), 13.

9. Ibid., 22.

10. L.M. Potter, 'East Indians Without Sugar — Essequibo, Guyana, 1923–39' (Conference on East Indians in the Caribbean, Trinidad, 1979).

11. L.A.A. de Verteuil, *Trinidad: Its Geography, Natural Resources, Administration and Prospects* (2nd ed., London: Ward and Lock, 1884), 349.

12. D.G. Mandelbaum, *Society in India* (2 Vols. Berkeley: University of California Press, 1972).

13. N.K. Mahabir, *The Still Cry: Personal Accounts of East Indians in Trinidad during Indentureship (1845–1911)* (New York: Calaloux Publications, 1985), 130–32.

14. De Verteuil, 351.

15. Ramnarine, 1979.

16. G. Tikasingh, 'The Establishment of the Indians in Trinidad, 1870–1900' (PhD. thesis, UWI, 1976), 400ff.

17. *Trinidad Council Papers, No.13 of 1906*, 'The Labour Question,' 6. Subsequently, it would become common for people to assert that Indians benefited from free grants of land. In reality, land was acquired by commutation of the return passage to India or, much more usually, by outright purchase. Nevertheless, the folklore of free grants persisted.

18. R.E. Frykenberg, *Land Control and Social Structure in Indian History* (Madison: University of Wisconsin Press, 1969).

19. Tikasingh, 229.

20. C.V. Prorok, 'Hindu Temples in Trinidad: Cultural Geography of Religious Structures and Ethnic Identity' (PhD. dissertation, Louisiana State University, 1987).

21. K. Bahadur Singh, *Temples and Mosques: an Illustrated Study of East Indian Places of Worship in Guyana* (Georgetown: Guyana Release, 1980).

22. M. Silverman, 'Resource Change and Village Factionalism in an East Indian Community, Guyana' (PhD. dissertation, McGill University,

1973).

23. Potter, 1977.

24. *Supreme Court Judgments, Trinidad and Tobago*, Vol. 5, 7–47.

25. A. Béteille, *Caste, Class and Power: Changing Patterns of Stratification in a Tanjore Village* (Berkeley: University of California Press, 1965).

26. Perhaps overseas Indians, some of whom doubtless had been induced to emigrate as a consequence of the effects on the Indian countryside of British revenue schemes, had internalised, more than they themselves recognised, the ideals of private property contained in those arrangements.

CHAPTER 19

The Roots of Survival: Agriculture in Trinidad and Tobago During World War II
Rita Pemberton

Introduction

It was characteristic of the sugar plantation colonies of the Caribbean to expend local resources on export-crop production and import essential food items. This pattern of activity developed in the early days of sugar production when the demand for sugar was so great that the resulting high prices encouraged planters to attempt to maximise production. It then seemed good economic sense to import food, which was presumably cheap, and use the existing resources to produce the export crop. This was one of the planks upon which the entire plantation system was organised. The practice was not flexible and was based on the assumption that external sources of food would always be available, accessible and affordable. Indeed, it was also assumed that the returns from export-crop production would continue to be high enough to pay for food imports, which would, presumably, remain cheap.

However, for the sugar colonies of the British West Indies, the weakness of such a practice had been constantly demonstrated, given the frequency of war in the age of sugar. Wartime conditions made the experience of food crises common for these colonies. In addition, hurricanes and storms, and the late arrival of ships added to their problems. At these times, the uncertainty of an imported food supply and the possibility of unanticipated price hikes were well demonstrated. Though they always produced panic in the colonies, such experiences were not translated into a practical policy for local food production. Under these conditions, coping strategies were devised to deal with the problem in the short term, for there was an underlying assumption that such crises would be temporary.

In the British West Indian plantation experience, severe threats to the normal method of operation had been posed by some wars, such as the War of American Independence (1776–83). Carrington reports that there were many casualties in this war as a result of the disruption of normal trading activity over the seven-year period. He also argues that the colonies faced further economic problems as a result of the war when adjustments to the trading system had to be made.[1] One school of historians dates the economic decline of the British West Indies to this war and its after-effects. Another war which posed serious problems for the region, and again raised the issue of the feasibility of locally-produced food, was World War II.

This essay examines the response of the agricultural sector of Trinidad and Tobago to the exiguous circumstances of war. It outlines the crisis faced in the colony and describes and assesses the strategies implemented to deal with it. It first discusses the state of agriculture and the nature of agricultural administration in the colony before the war broke out. Then the crisis in the colony and the agricultural measures formulated to deal with it are discussed. In this discussion focus will be placed on the participation of the various sub-sectors in agriculture and both the administrative and community response. The essay argues that policy framers were aware of and able to implement policies that could have assisted the formulation of a more flexible agricultural policy, which would have provided greater food security for the colony, but that these policies were only implemented during the exigencies of war or calamity.

The state of agriculture in the colony of Trinidad and Tobago, 1930–39

The agricultural sector of Trinidad and Tobago was made up of two sub-sectors, plantation and peasant. Sugar was the main plantation crop, followed by cocoa. A few estates in Tobago and in southeast Trinidad produced coconuts. The peasant sub-sector concentrated on food-crop production, though some of its members were involved in sugar cultivation, while others were small-scale cocoa producers. Sugar planters in both islands had been loud in their cries of distress in the industry since the middle of the nineteenth century. The last three decades of that century brought worsening conditions as British West Indian sugar faced stiff competition from European bounty-fed beet sugar. The resulting distress caused the British government to establish the Norman Commission to inquire into the state of the industry in the colonies in 1897. By the second decade of the twentieth century, the Trinidad sugar industry had recovered from the depression, and recorded some increase in production and improvements in field operation.[2] However, the Tobago sugar industry had declined beyond repair throughout the nineteenth century and was dead by the end of the century.[3]

After enjoying its golden age between 1870 and 1920, the cocoa industry crashed in 1922. Faced with stiff competition from West African producers, some Trinidadian cocoa planters abandoned their estates. The cocoa-producing districts of the colony suffered as workers migrated to other areas in search of employment. This situation contributed to the distress that was evident in the colony during the 1930s and by this time the Trinidad economy was heavily dependent on the petroleum sector.

Food imports into Trinidad and Tobago, 1930–46

Concerns were expressed about the colony's high food import bill during the 1930s,[4] but there was no change in the trend. Between 1937 and 1946, there were significant increases in the import quantities and prices of several basic food items. These included flour, ground provisions, meat and meat products. Food imports totalled $6,466,740 in 1937, increased to $17,865,571 in 1944 and reached $17,914,636 in 1946.[5] Although some of the increase in value is related to price inflation, there were significant increases in the purchased quantities of a number of items (see Table 19.1).

Table 19.1: Quantities of food imports, 1937, 1944 and 1946

| | Quantity | | | |
Item	1937	1944	1946	Unit
Flour	341,254	425,316	512,368	Bags
Rice	41,533,408	30,845,440	24,173,408	lb.
Potatoes	86,387	60,247	118,830	cwt.
Onions & garlic	79,288	28,090	85,728	bushel
Tea	276,077	391,790	359,327	lb.
Fruits, peas, dhall & spilt peas	4,531,699	5,273,428	4,180,736	lb.
Ground provisions	10,540	32,288	32,480	cwt.
Cattle	9,291	18,504	5,526	-
Other animals for slaughter	12,720	16,239	23,199	-
Fresh meat	114,594	131,536	1,818,279	lb.
Pickled or salted meat	2,927,456	5,759,040	3,018,960	lb.
Smoked or cured meat	2,291,296	3,282,524	1,902,768	lb.
Cured or salted fish	5,587,120	5,030,256	4,691,568	lb.
Condensed milk	75,691	102,152	107,524	cwt.

Source: Report of the Sub-Committee on Agriculture, 1948, 93–95.

Caribbean Commission

World War II presented a very severe crisis. This war led to a serious disruption of normal activities as all the major powers were involved. Such was the fear of serious regional distress because of the war that on March 9, 1942 Britain and the United States formed the Anglo-American Caribbean Commission to deal with the problems on a cooperative basis.[6] In its report for 1942-43 the commission agreed to deal with the problems of the Caribbean on a regional rather than a local basis. It sought to encourage greater diversification of agriculture, promote increased inter-island trade and improve the transportation of the region.[7] The commission assisted in the establishment of a system of bulk purchasing of imported essential foods and the organisation of a local administrative system of inter-island distribution through the schooner pool. This involved stockpiling emergency food supplies at strategic locations in order to safeguard against a total cut off of supplies. In addition, it made a major thrust into prodding government to increase local food production, especially to supply local substitutes for imported items. Also, its staff was involved in efforts to increase the production of protein foods in which Caribbean diets were very deficient.[8] It was also involved in the attempt to reduce unemployment by securing jobs for the locals on the United States bases in the region.[9] Once World War II had begun, the commission became preoccupied with the more immediate problem of supplying the islands with the essentials of life. To do this, it facilitated the coordination of shipping between the colonial shipping lines, the United States and Canada. Essential food was imported through the British Colonial Supply Commission in Washington, while American officials undertook investigations into the food situation in the territories.[10] It then became heavily involved in the promotion of food security in the region.

'Grow more food' campaign

The Trinidad and Tobago survival programme was an elaboration of that undertaken during World War I. A 'Grow More Food' campaign was again launched in 1939. The strategy was carefully explained to the public and popularised through leaflets, lectures and demonstrations. Land was made readily available for rent as Emergency War Gardens at low prices. The whole strategy was supervised by the Department of Agriculture, with assistance from the Trinidad and Tobago Agricultural Society, and consultants from the United States and Britain.[11]

During World War II, because of the demand for labour on the United States bases, there was a shortage of workers for agricultural purposes. Thus, the sugar and cocoa estates experienced problems with regard to their labour supply and it was difficult to maintain a system of planting between the canes in order to increase the area under food cultivation.[12] The American bases attracted workers, because they offered more remunerative employment than agricultural work. It was estimated that about 15,000 workers abandoned agriculture.[13] This development, which was facilitated by the provision of transportation to and from the bases to workers from the more remote areas, resulted in the attraction of workers from the more distant areas.[14] Workers flocked to the bases from Tobago as well, abandoning their gardens in the process.[15] This migration, in addition to population increases in Trinidad, led to such an increased consumer demand for local food that the Food Comptroller predicted a shortage of food during June, July and September 1941.[16] Further, there was an acute tyre shortage in the colony due to the war. Since this item could not be produced locally and was critical to the plan for food security and survival generally, a Tyre Board was formed. This Board controlled the issuing of tyres in the colony.[17] The tyre shortage, and the knowledge that it could not be alleviated without the arrival of shipments from abroad, affected the approach to the food production programme. Therefore, the Grow More Food campaign had to operate '. . . on lines making each district of Trinidad as self sufficient as possible during 1942–44, and giving people lands within reasonable distances from their existing homes.'[18] The Department of Agriculture laid out demonstration gardens across the country and school principals were drawn into the food-production activity.[19] In the face of a severe scarcity of poultry and eggs, a Poultry Committee was established to stimulate production of these items. Poultry production was also stimulated through the formation of Juvenile Clubs in Trinidad, which were patterned on those already existing in Tobago. Both the Departments of Education and Agriculture were involved in these clubs. Selected breeds of poultry were distributed to these clubs and to the peasantry, while government also increased its grants to the government farms to increase poultry production.[20] The demand for local foods increased and in November 1941 the arrangement with the Canadian Banana Company had to be suspended as both local demand and prices were high. Also, 900 acres of rice were planted, yielding a 25 per cent increase in local rice production.[21]

The initial response to the programme was not at all satisfactory. Over the first two years of the war, 1,400 war gardens were given out,[22] but the problems persisted, as some of these were abandoned by persons seeking jobs on the bases. Cessation of food supplies from Argentina and Brazil created further problems in Trinidad forcing the authorities to look to Venezuela to make up the shortage.[23] St Vincent and Barbados also reduced the quantities of food and planting material that were sold to Trinidad thus making the crisis worse.[24] There were shortages of all kinds in the colony. Frozen beef, salted fish, and fresh fish were short. This shortage of fish occurred because the fishermen were hampered by the closing of their traditional fishing grounds due to naval activity. Vendors, restauranteurs and hoteliers vied with each other for the limited supply of fish and shrimp that were available.[25] The situation became more complicated as transportation problems affected the supply of charcoal which itself became short, because supplies from both British Guiana and local sources were affected. Laundresses and those without electricity were seriously affected.[26] Hoarding and 'black marketing' became common, aggravating the problems. The Food Comptroller was given wider powers to locate excess food stock and laws against hoarding food in excess of two weeks' supply made this practice punishable by a fine of $480 or six months in prison.[27]

Food control department

There was such disquiet about the situation in the colony that a plan to arrest the state of affairs was formulated. A Food Control Department was established, whose objectives included appointing officers 'to visit small land holders and to impress on them the necessity of growing food, at least for the duration of the war and one year after,'[28] to advise on crops, distribute seeds and planting material, and report on developments in their areas. Officers of the Department of Agriculture convened meetings for propaganda purposes and also to find out land needs, in order to attempt to satisfy them and so assist the food-production process. This department included a food import section which was in charge of ensuring the acquisition of rice, flour and other essentials as reserve stock. There was also a Ground Provisions Committee.

The population was alerted to the full extent of the problem through a house-to-house campaign in the rural areas conducted by specially recruited officers. Employees at the American bases and their families were advised to plant food for their own needs. Radio programmes and newspapers helped to sensitise the public to the campaign. To indicate the urgency of the situation, public property was cultivated with food crops. Flower gardens in Port-of-Spain and other urban centres were diverted to food production.

Special laws, called the Sugar Short-Term Crop Regulations, mandated that all sugar estates plant short-term crops, such as peas, sweet potatoes and beans, on a portion of all new land planted in canes.[29] Government increased its nurseries to ensure an adequate supply of planting material throughout the colony.[30] Officers of the Department of Agriculture also supervised the sugar districts to ensure that the companies were complying with the regulations.[31]

The Food Control Department established a committee to deal with such other matters as costs, profit margins and selling prices of essential food items. The committee met every Thursday and was chaired by a food comptroller who was also the comptroller of customs and excise. After considering the submissions of producers, dealers and other interested groups, the committee submitted recommendations to the Legislative Council.[32]

Marketing and price control

There were several complaints about the system of price controls in the colony and the resulting hardships on rural shopkeepers, who faced high transportation costs which eroded their profits,[33] but were accused of dishonesty and exploitation by consumers. In turn, the shopkeepers and their sympathisers blamed the urban merchants for creating '. . . rogues and vagabonds out of the shopkeepers.'[34] They claimed that on occasions they purchased bags of rice only to find that they did not have the right weight, resulting in losses to them.[35] The job of the Food Committee was thus made extremely difficult. It was necessary to augment the supply of some items from time to time. As a result, rice was purchased from Brazil through the Ministry of Food in the United Kingdom.[36]

A marketing section was also set up. This section, which was administered from the Food Control Department, came under the jurisdiction of the controller of marketing.[37] The colony was divided into eight areas, each provided with a Food Control Marketing Depot and a number of sub-depots or buying stations, based on the existing divisions of counties and wards. For example, the County of St George was divided into three marketing areas — west, east and central. West served the Diego Martin and St Ann's Wards; east served Arima, Blanchisseuse and San Raphael Wards; and central served the Ward of Tacarigua. The sub-depots served as important collection centres in the outlying areas, to ensure that supplies reached areas of greatest demand.

The depots were under managers responsible for running an efficient organisation, according to specific instructions. Purchases were to be made only of items specified by the comptroller, with special emphasis on quality. In 1942, a list of guaranteed buying prices was issued by the comptroller to the depots and sub-depots (see Table 19.2).[38] These prices represented an increase in the market prices of the various items before the outbreak of the war. A guaranteed market and assured prices were incentives to increase cultivation. Items not on the guaranteed list were purchased under directions from the comptroller.

Table 19.2: Guaranteed prices at food depots

ITEM	PRICE (cents per lb)
Sweet potatoes	2.00
Eddoes	1.50
Tannias	2.25
Lisbon yams	3.00
Cush Cush	3.50
Black-eye peas (dry)	3.00
Gub-Gub peas (dry)	3.50
Red beans (dry)	5.00
Pigeon peas (dry)	5.00
Corn (dry)	2.50

Source: A.E. Trotman, Notes to Members of the Marketing Department, 1942, 2.

Since one of the main aims of the campaign was to ensure that each area was adequately served with food, it was the business of the depot manager to indicate the likely shortfall or surplus quantities of goods. All purchases from the sub-depots were to be sent to the main depots and only the surplus from these areas was re-directed for sale elsewhere. Tobago was the exception to this; all purchases were to be sent to Port-of-Spain.[39] All items were only to be sold to the government agencies in wholesale quantities[40] at prices to be determined by the comptroller. Every effort was made to recover costs but the operation was not intended to be profit-making. Sales were made first to vendors in established markets and after that to the public at the depots. Sales were on a cash-only basis, except with the written permission of the comptroller.[41] Public institutions were under instructions to buy all their supplies from the depot. Purchases by these institutions provided an assured market upon which the depots came to depend for they constituted the greater part of the depots' business.[42]

Other activities of the Food Control Department

The Food Control Department imported Lisbon yams from Barbados for use in the nurseries. It advised the oil companies to invest in food production to ensure that their employees were fed over the difficult period. Meetings were held all over the country to inform the public of the situation and the strategies that were being used. A Cocoa Subsidy Scheme was launched, under which a subsidy of $10.00 was paid for every acre withdrawn from cocoa cultivation to make way for provision gardens, but this did not achieve the expected response.[43]

The department maintained 30 acres of nurseries comprising other crops on sugar estates and other centres to allow farmers to obtain planting material. These were first planted only in sweet potatoes, but later on cassava and other crops were planted. Half-a-million sweet potato slips were brought to Trinidad from Tobago, while dasheen, tannia, yams, eddoes and corn were also brought from Tobago, Toco (Trinidad) and Barbados for distribution and sale in Port-of-Spain and San Fernando, to the oilfields and to sugar companies at cost. Cottage manufacturing of items such as cassava flour was demonstrated.[44]

The Legislative Council voted $50,000 for the acquisition of land, near to population centres, for the cultivation of food. Land was acquired in Manzanilla, Cumuto, Rio Claro, Talparo, Todds Road, Toco, Cumana and Sangre Grande. Additional land was obtained through an arrangement with the Agricultural Bank of Trinidad and Tobago for the rental to the Food Control Department of properties acquired by the bank. Trinidad Estates Limited rented several hundred acres of land close to heavily populated centres along the Eastern Main Road to the Food Control Department to assist the food effort. In general, the sugar interests were supportive. The Food Comptroller also sought to increase rice production, one of Trinidad's most essential foodstuffs, in the Nariva Lagoon, not only to meet present needs but on a permanent basis.[45] The various efforts to stave off the food crisis that seemed imminent in 1942 met with some success. This was indicated by the food comptroller in his statement of expenditure of the Special War Services Fund, where he indicated the increased acreage under cultivation (see table 19.3).

Table 19.3: Increased land cultivation in 1942

TYPE OF LAND	ACREAGE
Sugar companies and cane farmers	2,628
Professional gardeners & land settlement schemes	3,000
Allotment holdings	3,000
Extension of oilfield gardens	800

Source: NAMDEVCO Library, Trinidad and Tobago Department of Agriculture, Food Comptroller to the Colonial Secretary, August 4, 1942, 4.

Table 19.3 shows that the major agricultural and industrial operations in the colony were involved in the expanded food production programme. The cane farmers and the sugar companies operated under the Short-Term Crop Regulations Ordinance (1942) mentioned earlier. The professional gardeners included rice cultivators and small farmers in the Land Settlement Schemes. The system of giving out lots of land (referred to as allotments) for food cultivation extended cultivation to backyards, additional gardens, clay reserves and roadsides of Port-of-Spain, San Fernando and the villages. The area under increased cultivation by June 30, 1942 totalled over 9,400 acres.

The July 1942 crisis

The July 1942 crisis brought home the realities of the war situation and stimulated the need for an accelerated food production programme. This crisis developed as enemy action against shipping in the region in May/June 1942 interrupted food imports of flour, rice, potatoes, frozen meat and canned goods. By July 15, there were long queues waiting for limited supplies of bread, beef, condensed milk, flour, rice and fish in Port-of-Spain and the other main population centres. The demand for locally-produced food became even greater as time went by. Breadfruit lines were common in the Port-of-Spain market as the supply of rice and flour dwindled. Plantains, ground provisions, vegetables and pork were also scarce.[46] As a result, there was a significant increase in the prices of several items as indicated in table 19.4.

Table 19.4: Price increases as a result of wartime demand

ITEM	OLD PRICE	NEW PRICE
Breadfruit (each)	4 cents	20 cents
Bananas (bunch)	60 cents	$4.00
Sweet potatoes, yams & tannias (lb.)	4 cents	8-9 cents

Source: NAMDEVCO Library, Trinidad and Tobago Department of Agriculture, Food Comptroller to the Colonial Secretary March 1, 1943, Report on the Progress of Local Food Production in Trinidad for the Six Months to December 31, 1942, 2.

Market supplies in the capital were sold out within hours and country markets were also empty, as vendors sold on the 'black market,' cashing in on peoples' willingness to pay high prices rather than starve. The situation was worse in the country districts, which had no flour or rice, while small quantities of these could be obtained in the towns. This scarcity further affected the labour situation on estates, as some men were required to do the queuing up for food. There were problems even when the flour did arrive, for priority was given on the docks to supplies for the military. Then the tyre shortage disrupted the system of transport in the colony, making distribution difficult. Thus many areas were forced to become self-reliant in food.

Feverish efforts at cultivation were made by those who had, until then, ignored the call to cultivate. According to the Food Comptroller, by March 1943 there was a 50 per cent increase in the acreage planted in household gardens. There was also an increased interest in the subsidy scheme by cocoa estate owners who added approximately 1,700 acres to the cultivation of food crops under the scheme between the end of June 1942 and March 1943. By the latter date, the area cultivated under the cocoa subsidy scheme exceeded 1,950 acres. There was revived interest in land settlements and 650 additional acres were given out.[47]

Under the Short-Term Crop Regulations, by March 1943, 434 acres had been planted solely in food crops, and a further 4,376 acres were planted in quick cash crops intercalated between young canes. This brought the total area cultivated in food on the sugar estates to 2,892 acres, 1,000 of which were planted by the cane farmers.[48]

Rice received special attention because flooding in British Guiana in 1942 had resulted in limited shipments to Trinidad. In order to expand local production rapidly, the cultivation of hill rice was encouraged and a plan was drawn up for the further extension of the rice industry by the Drainage and Irrigation Department. The aim was to produce 50 per cent of local needs in the colony. It was therefore necessary to pay attention to the problem of disease. Hitherto of small consequence, this was a growing problem which received the attention of the mycologist of the Department of Agriculture.[49]

The size and price of bread to be sold was fixed by the Food Comptroller under the Baking and Sale of Bread Order of June 5, 1942. This order was enforced to prevent profiteering.[50] Between July and September, soap, sweet potatoes, corn, peas and cassava were scarce. Soap was included in the items involved in profiteering. The Food Comptroller took over all shipments of essential items for controlled distribution and all local fruits and food were put on a price schedule.[51] The colony's supply of protein was maintained by imports of cattle from Venezuela and a concerted effort to grow peas and beans. The supply of fish and chicken was unsatisfactory. Small livestock producers, who usually supplied 75 per cent of the chicken consumed in Trinidad, had to kill off their birds to survive the July crisis. This was also done to allow them to eat the corn, breadfruit and coconut normally fed to the birds. Thus, poultry and eggs were destined to remain in short supply for the duration of the war. Fishing continued to be curtailed by the use of some of the main fishing areas for naval purposes. Efforts to collect fish from those areas where fishing was possible and distribute to other areas were hampered by the shortage of tyres which affected transportation.[52]

The editor of the *Trinidad Guardian* noted in October 1942 that the dramatic rate of population increase in the colony contributed to the food shortage and to the problems of the Food Comptroller. He noted that despite an increase of over 10,000 acres under food crops, the food supply was still short, and exhorted the population to grow more food.[53] By November 1942, the situation was viewed as hopeless. The governor saw no possible solution to the rice shortage problem and suggested that an effective policy to satisfy both wartime and the permanent food needs of the colony should be pursued.[54] The policy adopted in December 1942 was to reduce the distribution of rice and flour by 25 per cent to encourage consumption of local foods and to build up a local reserve of these items. In this way Trinidad was following the pattern set by Barbados where imported rice was withheld to facilitate the consumption of locally produced sweet potatoes.[55] The population was being encouraged to consume the local items which were being produced in large quantities.

The years 1943 and 1944

The year 1943 began with 'serious' transportation problems, according to the governor. There was a shortage of all transport materials — tyres, tubes, motors, railway rolling stock, rails and trucks. The governor explained that the food problem was due to a number of factors. He stated that the population then enjoyed increased purchasing power and that the armed forces made purchases from civilian stocks. In addition, the population migrated from one area to the other in keeping with the demand for labour. This caused the demand for food to increase considerably in some areas. At the same time, the enlisting of agricultural workers in the fighting forces and the transfer of others to the military bases resulted in a fall in local food production. The situation was complicated by the fact that there was a severe water shortage in the colony at the same time that the need to intensify local food production was urgent.[56] However, it was necessary to continue to encourage the population to grow and consume more local food. To this end a War Cooking Centre was set up at Tragerite Road, Port-of-Spain, 'to help everybody, especially those who have the problem of cooking and serving meals from unfamiliar foods....'[57] The centre conducted classes, held demonstrations and sold food to the public.

The Food Production Department encouraged the production of cassava for making chips, and for the production of flour to mix with wheat flour. The Women's Voluntary Service for Civil Defence (WVS) gave demonstrations on the uses of cassava.[58] The shortage of rice continued but the department reported that Tobago had produced enough sweet potatoes to supply Trinidad for three months. The WVS demonstrated 52 different dishes in which sweet potatoes were used.[59]

The importation of a number of food items was made the direct responsibility of the Food Comptroller, through whom all orders were to be placed. These included red kidney beans , canned and salted beef, bran, cooking butter, frozen meat, condensed and evaporated milk, split peas, salmon, sardines, rice, pickled pork products, oats and linseed oil meal. Householders were forbidden from storing more than one week's supply of flour, condensed milk and rice, and two weeks' supply of all other food items. There was a prohibition on the sale of food in restaurants and clubs between the hours of 9.45 p.m. and 5.00 a.m. The making of cakes and pastry for sale was prohibited and ingredients to be put in bread for sale were specified. The weights and prices of bread to be sold were also specified and bakers were required to keep detailed records. There were regulations to prevent the slaughtering of young and breeding animals, and to ensure distribution of meat across the colony. Special days were fixed for the slaughtering of pigs. In response to heavy 'black marketing' of pork, restaurants were restricted to selling cooked pork only on Tuesdays and Fridays. To deal with the phenomenon of increased prices basic items, such as condensed milk, flour, canned and pickled meats and pickled pork products, were subsidised.[60]

Despite all these measures, by June 1943, the shortages of food became more acute. There was profiteering on chicken, pork and fish. The Trinidad situation was paralleled in Martinique where schools had been closed to allow students and teachers to take a more active part in the cultivation of local foods. This island faced a severe shortage of bread, milk, fish, oil, fats and tea, with the result that these commodities, and also bananas, yams and potatoes had to be rationed.[61]

The food strategy in Trinidad and Tobago was dependent upon easy access to land, underscoring the need for a greater change in the traditional land policy. This was formulated by 1943 and by the end of that year, the Food Control Department had brought over 10,500 acres under food cultivation. These included 2,044 acres of purchased lands, 2,634 acres of rented lands, 3,164 acres of land repossessed by the Agricultural Bank and handed to the department, 2,300 acres of land given out by the Wardens' Department and 438 acres of Crown land.[62] Even so, the private demand for cultivable land continued to increase, but not all the land made available by the department was arable.[63] During the period July 1, 1943 to March 31, 1944, a further 157 acres were purchased by the department, 1,553 acres were rented and 2,336 acres of Crown land were made available. Bank properties under food-crop cultivation totalled 3,550 acres, while the sugar estates offered householders an additional 2,000 acres. In this period, a total of 8,596 acres of land were either purchased or rented by government for its food production programme, while 5,444 acres were rented to the public.[64]

Despite bad weather, 1943 witnessed great improvement in local food production. The increase was timely since the Orinoco floods of May 1943, which wiped out the total production of the Penal area, seriously affected Venezuela and reduced its ability to export to Trinidad. Transportation problems also continued to aggravate the situation.[65] However, the colony's agriculture benefited from the closure of some of the bases located here, thus releasing more manpower for food production. For many, there was no alternative employment, since the cocoa industry was itself in crisis.

By March 30, 1944, the Food Control Department had placed 6,699 people on 7,491 acres of land which were directly under its control. This is quite apart from over 2,023 acres which remained under the control of the Wardens. The colony seemed to be within reach of its goal of a 30,000-acre increase in land under food production.[66]

Conclusion

This essay has examined the response of the agricultural sector of Trinidad and Tobago to the demanding circumstances of World War II. The war revealed the extent to which the colony was dependent on imported food and thus placed in such a circumstance. But the crisis threw the colony back on its own resources and caused it to devise local food-production strategies that were largely successful. For the first time urgent attention was given to the problems which the peasantry faced. Peasant agriculture, therefore, enjoyed a boom during the war period. Unfettered by the controls which the rival plantation sub-sector normally exercised over the colony's resources and the competition from imported foods, peasant agriculture thrived.

The response to the call to grow more food indicated that this could be done with the appropriate stimuli. The support of the planting and commercial sectors to this new food thrust helped to ensure its success, but this was given on the understanding that it was a temporary measure. It was their contribution to the war effort, not to have to depend on Britain for food supplies, and to help to defeat Hitler. These arrangements, then, would end when the situation returned to normal, despite the recognition of several public officers that the colony imported too much food that it could produce for itself. The structure of agricultural production had not changed since the inception of the sugar industry, despite the occurrence of food crises over the centuries. The essay shows that policy-makers were aware of and able to implement policies that could have resulted in greater food security for Trinidad and Tobago. However, these policies were only implemented in the exigencies of war or calamity, particularly World War II.

Notes

1. S. Carrington, *The British West Indies During the American Revolution* (Dordrecht: Foris Publications, 1988), 57–60, 166.
2. B. Brereton, *A History of Modern Trinidad 1783–1862* (Port of Spain: Heinemann, 1981), 205–07.
3. R. Pemberton, 'The Evolution of Agricultural Policy in Trinidad and Tobago, 1890–1945' (PhD. thesis, UWI, St Augustine Campus, 1996), 43–44.
4. Trinidad and Tobago Council Papers No. 33 of 1933, Report of the Director of Agriculture for 1932, 8.
5. Trinidad and Tobago. Report of the Sub-Committee on Agriculture, 1948, 93–95.
6. CO 318 /452/7 71265, 1943, Report of the Anglo-American Caribbean Commission to the Governments of the United States and Britain for the Years 1942–1943, Part III, 5.
7. US Section of the Anglo-American Caribbean Commission, *A Record of Progress in Facing Stern Realities* (Washington, 1943), 29.
8. CO 318/452/7 71265, Report of the Anglo-American Caribbean Commission, Part III, 11.
9. Ibid., 17.
10. E. J. Wortley, *Agricultural Development in Trinidad and Tobago* (The Wortley Report), (Port-of-Spain, 1940), 43.
11. CO 318/452/6 71265, Anglo-American Commission, 'International Action and the Colonies' (Fabian Publishers Ltd., Research Services No. 75, 1943), Part II, 4.

12. CO 318/452/6 71265/43, Comptroller of Development and Welfare to Secretary of State, August 6, 1943.
13. NAMDEVCO Library, Trinidad and Tobago Department of Agriculture, Food Comptroller to the Colonial Secretary, August 9, 1942. Report of the Food Comptroller on Local Food Production for the six Months ending June 30, 1942, 4.
14. Ibid., 1.
15. Ibid.
16. Ibid.
17. NAMDEVCO Library, Trinidad and Tobago Department of Agriculture, Food Comptroller to the Colonial Secretary, March 1, 1943, Progress Report on Local Food Production in Trinidad and Tobago for the Six Months Ending December 31, 1942, 6.
18. Ibid., 8.
19. Ibid., 615.
20. NAMDEVCO Library, Trinidad and Tobago Department of Agriculture, Food Comptroller to the Colonial Secretary, August 9, 1942. Report of the Food Comptroller on Local Food Production for the six Months ending June 30, 1942, 1.
21. Governor's Message to the Legislative Council, *Trinidad Guardian*, April 25, 1942.
22. *Sunday Guardian*, April 19, 1942.
23. *Trinidad Guardian*, May 22, 1942.
24. *Ibid.*, May 23, 1942.
25. *Ibid.*, April 23, 1942.
26. *Ibid.*, May 8, 1942.
27. *Ibid.*
28. NAMDEVCO Library, Trinidad and Tobago Department of Agriculture, Food Comptroller to the Colonial Secretary, August 9, 1942. Report of the Food Comptroller on Local Food Production for the six Months ending June 30, 1942, 1.
29. M.H. Fahey, 'Crop Prospects in Trinidad and Tobago,' Trinidad and Tobago Agricultural Society Paper 843 (1942): 13.
30. *Proceedings of the Agricultural Society of Trinidad and Tobago*, Vol. XLI, (Port-of-Spain, 1941), 555.
31. NAMDEVCO Library, Trinidad and Tobago Department of Agriculture, Food Comptroller to the Colonial Secretary, August 31, 1943, Progress Report on Local Food Production in Trinidad and Tobago in the Six Months ending June 1943, 1.
32. Debates in the Legislative Council, Trinidad and Tobago, *Hansard*, January – December. 1943, 350.
33. *Ibid.*, 347, 351.
34. *Ibid.*, 349.

35. *Ibid.*, 352.
36. *Hansard Debates*, Trinidad and Tobago, January–December 1943, No. 58 of 1942, 95.
37. NAMDEVCO Library, Trinidad and Tobago Department of Agriculture, A.E. Trotman, Controller of Marketing, 'Notes to Members of the Marketing Department,' September 8, 1942, 1.
38. Ibid., 1–3.
39. Ibid., 2.
40. These were in lots of 50 or 100 pounds.
41. Trotman, 'Notes,' 3.
42. NAMDEVCO Library, Trinidad and Tobago Department of Agriculture, A.E. Trotman, Memo. to the Acting Director of Agriculture from the Marketing and Cooperative Officer, January 24, 1942, Section 19.
43. NAMDEVCO Library, Trinidad and Tobago Department of Agriculture, Food Comptroller to Colonial Secretary, August 9, 1942, 1–2.
44. Ibid., 2.
45. Ibid., 4–5.
46. *Trinidad Guardian*, July 25, 1942.
47. NAMDEVCO Library, Trinidad and Tobago Department of Agriculture, Food Comptroller to the Colonial Secretary, March 1, 1943, 2–3.
48. Ibid., 3.
49. Ibid., August 31, 1943, 2.
50. *Sunday Guardian*, July 26, 1942.
51. *Ibid.*, September 13, 1942, 4; *Trinidad Guardian*, August 1, 1942.
52. NAMDEVCO Library, Trinidad and Tobago Department of Agriculture, Food Comptroller to the Colonial Secretary, March 1, 1943, 6.
53. *Trinidad Guardian*, October 2, 1942.
54. *Ibid.*, November 13, 1942.
55. *Sunday Guardian*, December 13, 1942.
56. *Trinidad Guardian*, January 7, 1943.
57. *Ibid.*, January 15, 1943.
58. *Ibid.*, February 5, 1943.
59. *Ibid.*, February 8, 1943.
60. *Sunday Guardian*, February 14, 1943.
61. *Ibid.*, June 27, 1943.
62. NAMDEVCO Library, Trinidad and Tobago Department of Agriculture, Food Comptroller to the Colonial Secretary, August 31, 1943, Report on the Progress of Local Food Production in Trinidad and Tobago for the Six Months Ending June 30, 1943, 4.
63. Ibid., 3–4.
64. Ibid. 4.
65. Ibid., 4–5; Food Comptroller to the Colonial Secretary, April 15, 1944, Progress Report on Local Food Production for the period ending March

30, 1944, 1.

66. NAMDEVCO Library, Trinidad and Tobago Department of Agriculture, Food Comptroller to the Colonial Secretary, April 15, 1944, 2-3.

Figure 17: *Campaining in the Ste. Madeline area, 1956.*
Figure 18*: Left, Mr. Ibbit Mosaheb; right, Dr. Eric Williams,*
at a political meeting in San Fernando
Figure 19: *Dr. Eric Williams. Sir Grantley Adams and Mr.*
Norman Manley at the hosting of the Federation flag after the
opening of the Federal Parliament, 1958.

CHAPTER 20

Preparing for Politics:
The Pre-PNM Years of Eric Williams
Brinsley Samaroo

The emergence of the Peoples National Movement (PNM) in January 1956 marked a major turning point in Caribbean development. For Trinidad and Tobago it signalled the beginning of the end of Crown Colony government initiated in 1801 when the British started to set up their formal institutions of governance replacing the Spanish Cabildo and its attendant agencies. The year 1956 also ushered in the era of the properly organised political party, replacing the politics of individualism which had characterised the previous political system. For the larger Caribbean population, Eric Williams, leader of the PNM, symbolised the capability of the West Indian to create a personal space in a world where coloured people were still regarded as hewers of wood and drawers of water. In the Pan-Caribbean context, Williams played a significant role in the creation of the short-lived British West Indies Federation, 1958–62, and of the more permanent University of the West Indies. The establishment of bicameralism in a number of Caribbean territories and the setting up of the Trinidad Senate established 'the mould for five copies to be made in the Commonwealth Caribbean, namely, Barbados (1966), Grenada (1973), St Lucia (1978), Antigua and Barbuda (1981) and Belize (1981).'[1] The party which Eric Williams founded at a public place which he re-christened 'the University of Woodford Square' has been able to survive even after his death in 1981 and today cannot be written off in the contest for national ascendancy. This is a remarkable feat in a region where it had become the pattern for a multiplicity of parties to be formed on the eve of every election only to wither on the vine after their defeat. This essay will argue that the PNM's longevity has been due to the fact that Williams, like John the Baptist, had spent years in the (political) wilderness preparing for the return of a viable political organisation. The PNM was long in gestation and what appeared in 1956 was the fruition of many ideas which were in Williams' mind long before that time.

The question of the genesis of Williams' decision to enter active public life in 1956 has long been a subject of intense debate in the Caribbean. Winston Mahabir, one of Williams' close colleagues since the forties and a minister in the first PNM administration, felt certain 'that the political ambitions of Williams were latent for as long I knew him. They were flogged into open activity by his dismissal from the [Caribbean] Commission.'[2] Paul Sutton is of the view that Williams had prepared himself well in advance of his dropping his bucket down in 1956; in fact in 1954, in a letter to Norman Manley, he had 'revealed an interest in office.'[3] It will be the argument of this essay that his knowledge of Caribbean history placed an enormous burden on his shoulder. His intimacy with the long-term effects of African slavery and of institutionalised racism left a heavy mark on his psyche. His observation, in his native land, of the lifestyle of the oil-rich barons juxtaposed against that of the poverty of those who drilled for the same oil, forced him to move inexorably towards a position in which he would be able to do something about it.

Early influences

The Eric Williams who burst upon the stage in 1956 was a leader whose thinking had been shaped by a number of events which had been taking place in the Caribbean environment as well as in his personal life. We will look very briefly at some of these influences; our first overview will be of the political climate into which he was born. Five years after its conquest by the British in 1797 the island had been set up as a pure Crown Colony, that is, one in which the controlling hand over legislation and administration rested with the Crown through the governor, its man on the spot. In 1801, the governor was given a Council of Advice which consisted entirely of nominated persons, mainly crown officers. From 1803, however, petition after petition from the merchant and planter oligarchy demanded a Legislative Council, to be chosen from among the island's vested interests. This petition was granted in 1831 when a fully nominated Legislative Council was established and an Executive Council replaced the Council of Advice. The nominated element in the island's unicameral legislature remained in place until 1961 when a wholly nominative body, namely the senate, was established as part of a bicameral legislature.

Trinidad and Tobago's first successful assault on its purely nominated legislature was in 1925 when the system was modified to allow for the election of six representatives out of a council of 24, excluding the governor who presided over its deliberations. But the period between 1925 and 1946 witnessed the continuing domination by the merchant and planter oligarchy and their increasing comprador colleagues. Voting for the six elected representatives was quite restrictive. High income and property qualifications for voters (and for candidates) ensured a small electorate. In 1938, for example, the Moyne

Commission reported that there was a registered electorate of only 30,911 persons or 6.6 per cent of the islands' estimated population. This report, with which Williams was very familiar, noted that these figures 'clearly indicate that at present qualifications have had, as they were no doubt intended to have, the effect of restricting the electorate to the comparatively well to do.'[4] This was the system under which the youthful Williams grew up until he left for England in 1932 at age 21. This was the very system to which he returned briefly, for the first time after his 1938 graduation, in April 1944. It was a mode of government which C.L.R. James, his then close friend and mentor, had described as an undiluted dictatorship wherein the governor was 'Father, Son and Holy Ghost.' It was a mode of government which Williams properly understood and that understanding gave him a solid basis for subsequent analysis of the political system.

The 1946 constitution reduced the size of the unicameral legislature to 18 members, excluding the governor who presided over it. There were now nine elected members, six nominated members and three members who were *ex-officio*. The governor retained a casting vote and had the reserve power of overriding any legislative measure passed by the council. The franchise was now extended to all persons who had attained the age of 21 and were resident for at least six months in the electoral district. Income and property qualifications for voters in legislative, borough and county elections were also abolished. For all these appearances of change, however, there were no real alterations in the power relationships existing in the colony. County councillors, for example, could exert themselves in campaigning but upon victory could exercise no executive power. Indeed in the very month of the 1946 elections, no fewer than nine pressure groups, including five trade unions, the Butler Party, the Indian Central Committee, the West Indian National Party and the Negro Welfare Cultural Association sent a letter to the secretary of state for the colonies expressing dissatisfaction with the 1946 constitution. In the proposed new legislature, they argued, 'the representatives of the people will still comprise no more than one half of the legislature without any new power and the executive council will still not be responsible to anyone but itself.'[5]

After his brief visit in 1944 Williams returned to Washington DC to continue working for the Anglo-American Caribbean Commission to which he had become a consultant in 1943 whilst teaching Social and Political Science at Howard University. In 1948 he returned to Trinidad on a more permanent basis, as deputy chairman of the commission and head of the Research Branch. During this longer stay he was able to analyse the operation of the 1946 constitution as well as observe the 1950 general elections conducted under yet another 'new' 1950 constitution. In the 1950 arrangement the size of the legislature was increased from 18 to 26. The number of elective seats was doubled from nine to 18; there were three crown officers as *ex-officio* members and five nominated members. An additional step was the enlargement of the executive council to nine members, five of whom were to be chosen by the Legislative Council. The others were to be all government nominees. The five executive council members serving from the Legislative Council were to hold key ministries assigned to them by the governor. These ministerial powers were to be shared with crown officers. Finally, under the 1950 constitution, the governor retained the discretionary powers of assent, reservation and certification, subject only to the authority of the secretary of state.[6]

The 1950–56 government which was formed as a result of this 1950 constitution was popularly known as the 'Gomes Government' because of the public perception of the enormous power wielded by Albert Gomes, minister of labour, commerce and industry. Gomes himself never denied this perception in public. Once he was out of office, however, he complained that ministers were reduced 'to a status so closely akin to that of a civil servant as gravely to impair the manoeuvrability every politician needs.'[7] Membership in the executive council, he claimed, was the government's 'most effective means of stripping the peoples' idols of their halos. The discipline it imposed on their demagogic proclivities was severe but cunningly unobtrusive.'[8] All business had to be funnelled through the governor. 'He was the only access to the Council.'[9] In Eric Williams, Gomes saw a way out. He sought Williams' assistance in the struggle for responsible government, hence his sponsoring of some of Williams' 1956 public lectures and the inclusion of Williams as an adviser on trade negotiations. Both of these events were to assist in catapulting Williams to national eminence. Despite his early closeness to Gomes, Williams realised that Gomes had become enmeshed within the imperialist framework. In the first draft of his resolution at the PNM's inaugural conference held at the Good Samaritan Friendly Society Hall on January 15, 1956 he summarised this trapped situation within which well-meaning politicians had inadvertently found themselves: 'The long period of colonialism to which we have been subjected has stunted our political growth by denying us the right to take part in the management of our own affairs while the nominated system absorbed the natural leaders of the people into the imperialist framework.'[10]

The meeting then resolved to change this situation. The problem, in Williams' view, was systemic, not personal. Having also looked at the pre-eminent role of individualism as it had operated in the recent past, Williams was able in January 1956 to speak in political terms which people readily understood; cleverly he did not separate himself or his party from the mistakes of the past. 'We were, all of us responsible,' he argued, 'and now we must together rectify the situation.' He stated further:

> Obviously we went wrong in 1950. Why did we go wrong? The answers to these questions are necessary if we are not to go wrong again in 1956. Our first error in 1950 was our choice of legislators. Our legislators presented themselves to us for the most part on an individual basis and we made our

selection for the most part on an individual basis. The individual's claims were based on personal attainments, charitable donations, racial origin. We did not stop to inquire how any one individual in a legislative body of 26 members could possibly fulfil his election promises.[11]

Another issue about which Williams felt passionately was that of racial discrimination. He was angrily aware of a European and North American epistemology which even in the twentieth century regarded non-Europeans as being lower in human civilisation. In the sphere of government, the British were very clear in their view that whereas white-dominated colonies such as Canada, New Zealand, Australia and South Africa could move rapidly towards responsible government and Dominion Status, the non-white colonies of South Asia, Africa and the Caribbean could not go the same route. These latter groups had to be carefully tutored under white supervision. In Williams' own island of Trinidad the Colonial Office was of the view that even a municipal authority such as the Port-of-Spain City Council could only be properly administered by whites:

> Purely local product is not of the calibre to run a show of this kind: on the other hand the European residents — businessmen, bankers, etc. are mostly too busy to take an active part in Municipal Government and would not in any case dream of being associated with the type of person in whose hands the present municipal corporation mostly rests.[12]

Williams was familiar with this kind of racism at both the personal and the societal levels. At the personal level, he appears to have had his fill of racial insults. At Oxford University he was incensed that he had not been awarded a fellowship at All Souls College. For him his rejection occurred because of his race: 'The entire episode, capped by the Warden's advice, convinced me that I would not get an All Souls' Fellowship and that the racial factor would dispose of me in 1936 as the examination factor had in 1935.'[13] Upon his graduation with a research degree the dean of his college was very surprised to see the young Trinidadian still hanging around: 'Are you still here? You had better go back home. You West Indians are too keen on trying to get posts here which take jobs away from Englishmen.'[14]

Williams' sojourn in the New World was not too different. On the many occasions when he had visited Puerto Rico he was never given a proper room, but always 'placed in the annex.'[15] The tone of the lengthy speech from which this quotation has been drawn quite clearly indicates that his race had much to do with the commission's decision against the renewal of his contract in 1955. During his teaching years at Howard he was also given 'the Puerto Rican treatment.' In Richmond, Virginia, for example, he and a group of West Indians were ordered to the back seats of a bus which was taking them further South.

And in Atlanta, to which city he had been invited to deliver a lecture, he was advised 'in his interest' to desist from going out for an after-dinner walk.[16] In the land of his birth racial discrimination in employment was clearly there for all to see. Trinidad's increasing oil wealth, particularly from the thirties, made it an attractive feeding ground for Europeans and white South Africans. But there was no level playing field for non-white Caribbean applicants who had studied in British or American universities. When, for example, an Indo-Trinidadian doctor domiciled in the USA applied to the Colonial Office indicating his desire to return home, the office sent him the minimum information and advised him to apply if he wished.[17] In that same year, an Englishman was dredged from his African retirement to a senior position in Trinidad. In January 1937 Dr R.G. Archibald sought to be re-hired: 'I returned from the Sudan in October but can't say that I am favourably impressed with the English winter and I am longing to go abroad again in any medical capacity. I feel I am too active mentally and physically to lapse into a slippered pantaloon stage, hence this letter.' On this occasion the Colonial Office's decision makers were exuberant. One minuted that 'Trinidad will be lucky indeed.' His colleague agreed: 'In every respect a great acquisition.' A third officer chimed in that 'Trinidad would, I think, be lucky to get him.'[18] Archibald was appointed superintendent of the Leper Asylum situated on an off-shore island, close to Port-of-Spain, gaining a new salary over and above his annual pension of £1,000. This was the Trinidad of Williams' youth, and when he entered public life he remembered what he had seen. This issue of the by-passing of West Indians for positions of employment in the region became a constantly recurring theme of Williams' advocacy. In what was possibly his first manifesto written for the Independent Labour Party (ILP) around 1954 the subject is mentioned twice. Among the goals of the ILP were '(2) The provision of greater opportunity for *everyone*, regardless of race, colour and creed to work, to be educated, and to live a healthy and useful life.' Later on, in the same manifesto, he elaborates on this major theme:

> Consistent with the democratic ideas which the ILP holds dear, the Party will insist on:
> The appointment of Trinidadians – and where necessary of other British West Indians – irrespective of race, colour or creed to all positions in the civil service from the head of state to the humblest caretaker.
> The opening of the doors of private employment to all Trinidadians irrespective of race, colour or creed.[19]

In another draft manifesto, written this time for the National Party, Williams reiterates the theme of the elimination of racism in employment, '(7) Appointment of suitably qualified West Indians to all positions in the public service. (8) Elimination of nepotism and of favouritism in appointments to public office.'[20] In his very first public 1956 Manifesto this matter once again takes a prominent place:

> PNM undertakes to pursue a policy towards the Public Service designed to:
> (1) Prevent favouritism, discrimination and political interference in appointments transfers and promotions.
> (2) Guarantee the appointment of qualified West Indians to the highest positions.[21]

Both before and after his entry into public life, Williams kept on hammering this topic of discrimination and the need for its elimination.[22]

There were two other guidelines which became major beacons in Williams' preparation for public political office. The first was his admiration for what was happening in Puerto Rico, another Caribbean island, and the relevance of the Puerto Rican model for the development of Trinidad and Tobago. The other influence was that of Jamaica's Norman Manley, and the Peoples National Party (PNP), the party which he co-founded in 1938. Because of his frequent travels to Puerto Rico on behalf of the Caribbean Commission Williams 'became persuaded of government-led modernization as the solution to the region's development policies.'[23] In his battles with the Caribbean Commission he had received strong support from Puerto Ricans who were associated with his work. He was also a great admirer of Muñoz Marin, 'now the first elected Governor of Puerto Rico who had come into power with a majority unequalled in any election in any democratic country' and had created '20,000 new jobs in industry to reduce the dependence on the sugar industry.' Marin had, in Williams' view, given to the people a new vitality and confidence which had no equal anywhere else in the Caribbean and had given Puerto Rico self-government.[24] Other references to Puerto Rico are frequent in his speeches: he had commissioned Arthur Lewis to do a study of industrial development in Puerto Rico and had mentioned to the commission a study of the incidence of malaria in Puerto Rico.

The importance of the Puerto Rican model in Williams' vision of development can be seen in the very first group which he formed in Trinidad as a sounding board for his ideas. The very first meeting of the 'Discussion Group' (later called the Bachacs) was held on January 8, 1954 at the home of Winston Mahabir, a practising physician in San Fernando. After brief preliminaries Williams led off a discussion on the topic 'The Industrialization of the West Indies.' In the West Indies, he argued, there were two models of development. In the British model, Colonial Office policy was opposed to industrialisation and therefore promoted agricultural enterprise, whereas in the Puerto Rican model this opposition to industrialisation was absent. Puerto

Rico had provided the answer that agriculture alone could absorb the surplus population, hence the urgent necessity to industrialise. Using the Puerto Rican model as the basis of his analysis, Williams then proceeded to recommend measures which he was to use later on in a framework which was described as 'industrialization by invitation.' The following excerpt from his discourse indicates his view of the advantages of the Puerto Rican model:

> What incentives can the Government give to Industrial Development? (a) Pioneer Status. (b) Promotional efforts by Government building factories. This has been the Puerto Rican pattern. What has been the secret of the success of the Puerto Rican efforts at industrialization? Duty free entry of Puerto Rican goods in the United States of America has been a great advantage which the Puerto Ricans enjoy over the British Caribbean territories.[25]

In order to achieve this Puerto Rican style of industrialisation Williams subsequently kept in close touch with Puerto Rican scholars, even inviting Theodoro Moscoso, a prominent economist, to advise on its implementation.

Equally important was the influence of Norman Manley. Williams had a long relationship with Manley which had started when they first met in 1944. In many ways he was similar to Manley. They both came from aspiring middle class homes which worshipped at the altar of education; both of them studied at prestigious secondary schools; both won scholarships to the same university; and both grew up in similar Crown Colonies in which there were stark inequalities and the continuous denial of political reform which placed power in the hands of elected representatives. Manley, born in 1893, was Williams' senior by almost two decades and after their initial meeting the older politician appears to have become a model for the aspiring one. Williams later asserted that during the decade after 1944 'we have been the closest of friends,' adding that Manley had been his constant defender against his detractors in the Caribbean Commission, even interceding on his behalf with British secretary of state, Creech-Jones, in 1948. Williams had successfully recommended Manley for an honorary doctorate at Howard and Manley's acceptance speech had been 'one of the greatest occasions during my long connection with Howard.'[26]

As he entered his first election campaign, Williams looked constantly to Manley and the PNP for guidance. At a mass meeting in Woodford Square on January 5, 1956 Williams piloted a resolution, later signed by thousands, demanding that in the upcoming federal negotiations every effort should be made to curtail the governor's financial and appointment powers, which formed the worst feature of Crown Colony government. The model for the Trinidad resolution was that of the Jamaican legislature of which Manley was the chief minister. The Jamaican legislature had given a unanimous mandate to its delegates to the forthcoming Federation Conference to seek revision of those colonial features of the draft federal constitution.[27] Six years later, as Williams prepared for his second national election, the first of 'our sister parties' to be recognised in his address to the Fifth Annual Convention of the PNM was the Peoples National Party of Jamaica. The 1961 general elections, he warned his party, would determine whether the PNM's 1956 victory was a mere flash in the pan or 'the first stage in that control by a progressive political party which had characterised the contemporary history of Puerto Rico, Antigua and more recently, Jamaica.'[28] In that address Williams dealt with the urgent matter of party reform; in this regard 'we studied very closely' the constitution and operation of the PNP in Jamaica. In 1958 Williams and Manley joined hands in contesting the federal elections under the banner of the West Indian Federal Labour Party. Manley believed, like Williams, that the life of the federation depended on two states, Trinidad and Jamaica.[29] Ironically, it was Williams' insistence on a strong centre in control of economic development which did much to alienate Jamaican enthusiasm for the federation. When Jamaica voted to withdraw from the federation in September 1961, Williams too signalled his intention to follow suit. The trust that had developed between Williams and Manley was not matched by any similar camaraderie in the southern Caribbean.

Laying the foundations, 1954–56

The two years leading up to the 1956 launching of the PNM constituted a period of intense activity for Williams and his group of activists who felt that the society needed re-direction. The 17 persons (five women and 12 men) who attended the first meeting on January 8, 1954 were informed by Winston Mahabir, the evening's host, that this group was 'neither a Dr Williams fan club nor a political group.' In order to prevent unwieldiness in the group, membership would be severely restricted and new admissions were to take place only when vacancies arose as a result of withdrawals from the group. Mahabir was elected chairman and the other office holders were Norman Girwar (secretary) and Ibbit Mosaheb (treasurer).[30] After this initial business, Williams took over the rest of the meeting and gave a lecture on 'Industrialization of the West Indies.' Similar meetings continued for the rest of 1954, with members meeting at each other's homes. At its eighth meeting, for example, held at Norman Girwar's home in San Fernando on April 23, 1954, it was decided that membership should be raised to 20 and Williams suggested that one of these new members should be a teacher. The rest of the session was taken up by a discussion led by Dennis Mahabir on whether the West Indian colonies which had broken away from the plantation system had done better (or worse) than those which had continued within the system. In the debate which followed Mahabir's presentation it was Williams who had the last word, defining the plantation system and recommending that the West Indies should look at the Australian model of sugar production in which the state subsidised its sugar producers. 'It is only the British West Indies who do not protect their agriculture.' The meeting ended at 11.10 p.m. with the announcement that the next session would take place in Port-of-Spain when Telford Georges would speak on 'the meaning of Political Stability.'[31]

As word spread of the existence of the discussion group there was an increasing demand for membership from middle class persons. This demand increased as Williams embarked on a series of public lectures on Caribbean and world affairs. One such lecture was given on May 28, 1954 at St George's Vocational School in Barataria. There Williams chatted with Kamaluddin Mohammed, the meeting's chairman and a local government leader at the time. The meeting marked the beginning of a lifelong personal and political relationship between the two. One year later Williams became a regular visitor to Mohammed's Dil Bahar restaurant on Queen Street, Port-of-Spain, discussing the formation of the PNM.[32] Williams was making other equally valuable contacts during this period. A major source of later strength was the Teachers' Economic and Cultural Association (TECA), a cooperative formed in 1935 by a group of black teachers who were very angry over 'the discriminatory manner in which the avenues of economic and social advancement were kept closed' to persons like themselves.[33] It was this group which had published Williams' *Education in the British West Indies* in 1950. Even at that time TECA appears to have found their hero. Its director-general, D.W. Rogers, praised Williams for setting West Indian history in its proper international context and for embarking on 'a vast programme' of public lectures and newspaper articles. Williams was not 'an ivory tower intellectual or an academic snob,' as was evident from the dedication of his book 'to the great masses of British West Indian people.'[34] A number of TECA's leaders became major political figures during the fifties and sixties: D.W. Rogers, J.S. Donaldson, W.J. Alexander, and Donald Pierre, to name a few. In fact, TECA's bookstore on Park Street, Port-of-Spain, was another regular meeting place for the plotting of strategy leading to the formation of the PNM.[35]

In May 1955, Williams received a letter from the Caribbean Commission informing him that his contract with that body was to be terminated by the end of June. As if in anticipation of that event, he had carefully prepared the ground for launching himself into the political fray. Even so, he moved cautiously. He invited some members of the discussion group, namely Winston Mahabir, Ibbit Mosaheb and Elton Richardson, to his home in Port-of-Spain to discuss his future and to read out his speech entitled 'My relations with the Caribbean Commission;' he even invited suggestions for amendment. That speech was delivered at Woodford Square for the first time, on June 21, 1955. In Richardson's estimation, 'the evening was an outstanding success and Eric was safely launched.'[36] This launching caused a major flurry of activity. One major initiative was the formation, apparently in July 1955, of the 'Political Education Group' (PEG), which now met regularly, mainly at Williams' home, then at 17 Lady Chancellor Road, Port-of-Spain. Later in 1955 when Williams moved to Cornelio Street, Woodbrook, the meetings continued there. The PEG contained very few of the Bachacs: Mosaheb, Richardson and Williams. The PEG, in effect, replaced the Bachacs. It represented a wider cross-section, a larger number of activists, and was based in the north of the island. The other 19 members were drawn from TECA, with a sprinkling of journalists, trade unionists, a lawyer, and an assortment of other middle class persons in various occupations. The PEG functioned at two levels — a general body of 22 members and an executive committee drawn from the general body. The first executive consisted of the following seven persons: Ibbit Mosaheb (chairman), Elton Richardson (vice chairman), Eric Williams, Donald Granado, Wilfred Alexander, Babsie Dolsingh, and David Nelson.[37]

The meetings of the PEG, unlike those of the Bachacs, had little to do with academic matters; these meetings were about political mobilisation. Academic matters were left in Williams' hand; he would do the lectures, but the physical arrangements were to be handled by the PEG. In July 1955 the group scheduled a series of public lectures on such topics as:

Historical background of race relations in the Caribbean
Analysis of political parties in the Caribbean
Federation
Education in Trinidad and Tobago.

These lectures were to be organised for Port-of-Spain (two venues), San Fernando, Arima, Tunapuna, San Juan, Sangre Grande, Rio Claro, Mayaro, Chaguanas, Couva, Gasparillo, Palo Seco, La Brea and Tobago. Most of these lectures did, in fact, take place.

S.B. Dolsingh submitted a report on the work of the Operations Committee which was collecting signatures for Williams' memorial on constitutional reform; many centres had been set up and 10,000 signatures had already been collected. That July meeting discussed the inclusion of other persons into the PEG and agreed to set up a research group to be headed by Williams. Six sub-committees were also set up to coordinate the following group activities:

programme and constitution
intelligence and propaganda
education
finance and economics
elections
operations.[38]

Both the executive and the general body of the PEG continued to meet regularly until Saturday December 31, 1955 when the final decisions were made regarding the launching of the PNM. It was decided that the inaugural conference would be held on January 15, 1956, that the launching of the party would take place on January 24, and that three foreign delegates be specially invited. Two of these were to come from Jamaica's Peoples National Party and the third from the Caribbean Area Division of the International Confederation of Free Trade Unions (CADORIT). The PEG also decided to request a message from James Griffiths, former secretary of state for the colonies, to be read at the launching.[39] In September, at the executive level, Williams successfully moved that membership of the PEG be increased to 50 in order to have a larger nucleus when going to the public and a broader general representation without compromising the criteria laid down by the group. When this resolution was presented to the general body, it was decided instead to expand the PEG to 100 members. At the same time it was decided that the party (the PNM) be launched with a membership of not less that 500. From this time there was a concerted drive to screen and admit suitable members. Persons who had previously belonged to other political parties were required to renounce publicly such membership before they could be admitted to the proposed new party. Dennis Mahabir, for example, was asked to renounce his membership in the ILP. During these months two lists of members of the proposed PNM were drawn up: the first 100 and the first 500. There was much jockeying for membership in the first 100 and as that list became filled, for the first 500. D. W. Rogers of TECA suggested that 'political clinics' be started for the benefit of all members and preparations were made for the collection of signatures to Williams' open letter to the Trinidad representatives at the forthcoming Federal Conference scheduled for London in February 1956. The first date for the collection of these signatures was January 5, 1956 at Williams' Woodford Square lecture on federation. A copy of this resolution was, of course, to be sent to Norman Manley.[40]

Lending credibility to the argument that Williams was preparing for politics before his severance from the Caribbean Commission is the fact that he participated in the devising of three manifestoes before the final PNM document. Around 1954 he wrote a manifesto for the ILP, then led by Raymond Hamel-Smith. From all accounts he wrote this manifesto for Elton Richardson who then presented it in his own name. According to Richardson, this document was 'ripped to bits.'[41] In his first draft of a 1960 speech, Williams made reference to this event, indicating that it was done whilst he was employed with the Caribbean Commission:

> I agreed to work with the group as an adviser in a private capacity. Their draft manifesto was so bad that I offered to write one for them — its worst feature was its sycophantic attitude to the oil industry. My draft was rejected by them. I took it away from them and it became the first draft of the Peoples Charter.[42]

The second manifesto was written for the United People's Movement (UPM). This too was to contribute to the People's Charter of 1956:

We are not an ordinary party in the accepted narrow sense of the word. We are a rally, a convention, a movement. We specialize in the mobilization of all the forces in the community, not only racial but also social — cutting across class and creed, uniting all those who believe that certain things must be done to save all of us. Our emphasis is in unity, in the people, in united action by the people. Hence our name the UNITED PEOPLE'S MOVEMENT.[43]

The third manifesto in which Williams appears to have had a hand was that of the National Party. Basing its philosophy on the UN Human Rights Charter and the much earlier American Declaration of Independence, the National Party proclaimed that it held certain 'truths to be self-evident.'

That every man and woman in Trinidad and Tobago is born with the inalienable right inherent in first-class citizenship. The state should therefore aim at promoting within the limits of its resources, the following services essential to the full development of its citizens.
    (i)   The opportunity to achieve a standard of living adequate for the health and well-being of the individual and his family.
    (ii) Social security indispensable for the dignity and the free development of the individual personality.
    (iii) Free primary and secondary education for their children.
The National Party's mission is to lift the people of Trinidad and Tobago out of the ditch in which they now find themselves.[44]

The PNM seemed the logical culmination of the visions created in the United People's Movement and the National Party. All the policies embraced by the PNM had been espoused by its two major forerunners. The mass of information offered in the pre-PNM manifestos, including that of the ILP, provided a rich cache of political ammunition which, despite serious setbacks, has been able to carry forward the party up to the present. Apart from the over-all theoretical bases which have been cited above, Williams was able to tabulate many of the nation's ills and to present them in a manner that appealed to the average voter. Some of these problems of 1954 remind us of the fact that so much has not changed since then:

- 250 applications for a $50.00 a month messenger's job
- Overcrowding in primary schools
- Resignation of doctors from Medical Services
- Shanty Town to be removed

- · Shanty Town to stay
- · High cost of training at University College of the West Indies
- · Teachers criticised as 'idle philosophers'
- · War between taxis and buses
- · Caura 'buball'; no prosecutions
- · Railway 'buball'; CID investigating.[45]

What emerged as the final PNM Manifesto and the People's Charter were not hastily assembled documents. They represent years of previous thought and research, now carefully organised, written and then re-written for greater effect. In the preparations leading to the formation of the party there was hardly any spontaneity; every detail was carefully planned, nothing being left to chance. The opposition of the day was scarcely organised. Individualism was the order of the day. In the 1950 elections, for example, there were 141 candidates for 18 elective seats.[46] In these elections there was little care for policy or programme, but every care for personal contacts, kin relations, financial reward and race.[47] Even Albert Gomes recounted that he was defeated in an election because he opposed his polling agent's advice to 'pass off' one Chinese voter for another 'because all Chinese look alike.' On Gomes' second foray, however, 'I put everything into the hands of those who permitted no scruple' and a few days afterwards he was duly installed as a municipal councillor.[48] Williams and the PNM brought some order into this disorder, thereby improving the quality of the politics. Even before the PNM, the People's Education Group sought to send a clear message that disloyalty would not be tolerated. In December 1955, for example, one of the PEG's executive members was expelled for accepting an appointment as public relations officer with the Gomes government, 'Since such an appointment (prospective or otherwise) qualifies your eligibility to membership in the Group in the light of criteria laid down, the Executive Committee had no alternative but to terminate your membership immediately.'[49]

Williams and the East Indian community

Our final examination of the political thought of Williams before 1956 concerns his attitude to the East Indian population in Trinidad and Tobago. Kusha Haraksingh, in an insightful paper on 'Indians in the intellectual perspective of Eric Williams,' strikes accurately at the premises which guided Williams *vis-à-vis* his political attitude to the East Indian population. Haraksingh points to two major faults which severely clouded Williams' analysis of the East Indian position. In the first place, Williams' immense scholarship in the area of the African experience in the New World did not find its match in his knowledge of the Indian dimension, 'the topic simply was tangential to his main concerns.'[50] Other commentators support this view. Linda Heywood calls

Williams 'a brilliant scholar of the black experience' and cites C.L.R. James' view that 'Williams was a lucky man. Nothing better for his future development could have happened than going to lecture at Howard, the Negro University in the United States.'[51] Heywood further points out that in 1940 Williams again emphasised that the work which he was doing on the Caribbean was 'in line with my consistent argument that societies in the Caribbean are of vital importance to the Negroes in the United States.'[52] Another researcher on Williams' life asserts that from 1955 Williams was 'now determined that his personal life-long struggles, as, and on behalf of the black man, would be converted in the struggle of all Trinidadians against foreign denomination.'[53]

Haraksingh's second major criticism of Williams' interpretation of the East Indian mind is that his analysis, based as it was on his Oxford experience, was seriously flawed. Williams had attended meetings of the Oxford Majliss (the Indian student body) in which there was constant debate on India's freedom struggle. There Williams felt privileged to listen to Nehru and Radhakrishan, among others. These formative intellectual contacts were to shape his attitude on this side of the water. But most Indian nationalists of the Oxford school had failed to take cognisance of the indivisibility between religion and politics in the Hindu and Muslim mind. Nehru and Congress seemed intent on demonstrating to the British that Congress was fit to govern India by British standards of judgement. This stressed the secular British approach to their own politics, influenced, as that was, by a strict separation of religion from politics. In this way the Congress neglected to take on board the salience of strong religious sentiment in the whole process. Thus they sought to absorb minorities such as Muslims and Sikhs into the larger secular frame, whilst the rank and file in their own party had other preoccupations.[54] This approach, as we now know, had very tragic consequences for the sub-continent. Focused so much on the African experience in the Americas, Williams failed to appreciate the rich civilisational heritage which Indians brought to their Caribbean homelands. He seemed to know little about their ancestral love for the land which they regarded as mother (Dharti Mata) or about the ways in which they had converted negative aspects of the plantation system to their own advantage, making the cane fields a rich habitation rather than a place to be shunned. Williams himself in the midst of his problems with the Caribbean Commission had indignantly asked Manley, 'What am I to do, cut sugar cane?'[55] Such a declaration could hardly have been expected to endear him to people who either worked in the fields or had ancestors who had been sugar workers.

At the same time it cannot be denied that Williams seemed aware of this inadequacy and tried to rectify the situation. When Winston Mahabir, one of his early Bachac colleagues, expressed curiosity about his selective emphasis on the African experience, Williams replied that the racial emphasis was purely incidental. In Mahabir's words, 'he was writing about Negro slavery. There was no reason why I should not document the story of Indian indenture.'[56]

Around the same time, a number of San Fernando East Indians encouraged Williams to research and write the story of their ancestors and Williams agreed. He indicated that this matter had been on his mind for some time and that he had even discussed it with Nehru's sister Vijayalakshmi Pandit in Washington and she had agreed to help in whatever way she could.[57] Williams then requested financial assistance for the work and a number of prominent San Fernandians subscribed to the project. However, as Williams became increasingly taken up with public activity at home and abroad, he found it impossible to continue with the project and refunded the monies earlier collected.[58] At the personal level, Williams apparently had no difficulties in dealing with 'the recalcitrant and hostile minority of the West Indian nation masquerading as "the Indian nation" and prostituting the name of India for its selfish reactionary political ends.'[59]

Williams' inability to understand fully the East Indian way of thinking and his consequent ham-fisted manner of dealing with this group in the political sphere has to be seen against the intersection of power and race relations from the late forties. The political leadership of the East Indian community was in a sour mood for a number of reasons. In the discussions which led to the granting of the 1946 constitution the local Franchise Committee made a strong recommendation that there should be a language qualification for voters; the result would have been the disqualification of the majority of the East Indian electorate. E.A. Robinson, a white planter who had been defeated by an East Indian candidate in the 1925 general elections, was clear in enunciating the reasons for this exclusion. If the franchise was widened 'the colony would be ruled by East Indians.'[60] This recommendation was the cause of widespread East Indian protest led by Adrian Cola Rienzi, president of the Trades Union Congress. In the end it was the secretary of state who had to intervene, instructing the governor to strike off the language qualification: 'A measure that savours of racial discrimination is politically objectionable even when it has tangible advantages; when it will be ineffective, it is surely, indefensible.'[61]

Anti-Indian sentiment was again perceived by the East Indian community when the colony's validating elite, consisting mainly of the white (foreign and local) ruling class, took the decision to postpone the general elections due in 1955. There was the widespread belief that 'the Hindu-based People's Democratic Party was likely to return the largest bloc of candidates to the Legislative if the elections were held in 1955.'[62] Postponement would give the non-Indian population sufficient time to mobilise against the Indians. As the colony moved towards independence and as the local prospect of power became real, the two major ethnic groups sought to claim their ethnic, political spaces, each seeking viciously to fend off the other. During the last few months of the pre-1956 organisation of the PNM this fear of East Indian dominance was so real among prospective PNM aspirants that, at a special meeting called to instruct canvassers, Party strategists asked the question and supplied the answer:

> Is Dr Williams pro-Indian?
> (i) Where the Party is concerned there is no race or class discrimination. Our members are all prepared to actively oppose racial and/or class discrimination in any form.
> (ii) Dr Williams and all our present members are neither pro-Indian, pro-Negro, pro-Chinese, pro-Portuguese or any other nationality; we are pro-West Indian, and our West Indian population comprises many races, classes, colours, religions and beliefs.[63]

Notwithstanding such assurances, the ethnic antagonism persisted. In October 1958 the *PNM Weekly* carried a letter from two teachers who were pursuing studies at the University College, Jamaica. These teachers were jubilant about the PNM's successes in Trinidad. They now advocated that both Nehru and Nkrumah should be invited to Trinidad and Tobago to engage in support of the party. At the same time, however, the party should strengthen ties with Tobago 'with a view to prevent the East Indian community from exploiting Tobagonians through economic means.'[64] This African/Indian conflict which preceded Williams and persisted after he died in 1981, continues unabated up to our own time. During the period that the PNM held power, from 1956 to 1986, the East Indian population were loud in their complaints about being left out of the power structure. Now that the Indian-based United National Congress (UNC) is in government it seems to be the PNM's turn to complain. In his address to the Thirty-seventh Annual Convention of the PNM on November 14, 1999, the party's political leader declared that chief executive officers were being fired from state boards simply because they 'looked PNM;' he also condemned 'their vulgar slogan of "is we time now"'.[65] This accusation of a racist UNC agenda was published in a New York based paper, *Black Diaspora*, in March of 2000 where the PNM leader claimed that 'there's been no shortage of charges that the Panday administration has pursued a course in which shameless favouritism towards the Indian element in the Society has been the norm.'[66] Needless to say, this charge has elicited a spirited response from East Indian writers who accuse Patrick Manning of having his own racial agenda.[67] The more things change, the more they remain the same! In the business of inter-ethnic relations we are exactly where we were 50 years ago and there appears to be no diminution of the rivalry at the political level. On the positive side, of course, is the consolation that the situation has not become as fragile as in Guyana. There may yet be some hope.

Conclusion

What, in the final analysis, can we say about Williams' preparedness for national politics when he launched the PNM in January of 1956? It has been the argument of this essay that history, the discipline which he chose, placed an enormous burden on his shoulder. His specialisation on the African experience in the Americas and the spiritual legacies of that sad experience caused him to dream of righting that enormous wrong. His personal experience of the legacy of prejudice, bequeathed by the plantation system, sharpened his desire to re-shape the Caribbean world nearer to his heart's desire. This vision became increasingly more clearly focused after his graduation in 1938, from which time he prepared himself in a number of ways for a later public political role. From around 1954, he earnestly set about laying the foundations for a philosophy (the Charter), a coherent listing of problems and their solutions, party discipline and a broad, British-derived, secular platform. By these methods he brought order into a chaotic political process and steered the nation to independence, in and out of federation, and onto a programme of industrialisation which started the modernisation of the economy.

Being an educator, he stressed the importance of learning and opened up this learning to thousands who had no access to the same. His own penchant for incessant hard work inspired a whole generation of the region's youth. On the other hand, he was entrapped in the same colonial process which he sought to unravel. He looked at a heterogeneous Caribbean world through British spectacles, failing to understand both the East Indian and the 'Black Power' aspirations. These were outside the European frame and therefore not sufficiently important to merit his serious attention; hence the revolution of 1970, when young blacks revolted against an ostensibly black government. Similarly, despite all the overt rituals of inter-ethnic harmony, the racial divide continues to widen in a brutal contest for political ascendancy.

Notes

The author wishes to express his sincere thanks to the staff of the UWI, St Augustine Library for use of the Eric Williams Collection, and to Dr. Ibbit Mosaheb for his assistance in the preparation of this essay.

1. H.A. Ghany, 'Constitution-making in the Commonwealth Caribbean with Special Reference to Trinidad and Tobago' (PhD. thesis, University of London, 1987), 17–18.
2. Winston Mahabir, *In and Out of Politics* (Port of Spain: Inprint Caribbean, 1978), 20.
3. Paul Sutton, 'The Historian as Politician. Eric Williams and Walter Rodney,' in *Intellectuals in the Twentieth Century Caribbean,* ed., A.

Hennessy. (London: Macmillan, 1992), 102.

4. Cmd. 6607. 1945, West India Royal Commission Report (London: HMSO, 1945), 379.
5. CO 295/630, See No. 8657 in File 7009.
6. Ann Spackmann, *Constitutional Development in the West Indies 1933–1968* (Kingston: Institute of Social and Economic Research, 1975), 155–56.
7. A. Gomes, *Through a Maze of Colour* (Port-of-Spain: Key Caribbean, 1974), x.
8. *Ibid.*, 118.
9. *Ibid.*, 121.
10. Eric Williams Collection (EWC), UWI, St Augustine Library, File 543, No. 3, Launching of the PNM.
11. EWC, File 541, 'The year 1950 in retrospect.'
12. CO 295/599, File 70285, PO 5, City Council Affairs, Memo. by A. Poynton, November 22, 1937.
13. Eric Williams, *Inward Hunger* (London: André Deutsch, 1969), 46.
14. *Ibid.*, 52.
15. Eric Williams, 'My Relations with the Caribbean Commission,' in *Eric Williams Speaks,* ed., S. Cudjoe. (Wellesley: Calaloux Publications, 1993), 126.
16. Interview with Dr Ibbit Mosaheb ((born 1919), on February 5, 2000. Mosaheb was Williams' student at Howard University during the 1940s. He was treasurer of the Bachacs (1954), Chairman of the Political Education Group (1955), a foundation member of the PNM, and the second PNM Mayor of San Fernando (1957–58).
17. CO 295/596, See Dr Jurawan's enquiry.
18. CO 295/598, R.G. Archibald to Stanton, January 20, 1937.
19. EWC, File 541, ILP Programme outline, 3 and 6. For Williams' connection with the ILP, see Elton Richardson, *Revolution or Evolution* (San Juan, Trinidad: Inprint Caribbean, 1984), 26.
20. See EWC, File 541, People's Party Programme, 21.
21. PNM General Elections Manifesto, September 24 , 1956, 3.
22. For examples, see Paul Sutton, ed., *Forged from the Love of Liberty: Selected Speeches of Dr Eric Williams* (London: Longman Caribbean, 1981), 203f.
23. Sutton, 'The Historian as Politician,' 102.
24. Eric Williams, 'My relations with the Caribbean Commission,' in *Eric Williams Speaks*, ed., Cudjoe, 132.
25. EWC, File 542, Minutes of first meeting.
26. Williams, 'My Relations with the Caribbean Commission,' 147–48
27. See Resolution in EWC, File 543.
28. EWC, File 547, Address to Fifth Party Convention.

29. See Manley's 'Our policy and federation,' in *Manley and the new Jamaica. Selected Speeches and Writings 1938-1968,* ed., R. Nettleford. (Trinidad and Jamaica: Longman Caribbean, 1971), 173.
30. EWC, File 542, Minutes of first meeting.
31. EWC, File 542, Minutes of eighth meeting.
32. H. Ghany, *Kamal, a Lifetime of Politics, Religion and Culture* (Port-of-Spain: K. Mohammed 1996), 67-69.
33. S. Ryan, *Race and Nationalism in Trinidad and Tobago* (University of Toronto Press, 1972), 106.
34. Eric Williams, *Education in the British West Indies* (Port-of-Spain: Guardian Commercial Printery, 1950), v. In this book Williams thanked Norman Manley for reading the manuscript.
35. Ivar Oxaal, *Black Intellectuals Come to Power* (Cambridge, Mass.:Schenkman, 1968), 103.
36. Richardson, 28; see also Mahabir, 18.
37. EWC, File 542, Minutes of PEG Executive Committee, September 18, 1955.
38. EWC, File 542, Minutes of PEG, July 28, 1955.
39. EWC, File 542, Minutes of Executive Committee, December 31, 1955.
40. This summary was obtained from Executive and General meetings for the period July to December 1955 (see EWC, File 542).
41. Richardson, 26. Mosaheb supports this account (Interview, March 5, 2000).
42. EWC, File 547, Responsibility of the party members, September 30, 1960.
43. See EWC, File 541, 'The Problem.'
44. EWC, File 541, National Party Manifesto.
45. EWC, 541, ILP programme outline.
46. Ryan, 86.
47. John La Guerre, 'The Race Factor and the Election of 1950 in Trinidad and Tobago,' UWI St Augustine Library, 1979, 9.
48. Gomes, 35.
49. EWC, File 542, D. Granado to David Nelson, December 24 , 1955.
50. Kusha Haraksingh, 'Image and Icon: Indians in the Intellectual Perspective of Eric Williams,' *Caribbean Issues*, 8.2 (1999): 62.
51. Linda M. Heywood, 'Eric Williams: the Howard Years, 1939-1948,' *Caribbean Issues*, 8.1 (1998): 14-15.
52. *Ibid.*, 18.
53. K. Boodhoo, ed., *Eric Williams: The Man and the Leader* (Lanham, MD.: University Press of America, 1986), xiv.
54. Haraksingh, 65.
55. Cited in Haraksingh, 71.
56. Mahabir, 14.

57. Interview with Ibbit Mosaheb, March 5, 2000. Mrs. Pandit had served as India's ambassador to the USA (1949–51), and to the United Kingdom (1955–61). In 1955 Williams discussed with her the possibility of the publication of a Caribbean edition of Nehru's autobiography (see *Inward Hunger*, 143).

58. Williams, *Inward Hunger*, 143; interview with Mosaheb, March 5, 2000.

59. Williams, *Inward Hunger*, 275.

60. UWI St Augustine Library, Council Paper (Minutes of the Legislative Council), 35 of 1944, 10.

61. CO 295/630, Stanley to Clifford, November 25, 1944.

62. Ryan, 101.

63. EWC, File 542, PEG meeting held at Dr Richardson's home, December 3, 1955.

64. *PNM Weekly*, October 20, 1958.

65. Office of Leader of the Opposition, Address by the Political Leader, Chaguaramas Convention Centre, November 14, 1999: 9, 12.

66. 'Manning charges racism in Panday Gov't,' *Sunday Guardian*, March 5, 2000.

67. See, for example, 'Manning's potshots from abroad,' *Sunday Guardian*, March 12, 2000; also 'Manning's statement threatens Indo-Trinis,' *Express*, March 13, 2000.

CHAPTER

Race, Class And Ideology in Post-Colonial Trinidad, 1956–91
Kelvin Singh

T he term 'post-colonial' in this paper is employed in a strictly political and chronological sense, meaning the period after the island of Trinidad (together with its political adjunct, the island of Tobago) was conceded almost complete political independence, 'almost' because it is a political independence still circumscribed by the retention of the British Privy Council as the final court of appeal in judicial matters (including the interpretation of the island's constitution).

'Ideology' refers to the corpus of ideas and values, whether logically integrated or not, promoted by representatives, self-appointed or not, of two or more competing groups, about how the society should be organised and towards what ends.

'Race' is employed largely as a sociological rather than a biological concept, though visible phenotypical group differences have been the main criteria employed by the local population to distinguish its major components: African, Indian, Chinese, Syrian-Lebanese and European, as well as the miscegenated components that have emerged from the 'cross-over' sexual merging of individuals from the major groups. These are popularly known by such creole designations as 'dougla,' (of Afro-Indian ancestry) or 'red' (of Afro-European ancestry and referred to in most anglophone post-colonial Caribbean histories as 'Coloureds,' though now officially categorised as 'mixed').

'Class' is used here as a strictly politico-economic category, based on the relationship of three major strata of the population to the ownership and/or control of the means of production and distribution and to the state. They comprise a ruling class of economic, political and professional elites, with shared basic material interests and ideological values; a middle class (a larger composite class made up of different occupational groups and ethnic fragments, generally literate, involved in the public services, the teaching profession, and small-scale commercial enterprises, but not politically united); and a working class (also occupationally differentiated and multi-ethnic, made up principally of skilled and unskilled manual workers, as well as small-scale food producers, but again not politically united). These classes are, of course, convenient analytical categories and do not imply any rigid demarcation in the population's perception of social reality. Indeed, most of the population were either not class conscious or only marginally so. The situation was quite different with regard to 'race' consciousness.

Of the three major classes categorised in this essay, the ruling class experienced a major change in its ethnic composition once political independence was conceded to the two-island colony by Great Britain in 1962. The black and coloured middle class at last gained a preponderant voice in the Legislative Council, though the former white colonial ruling class retained considerable political influence through the constitutional arrangements that allowed for a nominated rather than an elected Senate or upper house. They also maintained control over the private corporate sector, financial and commercial, as well as (before 1973) the plantation sector. They likewise retained some degree of influence over the coercive arm of the state and the judiciary. With the expansion of a light manufacturing sector, they became the leading investors, sometimes in collaboration with entrepreneurs of the Syrian-Lebanese community, whom they had perceived in the late colonial period as menacing commercial competitors.[1] In all these sectors, moreover, they continued and strengthened the external linkages they traditionally had with British and Canadian investors, who were shortly to be reinforced by American investors. In other words, the leading members of the former white colonial ruling class could count on powerful white allies in the North Atlantic economic, political and military environment within which the newly autonomous two-island state was enmeshed.

The transition to political independence between 1956 and 1962 was inevitably a tension-filled one. The Indian sector of the society comprised approximately 35 per cent of the population in 1956, the African population approximately 47 per cent, the population of mixed ancestry around 14 per cent, while the European sector, inclusive of the Portuguese, comprised a little less than three per cent, the Syrian/Lebanese less than one per cent and the Chinese approximately one per cent.[2] With the concession of adult franchise to the population in 1946, it was just a matter of time before the middle class leaders of the African and Indian sectors of the population would be presiding over two consolidated ethnic blocs reflecting the island's demography.

'Race,' or more accurately, 'ethnicity' (since the cultural dimension of 'race' was important, especially with regard to the Hindu and Muslim segments of the Indian population), had been the fundamental criterion of political and economic management during the colonial period. Race and class practically coincided during this period since non-Europeans were alleged by all the European colonial powers to be in various stages of unfitness for the exercise of political and economic management of their societies, and at best would have to undergo a long process of acculturation to European — in this case, British — standards and values. Only that minority of Africans and Indians fortunate enough to gain a secondary or tertiary education would be able to fulfil this requirement.[3] In this respect, Africans and those of mixed-African descent had a significant head-start over Indians, since the latter did not become numerically significant as permanent settlers in the society before the last decade of the nineteenth century. The latter were also largely confined to the rural areas, forming the bulk of the plantation labour force, and over half their numbers were functionally illiterate in the English language as late as 1956. Additionally, the majority remained firmly attached to the core elements of their Asian culture, particularly to the Hindu and Muslim religions, marriage patterns, music and dance. In all these respects, added to their phenotypical differences from both the African and European segments of the population, they were perceived by the latter as a distinctive and alien segment, except for the minority of westernised, largely Presbyterian-educated, middle class elements who were emerging from within the Indian segment of the population in the first half of the twentieth century.[4]

Had the emerging westernised middle class Indians in the crucial transition period between 1946 and 1956 retained the political hegemony they had exercised in the first half of the twentieth century over the Indian segment of the population, the subsequent political evolution of the society might have been significantly different in terms of ethnicity, for they were not the carriers of what the non-Indian population considered alien cultural symbols. Yet there was a certain inevitability about what subsequently happened. It was precisely because of their western acculturation that this Indian middle class would be rejected by the rural Indian masses as authentic representatives of their cultural interests, though they had often articulated their material and cultural grievances.[5] This was also a decade of fluid political alignments. The working class movement which initially appeared to be consolidating across ethnic boundaries in the late 1930s and early 1940s had begun to fragment, once strike and other protest action were contained within the imposed institutional framework of industry-specific trade unionism. The charismatic, but temperamental Tubal Uriah Butler, a working class leader, was presiding over an odd coalition of middle class Indians and African working class devotees located mostly in the island's oil belt. Trade unionism, western style, was proving to be a source of division rather than unification of the island's African and Indian working masses. Moreover, the colonial administration was making a last-ditch effort to preserve as much of the colonial order as it could in the new era of universal franchise, and this meant the containment of radical populists like Butler and the socialist-oriented trade union leaders like John

Rojas and Quintin O'Connor. Political competition between the Butlerites and their former colleagues in the Oilfield Workers Trade Union, whose ideology was basically socialist, only served to compound the fragmentation of the working class movement in this critical transition period. This, of course, worked to the advantage of the colonial elites who were able, through the governor, to put together a quasi-ministerial team of elected representatives who could be relied on to pursue economic and labour policies compatible with traditional colonial interests.[6]

Equally important, working class fragmentation also facilitated biracial political consolidation. The rural Indian population, over 70 per cent of whom were Hindu, locked into the plantation sector by white colonial policy, and the objects of contempt from western-acculturated Africans and those of mixed African ancestry, who had internalised the negative British imperialist stereotypes of Indian civilisation, had found a leader in Bhadase Sagan Maraj, a Brahmin caudillo, to represent their long-neglected cultural interests. Maraj was able to unify the major competing Hindu sanatanist factions under his leadership and, as an elected member of the Legislative Council in the period 1950–55, established a working alliance with the Syrian-descended Roy Joseph, minister of education, who supported a rapid school-building programme launched by Maraj's religious organisation, the Sanatan Dharma Maha Sabha (SDMS), in several rural districts with substantial Hindu residents who had long resented the proselytising role of the schools run by Christian denominations. Maraj also became a major player in the trade union rivalry taking place in the sugar industry and by 1956 would assume the leading role over the predominantly Indian sugar workers.[7]

With the approach of the 1956 general elections, by which time he had formed his own political organisation, the Peoples' Democratic Party (PDP), Maraj appeared to be a major contender for legislative influence in the period that was to usher in full internal self-government to the two-island colony. Like Butler, his African counterpart, he was a charismatic leader, but was clearly presiding over a more ethnically consolidated base, aligning an Indian *petite bourgeoisie*, an emergent Indian professional middle class (predominantly teachers), an influential Hindu priesthood and the sugar workers (the core of the Indian working class). The Port-of-Spain-based, western-acculturated African and mixed-African middle class saw the emergence of Maraj's party as the principal threat to their bid for political hegemony as the imperial power began its tactical retreat.[8] As they had done periodically since the 1880s, some members of the mixed-African middle class had entered into a loose coalition with *declassés* elements of the white segment of the Port-of-Spain population, led by Albert Gomes, a Portuguese creole, to form the Party of Political Progress Groups. It had the support of the colony's economic and professional elites, mostly of white and mixed ancestry, and was based primarily in Port-of-Spain, the colony's capital.[9] But the mass base that Gomes had enjoyed through his earlier involvement in trade unionism was being rapidly eroded as he increasingly appeared to have been co-opted by the colonial establishment. The political groups still espousing the ideology of socialism inherited from the 1920s and 1930s no longer had, ironically, a mass base in this transition period.[10]

It was into this scenario that Dr Eric Williams, the first local student to earn a doctorate in history, entered, carrying with him the kind of charisma that was bound to appeal to the urban middle class, inclusive of some Indian professionals, who had been nurtured in the culture of academic achievement as the principal avenue to upward mobility. The story of Williams' dismissal from the Anglo-American Caribbean Commission and his subsequent decision to enter the political arena, with the avid support of a middle class intelligentsia, is narrated elsewhere and need not be repeated here.[11] The critical factors in the subsequent evolution of the Trinidad and Tobago polity was the decision of his party, the People's National Movement (PNM), not to enter into any alliance with any other political faction, nor to accept any candidate who had formal links with the Hindu-based SDMS.[12] This set the stage for the strategy Williams would then employ to win the 1956 legislative council elections. This strategy consisted of projecting the ideology of West Indian nationalism, whose ethnic implications could not be missed by representatives of the Indian population; launching a bitter attack on the SDMS and its school-building programme, as well as its linkage with Bhadase Maraj's PDP; and at the same time signalling to the African population that he was about to terminate the era of white dominance in the two-island colony.[13] At first he did not succeed in winning the consolidated support of the African and mixed-African population, especially in the oil belt in the south of Trinidad, where there was still a lingering loyalty to Butler. Nor was he successful in the cocoa-growing districts in the north-east of Trinidad, where Victor Bryan, the leader of the revitalised Trinidad Labour Party (the legacy of the deceased Arthur Andrew Cipriani, that exceptional white creole), held his own. Nor did he as yet win over the island of Tobago, where Tobagonian *insularismo*, represented by A.P.T. James, prevailed over Williams' West Indian nationalism. But by focusing his attack on the SDMS, he was able to detach a substantial number of Muslim and Presbyterian Indians from Bhadase Maraj's Hindu-based PDP and win a slender majority for his PNM in the Legislative Council elections of 1956, enough to enable him to form a cabinet with the approval of Sir Edward Beetham, the colony's last governor, and the Colonial Office.[14]

The next five years, however, would witness a dramatic rally around Williams by the African and a large proportion of the mixed-African population, as Williams, smarting under his party's narrow defeat in the subsequent federal elections of 1958, and ignoring the feelings of those members of his party who were of Indian ancestry, widened the range of his attack beyond the Hindu-based SDMS to incorporate the whole Indian segment of the colony's population. They were now portrayed as a recalcitrant minority standing in the way of West Indian nationalism — despite the fact that the PDP was now part of a West Indian federal party, the Democratic Labour Party (DLP), led by the Jamaican, Alexander Bustamante.[15] Williams also engaged in menacing rhetoric against the white elite, which appeared to be aligning with the PDP (soon to be merged into a more trans-ethnic party named after the federal DLP) to contain the rise of Williams' Afro-centric nationalism.[16] It was in this period, too, that the first public signs of an element of political thuggery emerged as part of the PNM's electioneering strategy, intensifying in the run-up to the 1961 general elections, and culminating in the declaration by the PNM administration of a limited state of emergency in some of the constituencies heavily populated by Indians, when it appeared that communal violence might erupt there.[17]

Williams was engaged in *realpolitik*, calculating that political contestation between an Indian-based and an African-based party would virtually ensure an indefinite tenure in office of the African-based party by virtue of the numerical superiority of the African and mixed-African populations, and the ability of the governing party to gerrymander electoral boundaries on the basis of the geographical residency of the two largest voting blocs (Africans and Indians).[18] Such a polarised pattern of ethnic voting provided both opportunities and dangers for the smaller non-Indian ethnic groups. They could overtly or covertly support the Indian-based party to contain the drive towards African hegemony, as they were to do between 1956 and 1961. Their main interest was to ensure that Afro-political nationalism was not transformed into Afro-economic nationalism. So long as the African-controlled state did not espouse the socialist ideology in word or deed, they could abide by and indeed collaborate with it.

In this respect, despite his occasional threatening rhetoric, Williams had already indicated that he was impressed by the Puerto Rican model of development, and he looked forward to American investments.[19] This might not have been welcome to a white colonial elite which was historically tied to British lines of trade and investment, but it was certainly in their eyes a more attractive option than the socialist one or one based on an ideology of African political and economic hegemony. Besides, it was becoming obvious that the British, faced with their own post-war problems, were in a process of tactical retreat from the Caribbean. Indeed, as is well known, once the British West Indies Federation had collapsed in 1962, they quickly proceeded to grant Jamaica and Trinidad/Tobago, the two largest of their West Indian colonies, political independence, albeit circumscribed by the retention of the British Privy Council as the highest court of appeal and the British Crown as the highest nominal symbol of authority.[20]

The biracial system which pitted a succession of Indian-led parties, whose main electoral support was in the constituencies with high concentrations of

Indian voters, against the Williams-led PNM, whose base of support was in the constituencies with a high concentration of African and mixed-African voters, ensured the unbroken ascendancy of the PNM for a period of 30 years (1956–86). The politics of race played the major role in sustaining the PNM in power for this period. The Indian middle class leadership was drawn increasingly from a rising Indian professional elite after 1961, when Bhadase Maraj was jettisoned in favour Dr Rudranath Capildeo, a London-trained mathematician/physicist.[21] During the politics of transition to 'independence' the Indian-based DLP received support from the colonial white elite in undertaking the role of opposition party. In the circumstances that support was predictable, Williams' anti-white rhetoric coinciding as it did with his attack on the Indian-based political leadership.

However, once the Indian-based party had performed its role of containment of the African-based PNM, the white elite was able to effect a reconciliation with the latter as the first post-independence constitution permitted them nominated representation to the senate. Williams also co-opted a few whites as advisors and intermediaries with the white business world,[22] a necessary move if he hoped to attract foreign capital to fulfil his Puerto Rican development strategy. Indeed, Williams was also successful in co-opting the Chinese and the Syrian-Lebanese ethnic minorities into a collaborative role with the PNM. A substantial proportion of the Muslim sector of the Indian population also threw in their lot with the PNM when he made Kamaluddin Mohammed, an Indian Muslim, a key member of his cabinet. That meant that the electoral opposition was, for the most part, a Hindu-based opposition after 1962, when political independence was conceded to the two-island colony.

This is not to say that the PNM regime did not come under class challenge. From 1965 class-based challenges to the political system began to be mounted, mainly by disaffected trade unionists who recognised that Williams' government was failing to alter significantly the colonial social structure. His Puerto Rican model of development was, in fact, reinforcing the economically ascendant position of the white business elite, and the ethnic profile of business management remained unchanged in an economy that was still basically an oil- and sugar-based one. Investment in the oil and petrochemical sectors were capital-intensive and the enormous concessions granted to this sector were leading to a net outflow of foreign exchange.[23] The light manufacturing sector, while providing some additional jobs, was largely of the assembly-type, which required a substantial recurrent draw-down on foreign exchange reserves to pay for the necessary imported components and to facilitate profit remittances to parent companies abroad. With a rising population, reinforced by a steady stream of West Indian immigrants, and the expansion of a white-collar middle class that the PNM's programme of expanded secondary and tertiary education was creating, the Puerto Rican model could not solve the neo-colonial problems of dependency and underdevelopment, with their inevitable social concomitants of high unemployment and deficient social services.

It was in this context that working class ideologues within the trade union movement, as well as from an emergent post-independence intelligentsia, sought to transcend the limitations of race politics. Most of the new intelligentsia came from the newly established St Augustine campus of the University of the West Indies. Williams, however, had won over the key Port-of-Spain-based trade unions — those representing the dockworkers, the public service and a large section of the teachers. These unions were based in the capital city, the geographical core of the PNM. The industry-specific mode of trade union negotiation inherited from the colonial power allowed the state to reward collaborative unions while minimising concessions to opposing ones. Therefore, the trade union movement was never able to mount a unified challenge to the regime throughout the whole period of its ascendancy, and whenever it resorted to the anarcho-syndicalist tactic of strike action, Williams did not hesitate to pass restrictive industrial legislation and employ the armed apparatus of the state against the radical unions, even declaring a state of emergency if he thought it necessary.[24]

The radical unions also had to deal with a further complication: after 1965 Bhadase Maraj, already ousted from the leadership of the Indian-based opposition, began collaborating with Williams. But as boss of the sugar workers' union, Maraj failed to win any substantial concessions from Tate and Lyle, the British-based multinational corporation which still controlled the Trinidad sugar industry. When disgruntled workers finally overthrew him as their union boss, he was replaced by a young Indian lawyer/economist, Basdeo Panday, who proceeded to make the sugar workers' union the base of a new political party, the United Labour Front (ULF), in opposition to the PNM regime.[25] That meant, in effect, that although the new Panday-led political party had the support of the leading cadres of the radical African-led unions, especially the Oilfield Workers Trade Union, which since 1937 had repeatedly aligned itself with the sugar workers, the new party was still identified in the minds of the African population — including a substantial section of the membership of the radical unions — as an Indian-based party, and the PNM propaganda machine did not fail to remind them of this.[26] As the general elections of 1966 and 1976 were to demonstrate, the ideology of socialism based on the workers' state proved to be insufficient to break the pattern of racial solidarity as the basis of political mobilisation in the newly independent two-island state. In 1966 every candidate of the C.L.R. James-inspired Workers and Farmers Party lost his deposit, while in 1976 the ULF won just ten of the 36 seats contested and these were in the predominantly Indian-populated ones.[27]

We must now examine the other factors that contributed to the sustenance of the pattern of racial political mobilisation and voting. One such factor was the resurgence of the Garveyite movement under the name of Black Power. In its initial phase under Garvey himself during the 1920s and the 1930s, the movement had focused on African initiative and collective effort within the private sector of the economy, while preaching the virtues of Pan-African solidarity. In its post-independence phase, beginning in the late 1960s, the movement looked primarily to the African-controlled state to play a leading role in the economy, while facilitating the rise of an African bourgeoisie at corporate, retail and huckstering levels within the private sector. In a series of street demonstrations, led by a section of the new university-based African intelligentsia, the movement generated a local political environment, which coincided with, and drew inspiration from, a similar environment in the United States of America.[28] The movement was almost analogous to that which had been stimulated by Williams himself in the later 1950s and early 1960s. However, there was one significant difference from the tactics adopted by Williams: the new African intelligentsia avoided antagonising the Indian population and indeed sought to convince the latter that it was representing their cause as well. It focused its attack exclusively on the white economic power structure and the failure of the PNM regime to replace it with a black one. But only a minority of Indians were persuaded enough to participate actively in the demonstrations. Those in the historic sugar zone received the demonstrators with politeness and even offered hospitality. But the majority of Indians were uncertain, and some remained apprehensive about the real objectives of the Black Power Movement.[29] Historical and recently experienced antipathies between Africans and Indians could not be eradicated by a few days of symbolic street demonstrations urging African-Indian solidarity. Moreover, at the existential level, it was becoming evident that the movement, apart from its focus on the structure of economic control, was also preoccupied with other essentially African dilemmas: those of African cultural identity, aesthetics, and somatic norm image.[30] The symbolic appeal of the movement for the Indians was thus bound to be limited.

The Black Power Movement had no organic connection with the labour movement. Though some of the more radical union leaders, like George Weekes of the Oilfield Workers Trade Union, did identify with it, probably because they too wished for the state to assume control of the 'commanding heights' of the economy, most of the Port-of-Spain-based unions distanced themselves from it and, indeed, urged Williams to declare a state of emergency. Nor was the aborted uprising by the country's small military regiment an integral part of the movement, though the environment of unrest might have been a precipitating factor. The ill-fated insurgency by a small band of middle class *guerilleros*, known as the National Union of Freedom Fighters, probably was also inspired by the unrest but had little ideological connection to the Black Power Movement, which did not advocate armed struggle but was essentially a movement to put pressure on the African-based government to use the power of the state to pursue more African-oriented economic, social welfare and cultural policies.[31]

The unrest of the early 1970s was suppressed by the PNM regime without much difficulty. But Williams knew that unless he acceded to some of the demands of the movement, the political base of his party could be seriously eroded, especially among the younger generation of Africans. Already in the midst of the turmoil one of his young cabinet ministers, A.N.R. Robinson, had tendered his resignation and would henceforth become one of the leading opponents of the PNM regime with his own solid two-constituency base in the smaller island of Tobago. A wide cross section of the new African intelligentsia, even when they disagreed on ideology and tactics, were nevertheless entering the ranks of political opposition.[32] Williams' response was to convince the African electorate that he was identified with their aspirations and that he differed only in tactics. As evidence of this, he demanded and received from the white economic elite a place for the state in the banking sector. He set up a Workers' Bank in which the trade unions would be significant shareholders. He also established a state-owned National Commercial Bank and levied a special tax to promote an extensive public works programme to cater for the mainly urban unemployed. A stroke of luck, the surge in oil prices from late 1973, just when the local economy seemed to be in crisis and he had proffered his resignation as political leader of the PNM, enabled him to widen dramatically the area of state control in the economy, opening up in the process vast opportunities for the rise of an African managerial elite.[33] But even as the state was extending its range of economic ownership and management, Williams publicly repudiated socialist ideology and gave up economic planning, making in the process unfavourable comparisons between the capitalist and socialist countries.[34] Whether this was intended to pacify the western capitalist countries, especially the USA, on whose market the Trinidad petrochemical sector was heavily dependent, or was simply part of his much-vaunted 'pragmatist' ideology, is difficult to say.

As the ideological war in the Caribbean intensified, he consistently called for the reintegration of Cuba into the Caribbean and Latin American polity. When, however, Cuban troops went to the rescue of Angola from encroaching South African contingents in 1979, he refused to allow Cuban planes to land at Piarco International Airport,[35] although he had been one of the leading critics of the apartheid regime in South Africa. Again, when Maurice Bishop's New Jewel Movement overthrew the thuggish Gairy regime in Grenada and proceeded to establish a socialist regime on the Cuban model, he steadfastly refused to establish diplomatic relations with it.[36]

If all this was intended to reassure the United States government that his regime was not socialist, nevertheless the local white economic elite was becoming apprehensive at the steady incursion of the state into areas of the economy traditionally regarded as the proper sphere of private enterprise. It was in this context that the white economic elite gave covert support to a new political party, the Organisation of National Reconstruction (ONR). The latter quickly drew substantial support from the Indian middle class, which was becoming increasingly convinced that the politics of Indian opposition was leading only to the marginalisation of their interests. Led by Karl Hudson-Phillips, a former attorney-general in Williams' government, and containing a significant cadre of defectors from Williams' PNM, the new party appeared at one point to be gaining such momentum that it seemed that it would at least replace Basdeo Panday's Indian-based ULF (which itself suffered from a severe factional split) as the new official opposition.[37] Should that happen, it would be more difficult for the PNM and its newly entrenched state capitalist managerial elite to win African mass support by projecting the spectre of an Indian party as the only alternative to the PNM. But before that new political scenario could unfold, Williams died unexpectedly at the end of March1981, to be succeeded as leader of his party by George Chambers, one of his three deputy leaders and his minister of finance.[38]

Benefiting from a wave of shock and public sympathy from Williams' death, the leading cadres of the PNM were able to rally once more the African masses to the party's fold, helped by an overt and covert campaign that focused on the issue of race on the eve of the 1981 general elections.[39] Though receiving a larger percentage of the popular vote than the Indian-based ULF, the new party suffered from the ethnic demarcation of constituency boundaries and failed to win even one seat in the elections. But it could boast that it had a significant trans-ethnic base, even though that was mostly middle class and not concentrated enough in any one constituency.[40] The electoral humiliation made its supporters implacable opponents of the PNM regime, which was now to suffer from the down-swing of the petroleum-based economy.

If the white economic elite expected that the Chambers' administration, under the new adverse conditions in the petroleum-based economy, would begin a process of state retreat from the economic sectors it controlled, they were mistaken. Instead, the Chambers administration sought to widen the state's share holding stake in the private sector through the establishment of a stock exchange and a state investment agency known as the Unit Trust, a move which spokesmen for the large corporate sector interpreted as further evidence that the state was incrementally heading in a socialist direction without officially espousing socialist ideology.[41] Despite assurances from the new minister of finance that the Unit Trust would limit its shareholding to no more than 10 per cent of any company's shares, the private corporate sector feared that the linkage of the Central Bank with the National Insurance Board and the Unit Trust, all now under state control and African management, would give to the state a preponderance of economic power. When, in addition, the Chambers' administration passed a retrenchment and severance bill that would have given to retrenched workers a prior claim over stockholders and creditors on the assets of the companies with whom they had been employed, the private corporate sector saw this as a threat to the capitalist system.[42]

Not surprisingly the Chambers administration came under increasing attack from the private corporate sector as its five-year term wore on. The exception was a Chinese-led conglomerate, which appeared to be prospering under the administration.[43] In the meantime, some elements within the African intelligentsia emphasised the need for continued African support of the regime, arguing that Africans did not have an entrepreneurial culture and therefore had to depend on the state for employment and entrepreneurial support. There was good reason for adopting this position. The regime had not only expanded opportunities for an African managerial class in the proliferating state enterprises, but it had created a large public works programme for the urban, mostly African, unemployed, and had patronised the growth of an African retail sector in the heart of Port-of-Spain. In contrast, units of the police and military began a campaign of destroying the wayside stalls of Indian vendors, an action which was bound to keep the Indian masses in a state of alienation from the regime.[44]

If the intention of all this was to maintain the biracial system of party politics, it could only be sustained by efficient management of the state sector, especially in the context of declining petroleum prices. But corruption and mismanagement of the state sector had already become notorious. Press disclosures of corrupt deals, sometimes involving key cabinet ministers, coincided with a precipitous fall in oil revenues in the latter half of the Chambers administration.[45] Falling oil revenues not only made it more difficult for the state to maintain its patronage of the African lumpenproletariat through its extensive public works programme, but also forced it to devalue the local currency, with the consequent rise in consumer prices. At the same time, the weaker companies in the private sector began collapsing, thereby putting greater pressure on the labour force.[46]

These developments provided a new opportunity for opposing political factions to make another bid to topple the regime. Among these were not only the traditional Indian-based opposition, but the Tobago-based opposition (the Democratic Action Congress), led by A.N.R. Robinson, the former PNM finance minister; the middle class ONR, led by Karl Hudson-Phillips, the former PNM attorney-general; and the politically romantic African/mixed-African intelligentsia known as the Tapia House Movement. But they all understood that not one of them had as yet a sufficiently wide electoral base to defeat the PNM. They were therefore forced to merge their parties into a single entity known as the National Alliance for Reconstruction (NAR), entrusting the leadership to the Tobago-based Robinson. The formation of this 'party of parties,' as the Tapia House Movement described it, led to an overwhelming victory over the PNM in the 1986 general elections, the PNM winning just three seats out of the 36 contested. Attended by unprecedented scenes of euphoria from the mass of the NAR's trans ethnic supporters, the victory appeared to mark the end of the biracial system of politics.[47] But in their moments of euphoria few of the NAR's supporters bothered to consider whether the interests represented within the new party were compatible, especially if the leadership of the long-marginalised Indian sector was to demand equity in appointments to the new cabinet and to state boards, and if the strong corporate interests that lay behind the ONR were to press ahead with their demand for divestment of state enterprises and retrenchment in the public sector.

Within a year the 'party of parties' was in travail. Its sentimental slogan of 'one love' proved to be ideologically barren since it was intended simply to mask the race and class cleavages that existed in the society and were reproduced in the party. The struggle for the distribution of portfolios within the cabinet, state boards and state enterprises was both a race and a class struggle. It was a struggle between the African and Indian factions of the middle class.[48] In the context of the struggle over ministerial and statutory appointments, ethnic consciousness was heightened over the proposed construction of a cultural centre by the government of India, following precedents set by the Venezuelan and some other governments.[49] The Indian demand for equity in the distribution of portfolios was soon interpreted by the African faction as a 'ULF grab for power,' which was equated as a move towards 'the Indianisation of the Government.'[50] The distribution of the chairmanship of the state boards, however, did not reflect this. Out of 41 boards Indians were assigned to the chairmanship of six, and these were considered minor. Persons of African descent were assigned to 28, while seven, the really 'big plums,' according to Selwyn Ryan, the academic/feature columnist, were assigned to 'French Creoles,' the local collective designation for persons of European ancestry.[51]

In the cabinet, Indians at first fared somewhat better. Though they were in a minority there as well, the important Ministry of Energy was assigned to Kelvin Ramnath, an Indian member of the ULF; the Ministry of External Affairs and Immigration went to Basdeo Panday, the leader of the ULF; Local Government was also assigned to Brinsley Samaroo, an Indian. But the bickering continued and was precipitated by the personal animosity that developed between John Humphrey, the white Creole ULF minister of housing, and A.N.R. Robinson, the prime minister, over such issues as a harbour development contract for Tobago and the creation of a new local currency — the brainchild of Humphrey — to be called the 'Trinity Dollar.' Amidst the bickering, towards the end of his administration's first year, Robinson not only relieved Humphrey of his ministerial portfolio, but also took away the energy portfolio from Kelvin Ramnath, and the immigration section of Panday's portfolio, a move that was bound to be regarded as a personal affront by the ULF leader. This move by Robinson only served to intensify the public criticism of his leadership by the alienated members of his cabinet, to which Robinson responded in February

1988, by removing the ULF leader and his alienated colleagues from the cabinet. It was a move that won the approbation of the Trinidad and Tobago Chamber of Commerce, the Manufacturers Association, and the Employers Consultative Association — all representative of the larger business interests in the country. Also welcoming the move were the two leading newspapers, the *Trinidad Express* and the *Trinidad Guardian*.[52] The demoted ULF members did not resign from the party but proceeded the following month to form a party caucus called 'Club 88.' In March 1989, by which time it was clear that the NAR was becoming unpopular with African middle and working classes because of its economic policies, 'Club 88' was launched as a full-fledged political party called the United National Congress (UNC).

The NAR was nevertheless able to retain three prominent Indians, all former academics at the St Augustine campus of the University of the West Indies, while Robinson was able to co-opt from the campus' Department of History another who resigned his lectureship with alacrity to fill the ministerial position from which Panday, until then his political leader, was peremptorily removed. The fact was that with its overwhelming electoral victory in December 1986, the leadership of the NAR and its advisers could have risked losing the alienated ULF representatives without the NAR losing its parliamentary majority. But the leadership miscalculated on the electoral appeal of its remaining middle class Indian members and would pay a heavy price for this in the 1991 parliamentary elections. A sign of mass Indian disaffection with the NAR was the surge of Indian migrants to Canada between 1988 and 1990, seeking asylum as 'refugees.'[53] Adding to the racial polarisation between the two largest ethnic communities was the race-based mobilisation that was being urged on the African community by neo-Garveyites and other Black Power advocates, assisted by the Nigerian envoy, who urged the formation of an umbrella organisation of all African groups to promote African interests. This culminated in the formation of the Confederation of African Organisations of Trinidad and Tobago on August 1, 1988, coinciding with the celebration of Emancipation Day and the visit of the Oni of Ife, spiritual head of the Yorubas. At the same time, ethnocentric leaders of the Indian community began mobilising to demand a national holiday in recognition of the first arrival of Indians in Trinidad, completely oblivious to the conditions under which those Indians had arrived and to the indirect panegyric that was being cast on British imperialism.[54]

The rivalry and mutual apprehensions of the two largest ethnic groups helped to strengthen the leverage that was being exercised by the smaller ethnic groups, particularly those of European descent, who had the closest links with foreign corporate interests in trade, finance and industry. They now successfully pressured the NAR administration to reduce the public sector wage bill through a cut in public sector wages and retrenchment; to dispense with the cost-of-living allowance built into most industrial agreements; to abandon legislation that would have given retrenched workers a first claim on the assets of companies; to impose a 15 per cent sales tax (misnamed 'value added tax') on items of mass consumption; to engage in the phased transference of state enterprises to the private sector; and to devalue the Trinidad and Tobago currency.[55] While the mass of the population were required to bear these austerities, the banks and conglomerates continued to register substantial profits and to expand their economic power by destroying or absorbing weaker rivals.[56] In ethnically homogenous societies, such conditions would have inevitably led to class conflict. But in the ethnically polarised society of Trinidad and Tobago this was almost impossible. Attempts by the more radical unions to mount demonstrations and protests against the NAR's policies proved futile.[57]

Yet, in a most unexpected and dramatic way, the NAR administration was subjected in late July and early August 1990 to its most traumatic experience. In the context of an unresolved land dispute with the Jamaat al Muslimeen, a Black Muslim organisation, and an intense controversy over the signing of a maritime treaty with Venezuela that demarcated the waters of the Gulf of Paria between Trinidad/Tobago and Venezuela, the parliamentary building was stormed by armed members of the 'Jamaat,' who also bombed the nearby police headquarters and seized control of the country's sole television station. In the parliamentary building, a number of ministers, including the prime minister, were held hostage, as were the occupants of the television station.[58] During the insurgency, one policeman and several civilians were killed by the armed rebels. Prime Minister Robinson, and Selwyn Richardson, his attorney-general, had been physically abused during the ordeal. In the midst of the crisis, a wave of arson and looting engulfed Port-of-Spain. The uprising had no mass support, and it had no connection with organised labour; yet there was some grim satisfaction among the politically alienated and economically frustrated sections of the population at the turn of events. In return for the release of the hostages, the acting president and government ministers who were not in the parliamentary building at the time, agreed to an amnesty for the rebels. Subsequent attempts to keep the latter in indefinite detention were nullified by a British Privy Council decision, and it was later revealed that the rebels had received their military equipment from the United States, not from Libya as alleged in the local and international media during the crisis.[59]

Nothing, however, underscores the widespread unpopularity of the NAR administration, which was built on the nebulous ideology of 'one love' than its humiliating defeat as a political party in the parliamentary elections of the following year. The party lost every seat it had won in Trinidad in 1986 and retained only the two Tobago seats associated with Robinson's dissolved political component of the NAR, the Democratic Action Congress. As a political party, the NAR, the party of the trans-ethnic middle class and corporate business interests, was annihilated. But the result was not the emergence of a working class or populist party, but a return to the biracial form of political mobilisation associated with the African-based PNM and the latest incarnation of the Indian-based political formations, the UNC. The PNM won the 1991 parliamentary elections, but with a smaller majority than in its period of greatest ascendancy (1961–81). The UNC, like its previous incarnations, formed the opposition.[60] The two major ethnic groups were once again politically counterposed — not an unattractive political situation for the elite elements in the society and their foreign allies, since it had repeatedly proved to be the most effective antidote to working class mobilisation and socialist ideology.

Notes

1. Kelvin Singh, *Race and Class Struggles in a Colonial State: Trinidad 1917–1945* (Kingston: The Press, UWI., 1994), 101–04, 109–11.
2. These estimates are derived from the *Trinidad and Tobago Statistical Digest*, 1935–1955, Table 8, p. 7.
3. Bridget Brereton, *Race Relations in Colonial Trinidad, 1870–1900* (Cambridge: Cambridge University Press, 1979), Chap. 4 passim.
4. M.D.S. Ramesar, *Survivors of Another Crossing: A History of East Indians in Trinidad, 1880–1946* (Port-of-Spain: UWI School of Continuing Studies 1994), 141–43; Carl Campbell, *Colony and Nation: A Short History of Education in Trinidad and Tobago, 1834–1986* (Kingston: Ian Randle Publishers, 1992), 17–18.
5. Kelvin Singh, 'Conflict and Collaboration: Tradition and Modernizing Indo-Trinidadian Elites (1917-56),' *New West Indian Guide*, 70 (1996): 232.
6. Selwyn Ryan, *Race and Nationalism in Trinidad and Tobago* (St Augustine: Institute of Social and Economic Research, UWI, 1974), 89–99.
7. Singh, 'Conflict and Collaboration,' 244.
8. Ryan, *Race and Nationalism*, 130.
9. *Ibid.*, 86–87.
10. These were the West Indian Independence Party and the Caribbean National Labour Party.
11. Ryan, *Race and Nationalism*, 107–09; Paul Sutton, ed. *Forged From the Love of Liberty* (Port-of-Spain: Longman Caribbean, 1981), 269–80.
12. The candidature of Jang Bahadoorsingh, a Vice-President of the SDMS and an early member of the PNM, was rejected by the PNM group of Laventille, while S.B. Dolsingh, another member of the SDMS was expelled from the PNM, though Dolsingh claimed that he had resigned before he was expelled (*Guardian*, July 14, 1956).
13. For his attacks on the SDMS see the *Guardian*, August 1 & 2, 1956. Also *PNM Weekly Special Supplement*, August 9, 1956.
14. Bridget Brereton, *A History of Modern Trinidad, 1783–1962* (Port-of-

Spain: Heinemann, 1981), 237.

15. *Guardian*, April 3, 1958, editorial.

16. On white fears, see F.E. Brassington, *The Politics of Opposition* (Diego Martin: West Indian Publishing Company, 1976), 83-84.

17. On PNM thuggery, see *Ibid.*, 20; Ivar Oxaal, *Black Intellectuals Come to Power* (Cambridge Mass.: Schenkman, 1968), 172. Both give eye-witness accounts. See also the recollections of Margaret Hector in *Sunday Express*, January 11, 1987.

18. Williams' confidence about winning an election fought on a racial basis emerges in a 1961 campaign speech: 'Indians as a group may not be with us and may be against us. So what? We beat them in 1956 and we will beat them again' (Cited in H.P. Singh, *The Indian Struggle for Justice and Equality*, The India Review Press, 1993, 43).

19. *PNM. Weekly*, June 25, 1956.

20. In 1976, the PNM government adopted a republican constitution, but retained the Privy Council.

21. On the intrigues within the DLP and the replacement of Maraj by Capildeo, see Brassington, 87-89, 106-08.

22. Perhaps the most influential was John O'Halloran, who later became enmeshed in corruption scandals.

23. See, for example, details of the enormous concession made to Federation Chemicals in 1958, whose US-based parent company was W.R. Grace and Company. Under an agreement signed by John O'Halloran, the Trinidad and Tobago government even had to make foreign exchange available for the company to import plant and equipment (*Express*, February 1, 1981).

24. D. Abdulah, 'The Role of Labour in the Development Experience,' in Selwyn Ryan, ed., *The Independence Experience, 1962-1987* (St Augustine: Institute of Social and Economic Research, UWI, 1988), 118-19.

25. Basdeo Panday became President of the All Trinidad Sugar Estates and Factory Workers Union in March 1973. The ULF was formed in February 1975 and became a political party in March 1976 (Selwyn Ryan, *Pathways to Power*, St Augustine: Institute of. Social and Economic Research, UWI, 1996, 64).

26. Typical was the alarm sounded by J.A.Bain, and given prominence by the *Guardian*, who argued that if Indians captured political power they would merge it with economic power (*Guardian*, April 25, 1976). But the real fear of the interests represented by the paper was that the ULF might adopt socialist policies if it won the elections (See *Ibid.*, September 11, 1976, editorial).

27. For a comprehensive account of the 1976 elections, see Ryan, *Pathways to Power*, Chap. V passim.

28. James Millette, 'Towards the Black Power Revolt of 1970,' in *The Black*

Power Revolution of 1970, ed., Selwyn Ryan. (St Augustine: Insititute of Social and Economic Research, UWI, 1995), 70-71. Millette traces other influences as well, but judged by the clenched-fist symbol and such adopted names as 'Black Panthers,' it is clear that in Trinidad the Civil Rights Movement in the United States had the most influence.

29. John La Guerre, 'The Indian Response to Black Power,' in Ryan, ed., *The Black Power Revolution*, 273-307. La Guerre's insinuation that the movement operated within a partial Marxist framework is difficult to reconcile with the explicit repudiation of class struggle by the National Joint Action Committee (NJAC), the leading organisation in the movement.

30. African clothes, African hair styles and an appreciation of African physical beauty were all advocated (See the National Joint Action Committee's paper *East Dry River Speaks*, 1970).

31. The local Black Panthers Organisation best exemplified the pressure tactic when it declared that 'Williams must govern or get out' (see their 'White Paper,' in the *Express*, March 11, 1970).

32. A good example is the New World Group, which split in 1968, with its two leading members on the St Augustine campus forming their separate organisations. James Millette, of Marxist/Leninist persuasion, formed a political party, the United National Independence Party, while Lloyd Best, denouncing 'doctor politics' and 'conventional politics,' formed the Tapia House Movement.

33. J. Harewood, and R. Henry, *Inequality in a Post-Colonial Society: Trinidad and Tobago, 1956-1981* (St Augustine: Institute of Social and Economic Research, UWI, 1985), 73-74.

34. *Sunday Guardian*, October 17, 1976: Report of House of Representatives debate on President's Message.

35. *Express*, December 19, 1975.

36. Williams did not even open the letters written to him by Maurice Bishop. According to Senator John Donaldson, his Minister of National Security and External Affairs, Williams' action was guided by a Cabinet directive — a dubious claim made in the midst of local criticism both inside and outside the Trinidad and Tobago Parliament (see the *Guardian*, November 22, 1979).

37. The author was initially co-opted into the executive of the ONR as First Vice-Chairman, but withdrew when he became convinced that the party was being manipulated by big business.

38. It was alleged that Williams' corpse was left lying on a couch at his official residence for over fourteen hours, while the President and the PNM cabinet haggled over who should be his successor (*Express*, April 13, 1981: Letter from Martin Kavanaugh). For a more detailed examination of Williams' death see H. Ghany, ed., *Kamal: A Lifetime*

of Politics, Religion and Culture (Port-of-Spain: K. Mohammed, 1996), 376–77.

39. On the eve of the elections, Selwyn Ryan portrayed the contest essentially as one of 'White/Associate White vs African' (*Express*, October 25, 1981).

40. The PNM received 53 per cent of the popular vote, ONR 22 per cent and the Alliance (comprising the ULF, the Tapia House and the DAC) 20 per cent (*Express*, November 12, 1991).

41. See, for example, the charges made by Alvin Chow during the Senate debate on the Unit Trust Bill (*Guardian*, May 4 & 6 , 1981).

42. *Express*, October 20, 1985; also *Guardian*, November 7 , 1985. The bill was later emasculated by the High Court.

43. The Chinese business interests had formed a conglomerate, the Associated Brands Ltd., which attempted to take over the white-controlled McEarnerny/Alstons group *(Express*, August 6, 1986).

44. *Express*, May 28, 1984.

45. D. Alleyne, 'Petroleum and Development (1962–1987),' in *The Independence Experience 1962-1987*, ed., Selwyn Ryan. (St Augustine: Institute of Social and Economic Research, UWI., 1988), 22.

46. By October 1986, more than 20,000 persons had been retrenched in the private sector, according to Hilton Clarke, President of the Employers' Consultative Association (*Express*, October 16, 1986).

47. For a description of the euphoria, see Ramdath Jagessar's 'A Night to Remember,' *Guardian*, December 17, 1986.

48. For comments of Carl Parris on the composition of state boards see the *Guardian*, June 3, 1987; for Selwyn Ryan's comments on the growing rift within the NAR see *Sunday Express*, June 7, 1987.

49. See, for example, comments of G. Frankson in the *Express*, March 14, 1987. In September 1990 the issue was still unresolved (*Guardian*, September 15, 1990, editorial).

50. Interview with an anonymous technocrat, who argued that 'African technocrats were in the firing line' (*Sunday Express*, December 13, 1987). However, a spokesman for Lloyd Best's Tapia House Movement felt that the interview, given front-page headline by the newspaper, was an attempt 'to stampede Afro-Trinidadians into supporting the NAR and its political leader.' On the alleged 'Indianisation of the Government,' see the *Sunday Express*, April 19, 1987.

51. *Sunday Express*, January 17, 1988, Section 2.

52. *Express*, February 8, 1988; *Guardian*, February 10, 1988.

53. *Guardian*, December 11, 1990, editorial.

54. In November 1987, Mohammed Z. Anka, the Nigerian High Commissioner to Trinidad and Tobago, called on all African organisations to close ranks, promising that his Mission would 'firmly

collaborate with a formidable association of African people in this country' (*Guardian*, November 12, 1987). For the launching of the Confederation of African Organisations and the arrival of the Oni of Ife, see the *Express* August 1 & 14 , 1988. By June 1990, 'Indian Arrival Day' had become a major issue among ethnically-driven Indians (see comments of S. Capildeo in the *Guardian*, June 4, 1990).

55. See, for example, the praise lavished on the government's economic programme by David Renwick, the pro-business columnist (*Sunday Express*, July 30, 1989).

56. One of the victims of this economic war was the conglomerate of Ram Kirpalani, the pre-eminent Indian tycoon, whose entrepreneurial activities had gone beyond merchandising and into manufacturing and finance. On the collapse of his 'empire' following his death in a motor crash, see the *Express*, July 30, 1989.

57. *Express*, March 6, 1989; *Guardian*, April 7, 1989.

58. For a fairly detailed narrative of the uprising, see V.E.T. Furlonge-Kelly, *The Silent Victory* (Port of Spain: Golden Eagle Enterprises, 1991), Chapter 3 passim.

59. *Ibid.*. Chap. 4 passim. Mr. Robinson subsequently suggested that the uprising was connected to a concurrent debate on corruption, involving a former PNM minister and an American oil company. It is this writer's view, however, that the real linkage was the maritime treaty with Venezuela, which had serious economic and geo-strategic implications not only for Trinidad and Tobago, but also for US and British interests in the Gulf of Paria. For Robinson's views, see the *Guardian* and the *Express*, October 16, 1990. For the maritime treaty controversy, see the *Guardian*, July 21, 23 & 27, 1990.

60. The PNM won 21 of the 36 seats contested, the UNC 13, and the NAR 2 (both in Tobago). For an ethnic profile of the results, see Ryan's *Pathways to Power*, 215–19.

Bibliography

Books and Articles

Abdulah, D. 'The Role of Labour in the Development Experience.' In *The Independence Experience, 1962-1987,* ed., Selwyn Ryan. St Augustine: Institute of Social and Economic Research, 1988: 437-69.

Acworth, A.W. *Treasure in the Caribbean: A First Study of Georgian Buildings in the British West Indies.* London: Pleiades Books, 1949.

Adamson, Alan Herbert. *Sugar Without Slaves: The Political Economy of British Guiana 1838-1904.* New Haven: Yale University Press, 1972.

———. 'The Reconstruction of Plantation Labor After Emancipation: the Case of British Guiana.' In *Race and Slavery in the Western Hemisphere: Quantitative Studies,* edited by S.L. Engerman and E. Genovese. Princeton: Princeton University Press, 1975: 457-73.

Akroyd, W.R. *Sweet Malefactor: Sugar, Slavery and Human Society.* London: Heinemann, 1967.

Alleyne, D. 'Petroleum and Development (1962-1987).' In *The Independence Experience, 1962-1987,* ed. Selwyn Ryan. St Augustine: Institute of Social and Economic Research, 1988: 19-26.

Alleyne, Mervyn, *Roots of Jamaican Culture.* London: Pluto Press, 1988.

Alleyne, Warren. *Historic Bridgetown.* Bridgetown: Barbados National Trust, 1978.

Almanack and Local Guide of British Guiana Containing the Laws, Ordinances and Regulations of the Colony, the Civil and Military Lists with a List of Estates from Corentyne to Pomeroon Rivers. Demerary: The Royal Gazette Office, 1832.

Andic, F. and T. Matthews, eds. *The Caribbean in Transition.* Rio Piedras, Puerto Rico: Institute of Caribbean Studies, 1965.

[Anon.]. *Authentic History of the English West Indies.* London: Dean and Munday, Printed for the author, 1810.

[Anon.]. *Poems on Subjects Arising in England, and the West Indies.* London, 1783.

[Anon]. 'Treatment of Slaves in Barbadoes.' *The Christian Remembrancer,* 5 (1823).

[Anon.]. *Marly, Or a Planter's Life in Jamaica.* Glasgow: Richard Griffin, 1828.

[Anon]. 'Odd Pages from Old Records' [Letters between Seale Yearwood and

A. Frere, March 1796 and April 26, 1797]. *JBMHS*, 16 (1949): 113-17.

[Anon.] 'Old Plantation Customs.' *JBMHS*, 7 (1940): 109-15.

[Anon]. 'Hooper of Barbados.' *JBMHS*, 4 (1939): 32 32-41; & 6 (1939): 198-205.

[Anon.] 'Treatment of Slaves in Barbadoes.' *The Christian Remembrancer*, 5 (1823).

Andrade, Jacob. *A Record of the Jews in Jamaica From the English Conquest to the Present Time*. Kingston: The Jamaica Times Ltd., 1941.

Andrews, Charles M. *The Colonial Period of American History, Vol. 3: The Settlements*. New Haven: Yale University Press, 1936.

Anthony, M. *Port of Spain in a World of War 1939-1945: The Making of Port of Spain*. Port of Spain: Ministry of Sports, Culture and Youth Affairs, 1983.

Antrobus, Peggy. 'New Institutions and Programmes for Caribbean Women.' In *Women of the Caribbean*, edited by Pat Ellis. Kingston: Kingston Publishers Ltd., 1986: 131-34.

Archer, C.V. and W.K. Furgusson. *Laws of Barbados, Vol. 1, 1667-1895*. Bridgetown: Barbados Advocate,1994.

Armstrong, Douglas and Mark Fleischman. 'Analysis of Four House Area Burials from the African Jamaican Settlement of Seville.' *Syracuse University Archaeological Reports 6*, Syracuse: Department of Anthropology, Syracuse University, 1993.

Astley, Thomas. *A New General Collection of Voyages and Travels*. London: Printed for T. Astley, 1745.

Atkins, John. *A Voyage to Guinea, Brazil, & the West Indies in His Majesty's ships, the Swallow and Weymouth*. London: C. Ward and R. Chandler, 1735.

Augier, F.R. 'Before and After 1865.' *New World Quarterly*, 2.2 (1966): 21-40.

——, ed. *The University of the West Indies 40th Anniversary Lectures*. Mona: UWI, 1990.

——, S.C. Gordon, D. G. Hall, and M. Reckord. *The Making of the West Indies*. London: Longmans, Green and Co. Ltd., 1960.

Ausubel, Herman, J. Bartlet Brebner and Erling M. Hunt, eds. *Some Modern Historians of Britain: Essays in Honor of R. L. Schuyler*. New York: The Dryden Press, 1951.

Bacchus, M.K. 'Education as a Social Control Mechanism.' *The Alberta Journal of Educational Research*, 25.3 (1979): 160-173.

——. *Utilization, Misuse, and Development of Human Resources in the Early West Indian Colonies*. Ontario: Wilfrid Laurier University Press, 1990.

Baldwin, Robert E. 'Patterns of Development in Newly Settled Regions.' *The Manchester School of Economic and Social Studies* 24 (1956): 161-79.

Banbuck, C.A. *Histoire politique, économique et sociale de la Martinique sous l'Ancien Régime (1635-1789)*. Paris: Libraire des Sciences Politiques et Sociales, 1935.

Baptiste, Fitzroy. *War, Cooperation and Conflict: The European Possessions in the Caribbean, 1939 1945*. New York: Greenwood Press, 1988.

Barbados Legislature. House of Assembly. *Report from a Select Committee of the House of Assembly, Appointed to Inquire into the Origin, Causes and Progress of the Late Insurrection, 1817*. London: T. Cadell and W. Davies, 1818.

——. *Barbadoes: Report of a Committee of the General Assembly Upon the Several Heads of Enquiry &c. Relative to the Slave Trade*. London, 1790.

——. *Report of a Committee of the Council of Barbadoes, Appointed to Inquire into the Actual Condition of the Slaves in this Island*. London: W. Sior, 1824.

Barber, John. *A History of the Amistad Captives*. New York: Arno Press, 1969.

Barclay, Alexander. *A Practical View of the Present State of Slavery in the West Indies*. London: Smith Elder and Co., 1826.

Bayley, Frederick, W.N. *Four Years Residence in the West Indies, During the Years 1826, 7, 8, and 9*. London: William Kidd, 1832.

Beckles, Hilary McD. 'Slave Drivers' War: The 1816 Barbados Slave Uprising.' *Boletín de Estudios Latinoamericanos y del Caribe*, 39 (1985): 85–111.

——. *Natural Rebels: A Social History of Enslaved Black Women in Barbados*. New Jersey: Rutgers University Press, 1989.

——. *A History of Barbados. From Amerindian Settlement to Nation-State*. Cambridge: Cambridge University Press, 1990.

——. 'An Economic Life of Their Own: Slaves as Commodity Producers and Distributors in Barbados.' In *The Slaves' Economy: Independent Production by Slaves in the Americas*, edited by Ira Berlin and Philip D. Morgan. London: Frank Cass, 1991: 31–48.

——. 'Emancipation by Law or War! Wilberforce and the 1816 Barbados Slave Rebellion.' In *Abolition and its Aftermath*, ed., David Richardson. London: Frank Cass, 1985: 80–105.

——. *Centering Woman: Gender Discourses in Caribbean Slave Society*. Kingston: Ian Randle Publishers, 1999.

—— and Karl Watson. 'Social Protest and Labour Bargaining: The Changing Nature of Slaves' Responses to Plantation Life in 18th Century Barbados.' *Slavery and Abolition*, 8 (1987): 272–93.

—— and Verene Shepherd, eds. *Caribbean Freedom*. Kingston: Ian Randle Publishers, 1993.

Beecher, John Coleman. *Jamaica Cricket 1863–1926*. Kingston: Gleaner, 1926.

Beer, George Louis. *The Old Colonial System 1660–1754*. New York: Macmillan, 1912.

Belgrove, William. *A Treatise Upon Husbandry or Planting*. Boston, 1755.

Bell, Kenneth N. and W.P. Morrell. *Selected Documents on British Colonial Policy*. Oxford: Clarendon Press, 1968.

Benezet, Anthony. *Notes on the Slave Trade*. Philadelphia: Joseph Crukshank, 1781.

Bennett, J. Harry. *Bondsmen and Bishops*. Berkeley and Los Angeles: University of California Press, 1958.

Berlin, Ira. *Many Thousands Gone: The First Two Centuries of Slavery in North*

America. Cambridge, Mass.: Belknap Press of Harvard University Press, 1998.

—— and Philip D. Morgan, eds. *The Slaves' Economy: Independent Production by Slaves in the Americas.* London: Frank Cass, 1991.

—— and Philip D. Morgan, eds. *Cultivation and Culture: Labor and the Shaping of Slave Life in the Americas.* Charlottesville: University Press of Virginia, 1993.

—— and Philip D. Morgan. 'Labor and the Shaping of Slave Life in the Americas.' In *Cultivation and Culture: Labor and the Shaping of Slave Life in the Americas,* edited by Ira Berlin and Philip D. Morgan. Charlottesville: University Press of Virginia, 1993: 1–45.

Best, Lloyd. 'Outlines of a Model of Pure Plantation Economy,' *Social and Economic Studies,* 17.3 (1968): 283–326.

Béteille, A. *Caste, Class and Power: Changing Patterns of Stratification in a Tanjore Village.* Berkeley: University of California Press, 1965.

Bettelheim, Judith. 'Jamaica Jonkonu and Related Caribbean Festivals.' In *Africa in the Caribbean,* eds., Margaret Crahan and Franklin Knight. Baltimore: The Johns Hopkins University Press, 1979: 80–100.

Bohannan, Paul and Philip Curtin. *Africa and Africans.* Garden City, N.Y.: Natural History Press, 1971.

Bolingbroke, Henry. *A Voyage to Demerary.* 1807. Reprint. Georgetown: Daily Chronicle Ltd., 1947.

Bolland, O. Nigel. 'Systems of Domination After Slavery: The Control of Land and Labour in the British West Indies After 1838.' In *Caribbean Freedom,* edited by Hilary McD. Beckles and Verene A. Shepherd. Kingston: Ian Randle Publishers, 1993: 107–23.

——. *The Politics of Labour in the British Caribbean.* Kingston: Ian Randle Publishers, 2001.

Boodhoo, K., ed. *Eric Williams: The Man and the Leader.* Lanham, MD: University Press of America, 1986.

Bovell, James. 'Observations on the Climate of Barbadoes.' *The British American Journal of Medical and Physical Science,* 4 (1848).

Brandow, James C., comp. *Genealogies of Barbados Families.* Baltimore: Genealogical Publishing Co., Inc., 1983.

Brandow, James C., ed. 'Diary of Joseph Senhouse' [1776–1778]. *JBMHS,* 37 (1986): 381–414.

Brassington, F.E. *The Politics of Opposition.* Diego Martin: West India Publishing Co., 1976.

Brathwaite, Kamau. *The Folk Culture of the Slaves in Jamaica.* London: New Beacon Books, 1970.

——. *The Development of Creole Society in Jamaica, 1770–1820.* Oxford: Clarendon Press, 1971.

Braudel, Fernand. 'Antilles et Amérique,' *Annales ESC* 3 (1948): 537.

——. *La Méditerranée et le monde méditerranéen à l'époque de Philippe II*. Paris: Librairie Armand Colin, 1949.

Breen, T.H. *Tobacco Culture: The Mentality of the Great Tidewater Planters on the Eve of the Revolution*. Princeton: Princeton University Press, 1985.

Brereton, Bridget. *Race Relations in Colonial Trinidad, 1870-1900*. Cambridge: Cambridge University Press, 1979.

Brereton, Bridget. *A History of Modern Trinidad 1783-1862*. Port of Spain: Heinemann, 1981.

Bridenbaugh, Carl and Roberta Bridenbaugh. *No Peace Beyond the Line: The English in the Caribbean, 1624-1690*. New York: Oxford University Press, 1972.

Brugevin, Joseph. 'Journal de Traite du Vaisseau la Licorne de Bordeaux.' In *Traite des Noirs et Navires Négriers au XVIII Siècle*, edited by Patrick Villiers. Grenoble: Éditions des 4 Seigneurs, 1982: 127-62.

Burn, W.L. *The British West Indies*. London: Hutchinson, 1951.

Burnard, Trevor. 'A Failed Settler Society: Marriage and Demographic Failure in Early Jamaica.' *Journal of Social History*, 28 (1994): 63-82.

Burns, Sir Alan. *Colonial Civil Servant*. London: George Allen and Unwin Ltd., 1949.

——. *History of the British West Indies*. London: George Allen and Unwin Ltd, 1954.

Burton, Richard. *Afro-Creole: Power, Opposition and Play in the Caribbean*. London: Cornell University Press, 1997.

Bush, Barbara. *Slave Women in Caribbean Society 1650-1838*. Bloomington: Indiana University Press, 1990.

Cable, Mary. *Black Odyssey: The Case of the Slave Ship Amistad*. Baltimore: Penguin Books, 1977.

Cadbury, Henry J. ed. 'An Account of Barbados 200 Years Ago' [by John Smith]. *JBMHS*, 9 (1942): 81-83.

Campbell, Carl. 'Towards an Imperial Policy for the Education of Negroes in the West Indies after Emancipation.' *Jamaican Historical Review*, 7 (1967): 68-102.

——. 'Social and Economic Obstacles to the Development of Popular Education in post-Emancipation Jamaica 1834-1865.' *Journal of Caribbean History*, 1 (1970): 57-88.

——. 'Denominationalism and the Mico Schools in Jamaica 1835-1842.' *Caribbean Studies*, 10.4 (1971):152-84.

——. *Colony and Nation. A Short History of Education in Trinidad and Tobago*. Kingston: Ian Randle Publishers, 1992.

——. *The Young Colonials. A Social History of Education in Trinidad and Tobago 1834-1939*. Kingston: The University of the West Indies Press, 1996.

Campbell, Mavis. *The Dynamics of Change in a Slave Society: A Sociopolitical History of the Free Coloreds of Jamaica, 1800-1865*. Rutherford, New Jersey:

Associated Universities Press, 1976.

Carmichael, A.C. *Domestic Manners and Social Conditions of the White, Coloured and Negro Population of the West Indies.* 2 Vols. London: Whittaker, 1833.

Carrington, Selwyn. *The British West Indies During the American Revolution.* Dordrecht, Holland: Foris Publications, 1988.

Cashman, Richard. 'Cricket and Colonialism: Colonial Hegemony and Indigenous Subversion?' In *Pleasure, Profit and Proselytism: British Culture and Sport at Home and Abroad 1700-1914,* edited by J.A. Mangan. London: Frank Cass, 1988: 258-72.

Chambers, Douglas. 'Tracing Igbo into the Diaspora.' In *Identity in the Shadow of Slavery,* edited by Paul E. Lovejoy. London & New York: Continuum, 2000: 55-71.

Chandler, Alfred D. 'The Expansion of Barbados.' *Journal of the Barbados Museum and Historical Society,* 13 (1946): 106-30.

Chandler, John. 'Plantation Field Names in Barbados.' *JBMHS,* 32 (1968):133-43.

Churchill, A. and I. *Collection of Voyages and Travels.* 3rd ed. London: Printed for Henry Lintot and John Osborn, 1744-46.

Clarke, Forster. 'Plan of Treatment of the Negroes on the Estates in Barbados, 1823.' *JBMHS,* 2 (1934): 29-31.

Cochrane, Thomas. *Notes on the Minerology, Government and Condition of the British West India Islands.* London: J. Ridgeway 1851.

Coleman, D.C. *Myth, History and the Industrial Revolution.* London: The Hambledon Press, 1992.

Coleridge, Henry Nelson. *Six Months in the West Indies in 1825.* London: John Murray, 1832.

Connell, Neville, ed. 'Father Labat's Visit to Barbados in 1700.' *JBMHS,* 24 (1957): 160-74.

Coughtry, Jay. *The Notorious Triangle: Rhode Island and the African Slave Trade 1700-1807.* Philadelphia: Temple University Press, 1981.

Coupland, Reginald. *The British Anti-Slavery Movement.* 1933. Reprint. London: Frank Cass & Co., 1964.

Crahan, Margaret and Franklin Knight, eds. *Africa in the Caribbean.* Baltimore: The Johns Hopkins University Press, 1979.

Craton, Michael. *Searching For The Invisible Man.* Cambridge, Mass.: Harvard University Press, 1978.

——. 'Changing Patterns of Slave Families in the British West Indies.' *Journal of Interdisciplinary History,* 10 (1979): 1-35.

——. 'Proto-Peasant Revolts? The Late Slave Rebellions in the British West Indies, 1816-1832.' *Past and Present,* 85 (1979): 99-125.

——. *Testing the Chains: Resistance to Slavery in the British West Indies.* Ithaca: Cornell University Press, 1982.

—— and James Walvin. *A Jamaica Plantation: The History of Worthy Park, 1670-*

1970. London: W.H. Allen, 1970.

Crouse, Nellis M. *The French Struggle for the West Indies 1665-1713*. New York: Columbia University Press, 1943.

Crow, H. *Memoirs of the Late Capt. Crow of Liverpool*. London: Longman, Rees, Orme, Brown and Green, 1830.

Cruickshank, J. Graham. 'Field Names in Barbados.' *JBMHS*, 2 (1935): 166.

Cudjoe, S., ed. *Eric Williams Speaks*. Wellesley: Calaloux Publications, 1993.

Curtin, Philip D. *Africa Remembered: Narratives by West Africans from the Era of the Slave Trade*. Madison: University of Wisconsin Press, 1967.

——. *The Atlantic Slave Trade: A Census*. Madison: University of Wisconsin Press, 1969.

Cutrufelli, Maria R. *Women of Africa. Roots of Oppression*. London: Zed Books, 1983.

Da Costa, Emilia Viotti. *Crowns of Glory, Tears of Blood*. New York: Oxford University Press, 1994.

Dalton, Henry. *The History of British Guiana*. 2 Vols. London: Longman, 1855.

Davies, K.G. *The Royal African Company*. London: Longman, 1957.

——. 'Empire and Capital.' *Economic History Review*, 13 (1960): 105-10.

——. *The North Atlantic World in the Seventeenth Century*. Minneapolis: University of Minnesota Press, 1974.

Davis, David Brion. *The Problem of Slavery in Western Culture*. Harmondsworth: Penguin, 1970.

Davis, N. Darnell. *The Cavaliers and Roundheads of Barbados 1650-1652, with Some Account of the Early History of Barbados*. Georgetown, British Guiana: The 'Argosy' Press, 1887.

Davis, Ralph. 'English Foreign Trade, 1660-1700.' *Economic History Review*, 7 (1954): 150-66.

Davy, John. *The West Indies, Before and Since Slave Emancipation*. London: W. and F.G. Cash, 1854.

Debien, G. 'Les travaux d'histoire sur Saint-Domingue: Chronique bibliographique (1946-1950).' *Revue d'histoire des colonies*, 36 (1949): 282-330.

——. 'La société coloniale aux XVIIᵉ et XVIIIᵉ siècles: Les engagés pour les Antilles (1634-1715).' *Revue d'histoire des colonies*, 38 (1951): 1-280.

——. 'Richard Pares.' *Revue d'histoire de colonies*, 45 (1958): 300-06.

Deerr, Noel. *The History of Sugar*. 2 Vols. London: Chapman and Hall Ltd., 1949-50.

Delafosse, M. 'La Rochelle et les îles au XVIIᵉ siècle.' *Revue d'histoire des colonies*, 36 (1949): 238-81.

Denyer, Susan. *African Traditional Architecture*. New York: Africana Publishing, 1978.

De Verteuil, L.A.A. *Trinidad: Its Geography, Natural Resources, Administration and Prospects*. 2nd ed. London: Ward and Lock, 1884.

Dickson, Kwamina. *A Historical Geography of Ghana.* London: Cambridge University Press, 1969.

Dickson, William. *Letters on Slavery.* 1789. Reprint. Westport, Conn: Negro Universities Press, 1970.

——. *Mitigation of Slavery.* London: 1814. Reprint. Westport, Conn.: Negro Universities Press, 1970.

Dirks, Robert. 'John Canoe: Ethnohistorical and Comparative Analysis of a Carib Dance.' *Actes du XLII Congrés International des Americanistes,* 6 (1979): 487-501.

——. *The Black Saturnalia: Conflict and its Ritual Expression on British West Indian Slave Plantations.* Gainesville: University Presses of Florida, 1987.

Donnan, Elizabeth. *Documents Illustrative of the Slave Trade to America.* Washington, D.C.: Carnegie Institute of Washington, 1930.

Douglass, William. *A Summary, Historical, and Political of the . . . British Settlements in North America.* 2 Vols. Boston and London, 1755.

Downes, Aviston D. ' "Flannelled Fools" ' ? Cricket and the Political Economy of the British West Indies c.1895-1906.' *The International Journal of the History of Sport,* 17.4 (2000): 59-80.

Du Boisrourvay, X. and M. Konrat, ed. *La Traite des noirs à Nantes du XVIIe au XIXe siècle.* Nantes: CRDP Nantes, 1981.

Dunn, Richard S. *Sugar and Slaves: The Rise of the Planter Class in the English West Indies, 1624-1713.* Chapel Hill: University of North Carolina Press, 1972.

Du Tertre, J.B. *Histoire générale des Antilles habitées par les Français.* Paris: Th. Jolly, 1654.

Earle, Carville V. 'A Staple Interpretation of Slavery and Free Labor.' *Geographical Review,* 68 (1978): 51-65.

Easterbrook, W.T. and Hugh G. J. Aitken. *Canadian Economic History.* Toronto: University of Toronto Press, 1956.

Eddy, T.P. 'Food Shortage as a Health Catastrophe.' In *Health in Tropical Africa Africa During the Colonial Period. Based on the Proceedings of a Symposium held at New College, Oxford 21-23 March 1977,* edited by E.E. Sabben-Clarke, D.J. Bradley and K. Kirkwood. Oxford: Clarendon Press, 1980: 37-42.

Edwards, Bryan. *The History, Civil and Commercial of the British Colonies in the West Indies.* 1793, 1801, 1810. Reprint. London: J. Stockdale, 1819.

Edwards, Jay. 'The Evolution of Vernacular Architecture in the Western Caribbean.' In *Cultural Traditions and Caribbean Identity,* edited by S.J.K. Wilkerson. Gainesville: Center for Latin American Studies, University of Florida, 1980: 291-343.

Egerton, Hugh E. 'The Transference of Colonial Power to the United Provinces and England.' In *The Cambridge Modern History,* eds., A.W. Ward, G.W. Prothero and Stanley Leathes. Cambridge: Cambridge University Press, 1906, IV: 728-59.

Ellis, Pat, ed. *Women of the Caribbean*. Kingston: Kingston Publishers Ltd., 1986.

Eltis, David. *The Rise of African Slavery in the Americas*. Cambridge: Cambridge University Press, 2000.

Engerman, S.L. and E. Genovese. *Race and Slavery in the Western Hemisphere: Quantitative Studies*. Princeton: Princeton University Press, 1975.

Equiano, Olaudah. 'The Life of Olaudah Equiano' (excerpt). In *Caribbean Slavery in the Atlantic World*, edited by Verene A. Shepherd and Hilary McD. Beckles. Kingston & London: Ian Randle & James Currey, 2000: 822–28.

Erny, Pierre. *Childhood and Cosmos. The Social Psychology of the Black African Child*. New York: Media Intellectics Corp., 1973.

Fahey, M.H. 'Crop Prospects in Trinidad and Tobago.' Agricultural Society Paper No. 843, 1942.

Falconbridge, Alexander. *An Account of the Slave Trade on the Coast of Africa*. London: J. Phillips, 1788.

Farnie, D.A. 'The Commercial Empire of the Atlantic, 1607–1783.' *Economic History Review*, 15 (1962): 205–18.

Ferguson, Moira, ed. *The History of Mary Prince: A West Indian Slave Related by Herself*. 1831. Reprint. London: Pandora, 1987.

Fick, Carolyn E. *The Making of Haiti: The Saint Domingue Revolution from Below*. Knoxville: University of Tennessee Press, 1990.

Foner, Eric. *Slavery and Freedom in Nineteenth Century America*. Oxford: Clarendon Press, 1994.

Fortune, Stephen. *Merchants and Jews*. Gainesville: University of Florida Press, 1984.

Franck, Harry A. *Roaming through the West Indies*. London: T. Fisher Unwin, 1921.

Franklyn, Gilbert. Observations occassioned by the attempts made in England to effect the abolition of the slave trade: shewing the manner in which Negroes are treated in the British colonies in the West Indies: and also, some particular remarks on a letter addressed to the treasurer of the society for effecting such abolition, from Rev. Robert Boucher Nicholls. (London: Logographics Press, 1789).

Fraser, Henry, et al. *A–Z of Barbadian Heritage*. Kingston: Heinemann, 1990.

Frere, Henry. *A Short History of Barbados from its First Discovery and Settlement to the end of the Year 1767*. London: J. Dodsley, 1768.

Frykenberg, R.E. *Land Control and Social Structure in Indian History*. Madison: University of Wisconsin Press, 1969.

Furlonge, Kelly. V.E.T. *The Silent Victory*. Port of Spain: Golden Eagle Enterprises, 1991.

Gardiner, Richard. *An Account of the Expedition to the West Indies, against Martinico, Guadelupe, and the other Leeward Islands; subject to the French King, 1759*. London: Printed Z. Stuart, 1759.

Gardner, W.J. *A History of Jamaica*. 1873. Reprint. London: Frank Cass & Co.,

1971.

Galloway, J.H. 'The Sugar Industry in Barbados during the Seventeenth Century.' *Journal of Tropical Geography*, 19 (1964): 35-41.

Garrod, W.H. 'Our Water Supply.' *JBMHS*, 19 (1952): 107-11.

Gash, Norman. *Aristocracy and People. Britain 1815-1865.* London: Edward Arnold, 1976.

Gaspar, David Barry. *Bondmen and Rebels.* Baltimore: The Johns Hopkins University Press, 1985.

────── and Darlene Clark Hine, eds. *More Than Chattel. Black Women and Slavery in the Americas.* Bloomington: Indiana University Press, 1996.

Gaston-Martin. *Histoire de l'esclavage dans les colonies françaises.* Paris: Presses Universitaires de France, 1948.

Gaunt, Mary. *Harmony.* London: E. Benn Ltd., 1933.

Ghany, H. *Kamal, a Lifetime of Politics, Religion and Culture.* Port of Spain: K. Mohammed, 1996.

Gibbes, Philip. *Instructions for the Treatment of Negroes, etc. etc. etc.* 1786. Reprinted with additions. London: Printed for Shepperson and Reynolds, 1797.

Gilmore, John. *Queen's Park: A Brief History and Guide.* Bridgetown: National Cultural Foundation, 1990.

Gomes, A. *Through a Maze of Colour.* Port of Spain: Key Caribbean, 1974.

Gordon, Shirley. *A Century of West Indian Education.* London: Longmans, Green and Co., 1963.

──────. *Reports and Repercussions in West Indian Education 1835-1933.* London: Ginn and Co. Ltd., 1968.

Goveia, Elsa V. *A Study on the Historiography of the British West Indies to the End of the Nineteenth Century.* Mexico: Instituto Panamericano de Geografía e Historia, 1956.

──────. *The West Indian Slave Laws of the Eighteenth Century.* Bridgetown: Caribbean Universities Press, 1973.

Great Britain. Board of Trade. *Report of the Lords of the Committee of Council Appointed for the Consideration of all Matters Relating to Trade and Foreign Plantations, Submitting to His Majesty's Consideration the Evidence and Information they have Collected in Consequence of His Majesty's Order in Council dated 11th of February 1788, Concerning the Present State of the Trade to Africa and Particularly the Trade in Slaves.* London: 1789.

Great Britain. Parliament. *Abridgement of the Minutes of the Evidence, Taken Before a Committee of the House of Commons, Being a Committee of the Whole House, to Whom it was Referred to Consider of the Circumstances of the Slave Trade, Complained of in the Several Petitions Which were Presented to the House in the Last Session of Parliament, Relative to the State of the African Slave Trade.* 1789. Reprint. Chicago: Afro-Am Press, 1969.

──────. *Minutes of the Evidence Before a Committee of the House of Commons, Being a Committee of the Whole House, to Whom it was Referred to Consider of the*

473

Circumstances of the Slave Trade, Complained of in the Several Petitions Which were Presented to the House in the Last Session of Parliament, Relative to the State of the African Slave Trade. London: 1789.

——. *Minutes of the Evidence Taken Before the Committee of the House of Commons, being a Select Committee, Appointed on the 26th day of January 1790 for the Purpose of Taking the Examination of such Witnesses as Shall be Produced on the Part of the Several Petitioners who have Petitioned the House of Commons Against the Abolition of the Slave Trade.* London: 1790.

——. *Minutes of the Evidence Taken Before a Committee of the House of Commons Being a Select Committee, Appointed on the 23rd day of April 1790, to Take the Examination of the Several Witnesses Ordered by the House Respecting the African Slave Trade.* London: 1791.

Green, Benny. *A History of Cricket.* London: Barrie and Jenkins, 1988.

Green, William A. *British Slave Emancipation. The Sugar Colonies and the Great Experiment 1830-1865.* Oxford: Clarendon Press, 1976.

Greene, Jack P. and J.R. Pole, eds. *Colonial British America: Essays in the New History of the Early Modern Era.* Baltimore: The Johns Hopkins University Press, 1984.

Guerra y Sánchez, Ramiro. *Sugar and Society in the Caribbean: An Economic History of Cuban Agriculture.* New Haven: Yale University Press, 1964.

Gunkel, Alexander and Jerome Handler, eds. 'A Swiss Medical Doctor's Description of Barbados in 1661: The Account of Felix Christian Spoeri.' *JBMHS*, 33.1 (1969): 3-13.

——. 'A German Indentured Servant in Barbados in 1652: the Account of Heinrich von Uchteritz.' *JBMHS*, 33.3 (1970): 91-100.

Gutman, Herbert G. *The Black Family in Slavery and Freedom, 1750-1925.* New York: Pantheon Books, 1976.

Hall, Douglas. *Free Jamaica, 1838-1865: An Economic History.* London: Caribbean Universities Press, 1969.

——. 'The Flight from the Estates Reconsidered: The British West Indies, 1838-42.' *Journal of Caribbean History*, 10 & 11 (1978): 7-24.

——. *In Miserable Slavery, Thomas Thistlewood in Jamaica 1750-1900.* 1989. Reprint. Kingston: University of the West Indies Press, 1999.

Hall, Neville. 'Slaves' Use of their "Free" time in the Danish Virgin Islands in the Late Eighteenth and Early Nineteenth Century.' *Journal of Caribbean History*, 13 (1980): 21-43.

——. *Slave Society in the Danish West Indies.* Kingston: The Press, University of the West Indies, 1992.

Hall, Richard. *Acts Passed in the Island of Barbados from 1643-1762, Inclusive.* London: Printed for Hall, 1764.

Handbook of Jamaica for 1886-87. Kingston: Government Printing Establishment, 1886.

Handbook of Jamaica for 1921. Kingston: Government Printing Office, 1921.

Handler, Jerome S. *A Guide to Source Materials for the Study of Barbados History, 1627-1834.* Carbondale: Southern Illinois University Press, 1971.

——. *The Unappropriated People: Freedmen in the Slave Society of Barbados.* Baltimore: The Johns Hopkins University Press, 1974.

——. 'Sources for the Study of Preemancipation Sugar Plantations in Barbados: Manuscripts Relating to Newton and Seawell Plantations.' *Caribbean Archives*, 5 (1976): 11-21.

——. 'Slave Revolts and Conspiracies in Seventeenth Century Barbados.' *NWIG*, 56 (1982): 5-43.

——. *Searching for a Slave Cemetery in Barbados, West Indies: A Bioarchaeological and Ethnohistorical Investigation.* Research Paper No. 59. Carbondale: Center for Archaeological Investigations, Southern Illinois University, 1989.

——. *Supplement to a Guide for the Study of Barbados History.* Providence, Rhode Island: The John Carter Brown Library and the Barbados Museum and Historical Society, 1991.

——. 'A Prone Burial from a Plantation Cemetery in Barbados, West Indies: Possible Evidence for an African-type Witch or Other Negatively Viewed Person.' *Historical Archaeology*, 30 (1996): 76-86.

——. 'Escaping Slavery in a Caribbean Plantation Society: Marronage in Barbados, 1650s-1830s.' *NWIG*, 71 (1997): 183-225.

——. 'An African-Type Healer/Diviner and His Grave Goods: A Burial from a Plantation Slave Cemetery in Barbados, West Indies.' *International Journal of Historical Archaeology*, 1 (1997): 91-130.

——. 'Slave Medicine and Obeah in Barbados, ca. 1650-1834.' *NWIG*, 74 (2000): 57-90.

——, ed. 'Father Antoine Biet's Visit to Barbados in 1654.' *JBMHS*, 32 (1967): 56-76.

—— and Robert Corruccine. 'Plantation Slave Life in Barbados.' *Journal of Interdisciplinary History*, 14.1 (1983): 65-90.

—— and Kenneth Bilby. 'On the Early Use and Origin of the Term Obeah in Barbados and the Anglophone Caribbean.' *Slavery & Abolition*, 22 (2001): 87-100.

—— and Frederick W. Lange. *Plantation Slavery in Barbados: An Archaeological and Historical Investigation.* Cambridge, Mass.: Harvard University Press, 1978.

Hanotaux, Gabriel and Alfred Martineau, eds. *Histoire des colonies françaises et de l'expansion de la France dans le monde.* Paris: Société de l'Histoire Nationale, 1929.

Haraksingh, Kusha. 'Image and Icon: Indians in the Intellectual Perspective of Eric Williams.' *Caribbean Issues*, 8.2 (1999): 61-75.

Harewood, J. and R. Henry. *Inequality in a Post Colonial Society: Trinidad and Tobago, 1956-1981.* St Augustine: Institute of Social and Economic Research, 1985.

Harlow, Vincent T. *A History of Barbados 1625-1685*. Oxford: Clarendon Press, 1926.

Harper, Lawrence A. *The English Navigation Laws: A Seventeenth-Century Experiment in Social Engineering*. New York: Columbia University Press, 1939.

Harris, David R. 'The Invasion of Oceanic Islands by Alien Plants: An Example from the Leeward Islands, West Indies.' *Institute of British Geographers, Transactions and Papers*, 31 (1962): 67-82.

Harvey, Thomas and William Brewin. *Jamaica in 1866*. London: A. W. Bennett, 1866.

Hay, Douglas, et al. *Albion's Fatal Tree. Crime and Society in Eighteenth-Century England*. London: A. Lane, 1975.

Hendy, James. *A Treatise on the Glandular Disease of Barbados*. London: C. Dilly, 1784.

Hennessy, Alistair, ed. *Intellectuals in the Twentieth Century Caribbean*. London: Macmillan, 1992.

Herskovits, Melville J. *The Myth of the Negro PaSt* New York: Harper and Row, 1941.

Heuman, Gad. *Between Black and White: Race, Politics, and the Free Coloureds in Jamaica, 1792-1865*. Westport: Greenwood Press, 1981.

———. *'The Killing Time' The Morant Bay Rebellion in Jamaica*. London: The Macmillan Press Ltd., 1994.

Heywood, Linda M. 'Eric Williams: The Howard Years, 1939-1948.' *Caribbean Issues*, 8.1 (1998): 14-28.

Higham, C.S.S. *The Development of the Leeward Islands under the Restoration, 1660-1688: A Study of the Foundations of the Old Colonial System*. Cambridge: Cambridge University Press, 1921.

Higman, B.W. 'The Slave Family and Household in the British West Indies, 1800-1834.' *Journal of Interdisciplinary History*, 6.2 (1975): 261-87.

———. *Slave Population and Economy in Jamaica, 1807-1834*. Cambridge: Cambridge University Press, 1976.

———. *Slave Populations of the British Caribbean, 1807-1834*. Baltimore: The Johns Hopkins University Press, 1984.

———. *Jamaica Surveyed: Plantation Maps and Plans of the Eighteenth and Nineteenth Centuries*. Kingston: Institute of Jamaica Publications, 1988.

———. *Montpelier, Jamaica: A Plantation Community in Slavery and Freedom, 1739-1912*. Kingston, Jamaica: The Press, UWI, 1998.

———. *Writing West Indian Histories*. London: Macmillan, 1999.

———. 'The Sugar Revolution.' *Economic History Review*, 53 (2000): 213-36.

———, ed. *The Jamaica Census of 1844 and 1861*. Mona, Kingston: Department of History, UWI, Social History Project, 1980.

———, ed. *Trade, Government and Society in Caribbean History, 1700-1920*: Essays presented to Douglas Hall. Kingston: Heinemann, 1983.

———, ed. *Methodology and Historiography of the Caribbean*. Volume VI of the

General History of the Caribbean. London: Unesco Publishing/Macmillan Education, 1999.

Holder, Henry. *A Short Essay on the Subject of Negro Slavery with a Particular Reference to the Island of Barbadoes.* London: Couchman and Fry, for C. Dilly, 1788.

Holt, Richard. *Sport and the British: A Modern History.* Oxford: Oxford University Press, 1989.

Holt, Thomas. *The Problem of Freedom: Race, Labor, and Politics in Jamaica and Britain, 1832–1938.* Baltimore: The Johns Hopkins University Press, 1992.

Hoskins, William. *The Making of the English Landscape.* London: Hodder and Stoughton, 1988.

Hughes, Griffith. *The Natural History of Barbados in Ten Books.* London: Printed for the Author, 1750.

Hughes, Ronald. 'Sweet Bottom, St George, Barbados: An Early (1777) Non-White Freehold Village.' *JBMHS*, 36 [1981]: 266–78.

Hutton, Clinton. 'The Defeat of the Morant Bay Rebellion.' *The Jamaican Historical Review*, XIX (1996): 30–38.

Innis, Harold A. *The Fur Trade in Canada: An Introduction to Canadian Economic History.* New Haven: Yale University Press, 1930.

———. *The Cod Fisheries: The History of an International Economy.* New Haven: Yale University Press, 1940.

Jackson, Robert. *A Sketch of the History and Cure of Febrile Diseases; More Particularly as They Appear in the West-Indies Among the Soldiers of the British Army.* London: Baldwin, Craddock, and Joy, 1820.

Jakobsson, Stiv. *Am I not a Man and a Brother?* Uppsala: Gleerup, 1972.

James, C.L.R. *Beyond a Boundary.* 1963. Reprint. London: Stanley Paul, 1980.

Jemmott, Ralph A. 'A Brief History of Harrison College, 1733–1983.' *Harrisonian: 250th Anniversary Commemorative Issue.* Bridgetown: Harrison College, 1983.

Johnson, Edgar J.E. and Herman E. Krooss. *The American Economy: Its Origins, Development and Transformation.* Englewood Cliffs, New Jersey: Prentice Hall, 1960.

Johnson, Howard. *The Bahamas in Slavery and Freedom.* Kingston: Ian Randle Publishers,1991.

———. 'A Slow and Extended Abolition.' In *From Chattel Slaves to Wage Slaves: The Dynamics of Labour Bargaining in the Americas*, edited by Mary Turner. Kingston, London & Indianapolis: Ian Randle, James Currey & Indiana University Press, 1995: 165–81.

———. 'Richard B. Sheridan: The Making of a Caribbean Economic Historian.' In *West Indies Accounts: Essays on the History of the British Caribbean and the Atlantic Economy in Honour of Richard Sheridan*, edited by Roderick A. McDonald. Kingston: The Press, UWI, 1996: 1–28.

———. 'The "Jamaica 300" Celebrations of 1955: Commemoration in a Colonial Polity.' *Journal of Imperial and Commonwealth History*, 26 (1998): 120–37.

Jones, Howard. *Mutiny on the Amistad*. New York: Oxford University Press, 1987.

Jordan, J.W. *An Account of the Management of Certain Estates in the Island of Barbados*. London, 1824.

Katz, William. *Breaking the Chains: African-American Slave Resistance*. New York: Macmillan, 1990.

King, Wilma. ' "Suffer With Them Till Death." Slave Women and Their Children in Nineteenth-Century America.' In *More Than Chattel. Black Women and Slavery in the Americas*, edited by David Barry Gaspar and Darlene Clark Hine. Bloomington: Indiana University Press, 1996: 147–68.

Kingsley, Charles. *At Last: A Christmas in the West Indies*. London: Macmillan and Co., 1882.

Kiple, Kenneth. *The Caribbean Slave: A Biological History*. Cambridge: Cambridge University Press, 1984.

—— and Virginia Kiple. 'Deficiency Diseases in the Caribbean.' In *Caribbean Slavery in the Atlantic World*, edited by Verene A. Shepherd and Hilary McD. Beckles. Kingston & London: Ian Randle & James Currey, 2000: 785–94.

Klein, Herbert. *The Middle Passage: Comparative Studies in the Atlantic Slave Trade*. Princeton: Princeton University Press, 1978.

Klingberg, Frank J. 'The Lady Mico Charity Schools in the British West Indies 1835–1842.' *Journal of Negro History*, 24 (1939): 291-344.

——. *The Anti-Slavery Movement in England*. 1926. Reprint. Hamden, Conn: Archon Books, 1968.

Knight, Franklin W. *Slave Society in Cuba During the Nineteenth Century*. Madison: University of Wisconsin Press, 1970.

Kromer, Helen. *The Amistad Affair, 1839: The Slave Uprising Aboard the Spanish Schooner*. New York: Franklin Watts, 1973.

Kulikoff, Allan. *Tobacco and Slaves: The Development of Southern Cultures in the Chesapeake, 1680–1800*. Chapel Hill: University of North Carolina Press, 1986.

Kupperman, Karen Ordahl. *Providence Island, 1630–1641: The Other Puritan Colony*. Cambridge: Cambridge University Press, 1993.

Labat, Jean Baptiste. *Nouveau Voyage aux Isles de l'Amérique*, 6 Vols. Paris: Theodore et Guillaume Cavelier, 1722.

——. *Voyage du Chevalier des Marchais en Guinée, Iles Voisines, et a Cayenne; Fait en 1725, 1726 & 1727*. Paris: Guillaume Saugrain, 1730.

Lack, Paul D. 'An Urban Slave Community: Little Rock, 1831–1862.' *Arkansas Historical Quarterly*, 41.3 (1982): 258-87.

La Guerre, John. 'The Indian Response to Black Power.' In *The Black Power Revolution of 1970*, ed., Selwyn Ryan. St Augustine: Institute of Social and Economic Research, 1995: 273-307.

Lambert, Sheila, ed. *House of Commons Sessional Papers of the Eighteenth Century*. Vol. 69. Delaware: Scholarly Resources Inc., 1975.

Lasserre, Guy. *La Guadeloupe: Étude géographique*. Bordeaux: Union Française

D'Impression, 1961.

Lemoine, Maurice. *Bitter Sugar*. London: Zed Books, 1985.

Leroy-Beaulieu, Paul. *De la colonisation chez les peuples modernes*. Paris: Félix Alcan, 1908.

Levy, Claude. 'Slavery and the Emancipation Movement in Barbados, 1650–1833.' *Journal of Negro History*, 58 (1970): 1–12.

———. *Emancipation, Sugar and Federalism: Barbados and the West Indies, 1833–1876*. Gainesville: University of Florida Press, 1980.

Lewis, Matthew Gregory ('Monk'). *Journal of A West Indian Proprietor Kept During A Residence in the Island of Jamaica*. 1834. Reprint. Oxford: Oxford University Press, 1999.

Lewis, Rupert and Patrick Bryan, eds. *Garvey: His Work and Impact*. Kingston: Institute of Social and Economic Research and Dept. of Extra-Mural Studies, 1988.

Lewis, W. Arthur. 'Economic Development with Unlimited Supplies of Labour.' *The Manchester School of Economic and Social Studies*, 22 (1954): 139–91.

Ligon, Richard. *A True and Exact History of the Island of Barbados*. 1657. Reprint. London: Frank Cass & Co., 1970.

Littlefield, Daniel C. *Rice and Slaves: Ethnicity and the Slave Trade in Colonial South Carolina*. Baton Rouge: Louisiana State University Press, 1981.

Local Guide of British Guiana Containing Historical Sketches, Statistical Tables and the Entire Statute Laws of the Colony, in Force, January 1, 1843. Demerary: The Royal Gazette Office, 1843.

Lockmiller, David A. 'Agriculture in Cuba during the Second United States Intervention, 1906–1909.' *Agricultural History*, 11 (1937): 181–88.

London Missionary Society. *Report of the Proceedings against the late Rev. John Smith of Demerara*. 1824. Reprint. New York: Negro Universities Press, 1969.

Long, Edward. *The History of Jamaica*. 3 Vols. 1774. Reprint. London: Frank Cass, 1970.

Lovejoy, Paul E., ed. *Identity in the Shadow of Slavery*. London & New York: Continuum, 2000.

L'Ouverture, Toussaint. 'Speeches and Letters of Toussaint L'Ouverture' (excerpt). In *Caribbean Slavery in the Atlantic World*, edited by Verene A. Shepherd and Hilary McD. Beckles. Kingston & London: Ian Randle & James Currey, 2000: 858–67.

Lucas, C.P. *A Historical Geography of the British Colonies: Vol. 2, The West Indies*. Oxford: Clarendon Press, 1905.

Mair, Lucille Mathurin. *The Rebel Woman in the British West Indies During Slavery*. Kingston: Institute of Jamaica Publications, 1975.

MacInnes, C.M. *England and Slavery*. Bristol: J.W. Arrowsmith Ltd., 1934.

———. *An Introduction to the Economic History of the British Empire*. London: Rivingtons, 1935.

———. *A Gateway of Empire*. Bristol: Arrowsmith, 1939.

Mackintosh, W.A. 'Innis on Canadian Economic Development.' *Journal of Political Economy*, 61 (1953): 185-94.

Mahabir, N.K. *The Still Cry: Personal Accounts of East Indians in Trinidad During Indentureship (1845-1911)*. New York: Calaloux Publications, 1985.

Mahabir, Winston. *In and Out of Politics*. Port of Spain: Inprint Caribbean, 1978.

Mandelbaum, D.G. *Society in India*. 2 Vols. Berkeley: University of California Press, 1972.

Mangan, J.A. *The Games Ethic and Imperialism*. London: Viking, 1986.

——, ed. *Pleasure, Profit and Proselytism: British Culture and Sport at Home and Abroad 1700-1914*. London: Frank Cass, 1987.

Manley, Norman. 'Our Policy and Federation.' In *Manley and the New Jamaica. Selected Speeches and Writings 1938-1968*, edited by Rex Nettleford. Trinidad and Jamaica: Longman Caribbean, 1971.

Mannix, Daniel P. and Malcolm Cowley. *The Black Cargoes. A History of the Atlantic Slave Trade, 1518-1865*. London: Longmans, Green & Co., 1962.

Marshall, Woodville K. 'Social and Economic Problems in the Windward Islands, 1838-65.' In *The Caribbean in Transition*, edited by F. Andic and T. Matthews. Rio Piedras: University of Puerto Rico, 1965: 234-57.

——. 'Metayage in the Sugar Industry of the British West Indies, 1838-65.' *Jamaican Historical Review*, 5 (1965): 28-55.

——. 'Notes on Peasant Development in the West Indies Since 1838.' *Social and Economic Studies*, 17.3 (1968): 252-63.

——. 'The Termination of the Apprenticeship in Barbados and the Windward islands.' *Journal of Caribbean History*, 2 (1971): 1-45.

——. 'Aspects of the Development of the Peasantry.' *Caribbean Quarterly*, 18.1 (1972): 30-46, 53-57. Also published in *Les Mouvements paysans dans le monde contemporain* (Naples, 1976).

——. 'A Review of Historical Writing on the Commonwealth Caribbean since c. 1940.' *Social and Economic Studies*, 24.3 (1975): 271-307.

——. 'Commentary I' on S. Mintz, 'Slavery and the Rise of Peasantries.' In Michael Craton, ed. *Historical Reflections/Réflexions Historiques* 6.1 (1979): 243-48.

——. ' "Vox Populi": The St Vincent Riots and Disturbances of 1862.' In *Trade, Government and Society in Caribbean History, 1700-1920*, edited by B.W. Higman. Kingston: Heinemann, 1983: 85-115.

——. 'Apprenticeship and Labour Relations in Four Windward Islands.' In *Abolition and its Aftermath*, edited by David Richardson. London: Frank Cass, 1985: 203-24.

——. 'Amelioration and Emancipation (with special reference to Barbados).' In *Emancipation I. A Series of Lectures to Commemorate the 150th Anniversary of Emancipation*, edited by Alvin O. Thompson. Bridgetown: Department of History, UWI, Cave Hill and Barbados National Cultural Foundation, 1986: 72-87.

———. 'Nineteenth-Century Crises in the Barbadian Sugar Industry.' In *Emancipation II. A Series of Lectures to Commemorate the 150th Anniversary of Emancipation*, edited by Woodville K. Marshall, Bridgetown: Department of History, UWI, Cave Hill and Barbados National Cultural Foundation, 1987: 85–101.

———. 'Villages and Plantation Sub-Division.' In *Emancipation III. A Series of Lectures to Commemorate the 150th Anniversary of Emancipation*, edited by Woodville K. Marshall. Bridgetown: Department of History, UWI, Cave Hill and Barbados National Cultural Foundation, 1988: 1–19.

———. 'St Lucia in the Economic History of the Windward Islands: The Nineteenth Century Experience.' *Caribbean Quarterly*, 35.3 (1989): 25–33.

———. ' "We be wise to many more tings": Blacks' Hopes and Expectations of Emancipation.' In *The University of the West Indies 40th Anniversary Lectures*, edited by F.R. Augier. Mona: UWI, 1990: 31–46. Republished in *Caribbean Freedom*, edited by Hilary McD. Beckles and Verene A. Shepherd. Kingston: Ian Randle Publishers, 1993: 12–20.

———. 'Provision Ground and Plantation Labour in Four Windward Islands: Competition for Resources During Slavery.' *Slavery and Abolition*, 12.1 (1991): 48–67.

———. *The Post-Slavery Labour Problem Revisited.* The 1990 Elsa Goveia Memorial Lecture. Kingston: Department of History, UWI, Mona, Jamaica, 1991.

———. 'History Teaching in the University of the West Indies.' In *Before and After1865*, edited by Brian Moore and Swithin Wilmot. Kingston: Ian Randle Publishers, 1998: 49–76, 380–82.

———. 'The Historiography of Barbados and the Windward Islands,' Parts A and B of chapter 18. In *UNESCO General History of the Caribbean*, Vol. VI, edited by B.W. Higman. London and Oxford: UNESCO/Macmillan, 1999: 544–79.

———, ed. *The Colthurst Journal.* New York: Millwood, 1977.

———, Trevor Marshall and Bentley Gibbs. 'The Establishment of a Peasantry in Barbados, 1840–1920.' In *Social Groups and Institutions In the History of the Caribbean*. Proceedings of the Sixth Conference of the ACH, Rio Piedras, Puerto Rio, April 4–9, 1974. San Juan: ACH, 1975: 85–104.

Martin, Bernard and Mark Spurrell, eds. *The Journal of a Slave Trader 1750-54 with Newton's Thoughts upon the African Slave Trade.* London: Epworth Press, 1962.

Mathieson, William L. *British Slavery and Its Abolition, 1823–1838.* 1926. Reprint. New York: Octagon Books, 1967.

Matthews, John. *A Voyage to the River Sierra-Leone on the Coast of Africa.* London: Printed by B. White and Son, and J. Sewell, 1788.

May, Louis-Philippe. *Histoire économique de la Martinique (1635–1763).* Paris: Marcel Riviere, 1930.

Mayo, William. *A New and Exact Map of the Island of Barbadoes in America.*

London, 1722.

McCalman, Ian, ed. *The Horrors of Slavery and Other Writings by Robert Wedderburn.* Kingston & Princeton: Ian Randle & Markus Wiener, 1991.

McDonald, Roderick A. 'Urban Crime and Social Control in St Vincent During the Apprenticeship.' In *West Indian Accounts: Essays on the History of the British Caribbean and the Atlantic Economy in Honour of Richard Sheridan,* edited by Roderick A. McDonald. Kingston: The Press, UWI, 1996: 319–42.

——. *Between Slavery and Freedom.* Kingston: UWI Press, 2001.

——, ed. *West Indian Accounts: Essays on the History of the British Caribbean and the Atlantic Economy in Honour of Richard Sheridan.* Kingston: The Press, UWI, 1996.

McGowan, Winston. 'African Resistance to the Atlantic Slave Trade in West Africa.' *Slavery and Abolition,* 11.1 (1990): 5–29.

——. 'The Demerara Revolt, 1823.' In *Themes in African-Guyanese History,* edited by Winston F. McGowan, James G. Rose, and David A. Granger. Georgetown: Free Press, 1998: 107–40.

——, James Rose and David Granger, eds. *Themes in African-Guyanese History.* Georgetown: Free Press, 1998.

McLellan, George H.H. *Some Phases of Barbados Life: Tropical Scenes and Studies.* Georgetown: Argosy, 1909.

Meliora. *Letters on the Labouring Population of Barbadoes.* London, 1858.

Memoranda Respecting the French Slave Trade in 1820, Drawn up at the Close of that Year. London: Ellerton and Henderson, 1820.

Merivale, Herman. *Lectures on Colonization and Colonies.* London: Longmans, 1861.

Midgley, Clare. *Women Against Slavery; The British Campaigns, 1780-1870.* London: Routledge, 1992.

Millette, James. 'Towards the Black Power Revolt of 1970.' *The Black Power Revolution of 1970,* ed., Selwyn Ryan, St Augustine: Institute of Social and Economic Research, 1995: 625-60.

Milner, A.C. 'Colonial Records History: British Malaya.' *Modern Asian Studies,* 21.4 (1987): 773-92.

Mims, Stewart L. *Colbert's West India Policy.* New Haven: Yale University Press, 1912.

Mintz, Sidney W. 'The Culture History of a Puerto Rican Sugar Cane Plantation, 1876-1949.' *Hispanic American Historical Review,* 33 (1953): 224-51.

——. 'The Plantation as a Socio Cultural Type.' In *Plantation Systems of the New World.* Social Science Monograph, 7. Washington, D.C.: Pan American Union, 1959.

——. 'Caribbean Market Places and Caribbean History.' *Nova Americana,* 1 (1980-81): 333-44.

——. *Sweetness and Power: The Place of Sugar in Modern History.* New York: Viking, 1985.

―― and Richard Price. *An Anthropological Approach to the Afro-American Past: A Caribbean Perspective.* Philadelphia: ISHI., 1976.

Montejo, Esteban. 'The Autobiography of a Runaway Slave.' (excerpt) In *Caribbean Slavery in the Atlantic World*, edited by Verene A. Shepherd and Hilary McD. Beckles. Kingston & London: Ian Randle & James Currey, 2000: 829-42.

Moohr, Michael. 'The Economic Impact of Slave Emancipation in British Guiana 1832-1852.' *Economic History Review*, XXV (1972): 588-607.

Moore, Brian L. *Cultural Power, Resistance and Pluralism: Colonial Guyana 1838-1900.* Kingston: The Press, UWI, 1995.

――. 'Colonialism, Cricket Culture, and Afro-Creole Identity in the Caribbean After Emancipation: The Case of Guyana.' *Journal of Caribbean History*, 33.1 & 2 (1999): 54-73.

―― and Swithin Wilmot, eds. *Before and After 1865: Education, Politics and Regionalisation in the Caribbean: in honour of Sir Roy Augier* . Kingston: Ian Randle Publishers, 1998.

――and Michele A. Johnson. ' "Fallen Sisters": Attitudes to Female Prostitution in Jamaica at the turn of the Twentieth Century.' *Journal of Caribbean History*, 34.1 & 2 (2000): 46-70.

――and Michele A. Johnson, eds. *The Land We Live In: Jamaica in 1890.* Kingston: Social History Project, UWI, 2000.

―― and Michele A. Johnson, eds. *'Squalid Kingston,' 1890-1920: How the Poor Lived, Moved and Had Their Being.* Kingston: Social History Project, UWI, 2000.

Moore, Francis. *Travels into the Inland Parts of Africa.* London: Printed by E. Cave for the author, 1738.

Moreno Fraginals, Manuel. *El ingenio: complejo económico social cubano del azúcar.* Havana: Editorial de Ciencias Sociales, 1978.

Morgan, Philip D. *Slave Counterpoint: Black Culture in the Eighteenth-Century Chesapeake and Lowcountry.* Chapel Hill: University of North Carolina Press, for the Omohundro Institute of Early American History and Culture, Williamsburg, Virginia, 1998.

Morrissey, Marrietta. *Slave Women in the New World.* Lawrence: University Press of Kansas, 1989.

Mountfield, Anne. *The Slave Trade.* London: Wayland Publishers, 1973.

Mousnier, Jehan, ed. *Journal de la Traite des Noirs.* Paris: Éditions de Paris, 1957.

Moxly, J.H. Sutton. *A West Indian Sanatorium and a Guide to Barbados.* London: Sampson Low, Marston, Searle, & Rivington, 1886.

Munford, Clarence. *The Black Ordeal of Slavery and Slave Trading in the French West Indies, 1625-1715.* Lewiston: The Edwin Mellen Press, 1991.

Naipaul, Vidiadhar. *The Middle Passage: Impressions of Five Societies – British, French and Dutch – in the West Indies and South America.* London: André Deutsch, 1974.

[Naish, William ?]. 'Notes on Slavery, Made During a Recent Visit to Barbadoes.' *The Negro's Friend*, 18 (1830).

Nath, Dwarka. *A History of Indians in Guyana*. London: Nelsons, 1970.

Nettleford, Rex, ed. *Manley and the New Jamaica. Selected Speeches and Writings 1938-1968*. Trinidad and Jamaica: Longman Caribbean, 1971.

Newton, Arthur Percival. *The Colonising Activities of the English Puritans: The Last Phase of the Elizabethan Struggle with Spain*. New Haven: Yale University Press, 1914.

——. *The European Nations in the West Indies 1493-1688*. London: Adam and Charles Black, 1933.

Niddrie, David L. 'An Attempt at Planned Settlement in St Kitts in the Early Eighteenth Century.' *Caribbean Studies*, 5 (1966): 3-11.

Norris, Robert. *Memoirs of the Reign of Bossa Ahádee, King of Dahomey, an Inland Country of Guiney: to which are Added the Author's Journey to Abomey, the Capital; and a Short Account of the African Slave Trade*. 1789. Reprint. London: Frank Cass, 1968.

North, Douglass C. 'Location Theory and Regional Economic Growth.' *Journal of Political Economy*, 63 (1955): 243-58.

Northcott, Cecil. *Slavery's Martyr*. London: Epworth Press, 1976.

Oldmixon, John. *The British Empire in America, Containing the History of the Discovery, Settlement, Progress and Present State of all the British Colonies, on the Continent and Islands of America*. 2 Vols. 1708. Reprint. London: J. Brotherton and others, 1741.

Orderson, J. W. *Directions to Young Planters for their Care and Management of a Sugar Plantation in Barbadoes*. London: T. Bensley, 1800.

Ortiz, Fernando. *Contrapunteo Cubano del Tabaco y el Azúcar*. Havana: J. Montero, 1940. English translation: *Cuban Counterpoint: Tobacco and Sugar*. New York: Vintage Books, 1947, 1970.

Ott, Thomas O. *The Haitian Revolution, 1789-1804*. Knoxville: University of Tennessee Press, 1973.

Oxaal, Ivar. *Black Intellectuals Come to Power*. Cambridge Mass.: Schenkman, 1968.

Packwood, Cyril. *Chained to the Rock: Slavery in Bermuda*. New York: Eliseo Torres, 1975.

Paiewonsky, Isidor. *Eyewitness Accounts of Slavery in the Danish West Indies also Graphic Tales of Other Slave Happenings on Ships and Plantations*. New York: Fordham University Press, 1989.

Palmer, Colin. *Human Cargoes*. Chicago: University of Illinois Press, 1981.

Pares, Richard. *A West-India Fortune*. London: Longmans, Green and Co. Ltd., 1950.

——. *Merchants and Planters*. London: Economic History Society, 1960.

Park, Mungo. *Travels in the Interior Districts of Africa, Performed Under the Direction and Patronage of the African Association in the Years 1795, 1796 and 1797*.

London: Everyman's Library, 1969.

Parker, Geoffrey. *The Military Revolution: Military Innovation and the Rise of the WeSt* Cambridge: Cambridge University Press, 1988.

Parry, J.H. *Europe and a Wider World 1415–1715*. London: Hutchinson University Library, 1949.

——. 'Plantation and Provision Ground: An Historical Sketch of the Introduction of Food Crops into Jamaica.' *Revista de Historia de Americas*, 39 (1955): 1–20.

——. *The Age of Reconnaissance*. London: Weidenfeld and Nicolson, 1963.

——. *Trade and Dominion: The European Overseas Empires in the Eighteenth Century*. New York: Praeger Publishers, 1971.

——. *The Spanish Seaborne Empire*. Harmondsworth: Penguin Books, 1973.

—— and P.M. Sherlock. *A Short History of the West Indies*. London: Macmillan and Co. Ltd., 1956.

Patterson, Orlando. *The Sociology of Slavery: An Analysis of the Origins, Development and Structure of Negro Slave Society in Jamaica*. London: MacGibbon and Kee, 1967.

Phillips, Glen. 'The Stirrings of the Mercantile Community in the British West Indies Immediately After Emancipation.' *Journal of Caribbean History*, 23.1 (1989): 62–95.

Pinckard, George. *Notes on the West Indies and the Coast of Guiana*, 3 Vols. London: Longman, Hurst, Rees & Orme, 1806.

Pitman, Frank Wesley. *The Development of the British West Indies 1700–1763*. New Haven: Yale University Press, 1917.

Plimmer, Charlotte and Denis. *The Damn'd Master*. London: New English Library, 1971.

Poole, Robert. *The Beneficent Bee or Traveller's Companion.* 1753. Reprinted in *JBMHS*, 46 (2000): 188–89.

Porter, George R. *The Nature and Properties of the Sugar Cane*. London: Smith, Elder, and Co., 1830.

Porteus, Beilby. *An Essay Towards a Plan for the More Effectual Civilization and Conversion of the Negroe Slaves, on the Trust Estate in Barbadoes, Belonging to the Society for the Propagation of the Gospel in Foreign Parts*. London: Printed for T. Cadell and W. Davies, 1807.

Price, George. *Jamaica and the Colonial Office: Who Caused the Crisis?* London: Sampson, Low, Son and Marston, 1866.

Price, Jacob M. 'The Transatlantic Economy.' In *Colonial British America: Essays in the New History of the Early Modern Era*, edited by Jack P. Greene and J.R. Pole. Baltimore: The Johns Hopkins University Press, 1984: 18–42.

Prince, Mary. 'The History of Mary Prince: A West Indian Slave Related by Herself' (excerpt). In *Caribbean Slavery in the Atlantic World*, edited by Verene A. Shepherd and Hilary McD. Beckles. Kingston & London: Ian Randle & James Currey, 2000: 843–58.

Puckrein, Gary A. *Little England: Plantation Society and Anglo-American Politics 1627–1700*. New York: New York University Press, 1984.

Pullen-Burry, Bessie. *Jamaica As It Is, 1903*. London: T. Fisher Unwin, 1903.

Pyle, Howard . 'Jamaica, Old and New.' *Harper's New Monthly Magazine*, LXXX (January–February 1890): 391.

Radzinowicz, Sir Leon. *A History of English Criminal Law and Its Administration from 1750*. 5 Vols. London: Stevens, 1948–68.

Ragatz, Lowell J. *The Fall of the Planter Class in the British Caribbean, 1763–1833*. 1928. Reprint. New York: Octagon Press, 1971.

Rain, Thomas. *The Life and Labours of John Wray, Pioneer Missionary in British Guiana, Compiled from His Own Mss. and Diaries*. London: John Snow & Co., 1892.

Ramesar, M.D.S. *Survivors of Another Crossing: A History of East Indians in Trinidad, 1880 -1946*. Port of Spain: UWI Schoold of Continuing Studies, 1994.

Ramsey, Frank C. *Protein-Energy Malnutrition in Barbados*. New York: Josiah Macy Jr. Foundation, 1979.

Ratekin, Mervyn. 'The Early Sugar Industry in Española.' *Hispanic American Historical Review*, 34 (1954): 1–19.

Rath, Richard. 'African Music in Seventeenth Century Jamaica: Cultural Transit and Transmission.' *William and Mary Quarterly*, 3rd series, 50.4 (1993): 700–26.

Record of Progress in Facing Stern Realities. US Section of the Anglo-American Caribbean Commission. Washington, 1943.

Renard, Rosamunde. 'Labour Relations in Martinique and Guadeloupe 1848–70.' In *Caribbean Freedom*, edited by Hilary McD. Beckles and Verene A. Shepherd. Kingston: Ian Randle Publishers, 1993: 80–91.

Report of the Trial of Fourteen Negroes at the Court-House, Montego Bay, Jan. 28, 1824 and the two Following Days on a Charge of Rebellious Conspiracy, with the Arguments of the Advocates and the Speeches of the Judge. Montego Bay, 1824.

Rich, E.E. and C.H. Wilson, eds. *The Cambridge Economic History of Europe*, Vol. 4. Cambridge: Cambridge University Press, 1967.

——. 'Colonial Settlement and Its Labour Problems.' In *The Cambridge Economic History of Europe*, Vol.4, edited by E.E. Rich and C.H. Wilson. Cambridge: Cambridge University Press, 1967: 302–73.

Richards, Jimmy and Mervyn Wong. *Statistics of West Indies Cricket 1865–1989*. Kingston: Heinemann Caribbean, 1990.

Richardson, David, ed. *Abolition and its Aftermath: The Historical Context, 1790 1916*. London: Frank Cass, 1985.

Richardson, Elton. *Revolution or Evolution and Other Writings, Including the Scholarship of Eric Williams*. San Juan, Trinidad: Inprint Caribbean, 1984.

Riviere, W. Emanuel. 'Labour Shortage in the British West Indies After Emancipation.' *The Journal of Caribbean History*, 4 (1972): 1–30.

Roberts, Brian K. *Rural Settlement in Britain*. Folkestone, England: Dawson and Sons, 1977.

Roberts, W. Adolphe. *The Caribbean: The Story of Our Sea of Destiny*. New York: The Bobbs-Merrill Co., 1940.

Robertson, Glory (comp.). *Members of the Assembly of Jamaica from the General Election of 1830 to the Final Session January 1866*. Kingston: Institute of Jamaica, 1965.

Robinson, Derek. *A Shocking History of Bristol*. Bristol: Abson, 1973.

Rodney, Walter. *A History of the Guyanese Working People, 1881–1903*. Baltimore: The Johns Hopkins University Press, 1981.

Rolph, Thomas. *A Brief Account, Together with Observations made During a Visit in the West Indies . . . in Parts of the Years 1832–3*. Dundas, Upper Canada: Printed for G.H. Hackstaff, 1836.

Rose, J. Holland, A.P. Newton and E.A. Benians, eds. *The Cambridge History of the British Empire, Vol. 1: The Old Empire from the Beginnings to 1783*. Cambridge: Cambridge University Press, 1929.

Rose, James G. 'The Strikes of 1842 and 1848.' In *Themes in African-Guyanese History*, edited by Winston McGowan, James Rose and David Granger. Georgetown: Free Press, 1998: 158–200.

Rowley, Trevor. *Villages in the [English] Landscape*. London: Dent and Sons, 1978.

Royal Anthropological Institute of Great Britain and Ireland. *Notes and Queries on Anthropology*. 6th ed. London: Routledge and Kegan Paul, 1954.

Ryan, Selwyn. ed. *Race and Nationalism in Trinidad and Tobago*. St Augustine: Institute of Social and Economic Research, 1974.

—— *The Independence Experience, 1962- 1987*. St Augustine: Institute of Social and Economic Research, 1988.

—— ed. *The Black Power Revolution of 1970*. St Augustine: Institute of Socail and Economic Research, 1995.

—— Pathways to Power: Indians and the Politics of National Unity in Trinidad and Tobago. St Augustine, Institute of Social and Economic Research, 1996.

Ryder, Alan. *Benin and the Europeans, 1485–1897*. London: Longmans, 1969.

Sabben-Clarke, E.E., D. J. Bradley and K. Kirkwood, ed. *Health in Tropical Africa During the Colonial Period. Based on the Proceedings of a Symposium held at New College, Oxford 21–23 March 1977*. Oxford: Clarendon Press, 1980.

Saco, José Antonio. *Historia de la esclavitud de la raza africana en el Nuevo Mundo y en especial en los países Américo-Hispanos*. Havana: Cultural, 1938.

Salaman, Redcliffe N. *The History and Social Influence of the Potato*. Cambridge: Cambridge University Press, 1949.

Sandiford, Keith A.P. 'The Victorians at Play: Problems in Historiographical Methodology.' *Journal of Social History*. 15 (1981): 271–88.

——. 'Cricket and the Victorian Society.' *Journal of Social History*, 17 (1983): 303–17.

——. *Cricket Nurseries of Colonial Barbados: The Elite Schools 1865 1966*. Kingston:

The Press, UWI, 1998.

Satineau, Maurice. *Histoire de la Guadeloupe sous l'Ancien Régime 1635–1789.* Paris: Payot, 1928.

Sauer, C.O. 'The Agency of Man on the Earth.' In *Man's Role in Changing the Face of the Earth,* edited by William L. Thomas, Jr. Chicago: University of Chicago Press, 1956: 49–69.

Savary, Jacques. *Le Parfait Negociant, ou, Instruction Générale Pour Ce Qui Regarde le Commerce ...et L'Application des Ordinances.* Paris: J. Guignard 1675.

Schmidt, Louis Bernard. 'The Agricultural Revolution in the Prairies and the Great Plains of the United States.' *Agricultural History,* 4 (1934): 169–95.

Schnakenbourg, Christian. 'Note sur les origines de l'industrie sucrière en Guadeloupe au XVIIe siècle (1640-1670).' *Revue française d'histoire d'outre mer,* 55 (1968): 267–315.

Schomburgk, Robert H. *The History of Barbados.* London: Brown, Green and Longmans, 1847. Reprint London: Frank Cass, 1971.

Scott, Rebecca. 'Former Slaves Responses to Emancipation in Cuba.' In *Caribbean Freedom,* edited by Hilary McD. Beckles and Verene A. Shepherd. Kingston: Ian Randle Publishers, 1993: 21–27.

[Senhouse, William]. 'The Autobiographical Manuscript of William Senhouse' [1787]. *JBMHS,* 2 (1934–35): 61–79, 115–34, 191–209; & 3 (1935–36): 3–19, 87–99.

Senior, Bernard. *Jamaica As It Is, As It was and As It May Be.* London: T. Hurst, 1835.

Shepherd, Verene A. *Transients to Settlers: The Experience of Indians in Jamaica, 1845–1950.* Leeds & Warwick: Peepal Tree Press and the University of Warwick, 1994.

———. 'Liberation Struggles on Livestock Farms in Jamaica.' In *Caribbean Slavery in the Atlantic World,* edited by Verene A. Shepherd and Hilary McD. Beckles. Kingston: Ian Randle Publishers, 2000: 896–904.

——— et. al., eds. *Engendering History: Caribbean Women in Historical Perspective.* Kingston, London and New York: Ian Randle, James Currey and St Martin's, 1995.

———, ed./comp. *Women in Caribbean History.* Kingston: Ian Randle Publishers, 1999.

——— and Hilary McD. Beckles, eds. *Caribbean Slavery in the Atlantic World.* Kingston: Ian Randle Publishers, 2000.

Sheridan, Richard B. 'Samuel Martin, Innovating Sugar Planter of Antigua, 1750–1776.' *Agricultural History,* 34 (1960): 126–39.

———. 'The Rise of a Colonial Gentry: A Case Study of Antigua, 1730–1775.' *Economic History Review,* 13 (1961): 342–57.

———. 'The Wealth of Jamaica in the Eighteenth Century.' *Economic History Review,* 18 (1965): 292–311.

———. 'The Wealth of Jamaica in the Eighteenth Century: A Rejoinder.' *Economic*

History Review, 21 (1968): 46-68.

——. 'The Plantation Revolution and the Industrial Revolution.' *Caribbean Studies*, 9 (1969): 5-25.

——. *Sugar and Slavery: An Economic History of the British West Indies, 1623–1775*. Bridgetown, Barbados: Caribbean Universities Press, 1974.

——. 'The Crisis of Slave Subsistence in the B.W.I. during and after the American Revolution.' *William and Mary Quarterly*, XXXIII. 4 (1976): 615-41.

——. *Doctors and Slaves. A Medical and Demographic History of Slavery in the British West Indies*. Cambridge: Cambridge University Press, 1985.

Sherlock, Philip. *West Indies*. London: Thames and Hudson, 1966.

——. *West Indian Nations: A New History*. Kingston: Jamaica Publishing House Ltd., 1973.

—— and Hazel Bennett. *The Story of the Jamaican People*. Kingston: Ian Randle Publishers, 1998.

Singh, Bahadur. *Temples and Mosques: An Illustrated Study of East Indian Places of Worship in Guyana*. Georgetown: Guyana Release, 1980.

Singh, H.P. *The Indian Struggle for Justice and Equality*. Chaguanas: Indian Review Press, 1993.

Singh, Kelvin. *Race and Class Struggles in a Colonial State: Trinidad, 1917-1945*. Kingston: The Press, UWI, 1994.

—— 'Conflict and Collaboration: Tradidion and Modernizing Indo-Trinidadian Elites, 1917-56,' *New West Indian Guide*, 70 (1996): 229-53.

'Slave Holiday.' *Natural History*, 84.10 (1975): 84-90.

Smith, M.G. 'Community Organization in Rural Jamaica.' *Social and Economic Studies*, 5 (1956): 295-312.

Snelgrave, William. *A New Account of Some Parts of Guinea and the Slave Trade*. London: James, John and Paul Knapton, 1734.

Society for the Conversion and Religious Instruction and Education of the Negro Slaves in the British West India Islands. *Report for the Year 1828*. London, 1829.

Society for Improvement of Plantership in the Island of Barbados. *Minutes of the Society for the Improvement of Plantership in the Island of Barbados, Instituted December 8th, 1804*. Liverpool: Printed by Thos. Kaye, 1811.

Spackmann, A. *Constitutional Development in the West Indies 1933-1968*. Kingston: Institute of Social and Economic Research, 1975.

Spector, Margaret Marion. 'A.P. Newton.' In *Some Modern Historians of Britain: Essays in Honour of R.L. Schuyler*, edited by Herman Ausubel, J. Bartlet Brebner and Erling M. Hunt. New York: The Dryden Press, 1951: 286-305.

Stedman, John. *Narrative of a Five Years Expedition Against the Revolted Negroes of Surinam*. Transcribed for the first time from the original 1790 manuscript. Ed. Richard and Sally Price. Baltimore: The Johns Hopkins University Press, 1988.

Stephen, James. *The Slavery of the British West India Colonies*. 2 Vols. London:

Joseph Butterworth, 1824 and 1830.

Steward, Julian H. et al. *The People of Puerto Rico*. Urbana: University of Illinois Press, 1956.

Stewart, J. *A View of the Past and Present State of the Island of Jamaica*. 1823. Reprint. New York: Negro Universities Press, 1969.

Stewart, Robert. *Religion and Society in Post-Emancipation Jamaica*. Knoxville: University of Tennessee Press, 1992.

Stoddard, Charles Augustus. *Cruising Among the Caribbees: Summer Days in Winter Months*. New York: Charles Scribner's Sons, 1895.

Sturge, Joseph and Thomas Harvey. *The West Indies in 1837*. London: Hamilton, Adams, 1838.

Styles, John. 'Crime in 18th Century England.' *History Today*, 38 (1989): 36-42.

Sutton, Paul. 'The Historian as Politician: Eric Williams and Walter Rodney.' In *Intellectuals in the Twentieth Century Caribbean*, edited by Alistair Hennessy. London: Macmillan, 1992.

———, ed. *Forged from the Love of Liberty: Selected Speeches of Dr. Eric Williams*. Port of Spain: Longman Caribbean, 1981.

Tannenbaum, Frank. *Slave and Citizen: The Negro in the Americas*. New York: Alfred Knopf, 1946.

Taylor, Christopher. *Fields in the English Landscape*. London: Dent and Sons, 1975.

Thomas, Clive Y. *Plantations, Peasants and State: A Study of the Mode of Sugar Production in Guyana*. Los Angeles: Center for Afro-American Studies, University of California, 1984.

Thomas, William L. Jr., ed. *Man's Role in Changing the Face of the Earth*. Chicago: University of Chicago Press, 1956.

Thome, James A. and J. Horace Kimball. *Emancipation in the West Indies. A Six Months' Tour in Antigua, Barbados and Jamaica in the Year 1837*. New York: American Anti-Slavery Society, 1838.

Thompson, Alvin O. *Colonialism and Underdevelopment in Guyana 1580–1803*. Bridgetown: Carib Research and Publications, 1987.

———. 'The Chastisement of the Slave "America." ' *Journal of Caribbean History*, 33.1 & 2 (1999): 146-61.

———, ed. *Emancipation I. A Series of Lectures to Commemorate the 150th Anniversary of Emancipation*. Bridgetown: Department of History, UWI, Cave Hill and Barbados National Cultural Foundation, 1986: 72-87.

Thompson, E.P. 'The Moral Economy of the English Crowd in the Eighteenth Century.' *Past and Present*, 50 (1971): 76-136.

Thompson, Edgar T. 'The Climatic Theory of the Plantation.' *Agricultural History*, 15 (1941): 49-60.

Thornton, A.P. 'The Organization of the Slave Trade in the English West Indies, 1660-1685.' *William and Mary Quarterly*, 12 (1955): 399-409.

Titus, Noel. *Conflicts and Contradictions*. London: Minerva Press, 1998.

Towns, Thomas. 'An Extract of a Letter of Mr. Lister Containing Some Observations made at the Barbadoes [March 26,1675].' *Philosophical Transactions of the Royal Society of London,* X (1676).

Toynbee, Arnold. *Lectures on the Industrial Revolution in England.* London: Rivingtons, 1884.

T[ramond], J. 'Review of Harlow's "A History of Barbados 1625–1685." ' In *Revue d'histoire des colonies,* 20 (1927): 622–23.

Trinidad and Tobago. Agricultural Society. *Proceedings of the Agricultural Society of Trinidad and Tobago.* Vols. I and XLI. Port of Spain, 1894 and 1947.

Trinidad and Tobago. Department of Agriculture. *Annual Report of the Director of Agriculture, Trinidad and Tobago,* 1939–46.

———. *Agricultural Development in Trinidad and Tobago* (The E.J. Wortley Report). Port of Spain, 1940.

———. *Report of the Agricultural Policy Committee of Trinidad and Tobago. Part I.* Port of Spain, 1943.

———. *Report of the Agricultural Policy Committee of Trinidad and Tobago. Part II and Summary and Recommendations of Parts I and II.* Port of Spain, 1943.

———. *Report of the Food Controller on Local Food Production for the Six Months ending 31 December, 1942.* Port of Spain, 1943.

———. *Report of the Food Controller for the six Months ending 30 June 1943.* Port of Spain, 1943.

———. *Report of the Marketing of Ground Provisions, Vegetables and Fruit for Local Food Consumption.* Port of Spain, 1942.

———. *Report on Local Food Production for the Six Months ending 30 March 1944.* Port of Spain, 1944.

———. *Report of the Sub-Committee on Agriculture.* Port of Spain, 1948.

Trinidad and Tobago. Legislative Council. *Council Paper No.13 of 1906: Report of the Labour Committee, Legislative Council of Trinidad and Tobago.* Port of Spain, 1906.

Trotman, David. *Crime in Trinidad: Conflict and Control in a Plantation Society, 1838–1870.* Knoxville: University of Tennessee Press, 1986.

Trouillot, Michel-Rolph. *Silencing the Past: Power and the Production of History.* Boston: Beacon Press, 1995.

Turner, Mary. *Slaves and Missionaries: The Disintegration of Jamaican Slave Society, 1787–1834.* Urbana: University of Illinois Press, 1982.

———. 'Slave Workers, Subsistence and Labour Bargaining: Amity Hall, Jamaica, 1805–32.' In *The Slaves' Economy: Independent Production by Slaves in the Americas,* edited by Ira Berlin and Philip D. Morgan. London: Frank Cass, 1991.

———. 'Chattel Slaves into Wage Slaves.' In *From Chattel Slaves to Wage Slaves: The Dynamics of Labour Bargaining in the Americas,* edited by Mary Turner. Kingston, London and Indianapolis: Ian Randle, James Currey and Indiana University Press, 1995: 33–47.

———. 'The 11 o'clock Flog: Women, Work and Labour in the British Caribbean.' *Slavery and Abolition*, 20.1 (1999): 38-58.

———, ed. *From Chattel Slaves to Wage Slaves: The Dynamics of Labour Bargaining in the Americas*. Kingston, London and Indianapolis: Ian Randle, James Currey and Indiana University Press, 1995.

Van Lier, R.A.J. *Frontier Society*. The Hague: Martinus Nijhoff, 1971.

Vassell, Linnette. 'Women of the Masses.' In *Engendering History: Caribbean History in Historical Perspective*, edited by Verene A. Shepherd et. al. Kingston and London: Ian Randle Publishers and James Currey Press, 1995: 318-33.

———, comp. *Voices of Women in Jamaica, 1898-1939*. Kingston: Department of History, UWI, Mona, 1993.

Vignols, Léon. 'Une question mal posée: Le travail manuel des blancs et des esclaves aux Antilles (XVIIe-XVIIIe siècles).' *Revue historique*, 175 (1935): 308-15.

Villiers, Patrick. *Traite des Noirs et Navires Négriers au XVIIIe Siècle*. Grenoble: Éditions des 4 Seigneurs, 1982.

Waddell, D.A.G. *The West Indies and the Guianas*. Englewood Cliffs: Prentice-Hall Inc., 1967.

Walker, James. *Letters on the West Indies*. London: Camberwell Press, 1818.

Wallbridge, E.A. *The Demerara Martyr: Memoirs of the Reverend John Smith, Missionary in Demerara*. 1848. Reprint. New York: Negro Universities Press, 1969.

Waller, John A. *A Voyage in the West Indies*. London: Richard Phillips, 1820.

Ward, A.W., G.W. Prothero and Stanley Leathes, eds. *The Cambridge Modern History*, Vol. 4. Cambridge: Cambridge University Press, 1906.

Watkins, Melville H. 'A Staple Theory of Economic Growth.' *Canadian Journal of Economics and Political Science*, 29 (1963): 141-58.

Watson, Karl. *The Civilised Island, Barbados; A Social History, 1750-1816*. Ellerton, Barbados: Caribbean Graphic Production Ltd., 1979.

———. *A Kind of Right to be Idle: Old Doll Matriarch of Newton Plantation. Rewriting History No.3*. Cave Hill: Department of History, UWI, and Barbados Museum and Historical Society, 2000.

Watts, David. *Man's Influence on the Vegetation of Barbados 1627 to 1800*. Hull, England: University of Hull, Occasional Papers in Geography, No. 4, 1966.

———. *The West Indies: Patterns of Development, Culture and Environmental Change Since 1942*. Cambridge: Cambridge University Press, 1987.

Webber, A.R.F. *Centenary History and Handbook of British Guiana*. Georgetown: The Argosy Co. Ltd., 1931.

Welch, Pedro L.V. 'The Urban Context of Slave Life: Views from Bridgetown, Barbados, in the Eighteenth and Nineteenth Centuries.' *Plantation Society in the Americas*, 5.2 & 3 (1998): 281-96.

Wentworth, Trelawney. *The West India Sketch Book*, 2 Vols. London: Printed for Whittaker and Co., 1834.

West, Robert C. and John P. Augelli. *Middle America: Its Lands and Peoples.* Englewood Cliffs: Prentice-Hall Inc., 1966.

Westergaard, Waldemar. *The Danish West Indies under Company Rule (1671-1754).* New York: Macmillan, 1917.

Whitson, Agnes M. *The Constitutional Development of Jamaica, 1660 to 1729.* Manchester: Manchester University Press, 1929.

Wilkerson, S.J.K., ed. *Cultural Traditions and Caribbean Identity.* Gainesville: Center for Latin American Studies, University of Florida, 1980.

Williams, Cynric. *A Tour Through the Island of Jamaica.* London: Hunt and Clarke, 1823.

Williams, Eric. *The Negro in the Caribbean.* Washington: The Associates in Negro Folk Education, 1942.

———. *Capitalism and Slavery.* 1944,1967. Reprint. Chapel Hill: University of North Carolina Press, 1994.

———. *Education in the British West Indies.* Port of Spain: Guardian Commercial Printery, 1950.

———. *Documents on British West Indian History, 1807-1833.* Port of Spain: Trinidad Publishing Co., 1952.

———. *Inward Hunger.* London: André Deutsch., 1969.

———. 'My Relations with the Caribbean Commission.' In *Eric Williams Speaks,* edited by S. Cudjoe. Wellesley: Calaloux Publications, 1993.

Williamson, James A. *The Caribbee Islands under the Proprietary Patents.* London: Oxford University Press, 1926.

———. 'The Beginnings of an Imperial Policy, 1649-1660.' In *The Cambridge History of the British Empire, Vol.1: The Old Empire from the Beginnings to 1783,* edited by J. Holland Rose, A.P. Newton and E.A. Benians. Cambridge: Cambridge University Press, 1929: 207-38.

———. *Great Britain and the Empire: A Discursive History.* London: A. and C. Black, 1944.

Wilmot, Swithin. ' "Not Full Free": The Ex-Slaves and the Apprenticeship System in Jamaica, 1834-1838.' *Jamaica Journal,* 17.3 (1984): 2-10.

———. 'The Growth of Black Political Activity in Post-Emancipation Jamaica.' In *Garvey: His Work and Impact,* edited by Rupert Lewis and Patrick Bryan. Mona, Kingston: Institute of Social and Economic Research, and Dept. of Extra-Mural Studies, 1988: 39-46.

———. 'Emancipation in Action: Workers and Wage Conflict in Jamaica 1838-40.' In *Caribbean Freedom,* edited by Hilary McD. Beckles and Verene A. Shepherd. Kingston: Ian Randle Publishers, 1993: 48-53.

———. ' "Females of Abandoned Character?" Women and Protest in Jamaica, 1838-65.' In *Engendering History: Caribbean Women in Historical Perspective,* edited by Verene A. Shepherd, et. al. Kingston, London and New York: Ian Randle, James Currey and St Martin's, 1995: 279-95.

Woodroofe, J.M. 'A Brief History of the Pickwick C. C.' *Barbados Cricketers*

Annual, 1907–1908.

Wynter, Sylvia. 'Jonkonnu in Jamaica: Toward an Interpretation of Folk Dance as Cultural Process.' *Jamaica Journal,* 4.2 (1970): 34–38.

Unpublished Theses and Papers

Anderson, Juanita. 'Houses of the Enslaved Africans in the Caribbean and Southern United States.' Department of Anthropology, Southern Illinois University, Carbondale, 1978.

Beckles, Hilary McD. and Karl Watson. 'Concessionary Politics: Slave Resistance in Eighteenth Century Barbados.' Department of History, UWI, Mona, 1984.

Blake, Beverley. 'A History of Children in Nineteenth Century Jamaica.' M Phil. thesis, University of the West Indies, Mona, 1990.

Brown, Janet A. 'Black Versus White: An Analysis of the Slave Court of St Ann, 1787–1814.' Caribbean Studies paper, History Department, UWI, Mona, 1989.

Carter, Alvin. 'The Origins and Early Development of the Barbados Police Force 1835–45.' MA thesis, UWI, Cave Hill Campus, 1989.

Carter, Henderson. 'Resistance and Protest in Barbados, 1838–1904.' PhD. thesis, UWI, Cave Hill Campus, 2000.

Craton, Michael. 'Decoding Pitchy Patchy: The Roots, Branches and Essence of Junkanoo.' Paper presented at the Twenty-sixth Annual Conference of the ACH, Puerto Rico, 1994.

Eltis, David. 'The Volume and Structure of the Slave Trade.' Paper presented at the Conference on Enslaving Connections, York University, Toronto, October 2000.

Ghany, H.A. 'Constitution-making in the Commonwealth Caribbean with Special Reference to Trinidad and Tobago.' PhD. thesis, University of London, 1987.

Handler, Jerome S. 'Housing, House Types, and Furnishings of Barbados Plantation Slaves.' 1997. BDA.

——. 'Food and Nutrition of Barbados Plantation Slaves.' 1997. BDA.

——. 'The Domestic Economy of Barbados Plantation Slaves: Production and Distribution.' 1997. BDA.

——. 'Health and Medicine Among Barbadian Slaves: Diseases and Disabilities.' 1997. BDA.

——. 'Health and Medicine Among Barbadian Slaves: Medical Care and Treatment.' 1997. BDA.

Hughes, Ronald. 'Barbadian Sugar Plantations, 1640 to 1846.' Seminar Paper, 1977–78, Department of History, UWI, Cave Hill.

Hutton, Clinton. ' "Colour for Colour, Skin for Skin": The Ideological Foundations of Post-Slavery Society, 1838–1865.' PhD. thesis, UWI, Mona,

1992.

Johnson, Howard. 'Slave Life and Leisure in Nassau, Bahamas, 1783–1838.' Paper presented at the Twenty-sixth Annual Conference of the ACH, Puerto Rico, 1994.

Joseph, S. 'The Impact of World War II on Agriculture in Trinidad.' Caribbean Studies paper. UWI, St Augustine, Trinidad, 1986.

La Guerre, John. 'The Race Factor and the Election of 1950 in Trinidad and Tobago.' UWI St Augustine Library, 1979.

Mair, Lucille Mathurin. 'An Historical Study of Women in Jamaica from 1655 to 1844.' PhD. thesis, UWI, Mona, 1974.

Marshall, Woodville K. 'The Social and Economic Development of The Windward Islands, 1838–1865.' PhD. thesis, Cambridge University, 1963.

——. 'The Peasantry and the Sugar Industry.' Paper presented at Second Conference of the ACH, Barbados, 1970.

——. 'Rock Hall, St Thomas: The Search for the First Free Village in Barbados.' Paper presented at the Ninth Conference of the ACH, Barbados, 1977.

——. 'The Ex-slaves as Wage Labourers on the Sugar Estates in the British Windward Islands, 1838–46.' Paper presented at the Eleventh Conference of the ACH, Curaçao, 1979.

——. 'Caribbean Historiography: Anglophone and British West Indian Scholarship in the last 20 years.' Paper presented at the Twenty-first Conference of the ACH, Guadeloupe, 1989.

——. ' "It Is the Way We Live": the Village in Caribbean History.' Elsa Goveia Memorial Lecture, UWI, Cave Hill, Barbados, October 2000.

——. 'Henry James Ross of Grenada: A Pioneer of Tenant Farming Systems.' Paper presented at UWI School of Continuing Studies Conference on Grenada, Grenada, January 2002.

Moore, Brian L. and Michele A. Johnson. 'Conflicting Moralities: Sex and Illegitimacy in Jamaica at the Turn of the Twentieth Century.' Paper presented at the Workshop on Control and Resistance in the Post-emancipation Caribbean, University of Warwick, Coventry, U.K., July 2000.

Pemberton, Rita. 'The Evolution of Agricultural Policy in Trinidad and Tobago, 1890–1945.' PhD. thesis, UWI, St Augustine Campus, 1996.

Perkins, Francis. 'Busha's Mistress or Catherine the Fugitive: A Stirring Romance of the Days of Slavery in Jamaica.' Novel, Jamaica Archives, 1855.

Potter, Lesley M. 'The Paddy Proletariat and the Dependent Peasantry: East Indian Rice Growers in British Guiana, 1895–1920.' Paper presented at the Ninth Conference of the ACH, Barbados, 1977.

——. 'East Indians Without Sugar – Essequibo, Guyana, 1923–39.' Paper presented at the Conference on East Indians in the Caribbean, Trinidad, 1979.

Prorok, C.V. 'Hindu Temples in Trinidad: Cultural Geography of Religious Structures and Ethnic Identity.' PhD. dissertation, Louisiana State

University, 1987.

Ramnarine, Tyran. 'The Issue of East Indian Political Representation in British Guiana During the Latter Part of Indenture, 1890–1917.' Paper presented at the Eleventh Conference of the ACH, Curaçao, 1979.

Shepherd, Verene A. 'Pens and Penkeepers in a Plantation Society.' PhD. thesis, University of Cambridge, 1988.

——. 'Locating Enslaved Women's Voices in the Colonial Caribbean: The Promises and Pitfalls of Ventriloquism.' Paper presented at the Workshop on Atlantic Crossings: Women's Voices, Women's Stories in the Caribbean and the Nigerian Hinterland, Dartmouth College, New Hampshire, May 18-20, 2001.

Silverman, M. 'Resource Change and Village Factionalism in an East Indian Community, Guyana.' PhD. dissertation, McGill University, 1973.

Thompson, Alvin O. 'The Crown Slaves of Berbice: A Study of Official Mismanagement 1803–1831.' PhD. thesis, UWI, Cave Hill Campus, 1998.

Tikasingh, G. 'The Establishment of the Indians in Trinidad, 1870–1900.' PhD. thesis, UWI, 1976.

Welch, Pedro L.V. 'The Urban Context of the Slave Plantation System.' PhD. thesis, UWI, Cave Hill Campus, 1994.

Index